P9-CEE-517

IMPORTANT

HERE IS YOUR REGISTRATION CODE TO ACCESS MCGRAW-HILL PREMIUM CONTENT AND MCGRAW-HILL ONLINE RESOURCES

For key premium online resources you need THIS CODE to gain access. Once the code is entered, you will be able to use the web resources for the length of your course.

Access is provided only if you have purchased a new book.

If the registration code is missing from this book, the registration screen on our website, and within your WebCT or Blackboard course will tell you how to obtain your new code. Your registration code can be used only once to establish access. It is not transferable.

To gain access to these online resources

1. USE your web browser to go to: **mhhe.com/langan**

2. CLICK on "First Time User"

3. ENTER the Registration Code printed on the tear-off bookmark on the right

4. After you have entered your registration code, click on "Register"

5. FOLLOW the instructions to setup your personal UserID and Password

6. WRITE your UserID and Password down for future reference. Keep it in a safe place.

If your course is using WebCT or Blackboard, you'll be able to use this code to access the McGraw-Hill content within your instructor's online course.

To gain access to the McGraw-Hill content in your instructor's WebCT or Blackboard course simply log into the course with the user ID and Password provided by your instructor. Enter the registration code exactly as it appears to the right when prompted by the system. You will only need to use this code the first time you click on McGraw-Hill content.

These instructions are specifically for student access. Instructors are not required to register via the above instructions.

The McGraw-Hill Companies

Mc Graw Hill Higher Education

Thank you, and welcome to your McGraw-Hill Online Resources.

0-07-321274-1 T/A LANGAN: ENGLISH SKILLS WITH READINGS, 6/E

P5PX-15VU-AJDR-OD3W-C7RK

REGISTRATION CODE
REGISTRATION CODE

The McGraw-Hill Companies
Mc Graw Hill **Higher Education**

English Skills with Readings

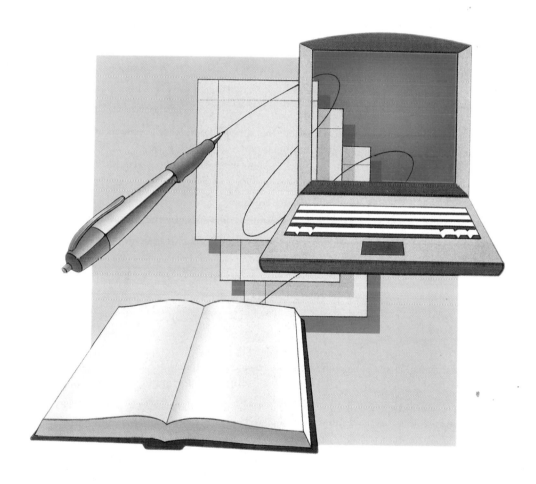

Copyright ©2005 The McGraw-Hill Companies, Inc. All rights reserved.

Praise for *English Skills with Readings, 6th Edition and English Skills, 8th Edition*

"Changing to this textbook is the single factor which has renewed my desire to teach this course."
—**Anneliese Homan, State Fair Community College**

"There can be no legitimate comparison between John Langan's McGraw-Hill developmental composition text series and any other texts available. Other texts are simply not as clear, precise, interesting, or comprehensive as *English Skills.*"
—**Candace C. Mesa, Dixie College**

"It is an outstanding text, good for discussion, individual work, or collaborative activities."
—**Patsy Krech, University of Memphis**

"A no-nonsense, accessible guide that gives students confidence . . . the most practical, student-friendly choice for a pre-college writing course."
—**Jennifer Leamy, Wake Technical Community College**

"A great choice for a developmental class with terrific supplementary materials like its CD-ROM and website. Well-written and logically organized."
—**Kathleen Shaw, Montgomery County Community College**

"I would tell my colleagues that if they reviewed it thoroughly, they would find *English Skills with Readings* to be an instructor's dream text."
—**Elizabeth W. Smith, Manatee Community College**

"I consider Langan to be the guru of writing instruction because he tells his students that writing is a skill that anyone can master with lots of hard work."
—**Rita Fork, El Camino College**

"The strength of the entire text is its comprehensiveness: it has qualities of a skills text and English handbook, of a composition and research and library guide."
—**Russell J. Gaudio, Gateway Community College**

"The greatest strengths of this text are its flexibility for the instructor, accessibility for the student, and clear focus on the writing needs of developmental students."
—**Michael A. Orlando, Bergen Community College**

"Full of valuable resources. I appreciate Langan's efforts to include readings with subject matter connected to students' experiences."
—**Starlette Vaughn, Sacramento City College**

"I love Langan's tone and style—direct and not condescending."
—**Jeanne Grandchamp, Bristol Community College**

"Very user-friendly."
—**Molly Emmons, College of the Redwoods – Del Norte**

English Skills with Readings

Copyright ©2005 The McGraw-Hill Companies, Inc. All rights reserved.

Sixth Edition

John Langan

Atlantic Cape Community College

Boston   Burr Ridge, IL   Dubuque, IA   Madison, WI   New York   San Francisco   St. Louis
Bangkok   Bogotá   Caracas   Kuala Lumpur   Lisbon   London   Madrid   Mexico City
Milan   Montreal   New Delhi   Santiago   Seoul   Singapore   Sydney   Taipei   Toronto

The McGraw·Hill Companies

Higher Education

ENGLISH SKILLS WITH READINGS
Published by McGraw-Hill, a business unit of The McGraw-Hill Companies, Inc., 1221 Avenue of the Americas, New York, NY, 10020. Copyright © 2006, 2002, 1999, 1995, 1991, 1988 by The McGraw-Hill Companies, Inc. All rights reserved. No part of this publication may be reproduced or distributed in any form or by any means, or stored in a database or retrieval system, without the prior written consent of The McGraw-Hill Companies, Inc., including, but not limited to, in any network or other electronic storage or transmission, or broadcast for distance learning.
Some ancillaries, including electronic and print components, may not be available to customers outside the United States.

This book is printed on acid-free paper.

1 2 3 4 5 6 7 8 9 0 DOC/DOC 0 9 8 7 6 5

ISBN   0-07-296270-4 (student edition)
ISBN   0-07-296274-7 (annotated instructor's edition)

Editor in Chief: *Emily Barrosse*
Publisher: *Lisa Moore*
Senior Sponsoring Editor: *Alexis Walker*
Senior Developmental Editor: *Paul Banks*
Marketing Manager: *Lori DeShazo*
Managing Editor: *Jean Dal Porto*
Project Manager: *Jean R. Starr*
Art Director: *Jeanne Schreiber*
Designer: *Cassandra J. Chu*
Text Designer: *Glenda King*
Cover Designer: *Glenda King*

Illustrator: *Paul Turnbaugh*
Photo Research Coordinator: *Natalia C. Peschiera*
Art Manager: *Robin K. Mouat*
Senior Media Producer: *Todd Vaccaro*
Lead Media Project Manager: *Marc Mattson*
Senior Production Supervisor: *Carol A. Bielski*
Composition: *11/13 Times New Roman*
    by Electronic Publishing Services, Inc., TN
Printing: *PMS Black, 45 # Pub Thin Bulk,*
    R.R.Donnelley/Crawfordsville

Credits: The credits section for this book begins on page 747 and is considered an extension of the copyright page.

Library of Congress Cataloging-in-Publication Data

Langan, John
    English skills with readings / John Langan. — 6th ed.
        p. cm.
        ISBN 0-07-296270-4 (softcover : alk. paper) — ISBN 0-07-296274-7 (softcover : alk. paper)
        1. English language—Rhetoric. 2. English language—Grammer. 3. College readers. I.
    Title.
PE1408.L3182 2006
808'.0427—dc22   2005041699

The Internet addresses listed in the text were accurate at the time of publication. The inclusion of a website does not indicate an endorsement by the authors of McGraw-Hill, and McGraw-Hill does not guarantee the accuracy of the information presented at these sites.

www.mhhe.com

About the Author

Copyright ©2005 The McGraw-Hill Companies, Inc. All rights reserved.

John Langan has taught reading and writing at Atlantic Cape Community College near Atlantic City, New Jersey, for over twenty-five years. The author of a popular series of college textbooks on both writing and reading, John enjoys the challenge of developing materials that teach skills in an especially clear and lively way. Before teaching, he earned advanced degrees in writing at Rutgers University and in reading at Rowan University. He also spent a year writing fiction that, he says, "is now at the back of a drawer waiting to be discovered and acclaimed posthumously." While in school, he supported himself by working as a truck driver, a machinist, a battery assembler, a hospital attendant, and an apple packer. John now lives with his wife, Judith Nadell, near Philadelphia. In addition to his wife and Philly sports teams, his passions include reading and turning on nonreaders to the pleasure and power of books. Through Townsend Press, his educational publishing company, he has developed the nonprofit "Townsend Library"—a collection of more than forty new and classic stories that appeal to readers of any age.

The Langan Series

Contents

Copyright ©2005 The McGraw-Hill Companies, Inc. All rights reserved.

Copyright ©2005 The McGraw-Hill Companies, Inc. All rights reserved.

Copyright ©2005 The McGraw-Hill Companies, Inc. All rights reserved.

Readings Listed by Rhetorical Mode

Copyright ©2005 The McGraw-Hill Companies, Inc. All rights reserved.

Note: Some selections are listed more than once because they illustrate more than one rhetorical method of development.

Examples

All the Good Things   *Sister Helen Mrosla*
Joe Davis: A Cool Man   *Beth Johnson*
What Good Families Are Doing Right   *Delores Curran*
Anxiety: Challenge by Another Name   *James Lincoln Collier*
Old before Her Time   *Katherine Barrett*
How They Get You to Do That   *Janny Scott*
Dealing with Feelings   *Rudolph F. Verderber*
Rudeness at the Movies   *Bill Wine*
The Most Hateful Words   *Amy Tan*
The Storyteller   *H. H. Munro ("Saki")*
Bullies in School   *Kathleen Berger*

Process

Anxiety: Challenge by Another Name   *James Lincoln Collier*
Let's Really Reform Our Schools   *Anita Garland*

Comparison-Contrast

Rowing the Bus   *Paul Logan*
Joe Davis: A Cool Man   *Beth Johnson*
Tickets to Nowhere   *Andy Rooney*
Old before Her Time   *Katherine Barrett*
The Most Hateful Words   *Amy Tan*

Definition

What Good Families Are Doing Right   *Delores Curran*
Anxiety: Challenge by Another Name   *James Lincoln Collier*
The Storyteller   *H. H. Munro ("Saki")*
Bullies in School   *Kathleen Berger*

To the Instructor

Key Features of the Book

English Skills with Readings will help students learn and apply the basic principles of effective composition. It will also help them master essential reading skills. It is a nuts-and-bolts book based on a number of assumptions or beliefs about the writing process:

- *First of all,* English Skills with Readings *assumes that four principles in particular are keys to effective writing:* **unity, support, coherence, and sentence skills.** These four principles are highlighted on the inside front cover and reinforced throughout the book.
  - Part One focuses on the first three principles and to some extent on sentence skills; Part Five serves as a concise handbook of sentence skills.
  - The four principles are applied in different types of paragraph development (Part Two) and in several-paragraph essays (Part Three).
- Part Four discusses research skills.
- Part Six presents seventeen reading selections.

The ongoing success of *English Skills with Readings* is evidence that the four principles are easily grasped, remembered, and followed by students.

- *The book also reflects a belief that, in addition to these four principles, there are other important factors in writing effectively.* The second chapter discusses *prewriting, rewriting, and editing.* Besides encouraging students to see *writing as a process*, the chapter also asks students to examine their *attitude toward writing*, to *write on what they know* about or can learn about, to consider keeping a *writing journal*, and to make *outlining* a part of the writing process.
- English Skills with Readings *assumes that the best way to begin writing is with personal experience.* After students have learned to support a point by providing material from their own experience, they are ready to develop an idea by drawing on their own reasoning abilities and on information in reports, articles, and

Copyright ©2005 The McGraw-Hill Companies, Inc. All rights reserved.

books. In Parts Two and Three, students are asked to write on *both experiential and objective topics.*

- *The book also assumes that beginning writers are more likely to learn composition skills through lively, engaging, and realistic models than through materials remote from the common experiences that are part of everyday life.* For example, when a writer argues that proms should be banned, or catalogs ways to harass an instructor, or talks about why some teenagers take drugs, students will be more apt to remember and follow the writing principles that are involved.

- *A related assumption is that students are especially interested in and challenged by the writing of their peers.* After reading vigorous papers composed by other students and understanding the power that good writing can have, students will be more encouraged to aim for similar honesty, realism, and detail in their own work.

- *Another premise of* English Skills with Readings *is that mastery of the paragraph should precede work on the several-paragraph essay.* Thus Part One illustrates the basic principles of composition writing using paragraph models, and the assignments in Part Two aim at developing the ability to support ideas within a variety of paragraph forms. The essential principles of paragraph writing are then applied to the several-paragraph essays in Part Three.

- *The grammar, punctuation, and usage skills that make up Part Five are explained clearly and directly, without unnecessary technical terms.* Here, as elsewhere, *abundant exercise material* is provided, especially for the mistakes that are most likely to interfere with clear communication.

- *A final assumption is that, since no two people will use an English text in exactly the same way, the material should be organized in a highly accessible manner.* Because each of the six parts of the book deals with a distinct area of writing, instructors can turn quickly and easily to the skills they want to present. At the same time, ideas for sequencing material are provided in a section titled "Using This Text" at the end of Chapter 1. And a detailed syllabus is provided in the Instructor's Manual.

I am very grateful for the ongoing popularity of *English Skills with Readings.* Instructors continue to say that the four bases really do help students learn to write effectively. And they continue to comment that students find the activities, assignments, model passages, and reading selections especially interesting and worthwhile.

The Readings

Copyright ©2005 The McGraw-Hill Companies, Inc. All rights reserved.

- The seventeen selections have been chosen for their content as much as for rhetorical mode. They are organized thematically into three groups: "Goals and Values," "Education and Self-Improvement," and "Human Groups and Society." Some selections reflect important contemporary concerns: for instance, "Let's Really Reform Our Schools," "Rudeness at the Movies," and "What Good Families Are Doing Right." Some provide information many students may find helpful: examples are "Anxiety: Challenge by Another Name," "How They Get You to Do That," and "Dealing with Feelings." Some recount profoundly human experiences: "All the Good Things," "Rowing the Bus," "Joe Davis: A Cool Man," and "A Drunken Ride, a Tragic Aftermath." (A list on pages xiii–xiv presents the readings by rhetorical mode.)

- Each reading begins with an overview that supplies background information where needed and stimulates interest in the piece.

- The ten reading comprehension questions that follow each selection give students practice in five key skills: understanding vocabulary in context, summarizing (by choosing an alternative title), determining the main idea, recognizing key supporting details, and making inferences. Reading educators agree that these are among the most crucial comprehension skills. A special chart in the Appendix enables students to track their progress as they practice these skills.

- Discussion questions following the reading comprehension questions deal with matters of content as well as aspects of structure, style, and tone. Through the questions on structure in particular, students will see that professional authors practice some of the same basic composing techniques (such as the use of transitions and emphatic order to achieve coherence) that they have been asked to practice in their own writing.

- Finally, two paragraph writing assignments and one essay writing assignment follow the discussion questions. The assignments range from personal narratives to expository and persuasive essays about issues in the world at large. Many assignments provide guidelines on how to proceed, including sample topic sentences or thesis statements and appropriate methods of development. In addition, five of the selections feature a fourth writing assignment requiring some simple Internet research.

When assigning a selection, instructors may find it helpful to ask students to read the overview as well as to answer the reading comprehension and discussion questions that follow the selection. Answers can then be gone over quickly in class. Through these activities, a writing instructor can contribute to the improvement of students' reading skills.

Changes in the Sixth Edition

Here is a list of what is new in the sixth edition of *English Skill with Readings:*

- *The new edition features a more visual design for today's students.* On the opening pages of the book, two *Peanuts* cartoons help reinforce the first and second steps in writing. More than thirty other cartoons, illustrations, posters, and photographs then appear throughout the book to reinforce writing principles or as incentives for writing. In each chapter on patterns of development in Part Two, two assignments are illustrated with visuals to give today's multimedia-trained students help in writing about a topic. Photos of many authors of the seventeen readings have been added to Part Six. In addition, a new full-color design adds visual appeal for students while helping to organize and highlight material.

- *Added practice materials reinforce the basic writing principles in the book.* In Chapter 3, "The First and Second Steps in Writing," instructors now have their choice of activities that sharply underscore the difference between point and support and that help illustrate just what is meant by being specific in writing.

- *Transitions in writing are treated in much more detail.* In Chapter 4, "The Third Step in Writing," instructors have at their disposal explanations and activities that will give students a much better sense of the use of transitions in writing.

- *An expanded treatment of purpose in writing and an introduction to tone* are now included in Chapter 7, "Introduction to Paragraph Development," in Part Two. Added attention is given to purpose and audience in the final assignment for each of the nine patterns of development.

- *A full set of activities and more writing assignments have been added to Part Three,* "Essay Development." With the help of these new materials, instructors who wish to provide students with a more substantial introduction to essay writing will be able to do so.

- *A completely revised Part Four offers students practical guidance on how to do research.* Chapter 19 consolidates and updates material on the library, the Internet, and the research paper. Students will quickly learn how to use their computer and a powerful search engine to look up material on almost any subject.

- *Chapter 39, "Using the Dictionary," has been expanded to help students take full advantage of online dictionaries.*

- Throughout the book, particularly in Part Five, *student models and practice materials have been updated and revised.*

- *Four new reading selections* are now included in the seventeen selections in Part Six: "The Most Hateful Words," by Amy Tan; "Joe Davis, A Cool Man," by Beth

Johnson; "The Scholarship Jacket," by Marta Salinas; and "The Storyteller," by H. H. Munro (Saki). The short story by Saki is the first fiction selection ever included in the readings; it is a timeless story that will delight students of any age. All seventeen selections have been class-tested; they engage the interest of students and make for interesting writing assignments.

About the Media Links

This edition of *English Skills with Readings* includes icons that link the text and its class-tested media supplements: *English Skills with Readings* Student CD-ROM and Online Learning Center. Each chapter in this edition features marginal icons that alert students to additional exercises, extended explanations, and supplemental resources for the topic at hand.

- **Learning Objectives/Chapter Outlines/Key Terms/Visuals:** A list of learning objectives, chapter outlines, definitions of key terms, and PowerPoint slides supplement each chapter of the textbook.
- **Writing On and Offline:** Online activities encourage students to activate new concepts in writing, applying what they've learned in class.
- **Interactive Exercises:** Crossword puzzles, matching exercises, and multiple-choice questions reinforce comprehension of key concepts and grammar rules.
- **Additional Resources:** Offerings include a comprehensive glossary; guides to using the Internet, avoiding plagiarism, and doing electronic research; a study skills primer, author links, and more.

Learning Aids Accompanying the Book

Supplements for Instructors

- An *Annotated Instructor's Edition* (ISBN 0-07-296274-7) consists of the student text complete with answers to all activities and tests, followed by an Instructor's Guide featuring teaching suggestions and a model syllabus.
- An *Online Learning Center* (www.mhhe.com/langan) offers a host of instructional aids and additional resources for instructors, including a comprehensive computerized test bank, the downloadable Instructor's Manual and Test Bank, online resources for writing instructors, and more.

Copyright ©2005 The McGraw-Hill Companies, Inc. All rights reserved.

- An *Instructor's CD-ROM* (0-07-296272-0) offers all of the above supplements in a convenient offline format.

- The *Classroom Performance System* (CPS by eInstruction) is an easy-to-use, wireless response system that allows instructors to conduct quizzes and polls in class and provide students with immediate feedback. McGraw-Hill provides a database of questions compatible with *English Skills* and *English Skills with Readings*. To download the database, go to the *English Skills* OLC at www.mhhe.com/langan. For further details on CPS, go to www.mhhe.com/einstruction.

- *PageOut!* helps instructors create graphically pleasing and professional web pages for their courses, in addition to providing classroom management, collaborative learning, and content management tools. *PageOut!* is **FREE** to adopters of McGraw-Hill textbooks and learning materials. Learn more at www.mhhe.com/pageout.

Supplements for Students

- An *Online Learning Center* (www.mhhe.com/langan), offers a host of instructional aids and additional resources for students, including self-correcting exercises, writing activities for additional practice, guides to doing research on the Internet and avoiding plagiarism, useful web links, and more. The site is powered by Catalyst, McGraw-Hill's innovative writing and research resource.

- A *Student CD-ROM* (0-07-296275-5) offers all the resources of the Student's Online Learning Center and more in a convenient offline format.

- *AllWrite! 2.1* is an interactive, browser-based tutorial program that provides an online handbook, comprehensive diagnostic pretests and posttests, and extensive practice exercises in every area.

Dictionary and Vocabulary Resources

- *Random House Webster's College Dictionary* (0-07-240011-0): This authoritative dictionary includes over 160,000 entries and 175,000 definitions. The most commonly used definitions are always listed first, so students can find what they need quickly.

- *The Merriam-Webster Dictionary* (0-07-310057-9), based on the best-selling Merriam-Webster's Collegiate Dictionary, contains over 70,000 definitions.

- *The Merriam-Webster Thesaurus* (0-07-310067-6): This handy paperback thesaurus contains over 157,000 synonyms, antonyms, related and contrasted words, and idioms.

Copyright ©2005 The McGraw-Hill Companies, Inc. All rights reserved.

- *Merriam-Webster's Vocabulary Builder* (0-07-310069-2) introduces 3,000 words, and includes quizzes to test progress.

- *Merriam-Webster's Notebook Dictionary* (0-07-299091-0): An extremely concise reference to the words that form the core of the English vocabulary, this popular dictionary, conveniently designed for 3-ring binders, provides words and information at students' fingertips.

- *Merriam-Webster's Notebook Thesaurus* (0-07-310068-4) is designed for 3-ring binders, and helps the student search for words they might need today. It provides concise, clear guidance for over 157,000 word choices.

- *Merriam-Webster's Collegiate Dictionary and Thesaurus, Electronic Edition* (0-07-310070-6): Available on CD-ROM, this online dictionary contains thousands of new words and meanings from all areas of human endeavor, including electronic technology, the sciences, and popular culture.

You can contact your local McGraw-Hill representative or consult McGraw-Hill's Web site at **www.mhhe.com/english** for more information on the supplements that accompany *English Skills with Readings, 6th Edition.*

Acknowledgments

Reviewers who have contributed to this edition through their helpful comments include

Vivian Brown-Carman, Bergen Community College

Anne J. Chamberlain, Community College of Baltimore County

Molly Emmons, College of the Redwoods – Del Norte

Rita Fork, El Camino College

Jeanne Grandchamp, Bristol Community College

Peggy F. Hopper, Walters State Community College

Christy Hughes, Orangeburg-Calhoun Technical College

Jennifer Leamy, Wake Technical Community College

Robert Miller, Terra Community College

Kathleen Shaw, Montgomery County Community College

Elizabeth W. Smith, Manatee Community College

Pam Smith, Copper Mountain College

Judy Stockstill, Central Christian College

Loretta S. Stribling, Whatcom Community College

Mary McCaslin Thompson, Anoka Ramsey Community College

Starlette Vaughn, Sacramento City College

I am also grateful for help provided by Janet M. Goldstein, Beth Johnson, and Paul Langan, as well as for the support of my McGraw-Hill editor, Alexis Walker.

John Langan

1 An Introduction to Writing

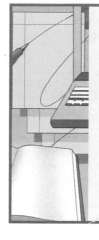

Copyright ©2006 The McGraw-Hill Companies, Inc. All rights reserved.

This chapter will

- introduce you to the basic principles of effective writing
- ask you to write a simple paragraph
- explain how the book is organized
- suggest a sequence for using the book

This chapter will also

- present writing as both a skill and a process of discovery
- suggest keeping a journal

English Skills with Readings grows out of experiences I had when learning how to write. My early memories of writing in school are not pleasant. In the middle grades I remember getting back paper after paper on which the only comment was "Handwriting very poor." In high school, the night before a book report was due, I would work anxiously at a card table in my bedroom. I was nervous and sweaty because I felt out of my element, like a person who knows only how to open a can of soup being asked to cook a five-course meal. The act of writing was hard enough, and my feeling that I wasn't any good at it made me hate the process all the more.

Luckily, in college I had an instructor who changed my negative attitude about writing. During my first semester in composition, I realized that my instructor repeatedly asked two questions about any paper I wrote: "What is your point?" and "What is your support for that point?" I learned that sound writing consists basically of making a point and then providing evidence to support or develop that point. As I understood, practiced, and mastered these and other principles, I began to write effective papers. By the end of the semester, much of my uneasiness and bad feelings about writing had disappeared. I knew that competent writing is a skill that I or anyone can learn with practice. It is a nuts-and-bolts process consisting of

3

a number of principles and techniques that can be studied and mastered. Further, I learned that while there is no alternative to the work required for competent writing, there is satisfaction to be gained through such work. I no longer feared or hated writing, for I knew I could work at it and be good at it.

English Skills with Readings explains in a clear and direct way the four basic principles you must learn to write effectively:

1   Start with a clearly stated point.

2   Provide logical, detailed support for your point.

3   Organize and connect your supporting material.

4   Revise and edit so that your sentences are effective and error-free.

Part One of this book explains each of these steps in detail and provides many practice materials to help you master them.

Understanding Point and Support

An Important Difference between Writing and Talking

In everyday conversation, you make all kinds of points, or assertions. You say, for example, "I hate my job"; "Sue's a really generous person"; or "That exam was unfair." The points that you make concern such personal matters as well as, at times, larger issues: "A lot of doctors are arrogant"; "The death penalty should exist for certain crimes"; "Tobacco and marijuana are equally dangerous."

The people you are talking with do not always challenge you to give reasons for your statements. They may know why you feel as you do, or they may already agree with you, or they simply may not want to put you on the spot; and so they do not always ask "Why?" But the people who *read* what you write may not know you, agree with you, or feel in any way obliged to you. If you want to communicate effectively with readers, you must provide solid evidence for any point you make. An important difference, then, between writing and talking is this: *In writing, any idea that you advance must be supported with specific reasons or details.*

Think of your readers as reasonable people. They will not take your views on faith, but they *are* willing to consider what you say as long as you support it. Therefore, remember to support with specific evidence any statement that you make.

Point and Support in Two Cartoons

The following two *Peanuts* cartoons will show you quickly and clearly what you need to write effectively. You need to know how to (1) make a point and (2) support the point.

Look for a moment at the following cartoon:

PEANUTS: © United Feature Syndicate, Inc.

See if you can answer the following questions:

- What is Snoopy's point in his paper?

  Your answer: His point is that _____

- What is his support for his point?

  Your answer: _____

Snoopy's point, of course, is that dogs are superior to cats. But he offers no support whatsoever to back up his point! There are two jokes here. First, he is a dog, so he is naturally going to believe that dogs are superior. The other joke is that his evidence ("They just are, and that's all there is to it!") is no more than empty words. His somewhat guilty look in the last panel suggests that he knows he has not proved his point. To write effectively, you must provide *real* support for your points and opinions.

Copyright ©2006 The McGraw-Hill Companies, Inc. All rights reserved.

Now look at this other cartoon about Snoopy as a writer.

PEANUTS: © United Feature Syndicate, Inc.

See if you can answer the following questions:

• What is Snoopy's point about the hero in his writing?

   Your answer: His point is that _____

• What is his support for his point?

   Your answer: _____

   Snoopy's point is that the hero's life has been a disaster. This time, Snoopy has an abundance of support for his point: the hapless hero never had any luck, money, friends, love, laughter, applause, fame, or answers. To write effectively, you must do what Snoopy has done here: make a clear point and provide plenty of support for that point.

Point and Support in a Paragraph

Suppose you and a friend are talking about jobs you have had. You might say about a particular job, "That was the worst one I ever had. A lot of hard work and not much money." For your friend, that might be enough to make your point, and you would not really have to explain your statement. But in writing, your point would have to be backed up with specific reasons and details.

Below is a paragraph, written by a student named Gene Hert, about his worst job. A *paragraph* is a short paper of 150 to 200 words. It usually consists of an opening point called a *topic sentence* followed by a series of sentences supporting that point.

My Job in an Apple Plant

Working in an apple plant was the worst job I ever had. First of all, the work was physically hard. For ten hours a night, I took cartons that rolled down a metal track and stacked them onto wooden skids in a tractor trailer. Each carton contained twenty-five pounds of bottled apple juice, and they came down the track almost nonstop. The second bad feature of the job was the pay. I was getting the minimum wage at that time, $3.65 an hour, plus a quarter extra for working the night shift. I had to work over sixty hours a week to get decent take-home pay. Finally, I hated the working conditions. We were limited to two ten-minute breaks and an unpaid half hour for lunch. Most of my time was spent outside on the loading dock in near-zero-degree temperatures. I was very lonely on the job because I had no interests in common with the other truck loaders. I felt this isolation especially when the production line shut down for the night, and I spent two hours by myself cleaning the apple vats. The vats were an ugly place to be on a cold morning, and the job was a bitter one to have.

Notice what the details in this paragraph do. They provide you, the reader, with a basis for understanding *why* the writer makes the point that is made. Through this specific evidence, the writer has explained and successfully communicated the idea that this job was his worst one.

The evidence that supports the point in a paragraph often consists of a series of reasons followed by examples and details that support the reasons. That is true of the paragraph above: three reasons are provided, with examples and details that back up those reasons. Supporting evidence in a paper can also consist of anecdotes, personal experiences, facts, studies, statistics, and the opinions of experts.

Copyright ©2006 The McGraw-Hill Companies, Inc. All rights reserved.

ACTIVITY 1

The paragraph on the apple plant, like almost any piece of effective writing, has two essential parts: (1) a point is advanced, and (2) that point is then supported. Taking a minute to outline the paragraph will help you understand these basic parts clearly. Add the words needed to complete the outline.

Point: Working in an apple plant is the worst job I ever had.

Reason 1: _____

    a. Loaded cartons onto skids for ten hours a night

    b. _____

Reason 2: _____

    a. _____

    b. Had to work sixty hours for decent take-home pay

Reason 3: _____

    a. Two ten-minute breaks and an unpaid lunch

    b. _____

    c. Loneliness on job

        (1) No interests in common with other workers

        (2) By myself for two hours cleaning the apple vats

ACTIVITY 2

See if you can complete the statements below.

1. An important difference between writing and talking is that in writing we absolutely must _____ any statement we make.

2. A _____ is made up of a point and a collection of specifics that support the point.

ACTIVITY 3

An excellent way to get a feel for the paragraph is to write one. Your instructor may ask you to do that now. The only guidelines you need to follow are the ones described here. There is an advantage to writing a paragraph right away, at a point where you have had almost no instruction. This first paragraph will give a

Copyright ©2006 The McGraw-Hill Companies, Inc. All rights reserved.

quick sense of your needs as a writer and will provide a baseline—a standard of comparison that you and your instructor can use to measure your writing progress during the semester.

Here, then, is your topic: Write a paragraph on the best or worst job you have ever had. Provide three reasons why your job was the best or the worst, and give plenty of details to develop each of your three reasons.

Notice that the sample paragraph, "My Job in an Apple Plant," has the same format your paragraph should have. You should do what this author has done:

- State a point in the first sentence.
- Give three reasons to support the point.
- Introduce each reason clearly with signal words (such as *First of all, Second,* and *Finally*).
- Provide details that develop each of the three reasons.

Write your paragraph on a separate sheet of paper. After completing the paragraph, hand it in to your instructor.

An Overview: How the Book Is Organized

English Skills with Readings is divided into six parts. Each part will be discussed briefly below. Questions appear, not to test you but simply to introduce you to the book's central ideas and organization. Your instructor may ask you to fill in the answers or just to note the answers in your head.

Part One (Pages 1–172) A good way to get a quick sense of any part of a book is to look at the table of contents. Turn back to the contents at the start of this book (pages vii–xi) to answer the following questions:

- What is the title of Part One? _____

- "An Introduction to Writing" is the opening chapter of Part One. How many

  subheads are included in this chapter? _____

- Chapter 2 describes the steps in the writing process. Fill in the two missing steps:

  Step 1: _____

  Step 2: Writing a First Draft

Step 3: _____

Step 4: Editing

- The title of the third chapter in Part One is "The First and Second Steps in Writing."
  What are the first and second steps in writing?

  _____

  _____

- The title of the fourth chapter in Part One is "The Third Step in Writing." What
  is the third step in writing?

  _____

- The next chapter introduces the fourth step in writing, which includes all the
  skills involved in writing clear, error-free sentences. Most of these sentence
  skills are covered later in the book, where they can be easily referred to as
  needed. In which part of the book are sentence skills treated?

  _____

- The title of the final chapter in Part One is "Four Bases for Revising Writing."
  Fill in the first four subheads following the title.

  Subhead 1. _____

  Subhead 2. _____

  Subhead 3. _____

  Subhead 4. _____

Inside Front Cover   Turn now to the inside front cover. You will see there a (*fill
in the missing word*) _____ of the four bases of effective writing.
These four standards can be used as a guide for every paper that you write. They
are summarized on the inside front cover for easy reference. If you follow them,
you are almost sure to write effective papers.

Part Two (Pages 173–298)   The title of Part Two is

_____

Part Two, as the title explains, is concerned with different ways to develop
paragraphs. Read the preview on page 174 and record here how many types of

paragraph development are explained: _____.

PART ONE **Preview**

Part One begins, in Chapter 1, by introducing you to the basic principles of effective writing. You learn that what is most important in writing is to make a point and support that point. This chapter next provides an overview of how the book is organized. It then goes on to discuss the benefits of paragraph writing and two key ideas about writing. The first key idea is that writing is a skill that anyone can learn with practice. The second key idea is that one can often discover a subject in the very process of writing about it. Finally, the chapter presents journal writing and offers some suggestions on how to use the text.

Chapter 2, "The Writing Process," explains and illustrates the sequence of steps in writing an effective paragraph. You learn how prewriting, revising, and editing will help with every paper that you write.

Chapter 3, "The First and Second Steps in Writing," shows you, in detail, how to begin your paper with a point and provide specific evidence to support that point.

Chapter 4, "The Third Step in Writing," shows you how to organize and connect the specific evidence in a paper.

Chapter 5, "The Fourth Step in Writing," shows you how to revise so that your sentences flow smoothly and clearly and how to edit so that your sentences are error-free.

Chapter 6, "Four Bases for Revising Writing," explains how four bases—unity, support, coherence, and sentence skills—will help you evaluate and revise papers.

Copyright ©2006 The McGraw-Hill Companies, Inc. All rights reserved.

PART ONE

Basic Principles of Effective Writing

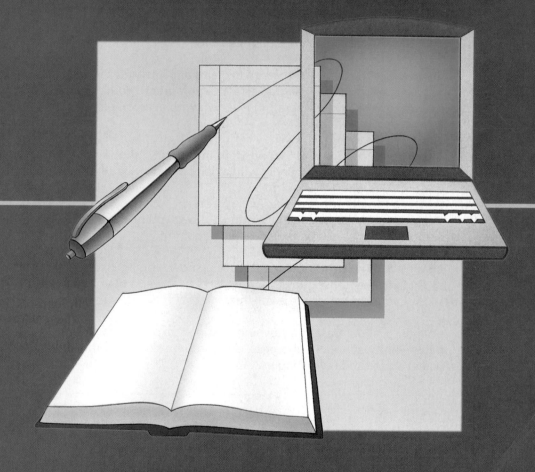

Turn to the first method of paragraph development, "Providing Examples," on page 185. You will see that the chapter opens with a brief introduction followed by several paragraphs written by students. Then you will see a series of six (*fill in the missing word*) _____ to help you evaluate the descriptive paragraphs in terms of unity, support, and coherence. Finally, there is a series of writing topics that can be developed by means of description. The same format is used for each of the other methods of paragraph development in Part Two.

Part Three (Pages 299–338) The title of Part Three is

_____

As the preview notes, in Part Two you were asked to write single paragraphs; in Part Three, you are asked to write papers of more than one (*fill in the missing word*) _____.

Part Four (Pages 339–352) The title of Part Four is

_____

Part Four gives you advice on a number of important skills that are related to writing. You can refer to this part of the book whenever the need arises.

• Which chapter will give you information about research?

_____

Part Five (Pages 353–584) The title of Part Five is

_____

Part Five is the longest part of the book. It gives you practice in skills needed to write clear and effective sentences. You will note from the table of contents that it contains a diagnostic test, the skills themselves, mastery tests, editing tests, and an achievement test. The skills are grouped into four sections:

"Grammar," "Mechanics," (*fill in the missing word*) "_____," and "Word Use."

Part Six (Pages 585–736) The title of Part Six is

_____

Part Six contains seventeen reading selections, along with activities that will help you improve both reading and writing skills. Turn to the first selection, "All the Good Things," on page 592. You will see that the selection begins with a short

Copyright ©2006 The McGraw-Hill Companies Inc. All rights reserved.

preview that gives you background information on the piece. Following the selection there are ten comprehension *(fill in the missing word)* _____ to help you practice important reading skills. Then, after a series of discussion questions that have to do with both reading and writing, there are several writing assignments.

Inside Back Cover   On the inside back cover is an alphabetical list of *(fill in the missing words)* _____.
Your instructor may use these symbols in marking your papers. In addition, you can use the page numbers in the list for quick reference to a specific sentence skill.

Charts in the Book   In addition to the guides on the inside front and back covers, several charts have been provided in the book to help you take responsibility for your own learning.

- What are the names of the charts on pages 742–745?

_____

_____

_____

Benefits of Paragraph Writing

Paragraph writing offers at least three benefits. First of all, mastering the structure of the paragraph will help make you a better writer. For other courses, you'll often do writing that will be variations on the paragraph form—for example, exam answers, summaries, response papers, and brief reports. In addition, paragraphs serve as the basic building blocks of essays, the most common form of writing in college. The basic structure of the traditional paragraph, with its emphasis on a clear point and well-organized, logical support, will help you write effective essays and almost every kind of paper that you will have to do.

Second, the discipline of writing a paragraph will strengthen your skills as a reader and listener. You'll become more critically aware of other writers' and speakers' ideas and the evidence they provide—or fail to provide—to support those ideas.

Most important, paragraph writing will make you a stronger thinker. Writing a solidly reasoned paragraph requires mental discipline and close attention to a set

Copyright ©2006 The McGraw-Hill Companies, Inc. All rights reserved.

of logical rules. Creating a paragraph in which there is an overall topic sentence supported by well-reasoned, convincing evidence is more challenging than writing a free-form or expressive paper. Such a paragraph obliges you to carefully sort out, think through, and organize your ideas. You'll learn to discover and express just what your ideas are and to develop those ideas in a sound and logical way. Traditional paragraph writing, in short, will train your mind to think clearly, and that ability will prove to be of value in every phase of your life.

Writing as a Skill

A sure way to wreck your chances of learning how to write competently is to believe that writing is a "natural gift" rather than a learned skill. People with such an attitude think that they are the only ones for whom writing is unbearably difficult. They feel that everyone else finds writing easy or at least tolerable. Such people typically say, "I'm not any good at writing" or "English was not one of my good subjects." They imply that they simply do not have a talent for writing, while others do. The result of this attitude is that people try to avoid writing, and when they do write, they don't try their best. Their attitude becomes a self-fulfilling prophecy: Their writing fails chiefly because they have brainwashed themselves into thinking that they don't have the "natural talent" needed to write. Unless their attitude changes, they probably will not learn how to write effectively.

A realistic attitude about writing must build on the idea that *writing is a skill.* It is a skill like driving, typing, or cooking, and like any skill, it can be learned. If you have the determination to learn, this book will give you the extensive practice needed to develop your writing skills.

Many people find it difficult to do the intense, active thinking that clear writing demands. (Perhaps television has made us all so passive that the active thinking necessary in both writing and reading now seems harder than ever.) It is frightening to sit down before a blank sheet of paper or a computer screen and know that an hour later, nothing on it may be worth keeping. It is frustrating to discover how much of a challenge it is to transfer thoughts and feelings from one's head into words. It is upsetting to find that an apparently simple writing subject often turns out to be complicated. But writing is not an automatic process: we will not get something for nothing—and we should not expect to. For almost everyone, competent writing comes from plain hard work—from determination, sweat, and head-on battle. The good news is that the skill of writing can be mastered, and if you are ready to work, you will learn what you need to know.

ACTIVITY

To get a sense of just how you regard writing, read the following statements. Put a check (✓) beside those statements with which you agree. This activity is not a test, so try to be as honest as possible.

_____ 1. A good writer should be able to sit down and write a paper straight through without stopping.

_____ 2. Writing is a skill that anyone can learn with practice.

_____ 3. I'll never be good at writing because I make too many mistakes in spelling, grammar, and punctuation.

_____ 4. Because I dislike writing, I always start a paper at the last possible minute.

_____ 5. I've always done poorly in English, and I don't expect that to change.

Now read the following comments about the five statements. The comments will help you see if your attitude is hurting or helping your efforts to become a better writer.

Comments

- Statement 1: *"A good writer should be able to sit down and write a paper straight through without stopping."*

    Statement 1 is not true. Writing is, in fact, a process. It is done not in one easy step but in a series of steps, and seldom at one sitting. If you cannot do a paper all at once, that simply means you are like most of the other people on the planet. It is harmful to carry around the false idea that writing should be easy.

- Statement 2: *"Writing is a skill that anyone can learn with practice."*

    Statement 2 is absolutely true. Writing is a skill, like driving or word processing, that you can master with hard work. If you want to learn to write, you can. It is as simple as that. If you believe this, you are ready to learn how to become a competent writer.

    Some people hold the false belief that writing is a natural gift, which some have and others do not. Because of this belief, they never make a truly honest effort to learn to write—and so they never learn.

- Statement 3: *"I'll never be good at writing because I make too many mistakes in spelling, grammar, and punctuation."*

The first concern in good writing should be content—what you have to say. Your ideas and feelings are what matter most. You should not worry about spelling, grammar, or punctuation while working on content.

Unfortunately, some people are so self-conscious about making mistakes that they do not focus on what they want to say. They need to realize that a paper is best done in stages, and that applying the rules can and should wait until a later stage in the writing process. Through review and practice, you will eventually learn how to follow the rules with confidence.

- Statement 4: *"Because I dislike writing, I always start a paper at the last possible minute."*

   This habit is all too common. You feel you are going to do poorly, and then behave in a way that ensures you *will* do poorly! Your attitude is so negative that you defeat yourself—not even allowing enough time to really try.

   Again, what you need to realize is that writing is a process. Because it is done in steps, you don't have to get it right all at once. If you allow yourself enough time, you'll find a way to make a paper come together.

- Statement 5: *"I've always done poorly in English, and I don't expect that to change."*

   How you may have performed in the *past* does not control how you can perform in the *present*. Even if you did poorly in English in high school, it is in your power to make English one of your best subjects in college. If you believe writing can be learned and then work hard at it, you *will* become a better writer.

   In conclusion, your attitude is crucial. If you believe you are a poor writer and always will be, chances are you will not improve. If you realize you can become a better writer, chances are you *will* improve. Depending on how you allow yourself to think, you can be your own best friend or your own worst enemy.

Writing as a Process of Discovery

In addition to believing that writing is a natural gift, many people believe, mistakenly, that writing should flow in a simple, straight line from the writer's head onto the page. But writing is seldom an easy, one-step journey in which a finished paper comes out in a first draft. The truth is that *writing is a process of discovery* which involves a series of steps, and those steps are very often a zigzag journey. Look at the following illustrations of the writing process:

Copyright ©2006 The McGraw-Hill Companies, Inc. All rights reserved.

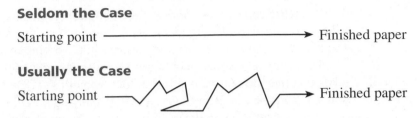

Very often, writers do not discover just what they want to write about until they explore their thoughts in writing. For example, Gene Hert had been asked to write about a best or worst job. Only after he did some freewriting on good and bad jobs did he realize that the most interesting details centered on his job at an apple plant. He discovered his subject in the course of writing.

Another student, Rhonda, talking afterward about a paper she wrote, explained that at first her topic was how she relaxed with her children. But as she accumulated details, she realized after a page of writing that the words *relax* and *children* simply did not go together. Her details were really examples of how she *enjoyed* her children, not how she *relaxed* with them. She sensed that the real focus of her writing should be what she did by herself to relax, and then she thought suddenly that the best time of her week was Thursday after school. "A light clicked on in my head," she explained. "I knew I had my paper." Then it was a matter of detailing exactly what she did to relax on Thursday evenings. Her paper, "How I Relax," is on page 89.

The point is that writing is often a process of continuing discovery. As you write, you may suddenly switch direction or double back. You may be working on a topic sentence and realize suddenly that it could be your concluding thought. Or you may be developing a supporting idea and then decide that it should be the main point of your paper. Chapter 2 will treat the writing process directly. What is important to remember here is that writers frequently do not know their exact destination as they begin to write. Very often they discover the direction and shape of a paper during the process of writing.

Keeping a Journal

Because writing is a skill, it makes sense that the more you practice writing, the better you will write. One excellent way to get practice in writing, even before you begin composing formal paragraphs, is to keep a daily or almost daily journal. Writing a journal will help you develop the habit of thinking on paper and will show you how ideas can be discovered in the process of writing. A journal can make writing a familiar part of your life and can serve as a continuing source of ideas for papers.

Copyright ©2006 The McGraw-Hill Companies, Inc. All rights reserved.

At some point during the day—perhaps during a study period after your last class of the day, or right before dinner, or right before going to bed—spend fifteen minutes or so writing in your journal. Keep in mind that you do not have to plan what to write about, or be in the mood to write, or worry about making mistakes as you write; just write down whatever words come out. You should write at least one page in each session.

You may want to use a notebook that you can easily carry with you for on-the-spot writing. Or you may decide to write on loose-leaf paper that can be transferred later to a journal folder on your desk. No matter how you proceed, be sure to date all entries.

Your instructor may ask you to make journal entries a specific number of times a week, for a specific number of weeks. He or she may have you turn in your journal every so often for review and feedback. If you are keeping the journal on your own, try to make entries three to five times a week every week of the semester. Your journal can serve as a sourcebook of ideas for possible papers. More important, keeping a journal will help you develop the habit of thinking on paper, and it can help you make writing a familiar part of your life.

ACTIVITY

Following is an excerpt from one student's journal. (Sentence-skills mistakes have been corrected to improve readability.) As you read, look for a general point and supporting material that could be the basis for an interesting paper.

October 6

Today a woman came into our department at the store and wanted to know if we had any scrap lumber ten feet long. Ten feet! "Lady," I said, "anything we have that's ten feet long sure as heck isn't scrap." When the boss heard me say that, he almost canned me. My boss is a company man, down to his toe tips. He wants to make a big impression on his bosses, and he'll run us around like mad all night to make himself look good. He's the most ambitious man I've ever met. If I don't transfer out of Hardware soon, I'm going to go crazy on this job. I'm not ready to quit, though. The time is not right. I want to be here for a year and have another job lined up and have other things right before I quit. It's good the boss wasn't around tonight when another customer wanted me to carry a bookcase he had bought out to his car. He didn't ask me to help him—he <u>expected</u> me to help him. I hate that kind of "You're my servant" attitude, and I told him that carrying stuff out to cars wasn't my job. Ordinarily I go out of my way to give people a hand, but not guys like him. . . .

- If the writer of this journal is looking for an idea for a paper, he can probably find several in this single entry. For example, he might write a narrative supporting the point that "In my sales job I have to deal with some irritating customers." See if you can find another idea in this entry that might be the basis for an interesting paragraph. Write your point in the space below.

_____

- Take fifteen minutes to prepare a journal entry right now on this day in your life. On a separate sheet of paper, just start writing about anything that you have said, heard, thought, or felt, and let your thoughts take you where they may.

Using This Text

Here is a suggested sequence for using this book if you are working on your own.

1   After completing this introduction, read the remaining five chapters in Part One and work through as many of the activities as you need to master the ideas in these chapters. By the end of Part One, you will have covered all the basic theory needed to write effective papers.

2   Turn to Part Five and take the diagnostic test. The test will help you determine what sentence skills you need to review. Study those skills one or two at a time while you continue to work on other parts of the book. These skills will help you write effective, error-free sentences.

3   What you do next depends on course requirements, individual needs, or both. You will want to practice at least several different kinds of paragraph development in Part Two. If your time is limited, be sure to include "Providing Examples," "Explaining a Process," "Comparing or Contrasting," and "Arguing a Position."

4   After you develop skill in writing effective paragraphs, go on to practice writing one or more of the several-paragraph essays described in Part Three.

5   Turn to Part Four as needed for help with projects that involve research.

6   Read at least one of the seventeen selections in Part Six every week, always being sure to work through the two sets of questions that follow each reading.

Remember that, for your convenience, the book includes the following:

- On the inside front cover, there is a checklist of the four basic steps in effective writing.

- On the inside back cover, there is a list of commonly used correction symbols.

Get into the habit of referring to these guides on a regular basis; they'll help you produce clearly thought-out, well-written papers.

English Skills with Readings will help you learn, practice, and apply the thinking and writing skills you need to communicate effectively. But the starting point must be your determination to do the work needed to become a strong writer. The ability to express yourself clearly and logically can open doors of opportunity for you, both in school and in your career. If you decide—*and only you can decide*—that you want such language power, this book will help you reach that goal.

Copyright ©2006 The McGraw-Hill Companies, Inc. All rights reserved.

2 The Writing Process

> *This chapter will explain and illustrate*
> - the sequence of steps in writing an effective paragraph
> - prewriting
> - revising
> - editing

Chapter 1 introduced you to the paragraph form and some basics of writing. This chapter will explain and illustrate the sequence of steps in writing an effective paragraph. In particular, the chapter will focus on prewriting and revising— strategies that can help with every paper that you write.

For many people, writing is a process that involves the following steps:

1   Discovering a point—often through prewriting.

2   Developing solid support for the point—often through more prewriting.

3   Organizing the supporting material and writing it out in a first draft.

4   Revising and then editing carefully to ensure an effective, error-free paper.

Learning this sequence will help give you confidence when the time comes to write. You'll know that you can use prewriting as a way to think on paper (or at the keyboard) and to discover gradually just what ideas you want to develop. You'll understand that there are four clear-cut goals to aim for in your writing—unity, support, organization, and error-free sentences. You'll realize that you can use revising to rework a paper until it is strong and effective. And you'll be able to edit a paper so that your sentences are clear and error-free.

Prewriting

Copyright ©2006 The McGraw-Hill Companies, Inc. All rights reserved.

If you are like many people, you may have trouble getting started writing. A mental block may develop when you sit down before a blank sheet of paper or a blank screen. You may not be able to think of an interesting topic or a point to make about your topic. Or you may have trouble coming up with specific details to support your point. And even after starting a paper, you may hit snags—moments when you wonder "What else can I say?" or "Where do I go next?"

The following pages describe five techniques that will help you think about and develop a topic and get words on paper: (1) freewriting, (2) questioning, (3) making a list, (4) clustering, and (5) preparing a scratch outline. These prewriting techniques help you think about and create material, and they are a central part of the writing process.

Technique 1: Freewriting

When you do not know what to write about a subject or when you are blocked in writing, freewriting sometimes helps. In *freewriting,* you write on your topic for ten minutes. You do not worry about spelling or punctuating correctly, about erasing mistakes, about organizing material, or about finding exact words. You just write without stopping. If you get stuck for words, you write "I am looking for something to say" or repeat words until something comes. There is no need to feel inhibited, since mistakes *do not count* and you do not have to hand in your paper.

Freewriting will limber up your writing muscles and make you familiar with the act of writing. It is a way to break through mental blocks about writing. Since you do not have to worry about mistakes, you can focus on discovering what you want to say about a subject. Your initial ideas and impressions will often become clearer after you have gotten them down on paper, and they may lead to other impressions and ideas. Through continued practice in freewriting, you will develop the habit of thinking as you write. And you will learn a technique that is a helpful way to get started on almost any paper.

Freewriting: A Student Model

Gene Hert's essay "My Job in an Apple Plant" on page 7 was written in response to an assignment to write a paper on the best or worst job he ever had. Gene began by doing some general freewriting and thinking about his jobs. Here is his freewriting:

I have had good and bad jobs, that's for sure. It was great earning money for the first time. I shoveled snow for my neighbor, a friend of mine and I did the work and had snowball fights along the way. I remember my neighbor reaching into his pocket and pulling out several dollars and handing us the money, it was like magic. Then there was the lawnmowing, which was also a good job. I mowed my aunts lawn while she was away at work. Then I'd go sit by myself in her cool living room and have a coke she left in the refrigarator for me. And look through all her magazines. Then there was the apple plant job I had after high school. That was a worst job that left me totaly wiped out at the end of my shift. Lifting cartons and cartons of apple juice for bosses that treated us like slaves. The cartons coming and coming all night long. I started early in the evening and finished the next morning. I still remember how tired I was. Driving back home the first time. That was a lonely job and a hard job and I don't eat apples anymore.

At this point, Gene read over his notes, and as he later commented, "I realized that I had several potential topics. I said to myself, 'What point can I make that I can cover in a paragraph? What do I have the most information about?' I decided to narrow my topic down to my awful job at the apple plant. I figured I would have lots of interesting details for that topic." Gene then did a more focused freewriting to accumulate details for a paragraph on his bad job:

The job I remember most is the worst job I ever had. I worked in an apple plant, I put in very long hours and would be totaly beat after ten hours of work. All the time lifting cartons of apple juice which would come racing down a metal track. The guy with me was a bit lazy at times, and I would be one man doing a two-man job. The cartons would go into a tracter trailer, we would have to throw down wooden skids to put the cartons on, then wed have to move the metal track as we filled up the truck. There is no other job I have had that even compares to this job, it was a lot worse than it seems. The bosses treated us like slaves and the company paid us like slaves. I would work all night from 7 p.m. and drive home in the morning at 5 a.m. and be bone tired. I remember my arms and sholders were so tired after the first night. I had trouble turning the steering wheel of my father's car.

Comment   Notice that there are problems with spelling, grammar, and punctuation in Gene's freewriting. Gene was not worried about such matters, nor should he have been. At this stage, he just wanted to do some thinking on paper and get some material down on the page. He knew that this was a good first step, a good way of getting started, and that he would then be able to go on and shape that material.

You should take the same approach when freewriting: explore your topic without worrying at all about being "correct." Figuring out what you want to say and getting raw material down on the page should have all of your attention at this early stage of the writing process.

Copyright ©2006 The McGraw-Hill Companies, Inc. All rights reserved

ACTIVITY

To get a sense of the freewriting process, take a sheet of paper and freewrite about different jobs you have had and what you liked or did not like about them. See how much material you can accumulate in ten minutes. And remember not to worry about "mistakes"; you're just thinking on paper.

Technique 2: Questioning

In *questioning*, you generate ideas and details by asking as many questions as you can think of about your subject. Such questions include *Why? When? Where? Who? How? In what ways?*

Here are questions that Gene Hert asked while further developing his paper:

Questioning: A Student Model

Questions	Answers
What did I hate about the job?	Very hard work. Poor pay. Mean bosses.
How was the work hard?	Nonstop cartons of apple juice. Cartons became very heavy.
Why was pay poor?	$3.65 an hour (minimum wage at the time). Only a quarter more for working the second shift. Only good money was in overtime—where you got time-and-a-half. No double time.
How were the bosses mean?	Yelled at some workers. Showed no appreciation. Created bad working conditions.
In what ways were working conditions bad?	Unheated truck in zero-degree weather. Floor of tractor trailer was cold steel. Breaks were limited—only two of them. Lonely job.

Comment Asking questions can be an effective way of getting yourself to think about a topic from different angles. The questions can help you generate details about a topic and get ideas on how to organize those details. Notice how asking questions gives Gene a better sense of the different reasons why he hated the job.

ACTIVITY

To get a feel for the questioning process, use a sheet of paper to ask yourself a series of questions about your best and worst jobs. See how many details you can accumulate in ten minutes. And remember again not to be concerned about "mistakes," because you are just thinking on paper.

Technique 3: Making a List

In *making a list,* also known as *brainstorming*, you create a list of ideas and details that relate to your subject. Pile these items up, one after another, without trying to sort out major details from minor ones, or trying to put the details in any special order, or even trying to spell words correctly. Your goal is to accumulate raw material by making up a list of everything about your subject that occurs to you.

After freewriting and questioning, Gene made up the following list of details.

Making a List: A Student Model

Apple factory job—worst one I ever had
Bosses were mean
Working conditions were poor
Went to work at 5 P.M., got back at 7 A.M.
Lifted cartons of apple juice for ten hours
Cartons were heavy
Only two ten-minute breaks a night
Pay was only $3.65 an hour
Just quarter extra for night shift
Cost of gas money to and from work
No pay for lunch break
Had to work 60 hours for good take-home pay
Loaded onto wooden skids in a truck
Bosses yelled at some workers
Temperature zero outside
Floors of trucks ice-cold metal
Nonstop pace
Had to clean apple vats after work
Slept, ate, and worked—no social life
No real friends at work

Copyright ©2006 The McGraw-Hill Companies, Inc. All rights reserved.

Comment   One detail led to another as Gene expanded his list. Slowly but surely, more details emerged, some of which he could use in developing his paragraph. By the time he had finished his list, he was ready to plan an outline of his paragraph and then to write his first draft.

ACTIVITY

To get a sense of making a list, use a sheet of paper to list a series of details about one of the best or worst jobs you ever had. Don't worry about deciding whether the details are major or minor; instead, just get down as many details as you can think of in five or ten minutes.

Technique 4: Clustering

Clustering, also known as *diagramming* or *mapping*, is another strategy that can be used to generate material for a paper. This method is helpful for people who like to think in a visual way. In clustering, you use lines, boxes, arrows, and circles to show relationships among the ideas and details that occur to you.

Begin by stating your subject in a few words in the center of a blank sheet of paper. Then, as ideas and details occur to you, put them in boxes or circles around the subject and draw lines to connect them to each other and to the subject. Put minor ideas or details in smaller boxes or circles, and use connecting lines to show how they relate as well.

Keep in mind that there is no right or wrong way of clustering. It is a way to think on paper about how various ideas and details relate to one another. Below is an example of what Gene might have done to develop his ideas:

Clustering: A Student Model

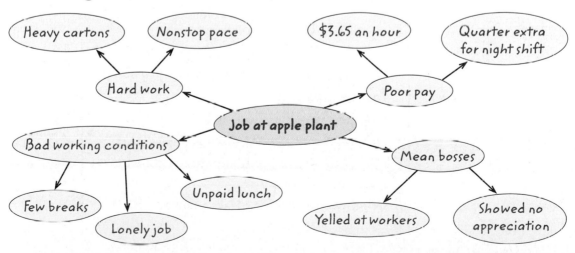

Comment   In addition to helping generate material, clustering often suggests ways to organize ideas and details.

ACTIVITY

Use clustering or diagramming to organize the details about a best or worst job that you created for the previous activity (page 25).

Technique 5: Preparing a Scratch Outline

A scratch outline can be the *single most helpful technique* for writing a good paper. A scratch outline often follows freewriting, questioning, making a list, or clustering, but it may also gradually emerge in the midst of these strategies. In fact, trying to make a scratch outline is a good way to see if you need to do more prewriting. If you cannot come up with a solid outline, then you know you need to do more prewriting to clarify your main point and its several kinds of support.

In a scratch outline, you think carefully about the point you are making, the supporting items for that point, and the order in which you will arrange those items. The scratch outline is a plan or blueprint to help you achieve a unified, supported, and well-organized composition.

Scratch Outline: A Student Model

In Gene's case, as he was working on his list of details, he suddenly realized what the plan of his paragraph could be. He could organize many of his details into one of three supporting groups: (1) the job itself, (2) the pay, and (3) the working conditions. He then went back to the list, crossed out items that he now saw did not fit, and numbered the items according to the group where they fit. Here is what Gene did with his list:

> Apple factory job—worst one I ever had
>
> ~~Bosses were mean~~
>
> 3 Working conditions were poor
>
> ~~Went to work at 5 P.M., got back at 7 A.M.~~
>
> 1 Lifted cartons of apple juice for ten hours
>
> 1 Cartons were heavy
>
> 3 Only two ten-minute breaks a night

Copyright ©2006 The McGraw-Hill Companies, Inc. All rights reserved.

2 Pay was only $3.65 an hour

2 Just quarter extra for night shift

~~Cost of gas money to and from work~~

2 Had to work 60 hours for good take-home pay

1 Loaded onto wooden skids in a truck

~~Bosses yelled at some workers~~

3 Temperature zero outside

~~Floors of trucks ice-cold metal~~

1 Nonstop pace

3 No pay for lunch break

3 Had to clean apple vats after work

~~Slept, ate, and worked—no social life~~

3 No real friends at work

Under the list, Gene was now able to prepare his scratch outline:

The apple plant was my worst job.

1. Hard work

2. Poor pay

3. Poor working conditions

Comment   After all his prewriting, Gene was pleased. He knew that he had a promising paper—one with a clear point and solid support. He saw that he could organize the material into a paragraph with a topic sentence, supporting points, and vivid details. He was now ready to write the first draft of his paragraph, using his outline as a guide. Chances are that if you do enough prewriting and thinking on paper, you will eventually discover the point and support of your paragraph.

ACTIVITY

Create a scratch outline that could serve as a guide if you were to write a paragraph on your best or worst job experience.

Writing a First Draft

When you write a first draft, be prepared to put in additional thoughts and details that did not emerge during prewriting. And don't worry if you hit a snag. Just leave a blank space or add a comment such as "Do later" and press on to finish the paper. Also, don't worry yet about grammar, punctuation, or spelling. You don't want to take time correcting words or sentences that you may decide to remove later. Instead, make it your goal to state your main idea clearly and develop the content of your paper with plenty of specific details.

Writing a First Draft: A Student Model

Here is Gene's first draft, done in longhand:

> ~~The apple plant job was my worst.~~ Working in an apple plant was the worst job I ever had. The work was physicaly hard. For ~~a long time~~ ten hours a night, I stacked cartons that rolled down a metal track in a tracter trailer. Each carton had cans or bottles of apple juice, and they were heavy. At the same time, I had to keep a mental count of all the cartons I had loaded. The pay for the job was a bad feature. I was getting the minamum wage at that time plus a quarter extra for night shift. I had to work a lot to get a decent take-home pay. Working conditions were poor at the apple plant, we were limited to ~~short breaks~~ two ten-minute breaks. The truck-loading dock where I was most of the time was a cold and lonely place. Then by myself cleaning up. DETAILS!

Comment   After Gene finished the first draft, he was able to put it aside until the next day. You will benefit as well if you can allow some time between finishing a draft and starting to revise.

ACTIVITY

See if you can fill in the missing words in the following explanation of Gene's first draft.

1. Gene presents his _____ in the first sentence and then crosses it out and revises it right away to make it read smoothly and clearly.

2. Notice that he continues to accumulate specific supporting details as he writes the draft. For example, he crosses out and replaces "a long time" with the more specific _____; he crosses out and replaces "short breaks" with the more specific _____.

3. There are various misspellings—for example, _____. Gene doesn't worry about spelling at this point. He just wants to get down as much of the substance of his paper as possible.

4. There are various punctuation errors, especially the run-on and the fragment near the (*beginning, middle, end*) _____ of the paragraph.

5. Near the close of his paragraph, Gene can't think of added details to insert, so he simply prints "_____ _____" as a reminder to himself for the next draft.

Revising

Revising is as much a stage in the writing process as prewriting, outlining, and doing the first draft. *Revising* means that you rewrite a paper, building upon what has already been done, in order to make it stronger. One writer has said about revision, "It's like cleaning house—getting rid of all the junk and putting things in the right order." It is not just "straightening up"; instead, you must be ready to roll up your sleeves and do whatever is needed to create an effective paper. Too many students think that a first draft *is* the paper. They start to become writers when they realize that revising a rough draft three or four times is often at the heart of the writing process.

Here are some quick hints that can help make revision easier. First, set your first draft aside for a while. You can then come back to it with a fresher, more objective point of view. Second, work from typed or printed text, preferably double-spaced so you'll have room to handwrite changes later. You'll be able to see the paper more impartially if it is typed than if you were just looking at your own familiar handwriting. Next, read your draft aloud. Hearing how your writing sounds will help you pick up problems with meaning as well as with style. Finally, as you do all these things, write additional thoughts and changes above the lines or in the margins of your paper. Your written comments can serve as a guide when you work on the next draft.

Copyright ©2006 The McGraw-Hill Companies, Inc. All rights reserved.

There are two stages to the revision process:

- Revising content
- Revising sentences

Revising Content

To revise the content of your paper, ask the following questions:

1   Is my paper **unified**?
    - Do I have a main idea that is clearly stated at the beginning of my paragraph?
    - Do all my supporting points truly support and back up my main idea?

2   Is my paper **supported**?
    - Are there separate supporting points for the main idea?
    - Do I have *specific* evidence for each supporting point?
    - Is there *plenty of* specific evidence for the supporting points?

3   Is my paper **organized**?
    - Do I have a clear method of organizing my paper?
    - Do I use transitions and other connecting words?

The next two chapters (Chapters 3 and 4) will give you practice in achieving **unity**, **support**, and **organization** in your writing.

Revising Sentences

To revise individual sentences in your essay, ask the following questions:

1   Do I use *parallelism* to balance my words and ideas?

2   Do I have a *consistent point of view*?

3   Do I use *specific* words?

4   Do I use *active* verbs?

5   Do I use words effectively by *avoiding slang, clichés, pretentious language,* and *wordiness*?

6   Do I *vary my sentences* in length and structure?

Chapter 5 will give you practice in revising sentences.

Revising: A Student Model

For his second draft, Gene used a word-processing program on a computer. He then printed out a double-spaced version of his paragraph, leaving himself plenty of room for handwritten revisions. Here is Gene's second draft plus the handwritten changes and additions that became his third draft:

Working in an apple plant was the worst job I ever had. ~First of all~ The work was

physicaly hard. For ten hours a night, I stacked cartons that rolled down a

metal track in a tracter trailer. Each carton contained ~bottles of~ 25 pounds of bottled apple juice,

and they came ~down the track~ nonstop. ~At the same time, I had to keep a mental count of~

~all the cartons I had loaded.~ The second bad feature ~that made the job a~

~worst one~ was the pay. I was getting the minamum wage at that time, $3.65

an hour. Plus ~just~ a quarter extra for night shift. I had to work ~a lot of hours~ over sixty hours a week

to get decent take-home pay. ~Finally~ I hated the working conditions. We were

limited to two ten-minute breaks and ~the half hour for lunch was not paid.~ an unpaid half hour for lunch

Most of my time was spent outside on the ~loading~ dock in ~cold~ near-zero-degree temperatures. And

I was very lonely on the job, ~because~ I had nothing in common with the other

workers. ~You~ I felt this isolation especially when the production line shut

down for the night, and I had to clean the apple vats. The vats were ~a bad~ an ugly place

to be on a cold morning and the job was a ~bad~ bitter one to have.

Comment   Gene made his changes in longhand as he worked on the second draft. As you will see when you complete the activity below, his revision serves to make the paragraph more unified, supported, and organized.

Copyright ©2006 The McGraw-Hill Companies, Inc. All rights reserved.

ACTIVITY

Fill in the missing words.

1. To clarify the organization, Gene adds at the beginning of the first supporting
    point the transitional phrase "_____," and he sets off
    the third supporting point with the word "_____."

2. In the interest of (*unity, support, organization*) _____,
    he crosses out the sentence "_____." He realizes that
    this sentence is not a relevant detail to support the idea that the work was
    physically hard.

3. To add more (*unity, support, organization*) _____,
    he changes "a lot of hours" to "_____"; he
    changes "on the dock" to "_____"; he changes
    "cold temperatures" to "_____."

4. In the interest of eliminating wordiness, he removes the words
    "_____" from the sixth sentence.

5. To achieve parallelism, Gene changes "the half hour for lunch was not paid"
    to "_____."

6. For greater sentence variety, Gene combines two short sentences,
    beginning the second part of the sentence with the subordinating word
    "_____."

7. To create a consistent point of view, Gene changes "You felt this isolation" to
    "_____."

8. Finally, Gene replaces the somewhat vague "bad" in "The vats were a bad
    place to be on a cold morning, and the job was a bad one to have" with two
    more precise words: "_____" and "_____."

Editing

The last major stage in the writing process is editing—checking a paper for mistakes in grammar, punctuation, usage, and spelling. Editing as well as proofreading (checking a paper for typos and other careless errors) is explained in detail on pages 128–130.

Editing: A Student Model

After typing into his word-processing file all the revisions in his paragraph, Gene printed out another clean draft of the paper. He now turned his attention to editing changes, as shown below:

My Job in an Apple Plant

Working in an apple plant was the worst job I ever had. First of all, the

work was ~~physicaly~~ *physically* hard. For ten hours a night, I took cartons that rolled down

a metal track and stacked them onto wooden skids in a ~~tracter~~ *tractor* trailer. Each

carton contained ~~25~~ *twenty-five* pounds of bottled apple juice, and they came down the

track almost nonstop. The second bad feature of the job was the pay. I was

getting the ~~minamum~~ *minimum* wage at that time, $3.65 an hour, *P*lus just a quarter

extra for working the night shift. I had to work over sixty hours a week to get a

decent take-home pay. Finally, I hated the working conditions. We were limited

to two ten-minute breaks and an unpaid half hour for lunch. Most of my time

was spent outside on the loading dock in near-zero-degree temperatures.

And I was very lonely on the job because I had no interests in common with

the other workers. I felt this isolation especially when the production line

shut down for the night, and ~~I had to clean~~ *spent two hours by myself cleaning* the apple vats. The vats were an

ugly place to be on a cold morning, and the job was a bitter one to have.

Comment   Once again, Gene made his changes in longhand right on the printout of his paper. To note these changes, complete the activity below.

Copyright ©2006 The McGraw-Hill Companies, Inc. All rights reserved.

ACTIVITY

Fill in the missing words.

1. As part of his editing, Gene checked and corrected the _____ of three words, *physically, tractor,* and *minimum.*

2. He added _____ to set off an introductory phrase ("First of all") and an introductory word ("Finally") and also to connect the two complete thoughts in the final sentence.

3. He corrected a fragment ("_____") by using a comma to attach it to the preceding sentence.

4. He realized that a number like "25" should be _____ as "twenty-five."

5. And since revision can occur at any stage of the writing process, including editing, Gene makes one of his details more vivid by adding the descriptive words "_____."

All that remained for Gene to do was to enter his corrections, print out the final draft of the paper, and proofread it for any typos or other careless errors. He was then ready to hand it in to his instructor.

Review Activities

You now have a good overview of the writing process, from prewriting to first draft to revising to editing. The remaining chapters in Part One will deepen your sense of the four goals of effective writing: unity, support, organization or coherence, and sentence skills.

To reinforce much of the information about the writing process that you have learned in this chapter, you can now work through the following activities:

1   Taking a writing inventory

2   Prewriting

3   Outlining

4   Revising

1 Taking a Writing Inventory

Copyright ©2006 The McGraw-Hill Companies, Inc. All rights reserved.

ACTIVITY

To evaluate your approach to the writing process, answer the questions below. This activity is not a test, so try to be as honest as possible. Becoming aware of your writing habits can help you make helpful changes in your writing.

1. When you start work on a paper, do you typically do any prewriting?

   _____ Yes   _____ Sometimes   _____ No

2. If so, which of the prewriting techniques do you use?

   _____ Freewriting   _____ Clustering

   _____ Questioning   _____ Scratch outline

   _____ List making   _____ Other (please describe)

3. Which prewriting technique or techniques work best for you or do you think will work best for you?

4. Many students have said they find it helpful to handwrite a first draft and then type that draft on a computer. They then print the draft out and revise it by hand. Describe your own way of drafting and revising a paper.

5. After you write the first draft of a paper, do you have time to set it aside for a while, so you can come back to it with a fresh eye?

6. How many drafts do you typically write when doing a paper?

7. When you revise, are you aware that you should be working toward a paper that is unified, solidly supported, and clearly organized? Has this chapter given you a better sense that unity, support, and organization are goals to aim for?

8. Do you revise a paper for the effectiveness of its sentences as well as for its content?

9. What (if any) information has this chapter given you about prewriting that you will try to apply in your writing?

10. What (if any) information has this chapter given you about revising that you will try to apply in your writing?

2 Prewriting

ACTIVITY

Below are examples of how the five prewriting techniques could be used to develop the topic "Inconsiderate Drivers." Identify each technique by writing F (for freewriting), Q (for questioning), L (for listing), C (for clustering), or SO (for the scratch outline) in the answer space.

_____   High beams on
Weave in and out at high speeds
Treat street like a trash can
Open car door onto street without looking
Stop on street looking for an address
Don't use turn signals
High speeds in low-speed zones
Don't take turns merging
Use horn when they don't need to
Don't give walkers the right of way
More attention to cell phone than the road

_____

What is one example of an inconsiderate driver?	A person who turns suddenly without signaling.
Where does this happen?	At city intersections or on smaller country roads.
Why is this dangerous?	You have to be alert and slow down yourself to avoid rear-ending the car in front.
What is another example of inconsideration on the road?	Drivers who come toward you at night with their high beams on.

_____ Some people are inconsiderate drivers.
1. In city:
   a. Stop in middle of street
   b. Turn without signaling
2. On highway:
   a. Leave high beams on
   b. Stay in passing lane
   c. Cheat during a merge
3. Both in city and on highway:
   a. Throw trash out of window
   b. Pay more attention to cell phone than to road

_____

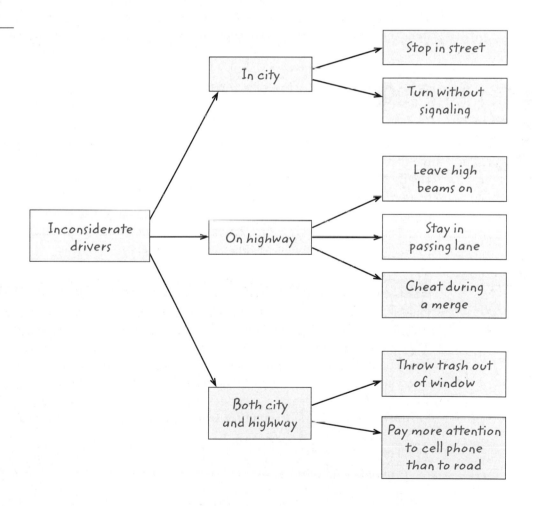

Copyright ©2006 The McGraw-Hill Companies, Inc. All rights reserved.

I was driving home last night after class and had three people try to blind me by coming at me with their high beams on. I had to zap them all with my high beams. Rude drivers make me crazy. The worst are the ones that use the road as a trash can. People who throw butts and cups and hamburger wrappings and other stuff out the car windows should be tossed into a trash dumpster. If word got around that this was the punishment maybe they would wise up. Other drivers do dumb things as well. I hate the person who will just stop in the middle of the street and try to figure out directions or look for a house address. Why don't they pull over to the side of the street? That hardly seems like too much to ask. Instead, they stop all traffic while doing their own thing. Then there are the people who keep what they want to do a secret. They're not going to tell you they plan to make a right- or left-hand turn. You've got to figure it out yourself when they suddenly slow down in front of you. Then there are all the people on their cell phones yakking away and not paying attention to their driving.

3 Outlining

As already mentioned (see page 26), outlining is central to writing a good paragraph. An outline lets you see, and work on, the bare bones of a paper, without the distraction of cluttered words and sentences. It develops your ability to think clearly and logically. Outlining provides a quick check on whether your paper will be *unified*. It also suggests right at the start whether your paper will be adequately *supported*. And it shows you how to plan a paper that is *well organized*.

The following series of exercises will help you develop the outlining skills so important to planning and writing a solid paragraph.

ACTIVITY 1

One key to effective outlining is the ability to distinguish between general ideas and specific details that fit under those ideas. Read each group of specific ideas below. Then circle the letter of the general idea that tells what the specific ideas have in common. Note that the general idea should not be too broad or too narrow. Begin by trying the example item, and then read the explanation that follows.

EXAMPLE   *Specific ideas:* runny nose, coughing, sneezing, sore throat

The general idea is:
a. cold symptoms.
b. symptoms.
c. throat problems.

Explanation   It is true that the specific ideas are all symptoms, but they have in common something even more specific—they are all symptoms of the common cold. Therefore, answer *b* is too broad; the correct answer is *a*. Answer *c* is too narrow because it doesn't cover all the specific ideas; it covers only the final item in the list ("sore throat").

1. *Specific ideas:* leaking toilet, no hot water, broken window, roaches
   The general idea is:
   a.   problems.
   b.   kitchen problems.
   c.   apartment problems.

2. *Specific ideas:* count to ten, take a deep breath, go for a walk
   The general idea is:
   a.   actions.
   b.   ways to calm down.
   c.   ways to calm down just before a test.

3. *Specific ideas:* putting sticky tape on someone's chair, putting a "kick me" sign on someone's back, putting hot pepper in someone's cereal
   The general idea is:
   a.   jokes.
   b.   practical jokes.
   c.   practical jokes played on teachers.

4. *Specific ideas:* going to bed earlier, eating healthier foods, reading for half an hour each day, trying to be kinder
   The general idea is:
   a.   resolutions.
   b.   problems.
   c.   solutions.

5. *Specific ideas:* money problems, family problems, relationship problems, health problems
   The general idea is:
   a.   poor grades.
   b.   causes of poor grades.
   c.   effects of poor grades.

Copyright ©2006 The McGraw-Hill Companies, Inc. All rights reserved.

ACTIVITY 2

In the following items, the specific ideas are given but the general ideas are unstated. Fill in each blank with a general heading that accurately describes the list provided.

EXAMPLE

General idea: Household Chores

Specific ideas: washing dishes
preparing meals
taking out trash
dusting

1. *General idea:* _____

   Specific ideas: convenient work hours
   short travel time to job
   good pay
   considerate boss

2. *General idea:* _____

   Specific ideas: greed
   cowardice
   selfishness
   dishonesty

3. *General idea:* _____

   Specific ideas: order the invitations
   get the bride's gown
   rent the tuxedos
   hire a photographer

4. *General idea:* _____

   Specific ideas: "Your mother stinks."
   "Your father's a bum."
   "You look like an ape."
   "Your car is a real piece of junk."

5. *General idea:* _____

   Specific ideas: "I like your dress."
   "You look great in red."
   "Your new haircut looks terrific."
   "You did very well on the exam."

ACTIVITY 3

Major and minor ideas are mixed together in the two paragraphs outlined below.
Put the ideas in logical order by filling in the outlines.

1. *Topic sentence:* People can be classified by how they treat their cars.

   Seldom wax or vacuum car
   Keep every mechanical item in top shape
   Protective owners
   Deliberately ignore needed maintenance
   Indifferent owners
   Wash and polish car every week
   Never wash, wax, or vacuum car
   Abusive owners
   Inspect and service car only when required by state law

   a. _____
      (1) _____
      (2) _____
   b. _____
      (1) _____
      (2) _____
   c. _____
      (1) _____
      (2) _____

2. *Topic sentence:* Living with an elderly parent has many benefits.

   Advantages for elderly person
   Live-in baby-sitter
   Learn about the past
   Advantages for adult children
   Serve useful role in family
   Help with household tasks
   Advantages for grandchildren
   Stay active and interested in young people
   More attention from adults

Copyright ©2006 The McGraw-Hill Companies, Inc. All rights reserved.

a. _____

    (1) _____

    (2) _____

b. _____

    (1) _____

    (2) _____

c. _____

    (1) _____

    (2) _____

ACTIVITY 4

Again, major and minor ideas are mixed together. In addition, in each outline one of the three major ideas is missing and must be added. Put the ideas in logical order by filling in the outlines that follow (summarizing as needed) and adding a third major idea.

1. *Topic sentence:* Extending the school day would have several advantages.

    Help children academically

    Parents know children are safe at the school

    More time to spend on basics

    Less pressure to cover subjects quickly

    More time for extras like art, music, and sports

    Help working parents

    More convenient to pick up children at 4 or 5 P.M.

    Teachers' salaries would be raised

a. _____

    (1) _____

    (2) _____

b. _____

    (1) _____

    (2) _____

Copyright ©2006 The McGraw-Hill Companies, Inc. All rights reserved.

c. _____

    (1) _____

    (2) _____

2. *Topic sentence:* By following certain hints about food, exercise, and smoking, you can increase your chances of dying young.

Don't ever walk if you can ride instead.

Choose foods such as bacon and lunch meats that are laced with nitrites and other preservatives.

Be very selective about what you eat.

If you begin to cough or feel short of breath, keep smoking.

If a friend invites you to play an outdoor sport, open a beer instead and head for your La-Z-Boy recliner.

Resist the urge to exercise.

Choose foods from one of four essential groups: fat, starch, sugar, and grease.

Smoke on a regular basis.

a. _____

    (1) _____

    (2) _____

b. _____

    (1) _____

    (2) _____

c. _____

    (1) _____

    (2) _____

ACTIVITY 5

Read the following two paragraphs. Then outline each one in the space provided. Write out the topic sentence in each case and summarize in a few words the primary and secondary supporting material that fits under the topic sentence.

1.
Why I'm a Stay-at-Home Baseball Fan

I'd much rather stay at home and watch ball games on television than go to the ballpark. First, it's cheaper to watch a game at home. I don't have to spend fifteen dollars for a ticket and another ten dollars for a parking space. If I want some refreshments, I can have what's already in the refrigerator instead of shelling out another six dollars for a limp, lukewarm hot dog and a watery Coke. Also, it's more comfortable at home. I avoid a bumper-to-bumper drive to the ballpark and pushy crowds who want to go through the same gate I do. I can lie quietly on my living-room sofa instead of sitting on a hard stadium seat with noisy people all around me. Most of all, watching a game on television is more informative. Not only do I see all the plays that I might miss from my fifteen-dollar seat, but I see some of them two and three times in instant replay. In addition, I get each play explained to me in glorious detail. If I were at the ballpark, I wouldn't know that the pitch our third baseman hit was a high and inside slider or that his grand-slam home run was a record-setting seventh in his career. The other fans can spend their money; put up with traffic, crowds, and hard seats; and guess at the plays. I'll take my baseball lying down—at home.

Topic sentence: _____

_____

a.   _____

   (1) _____

   (2) _____

b.   _____

   (1) _____

   (2) _____

c.   _____

   (1) _____

   (2) _____

2.

Why Teenagers Take Drugs

There are several reasons why teenagers take drugs. First of all, it is easy for young people to get drugs. Drugs are available almost anywhere, from a school cafeteria to a movie line to a football game. Teens don't have to risk traveling to the slums or dealing with shady types on street corners. It is also easy to get drugs because today's teens have spending money, which comes from allowances or earnings from part-time jobs. Teens can use their money to buy the luxuries they want—music, makeup, clothes, or drugs. Second, teens take drugs because the adolescent years are filled with psychological problems. For a teenager, one of these problems is the pressure of making important life decisions, such as choosing a career path. Another problem is establishing a sense of self. The teen years are the time when young people must become more independent from their parents and form their own values. The enormous mental pressures of these years can make some people turn to drugs. A final, and perhaps most important, reason why teenagers take drugs is peer pressure to conform. Teens often become very close to special friends, for one thing, and they will share a friend's interests, even if one interest is drugs. Teenagers also attend parties and other social events where it's all-important to be one of the crowd, to be "cool." Even the most mature teenager might be tempted to use drugs rather than risk being an outcast. For all these reasons, drugs are a major problem facing teenagers.

Topic sentence: _____

_____

a. _____

   (1) _____

   (2) _____

b. _____

   (1) _____

   (2) _____

c. _____

   (1) _____

   (2) _____

Copyright ©2006 The McGraw-Hill Companies, Inc. All rights reserved.

4 Revising

Listed in the box below are five stages in the process of composing a paragraph titled "Dangerous Places."

1. Prewriting (list)
2. Prewriting (freewriting, questioning, list, and scratch outline)
3. First draft
4. Revising (second draft)
5. Revising (final draft)

The five stages appear in scrambled order below and on the next page. Write the number 1 in the blank space in front of the first stage of development and number the remaining stages in sequence.

_____   There are some places where I never feel safe. For example, public rest rooms. The dirt and graffiti dirt on the floors and the graffiti scrawled on the walls make the room seem dangerous create a sense of danger. I'm also afraid in parking lots. Late at night, I don't like walking in the lot After class, I don't like the parking lot. When I leave my night class or the shopping mall late the walk to the car is scary. Most parking lots have large lights which make me feel at least a little better. I feel least safe in our laundry room. . . . It is a depressing place . . . Bars on the windows, . . . pipes making noises, . . . cement steps the only way out. . . .

_____   Dangerous Places
Highways
Cars—especially parking lots
Feel frightened in our laundry room
Big crowds—concerts, movies
Closed-in places
Bus and train stations
Airplane
Elevators and escalators

Dangerous Places

There are some places where I never feel completely safe. For example, I seldom feel safe in public rest rooms. I worry that I'll suddenly be alone there and that someone will come in to mug me. The ugly graffiti often scrawled on the walls, along with the grime and dirt in the room and crumpled tissues and paper towels on the floor, add to my sense of unease and danger. I also feel unsafe in large, dark, parking lots. When I leave my night class a little late, or I am one of the few leaving the mall at 10 P.M., I dread the walk to my car. I am afraid that someone may be lurking behind another car, ready to mug me. And I fear that my car will not start, leaving me stuck in the dark parking lot. The place where I feel least safe is the basement laundry room in our apartment building. No matter what time I do my laundry, I seem to be the only person there. The windows are barred, and the only exit is a steep flight of cement steps. While I'm folding the clothes, I feel trapped. If anyone unfriendly came down those steps, I would have nowhere to go. The pipes in the room make sudden gurgles, clanks, and hisses, adding to my unsettledness. Places like public rest rooms, dark parking lots, and the basement laundry room give me the shivers.

There are some places where I never feel completely safe. For example, I never feel safe in public rest rooms. If I'm alone there, I worry that someone will come in to rob and mug me. The dirt on the floors and the graffiti scrawled on the walls create a sense of danger. I feel unsafe in large, dark parking lots. When I leave my night class a little late or I leave the mall at 10 P.M., the walk to the car is scary. I'm afraid that someone may be behind a car. Also that my car won't start. Another place I don't feel safe is the basement laundry room in our apartment building. No matter when I do the laundry, I'm the only person there. The windows are barred and there are steep steps. I feel trapped when I fold the clothes. The pipes in the room make frightening noises such as hisses and clanks. Our laundry room and other places give me the shivers.

Some places seem dangerous and unsafe to me. For example, last night I stayed till 10:15 after night class and walked out to parking lot alone. Very scary. Also, other places I go to every day, such as places in my apartment building. Also frightened by big crowds and public rest rooms.

Why was the parking lot scary?	What places in my building scare me?
Dark	Laundry room (especially)
Only a few cars	Elevators
No one else in lot	Lobby at night sometimes
Could be someone behind a car	Outside walkway at night
Cold	

Copyright ©2006 The McGraw-Hill Companies, Inc. All rights reserved.

2 Parking lots

3 Laundry room

1 Public rest rooms

ACTIVITY 2

The author of "Dangerous Places" in Activity 1 made a number of editing changes between the second draft and the final draft. Compare the two drafts and, in the spaces provided below, identify five of the changes.

1. _____

2. _____

3. _____

4. _____

5. _____

3 The First and Second Steps in Writing

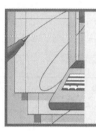

Copyright ©20C6 The McGraw-Hill Companies, Inc. All rights reserved.

> *This chapter will show you how to*
> - begin a paper by making a point of some kind
> - provide specific evidence to support that point
> - write a simple paragraph

Chapter 2 emphasized how prewriting and revising can help you become an effective writer. This chapter will focus on the first two steps in writing an effective paragraph:

1 Begin with a point.

2 Support the point with specific evidence.

Chapters 4 and 5 will then look at the third and fourth steps in writing:

3 Organize and connect the specific evidence (pages 75–109).

4 Write clear, error-free sentences (pages 110–143).

Step 1: Begin with a Point

Your first step in writing is to decide what point you want to make and to write that point in a single sentence. The point is commonly known as a *topic sentence*. As a guide to yourself and to the reader, put that point in the first sentence of your paragraph. Everything else in the paragraph should then develop and support in specific ways the single point given in the first sentence.

49

ACTIVITY

Read the two student paragraphs below about families today. Which paragraph clearly supports a single point? Which paragraph rambles on in many directions, introducing a number of ideas but developing none of them?

Paragraph A

Changes in the Family

Changes in our society in recent years have weakened family life. First of all, today's mothers spend much less time with their children. A generation or two ago, most households got by on Dad's paycheck, and Mom stayed home. Now many mothers work, and their children attend an after-school program, stay with a neighbor, or go home to an empty house. Another change is that families no longer eat together. In the past, Mom would be home and fix a full dinner—salad, pot roast, potatoes, and vegetables, with homemade cake or pie to top it off. Dinner today is more likely to be takeout food or frozen dinners eaten at home, or fast food eaten out, with different members of the family eating at different times. Finally, television has taken the place of family conversation and togetherness. Back when there were traditional meals, family members would have a chance to eat together, talk with each other, and share events of the day in a leisurely manner. But now families are more likely to be looking at the TV set than talking to one another. Many homes even have several TV sets, which people watch in separate rooms. Clearly, modern life is a challenge to family life.

Paragraph B

The Family

Family togetherness is very important. However, today's mothers spend much less time at home than their mothers did, for several reasons. Most fathers are also home much less than they used to be. In previous times, families had to work together running a farm. Now children are left at other places or are home alone much of the time. Some families do find ways to spend more time together despite the demands of work. Another problem is that with parents gone so much of the day, nobody is at home to prepare wholesome meals for the family to eat together. The meals Grandma used to

Copyright ©2006 The McGraw-Hill Companies, Inc. All rights reserved.

make would include pot roast and fried chicken, mashed potatoes, salad, vegetables, and delicious homemade desserts. Today's takeout foods and frozen meals can provide good nutrition. Some menu choices offer nothing but high-fat and high-sodium choices. People can supplement prepared foods by eating sufficient vegetables and fruit. Finally, television is also a big obstacle to togetherness. It sometimes seems that people are constantly watching TV and never talking to each other. Even when parents have friends over, it is often to watch something on TV. TV must be used wisely to achieve family togetherness.

Complete the following statement: Paragraph _____ is effective because it makes a clear, single point in the first sentence and goes on in the remaining sentences to support that single point.

Paragraph A starts with a point—that changes in our society in recent years have weakened family life—and then supports that idea with examples about mothers' working, families' eating habits, and television.

Paragraph B, on the other hand, does not make and support a single point. At first we think the point of the paragraph may be that "family togetherness is very important." But there is no supporting evidence showing how important family togetherness is. Instead, the line of thought in paragraph B swerves about like a car without a steering wheel. In the second sentence, we read that "today's mothers spend much less time at home than their mothers did, for several reasons." Now we think for a moment that this may be the main point and that the author will go on to list and explain some of those reasons. But the paragraph then goes on to comment on fathers, families in previous times, and families who find ways to spend time together. Any one of those ideas could be the focus of the paragraph, but none is. By now we are not really surprised at what happens in the rest of the paragraph. We are told about the absence of anyone "to prepare wholesome meals for the family," about what "the meals Grandma used to make" would be like, and about nutrition. The author then goes on to make a couple of points about how much people watch TV. The paragraph ends with yet another idea that does not support any previous point and that itself could be the point of a paragraph: "TV must be used wisely to achieve family togetherness." No single idea in this paragraph is developed, and the result for the reader is confusion.

In summary, while paragraph A is unified, paragraph B shows a complete lack of unity.

Step 2: Support the Point with Specific Evidence

The first essential step in writing effectively is to start with a clearly stated point. The second basic step is to support that point with specific evidence. Consider the supported point that you just read:

Point

Changes in our society in recent years have weakened family life.

Support

(1) Mothers
   (a) Most stayed home a generation ago
   (b) Most work now, leaving children at an after-school program, or with a neighbor, or in an empty house
(2) Eating habits
   (a) Formerly full homemade meals, eaten together
   (b) Now prepared foods at home or fast food out, eaten separately
(3) Television
   (a) Watching TV instead of conversing
   (b) Watching in separate rooms instead of being together

The supporting evidence is needed so that we can *see and understand for ourselves* that the writer's point is sound. The author of "Changes in the Family" has supplied specific supporting examples of how changes in our society have weakened family life. The paragraph has provided the evidence that is needed for us to understand and agree with the writer's point.

Now consider the following paragraph:

Good-Bye, Tony

I have decided not to go out with Tony anymore. First of all, he was late for our first date. He said that he would be at my house by 8:30, but he did not arrive until 9:30. Second, he was bossy. He told me that it would be too late to go to the new Chris Rock comedy that I wanted to see, and that we would go instead to a new action film with Johnny Depp. I told him that I didn't like violent movies, but he said that I could shut my eyes during the bloody parts. Only because it was a first date did I let him have his way. Finally, he was abrupt. After the movie, rather than suggesting a hamburger or a drink, he drove right out to a back road near Oakcrest High School and started necking with me. What he did a half hour later angered me most of all. He cut his finger on a pin I was wearing and immediately said we had to go right home. He was afraid the scratch would get infected if he didn't put Bactine and a Band-Aid on it. When he dropped me off, I said, "Good-bye, Tony," in a friendly enough way, but in my head I thought, "Good-bye <u>forever,</u> Tony."

The author's point is that she has decided not to go out with Tony anymore. See if you can summarize in the spaces below the three reasons she gives to support her decision:

Reason 1: _____

Reason 2: _____

Reason 3: _____

Notice what the supporting details in this paragraph do. They provide you, the reader, with a basis for understanding why the writer made the decision she did. Through specific evidence, the writer has explained and communicated her point successfully. The evidence that supports the point in a paragraph often consists of a series of reasons introduced by signal words (the author here uses *First of all, Second,* and *Finally*) and followed by examples and details that support the reasons. That is true of the sample paragraph above: three reasons are provided, followed by examples and details that back up those reasons.

The Point as an "Umbrella" Idea

You may find it helpful to think of the point as an "umbrella" idea. Under the writer's point fits all of the other material of the paragraph. That other material is made up of specific supporting details—evidence such as examples, reasons, or facts. The diagram to the right shows the relationship for the paragraph "Good-Bye, Tony":

Copyright ©2006 The McGraw-Hill Companies, Inc. All rights reserved.

ACTIVITY

Both of the paragraphs that follow resulted from an assignment to "Write a paper that details your reasons for being in college." Both writers make the point that they have various reasons for attending college. Which paragraph then goes on to provide plenty of specific evidence to back up its point? Which paragraph is vague and repetitive and lacks the concrete details needed to show us exactly why the author decided to attend college?

Hint   Imagine that you've been asked to make a short film based on each paragraph. Which one suggests specific pictures, locations, words, and scenes you could shoot?

Paragraph A

Reasons for Going to College

I decided to attend college for various reasons. One reason is self-respect. For a long time now, I have had little self-respect. I spent a lot of time doing nothing, just hanging around or getting into trouble, and eventually I began to feel bad about it. Going to college is a way to start feeling better about myself. By accomplishing things, I will improve my self-image. Another reason for going to college is that things happened in my life that made me think about a change. For one thing, I lost the part-time job I had. When I lost the job, I realized I would have to do something in life, so I thought about school. I was in a rut and needed to get out of it but did not know how. But when something happens that is out of your control, then you have to make some kind of decision. The most important reason for college, though, is to fulfill my dream. I know I need an education, and I want to take the courses I need to reach the position that I think I can handle. Only by qualifying yourself can you get what you want. Going to college will help me fulfill this goal. These are the main reasons why I am attending college.

Paragraph B

Why I'm in School

There are several reasons I'm in school. First of all, my father's attitude made me want to succeed in school. One night last year, after I had come in at 3 A.M., my father said, "Mickey, you're a bum. When I look at my son, all I see is a good-for-nothing bum." I was angry, but I knew my father was right

Copyright ©2006 The McGraw-Hill Companies, Inc. All rights reserved.

in a way. I had spent the last two years working at odd jobs at a pizza parlor and luncheonette, taking "uppers" and "downers" with my friends. That night, though, I decided I would prove my father wrong. I would go to college and be a success. Another reason I'm in college is my girlfriend's encouragement. Marie has already been in school for a year, and she is doing well in her computer courses. Marie helped me fill out my application and register for courses. She even lent me sixty-five dollars for textbooks. On her day off, she lets me use her car so I don't have to take the college bus. The main reason I am in college is to fulfill a personal goal: for the first time in my life, I want to finish something. For example, I quit high school in the eleventh grade. Then I enrolled in a government job-training program, but I dropped out after six months. I tried to get a high school equivalency diploma, but I started missing classes and eventually gave up. Now I am in a special program where I will earn my high school degree by completing a series of five courses. I am determined to accomplish this goal and to then go on and work for a degree in hotel management.

Complete the following statement: Paragraph _____ provides clear, vividly detailed reasons why the writer decided to attend college.

Paragraph B is the one that solidly backs up its point. The writer gives us specific reasons he is in school. On the basis of such evidence, we can clearly understand his opening point. The writer of paragraph A offers only vague, general reasons for being in school. We do not get specific examples of how the writer was "getting into trouble," what events occurred that forced the decision, or even what kind of job he or she wants to qualify for. We sense that the feeling expressed is sincere; but without particular examples we cannot really see why the writer decided to attend college.

Reinforcing Point and Support

You have now learned the two most important steps in writing effectively: making a point and supporting that point. Take a few minutes now to do the following activity. It will strengthen your ability to recognize a *point* and the *support* for that point.

ACTIVITY

In the following groups, one statement is the general point and the other statements are specific support for the point. Identify each point with a P and each statement of support with an S.

EXAMPLE

   _S_ My mother has cancer.

   _S_ My fourteen-year-old sister is pregnant.

   _S_ I lost my job.

   _P_ My family has real problems.

The point—that the family has real problems—is strongly supported by the three specific problems stated.

1. ____ The kitchen is so small that only one person can be there.

   ____ A nearby bus station fills the apartment with exhaust fumes every morning.

   ____ The apartment has some real drawbacks.

   ____ There are no closets.

2. ____ Some people skip breakfast.

   ____ Some people have poor eating habits.

   ____ Some people always order supersize portions.

   ____ Some people eat almost no fruits or vegetables.

3. ____ Children are at risk at the school.

   ____ There are two active gangs in the school.

   ____ Knives and guns have been found in lockers.

   ____ Drug busts have been made at the school.

4. ____ Cats are clean and do not require much attention.

   ____ Cats like living indoors and are safe to have around children

   ____ Cats are inexpensive to feed and easy to keep healthy.

   ____ There are definite advantages to having a cat as a pet.

5. ____ Ron feels short of breath.

   ____ Ron is getting dizzy and sweaty.

   ____ Ron might be having a heart attack.

   ____ Ron has pain in his chest.

Copyright ©2006 The McGraw-Hill Companies, Inc All rights reserved.

6. ____ The couple had different goals.

____ The couple disliked each other's friends.

____ The couple shared few interests in common.

____ The couple had good reasons to break up.

7. ____ The bread the waiter brought us is stale.

____ We've been waiting for our main course for over an hour.

____ It is time to speak to the restaurant manager.

____ The people next to us are awfully loud.

8. ____ Carla asks you questions about yourself.

____ Carla is a pleasure to be around.

____ Carla has a great smile.

____ Carla really listens when you talk.

9. ____ My boss is hard to work for.

____ She lacks a sense of humor.

____ She never gives praise.

____ She times all our breaks to the second.

10. ____ The man doesn't use his turn signals.

____ The man drives too fast down narrow residential streets.

____ The man doesn't come to a complete stop at stop signs.

____ The man is an unsafe driver.

11. ____ Though a mosquito is small, it has power.

____ A mosquito can find you in the dark.

____ A mosquito can keep you awake all night.

____ A mosquito can make you scratch yourself until you bleed.

12. ____ Because sending E-mail is so simple, family and friends may use it to stay in close touch.

____ When people are upset, they may send off an angry E-mail before they consider the consequences.

____ The jokes, petitions, and other E-mails that friends so easily forward can become a real nuisance.

____ The ease of using E-mail can be both a blessing and a curse.

13. ____ When answering the phone, some people's first words are "Who's this?"

____ Some people never bother to identify themselves when calling someone.

____ Some people have terrible telephone manners.

____ Some people hang up without even saying good-bye.

14. ____ One mother created what she called the homework zone—the kitchen table after dinner—where she and her young children did their assignments.

____ Some adult students have taken classes at a nearby community college during their lunch hour.

____ Adult students often find creative ways to balance school, employment, and family responsibilities.

____ By listening to taped lectures in the car, working students turn travel time into learning time.

15. ____ Moviegoers can take several simple steps to save money at the movie theater.

____ Bringing homemade popcorn to the movies is cheaper than buying expensive theater popcorn.

____ Buying candy at a grocery store, not a theater, cuts candy costs in half.

____ Going to movies early in the day reduces ticket prices by as much as $3 each.

The Importance of *Specific* Details

The point that opens a paper is a general statement. The evidence that supports a point is made up of specific details, reasons, examples, and facts.

Specific details have two key functions. First of all, details *excite the reader's interest.* They make writing a pleasure to read, for we all enjoy learning particulars about other people—what they do and think and feel. Second, details *support and explain a writer's point;* they give the evidence needed for us to see and understand a general idea. For example, the writer of "Good-Bye, Tony" provides details that make vividly clear her decision not to see Tony anymore. She specifies the exact time Tony was supposed to arrive (8:30) and when he actually arrived (9:30). She mentions the kind of film she wanted to see (a new Chris Rock movie) and the

Copyright ©2006 The McGraw-Hill Companies, Inc. All rights reserved.

one that Tony took her to instead (a violent movie). She tells us what she may have wanted to do after the movie (have a hamburger or a drink) and what Tony did instead (went necking); she even specifies the exact location of the place Tony took her (a back road near Oakcrest High School). She explains precisely what happened next (Tony "cut his finger on a pin I was wearing") and even mentions by name (Bactine and a Band-Aid) the treatments he planned to use.

The writer of "Why I'm in School" provides equally vivid details. He gives clear reasons for being in school (his father's attitude, his girlfriend's encouragement, and his wish to fulfill a personal goal) and backs up each reason with specific details. His details give us many sharp pictures. For instance, we hear the exact words his father spoke: "Mickey, you're a bum." He tells us exactly how he was spending his time ("working at odd jobs at a pizza parlor and luncheonette, taking 'uppers' and 'downers' with my friends"). He describes how his girlfriend helped him (filling out the college application, lending money and her car). Finally, instead of stating generally that "you have to make some kind of decision," as the writer of "Reasons for Going to College" does, he specifies that he has a strong desire to finish college because he dropped out of many schools and programs in the past: high school, a job-training program, and a high school equivalency course.

In both "Good-Bye, Tony" and "Why I'm in School," then, the vivid, exact details capture our interest and enable us to share in the writer's experience. We see people's actions and hear their words; the details provide pictures that make each of us feel "I am there." The particulars also allow us to understand each writer's point clearly. We are shown exactly why the first writer has decided not to see Tony anymore and exactly why the second writer is attending college.

ACTIVITY 1

Each of the five points below is followed by two attempts at support (*a* and *b*). Write S (for *specific*) in the space next to the one that succeeds in providing specific support for the point. Write X in the space next to the one that lacks supporting details.

1. My two-year-old son was in a stubborn mood today.

   _____ a. When I asked him to do something, he gave me nothing but trouble. He seemed determined to make things difficult for me, for he had his mind made up.

   _____ b. When I asked him to stop playing in the yard and come indoors, he looked me square in the eye and shouted "No!" and then spelled it out, "N . . . O!"

2. The prices in the amusement park were outrageously high.

_____ a. The food seemed to cost twice as much as it would in a supermarket and was sometimes of poor quality. The rides also cost a lot, and so I had to tell the children that they were limited to a certain number of them.

_____ b. The cost of the log flume, a ride that lasts roughly three minutes, was ten dollars a person. Then I had to pay four dollars for an eight-ounce cup of Coke and six dollars for a hot dog.

3. My brother-in-law is accident-prone.

_____ a. Once he tried to open a tube of Krazy Glue with his teeth. When the cap came loose, glue squirted out and sealed his lips shut. They had to be pried open in a hospital emergency room.

_____ b. Even when he does seemingly simple jobs, he seems to get into trouble. This can lead to hilarious, but sometimes dangerous, results. Things never seem to go right for him, and he often needs the help of others to get out of one predicament or another.

4. The so-called "bargains" at the yard sale were junk.

_____ a. The tables were filled with useless stuff no one could possibly want. They were the kinds of things that should be thrown away, not sold.

_____ b. The "bargains" included two headless dolls, blankets filled with holes, scorched potholders, and a plastic Christmas tree with several branches missing.

5. The key to success in college is organization.

_____ a. Knowing what you're doing, when you have to do it, and so on is a big help for a student. A system is crucial in achieving an ordered approach to study. Otherwise, things become very disorganized, and it is not long before grades will begin to drop.

_____ b. Organized students never forget paper or exam dates, which are marked on a calendar above their desks. And instead of having to cram for exams, they study their clear, neat classroom and textbook notes on a daily basis.

Comments   The specific support for point 1 is answer *b*. The writer does not just tell us that the little boy was stubborn but provides an example that shows us. In particular, the detail of the son's spelling out "N . . . O!" makes his stubbornness

Copyright ©2006 The McGraw-Hill Companies, Inc. All rights reserved.

vividly real for the reader. For point 2, answer *b* gives specific prices (ten dollars for a ride, four dollars for a Coke, and six dollars for a hot dog) to support the idea that the amusement park was expensive. For point 3, answer *a* vividly backs up the idea that the brother-in-law is accident-prone by detailing an accident with Krazy Glue. Point 4 is supported by answer *b*, which lists specific examples of useless items that were offered for sale—from headless dolls to a broken plastic Christmas tree. We cannot help agreeing with the writer's point that the items were not bargains but junk. Point 5 is backed up by answer *b*, which identifies two specific strategies of organized students: they mark important dates on calendars above their desks, and they take careful notes and study them on a daily basis.

In each of the five cases, the specific evidence enables us to *see for ourselves* that the writer's point is valid.

ACTIVITY 2

Follow the directions for Activity 1.

1. The house has been neglected by its owners.

   _____ a. As soon as you look at the house from the outside, you can tell that repairs need to be made. The roof is badly in need of attention. But it is very obvious that other outside parts of the house also are badly in need of care.

   _____ b. The roof is missing a number of shingles. The house's paint is peeling and spotted with mold. Two windows have been covered with plywood.

2. Students have practical uses for computers.

   _____ a. Students stay in touch with friends by E-mail. They often shop over the Internet. They do all their research online.

   _____ b. Students have an easier way now to communicate with their friends. They can also save time now: they have no need to go out and buy things but can do it at home. Also, getting information they need for papers no longer requires spending time in the library.

3. Rico knew very little about cooking when he got his first apartment.

   _____ a. He had to live on whatever he had in the freezer for a while. He was not any good in the kitchen and had to learn very slowly. More often than not, he would learn how to cook something only by making mistakes first.

_____ b. He lived on macaroni and cheese TV dinners for three weeks. His idea of cooking an egg was to put a whole egg in the microwave, where it exploded. Then he tried to make a grilled cheese sandwich by putting slices of cheese and bread in a toaster.

4. Speaking before a group is a problem for many people.

_____ a. They become uncomfortable even at the thought of speaking in public. They will go to almost any length to avoid speaking to a group. If they are forced to do it, they can feel so anxious that they actually develop physical symptoms.

_____ b. Stage fright, stammering, and blushing are frequent reactions. Some people will pretend to be ill to avoid speaking publicly. When asked to rank their worst fears, people often list public speaking as even worse than death.

5. Small children can have as much fun with ordinary household items as with costly toys.

_____ a. A large sheet thrown over a card table makes a great hideout or playhouse. Banging pot covers together makes a tremendous crash that kids love. Also, kids like to make long, winding fences out of wooden clothespins.

_____ b. Kids can make musical instruments out of practically anything. The result is a lot of noise and fun. They can easily create their own play areas as well by using a little imagination. There is simply no need to have to spend a lot of money on playthings.

The Importance of *Adequate* Details

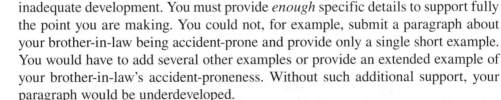

One of the most common and most serious problems in students' writing is inadequate development. You must provide *enough* specific details to support fully the point you are making. You could not, for example, submit a paragraph about your brother-in-law being accident-prone and provide only a single short example. You would have to add several other examples or provide an extended example of your brother-in-law's accident-proneness. Without such additional support, your paragraph would be underdeveloped.

At times, students try to disguise an undersupported point by using repetition and wordy generalities. You saw this, for example, in paragraph A ("Reasons for Going to College") on page 54. Be prepared to do the plain hard work needed to ensure that each of your paragraphs has full, solid support.

Copyright ©2006 The McGraw-Hill Companies, Inc. All rights reserved.

ACTIVITY

The following paragraphs were written on the same topic, and each has a clear opening point. Which one is adequately developed? Which one has few particulars and uses mostly vague, general, wordy sentences to conceal the fact that it is starved for specific details?

Paragraph A

Abuse of Public Parks

Some people abuse public parks. Instead of using the park for recreation, they go there, for instance, to clean their cars. Park caretakers regularly have to pick up the contents of dumped ashtrays and car litter bags. Certain juveniles visit parks with cans of spray paint to deface buildings, fences, fountains, and statues. Other offenders are those who dig up and cart away park flowers, shrubs, and trees. One couple were even arrested for stealing park sod, which they were using to fill in their lawn. Perhaps the most widespread offenders are the people who use park tables and benches and fireplaces but do not clean up afterward. Picnic tables are littered with trash, including crumpled bags, paper plates smeared with ketchup, and paper cups half-filled with stale soda. On the ground are empty beer bottles, dented soda cans, and sharp metal pop-tops. Parks are made for people, and yet—ironically—their worst enemy is "people pollution."

Paragraph B

Mistreatment of Public Parks

Some people mistreat public parks. Their behavior is evident in many ways, and the catalog of abuses could go on almost without stopping. Different kinds of debris are left by people who have used the park as a place for attending to their automobiles. They are not the only individuals who mistreat public parks, which should be used with respect for the common good of all. Many young people come to the park and abuse it, and their offenses can occur in any season of the year. The reason for their inconsiderate behavior is known only to themselves. Other visitors lack personal cleanliness in their personal habits when they come to the park, and the park suffers because of it. Such people seem to have the attitude that someone else should clean up after them. It is an undeniable fact that people are the most dangerous thing that parks must contend with.

Complete the following statement: Paragraph _____ provides an adequate number of specific details to support its point.

Paragraph A offers a series of detailed examples of how people abuse parks. Paragraph B, on the other hand, is underdeveloped. Paragraph B speaks only of "different kinds of debris," while paragraph A refers specifically to "dumped ashtrays and car litter bags"; paragraph B talks in a general way of young people abusing the park, while paragraph A supplies such particulars as "cans of spray paint" and defacing "buildings, fences, fountains, and statues." And there is no equivalent in paragraph B for the specifics in paragraph A about people who steal park property and litter park grounds. In summary, paragraph B lacks the full, detailed support needed to develop its opening point convincingly.

■ **Review Activity**

To check your understanding of the chapter so far, see if you can answer the following questions.

1. It has been observed: "To write well, the first thing that you must do is decide what nail you want to drive home." What is meant by *nail?*

   _____

2. How do you drive home the nail in the paper?

   _____

3. What are the two reasons for using specific details in your writing?

   a. _____

   b. _____

Practice in Making and Supporting a Point

You now know the two most important steps in competent writing: (1) making a point and (2) supporting that point with specific evidence. The purpose of this section is to expand and strengthen your understanding of these two basic steps.

You will first work through a series of activities on *making* a point:

1 Identifying Common Errors in Topic Sentences

2 Understanding the Two Parts of a Topic Sentence

3 Selecting a Topic Sentence

You will then sharpen your understanding of specific details by working through a series of activities on *supporting* a point:

1 Identifying Common Errors in Topic Sentences

When writing a point, or topic sentence, people sometimes make mistakes that undermine their chances of producing an effective paper. One mistake is to substitute an announcement of the topic for a true topic sentence. Other mistakes include writing statements that are too broad or too narrow. Following are examples of all three errors, along with contrasting examples of effective topic sentences.

Announcement

My Ford Focus is the concern of this paragraph.

The statement above is a simple announcement of a subject, rather than a topic sentence expressing an idea about the subject.

Statement That Is Too Broad

Many people have problems with their cars.

The statement is too broad to be supported adequately with specific details in a single paragraph.

Statement That Is Too Narrow

My car is a Ford Focus.

Copyright ©2006 The McGraw-Hill Companies, Inc. All rights reserved.

The statement above is too narrow to be expanded into a paragraph. Such a narrow statement is sometimes called a *dead-end statement* because there is no place to go with it. It is a simple fact that does not need or call for any support.

Effective Topic Sentence

I hate my Ford Focus.

The statement above expresses an opinion that could be supported in a paragraph. The writer could offer a series of specific supporting reasons, examples, and details to make it clear why he or she hates the car.

Here are additional examples:

Announcements

The subject of this paper will be my apartment.

I want to talk about increases in the divorce rate.

Statements That Are Too Broad

The places where people live have definite effects on their lives.

Many people have trouble getting along with others.

Statements That Are Too Narrow

I have no hot water in my apartment at night.

Almost one of every two marriages ends in divorce.

Effective Topic Sentences

My apartment is a terrible place to live.

The divorce rate is increasing for several reasons.

ACTIVITY 1

For each pair of sentences below, write A beside the sentence that only *announces* a topic. Write OK beside the sentence that *advances an idea* about the topic.

1. ____ a. This paper will deal with flunking math.

   ____ b. I flunked math last semester for several reasons.

2. ____ a. I am going to write about my job as a gas station attendant.

____ b. Working as a gas station attendant was the worst job I ever had.

3. ____ a. Obscene phone calls are the subject of this paragraph.

____ b. People should know what to do when they receive an obscene phone call.

4. ____ a. In several ways, my college library is inconvenient to use.

____ b. This paragraph will deal with the college library.

5. ____ a. My paper will discuss the topic of procrastinating.

____ b. The following steps will help you stop procrastinating.

ACTIVITY 2

For each pair of sentences below, write TN beside the statement that is *too narrow* to be developed into a paragraph. Write OK beside the statement in each pair that could be developed into a paragraph.

1. ____ a. I do push-ups and sit-ups each morning.

____ b. Exercising every morning has had positive effects on my health.

2. ____ a. José works nine hours a day and then goes to school three hours a night.

____ b. José is an ambitious man.

3. ____ a. I started college after being away from school for seven years.

____ b. Several of my fears about returning to school have proved to be groundless.

4. ____ a. Parts of Walt Disney's *Bambi* make the movie frightening for children.

____ b. Last summer I visited Disneyland in Anaheim, California.

5. ____ a. My brother was depressed yesterday for several reasons.

____ b. Yesterday my brother had to pay fifty-two dollars for a motor tune-up.

Copyright ©2006 The McGraw-Hill Companies, Inc. All rights reserved.

ACTIVITY 3

For each pair of sentences below, write TB beside the statement that is *too broad* to be supported adequately in a short paper. Write OK beside the statement that makes a limited point.

1. ____ a. Professional football is a dangerous sport.

____ b. Professional sports are violent.

2. ____ a. Married life is the best way of living.

____ b. Teenage marriages often end in divorce for several reasons.

3. ____ a. Aspirin can have several harmful side effects.

____ b. Drugs are dangerous.

4. ____ a. I've always done poorly in school.

____ b. I flunked math last semester for several reasons.

5. ____ a. Computers are changing our society.

____ b. Using computers to teach schoolchildren is a mistake.

2 Understanding the Two Parts of a Topic Sentence

As stated earlier, the point that opens a paragraph is often called a *topic sentence*. When you look closely at a point, or topic sentence, you can see that it is made up of two parts:

1 The *limited topic*

2 The writer's *attitude* toward or idea about the limited topic

The writer's attitude, point of view, or idea is usually expressed in one or more *key words*. All the details in a paragraph should support the idea expressed in the key words. In each of the topic sentences below, a single line appears under the topic and a double line under the idea about the topic (expressed in a key word or key words):

My girlfriend is very aggressive.

Highway accidents are often caused by absentmindedness.

The kitchen is the most widely used room in my house.

Copyright ©2006 The McGraw-Hill Companies, Inc. All rights reserved.

<u>Voting</u> should be <u>required by law</u> in the United States.

My <u>pickup truck</u> is the most <u>reliable</u> vehicle I have ever owned.

In the first sentence, the topic is *girlfriend,* and the key word that expresses the writer's idea about his topic is that his girlfriend is *aggressive.* In the second sentence, the topic is *highway accidents,* and the key word that determines the focus of the paragraph is that such accidents are often caused by *absentmindedness.* Notice each topic and key word or key words in the other three sentences as well.

ACTIVITY

For each point below, draw a single line under the topic and a double line under the idea about the topic.

1. Billboards should be abolished.
2. My boss is an ambitious man.
3. Politicians are often self-serving.
4. The apartment needed repairs.
5. Television commercials are often insulting.
6. My parents have rigid racial attitudes.
7. The middle child is often a neglected member of the family.
8. The language in many movies today is offensive.
9. Doctors are often insensitive.
10. Homeowners today are more energy-conscious than ever before.
11. My car is a temperamental machine.
12. My friend Debbie, who is only nineteen, is extremely old-fashioned.
13. Looking for a job can be a degrading experience.
14. The daily life of students is filled with conflicts.
15. Regulations in the school cafeteria should be strictly enforced.
16. The national speed limit should be raised.
17. Our vacation turned out to be a disaster.
18. The city's traffic-light system has both values and drawbacks.
19. Insects serve many useful purposes.
20. Serious depression often has several warning signs.

3 Selecting a Topic Sentence

Remember that a paragraph is made up of a topic sentence and a group of related sentences developing the topic sentence. It is also helpful to remember that the topic sentence is a *general* statement. The other sentences provide specific support for the general statement.

ACTIVITY

Each group of sentences below could be written as a short paragraph. Circle the letter of the topic sentence in each case. To find the topic sentence, ask yourself, "Which is a general statement supported by the specific details in the other three statements?"

Begin by trying the example item below. First circle the letter of the sentence you think expresses the main idea. Then read the explanation.

EXAMPLE   a. If you stop carrying matches or a lighter, you can cut down on impulse smoking.

b. If you sit in no-smoking areas, you will smoke less.

c. You can behave in ways that will help you smoke less.

d. By keeping a record of when and where you smoke, you can identify the most tempting situations and then avoid them.

Explanation   Sentence *a* explains one way to smoke less. Sentences *b* and *d* also provide specific ways to smoke less. In sentence *c*, however, no one specific way is explained. The words *ways that will help you smoke less* refer only generally to such methods. Therefore, sentence *c* is the topic sentence; it expresses the author's main idea. The other sentences support that idea by providing examples.

1. a. "I couldn't study because I forgot to bring my textbook home."

   b. "I couldn't take the final because my grandmother died."

   c. Students give instructors some common excuses.

   d. "I couldn't come to class because I had a migraine headache."

2. a. Its brakes are badly worn.

   b. My old car is ready for the junk pile.

   c. Its floor has rusted through, and water splashes on my feet when the highway is wet.

   d. My mechanic says its engine is too old to be repaired, and the car isn't worth the cost of a new engine.

Copyright ©2006 The McGraw-Hill Companies, Inc. All rights reserved.

3. a. The last time I ate at the diner, I got food poisoning and was sick for two days.

   b. The city inspector found roaches and mice in the diner's kitchen.

   c. Our town diner is a health hazard and ought to be closed down.

   d. The toilets in the diner often back up, and the sinks have only a trickle of water.

4. a. Part-time workers can be easily laid off.

   b. Most part-time workers get no fringe benefits.

   c. The average part-timer earns three dollars less an hour than a full-timer.

   d. Part-time workers have second-class status.

5. a. In early colleges, students were mostly white males.

   b. Colleges of two centuries ago were quite different from today's schools.

   c. All students in early colleges had to take the same courses.

   d. The entire student body at early schools would be only a few dozen people.

4 Writing a Topic Sentence: I

ACTIVITY

The following activity will give you practice in writing an accurate point, or topic sentence—one that is neither too broad nor too narrow for the supporting material in a paragraph. Sometimes you will construct your topic sentence after you have decided which details you want to discuss. An added value of this activity is that it shows you how to write a topic sentence that will exactly match the details you have developed.

1. *Topic sentence:* _____

   _____

   a.   When we brought a "welcome to the neighborhood" present, the family next door didn't even say thank you.

   b.   The family never attends the annual block party.

   c.   The family's children aren't allowed to play with other neighborhood kids.

   d.   Our neighbors keep their curtains closed and never sit out in their yard.

2.   *Topic sentence:* _____

_____

a.   Only about thirty people came to the dance, instead of the expected two hundred.
b.   The band arrived late and spent an hour setting up.
c.   There were at least three males at the dance to every female.
d.   An hour after the dance started, it ended because of a power failure.

3.   *Topic sentence:* _____

_____

a.   We had to wait half an hour even though we had reserved a table.
b.   Our appetizer and main course arrived at the same time.
c.   The busboy ignored our requests for more water.
d.   The wrong desserts were served to us.

4.   *Topic sentence:* _____

_____

a.   In early grades we had spelling bees, and I would be among the first to sit down.
b.   In sixth-grade English, my teacher kept me busy diagramming sentences on the board.
c.   In tenth grade we had to recite poems, and I always forgot my lines.
d.   In my senior year, my compositions had more red correction marks than anyone else's.

5. | *Topic sentence:* _____

_____

a.   The crowd scenes were crudely spliced from another film.

b.   Mountains and other background scenery were just painted cardboard cutouts.

c.   The "sync" was off, so that you heard voices even when the actors' lips were not moving.

d.   The so-called "monster" was just a spider that had been filmed through a magnifying lens.

5 Writing a Topic Sentence: II

Often you will start with a general topic or a general idea of what you want to write about. You may, for example, want to write a paragraph about some aspect of school life. To come up with a point about school life, begin by limiting your topic. One way to do this is to make a list of all the limited topics you can think of that fit under the general topic.

ACTIVITY

Following are five general topics and a series of limited topics that fit under them. Make a point out of *one* of the limited topics in each group.

Hint   To create a topic sentence, ask yourself, "What point do I want to make about _____ (*my limited topic*)?"

EXAMPLE   Recreation

- Movies
- Dancing
- TV shows
- Reading
- Sports parks

Your point: _Sports parks today have some truly exciting games._

Copyright ©2006 The McGraw-Hill Companies, Inc. All rights reserved.

1. Your school
   - Instructor
   - Cafeteria
   - Specific course
   - Particular room or building
   - Particular policy (attendance, grading, etc.)
   - Classmate

   Your point: _____

   _____

2. Job
   - Pay
   - Boss
   - Working conditions
   - Duties
   - Coworkers
   - Customers or clients

   Your point: _____

   _____

3. Money
   - Budgets
   - Credit cards
   - Dealing with a bank
   - School expenses
   - Ways to get it
   - Ways to save it

   Your point: _____

   _____

4. Cars
   - First car
   - Driver's test
   - Road conditions
   - Accident

- Mandatory speed limit
- Safety problems

Your point: _____

_____

5. Sports
   - A team's chances
   - At your school
   - Women's team
   - Recreational versus spectator
   - Favorite team
   - Outstanding athlete

   Your point: _____

   _____

6 Recognizing Specific Details: I

Specific details are examples, reasons, particulars, and facts. Such details are needed to support and explain a topic sentence effectively. They provide the evidence needed for readers to understand, as well as to feel and experience, a writer's point.

Here is a topic sentence followed by two sets of supporting sentences. Which set provides sharp, specific details?

Topic Sentence

Some poor people must struggle to make meals for themselves.

Set A

They gather up whatever free food they can find in fast-food restaurants and take it home to use however they can. Instead of planning well-balanced meals, they base their diet on anything they can buy that is cheap and filling.

Set B

Some make tomato soup by adding hot water to the free packets of ketchup they get at McDonald's. Others buy cans of cheap dog food and fry it like hamburger.

Copyright ©2006 The McGraw-Hill Companies, Inc. All rights reserved.

Set B provides specific details: instead of a general statement about "free food they find in fast-food restaurants and take . . . home to use however they can," we get a vivid detail we can see and picture clearly: "make tomato soup [from] free packets of ketchup." Instead of a general statement about how the poor will "base their diet on anything they can buy that is cheap and filling," we get exact and vivid details: "Others buy cans of cheap dog food and fry it like hamburger."

Specific details are often like the information we might find in a movie script. They provide us with such clear pictures that we could make a film of them if we wanted to. You would know just how to film the information given in set B. You would show a poor person breaking open a packet of ketchup from McDonald's and mixing it with water to make a kind of tomato soup. You would show someone opening a can of dog food and frying its contents like hamburger.

In contrast, the writer of set A fails to provide the specific information needed. If you were asked to make a film based on set A, you would have to figure out for yourself just what particulars you were going to show.

When you are working to provide specific supporting information in a paper, it might help to ask yourself, "Could someone easily film this information?" If the answer is "yes," you probably have good details.

ACTIVITY

Each topic sentence below is followed by two sets of supporting details (*a* and *b*). Write S (for *specific)* in the space next to the set that provides specific support for the point. Write G (for *general)* next to the set that offers only vague, general support.

1. *Topic sentence:* My roommate is messy.

   _____ a. He doesn't seem to mind that he can't find any clean clothes or dishes. He never puts anything back in its proper place; he just drops it wherever he happens to be. His side of the room looks as if a hurricane has gone through.

   _____ b. His coffee cup is covered inside with a thick layer of green mold. I can't tell you what color his easy chair is; it has disappeared under a pile of dirty laundry. When he turns over in bed, I can hear the crunch of cracker crumbs beneath his body.

2. *Topic sentence:* Roberta is very aggressive.

   _____ a. Her aggressiveness is apparent in both her personal and her professional life. She is never shy about extending social invitations. And while some people are turned off by her aggressive attitude, others are impressed by it and enjoy doing business with her.

_____ b. When she meets a man she likes, she is quick to say, "Let's go out sometime. What's your phone number?" In her job as a furniture salesperson, she will follow potential customers out onto the sidewalk as she tries to persuade them to buy.

3. *Topic sentence:* Our new kitten causes us lots of trouble.

_____ a. He has shredded the curtains in my bedroom with his claws. He nearly drowned when he crawled into the washing machine. And my hands look like raw hamburger from his playful bites and scratches.

_____ b. He seems to destroy everything he touches. He's always getting into places where he doesn't belong. Sometimes he plays too roughly, and that can be painful.

4. *Topic sentence:* My landlord is softhearted.

_____ a. Even though he wrote them himself, he sometimes ignores the official apartment rules in order to make his tenants happy.

_____ b. Although the lease states "No pets," he brought my daughter a puppy after she told him how much she missed having one.

5. *Topic sentence:* The library is a distracting place to try to study.

_____ a. It's hard to concentrate when a noisy eight-person poker game is going on on the floor beside you. It's also distracting to overhear remarks like, "Hey, Baby, what's your mother's address? I want to send her a thank-you card for having such a beautiful daughter."

_____ b. Many students meet in the library to do group activities and socialize with one another. Others go there to flirt. It's easy to get more interested in all that activity than in paying attention to your studies.

7 Recognizing Specific Details: II

ACTIVITY

At several points in the following paragraphs you are given a choice of two sets of supporting details. Write S (for *specific*) in the space next to the set that provides specific support for the point. Write G (for *general*) next to the set that offers only vague, general support.

Copyright ©2006 The McGraw-Hill Companies, Inc. All rights reserved.

Paragraph 1

My daughter's boyfriend is a good-for-nothing young man. After knowing him for just three months, everyone in our family is opposed to the relationship. For one thing, Russell is lazy.

_____ a. He is always finding an excuse to avoid putting in an honest day's work. He never pitches in and helps with chores around our house, even when he's asked directly to do so. And his attitude about his job isn't any better. To hear him tell it, he deserves special treatment in the workplace. He thinks he's gone out of his way if he just shows up on time.

_____ b. After starting a new job last week, he announced this Monday that he wasn't going to work because it was his _birthday_—as if he were somebody special. And when my husband asked Russell to help put storm windows on the house next Saturday, Russell answered that he uses his weekends to catch up on sleep.

Another quality of Russell's which no one likes is that he is cheap.

_____ c. When my daughter's birthday came around, Russell said he would take her out to Baldoni's, a fancy Italian restaurant. Then he changed his mind. Instead of spending a lot of money on a meal, he said, he wanted to buy her a really nice pair of earrings. So my daughter cooked dinner for him at her apartment. But there was no present, not even a little one. He claims he's waiting for a jewelry sale at Macy's. I don't think my daughter will ever see that "really nice" gift.

_____ d. He makes big promises about all the nice things he's going to do for my daughter, but he never comes through. His words are cheap, and so is he. He's all talk and no action. My daughter isn't greedy, but it hurts her when Russell says he's going to take her someplace nice or give her something special and then nothing happens.

Worst of all, Russell is mean.

_____ e. Russell seems to get special pleasure from hurting people when he feels they have a weak point. I have heard him make remarks that to him were funny but were really very insensitive. You've got to wonder about someone who needs to be ugly to other people just for the sake of being powerful. Sometimes I want to let him know how I feel.

Copyright ©2C06 The McGraw-Hill Companies, Inc. All rights reserved.

_____ f. When my husband was out of work, Russell said to him, "Well, you've got it made now, living off your wife." After my husband glared at him, he said, "Why're you getting sore? I'm just kidding." Sometimes he snaps at my daughter, saying things like "Don't make me wait—there are plenty of other babes who would like to take your place." At such times I want to toss him out to the curb.

Everyone in the family is waiting anxiously for the day when my daughter will see Russell the way the rest of us see him.

Paragraph 2

Many adult children move back in with their parents for some period of time. Although living with Mom and Dad again has some advantages, there are certain problems that are likely to arise. One common problem is that children may expect their parents to do all the household chores.

_____ a. They never think that they should take on their share of work around the house. Not only do they not help with their parents' chores; they don't even take responsibility for the extra work that their presence creates. Like babies, they go through the house making a mess that the parents are supposed to clean up. It's as if they think their parents are their servants.

_____ b. They expect meals to appear on the table as if by magic. After they've eaten, they go off to work or play, never thinking about who's going to do the dishes. They drop their dirty laundry beside the washing machine, assuming that Mom will attend to it and return clean, folded clothes to their bedroom door. And speaking of their bedrooms: every day they await the arrival of Mom's Maid Service to make the bed, pick up the floor, and dust the furniture.

Another frequent problem is that parents forget their adult children are no longer adolescents.

_____ c. Parents like this want to know everything about their adult children's lives. They don't think their kids, even though they are adults, should have any privacy. Whenever they see their children doing anything, they want to know all the details. It's as though their children are still teenagers who are expected to report all their activities. Naturally, adult children get irritated when they are treated as if they were little kids.

_____ d. They may insist upon knowing far more about their children's comings and goings than the children want to share. For example, if such parents see their adult son heading out the door, they demand to know: "Where are you going? Who will you be with? What will you be doing? What time will you be back?" In addition, they may not let their adult child have any privacy. If their daughter and a date are sitting in the living room, for instance, they may join them there and start peppering the young man with questions about his family and his job, as if they were interviewing him for the position of son-in-law.

Finally, there may be financial problems when an adult child returns to live at home.

_____ e. Having an extra adult in the household creates extra expenses. But many adult children don't offer to help deal with those extra costs. Adult children often eat at home, causing the grocery bill to climb. They may stay in a formerly unused room, which now needs to be heated and lit. They produce extra laundry to be washed. They use the telephone, adding to the long-distance bill. For all these reasons, adult children should expect to pay a reasonable fee to their parents for room and board.

_____ f. It's expensive to have another adult living in the household. Adult children would be paying a lot of bills on their own if they weren't staying with their parents. It's only fair that they share the expenses at their parents' house. They should consider all the ways that their living at home is increasing their parents' expenses. Then they should insist on covering their share of the costs.

8 Providing Supporting Evidence

ACTIVITY

Provide three details that logically support each of the following points, or topic sentences. Your details can be drawn from your own experience, or they can be invented. In each case, the details should show in a specific way what the point expresses in only a general way. You may state your details briefly in phrases, or as complete sentences.

EXAMPLE   The student had several ways of passing time during the dull lecture.

Shielded his eyes with his hand and dozed awhile.

Read the sports magazine he had brought to class.

Made an elaborate drawing on a page of his notebook.

1. I could tell I was coming down with the flu.

   _____

   _____

   _____

2. The food at the cafeteria was terrible yesterday.

   _____

   _____

   _____

3. I had car problems recently.

   _____

   _____

   _____

4. When your money gets tight, there are several ways to economize.

   _____

   _____

   _____

5. Some people have dangerous driving habits.

   _____

   _____

   _____

Copyright ©2006 The McGraw-Hill Companies, Inc. All rights reserved.

9 Identifying Adequate Supporting Evidence

ACTIVITY

Two of the following paragraphs provide sufficient details to support their topic sentences convincingly. Write AD, for *adequate development,* beside those paragraphs. There are also three paragraphs that, for the most part, use vague, general, or wordy sentences as a substitute for concrete details. Write U, for *underdeveloped,* beside those paragraphs.

_____   1.   **My Husband's Stubbornness**

My husband's worst problem is his stubbornness. He simply will not let any kind of weakness show. If he isn't feeling well, he refuses to admit it. He will keep on doing whatever he is doing and will wait until the symptoms get almost unbearable before he will even hint that anything is the matter with him. Then things are so far along that he has to spend more time recovering than he would if he had a different attitude. He also hates to be wrong. If he is wrong, he will be the last to admit it. This happened once when we went shopping, and he spent an endless amount of time going from one place to the next. He insisted that one of them had a fantastic sale on things he wanted. We never found a sale, but the fact that this situation happened will not change his attitude. Finally, he never listens to anyone else's suggestions on a car trip. He always knows he's on the right road, and the results have led to a lot of time wasted getting back in the right direction. Every time one of these incidents happens, it only means that it is going to happen again in the future.

_____   2.   **Dangerous Games**

Because they feel compelled to show off in front of their friends, some teenagers play dangerous games. In one incident, police found a group of boys performing a dangerous stunt with their cars. The boys would perch on the hoods of cars going thirty-five or forty miles an hour. Then the driver would brake sharply, and the boy who flew the farthest off the car would win. Teenagers also drive their cars with the lights off and pass each other on hills or curves as ways of challenging each other. In addition to cars, water seems to tempt young people to invent dangerous contests. Some students dared each other to swim through a narrow pipe under a four-lane highway. The pipe carried water from a stream to a pond, and the swimmer would have to hold his or her breath for several minutes before coming out on the other side. Another contest involved diving off the rocky sides of a quarry. Because large stones sat under the water in certain places, any dive could result in a broken neck. But the

Copyright ©2006 The McGraw-Hill Companies Inc. All rights reserved.

students would egg each other on to go "rock diving." Playing deadly games like these is a horrifying phase of growing up for some teenagers.

_____ 3.

Attitudes toward Food

As children, we form attitudes toward food that are not easily changed. In some families, food is love. Not all families are like this, but some children grow up with this attitude. Some families think of food as something precious and not to be wasted. The attitudes children pick up about food are hard to change in adulthood. Some families celebrate with food. If a child learns an attitude, it is hard to break this later. Someone once said: "As the twig is bent, so grows the tree." Children are very impressionable, and they can't really think for themselves when they are small. Children learn from the parent figures in their lives, and later from their peers. Some families have healthy attitudes about food. It is important for adults to teach their children these healthy attitudes. Otherwise, the children may have weight problems when they are adults.

_____ 4.

Qualities in a Friend

There are several qualities I look for in a friend. A friend should give support and security. A friend should also be fun to be around. Friends can have faults, like anyone else, and sometimes it is hard to overlook them. But a friend can't be dropped because he or she has faults. A friend should stick to you, even in bad times. There is a saying that "a friend in need is a friend indeed." I believe this means that there are good friends and fair-weather friends. The second type is not a true friend. He or she is the kind of person who runs when there's trouble. Friends don't always last a lifetime. Someone you believed to be your best friend may lose contact with you if you move to a different area or go around with a different group of people. A friend should be generous and understanding. A friend does not have to be exactly like you. Sometimes friends are opposites, but they still like each other and get along. Since I am a very quiet person, I can't say that I have many friends. But these are the qualities I believe a friend should have.

_____ 5.

An Unsafe Place

We play touch football on an unsafe field. First of all, the grass on the field is seldom mowed. The result is that we have to run through tangled weeds that wrap around our ankles like trip wires. The tall grass also hides some gaping holes lurking beneath. The best players know the exact positions of all the holes and manage to detour around them like soldiers zigzagging across a minefield. Most of us, though, endure at least one sprained ankle per game. Another danger is the old baseball infield that we use as the last twenty yards of our gridiron. This area is covered with stones and broken glass. No matter how often we clean it up, we can never keep pace with the broken bottles hurled on the field by the teenagers we call the "night shift." These people apparently hold drinking parties every night in the abandoned dugout and enjoy throwing the empties out on the field. During every game, we try to avoid falling on especially big chunks of Budweiser bottles. Finally, encircling the entire field is an old, rusty chain-link fence full of tears and holes. Being slammed into the fence during the play can mean a painful stabbing by the jagged wires. All these dangers have made us less afraid of opposing teams than of the field where we play.

10 Adding Details to Complete a Paragraph

ACTIVITY

Each of the following paragraphs needs specific details to back up its supporting points. In the spaces provided, add a sentence or two of realistic details for each supporting point. The more specific you are, the more convincing your details are likely to be.

1.
A Pushover Instructor

We knew after the first few classes that the instructor was a pushover. First of all, he didn't seem able to control the class.

_____

_____

_____

In addition, he made some course requirements easier when a few students complained.

_____

_____

_____

Finally, he gave the easiest quiz we had ever taken.

_____

_____

_____

CHAPTER 3   The First and Second Steps in Writing   85

Copyright ©2006 The McGraw-Hill Companies, Inc. All rights reserved.

2.

Helping a Parent in College

There are several ways a family can help a parent who is attending college. First, family members can take over some of the household chores that the parent usually does.

_____

_____

_____

Also, family members can make sure that the student has some quiet study time.

_____

_____

_____

Last, families can take an interest in the student's problems and accomplishments.

_____

_____

_____

11 Writing a Simple Paragraph

You know now that an effective paragraph does two essential things: (1) it makes a point, and (2) it provides specific details to support that point. You have considered a number of paragraphs that are effective because they follow these two basic steps or ineffective because they fail to follow them.

You are ready, then, to write a simple paragraph of your own. Choose one of the three assignments below, and follow carefully the guidelines provided.

ASSIGNMENT 1

Turn back to the activity on page 80 and select the point for which you have the best supporting details. Develop that point into a paragraph by following these steps:

a   If necessary, rewrite the point so that the first sentence is more specific or suits your purpose more exactly. For example, you might want to rewrite the second point so that it includes a specific time and place: "Dinner at the Union Building Cafeteria was terrible yesterday."

b   Provide several sentences of information to develop each of your three supporting details fully. Make sure that all the information in your paragraph truly supports your point. As an aid, use the paragraph form on page 745.

c   Use the words *First of all, Second,* and *Finally* to introduce your three supporting details.

d   Conclude your paragraph with a sentence that refers to your opening point. This last sentence "rounds off" the paragraph and lets the reader know that your discussion is complete. For example, the paragraph "Changes in the Family" on page 50 begins with "Changes in our society in recent years have weakened family life." It closes with a statement that refers to, and echoes, the opening point: "Clearly, modern life is a challenge to family life."

e   Supply a title based on your point. For instance, point 4 on page 81 might have the title "Ways to Economize."

Use the following list to check your paragraph for each of the above items:

Yes   No

_____ _____   Do you begin with a point?

_____ _____   Do you provide relevant, specific details that support the point?

_____ _____   Do you use the words *First of all, Second,* and *Finally* to introduce your three supporting details?

_____ _____   Do you have a closing sentence?

_____ _____   Do you have a title based on your point?

_____ _____   Are your sentences clear and free of obvious errors?

ASSIGNMENT 2

In this chapter you have read two paragraphs (pages 54–55) on reasons for being in college. For this assignment, write a paragraph describing your own reasons for being in college. You might want to look first at the following list of common reasons students give for going to school. Write a check mark next to each reason that applies to you. If you have different reasons for being in college that are not listed here, add them to the list. Then select your three most important reasons for being in school and generate specific supporting details for each reason.

Before starting, reread paragraph B on page 54. *You must provide comparable specific details of your own.* Make your paragraph truly personal; do not fall back on vague generalities like those in paragraph A on page 54. As you work on your paragraph, use the checklist for Assignment 1 as a guide.

Copyright ©2006 The McGraw-Hill Companies, Inc. All rights reserved.

Apply in
My Case

Reasons Students Go to College

_____   To have some fun before getting a job

_____   To prepare for a specific career

_____   To please their families

_____   To educate and enrich themselves

_____   To be with friends who are going to college

_____   To take advantage of an opportunity they didn't have before

_____   To find a husband or wife

_____   To see if college has anything to offer them

_____   To do more with their lives than they've done so far

_____   To take advantage of Veterans Administration benefits or other special funding

_____   To earn the status that they feel comes with a college degree

_____   To get a new start in life

_____   Other: _____

ASSIGNMENT 3

Write a paragraph about stress in your life. Choose three of the following stressful areas and provide specific examples and details to develop each area.

Stress at school

Stress at work

Stress at home

Stress with a friend or friends

Use the checklist for Assignment 1 as a guide while you are working on the paragraph.

4 The Third Step in Writing

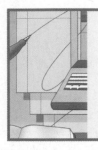

This chapter will show you how to

- organize specific evidence in a paper by using a clear method of organization
- connect the specific evidence by using transitions and other connecting words

You know from Chapter 3 that the first two steps in writing an effective paragraph are making a point and supporting the point with specific evidence. This chapter will deal with the third step. You'll learn the chief ways to organize and connect the supporting information in a paper.

Step 3: Organize and Connect the Specific Evidence

At the same time that you are generating the specific details needed to support a point, you should be thinking about ways to organize and connect those details. All the details in your paper must cohere, or stick together; when they do, your reader is able to move smoothly from one bit of supporting information to the next. This chapter will discuss the following ways to organize and connect supporting details: (1) common methods of organization, (2) transition words, and (3) other connecting words.

Common Methods of Organization: Time Order and Emphatic Order

Copyright ©2006 The McGraw-Hill Companies, Inc. All rights reserved.

Time order and emphatic order are common methods used to organize the supporting material in a paper. (You will learn more specialized methods of development in Part Two of the book.)

Time order simply means that details are listed as they occur in time. *First* this is done; *next* this; *then* this; *after* that, this; and so on. Here is a paragraph that organizes its details through time order.

How I Relax

The way I relax when I get home from school on Thursday night is, first of all, to put my three children to bed. Next, I run hot water in the tub and put in lots of scented bubble bath. As the bubbles rise, I undress and get into the tub. The water is relaxing to my tired muscles, and the bubbles are tingly on my skin. I lie back and put my feet on the water spigots, with everything but my head under the water. I like to stick my big toe up the spigot and spray water over the tub. After about ten minutes of soaking, I wash myself with scented soap, get out and dry myself off, and put on my nightgown. Then I go downstairs and make myself a ham, lettuce, and tomato sandwich on rye bread and pour myself a tall glass of iced tea with plenty of sugar and ice cubes. I carry these into the living room and turn on the television. To get comfortable, I sit on the couch with a pillow behind me and my legs under me. I enjoy watching The Tonight Show or a late movie. The time is very peaceful after a long, hard day of housecleaning, cooking, washing, and attending night class.

Fill in the missing words: "How I relax" uses the following words to help show time order: _____, _____, _____, _____, and _____.

Emphatic order is sometimes described as "save-the-best-till-last" order. It means that the most interesting or important detail is placed in the last part of a paper. (In cases where all the details seem equal in importance, the writer should impose a personal order that seems logical or appropriate to the details.) The last position in a paper is the most emphatic position because the reader is most likely to remember the last thing read. *Finally, last of all,* and *most important* are typical words showing emphasis. The following paragraph organizes its details through emphatic order.

The <u>National Enquirer</u>

There are several reasons why the <u>National Enquirer</u> is so popular. First of all, the paper is advertised on television. In the ads, attractive-looking people say, with a smile, "I want to know!" as they scan the pages of the <u>Enquirer</u>. The ads reassure people that it's all right to want to read stories such as "Heartbreak for Jennifer Lopez" or "Prince's Fiancée in New Royal Topless Scandal." In addition, the paper is easily available. In supermarkets, convenience stores, and drugstores, the <u>Enquirer</u> is always displayed in racks close to the cash register. As customers wait in line, they can't help being attracted to the paper's glaring headlines. Then, on impulse, customers will add the paper to their other purchases. Most of all, people read the <u>Enquirer</u> because they love gossip. We find other people's lives fascinating, especially if those people are rich and famous. We want to see and read about their homes, their clothes, and their friends, lovers, and families. We also take a kind of mean delight in their unflattering photos and problems and mistakes, perhaps because we envy them. Even though we may be ashamed of our interest, it's hard to resist buying a paper that promises "The Forbidden Love of Julia Roberts" or "Film Star Who Now Looks Like a Cadaver" or even "Hollywood Star Wars: Who Hates Whom and Why." The <u>Enquirer</u> knows how to get us interested and make us buy.

Fill in the missing words: The paragraph lists a total of _____ different reasons people read the *National Enquirer.* The writer of the paragraph feels that the most important reason is _____. He or she signals this reason by using the emphasis words _____.

Some paragraphs use a *combination of time order and emphatic order.* For example, "Good-Bye, Tony" on page 52 includes time order: it moves from the time Tony arrived to the end of the evening. In addition, the writer uses emphatic order, ending with her most important reason (signaled by the words *most of all)* for not wanting to see Tony anymore.

Transitions

Look at the following items. Then check (✓) the one that is easier to read and understand.

_____ Our landlord repainted our apartment. He replaced the dishwasher.

_____ Our landlord repainted our apartment. Also, he replaced the dishwasher.

Copyright ©2006 The McGraw-Hill Companies, Inc. All rights reserved.

You probably found the second item easier to understand. The word *also* makes it clear that the writer is adding a second way the landlord has been of help. *Transitions,* or *transition words,* are signal words that help readers follow the direction of the writer's thought. They show the relationship between ideas, connecting one thought to the next. They are "bridge" words, carrying the reader across from one idea to the next.

Paperback books cost less than hardbacks. ⎯⎯⎯ **ALSO** ⎯⎯⎯ , they are easier to carry.

Two major types of transitions are of particular help when you write: words that show *addition* and words that show *time.*

Words That Show Addition

Check (✓) the item that is easier to read and understand.

1. _____ a. A drinking problem can destroy a person's life. It can tear a family apart.

   _____ b. A drinking problem can destroy a person's life. In addition, it can tear a family apart.

2. _____ a. One way to lose friends is always to talk and never to listen. A way to end friendships is to borrow money and never pay it back.

   _____ b. One way to lose friends is always to talk and never to listen. Another way to end friendships is to borrow money and never pay it back.

In the pair of sentences about a drinking problem, the words *In addition* help make the relationship betwen the two sentences clear. The author is describing two effects of a drinking problem: it can destroy a life and a family. *In addition* and words like it are know as addition words. In the pair of sentences about losing friends, you probably found the second item easier to understand. The word *Another* is an addition word that makes it clear that the writer is describing a second way to lose friends.

Addition words signal added ideas. They help writers organize information and present it clearly to readers. Some common words that show addition are on the following page.

> **Addition words**
>
> | | | |
> |---|---|---|
> | one | to begin with | in addition |
> | first | another | next |
> | first of all | second | last (of all) |
> | for one thing | also | finally |

Words That Show Time

Check (✓) the item that is easier to read and understand.

1. _____ a. I had blood work done. I went to the doctor.

   _____ b. I had blood work done. Then I went to the doctor.

The word *Then* in the second item makes clear the relationship between the sentences. After having blood work done, the writer goes to the doctor. *Then* and words like it are time words, carrying the reader from one idea to the next.

I had blood work done. _____ I went to the doctor.

Here are some more pairs of sentences. Check (✓) the item in each pair that contains a time word and so is easier to read and understand.

2. _____ a. Every week my uncle studies the food ads to see which stores have the best specials. He clips all the coupons.

   _____ b. Every week my uncle studies the food ads to see which stores have the best specials. Next, he clips all the coupons.

3. _____ a. Carmen took a very long shower. There was no hot water left for anyone else in the house.

   _____ b. Carmen took a very long shower. After that, there was no hot water left for anyone else in the house.

Copyright ©2006 The McGraw-Hill Companies, Inc. All rights reserved.

In the pair of sentences about the uncle, the word *Next* helps make the relationship between the two sentences clear. The uncle studies ads, and then he clips coupons. In the second pair of sentences, the word *after* makes the relationship clear: after Carmen's long shower, there was no hot water left for anyone else.

Time words tell us *when* something happened in relation to when something else happened. They help writers organize and make clear the order of events, stages, and steps in a process. Below are some common words that show time.

Time words		
before	next	later
first	as	after
second	when	finally
third	while	then

ACTIVITY

1. Fill in each blank with the appropriate addition transition from the box. Use each transition once.

another	finally	one

There are some widely popular but inappropriate methods that people

have to combat stress. _____ common strategy is to consume massive quantities of junk food, which is easily done thanks to all the ever-

present convenience stores and fast-food restaurants. _____ way to deal with stress is to doze or sleep for hours and hours, even during the

day. _____, watching hours of nonstop TV can put people in a stupor that helps them forget the problems of everyday life.

2. Fill in each blank with the appropriate time transition from the box. Use each transition once.

then	next	before
first	after	

I do not like to write. In fact, I dislike writing so much that I have developed a series of steps for postponing the agony of doing writing assignments. _____ I tell myself that to proceed without the proper equipment would be unwise. So I go out to buy a new pen, and this kills at least an hour. _____ , I begin to stare at the blank page. _____ long, however, I realize that writing may also require thought, so I begin to think deeply about my subject. Soon I feel drowsy. This naturally leads to the conclusion that I need a nap because I can't throw myself into my writing until I am at my very best. _____ a refreshing nap, I again face the blank page. It is usually at this stage that I actually write a sentence or two—disappointing ones. I _____ wisely decide that I need inspiration, perhaps from an interesting magazine or a television movie. If I feel a bit guilty, I comfort myself with the knowledge that, as any artist knows, you can't rush these things.

3. Underline the three *addition* signals in the following paragraph:

I am opposed to state-supported lotteries for a number of reasons. First of all, by supporting lotteries, states are supporting gambling. I don't see anything morally wrong with gambling, but it is a known cause of suffering for many people who do it to excess. The state should be concerned with relieving suffering, not causing it. Another objection I have to state lotteries is the kind of advertising they do on television. The commercials promote the lotteries as an easy way to get rich. In fact, the odds against getting rich are astronomical. Last, the lotteries take advantage of the people who can least afford them. Studies have shown that people with lower incomes are more likely to play the lottery than people with higher incomes. This is the harshest reality of the lotteries: the state is encouraging people of limited means not to save their money but to throw it away on a state-supported pipe dream.

Copyright ©2006 The McGraw-Hill Companies, Inc. All rights reserved.

4. Underline the four *time* signals in the following paragraph:

It is often easy to spot bad drivers on the road because they usually make more than one mistake: they make their mistakes in series. First, for example, you notice that a man is tailgating you. Then, almost as soon as you notice, he has passed you in a no-passing zone. That's two mistakes already in a matter of seconds. Next, almost invariably, you see him speed down the road and pass someone else. Finally, as you watch in disbelief, glad that he's out of your way, he speeds through a red light or cuts across oncoming traffic in a wild left turn.

Other Kinds of Transitions

In the following box are other common transitional words, grouped according to the kind of signal they give readers. In the paragraphs you write, you will most often use addition signals (words like *first, also, another,* and *finally*), but all of the following signals are helpful to know as well.

Other Common Transitional Words

Space signals: next to, across, on the opposite side, to the left, to the right, in front, in back, above, below, behind, nearby

Change-of-direction signals: but, however, yet, in contrast, otherwise, still, on the contrary, on the other hand

Illustration signals: for example, for instance, specifically, as an illustration, once, such as

Conclusion signals: therefore, consequently, thus, then, as a result, in summary, to conclude, last of all, finally

---

ACTIVITY

1. Underline the three *space* signals in the following paragraph:

Standing in the burned-out shell of my living room was a shocking experience. Above my head were charred beams, all that remained of our ceiling. In front of me, where our television and stereo had once stood, were twisted pieces of metal and chunks of blackened glass. Strangely, some items seemed little damaged by the fire. For example, I could see the TV tuner knob and a dusty CD under the rubble. I walked through the gritty ashes until I came to what was left of our sofa. Behind the sofa had been a wall of family photographs. Now, the wall and the pictures were gone. I found only a waterlogged scrap of my wedding picture.

2. Underline the four *change-of-direction* signals in the following paragraph:

In some ways, train travel is superior to air travel. People always marvel at the speed with which airplanes can zip from one end of the country to another. Trains, on the other hand, definitely take longer. But sometimes longer can be better. Traveling across the country by train allows you to experience the trip more completely. You get to see the cities and towns, mountains and prairies that too often pass by unnoticed when you fly. Another advantage of train travel is comfort. Traveling by plane means wedging yourself into a narrow seat with your knees bumping the back of the seat in front of you and being handed a "snack" consisting of a bag of ten roasted peanuts. In contrast, the seats on most trains are spacious and comfortable, permitting even the longest-legged traveler to stretch out and watch the scenery just outside the window. And when train travelers grow hungry, they can get up and stroll to the dining car, where they can order anything from a simple snack to a gourmet meal. There's no question that train travel is definitely slow and old-fashioned compared with air travel. However, in many ways it is much more civilized.

3. Underline the three *illustration* signals in the following selection:

Status symbols are all around us. The cars we drive, for instance, say something about who we are and how successful we have been. The auto makers depend on this perception of automobiles, designing their commercials to show older, well-established people driving luxury sedans and young, fun-loving people driving to the beach in sports cars. Clothing, too, has always been a status symbol. Specifically, schoolchildren are often rated by their classmates according to the brand names of their clothing. Another example of a status symbol is the cell phone. This device, not so long ago considered a novelty, is now used by almost everyone. Being without a cell phone today is like being without a regular phone in the 1990s.

4. Underline the *conclusion* signal in the following paragraph:

A hundred years ago, miners used to bring caged canaries down into the mines with them to act as warning signals. If the bird died, the miners knew that the oxygen was running out. The smaller animal would be affected much more quickly than the miners. In the same way,

Copyright ©2006 The McGraw-Hill Companies, Inc. All rights reserved.

animals are acting as warning signals to us today. Baby birds die before they can hatch because pesticides in the environment cause the adults to lay eggs with paper-thin shells. Fish die when lakes are contaminated with acid rain or poisonous mercury. The dangers in our environment will eventually affect all life on earth, including humans. Therefore, we must pay attention to these early warning signals. If we don't, we will be as foolish as a miner who ignored a dead canary—and we will die.

Other Connecting Words

In addition to transitions, there are three other kinds of connecting words that help tie together the specific evidence in a paper: *repeated words, pronouns,* and *synonyms.* Each will be discussed in turn.

Repeated Words

Many of us have been taught by English instructors—correctly so—not to repeat ourselves in our writing. On the other hand, repeating key words can help tie ideas together. In the paragraph that follows, the word *retirement* is repeated to remind readers of the key idea on which the discussion is centered. Underline the word the five times it appears.

Oddly enough, retirement can pose more problems for the spouse than for the retired person. For a person who has been accustomed to a demanding job, retirement can mean frustration and a feeling of uselessness. This feeling will put pressure on the spouse to provide challenges at home equal to those of the workplace. Often, these tasks will disrupt the spouse's well-established routine. Another problem arising from retirement is filling up all those empty hours. The spouse may find himself or herself in the role of social director or tour guide, expected to come up with a new form of amusement every day. Without sufficient challenges or leisure activities, a person can become irritable and take out the resulting boredom and frustration of retirement on the marriage partner. It is no wonder that many of these partners wish their spouses would come out of retirement and do something—anything—just to get out of the house.

Pronouns

Pronouns (*he, she, it, you, they, this, that,* and others) are another way to connect ideas as you develop a paper. Using pronouns to take the place of other words or ideas can help you avoid needless repetition. (Be sure, though, to use pronouns with care in order to avoid the unclear or inconsistent pronoun references described in Chapters 27 and 28 of this book.) Underline the eight pronouns in the passage below, noting at the same time the words that the pronouns refer to.

> A professor of nutrition at a major university recently advised his students that they could do better on their examinations by eating lots of sweets. He told them that the sugar in cakes and candy would stimulate their brains to work more efficiently, and that if the sugar was eaten for only a month or two, it would not do them any harm.

Synonyms

Using synonyms—words that are alike in meaning—can also help move the reader from one thought to the next. In addition, the use of synonyms increases variety and interest by avoiding needless repetition of the same words. Underline the three words used as synonyms for *false ideas* in the following passage.

> There are many false ideas about suicide. One wrong idea is that a person who talks about suicide never follows through. The truth is that about three out of every four people who commit suicide notify one or more other persons ahead of time. Another misconception is that a person who commits suicide is poor or downtrodden. Actually, poverty appears to be a deterrent to suicide rather than a predisposing factor. A third myth about suicide is that people bent on suicide will eventually take their lives one way or another, whether or not the most obvious means of suicide is removed from their reach. In fact, since an attempt at suicide is a kind of cry for help, removing a convenient means of taking one's life, such as a gun, shows people bent on suicide that someone cares enough about them to try to prevent it.

ACTIVITY

Read the selection below and then answer the questions about it that follow.

My Worst Experience of the Week

[1]The registration process at State College was a nightmare. [2]The night before registration officially began, I went to bed anxious about the whole matter, and nothing that happened the next day served to ease my tension. [3]First, even though I had paid my registration fee early last spring, the people at the bursar's office had no record of my payment. [4]And for some bizarre reason, they wouldn't accept the receipt I had. [5]Consequently, I had to stand in line for two hours, waiting for someone to give me a slip of paper which

Copyright ©2006 The McGraw-Hill Companies, Inc. All rights reserved.

stated that I had, in fact, paid my registration fee. ⁶The need for this new receipt seemed ludicrous to me, since all along I had proof that I had paid. ⁷I was next told that I had to see my adviser in the Law and Justice Department and that the department was in Corridor C of the Triad Building. ⁸I had no idea what or where the Triad was. ⁹But, finally, I found my way to the ugly gray-white building. ¹⁰Then I began looking for Corridor C. ¹¹When I found it, everyone there was a member of the Communications Department. ¹²No one seemed to know where Law and Justice had gone. ¹³Finally, one instructor said she thought Law and Justice was in Corridor A. ¹⁴"And where is Corridor A?" I asked. ¹⁵"I don't know," the teacher answered. ¹⁶"I'm new here." ¹⁷She saw the bewildered look on my face and said sympathetically, "You're not the only one who's confused." ¹⁸I nodded and walked numbly away. ¹⁹I felt as if I were fated to spend the rest of the semester trying to complete the registration process, and I wondered if I would ever become an official college student.

Questions

1. How many times is the key word *registration* used? _____

2. Write here the pronoun that is used for *people at the bursar's office* (sentence 4): _____; *Corridor C* (sentence 11): _____; *instructor* (sentence 17): _____.

3. Write here the words that are used as a synonym for *receipt* (sentence 5):

_____

the words that are used as a synonym for *Triad* (sentence 9):

_____

the word that is used as a synonym for *instructor* (sentence 15).

_____

■ Review Activity

Complete the following statements.

1. *Time order* means _____

_____

2. *Emphatic order* means _____

_____

3. _____ are signal words that help readers follow the direction of a writer's thought.

4. In addition to transitions, three other kinds of connecting words that help link sentences and ideas are repeated words, _____, and _____.

Practice in Organizing and Connecting Specific Evidence

You now know the third step in effective writing: organizing and connecting the specific evidence used to support the main point of a paper. This closing section will expand and strengthen your understanding of the third step in writing.

You will work through the following series of activities:

1 Organizing through Time Order

2 Organizing through Emphatic Order

3 Organizing through a Combination of Time Order and Emphatic Order

4 Identifying Transitions

5 Identifying Transitions and Other Connecting Words

1 Organizing through Time Order

ACTIVITY

Use time order to organize the scrambled list of sentences below. Write the number 1 beside the point that all the other sentences support. Then number each supporting sentence as it occurs in time.

_____ The table is right near the garbage pail.

_____ So you reluctantly select a gluelike tuna-fish sandwich, a crushed apple pie, and watery, lukewarm coffee.

_____ You sit at the edge of the table, away from the garbage pail, and gulp down your meal.

_____   Trying to eat in the cafeteria is an unpleasant experience.

_____   Suddenly you spot a free table in the center.

_____   With a last swallow of the lukewarm coffee, you get up and leave the cafeteria as rapidly as possible.

_____   Flies are flitting into and out of the pail.

_____   By the time it is your turn, the few things that are almost good are gone.

_____   There does not seem to be a free table anywhere.

_____   Unfortunately, there is a line in the cafeteria.

_____   The hoagies, coconut-custard pie, and iced tea have all disappeared.

_____   You hold your tray and look for a place to sit down.

_____   You have a class in a few minutes, and so you run in to grab something to eat quickly.

2 Organizing through Emphatic Order

ACTIVITY

Use emphatic order (order of importance) to arrange the following scrambled list of sentences. Write the number 1 beside the point that all the other sentences support. Then number each supporting sentence, starting with what seems to be the least important detail and ending with the most important detail.

_____   The people here are all around my age and seem to be genuinely friendly and interested in me.

_____   The place where I live has several important advantages.

_____   The schools in this neighborhood have a good reputation, so I feel that my daughter is getting a good education.

_____   The best thing of all about this area, though, is the school system.

_____   Therefore, I don't have to put up with public transportation or worry about how much it's going to cost to park each day.

_____   The school also has an extended day-care program, so I know my daughter is in good hands until I come home from work.

_____   First of all, I like the people who live in the other apartments near mine.

Copyright ©2006 The McGraw-Hill Companies, Inc. All rights reserved.

_____   Another positive aspect of this area is that it's close to where I work.

_____   That's more than I can say for the last place I lived, where people stayed behind locked doors.

_____   The office where I'm a receptionist is only a six-block walk from my house.

_____   In addition, I save a lot of wear and tear on my car.

3 Organizing through a Combination of Time Order and Emphatic Order

ACTIVITY

Use a combination of time and emphatic order to arrange the scrambled list of sentences below. Write the number 1 beside the point that all the other sentences support. Then number each supporting sentence. Paying close attention to transitional words and phrases will help you organize and connect the supporting sentences.

_____   I did not see the spider but visited my friend in the hospital, where he suffered through a week of nausea and dizziness because of the poison.

_____   We were listening to the radio when we discovered that nature was calling.

_____   As I got back into the car, I sensed, rather than felt or saw, a presence on my left hand.

_____   After my two experiences, I suspect that my fear of spiders will be with me until I die.

_____   The first experience was the time when my best friend received a bite from a black widow spider.

_____   I looked down at my hand, but I could not see anything because it was so dark.

_____   I had two experiences when I was sixteen that are the cause of my *arachnophobia,* a terrible and uncontrollable fear of spiders.

_____   We stopped the car at the side of the road, walked into the woods a few feet, and watered the leaves.

_____   My friend then entered the car, putting on the dashboard light, and I almost passed out with horror.

_____   I saw the bandage on his hand and the puffy swelling when the bandage was removed.

_____   Then it flew off my hand and into the dark bushes nearby.

_____ I sat in the car for an hour afterward, shaking and sweating and constantly rubbing the fingers of my hand to reassure myself that the spider was no longer there.

_____ But my more dramatic experience with spiders happened one evening when another friend and I were driving around in his car.

_____ Almost completely covering my fingers was a monstrous brown spider, with white stripes running down each of a seemingly endless number of long, furry legs.

_____ Most of all, I saw the ugly red scab on his hand and the yellow pus that continued oozing from under the scab for several weeks.

_____ I imagined my entire hand soon disappearing as the behemoth relentlessly devoured it.

_____ At the same time I cried out "Arghh!" and flicked my hand violently back and forth to shake off the spider.

_____ For a long, horrible second it clung stickily, as if intertwined for good among the fingers of my hand.

4 Identifying Transitions

ACTIVITY 1

Fill in each blank with the appropriate addition transition from the box. Use each transition once.

also	second	for one thing	last of all

Why School May Frighten a Young Child

School may be frightening to young children for a number of reasons.

_____, the regimented environment may be a new and disturbing experience. At home, children may have been able to do what they wanted when they wanted to do it. In school, however, they are given set times for talking, working, playing, eating, and even going to the toilet. A

_____ source of anxiety may be the public method of discipline that some teachers use. Whereas at home children are scolded in private, in school they may be held up to embarrassment and ridicule in front of

Copyright ©2006 The McGraw-Hill Companies, Inc. All rights reserved.

their peers. "Bonnie," the teacher may say, "why are you the only one in class who didn't do your homework?" Or, "David, why are you the only

one who can't work quietly at your seat?" Children may _____ be frightened by the loss of personal attention. Their little discomforts or mishaps, such as tripping on the stairs, may bring instant sympathy from a parent; in school, there is often no one to notice, or the teacher is frequently too busy to care and just says, "Go do your work. You'll be

all right." _____, a child may be scared by the competitive environment of the school. At home, one hopes, such competition for attention is minimal. But in school, children may vie for the teacher's approving glance or tone, or for stars on a paper, or for favored seats in the front row. For these and other reasons, it is not surprising that children may have difficulty adjusting to school.

ACTIVITY 2

Fill in each blank with the appropriate time transition from the box. Use each transition once.

then	first	after
as	later	

A Victory for Big Brother

In one of the most terrifying scenes in all of literature, George Orwell in his classic novel *1984* describes how a government known as Big Brother destroys a couple's love. The couple, Winston and Julia, fall in love and meet

secretly, knowing the government would not approve. _____ informers turn them in, a government agent named O'Brien takes steps

to end their love. _____ he straps Winston down and explains

that he has discovered Winston's worst fear. _____ he sets a cage with two giant, starving sewer rats on the table next to Winston. He says that when he presses a lever, the door of the cage will slide up, and the rats will shoot out like bullets and bore straight into Winston's face.

_____ Winston's eyes dart back and forth, revealing his terror,

O'Brien places his hand on the lever. Winston knows that the only way out is for Julia to take his place. Suddenly, he hears his own voice screaming, "Do it to Julia! Not me! Julia!" Orwell does not describe Julia's interroga-

tion, but when Julia and Winston see each other _____, they realize that each has betrayed the other. Their love is gone. Big Brother has won.

ACTIVITY 3

Fill in each blank with the appropriate addition or change-of-direction transition from the box. Use each transition once.

however	also	next
finally	but	first

Watching TV Football

Watching a football game on television may seem like the easiest thing

in the world. _____, like the game of football itself, watching

a game correctly is far more complicated than it appears. _____ is the matter of what company you invite. The ideal number of people

depends on the size of your living room. You should _____ invite at least one person who will be rooting for the opposite team. There's nothing like a little rivalry to increase the enjoyment of a football game.

_____, you must attend to the refreshments. Make sure to have on hand plenty of everyone's favorite drinks, along with the essential chips, dips, and pretzels. You may even want something more substantial on hand, like sandwiches or pizza. If you do, make everyone wait until the moment of kickoff before eating. Waiting will make everything taste much

better. _____, there is one bit of sports equipment you should have on hand: a football. In the spirit of the occasion, it is good to have a

football to toss around outside during halftime. _____ if your team happens to be getting trounced, you may decide not to wait until halftime.

Copyright ©2006 The McGraw-Hill Companies, Inc. All rights reserved.

ACTIVITY 4

Fill in each blank with the appropriate addition or change-of-direction transitions from the box. Use each transition once.

fourth	but	yet	another
for one thing	second	however	last

Avoidance Tactics

Getting down to studying for an exam or writing a paper is hard, and so it is tempting for students to use one of the following five avoidance tactics

in order to put the work aside. _____, students may say to themselves, "I can't do it." They adopt a defeatist attitude at the start and give up without a struggle. They could get help with their work by using such

college services as tutoring programs and skill labs, _____ they

refuse even to try. A _____ avoidance technique is to say, "I'm too busy." Students may take on an extra job, become heavily involved in social activities, or allow family problems to become so time-consuming

that they cannot concentrate on their studies. _____ if college really matters to a student, he or she will make sure that there is enough

time to do the required work. _____ avoidance technique is expressed by the phrase, "I'm too tired." Typically, sleepiness occurs when it is time to study or go to class and then vanishes when the pressure of

school is off. This sleepiness is a sign of work avoidance. A _____ excuse is to say, "I'll do it later." Putting things off until the last minute is practically a guarantee of poor grades on tests and papers. When everything else—watching TV, calling a friend, or even cleaning the oven— seems more urgent than studying, a student may simply be escaping

academic work. _____, some students avoid work by saying to themselves, "I'm here and that's what counts." Some students live under the dangerous delusion that, since they possess a college ID, a parking sticker, and textbooks, the course work will somehow take care of itself.

_____ once a student has a college ID in a pocket, he or she has only just begun. Doing the necessary studying, writing, and reading will bring real results: good grades, genuine learning, and a sense of accomplishment.

ACTIVITY 5

Fill in each blank with the appropriate transition from the box. Use each transition once.

Addition transitions: first of all, second, finally

Time transition: when

Illustration transition: once

Change-of-direction transition: however

Conclusion transition: as a result

Joining a Multicultural Club

One of the best things I've done in college is to join a multicultural club. _____, the club has helped me become friendly with a diverse group of people. At any time in my apartment, I can have someone from Pakistan chatting about music to someone from Sweden, or someone from Russia talking about politics to someone from Uganda. _____, I watched a Mexican student give tacos to three students from China. They had never tasted such a thing before, but they liked it. A _____ benefit of the club is that it's helped me realize how similar people are.

_____ the whole club first assembled, we wound up having a conversation about dating and sex that included the perspectives of fifteen countries and six continents! It was clear we all shared the feeling that sex was fascinating. The talk lasted for hours, with many different people describing the wildest or funniest experience they had had with the opposite sex. Only a few students, particularly those from the United States and Japan, seemed bashful. _____, the club has reminded me about the dangers of stereotyping. Before I joined the club, my only direct experience with people from China was ordering meals in the local Chinese restaurant. _____, I believed that most Chinese people ate lots of rice and worked in restaurants. In the club, _____ I met Chinese people who were soccer players, English majors, and math teachers. I've also seen Jewish and Muslim students—people who I thought would never get along—drop their preconceived notions and become friends. Even more than my classes, the club has been an eye-opener for me.

Copyright ©2006 The McGraw-Hill Companies, Inc. All rights reserved.

5 Identifying Transitions and Other Connecting Words

ACTIVITY

This activity will give you practice in identifying transitions and other connecting words that are used to help tie ideas together.

Section A—Transitions: Locate the transitional word in each sentence and write it in the space provided.

1. I decided to pick up a drop-add form from the registrar's office. However, I changed my mind when I saw the long line of students waiting there.

   _____

2. In England, drivers use the left-hand side of the road. Consequently, in a car the steering wheel is on the right side.

   _____

3. Crawling babies will often investigate a new object by putting it in their mouth. Therefore, parents should be alert for any pins, tacks, or other dangerous items on floors and carpets.

   _____

4. One technique that advertisers use is to have a celebrity endorse a product. The consumer then associates the product with the star qualities of the celebrity.

   _____

Section B—Repeated Words: In the space provided, write the repeated words.

5. We absorb radiation from many sources in our environment. Our color television sets and microwave ovens, among other things, give off low-level radiation.

   _____

6. Many researchers believe that people have weight set-points their bodies try to maintain. This may explain why many dieters return to their original weight.

   _____

7. At the end of the rock concert, thousands of fans held up lighters in the darkened area. The sea of lighters signaled that the fans wanted an encore.

   _____

8. Establishing credit is important for everyone. A good credit history is often necessary when applying for a loan or charge account.

    _____

Section C—Synonyms: In the space provided, write in the synonym for the underlined word.

9. I checked my <u>car</u>'s tires, oil, water, and belts before the trip. But the ungrateful machine sputtered and died about fifty miles from home.

    _____

10. Women's <u>clothes</u>, in general, use less material than men's clothes. Yet women's garments usually cost more than men's.

    _____

11. The temperance movement in this country sought to ban <u>alcohol</u>. Drinking liquor, movement leaders said, led to violence, poverty, prostitution, and insanity.

    _____

12. For me, <u>apathy</u> quickly sets in when the weather becomes hot and sticky. This listlessness disappears when the humidity decreases.

    _____

Section D—Pronouns: In the space provided, write in the word referred to by the underlined pronoun.

13. At the turn of the century, bananas were still an oddity in the United States. Some people even attempted to eat <u>them</u> with the skin on.

    _____

14. Canning vegetables is easy and economical. <u>It</u> can also be very dangerous.

    _____

15. There are a number of signs that appear when students are under stress. For example, <u>they</u> start to have trouble studying, eating, and even sleeping.

    _____

Copyright ©2006 The McGraw-Hill Companies, Inc. All rights reserved.

5 The Fourth Step in Writing

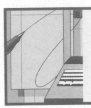

> *This chapter will show you how to*
> - revise so that your sentences flow smoothly and clearly
> - edit so that your sentences are error-free

Step 4: Write Clear, Error-Free Sentences

Up to now this book has emphasized the first three steps in writing an effective paragraph: making a point, supporting the point, and organizing and connecting the evidence. This chapter will focus on the fourth step: writing clear, error-free sentences. You'll learn how to revise a paragraph so that your sentences flow smoothly and clearly. Then you'll review how to edit a paragraph for mistakes in grammar, punctuation, and spelling.

Revising Sentences

The following strategies will help you to revise your sentences effectively.

- Use parallelism.
- Use a consistent point of view.
- Use specific words.
- Use concise wording.
- Vary your sentences.

Use Parallelism

Words in a pair or a series should have a parallel structure. By balancing the items in a pair or a series so that they have the same kind of structure, you will make a sentence clearer and easier to read. Notice how the parallel sentences that follow read more smoothly than the nonparallel ones.

Nonparallel (Not Balanced)	**Parallel (Balanced)**
I resolved to lose weight, to study more, and *watching* less TV.	I resolved to lose weight, to study more, and to watch less TV. (A balanced series of *to* verbs: *to lose, to study, to watch*)
A consumer group rates my car as noisy, expensive, and *not having much safety.*	A consumer group rates my car as noisy, expensive, and unsafe. (A balanced series of descriptive words: *noisy, expensive, unsafe*)
Lola likes wearing soft sweaters, eating exotic foods, and *to bathe* in scented bath oil.	Lola likes wearing soft sweaters, eating exotic foods, and bathing in scented bath oil. (A balanced series of *-ing* words: *wearing, eating, bathing*)
Single life offers more freedom of choice; *more security is offered by marriage.*	Single life offers more freedom of choice; marriage offers more security. (Balanced verbs and word order: *single life offers . . . ; marriage offers . . .*)

You need not worry about balanced sentences when writing first drafts. But when you rewrite, you should try to put matching words and ideas into matching structures. Such parallelism will improve your writing style.

ACTIVITY

Cross out and revise the unbalanced part of each of the following sentences.

EXAMPLE When Gail doesn't have class, she uses her time to clean house, ~~getting~~ *to get* her laundry done, and to buy groceries.

1. Lola plans to become a model, a lawyer, or to go into nursing.

Copyright ©2006 The McGraw-Hill Companies, Inc. All rights reserved.

2. Filling out an income tax form is worse than wrestling a bear or to walk on hot coals.

3. The study-skills course taught me how to take more effective notes, to read a textbook chapter, and preparing for exams.

4. Home Depot has huge sections devoted to plumbing equipment, electrical supplies, and tools needed for carpentry.

5. Martha Grencher likes to water her garden, walking her fox terrier, and arguing with her husband.

6. Filled with talent and ambitious, Eduardo plugged away at his sales job.

7. When I saw my roommate with my girlfriend, I felt worried, angry, and embarrassment as well.

8. Cindy's cat likes sleeping in the dryer, lying in the bathtub, and to chase squirrels.

9. The bacon was fatty, grease was on the potatoes, and the eggs were cold.

10. People in the lobby munched popcorn, sipped sodas, and were shuffling their feet impatiently.

Use a Consistent Point of View

Consistency with Verbs

Do not shift verb tenses unnecessarily. If you begin writing a paper in the present tense, don't shift suddenly to the past. If you begin in the past, don't shift without reason to the present. Notice the inconsistent verb tenses in the following example:

> The shoplifter *walked* quickly toward the front of the store. When a clerk *shouts* at him, he *started* to run.

The verbs must be consistently in the present tense:

The shoplifter *walks* quickly toward the front of the store. When a clerk *shouts* at him, he *starts* to run.

Or the verbs must be consistently in the past tense:

The shoplifter *walked* quickly toward the front of the store. When a clerk *shouted* at him, he *started* to run.

ACTIVITY

In each item, one verb must be changed so that it agrees in tense with the other verbs. Cross out the incorrect verb and write the correct form above each crossed-out verb.

EXAMPLE   Kareem wanted to be someplace else when the dentist ~~carries~~ *carried* in a long needle.

1. I played my stereo and surfed the Internet before I decide to do some homework.

2. The hitchhiker stopped me as I walks from the turnpike rest station and said, "Are you on your way to San Jose?"

3. Some students attend all their classes in school and listen carefully during lectures, but they don't take notes. As a result, they often failed tests.

4. His parents stayed together for his sake; only after he graduates from college were they divorced.

5. In the movie, artillery shells exploded on the hide of the reptile monster. It just grinned, tosses off the shells, and kept eating people.

6. Several months a year, monarch butterflies come to live in a spot along the California coast. Thousands and thousands of them hang from the trees and fluttered through the air in large groups.

7. After waking up each morning, Harry stays in bed for a while. First he stretches and yawned loudly, and then he plans his day.

Copyright ©2006 The McGraw-Hill Companies, Inc. All rights reserved.

8. The salespeople at Biggs's Department Store are very helpful. When people asked for a product the store doesn't carry or is out of, the salesperson recommends another store.

9. Part-time workers at the company are the first to be laid off. They are also paid less, and they received no union representation.

10. Smashed cars, ambulances, and police cars blocked traffic on one side of the highway. On the other side, traffic slows down as drivers looked to see what had happened.

Consistency with Pronouns

Pronouns should not shift point of view unnecessarily. When writing a paper, be consistent in your use of first-, second-, or third-person pronouns.

Type of Pronoun	Singular	Plural
First-person pronouns	I (my, mine, me)	we (our, us)
Second-person pronouns	you (your)	you (your)
Third-person pronouns	he (his, him) she (her) it (its)	they (their, them)

Note   Any person, place, or thing, as well as any indefinite pronoun like *one, anyone, someone,* and so on (page 429), is a third-person word.

For instance, if you start writing in the third person *she*, don't jump suddenly to the second person *you*. Or if you are writing in the first person *I*, don't shift unexpectedly to *one*. Look at the examples.

Inconsistent

I enjoy movies like *The Return of the Vampire* that frighten *you*.
(A very common mistake people make is to let *you* slip into their writing after they start with another pronoun.)

As soon as a person walks into Helen's apartment, *you* can tell that Helen owns a cat.
(Again, *you* is a shift in point of view.)

Consistent

I enjoy movies like *The Return of the Vampire* that frighten me.

As soon as a person walks into Helen's apartment, *he or she* can tell that Helen owns a cat.
(See also the note on *his or her* references on pages 429–430.)

ACTIVITY

Cross out inconsistent pronouns in the following sentences and write the correct form of the pronoun above each crossed-out word. You may have to change the form of the verb as well.

EXAMPLE My dreams are always the kind that haunt ~~you~~ *me* the next day.

1. Whenever we take our children on a trip, you have to remember to bring snacks, tissues, and toys.

2. In our society, we often need a diploma before you are hired for a job.

3. I work at a company where the owners don't provide you with any health insurance.

4. If a student organizes time carefully, you can accomplish a great deal of work.

5. Although I know you should watch your cholesterol intake, I can never resist an ear of corn dripping with melted butter.

6. Good conversationalists have the ability to make a person they are talking to feel as if they are the only other person in the room.

Copyright ©2006 The McGraw-Hill Companies, Inc. All rights reserved.

7. We never go to the Salad Bowl anymore, because you wait so long to be seated and the waiters usually make mistakes with the order.

8. I'm careful about talking to people on the subway because one can get into some really weird situations.

9. We can't afford to move right now, because you need not only the first month's rent but also an extra month's security deposit.

10. In my job as store manager, I'm supposed to be nice to the customer even if they are being totally unreasonable.

Use Specific Words

To be an effective writer, you must use specific words rather than general words. Specific words create pictures in the reader's mind. They help capture interest and make your meaning clear. Compare the following sentences:

General	Specific
The boy came down the street.	Theo ran down Woodlawn Avenue.
A bird appeared on the grass.	A blue jay swooped down onto the frost-covered lawn.
She stopped the car.	Jackie slammed on the brakes of her Camry.

The specific sentences create clear pictures in our minds. The details *show* us exactly what has happened.

Here are four ways to make your sentences specific.

1   Use exact names.

   She loves her *car.*

   Renée loves her *Honda.*

2   Use lively verbs.

   The garbage truck *went* down Front Street.

   The garbage truck *rumbled* down Front Street.

3   Use descriptive words (modifiers) before nouns.

A girl peeked out the window.

A *chubby six-year-old* girl peeked out the *dirty kitchen* window.

4   Use words that relate to the five senses: sight, hearing, taste, smell, and touch.

That woman is a karate expert.
That *tiny, silver-haired* woman is a karate expert. (*Sight*)

When the dryer stopped, a signal sounded.
When the *whooshing* dryer stopped, a *loud buzzer* sounded. (*Hearing*)

Lola offered me an orange slice.
Lola offered me a *sweet, juicy* orange slice. (*Taste*)

The real estate agent opened the door of the closet.
The real estate agent opened the door of the *cedar-scented* closet. (*Smell*)

I pulled the blanket around me to fight off the wind.
I pulled the *fluffy* blanket around me to fight off the *chilling* wind. (*Touch*)

ACTIVITY 1

This activity will give you practice in replacing vague, indefinite words with sharp, specific words. Add three or more specific words to replace the general word or words underlined in each sentence. Make changes in the wording of a sentence as necessary.

EXAMPLE   My bathroom cabinet contains <u>many drugs</u>.

My bathroom cabinet contains aspirin, antibiotics, tranquilizers, and codeine cough medicine.

1. At the shopping center, we visited <u>several stores</u>.

   _____

   _____

2. Sunday is my day to take care of <u>chores</u>.

   _____

   _____

Copyright ©2006 The McGraw-Hill Companies, Inc. All rights reserved.

3. Lola enjoys various activities in her spare time.

    _____

    _____

4. I spent most of my afternoon doing homework.

    _____

    _____

5. We returned home from vacation to discover that several pests had invaded the house.

    _____

    _____

ACTIVITY 2

Again, you will practice changing vague, indefinite writing into lively, image-filled writing that helps capture the reader's interest and makes your meaning clear. With the help of the four methods described on pages 116–117, add specific details to the sentences that follow. Note the examples.

EXAMPLES   The person got out of the car.

The elderly man painfully lifted himself out of the white Buick

station wagon.

The fans enjoyed the victory.

Many of the fifty thousand fans stood, waved banners, and

cheered wildly when Barnes scored the winning touchdown.

1. The lunch was not very good.

    _____

    _____

2. The animal ran away.

    _____

    _____

3. An accident occurred.

_____

_____

4. The instructor came into the room.

_____

_____

5. The machine did not work.

_____

_____

Copyright ©2006 The McGraw-Hill Companies, Inc. All rights reserved.

Use Concise Wording

Wordiness—using more words than necessary to express a meaning—is often a sign of lazy or careless writing. Your readers may resent the extra time and energy they must spend when you have not done the work needed to make your writing direct and concise.

Here are examples of wordy sentences:

Anne is of the opinion that the death penalty should be allowed.

I would like to say that my subject in this paper will be the kind of generous person that my father was.

Omitting needless words improves the sentences:

Anne supports the death penalty.

My father was a generous person.

The following box lists some wordy expressions that could be reduced to single words.

Wordy Form	Short Form
a large number of	many
a period of a week	a week
arrive at an agreement	agree
at an earlier point in time	before
at the present time	now
big in size	big
owing to the fact that	because
during the time that	while
five in number	five
for the reason that	because
good benefit	benefit
in every instance	always
in my own opinion	I think
in the event that	if
in the near future	soon
in this day and age	today
is able to	can
large in size	large
plan ahead for the future	plan
postponed until later	postponed
red in color	red
return back	return

Copyright ©2006 The McGraw-Hill Companies, Inc. All rights reserved.

ACTIVITY

Rewrite the following sentences, omitting needless words.

1. After a lot of careful thinking, I have arrived at the conclusion that drunken drivers should receive jail terms.

   _____

   _____

2. The movie that I went to last night, which was fairly interesting, I must say, was enjoyed by me and my girlfriend.

   _____

   _____

3. Ben finally made up his mind after a lot of indecisions and decided to look for a new job.

   _____

   _____

4. Owing to inclement weather conditions of wind and rain, we have decided not to proceed with the athletic competition about to take place on the baseball diamond.

   _____

   _____

5. Beyond a doubt, the only two things you can rely or depend on would be the fact that death comes to everyone and also that the government will tax your yearly income.

   _____

   _____

Vary Your Sentences

One aspect of effective writing is to vary your sentences. If every sentence follows the same pattern, writing may become monotonous. This chapter explains four ways you can create variety and interest in your writing style. The first two ways involve coordination and subordination—important techniques for achieving different kinds of emphasis.

The following are four methods you can use to make your sentences more varied and more sophisticated:

1   Add a second complete thought (coordination).

2   Add a dependent thought (subordination).

3   Begin with a special opening word or phrase.

4   Place adjectives or verbs in a series.

Revise by Adding a Second Complete Thought

When you add a second complete thought to a simple sentence, the result is a *compound* (or double) sentence. The two complete statements in a compound sentence are usually connected by a comma plus a joining, or *coordinating*, word (*and, but, for, or, nor, so, yet*).

Use a compound sentence when you want to give equal weight to two closely related ideas. The technique of showing that ideas have equal importance is called *coordination*. Following are some compound sentences. Each contains two ideas that the writer regards as equal in importance.

Bill has stopped smoking cigarettes, but he is now addicted to chewing gum.

I repeatedly failed the math quizzes, so I decided to drop the course.

Darrell turned all the lights off, and then he locked the office door.

ACTIVITY

Combine the following pairs of simple sentences into compound sentences. Use a comma and a logical joining word (*and, but, for, so*) to connect each pair.

Note   If you are not sure what *and, but, for,* and *so* mean, review pages 391–393.

EXAMPLE   •   The cars crept along slowly.

   •   Visibility was poor in the heavy fog.

   The cars crept along slowly, for visibility was poor in the heavy fog.

1. •   Lee thought she would never master the computer.

   •   In two weeks she was using it comfortably.

   _____

   _____

2. • Vandals smashed the car's headlights.
   • They slashed the tires as well.

   _____

   _____

3. • I married at age seventeen.
   • I never got a chance to live on my own.

   _____

   _____

4. • Mold grew on my leather boots.
   • The closet was warm and humid.

   _____

   _____

5. • My father has a high cholesterol count.
   • He continues to eat red meat almost every day.

   _____

   _____

Revise by Adding a Dependent Thought

When you add a dependent thought to a simple sentence, the result is a complex sentence.*
A dependent thought begins with a word or phrase like one of the following:

Dependent Words

after	if, even if	when, whenever
although, though	in order that	where, wherever
as	since	whether
because	that, so that	which, whichever
before	unless	while
even though	until	who, whoever
how	what, whatever	whose

*The two parts of a complex sentence are sometimes called an *independent clause* and a *dependent clause*. A *clause* is simply a word group that contains a subject and a verb. An independent clause expresses a complete thought and can stand alone. A dependent clause does not express a complete thought in itself and "depends on" the independent clause to complete its meaning. Dependent clauses always begin with a dependent, or subordinating, word.

Copyright ©2006 The McGraw-Hill Companies, Inc. All rights reserved.

A *complex* sentence is used to emphasize one idea over another. Look at the following complex sentence:

Although I lowered the thermostat, my heating bill remained high.

The idea that the writer wants to emphasize here—*my heating bill remained high*—is expressed as a complete thought. The less important idea—*Although I lowered my thermostat*—is subordinated to this complete thought. The technique of giving one idea less emphasis than another is called *subordination*.

Following are other examples of complex sentences. In each case, the part starting with the dependent word is the less emphasized part of the sentence.

Even though I was tired, I stayed up to watch the horror movie.

Before I take a bath, I check for spiders in the tub.

When Vera feels nervous, she pulls on her earlobe.

ACTIVITY

Use logical subordinating words to combine the following pairs of simple sentences into sentences that contain a dependent thought. Place a comma after a dependent statement when it starts the sentence.

EXAMPLE • Our team lost.
       • We were not invited to the tournament.

       Because our team lost, we were not invited to the tournament.

_____

1. • I receive my degree in June.
   • I will begin applying for jobs.

_____

_____

2. • Lola doesn't enjoy cooking.
   • She often eats at fast-food restaurants.

_____

_____

3. • I sent several letters of complaint.
    • The electric company never corrected my bill.

      _____

      _____

4. • Neil felt his car begin to skid.
    • He took his foot off the gas pedal.

      _____

      _____

5. • The final exam covered sixteen chapters.
    • The students complained.

      _____

      _____

Revise by Beginning with a Special Opening Word or Phrase

Among the special openers that can be used to start sentences are (1) -*ed* words, (2) -*ing* words, (3) -*ly* words, (4) *to* word groups, and (5) prepositional phrases. Here are examples of all five kinds of openers:

-ed *word*

Tired from a long day of work, Sharon fell asleep on the sofa.

-ing *word*

Using a thick towel, Mel dried his hair quickly.

-ly *word*

Reluctantly, I agreed to rewrite the paper.

to *word group*

To get to the church on time, you must leave now.

Prepositional phrase

With Fred's help, Martha planted the evergreen shrubs.

Copyright ©2006 The McGraw-Hill Companies, Inc. All rights reserved.

ACTIVITY

Combine the simple sentences into one sentence by using the opener shown at the left and omitting repeated words. Use a comma to set off the opener from the rest of the sentence.

EXAMPLE   *-ing* word   • The toaster refused to pop up.

• It buzzed like an angry hornet.

Buzzing like an angry hornet, the toaster refused to pop up.

-ed word   1. • Nate dreaded the coming holidays.

• He was depressed by his recent divorce.

_____

_____

-ing word   2. • The star player glided down the court.

• He dribbled the basketball like a pro.

_____

_____

-ly word   3. • I waited in the packed emergency room.

• I was impatient.

_____

_____

to word group   4. • The little boy likes to annoy his parents.

• He pretends not to hear them.

_____

_____

Prepositional phrase   5. • People must wear rubber-soled shoes.

• They must do this in the gym.

_____

_____

Revise by Placing Adjectives or Verbs in a Series

Various parts of a sentence may be placed in a series. Among these parts are adjectives (descriptive words) and verbs. Here are examples of both in a series.

Adjectives

The *black, smeary* newsprint rubbed off on my *new butcher-block* table.

Verbs

The quarterback *fumbled* the ball, *recovered* it, and *sighed* with relief.

ACTIVITY

Combine the simple sentences in each group into one sentence by using adjectives or verbs in a series and by omitting repeated words. In most cases, use a comma between the adjectives or verbs in a series.

EXAMPLE • Before Christmas, I made fruitcakes.
  • I decorated the house.
  • I wrapped dozens of toys.

  Before Christmas, I made fruitcakes, decorated the house, and
  wrapped dozens of toys.

1. • My lumpy mattress was giving me a cramp in my neck.
   • It was causing pains in my back.
   • It was making me lose sleep.

   _____

   _____

2. • Lights appeared in the fog.
   • The lights were flashing.
   • The lights were red.
   • The fog was soupy.
   • The fog was gray.

   _____

   _____

Copyright ©2006 The McGraw-Hill Companies, Inc. All rights reserved.

3. • Before going to bed, I locked all the doors.
   • I activated the burglar alarm.
   • I slipped a kitchen knife under my mattress.

   _____

   _____

4. • Lola picked sweater hairs off her coat.
   • The hairs were fuzzy.
   • The hairs were white.
   • The coat was brown.
   • The coat was suede.

   _____

   _____

5. • The contact lens fell onto the floor.
   • The contact lens was thin.
   • The contact lens was slippery.
   • The floor was dirty.
   • The floor was tiled.

   _____

   _____

Editing Sentences

After revising sentences in a paragraph so that they flow smoothly and clearly, you need to edit the paragraph for mistakes in grammar, punctuation, mechanics, usage, and spelling. Even if a paragraph is otherwise well-written, it will make an unfavorable impression on readers if it contains such mistakes. To edit a paragraph, check it against the agreed-upon rules or conventions of written English—simply called *sentence skills* in this book. Here are the most common of these conventions:

1 Write complete sentences rather than fragments.

2 Do not write run-ons.

3 Use verb forms correctly.

4 Make sure that subject, verbs, and pronouns agree.

5 Eliminate faulty modifiers.

6 Use pronoun forms correctly.

7 Use capital letters where needed.

8 Use the following marks of punctuation correctly: apostrophe, quotation marks, comma, semicolon, colon, hyphen, dash, parentheses.

9 Use correct manuscript form.

10 Eliminate slang, clichés, and pretentious words.

11 Check for possible spelling errors.

12 Eliminate careless errors.

 These sentence skills are treated in detail in Part Five of this book, and they can be referred to easily as needed. Both the list of sentence skills on the inside front cover and the correction symbols on the inside back cover include page references so that you can turn quickly to any skill you want to check.

Hints for Editing

Here are hints that can help you edit the next-to-final draft of a paper for sentence-skills mistakes:

1 Have at hand two essential tools: a good dictionary (see page 504) and a grammar handbook (you can use the one in this book on pages 353–583).

2 Use a sheet of paper to cover your paragraph so that you will expose only one sentence at a time. Look for errors in grammar, spelling, and typing. It may help to read each sentence out loud. If a sentence does not read clearly and smoothly, chances are something is wrong.

3 Pay special attention to the kinds of errors you tend to make. For example, if you tend to write run-ons or fragments, be especially on the lookout for those errors.

4 Try to work on a printed draft, where you'll be able to see your writing more objectively than you can on a handwritten page; use a pen with colored ink so that your corrections will stand out.

Copyright ©2006 The McGraw-Hill Companies, Inc. All rights reserved.

A Note on Proofreading

Proofreading means checking the final, edited draft of your paragraph closely for typos and other careless errors. A helpful strategy is to read your paper backward, from the last sentence to the first. This helps keep you from getting caught up in the flow of the paper and missing small mistakes. Here are six helpful proofing symbols:

Proofing Symbol	Meaning	Example
∧	insert missing letter or word	bel*i*eve
℘	omit	in the ~~the~~ meantime
∪∩	reverse order of words or letters	once a upon time
#	add space	alltogether #
⌣	close up space	foot ball
cap, lc	Add a capital (or a lowercase) letter	(cap) My persian Cat (lc)

If you make too many corrections, type in the corrections and reprint the page.

ACTIVITY

In the spaces at the bottom, write the numbers of the ten word groups that contain fragments or run-ons. Then, in the spaces between the lines, edit by making the necessary corrections. One is done for you as an example.

[1]Two groups of researchers have concluded that "getting cold" has little to do with

"catching a cold." [2]When the experiment was done for the first time. [3]Researchers exposed

more than four hundred people to the cold virus. [4]Then divided those people into three

groups. [5]One group, wearing winter coats, sat around in ten-degree temperatures the

second group was placed in sixty-degree temperatures. [6]With the third group staying in

a room. [7]Where it was eighty degrees. [8]The number of people who actually caught colds was the same. [9]In each group. [10]Other researchers repeated this experiment ten years later. [11]This time they kept some subjects cozy and warm they submerged others in a tank filled with water. [12]Whose temperature had been lowered to seventy-five degrees. [13]They made others sit around in their underwear in forty-degree temperatures. [14]The results were the same, the subjects got sick at the same rate. [15]Proving that people who get cold do not always get colds.

1. _____   2. _____   3. _____   4. _____   5. _____

6. _____   7. _____   8. _____   9. _____   10. _____

Note   A series of editing tests appears on pages 565–577. You will probably find it most helpful to take these tests after reviewing the sentence skills in Part Five.

Practice in Revising Sentences

You now know the fourth step in effective writing: revising and editing sentences. You also know that practice in *editing* sentences is best undertaken after you have worked through the sentence skills in Part Five. The focus in this closing section, then, will be on *revising* sentences—using a variety of methods to ensure that your sentences flow smoothly and are clear and interesting. You will work through the following series of review tests:

1   Using parallelism.

2   Using a consistent point of view.

3   Using specific words.

4   Using concise wording.

5   Varying your sentences.

Copyright ©2006 The McGraw-Hill Companies, Inc. All rights reserved.

1 Using Parallelism

■ **Review Test 1**

Cross out the unbalanced part of each sentence. In the space provided, revise the unbalanced part so that it matches the other item or items in the sentence. The first one is done for you as an example.

1. Our professor warned us that he would give surprise tests, ~~the assignment of term papers,~~ and allow no makeup exams.

   assign term papers

2. Making a big dinner is a lot more fun than to clean up after it.

   _____

3. The street-corner preacher stopped people walking by, was asking them questions, and handed them a pamphlet.

   _____

4. My teenage daughter enjoys shopping for new clothes, to try different cosmetics, and reading beauty magazines.

   _____

5. Many of today's action movies have attractive actors, fantastic special effects, and dialogue that is silly.

   _____

6. While you're downtown, please pick up the dry cleaning, return the library books, and the car needs washing too.

   _____

7. I want a job that pays high wages, provides a complete benefits package, and offering opportunities for promotion.

   _____

8. As the elderly woman climbed the long staircase, she breathed hard and was grabbing the railing tightly.

   _____

9. I fell into bed at the end of the hard day, grateful for the sheets that were clean, soft pillow, and cozy blanket.

   _____

10. Ray's wide smile, clear blue eyes, and expressing himself earnestly all make him seem honest, even though he is not.

_____

■ Review Test 2

Cross out the unbalanced part of each sentence. In the space provided, revise the unbalanced part so that it matches the other item or items in the sentence.

1. The neighborhood group asked the town council to repair the potholes and that a traffic light be installed.

_____

2. Pesky mosquitoes, humidity that is high, and sweltering heat make summer an unpleasant time for me.

_____

3. The afternoon mail brought advertisements that were unwanted, bills I couldn't pay, and magazines I didn't like.

_____

4. Our house has a broken garage door, shutters that are peeling, and a crumbling chimney.

_____

5. My car needed the brakes replaced, the front wheels aligned, and recharging of the battery.

_____

6. I had to correct my paper for fragments, misplaced modifiers, and there were apostrophe mistakes.

_____

7. We do not want to stay home during our vacation, but a trip is not something we can afford.

_____

8. Stumbling out of bed, a cup of coffee that he drinks, and listening to the weather report make up Roy's early-morning routine.

_____

Copyright ©2006 The McGraw-Hill Companies, Inc. All rights reserved.

9. Having a headache, my stomach being upset, and a bad case of sunburn did not put me in a good mood for the evening.

_____

10. The Gray Panthers is an organization that not only aids older citizens but also providing information for their families.

_____

2 Using a Consistent Point of View

■ **Review Test 1**

Change verbs as needed in the following passage so that they are consistently in the past tense. Cross out each incorrect verb and write the correct form above it, as shown in the example. You will need to make nine corrections.

Late one rainy night, Mei Ling woke to the sound of steady dripping. When she got out of bed to investigate, a drop of cold water ~~splashes~~ *splashed* onto her arm. She looks up just in time to see another drop form on the ceiling, hang suspended for a moment, and fall to the carpet. Stumbling to the kitchen, Mei Ling reaches deep into one of the cabinets and lifts out a large roasting pan. As she did so, pot lids and baking tins clattered out and crash onto the counter. Mei Ling ignored them, stumbled back to the bedroom, and places the pan on the floor under the drip. But a minute after sliding her icy feet under the covers, Mei Ling realized she is in trouble. The sound of each drop hitting the metal pan echoed like a gunshot in the quiet room. Mei Ling feels like crying, but she finally thought of a solution. She got out of bed and returns a minute later with a thick bath towel. She lined the pan with the towel and crawls back into bed.

■ Review Test 2

Cross out the inconsistent pronouns in the following sentences and revise by writing the correct form of the pronoun above each crossed-out word.

I

EXAMPLE I dislike waitressing, for ~~you~~ can never count on a fair tip.

1. My kitchen is so narrow that one can't open the refrigerator without turning sidewise first.

2. Wanting relief from her headaches, Carla asked her doctor if acupuncture could really do you any good.

3. I drink coffee at work because you need a regular jolt of energy.

4. As we entered the house, you could hear someone giggling in the hallway.

5. I hate going to the supermarket because you always have trouble finding a parking space there.

6. In this company, a worker can take a break only after a relief person comes to take your place.

7. Sometimes the Bradleys take the turnpike route, but it costs you five dollars in tolls.

8. As we sat in class waiting for the test results, you could feel the tension.

9. My brother doesn't get enough regular exercise, even though he knows exercise is good for you.

10. My favorite subject is abnormal psychology because the case studies make one seem so normal by comparison.

Copyright ©2006 The McGraw-Hill Companies, Inc. All rights reserved.

3 Using Specific Words

■ **Review Test 1**

Revise the following sentences, replacing vague, indefinite words with sharp, specific ones.

1. When I woke up this morning, I had *several signs of a cold.*

   _____

   _____

2. Lin brought *lots of reading materials* to keep her busy in the hospital waiting room.

   _____

   _____

3. To do well in school, a student needs *certain qualities.*

   _____

   _____

4. The table at the wedding reception was full of *a variety of appetizers.*

   _____

   _____

5. As I grew older and less stupid, I realized that money cannot buy *certain things.*

   _____

   _____

■ **Review Test 2**

With the help of the methods described on pages 116–117 and summarized below, add specific details to the sentences that follow.

1   Use exact names.

2   Use lively verbs.

3   Use descriptive words (modifiers) before nouns.

4   Use words that relate to the senses—sight, hearing, taste, smell, touch.

1. The crowd grew restless.

   _____

   _____

2. I relaxed.

   _____

   _____

3. The room was cluttered.

   _____

   _____

4. The child threw the object.

   _____

   _____

5. The driver was angry.

   _____

   _____

4 Using Concise Wording

■ Review Test 1

Rewrite the following sentences, omitting needless words.

1. There was this one girl in my class who rarely if ever did her homework.

   _____

   _____

2. Judging by the looks of things, it seems to me that it will probably rain very soon.

   _____

   _____

Copyright ©2006 The McGraw-Hill Companies, Inc. All rights reserved.

3. Seeing as how the refrigerator is empty of food, I will go to the supermarket in the very near future.

_____

_____

4. In this day and age it is almost a certainty that someone you know will be an innocent victim of criminal activity.

_____

_____

5. In my personal opinion it is correct to say that the spring season is the most beautiful period of time in the year.

_____

_____

■ Review Test 2

Rewrite the following sentences, omitting needless words.

1. Workers who are on a part-time basis are attractive to a business because they do not have to be paid as much as full-time workers for a business.

_____

_____

2. During the time that I was sick and out of school, I missed a total of three math tests.

_____

_____

3. The game, which was scheduled for later today, has been canceled by the officials because of the rainy weather.

_____

_____

4. At this point in time, I am quite undecided and unsure about just which classes I will take during this coming semester.

_____

_____

Copyright ©2006 The McGraw-Hill Companies, Inc. All rights reserved.

5. An inconsiderate person located in the apartment next to mine keeps her radio on too loud a good deal of the time, with the result being that it is disturbing to everyone in the neighboring apartments.

_____

_____

5 Varying Your Sentences

▪ Review Test 1

Using coordination, subordination, or both, combine each of the following groups of simple sentences into one longer sentence. Omit repeated words. Various combinations are possible, so for each group, try to find the combination that flows most smoothly and clearly.

1. • My grandmother is eighty-six.
   • She drives to Florida alone every year.
   • She believes in being self-reliant.

   _____

   _____

2. • They left twenty minutes early for class.
   • They were late anyway.
   • The car overheated.

   _____

   _____

3. • John failed the midterm exam.
   • He studied harder for the final.
   • He passed it.

   _____

   _____

4. • A volcano erupts.
    • It sends tons of ash into the air.
    • This creates flaming orange sunsets.

    _____

    _____

5. • A telephone rings late at night.
    • We answer it fearfully.
    • It could bring tragic news.

    _____

    _____

■ Review Test 2

Using coordination, subordination, or both, combine each of the following groups of simple sentences into two longer sentences. Omit repeated words. Various combinations are possible, so for each group, try to find the combination that flows most smoothly and clearly.

1. • Wendy pretended not to overhear her coworkers.
    • She couldn't stop listening.
    • She felt deeply embarrassed.
    • They were criticizing her work.

    _____

    _____

    _____

2. • Tony got home from the shopping mall.
    • He discovered that his rented tuxedo did not fit.
    • The jacket sleeves covered his hands.
    • The pants cuffs hung over his shoes.

    _____

    _____

    _____

Copyright ©2006 The McGraw-Hill Companies, Inc. All rights reserved.

3. • The boys waited for the bus.
   • The wind shook the flimsy shelter.
   • They shivered with cold.
   • They were wearing thin jackets.

   _____

   _____

   _____

4. • The engine almost started.
   • Then it died.
   • I realized no help would come.
   • I was on a lonely road.
   • It was very late.

   _____

   _____

   _____

5. • Gary was leaving the store.
   • The shoplifting alarm went off.
   • He had not stolen anything.
   • The clerk had forgotten to remove the magnetic tag.
   • The tag was on a shirt Gary had bought.

   _____

   _____

   _____

■ Review Test 3

Part A   Combine the simple sentences into one sentence by using the opener shown in the margin and omitting repeated words. Use a comma to set off the opener from the rest of the sentence.

-ed word

1. • We were exhausted from four hours of hiking.
   • We decided to stop for the day.

   _____

   _____

-ing word

2. • Gus was staring out the window.
   • He didn't hear the instructor call on him.

   _____

   _____

-ly word

3. • Nobody saw the thieves steal our bikes.
   • This was unfortunate.

   _____

   _____

to word
group

4. • Wayne rented a limousine for the night.
   • He wanted to make a good impression.

   _____

   _____

Prepositional
phrase

5. • Joanne goes online to visit her friends.
   • She does this during her lunch breaks.

   _____

   _____

Part B Combine the simple sentences in each group into one sentence by using adjectives or verbs in a series and by omitting repeated words. In most cases, use a comma between the adjectives or verbs in a series.

6. The photographer waved a teddy bear at the baby.
   He made a funny face.
   He quacked like a duck.

   _____

   _____

7. The bucket held a bunch of daisies.
   The bucket was shiny.
   The bucket was aluminum.
   The daisies were fresh.
   The daisies were white.

   _____

   _____

8. Amy poured herself a cup of coffee.
   She pulled her hair back into a ponytail.
   She opened her textbook.
   She sat down at her desk.
   She fell asleep.

   _____

   _____

9. The box in the dresser drawer was stuffed with letters.
   The box was cardboard.
   The dresser drawer was locked.
   The letters were faded.
   The letters were about love.

   _____

   _____

10. The boy asked the girl to dance.
    The boy was short.
    The boy was self-confident.
    The girl was tall.
    The girl was shy.

    _____

    _____

Copyright ©2006 The McGraw-Hill Companies, Inc. All rights reserved.

6 Four Bases for Revising Writing

> *This chapter will show you how to evaluate a paragraph for*
> * unity
> * support
> * coherence
> * sentence skills

In the preceding chapters, you learned four essential steps in writing an effective paragraph. The box below shows how these steps lead to four standards, or bases, you can use in revising a paper.

Four Steps ⟶	Four Bases
1 If you make one point and stick to that point,	your writing will have *unity*.
2 If you back up the point with specific evidence,	your writing will have *support*.
3 If you organize and connect the specific evidence,	your writing will have *coherence*.
4 If you write clear, error-free sentences,	your writing will demonstrate effective *sentence skills*.

This chapter will discuss the four bases—unity, support, coherence, and sentence skills—and will show how these four bases can be used to evaluate and revise a paragraph.

Base 1: Unity

Understanding Unity

The following two paragraphs were written by students on the topic "Why Students Drop Out of College." Read them and decide which one makes its point more clearly and effectively, and why.

Paragraph A

Why Students Drop Out

Students drop out of college for many reasons. First of all, some students are bored in school. These students may enter college expecting nonstop fun or a series of fascinating courses. When they find out that college is often routine, they quickly lose interest. They do not want to take dull required courses or spend their nights studying, and so they drop out. Students also drop out of college because the work is harder than they thought it would be. These students may have made decent grades in high school simply by showing up for class. In college, however, they may have to prepare for two-hour exams, write fifteen-page term papers, or make detailed presentations to a class. The hard work comes as a shock, and students give up. Perhaps the most common reason students drop out is that they are having personal or emotional problems. Younger students, especially, may be attending college at an age when they are also feeling confused, lonely, or depressed. These students may have problems with roommates, family, boyfriends, or girlfriends. They become too unhappy to deal with both hard academic work and emotional troubles. For many types of students, dropping out seems to be the only solution they can imagine.

Paragraph B

Student Dropouts

There are three main reasons students drop out of college. Some students, for one thing, are not really sure they want to be in school and lack the desire to do the work. When exams come up, or when a course requires a difficult project or term paper, these students will not do the required studying or research. Eventually, they may drop out because their grades are so poor they are about to flunk out anyway. Such students sometimes come back to school later with a completely different attitude about school. Other students drop out for financial reasons. The pressures

Copyright ©2006 The McGraw-Hill Companies, Inc. All rights reserved.

of paying tuition, buying textbooks, and possibly having to support themselves can be overwhelming. These students can often be helped by the school because financial aid is available, and some schools offer work-study programs. Finally, students drop out because they have personal problems. They cannot concentrate on their courses because they are unhappy at home, they are lonely, or they are having trouble with boyfriends or girlfriends. Instructors should suggest that such troubled students see counselors or join support groups. If instructors would take a more personal interest in their students, more students would make it through troubled times.

ACTIVITY

Fill in the blanks: Paragraph _____ makes its point more clearly and effectively

because _____

_____

_____

Comment   Paragraph A is more effective because it is *unified.* All the details in paragraph A are *on target;* they support and develop the single point expressed in the first sentence—that there are many reasons students drop out of college.

On the other hand, paragraph B contains some details irrelevant to the opening point—that there are three main reasons students drop out. These details should be omitted in the interest of paragraph unity. Go back to paragraph B and cross out the sections that are off target—the sections that do not support the opening idea.

You should have crossed out the following sections: "Such students sometimes . . . attitude about school"; "These students can often . . . work-study programs"; and "Instructors should suggest . . . through troubled times."

The difference between these two paragraphs leads us to the first base, or standard, of effective writing: *unity.* To achieve unity is to have all the details in your paper related to the single point expressed in the topic sentence, the first sentence. Each time you think of something to put in, ask yourself whether it relates to your main point. If if does not, leave it out. For example, if you were writing about a certain job as the worst job you ever had and then spent a couple of sentences talking about the interesting people that you met there, you would be missing the first and most essential base of good writing.

Checking for Unity

To check a paper for unity, ask yourself these questions:

1   Is there a clear opening statement of the point of the paper?

2   Is all the material on target in support of the opening point?

Base 2: Support

Understanding Support

The following student paragraphs were written on the topic "A Quality of Some Person You Know." Both are unified, but one communicates more clearly and effectively. Which one, and why?

Paragraph A

My Quick-Tempered Father

My father is easily angered by normal everyday mistakes. One day my father told me to wash the car and cut the grass. I did not hear exactly what he said, and so I asked him to repeat it. Then he went into a hysterical mood and shouted, "Can't you hear?" Another time he asked my mother to go to the store and buy groceries with a fifty-dollar bill, and he told her to spend no more than twenty dollars. She spent twenty-two dollars. As soon as he found out, he immediately took the change from her and told her not to go anywhere else for him; he did not speak to her the rest of the day. My father even gives my older brothers a hard time with his irritable moods. One day he told them to be home from their dates by midnight; they came home at 12:15. He informed them that they were grounded for three weeks. To my father, making a simple mistake is like committing a crime.

Paragraph B

My Generous Grandfather

My grandfather is the most generous person I know. He gave up a life of his own in order to give his children everything they wanted. Not only did he give up many years of his life to raise his children properly, but he is

Copyright ©2006 The McGraw-Hill Companies, Inc. All rights reserved.

now sacrificing many more years to his grandchildren. His generosity is also evident in his relationship with his neighbors, his friends, and the members of his church. He has been responsible for many good deeds and has always been there to help all the people around him in times of trouble. Everyone knows that he will gladly lend a helping hand. He is so generous that you almost have to feel sorry for him. If one day he suddenly became selfish, it would be earthshaking. That's my grandfather.

ACTIVITY

Fill in the blanks: Paragraph _____ makes its point more clearly and effectively

because _____

_____

_____

Comment   Paragraph A is more effective, for it offers specific examples that show us the father in action. We see for ourselves why the writer describes the father as quick-tempered.

Paragraph B, on the other hand, gives us no specific evidence. The writer of paragraph B tells us repeatedly that the grandfather is generous but never shows us examples of that generosity. Just how, for instance, did the grandfather sacrifice his life for his children and grandchildren? Did he hold two jobs so that his son could go to college, or so that his daughter could have her own car? Does he give up time with his wife and friends to travel every day to his daughter's house to baby-sit, go to the store, and help with the dishes? Does he wear threadbare suits and coats and eat Hamburger Helper and other inexpensive meals (with no desserts) so that he can give money to his children and toys to his grandchildren? We want to see and judge for ourselves whether the writer is making a valid point about the grandfather, but without specific details we cannot do so. In fact, we have almost no picture of him at all.

Consideration of these two paragraphs leads us to the second base of effective writing: *support.* After realizing the importance of specific supporting details, one student writer revised a paper she had done on a restaurant job as the worst job she ever had. In the revised paper, instead of talking about "unsanitary conditions in the kitchen," she referred to such specifics as "green mold on the bacon" and "ants in the potato salad." All your papers should include many vivid details!

Checking for Support

To check a paper for support, ask yourself these questions:

1   Is there *specific* evidence to support the opening point?

2   Is there *enough* specific evidence?

Base 3: Coherence

Understanding Coherence

The following two paragraphs were written on the topic "The Best or Worst Job You Ever Had." Both are unified and both are supported. However, one communicates more clearly and effectively. Which one, and why?

Paragraph A

Pantry Helper

My worst job was as a pantry helper in one of San Diego's well-known restaurants. I had an assistant from three to six in the afternoon who did little but stand around and eat the whole time she was there. She would listen for the sound of the back door opening, which was a sure sign the boss was coming in. The boss would testily say to me, "You've got a lot of things to do here, Alice. Try to get a move on." I would come in at two o'clock to relieve the woman on the morning shift. If her day was busy, that meant I would have to prepare salads, slice meat and cheese, and so on. Orders for sandwiches and cold platters would come in and have to be prepared. The worst thing about the job was that the heat in the kitchen, combined with my nerves, would give me an upset stomach by seven o'clock almost every night. I might be going to the storeroom to get some supplies, and one of the waitresses would tell me she wanted a bacon, lettuce, and tomato sandwich on white toast. I would put the toast in and head for the supply room, and a waitress would holler out that her customer was in a hurry. Green flies would come in through the torn screen in the kitchen window and sting me. I was getting paid only $5.05 an hour. At five o'clock, when the dinner rush began, I would be dead tired. Roaches scurried in all directions whenever I moved a box or picked up a head of lettuce to cut.

Copyright ©2006 The McGraw-Hill Companies, Inc. All rights reserved.

Paragraph B

My Worst Job

The worst job I ever had was as a waiter at the Westside Inn. First of all, many of the people I waited on were rude. When a baked potato was hard inside or a salad was flat or their steak wasn't just the way they wanted it, they blamed me, rather than the kitchen. Or they would ask me to light their cigarettes, or chase flies from their tables, or even take their children to the bathroom. Also, I had to contend not only with the customers but with the kitchen staff as well. The cooks and busboys were often undependable and surly. If I didn't treat them just right, I would wind up having to apologize to customers because their meals came late or their water glasses weren't filled. Another reason I didn't like the job was that I was always moving. Because of the constant line at the door, as soon as one group left, another would take its place. I usually had only a twenty-minute lunch break and a ten-minute break in almost nine hours of work. I think I could have put up with the job if I had been able to pause and rest more often. The last and most important reason I hated the job was my boss. She played favorites, giving some of the waiters and waitresses the best-tipping repeat customers and preferences on holidays. She would hover around during my break to make sure I didn't take a second more than the allotted time. And even when I helped out by working through a break, she never had an appreciative word but would just tell me not to be late for work the next day.

ACTIVITY

Fill in the blanks: Paragraph _____ makes its point more clearly and effectively because _____

_____

_____

Comment   Paragraph B is more effective because the material is organized clearly and logically. Using emphatic order, the writer gives us a list of four reasons why the job was so bad: rude customers, an unreliable kitchen staff, constant motion, and—most of all—an unfair boss. Further, the writer includes transitional words that act as signposts, making movement from one idea to the next easy to follow. The major transitions are *First of all, Also, Another reason,* and *The last and most important reason.*

Copyright ©2005 The McGraw-Hill Companies, Inc. All rights reserved.

While paragraph A is unified and supported, the writer does not have any clear and consistent way of organizing the material. Partly, emphatic order is used, but this is not made clear by transitions or by saving the most important reason for last. Partly, time order is used, but it moves inconsistently from two to seven to five o'clock.

These two paragraphs lead us to the third base of effective writing: *coherence*. The supporting ideas and sentences in a composition must be organized so that they cohere, or "stick together." As has already been mentioned, key techniques for tying material together are a clear method of organization (such as time order or emphatic order), transitions, and other connecting words.

Checking for Coherence

To check a paper for coherence, ask yourself these questions:

1   Does the paper have a clear method of organization?

2   Are transitions and other connecting words used to tie the material together?

Base 4: Sentence Skills

Understanding Sentence Skills

Two versions of a paragraph are given below. Both are unified, supported, and organized, but one version communicates more clearly and effectively. Which one, and why?

Paragraph A

Falling Asleep Anywhere

[1]There are times when people are so tired that they fall asleep almost anywhere. [2]For example, there is a lot of sleeping on the bus or train on the way home from work in the evenings. [3]A man will be reading the newspaper, and seconds later it appears as if he is trying to eat it. [4]Or he will fall asleep on the shoulder of the stranger sitting next to him. [5]Another place where unplanned naps go on is the lecture hall. [6]In some classes, a student will start snoring so loudly that the professor has to ask another student to shake the sleeper awake. [7]A more embarrassing situation occurs when a student leans

on one elbow and starts drifting off to sleep. [8]The weight of the head pushes the elbow off the desk, and this momentum carries the rest of the body along. [9]The student wakes up on the floor with no memory of getting there. [10]The worst place to fall asleep is at the wheel of a car. [11]Police reports are full of accidents that occur when people lose consciousness and go off the road. [12]If the drivers are lucky, they are not seriously hurt. [13]One woman's car, for instance, went into a river. [14]She woke up in four feet of water and thought it was raining. [15]When people are really tired, nothing will stop them from falling asleep—no matter where they are.

Paragraph B

"Falling Asleep Anywhere"

[1]There are times when people are so tired that they fall asleep almost anywhere. [2]For example, on the bus or train on the way home from work. [3]A man will be reading the newspaper, seconds later it appears as if he is trying to eat it. [4]Or he will fall asleep on the shoulder of the stranger sitting next to him. [5]Another place where unplanned naps go on are in the lecture hall. [6]In some classes, a student will start snoring so loudly that the professor has to ask another student to shake the sleeper awake. [7]A more embarrassing situation occurs when a student leans on one elbow and starting to drift off to sleep. [8]The weight of the head push the elbow off the desk, and this momentum carries the rest of the body along. [9]The student wakes up on the floor with no memory of getting there. [10]The worst time to fall asleep is when driving a car. [11]Police reports are full of accidents that occur when people conk out and go off the road. [12]If the drivers are lucky they are not seriously hurt. [13]One womans car, for instance, went into a river. [14]She woke up in four feet of water. [15]And thought it was raining. [16]When people are really tired, nothing will stop them from falling asleep—no matter where they are.

ACTIVITY 1

Fill in the blanks: Paragraph _____ makes its point more clearly and effectively

because _____

_____

_____

Comment   Paragraph A is more effective because it incorporates *sentence skills,* the fourth base of competent writing.

Copyright ©2006 The McGraw-Hill Companies, Inc. All rights reserved.

ACTIVITY 2

See if you can identify the ten sentence-skills mistakes in paragraph B. Do this, first of all, by going back and underlining the ten spots in paragraph B that differ in wording or punctuation from paragraph A. Then try to identify the ten sentence-skills mistakes by circling what you feel is the correct answer in each of the ten statements below.

Note   Comparing paragraph B with the correct version may help you guess correct answers even if you are not familiar with the names of certain skills.

1. The title should not be set off with
   a.   capital letters.
   b.   quotation marks.

2. In word group 2, there is a
   a.   missing comma.
   b.   missing apostrophe.
   c.   sentence fragment.
   d.   dangling modifier.

3. In word group 3, there is a
   a.   run-on.
   b.   sentence fragment.
   c.   mistake in subject-verb agreement.
   d.   mistake involving an irregular verb.

4. In word group 5, there is a
   a.   sentence fragment.
   b.   spelling error.
   c.   run-on.
   d.   mistake in subject-verb agreement.

5. In word group 7, there is a
   a.   misplaced modifier.
   b.   dangling modifier.
   c.   mistake in parallelism.
   d.   run-on.

6. In word group 8, there is a
   a.   nonstandard English verb.
   b.   run-on.
   c.   comma mistake.
   d.   missing capital letter.

7. In word group 11, there is a
   a.   mistake involving an irregular verb.
   b.   sentence fragment.
   c.   slang phrase.
   d.   mistake in subject-verb agreement.

8. In word group 12, there is a
   a.   missing apostrophe.
   b.   missing comma.
   c.   mistake involving an irregular verb.
   d.   sentence fragment.

9. In word group 13, there is a
    a. mistake in parallelism.
    b. mistake involving an irregular verb.
    c. missing apostrophe.
    d. missing capital letter.

10. In word group 15, there is a
    a. missing quotation mark.
    b. mistake involving an irregular verb.
    c. sentence fragment.
    d. mistake in pronoun point of view.

Comment   You should have chosen the following answers:

1. b   2. c   3. a   4. d   5. c
6. a   7. c   8. b   9. c   10. c

Part Five of this book explains these and other sentence skills. You should review all the skills carefully. Doing so will ensure that you know the most important rules of grammar, punctuation, and usage—rules needed to write clear, error-free sentences.

Checking for Sentence Skills

Sentence skills and the other bases of effective writing are summarized in the following chart and on the inside front cover of the book.

A Summary of the Four Bases of Effective Writing

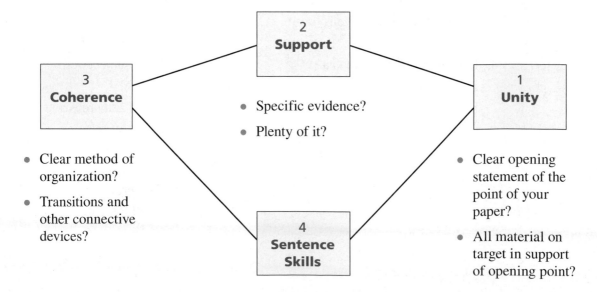

2 Support

3 Coherence

1 Unity

• Specific evidence?
• Plenty of it?

• Clear method of organization?
• Transitions and other connective devices?

• Clear opening statement of the point of your paper?
• All material on target in support of opening point?

4 Sentence Skills

- Fragments eliminated? (page 369)
- Run-ons eliminated? (386)
- Correct verb forms? (402, 412)
- Subject and verb agreement? (420)
- Faulty parallelism and faulty modifiers eliminated? (111, 445, 449)
- Faulty pronouns eliminated? (427, 434)
- Capital letters used correctly? (459)
- Punctuation marks where needed?

  (a) Apostrophe (472)   (d) Semicolon; colon (500)

  (b) Quotation marks (481)   (e) Hyphen; dash (501–502)

  (c) Comma (490)   (f) Parentheses (503)

- Correct paper format? (454)
- Needless words eliminated? (119)
- Effective word choices? (536)
- Possible spelling errors checked? (514)
- Careless errors eliminated through proofreading? (128–130, 182, 565)
- Sentences varied? (121–127)

Practice in Using the Four Bases

You are now familiar with four bases, or standards, of effective writing: unity, support, coherence, and sentence skills. In this closing section, you will expand and strengthen your understanding of the four bases as you work through the following activities:

1   Evaluating Scratch Outlines for Unity

2   Evaluating Paragraphs for Unity

3   Evaluating Paragraphs for Support

4   Evaluating Paragraphs for Coherence

5   Revising Paragraphs for Coherence

6   Evaluating Paragraphs for All Four Bases: Unity, Support, Coherence, and Sentence Skills

Copyright ©2006 The McGraw-Hill Companies, Inc All rights reserved.

1 Evaluating Scratch Outlines for Unity

The best time to check a paper for unity is at the outline stage. A scratch outline, as explained on page 26, is one of the best techniques for getting started with a paper.

Look at the following scratch outline that one student prepared and then corrected for unity:

I had a depressing weekend.

1. Hay fever bothered me
2. Had to pay seventy-seven-dollar car bill
3. ~~Felt bad~~
4. Boyfriend and I had a fight
5. ~~Did poorly in my math test today as a result~~
6. My mother yelled at me unfairly

Four reasons support the opening statement that the writer was depressed over the weekend. The writer crossed out "Felt bad" because it was not a reason for her depression. (Saying that she felt bad is only another way of saying that she was depressed.) She also crossed out the item about the math test because the point she is supporting is that she was depressed over the weekend.

ACTIVITY

In each outline, cross out the items that do not support the opening point. These items must be omitted in order to achieve paragraph unity.

1. The cost of raising a child keeps increasing.

   a. School taxes get higher every year.

   b. A pair of children's sneakers can now cost over $100.

   c. Overpopulation is a worldwide problem.

   d. Providing nutritious food is more costly because of inflated prices.

   e. Children should work at age sixteen.

2. My father's compulsive gambling hurt our family life.

   a. We were always short of money for bills.

   b. Luckily, my father didn't drink.

   c. My father ignored his children to spend time at the racetrack.

   d. Gamblers' Anonymous can help compulsive gamblers.

   e. My mother and father argued constantly.

3. There are several ways to get better mileage in your car.

   a. Check air pressure in tires regularly.

   b. Drive at no more than fifty-five miles per hour.

   c. Orange and yellow cars are the most visible.

   d. Avoid jackrabbit starts at stop signs and traffic lights.

   e. Always have duplicate ignition and trunk keys.

4. My swimming instructor helped me overcome my terror of the water.

   a. He talked with me about my fears.

   b. I was never good at sports.

   c. He showed me how to hold my head under water and not panic.

   d. I held on to a floating board until I was confident enough to give it up.

   e. My instructor was on the swimming team at his college.

5. Fred Wilkes is the best candidate for state governor.

   a. He has fifteen years' experience in the state senate.

   b. His son is a professional football player.

   c. He has helped stop air and water pollution in the state.

   d. His opponent has been divorced.

   e. He has brought new industries and jobs to the state.

2 Evaluating Paragraphs for Unity

ACTIVITY

Each of the following five paragraphs contains sentences that are off target—sentences that do not support the opening point—and so the paragraphs are not unified. In the interest of paragraph unity, such sentences must be omitted.

Cross out the irrelevant sentences and write the numbers of those sentences in the spaces provided. The number of spaces will tell you the number of irrelevant sentences in each paragraph.

Copyright ©2006 The McGraw-Hill Companies, Inc. All rights reserved.

1.
A Kindergarten Failure

[1]In kindergarten I experienced the fear of failure that haunts many schoolchildren. [2]My moment of panic occurred on my last day in kindergarten at Charles Foos Public School in Riverside, California. [3]My family lived in California for three years before we moved to Omaha, Nebraska, where my father was a personnel manager for Mutual of Omaha. [4]Our teacher began reading a list of names of all those students who were to line up at the door in order to visit the first-grade classroom. [5]Our teacher was a pleasant-faced woman who had resumed her career after raising her own children. [6]She called off every name but mine, and I was left sitting alone in the class while everyone else left, the teacher included. [7]I sat there in absolute horror. [8]I imagined that I was the first kid in human history who had flunked things like crayons, sandbox, and sliding board. [9]Without getting the teacher's permission, I got up and walked to the bathroom and threw up into a sink. [10]Only when I ran home in tears to my mother did I get an explanation of what had happened. [11]Since I was to go to a parochial school in the fall, I had not been taken with the other children to meet the first-grade teacher at the public school. [12]My moment of terror and shame had been only a misunderstanding.

The numbers of the irrelevant sentences: _____   _____

2.
How to Prevent Cheating

[1]Instructors should take steps to prevent students from cheating on exams. [2]To begin with, instructors should stop reusing old tests. [3]A test that has been used even once is soon known on the student grapevine. [4]Students will check with their friends to find out, for example, what was on Dr. Thompson's biology final last term. [5]They may even manage to find a copy of the test itself, "accidentally" not turned in by a former student of Dr. Thompson's. [6]Instructors should also take some commonsense precautions at test time. [7]They should make students separate themselves—by at least one seat—during an exam, and they should watch the class closely. [8]The best place for the instructor to sit is in the rear of the room, so that a student is never sure if the instructor is looking at him or her. [9]Last of all, instructors must make it clear to students that there will be stiff penalties for cheating. [10]One of the problems with our school systems is a lack of discipline. [11]Instructors never used to give in to students' demands or put up with bad behavior, as they do today. [12]Anyone caught cheating should immediately

receive a zero for the exam. [13]A person even suspected of cheating should be forced to take an alternative exam in the instructor's office. [14]Because cheating is unfair to honest students, it should not be tolerated.

The numbers of the irrelevant sentences: _____ _____

Copyright ©2005 The McGraw-Hill Companies, Inc. All rights reserved.

3. **Other Uses for Cars**

[1]Many people who own a car manage to turn the vehicle into a trash can, a clothes closet, or a storage room. [2]People who use their cars as trash cans are easily recognized. [3]Empty snack bags, hamburger wrappers, pizza cartons, soda cans, and doughnut boxes litter the floor. [4]On the seats are old scratched CDs, blackened fruit skins, crumpled receipts, crushed cigarette packs, and used tissues. [5]At least the trash stays in the car, instead of adding to the litter on our highways. [6]Other people use a car as a clothes closet. [7]The car contains several pairs of shoes, pants, or shorts, along with a suit or dress that's been hanging on the car's clothes hanger for over a year. [8]Sweaty, smelly gym clothes will also find a place in the car, a fact passengers quickly discover. [9]The world would be better off if people showed more consideration of others. [10]Finally, some people use a car as a spare garage or basement. [11]In the backseats or trunks of these cars are bags of fertilizer, beach chairs, old textbooks, chainsaws, or window screens that have been there for months. [12]The trunk may also contain an extra spare tire, a dented hubcap, a gallon container of window washer fluid, and old stereo equipment. [13]If apartments offered more storage space, probably fewer people would resort to using their cars for such storage purposes. [14]All in all, people get a lot more use out of their cars than simply the miles they travel on the road.

The numbers of the irrelevant sentences: _____ _____ _____

4. **Why Adults Visit Amusement Parks**

[1]Adults visit amusement parks for several reasons. [2]For one thing, an amusement park is a place where it is acceptable to "pig out" on junk food. [3]At the park, everyone is drinking soda and eating popcorn, ice cream, or hot dogs. [4]No one seems to be on a diet, and so buying all the junk food you can eat is a guilt-free experience. [5]Parks should provide stands where healthier food, such as salads or cold chicken, would be sold. [6]Another reason people visit amusement parks is to prove themselves. [7]They want

to visit the park that has the newest, scariest ride in order to say that they went on the Parachute Drop, the seven-story Elevator, the Water Chute, or the Death Slide. [8]Going on a scary ride is a way to feel courageous and adventurous without taking much of a risk. [9]Some rides, however, can be dangerous. [10]Rides that are not properly inspected or maintained have killed people all over the country. [11]A final reason people visit amusement parks is to escape from everyday pressures. [12]When people are poised at the top of a gigantic roller coaster, they are not thinking of bills, work, or personal problems. [13]A scary ride empties the mind of all worries—except making it to the bottom alive. [14]Adults at an amusement park may claim they have come for their children, but they are there for themselves as well.

The numbers of the irrelevant sentences: _____   _____   _____

5.   **A Dangerous Cook**

[1]When my friend Tom sets to work in the kitchen, disaster often results. [2]Once he tried to make toasted cheese sandwiches for us by putting slices of cheese in the toaster along with the bread; he ruined the toaster. [3]Unfortunately, the toaster was a fairly new one that I had just bought for him three weeks before, on his birthday. [4]On another occasion, he had cut up some fresh beans and put them in a pot to steam. [5]I was really looking forward to the beans, for I eat nothing but canned vegetables in my dormitory. [6]I, frankly, am not much of a cook either. [7]The water in the Teflon pan steamed away while Tom was on the telephone, and both the beans and the Teflon coating in the pan were ruined. [8]Finally, another time Tom made spaghetti for us, and the noodles stuck so tightly together that we had to cut off slices with a knife and fork. [9]In addition, the meatballs were burned on the outside but almost raw inside. [10]The tomato sauce, on the other hand, turned out well. [11]For some reason, Tom is very good at making meat and vegetable sauces. [12]Because of Tom's kitchen mishaps, I never eat at his place without an Alka-Seltzer in my pocket, or without money in case we have to go out to eat.

The numbers of the irrelevant sentences: _____   _____   _____

_____   _____

Copyright ©2006 The McGraw-Hill Companies, Inc. All rights reserved.

3 Evaluating Paragraphs for Support

ACTIVITY

The five paragraphs that follow lack sufficient supporting details. In each paragraph, identify the spot or spots where more specific details are needed.

1.   **Chicken: Our Best Friend**

   ¹Chicken is the best-selling meat today for a number of good reasons. ²First of all, its reasonable cost puts it within everyone's reach. ³Chicken is popular, too, because it can be prepared in so many different ways. ⁴It can, for example, be cooked by itself, in spaghetti sauce, or with noodles and gravy. ⁵It can be baked, boiled, broiled, or fried. ⁶Chicken is also convenient. ⁷Last and most important, chicken has a high nutritional value. ⁸Four ounces of chicken contain twenty-eight grams of protein, which is almost half the recommended daily dietary allowance.

Fill in the blanks: The first spot where supporting details are needed occurs after sentence number _____. The second spot occurs after sentence number _____.

2.   **A Car Accident**

   ¹I was on my way home from work when my terrible car accident took place. ²As I drove my car around the curve of the expressway exit, I saw a number of cars ahead of me. ³They were backed up because of a red light at the main road. ⁴I slowly came to a stop behind a dozen or more cars. ⁵In my rearview mirror, I then noticed a car coming up behind me that did not slow down or stop. ⁶I had a horrible, helpless feeling as I realized the car would hit me. ⁷I knew there was nothing I could do to signal the driver in time, nor was there any way I could get away from the car. ⁸Minutes after the collision, I picked up my glasses, which were on the seat beside me. ⁹My lip was bleeding, and I got out a tissue to wipe it. ¹⁰The police arrived quickly, along with an ambulance for the driver of the car that hit me. ¹¹My car was so damaged that it had to be towed away. ¹²Today, eight years after the accident, I still relive the details of the experience whenever a car gets too close behind me.

Fill in the blank: The point where details are needed occurs after sentence number _____.

3.   **Tips on Bringing Up Children**

¹In some ways, children should be treated as mature people. ²For one thing, adults should not use baby talk with children. ³Using real words with children helps them develop language skills more quickly. ⁴Baby talk makes children feel patronized, frustrated, and confused, for they want to understand and communicate with adults by learning their speech. ⁵So animals should be called cows and dogs, not "moo-moos" and "bow-wows." ⁶Second, parents should be consistent when disciplining children. ⁷For example, if a parent tells a child, "You cannot have dessert unless you put away your toys," it is important that the parent follow through on the warning. ⁸By being consistent, parents will teach children responsibility and give them a stable center around which to grow. ⁹Finally, and most important, children should be allowed and encouraged to make simple decisions. ¹⁰Parents will thus be helping their children prepare for the complex decisions that they will have to deal with in later life.

Fill in the blank: The spot where supporting details are needed occurs after sentence number _____.

4.   **Being on TV**

¹People act a little strangely when a television camera comes their way. ²Some people behave as if a crazy puppeteer were pulling their strings. ³Their arms jerk wildly about, and they begin jumping up and down for no apparent reason. ⁴Often they accompany their body movements with loud screams, squeals, and yelps. ⁵Another group of people engage in an activity known as the cover-up. ⁶They will be calmly watching a sports game or other televised event when they realize the camera is focused on them. ⁷The camera operator can't resist zooming in for a close-up of these people. ⁸Then there are those who practice their funny faces on the unsuspecting public. ⁹They take advantage of the television time to show off their talents, hoping to get that big break that will carry them to stardom. ¹⁰Finally, there are those who pretend they are above reacting for the camera. ¹¹They wipe an expression from their faces and appear to be interested in something else. ¹²Yet if the camera stays on them long enough, they will slyly check to see if they are still being watched. ¹³Everybody's behavior seems to be slightly strange in front of a TV camera.

Fill in the blanks: The first spot where supporting details are needed occurs after sentence number _____. The second spot occurs after sentence number _____.

develops after you move in, you want to know that a decent and capable person will be there to handle the matter. ⁸Find out what's available that matches your interests. ⁹Your town newspaper and local real estate offices can provide you with a list of apartments for rent. ¹⁰Family and friends may be able to give you leads. ¹¹And your school may have a housing office that keeps a list of approved apartments for rent. ¹²Decide just what you need. ¹³If you can afford no more than $400 a month, you need to find a place that will cost no more than that. ¹⁴If you want a location that's close to work or school, you must take that factor into account. ¹⁵If you plan to cook, you want a place with a workable kitchen. ¹⁶By taking these steps, you should be ready to select the apartment that is best for you.

a. The paragraph should use time order. Write 1 before the step that should come first, 2 before the intermediate step, and 3 before the final step.

_____ Visit and carefully inspect the most promising apartments.

_____ Decide just what you need.

_____ Find out what's available that matches your interests.

b. Before which of three steps could the transitional words *The first step is to* be added? _____

c. Before which step could the transitional words *After you have decided what you are looking for, the next step is to* be added? _____

d. Before which step could the transitional words *The final step* be added?

_____

e. To whom does the pronoun *him or her* in sentence 6 refer to?

_____

f. What is a synonym for *landlord* in sentence 7? _____

g. What is a synonym for *apartment* in sentence 13? _____

5 Revising Paragraphs for Coherence

The two paragraphs in this section begin with a clear point, but in each case the supporting material that follows the point is not coherent. Read each paragraph and the comments that follow it on how to organize and connect the supporting material. Then do the activity for the paragraph.

Copyright ©2006 The McGraw-Hill Companies, Inc. All rights reserved.

Paragraph 1

A Difficult Period

Since I arrived in the Bay Area in midsummer, I have had the most difficult period of my life. I had to look for an apartment. I found only one place that I could afford, but the landlord said I could not move in until it was painted. When I first arrived in San Francisco, my thoughts were to stay with my father and stepmother. I had to set out looking for a job so that I could afford my own place, for I soon realized that my stepmother was not at all happy having me live with them. A three-week search led to a job shampooing rugs for a housecleaning company. I painted the apartment myself, and at least that problem was ended. I was in a hurry to get settled because I was starting school at the University of San Francisco in September. A transportation problem developed because my stepmother insisted that I return my father's bike, which I was using at first to get to school. I had to rely on a bus that often arrived late, with the result that I missed some classes and was late for others. I had already had a problem with registration in early September. My counselor had made a mistake with my classes, and I had to register all over again. This meant that I was one week late for class. Now I'm riding to school with a classmate and no longer have to depend on the bus. My life is starting to order itself, but I must admit that at first I thought it was hopeless to stay here.

Comments on Paragraph 1   The writer of this paragraph has provided a good deal of specific evidence to support the opening point. The evidence, however, needs to be organized. Before starting the paragraph, the writer should have decided to arrange the details by using time order. He or she could then have listed in a scratch outline the exact sequence of events that made for such a difficult period.

ACTIVITY 1

Here is a list of the various events described by the writer of paragraph 1. Number the events in the correct time sequence by writing 1 in front of the first event that occurred, 2 in front of the second event, and so on.

Since I arrived in the Bay Area in midsummer, I have had the most difficult period of my life.

_____ I had to search for an apartment I could afford.

_____ I had to find a job so that I could afford my own place.

_____ My stepmother objected to my living with her and my father.

_____ I had to paint the apartment before I could move in.

_____ I had to find an alternative to unreliable bus transportation.

_____ I had to register again for my college courses because of a counselor's mistake.

Your instructor may now have you rewrite the paragraph on separate paper. If so, be sure to use time signals such as *first, next, then, during, when, after,* and *now* to help guide your reader from one event to the next.

Paragraph 2

Childhood Cruelty

When I was in grade school, my classmates and I found a number of excuses for being cruel to a boy named Andy Poppovian. Sometimes Andy gave off a strong body odor, and we knew that several days had passed since he had taken a bath. Andy was very slow in speaking, as well as very careless in personal hygiene. The teacher would call on him during a math or grammar drill. He would sit there silently for so long before answering that she sometimes said, "Are you awake, Andy?" Andy had long fingernails that he never seemed to cut, with black dirt caked under them. We called him "Poppy," or we accented the first syllable in his name and mispronounced the rest of it and said to him, "How are you today, POP-o-van?" His name was funny. Other times we called him "Popeye," and we would shout at him. "Where's your spinach today, Popeye?" Andy always had sand in the corners of his eyes. When we played tag at recess, Andy was always "it" or the first one who was caught. He was so physically slow that five guys could dance around him and he wouldn't be able to touch any of them. Even when we tried to hold a regular conversation with him about sports or a teacher, he was so slow in responding to a question that we got bored talking with him. Andy's hair was always uncombed, and it was often full of white flakes of dandruff. Only when Andy died suddenly of spinal meningitis in seventh grade did some of us begin to realize and regret our cruelty toward him.

Comments on Paragraph 2   The writer of this paragraph provides a number of specifics that support the opening point. However, the supporting material has not been organized clearly. Before writing this paragraph, the author should have (1) decided to arrange the supporting evidence by using emphatic order and (2) listed in a scratch outline the reasons for the cruelty to Andy Poppovian and the supporting details for each reason. The writer could also have determined which reason to use in the emphatic final position of the paper.

Copyright: ©2006 The McGraw-Hill Companies, Inc. All rights reserved.

ACTIVITY 2

Create a clear outline for paragraph 2 by filling in the scheme below. The outline is partially completed.

> When I was in grade school, my classmates and I found a number of excuses for being cruel to a boy named Andy Poppovian.

Reason	1.	*Funny name*
Details	a.	
	b.	
	c.	
Reason	2.	*Physically slow*
Details	a.	
	b.	*Five guys could dance around him*
Reason	3.	
Details	a.	
	b.	*In regular conversation*
Reason	4.	
Details	a.	
	b.	*Sand in eyes*
	c.	
	d.	

Your instructor may have you rewrite the paragraph on separate paper. If so, be sure to introduce each of the four reasons with transitions such as *First, Second, Another reason,* and *Finally.* You may also want to use repeated words, pronouns, and synonyms to help tie your sentences together.

6 Evaluating Paragraphs for All Four Bases: Unity, Support, Coherence, and Sentence Skills

ACTIVITY

In this activity, you will evaluate paragraphs in terms of all four bases: unity, support, coherence, and sentence skills. Evaluative comments follow each paragraph below. Circle the letter of the statement that best applies in each case.

1.
Drunk Drivers

People caught driving while drunk—even first offenders—should be jailed. Drunk driving, first of all, is more dangerous than carrying around a loaded gun. In addition, a jail term would show drivers that society will no longer tolerate such careless and dangerous behavior. Finally, severe penalties might encourage solutions to the problem of drinking and driving. People who go out for a good time and intend to have several drinks would always designate one person, who would stay completely sober, as the driver.

a. The paragraph is not unified.

b. The paragraph is not adequately supported.

c. The paragraph is not well organized.

d. The paragraph does not show a command of sentence skills.

e. The paragraph is well written in terms of the four bases.

2.
A Frustrating Moment

A frustrating moment happened to me several days ago. When I was shopping. I had picked up a tube of crest toothpaste and a jar of noxema skin cream. After the cashier rang up the purchases, which came to $4.15. I handed her $10. Then got back my change, which was only $0.85. I told the cashier that she had made a mistake. Giving me change for $5 instead of $10. But she insist that I had only gave her $5, I became very upset and demand that she return the rest of my change. She refused to do so instead she asked me to step aside so she could wait on the next customer. I stood very rigid, trying not to lose my temper. I simply said to her, I'm not going to leave here, Miss, without my change for $10. Giving in at this point a bell

Copyright: ©2006 The McGraw-Hill Companies, Inc. All rights reserved.

was rung and the manager was summoned. After the situation was explain to him, he ask the cashier to ring off her register to check for the change. After doing so, the cashier was $5 over her sale receipts. Only then did the manager return my change and apologize for the cashier mistake.

a. The paragraph is not unified.

b. The paragraph is not adequately supported.

c. The paragraph is not well organized.

d. The paragraph does not show a command of sentence skills.

e. The paragraph is well written in terms of the four bases.

3.   **Asking Girls Out**

There are several reasons I have trouble asking girls to go out with me. I have asked some girls out and have been turned down. This is one reason that I can't talk to them. At one time I was very shy and quiet, and people sometimes didn't even know I was present. I can talk to girls now as friends, but as soon as I want to ask them out, I usually start to become quiet, and a little bit of shyness comes out. When I finally get the nerve up, the girl will turn me down, and I swear that I will never ask another one out again. I feel sure I will get a refusal, and I have no confidence in myself. Also, my friends mock me, though they aren't any better than I am. It can become discouraging when your friends get on you. Sometimes I just stand there and wait to hear what line the girl will use. The one they use a lot is "We like you as a friend, Ted, and it's better that way." Sometimes I want to have the line put on a tape recorder, so they won't have to waste their breath on me. All my past experiences with girls have been just as bad. One girl used me to make her old boyfriend jealous. Then when she succeeded, she started going out with him again. I had a bad experience when I took a girl to the prom. I spent a lot of money on her. Two days later, she told me that she was going steady with another guy. I feel that when I meet a girl I have to be sure I can trust her. I don't want her to turn on me.

a. The paragraph is not unified.

b. The paragraph is not adequately supported.

c. The paragraph is not well organized.

d. The paragraph does not show a command of sentence skills.

e. The paragraph is well written in terms of the four bases.

4.   **A Change in My Writing**

A technique in my present English class has corrected a writing problem that I've always had. In past English courses, I had major problems with commas in the wrong places, bad spelling, capitalizing the wrong words, sentence fragments, and run-on sentences. I never had any big problems with unity, support, or coherence, but the sentence skills were another matter. They were like little bugs that always appeared to infest my writing. My present instructor asked me to rewrite papers, just concentrating on sentence skills. I thought that the instructor was crazy because I didn't feel that rewriting would do any good. I soon became certain that my instructor was out of his mind, for he made me rewrite my first paper four times. It was very frustrating, for I became tired of doing the same paper over and over. I wanted to belt my instructor against the wall when I'd show him each new draft and he'd find skills mistakes and say, "Rewrite." Finally, my papers began to improve and the sentence skills began to fall into place. I was able to see them and correct them before turning in a paper, whereas I couldn't before. Why or how this happened I don't know, but I think that rewriting helped a lot. It took me most of the semester, but I stuck it out and the work paid off.

a. The paragraph is not unified.

b. The paragraph is not adequately supported.

c. The paragraph is not well organized.

d. The paragraph does not show a command of sentence skills.

e. The paragraph is well written in terms of the four bases.

5.   **Luck and Me**

I am a very lucky man, though the rest of my family has not always been lucky. Sometimes when I get depressed, which is too frequently, it's hard to see just how lucky I am. I'm lucky that I'm living in a country that is free. I'm allowed to worship the way I want to, and that is very important to me. Without a belief in God a person cannot live with any real certainty in life. My relationship with my wife is a source of good fortune for me. She gives me security, and that's something I need a lot. Even with these positive realities in my life, I still seem to find time for insecurity, worry, and, worst

Copyright ©200⁵ The McGraw-Hill Companies. Inc. All rights reserved.

of all, depression. At times in my life I have had bouts of terrible luck. But overall, I'm a very lucky guy. I plan to further develop the positive aspects of my life and try to eliminate the negative ones.

a. The paragraph is not unified.

b. The paragraph is not adequately supported.

c. The paragraph is not well organized.

d. The paragraph does not show a command of sentence skills.

e. The paragraph is well written in terms of the four bases.

Paragraph
Development

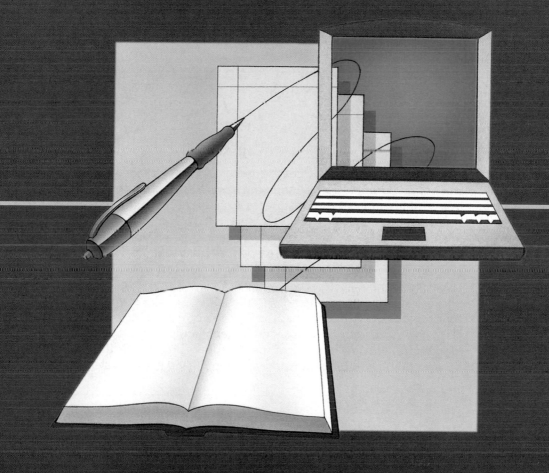

Copyright ©2006 The McGraw-Hill Companies, Inc. All rights reserved.

PREVIEW

Part Two introduces you to paragraph development and gives you practice in the following common types of paragraph development:

Providing Examples

Explaining a Process

Examining Cause and Effect

Comparing or Contrasting

Defining a Term

Dividing and Classifying

Describing a Scene or Person

Narrating an Event

Arguing a Position

After a brief explanation of each type of paragraph development, student paragraphs illustrating each type are presented, followed by questions about those paragraphs. The questions relate to the standards of effective writing described in Part One. You are then asked to write your own paragraph. In each case, writing assignments progress from personal-experience topics to more formal and objective topics; some topics require simple research, and the last assignment in each section asks you to write with a specific purpose and audience in mind. At times, points or topic sentences for development are suggested, so that you can concentrate on (1) making sure your evidence is on target in support of your opening idea, (2) providing plenty of specific supporting details to back up your point, and (3) organizing your supporting material clearly.

7 Introduction to Paragraph Development

Nine Patterns of Paragraph Development

Traditionally, writing has been divided into the following patterns of development:

- Exposition

Examples	Comparison and contrast
Process	Definition
Cause and effect	Division and classification

- Description

- Narration

- Argumentation

In *exposition*, the writer provides information about and explains a particular subject. Patterns of development within exposition include giving *examples*, detailing a *process* of doing or making something, analyzing *causes and effects*, *comparing* and *contrasting*, *defining* a term or concept, and *dividing* something into parts or *classifying* it into categories.

In addition to exposition, three other patterns of development are common: description, narration, and argumentation. A *description* is a verbal picture of a person, place, or thing. In *narration*, a writer tells the story of something that happened. Finally, in *argumentation*, a writer attempts to support a controversial point or defend a position on which there is a difference of opinion.

The pages ahead present individual chapters on each pattern. You will have a chance, then, to learn nine different patterns or methods for organizing material in your papers. Each pattern has its own internal logic and provides its own special strategies for imposing order on your ideas. As you practice each pattern, you should remember two points:

- *Point 1:* While each paragraph that you write will involve one predominant pattern, very often one or more additional patterns may be involved as well. For

Copyright ©2006 The McGraw-Hill Companies, Inc. All rights reserved

instance, the paragraph "Good-Bye, Tony" that you have already read (page 52) presents a series of causes leading to an effect—that the writer will not go out with Tony again. But the writer also presents examples to explain each of the causes (Tony was late, he was bossy, he was abrupt). And there is an element of narration, as the writer presents examples that occur from the beginning to the end of the date.

- *Point 2:* No matter which pattern or patterns you use, each paragraph will probably involve some form of argumentation. You will advance a point and then go on to support your point. To convince the reader that your point is valid, you may use a series of examples, or narration, or description, or some other pattern of organization. Among the paragraphs you will read in Part Two, one writer supports the point that a certain pet shop is depressing by providing a number of descriptive details. Another writer labels a certain experience in his life as heartbreaking and then uses a narrative to demonstrate the truth of his statement. A third writer advances the opinion that good horror movies can be easily distinguished from bad horror movies and then supplies comparative information about both to support her claim. Much of your writing, in short, will have the purpose of persuading your reader that the idea you have advanced is valid.

The Progression in Each Chapter

After each type of paragraph development is explained, student papers illustrating that type are presented, followed by questions about the paragraphs. The questions relate to unity, support, and coherence—principles of effective writing explained earlier in this book. You are then asked to write your own paragraph. In most cases, the first assignment is fairly structured and provides a good deal of guidance for the writing process. The other assignments offer a wide choice of writing topics. The fourth assignment always requires some simple research, and the fifth assignment requires writing with a specific purpose and for a specific audience.

Important Considerations in Paragraph Development

Before you begin work on particular types of paragraphs, there are several general considerations about writing to keep in mind. They will be discussed in turn.

Copyright ©2006 The McGraw-Hill Companies, Inc. All rights reserved.

Knowing Your Subject

Whenever possible, write on a subject that interests you. You will then find it easier to put more time into your work. Even more important, try to write on a subject that you already know something about. If you do not have direct experience with the subject, you should at least have indirect experience—knowledge gained through thinking, prewriting, reading, or talking about the subject.

If you are asked to write on a topic about which you have no experience or knowledge, you should do whatever research is required to gain the information you need. Chapter 19, "A Quick Guide to Research," will show you how to look up relevant information. Without direct or indirect experience, or the information you gain through research, you may not be able to provide the specific evidence needed to develop whatever point you are trying to make. Your writing will be starved for specifics.

Knowing Your Purpose and Audience

The three most common purposes of writing are to inform, to persuade, and to entertain. Each is described briefly below.

- To **inform**—to give information about a subject. Authors who are writing to inform want to provide facts that will explain or teach something to readers. For example, an informative paragraph about sandwiches might begin, "Eating food between two slices of bread—a sandwich—is a practice that has its origins in eighteenth-century England."

- To **persuade**—to convince the reader to agree with the author's point of view on a subject. Authors who are writing to persuade may give facts, but their main goal is to argue or prove a point to readers. A persuasive paragraph about sandwiches might begin, "There are good reasons why every sandwich should be made with whole grain bread."

- To **entertain**—to amuse and delight; to appeal to the reader's senses and imagination. Authors write to entertain in various ways, through fiction and nonfiction. An entertaining paragraph about sandwiches might begin, "What I wanted was a midnight snack, but what I got was better—the biggest, most magical sandwich in the entire world."

As already noted, much of the writing assigned in this book will involve some form of argumentation or persuasion. You will advance a point or thesis and then support it in a variety of ways. To some extent, also, you will write papers to inform—to provide readers with information about a particular subject. And since, in practice, writing often combines purposes, you might find yourself at times providing vivid or humorous details in order to entertain your readers as well.

Your audience will be primarily your instructor and sometimes other students. Your instructor is really a symbol of the larger audience you should see yourself writing for—an audience of educated adults who expect you to present your ideas in a clear, direct, organized way. If you can learn to write to persuade or inform such a general audience, you will have accomplished a great deal.

A Note on Tone

It will also be helpful for you to write some papers for a more specific audience. By so doing, you will develop an ability to choose words and adopt a tone of voice that is just right for a given purpose and a given group of people. *Tone* reveals the attitude that a writer has toward a subject. It is expressed through the words and details the writer selects. Just as a speaker's voice can project a range of feelings, a writer's voice can project one or more tones, or feelings: anger, sympathy, hopefulness, sadness, respect, dislike, and so on.

ACTIVITY

To appreciate differences in tone, look at the six statements below, which express different attitudes about a shabby apartment. Six different tones are used. Label each statement with the tone you think is present.

a. bitter	c. matter-of-fact	e. tolerant and accepting
b. sentimental	d. humorous	f. optimistic and hopeful

_____ 1. This place may be shabby, but since both of my children were born while we lived here, it has a special place in my heart.

_____ 2. This isn't the greatest apartment in the world, but it's not really that bad.

_____ 3. If only there were some decent jobs out there, I wouldn't be reduced to living in this miserable dump.

_____ 4. This place does need some repairs, but I'm sure the landlord will be making improvements sometime soon.

Copyright ©2006 The McGraw-Hill Companies, Inc. All rights reserved.

_____ 5. When we move away, we're planning to release three hundred cockroaches and two mice so we can leave the place exactly as we found it.

_____ 6. It's a small two-bedroom apartment that needs to be repainted and have the kitchen plumbing repaired.

Explanation The tone of item 1 is sentimental. "It has a special place in my heart" expresses tender emotions. In item 2, the words "not really that bad" show that the writer is tolerant, accepting the situation while recognizing that it could be better. We could describe the tone of item 3 as bitter. The writer resents a situation that forces him or her to live in a "miserable dump." Item 4 is optimistic and hopeful, since the writer is expecting the apartment to be improved soon. The tone of item 5 is humorous. Its writer claims to be planning a comic revenge on the landlord. The tone of item 6 is matter-of-fact and objective, simply describing what needs to be done.

The "Purpose and Audience" Assignment in Each Chapter

In this part of the book, there is an assignment at the end of each chapter that asks you to write with a very specific purpose in mind and for a very specific audience. You will be asked, for example, to imagine yourself as an employee writing a description of a new job opening at your workplace, as a graduate of a local high school advising a counselor there about a drug problem, as an aide at a day-care center preparing instructions for children, as an apartment tenant complaining to a landlord about neighbors, or as a travel agent providing suggestions for different kinds of family vacations. Through these and other assignments, you will learn how to adjust your style and tone of voice to a given writing situation.

Using a Computer

If you don't yet write on a computer, it's time to start. In today's world, word processing is an essential mechanical skill, just as effective writing is a vital communication skill.

The computer can be a real aid in the writing process. You can quickly add or delete anything, from a word to an entire section. You can "cut" material and "paste" it elsewhere in seconds. A word-processing program makes it easy to set margins, space lines, and number pages. It can also help you check your spelling, your grammar, and to some extent your style. And at any point during your work, you can print out one or more copies of your text.

Word processing is not hard to learn. Just as you don't need to know how a car works to drive one, you don't need to understand how a computer functions to use it. With a few simple keystrokes under your belt, you can begin. You do not even need to own your own computer. Nearly every college has at least one computer center, complete with rows of computers and staff members to provide assistance. Free classes in word processing may be available as well.

Tips on Using a Computer

- If you are using your school's computer center, allow yourself enough time. You may have to wait for a computer or printer to be free. In addition, you may need several sessions at the computer and printer to complete your paper.

- Every word-processing program allows you to "save" your writing by hitting one or more keys. Save your work frequently as you work on a draft. Work that is saved is preserved by the computer. Work that is not saved is lost when the file you are working on is closed, when the computer is turned off—or if there's a power or system failure.

- Keep your work in two places—the hard drive or disk you are working on and a backup disk. At the end of each session with the computer, copy your work onto the backup disk. Then if the hard drive or working disk becomes damaged, you'll have the backup copy.

- Print out your work at least at the end of every session. Then you'll not only have your most recent draft to work on away from the computer; you'll also have a copy in case something should happen to your disks.

- Work in single spacing so you can see as much of your writing on the screen at one time as possible. Just before you print out your work, change to double spacing.

- Before making major changes in a paper, create a copy of your file. For example, if your file is titled "Worst Job," create a file called "Worst Job 2." Then make all your changes in that file. If the changes don't work out, you can always go back to the original file.

Ways to Use a Computer at Each Stage of the Writing Process

Following are some ways to make word processing a part of your writing. Note that the sections that follow correspond to the stages of the writing process described in Chapter 2, pages 20–48.

Copyright ©2006 The McGraw-Hill Companies, Inc. All rights reserved.

Prewriting

If you're a fast typist, many kinds of prewriting will go well on the computer. With freewriting in particular, you can get ideas onto the screen almost as quickly as they occur to you. A passing thought that could be productive is not likely to get lost. You may even find it helpful, when freewriting, to dim the screen of your monitor so that you can't see what you're typing. If you temporarily can't see the screen, you won't have to worry about grammar or spelling or typing errors (none of which matter in prewriting); instead, you can concentrate on getting down as many ideas and details as possible about your subject.

After any initial freewriting, questioning, and list-making on a computer, it's often very helpful to print out a hard copy of what you've done. With a clean printout in front of you, you'll be able to see everything at once and revise and expand your work with handwritten comments in the margins of the paper.

If you have prepared a list of items, you may be able to turn that list into an outline right on the screen. Delete the ideas you feel should not be in your paper (saving them at the end of the file in case you change your mind), and add any new ideas that occur to you. Then use the cut and paste functions to shuffle the supporting ideas around until you find the best order for your paper.

Word processing also makes it easy for you to experiment with the wording of the point of your paper. You can try a number of versions in a short time. After you have decided on the version that works best, you can easily delete the other versions—or simply move them to a temporary "leftover" section at the end of the paper.

Writing Your First Draft

Some people like to write out a first draft by hand and then type it into the computer for revision. If you do this, you may find yourself making some changes and improvements as you type your handwritten draft. And once you have a draft on the screen, or printed out, you will find it much easier to revise than a handwritten draft.

If you feel comfortable composing directly on the screen, you can benefit from the computer's special features. For example, if you have written an anecdote in your freewriting that you plan to use in your paper, simply copy the story from your freewriting file and insert it where it fits in your paper. You can refine it then or later. Or if you discover while typing that a sentence is out of place, cut it out from where it is and paste it wherever you wish. And if while writing you realize that an earlier sentence can be expanded, just move your cursor back to that point and type in the added material.

Revising

It is during revision that the virtues of word processing really shine. All substituting, adding, deleting, and rearranging can be done easily within an existing file. All changes instantly take their proper places within the paper, not scribbled above the line or squeezed into the margin. You can concentrate on each change you want to make, because you never have to type from scratch or work on a messy draft. You can carefully go through your paper to check that all your supporting evidence is relevant and to add new support here and there where needed. Anything you decide to eliminate can be deleted in a keystroke. Anything you add can be inserted precisely where you choose. If you change your mind, all you have to do is delete or cut and paste. Then you can sweep through the paper focusing on other changes: improving word choice, increasing sentence variety, eliminating wordiness, and so on.

If you are like some students, you will find it convenient to print out a hard copy of your file at various points throughout the revision. You can then revise in longhand—adding, crossing out, and indicating changes—and later quickly make those changes in the document.

Editing and Proofreading

Editing and proofreading also benefit richly from word processing. Instead of crossing out or whiting out mistakes, or rewriting an entire paper to correct numerous errors, you can make all necessary changes within the most recent draft. If you find editing or proofreading on the screen hard on your eyes, print out a copy. Mark any corrections on that copy, and then transfer them to the final draft.

If the word-processing program you're using includes spelling and grammar checks, by all means use them. The spell-check function tells you when a word is not in the computer's dictionary. Keep in mind, however, that the spell-check cannot tell you how to spell a name correctly or when you have mistakenly used, for example, *their* instead of *there*. To a spell-check, *Thank ewe four the complement* is as correct as *Thank you for the compliment*. Also use the grammar check with caution. Any errors it doesn't uncover are still your responsibility.

A word-processed paper, with its clean appearance and attractive formatting, looks so good that you may think it is in better shape than it really is. Do not be fooled by your paper's appearance. Take sufficient time to review your grammar, punctuation, and spelling carefully.

Even after you hand in your paper, save the computer file. Your teacher may ask you to do some revising, and then the file will save you from having to type the paper from scratch.

Using Peer Review

In addition to having your instructor as an audience for your writing, you will benefit by having another student in your class as an audience. On the day a paper is due, or on a day when you are writing papers in class, your instructor may ask

Copyright ©2006 The McGraw-Hill Companies, Inc. All rights reserved.

you to pair up with another student. That student will read your paper, and you will read his or her paper.

Ideally, read the other paper aloud while your partner listens. If that is not practical, read it in a whisper while he or she looks on. As you read, both you and your partner should look and listen for spots where the paper does not read smoothly and clearly. Check or circle the trouble spots where your reading snags.

Your partner should then read your paper, marking possible trouble spots while doing so. Then each of you should do three things:

1 Identification

On a separate sheet of paper, write at the top the title and author of the paper you have read. Under it, put your name as the reader of the paper.

2 Scratch Outline

"X-ray" the paper for its inner logic by making up a scratch outline. The scratch outline need be no more than twenty words or so, but it should show clearly the logical foundation on which the essay is built. It should identify and summarize the overall point of the paper and the three areas of support for the point.

Your outline can look as follows.

Point: _____

Support:

1. _____

2. _____

3. _____

For example, here is a scratch outline of the paper on page 210 about a new puppy in the house:

Point: _A new puppy can have dramatic effects on a house._

Support:

1. _Keeps family awake at night_

2. _Destroys possessions_

3. _Causes arguments_

3 Comments

Under the outline, write the heading "Comments." Here is what you should comment on:

- Look at the spots where your reading of the paper snagged: Are words missing or misspelled? Is there a lack of parallel structure? Are there mistakes with punctuation? Is the meaning of a sentence confused? Try to figure out what the problems are and suggest ways of fixing them.

- Are there spots in the paper where you see problems with *unity*, *support*, or *organization*? (You'll find it helpful to refer to the checklist on the inside front cover of this book.) If so, offer comments. For example, you might say, "More details are needed in the first supporting paragraph," or "Some of the details in the last supporting paragraph don't really back up your point."

- Finally, make note of something you really liked about the paper, such as good use of transitions or an especially realistic or vivid specific detail.

After you have completed your evaluation of the paper, give it to your partner. Your instructor may provide you with the option of rewriting a paper in light of this feedback. Whether or not you rewrite, be sure to hand in the peer evaluation form with your paper.

Doing a Personal Review

1   While you're writing and revising an essay, you should be constantly evaluating it in terms of *unity, support,* and *organization*. Use as a guide the detailed checklist on the inside front cover of this book.

2   After you've finished the next-to-final draft of an essay, check it for the *sentence skills* listed on the inside front cover. It may also help to read the paper out loud. If a given sentence does not sound right—that is, if it does not read clearly and smoothly—chances are something is wrong. In that case, revise or edit as necessary until your paper is complete.

8 Providing Examples

Copyright ©2005 The McGraw-Hill Companies, Inc. All rights reserved.

In our daily conversations, we often provide *examples*—that is, details, particulars, specific instances—to explain statements that we make. Consider the several statements and supporting examples in the box below:

Statement	Examples
Wal-Mart was crowded today.	There were at least four carts waiting at each of the checkout counters, and it took me forty-five minutes to get through a line.
The corduroy shirt I bought is poorly made.	When I washed it, the colors began to fade, one button cracked and another fell off, a shoulder seam opened, and the sleeves shrank almost two inches.
My son Peter is unreliable.	If I depend on him to turn off a pot of beans in ten minutes, the family is likely to eat burned beans. If I ask him to turn down the thermostat before he goes to bed, the heat is likely to stay on all night.

In each case, the examples help us *see for ourselves* the truth of the statement that has been made. In paragraphs, too, explanatory examples help the audience fully understand a point. Lively, specific examples also add interest to a paper.

In this chapter, you will be asked to provide a series of examples to support a topic sentence. Providing examples to support a point is one of the most common and simplest methods of paragraph development. First read the paragraphs ahead; they all use examples to develop their points. Then answer the questions that follow.

Paragraphs to Consider

Inconsiderate Drivers

[1]Some people are inconsiderate drivers. [2]In the city, they will at times stop right in the middle of the street while looking for a certain home or landmark. [3]If they had any consideration for the cars behind them, they would pull over to the curb first. [4]Other drivers will be chatting on their cell phones and then slow down unexpectedly at a city intersection to make a right or left turn. [5]The least they could do is use their turn signals to let those behind them know in advance of their intention. [6]On the highway, a common example of inconsiderateness is night drivers who fail to turn off their high beams, creating glare for cars approaching in the other direction. [7]Other rude highway drivers move to the second or passing lane and then stay there, making it impossible for cars behind to go around them. [8]Yet other drivers who act as if they have special privileges are those who do not wait their turn in bottleneck situations where the cars in two lanes must merge alternately into one lane. [9]Perhaps the most inconsiderate drivers are those who throw trash out their windows, creating litter that takes away some of the pleasure of driving and that must be paid for with everyone's tax dollars.

Office Politics

[1]Office politics is a destructive game played by several types of people. [2]For instance, two supervisors may get into a conflict over how to do a certain job. [3]Instead of working out an agreement like adults, they carry on a power struggle that turns the poor employees under them into human Ping-Pong balls being swatted between two angry players. [4]Another common example of office politics is the ambitious worker who takes credit for other people's ideas. [5]He or she will chat in a "friendly" fashion with inexperienced employees, getting their ideas about how to run the office more smoothly. [6]Next thing you know, Mr. or Ms. Idea-Stealer is having a closed-door session with the boss and getting promotion points for his or her "wonderful creativity." [7]Yet another illustration of office politics is the spy. [8]This employee acts very buddy-buddy with other workers, often dropping little comments about things he or she doesn't like in the workplace. [9]The spy encourages people to talk about their problems at work, how they don't like their boss, the pay, and the working conditions. [10]Then the spy goes straight back and repeats all he or she has heard to the boss, and the employees get blamed for their "poor attitude." [11]A final example of office politics is people who gossip. [12]Too often, office politics can turn a perfectly fine work situation into a stressful one.

An Egotistical Neighbor

¹I have an egotistical neighbor named Alice. ²If I tell Alice how beautiful her dress is, she will take the time to tell me the name of the store where she bought it, the type of material that was used in making it, and the price. ³Alice is also egotistical when it comes to her children. ⁴Because they are hers, she thinks they just have to be the best children on the block. ⁵I am wasting my time by trying to tell her I have seen her kids expose themselves on the street or take things from parked cars. ⁶I do not think parents should praise their children too much. ⁷Kids have learned how to be good at home and simply awful when they are not at home. ⁸Finally, Alice is quick to describe the furnishings of her home for someone who is meeting her for the first time. ⁹She tells how much she paid for the paneling in her dining room. ¹⁰She mentions that she has three flat-screen television sets and that they were bought at an expensive electronics store. ¹¹She lets the person know that the entertainment system in her living room cost more than two thousand dollars, and that she has such a large collection of DVDs that she would not be able to watch them all in one week. ¹²Poor Alice is so self-centered that she never realizes how boring she can be.

■ Questions

About Unity

1. Which two sentences in "An Egotistical Neighbor" are irrelevant to the point that Alice is egotistical? (*Write the sentence numbers here.*)

   _____   _____

About Support

2. In "Inconsiderate Drivers," how many examples are given of inconsiderate drivers?

   _____ two _____ four _____ six _____ seven

3. After which sentence in "Office Politics" are specific details needed?

   _____

About Coherence

4. What are the four transition words or phrases that are used to introduce each new example in "Office Politics"?

   _____   _____   _____   _____

Copyright ©2006 The McGraw-Hill Companies, Inc. All rights reserved.

5. What two transition words are used to introduce examples in "An Egotistical Neighbor"?

_____   _____

6. Which paragraph clearly uses emphatic order to organize its details, saving for last what the writer regards as the most important example?

_____

Developing an Examples Paragraph

Development through Prewriting

Backing up your statements with clear, specific illustrations is the key to a successful examples paragraph. When Charlene, the writer of "Office Politics," was assigned an examples paragraph, she at first did not know what to write about.

Then her teacher made a suggestion. "Imagine yourself having lunch with some friends," the teacher said. "You're telling them *how* you feel about something and *why*. Maybe you're saying, 'I am so mad at my boyfriend!' or 'My new apartment is really great.' You wouldn't stop there—you'd continue by saying what your boyfriend does that is annoying, or in what way your apartment is nice. In other words, you'd be making a general point and backing it up with examples. That's what you need to do in this paper."

That night, Charlene was on the telephone with her brother. She was complaining about the office where she worked. "Suddenly I realized what I was doing," Charlene said. "I was making a statement—I hate the politics in my office—and giving examples of those politics. I knew what I could write about!"

Charlene began preparing to write her paragraph by freewriting. She gave herself ten minutes to write down everything she could think of on the subject of politics in her office. This is what she wrote:

> Of all the places I've ever worked this one is the worst that way. Can't trust anybody there—everybody's playing some sort of game. Worst one of all is Bradley and the way he pretends to be friendly with people. Gets them to complain about Ms. Bennett and Mr. Hankins and then runs back to them and reports everything. He should realize that people are catching on to his game and figuring out what a jerk he is. Melissa steals people's ideas and then takes credit for them. Anything to get brownie points. She's always out for herself first, you can tell. Then there's all the gossip

that goes on. You think you're in a soap opera or something, and it's kind of fun in a way but it also is very distracting people always talking about each other and worrying about what they say about you. And people talk about our bosses a lot. Nobody knows why Ms. Bennett and Mr. Hankins hate each other so much but they each want the workers on their side. You do something one boss's way, but then the other boss appears and is angry that you're not doing it another way. You don't know what to do at times to keep people happy.

Charlene read over her freewriting and then spent some time asking questions about her paragraph. "Exactly what do I want my point to be?" she asked. "And exactly how am I going to support that point?" Keeping those points in mind, she worked on several scratch outlines and wound up with the following:

Office politics are ruining the office.
1.   Bradley reports people's complaints.
2.   Melissa steals ideas.
3.   People gossip.
4.   Ms. Bennett and Mr. Hankins make workers choose sides.

Working from this outline, she then wrote the following first draft:

My office is being ruined by office politics. It seems like everybody is trying to play some sort of game to get ahead and don't care what it does to anybody else. One example is Bradley. Although he pretends to be friendly with people he isn't sincere. What he is trying to do is get them to complain about their bosses. Once they do, he goes back to the bosses and tells them what's been said and gets the worker in trouble. I've seen the same kind of thing happen at two other offices where I've worked. Melissa is another example of someone who plays office politics games. She steals other people's ideas and takes the credit for them. I had a good idea once on how to reduce office memos. I told her we ought to use E-mail to send office memos instead of typing them on paper. She went to Ms. Bennett and pretended the idea was hers. I guess I was partly to blame for not acting on the idea myself. And Ms. Bennett and Mr. Hankins hate each other and try to get us to take sides in their conflict. Then there is all the gossip that goes on. People do a lot of backbiting, and you have to be very careful about your behavior or people will start talking about you. All in all, office politics is really a problem where I work.

Copyright ©2006 The McGraw-Hill Companies, Inc. All rights reserved.

Development through Revising

After completing her first draft, Charlene put it aside until the next day. When she reread it, this was her response:

> "I think the paragraph would be stronger if I made it about office politics in general instead of just politics in my office. The things I was writing about happen in many offices, not just in mine. And our instructor wants us to try some third-person writing. Also, I need to make better use of transitions to help the reader follow as I move from one example to another."

With these thoughts in mind, Charlene began revising her paper, and after several drafts she produced the paragraph that appears on page 186.

Writing an Examples Paragraph

WRITING ASSIGNMENT 1

The assignment here is to complete an unfinished paragraph (in the box), which has as its topic sentence, "My husband Roger is a selfish person." Provide the supporting details needed to develop the examples of Roger's selfishness. The first example has been done for you.

A Selfish Person

My husband Roger is a selfish person. For one thing, he refuses to move out of the city, even though it is a bad place to raise the children. *We inherited some money when my parents died, and it might be enough for a down payment on a small house in a nearby town. But Roger says he would miss his buddies in the neighborhood.*

_____

Also, when we go on vacation, we always go where Roger wants to go. _____

Another example of Roger's selfishness is that he always spends any budget money that is left over. _____

_____

_____

_____

Finally, Roger leaves all the work of caring for the children to me.

_____

_____

_____

_____

Prewriting

a   On a separate piece of paper, jot down a couple of answers for each of the following questions:

- What specific vacations did the family go on because Roger wanted to go? Write down particular places, length of stay, time of year. What vacations has the family never gone on (for example, to visit the wife's relatives), even though the wife wanted to?

- What specific items has Roger bought for himself (rather than for the whole family's use) with leftover budget money?

- What chores and duties involved in the everyday caring for the children has Roger never done?

Note   Your instructor may ask you to work with one or two other students in generating the details needed to develop the three examples in the paragraph. The groups may then be asked to read their details aloud, with the class deciding which details are the most effective for each example.

Copyright ©2006 The McGraw-Hill Companies, Inc. All rights reserved.

Here and in general in your writing, try to generate *more* supporting material than you need. You are then in a position to choose the most convincing details for your paper.

b Read over the details you have generated and decide which sound most effective. Jot down additional details as they occur to you.

c Take your best details, reshape them as needed, and use them to complete the paragraph about Roger.

Revising

Read over the paragraph you have written. Ask yourself these questions:

- Do the examples I have provided really support the idea that Roger is selfish?
- Are there enough examples to make my point about Roger and have people agree with me?
- Have I checked my paper for spelling and other sentence skills, as listed on the inside front cover of the book?

Continue revising your work until you can answer "yes" to all these questions.

WRITING ASSIGNMENT 2

Write an examples paragraph about one quality of a person you know well. The person might be a member of your family, a friend, a roommate, a boss or supervisor, a neighbor, an instructor, or someone else. Here is a list of descriptions that you might consider choosing from. Feel free to choose another description that does not appear here.

Honest	Hardworking	Jealous
Bad-tempered	Supportive	Materialistic
Ambitious	Suspicious	Sarcastic
Prejudiced	Open-minded	Self-centered
Considerate	Lazy	Spineless
Argumentative	Independent	Good-humored
Softhearted	Stubborn	Cooperative
Energetic	Flirtatious	Self-disciplined
Patient	Irresponsible	Sentimental

Reliable	Stingy	Defensive
Generous	Trustworthy	Dishonest
Persistent	Aggressive	Insensitive
Shy	Courageous	Unpretentious
Sloppy	Compulsive	Tidy

Prewriting

a Select the individual you will write about and the quality of this person that you will focus on. For example, you might choose a self-disciplined cousin. Her quality of self-discipline will then be the point of your paper.

b Make a list of examples that will support your point. A list for the self-disciplined cousin might look like this:

> Exercises every day for forty-five minutes
>
> Never lets herself watch TV until homework is done
>
> Keeps herself on a strict budget
>
> Organizes her school papers in color-coordinated notebooks
>
> Eats no more than one dessert every week
>
> Balances her checkbook the day her statement arrives

c Read over your list and see how you might group the items into categories. The list above, for example, could be broken into three categories: schoolwork, fitness, and money.

> Exercises every day for forty-five minutes (fitness)
>
> Never lets herself watch TV until homework is done (schoolwork)
>
> Keeps herself on a strict budget (money)
>
> Organizes her school papers in color-coordinated notebooks (schoolwork)
>
> Eats no more than one dessert every week (fitness)
>
> Balances her checkbook the day her bank statement arrives (money)

d Prepare a scratch outline made up of the details you've generated, with those details grouped into appropriate categories.

1. Self-disciplined about fitness
    A. Exercises every day for forty-five minutes
    B. Eats no more than one dessert every week

Copyright ©2006 The McGraw-Hill Companies, Inc. All rights reserved.

2.   Self-disciplined about schoolwork
      A.   Never lets herself watch TV until homework is done
      B.   Organizes her school papers in color-coordinated notebooks
3.   Self-disciplined about money
      A.   Keeps herself on a strict budget
      B.   Balances her checkbook the day her bank statement arrives

e   Write the topic sentence of your paragraph. You should include the name of the person you're writing about, your relationship to that person, and the specific quality you are focusing on. For example, you might write, "Keisha, a school-mate of mine, is very flirtatious," or "Stubbornness is Uncle Carl's outstanding characteristic." And a topic sentence for the paragraph about the self-disciplined cousin might be: "My cousin Mari is extremely self-disciplined."

Remember to focus on only *one* characteristic. Also remember to focus on a *specific* quality, not a vague, general quality. For instance, "My English instructor is a nice person" is too general.

f   Now you have a topic sentence and an outline and are ready to write the first draft of your paragraph. Remember, as you flesh out the examples, that your goal is not just to *tell* us about the person but to *show* us the person by detailing his or her words, actions, or both. In preparation for this writing assignment, you might want to go back and reread the examples provided in "An Egotistical Neighbor."

Revising

It's hard to criticize your own work honestly, especially just after you've finished writing. If at all possible, put your paragraph away for a day or so and then return to it. Better yet, wait a day and then read it aloud to a friend whose judgment you trust.

Read the paragraph with these questions in mind:

• Does my topic sentence clearly state whom I am writing about, what that person's relationship is to me, and what quality of that person I am going to focus on?

• Do the examples I provide truly show that my subject has the quality I'm writing about?

• Have I provided enough specific details to solidly support my point that my subject has a certain quality?

• Have I organized the details in my paragraph into several clearly defined categories?

- Have I used transitional words such as *also, in addition, for example,* and *for instance* to help the reader follow my train of thought?

- Have I checked my paper for sentence skills, as listed on the inside front cover of the book?

Continue revising your work until you and your reader can answer "yes" to all these questions.

WRITING ASSIGNMENT 3

Write a paragraph that uses examples to develop one of the following statements or a related statement of your own.

1. _____ is a distracting place to try to study.

2. The daily life of a student is filled with conflicts.

3. Abundant evidence exists that the United States has become a health-conscious nation.

4. Despite modern appliances, many household chores are still drudgery.

5. One of my instructors, _____, has some good (*or* unusual) teaching techniques.

6. Wasted electricity is all around us.

7. Life in the United States is faster-paced today than ever before.

8. Violence on television is widespread.

9. Today, some people are wearing ridiculous fashions.

10. Some students here at _____ do not care about learning (*or* are overly concerned about grades).

Be sure to choose examples that truly support your topic sentence. They should be relevant facts, statistics, personal experiences, or incidents you have heard or read about. Organize your paragraph by listing several examples that support your point. Save the most vivid, most convincing, or most important example for last.

WRITING ASSIGNMENT 4

As the following cartoon suggests, the diet of many Americans is not healthy. We eat too much junk food and far too much cholesterol. Write a paragraph with a topic sentence like one of the following:

Copyright ©2006 The McGraw-Hill Companies, Inc All rights reserved.

© The New Yorker Collection 1988 Tom Cheney from cartoonbank.com. All Rights Reserved.

The diet of the average American is unhealthy.

The diet of many American families is unhealthy.

Many schoolchildren in America do not have a healthy diet.

Using strategies described in Chapter 19, "A Quick Guide to Research" (pages 339–352), research the topic with keywords such as "unhealthy American diets." Combine information you find with your own observations to provide a series of examples that support your point.

WRITING ASSIGNMENT 5

Writing for a Specific Purpose and Audience

In this examples paragraph, you will write with a specific purpose and for a specific audience. Imagine that you are a television critic for a daily newspaper. Your job is to recommend to viewers, every day, the programs most worth watching. You've decided that there is nothing particularly good on TV today. Therefore, your plan is to write a one-paragraph article about TV commercials, supporting this point: "Television advertisements are more entertaining than the programs they interrupt." To prepare for this article, spend some time watching television, taking detailed notes on several ads. Decide on two or three ways in which the ads are entertaining; these ways will be the main supporting points in your outline. Then choose at least one ad to use as a specific example to illustrate each of those points. Here are some entertaining qualities that may be seen in ads:

Humor	Drama	Suspense
Cleverness	Emotion	Beauty
Music		

9 Explaining a Process

Every day we perform many activities that are *processes*—that is, series of steps carried out in a definite order. Many of these processes are familiar and automatic: for example, tying shoelaces, changing bed linen, using a vending machine, and starting a car. We are thus seldom aware of the sequence of steps making up each activity. In other cases, such as when we are asked for directions to a particular place, or when we try to read and follow the directions for a new table game, we may be painfully conscious of the whole series of steps involved in the process.

In this section, you will be asked to write a process paragraph—one that explains clearly how to do or make something. To prepare for this assignment, you should first read the student process papers below and then respond to the questions that follow.

Note In process writing, you are often giving instruction to the reader, and so the pronoun *you* can appropriately be used. Two of the model paragraphs here use *you*—as indeed does much of this book, which gives instruction on how to write effectively. As a general rule, though, do not use *you* in your writing.

Paragraphs to Consider

Sneaking into the House at Night

[1]The first step I take is bringing my key along with me. [2]Obviously, I don't want to have to knock on the door at 1:30 in the morning and rouse my parents out of bed. [3]Second, I make it a point to stay out past midnight. [4]If I come in before then, my father is still up, and I'll have to face his disapproving look. [5]All I need in my life is for him to make me feel guilty. [6]Trying to make it as a college student is as much as I'm ready to handle. [7]Next, I am careful to be very quiet upon entering the house. [8]This involves lifting the front door up slightly as I open it, so that it does not creak. [9]It also means treating the floor and steps to the second floor like a minefield, stepping carefully over the spots that squeak. [10]When I'm upstairs, I stop

Copyright ©2006 The McGraw-Hill Companies, inc. All rights reserved.

briefly in the bathroom without turning on the light. [11]Finally, I tiptoe to my room, put my clothes in a pile on a chair, and slip quietly into bed. [12]With my careful method of sneaking into the house at night, I have avoided some major hassles with my parents.

How to Harass an Instructor

[1]There are several steps you can take to harass an instructor during a class. [2]First of all, show up late, so that you can interrupt the beginning of the instructor's presentation. [3]Saunter in nonchalantly and try to find a seat next to a friend. [4]In a normal tone of voice, speak some words of greeting to your friends as you sit down, and scrape your chair as loudly as possible while you make yourself comfortable in it. [5]Then just sit there and do anything but pay attention. [6]When the instructor sees that you are not involved in the class, he or she may pop a quick question, probably hoping to embarrass you. [7]You should then say, in a loud voice, "I DON'T KNOW THE ANSWER." [8]This declaration of ignorance will throw the instructor off guard. [9]If the instructor then asks you why you don't know the answer, say, "I don't even know what page we're on" or "I thought the assignment was boring, so I didn't do it." [10]After the instructor calls on someone else, get up loudly from your seat, walk to the front of the classroom, and demand to be excused for an emergency visit to the washroom. [11]Stay there at least fifteen minutes and take your time coming back. [12]If the instructor asks you where you've been when you reenter the room, simply ignore the question and go to your seat. [13]Flop into your chair, slouching back and extending your legs as far out as possible. [14]When the instructor informs you of the assignment that the class is working on, heave an exaggerated sigh and very slowly open up your book and start turning the pages. [15]About a half hour before class is over, begin to look at the clock every few minutes. [16]Ten minutes before dismissal time, start noisily packing up your books and papers. [17]Then get up and begin walking to the door a couple of minutes before the class is supposed to end. [18]The instructor will look at you and wonder whether it wouldn't have been better to go into business instead of education.

Dealing with Verbal Abuse

[1]If you are living with a man who abuses you verbally with criticism, complaints, and insults, you should take steps to change your situation. [2]First, realize that you are not to blame for his abusive behavior. [3]This may be difficult for you to believe. [4]Years of verbal abuse have probably convinced you that you're responsible for everything that's wrong with your relationship. [5]But that is a lie. [6]If your partner is verbally abusive, it is his responsibility to learn why he chooses to deal with his problems by

3 Offer to go with him to counseling.

1 Realize you're not to blame.

5 Learn to stand up for yourself.

4 Go into counseling yourself if he won't do it.

~~Call the police if he ever becomes violent.~~

6 Leave him if he refuses to change.

Then Selma grouped her items into four steps. Those steps were (1) realize you're not to blame; (2) tell the abuser you won't accept more abuse; (3) get into counseling, preferably with him; and (4) if necessary, leave him.

Selma was ready to write her first draft. Here it is:

Some people think that "abuse" has to mean getting punched and kicked, but that's not so. Verbal abuse can be as painful inside as physical abuse is on the outside. It can make you feel worthless and sad. I know because I lived with a verbally abusive man for years. Finally I found the courage to deal with the situation. Here is what I did. With the help of friends, I finally figured out that I wasn't to blame. I thought it was my fault because that's what he always told me—that if I wasn't so stupid, he wouldn't criticize and insult me. When I told him I wanted him to stop insulting and criticizing me, he just laughed at me and told me I was a crybaby. One of my friends suggested a counselor, and I asked Harry to go talk to him with me. We went together once but Harry wouldn't go back. He said he didn't need anyone to tell him how to treat his woman. I wasn't that surprised because Harry grew up with a father who treated his mother like dirt and his mom just accepts it to this day. Even after Harry refused to go see the counselor, though, I kept going. The counselor helped me see that I couldn't make Harry change, but I was still free to make my own choices. If I didn't want to live my life being Harry's verbal punching bag, and if he didn't want to change, then I would have to. I told Harry that I wasn't going to live that way anymore. I told him if he wanted to work together on better ways to communicate, I'd work with him. But otherwise, I would leave. He gave me his usual talk about "Oh, you know I don't really mean half the stuff I say when I'm mad." I said that wasn't a good enough excuse, and that I did mean what I was saying. He got mad all over again and called me every name in the book. I stuck around for a little while after that but then realized "This is it. I can stay here and take this or I can do what I know is right for me." So I left. It was a really hard decision but it was the right one. Harry may be angry at me forever but I know now that his anger and his verbal abuse are his problem, not mine.

Copyright ©2006 The McGraw-Hill Companies, Inc. All rights reserved.

Development through Revising

After Selma had written her first draft, she showed it to a classmate for her comments. Here is what the classmate wrote in response:

> In order for this to be a good process essay, I think you need to do a couple of things.
>
> First, although the essay is based on what you went through, I think it's too much about your own experience. I'd suggest you take yourself out of it and just write about how any person could deal with any verbally abusive situation. Otherwise this paper is about you and Harry, not the process.
>
> Second, you need a clear topic sentence that tells the reader what process you're going to explain.
>
> Third, I'd use transitions like 'first' and 'next' to make the steps in the process clearer. I think the steps are all there, but they get lost in all the details about you and Harry.

When Selma reread her first draft, she agreed with her classmate's suggestions. She then wrote the version of "Dealing with Verbal Abuse" that appears on page 198.

Writing a Process Paragraph

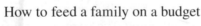
WRITING ASSIGNMENT 1

Choose one of the topics below to write about in a process paper.

How to feed a family on a budget

How to break up with a boyfriend or girlfriend

How to balance a checkbook

How to change a car or bike tire

How to get rid of house or garden pests, such as mice, roaches, or wasps

How to play a simple game like checkers, or tic-tac-toe, or an easy card game

How to shorten a skirt or pants

How to meet new people, for either dating or friendship

How to plant a garden

How to deal with a nosy person

How to fix a leaky faucet, a clogged drain, or the like

How to build a campfire or start a fire in a fireplace

How to study for an important exam

How to conduct a yard or garage sale

How to wash dishes efficiently, clean a bathroom, do laundry, or the like

Prewriting

a   Begin by freewriting on your topic for ten minutes. Do not worry about spelling, grammar, organization, or other matters of form. Just write whatever comes into your head regarding the topic. Keep writing for more than ten minutes if ideas keep coming to you. This freewriting will give you a base of raw material to draw from during the next phase of your work on the paragraph. After freewriting, you should have a sense of whether there is enough material available for you to write a process paragraph about the topic. If so, continue as explained below. If there is not enough material, choose another topic and freewrite about *it* for ten minutes.

b   Write a clear, direct topic sentence stating the process you are going to describe. For instance, if you are going to describe a way to study for major exams, your topic sentence might be "My study-skills instructor has suggested a good way to study for major exams." Or you can state in your topic sentence the process and the number of steps involved: "My technique for building a campfire involves four main steps."

c   List all the steps you can think of that may be included in the process. Don't worry, at this point, about how each step fits or whether two steps overlap. Here, for example, is the list prepared by the author of "Sneaking into the House at Night":

Quiet on stairs

Come in after Dad's asleep

House is freezing at night

Bring key

Know which steps to avoid

Lift up front door

Late dances on Saturday night

Don't turn on bathroom light

Avoid squeaky spots on floor

Get into bed quietly

Copyright ©2006 The McGraw-Hill Companies, Inc. All rights reserved.

d   Number your items in the order in which they occur; strike out items that do not fit in the list; add others that come to mind. The author of "Sneaking into the House at Night" did this step as follows:

~~Quiet on stairs~~

2 Come in after Dad's asleep

~~House is freezing at night~~

1 Bring key

5 Know which steps to avoid

3 Lift up front door

~~Late dances on Saturday night~~

6 Don't turn on bathroom light

4 Avoid squeaky spots on floor

8 Get into bed quietly

7 Undress quietly

e   Use your list as a guide to write the first draft of your paper. As you write, try to think of additional details that will support your opening sentence. Do not expect to finish your paper in one draft. After you complete your first rough draft, in fact, you should be ready to write a series of drafts as you work toward the goals of unity, support, and coherence.

Revising

After you have written the first draft of your paragraph, set it aside for a while if you can. Then read it out loud, either to yourself or (better yet) to a friend or classmate who will be honest with you about how it sounds. You (or you and your friend) should keep these points in mind:

- An effective process paper describes a series of activities in a way that is clear and easy to follow. Are the steps in your paper described in a clear, logical way? Have you used transitions such as *first, next, also, then, after, now, during,* and *finally* to make the paper move smoothly from one step to another?

- Does the paragraph explain every necessary step so that a reader could perform the task described?

- Can you answer "yes" to other questions about unity, support, and coherence on the inside front cover of this book?

Copyright ©2006 The McGraw-Hill Companies, Inc. All rights reserved.

- Is the point of view consistent? For example, if you begin by writing "This is how I got rid of mice" (first person), do not switch to "You must buy the right traps" (second person). Write your paragraph either from the first-person point of view (using *I* and *we*) or from the second-person point of view (*you*)—do not jump back and forth between the two.

- Have you corrected any sentence-skills mistakes that you noticed while reading the paper out loud? Have you checked the paper carefully for sentence skills, including spelling, as listed on the inside front cover of the book?

Continue revising your work until you and your reader can answer "yes" to all these questions.

WRITING ASSIGNMENT 2

Write a paragraph about one of the following processes. For this assignment, you will be working with more general topics than those in Writing Assignment 1. In fact, many of the topics are so broad that entire books have been written about them. A big part of your task, then, will be to narrow the topic down enough so that it can be covered in one paragraph. Then you'll have to invent your own steps for the process. In addition, you'll need to make decisions about how many steps to include and the order in which to present them.

How to break a bad habit such as smoking, overeating, or excess drinking
How to improve a course you have taken
How to make someone you know happy
How to discipline a child
How to improve the place where you work
How to show appreciation to others
How to make someone forgive you
How to make yourself depressed
How to get over a broken relationship
How to procrastinate
How to flirt

Prewriting

a   Choose a topic that appeals to you. Then ask yourself, "How can I make this broad, general topic narrow enough to be covered in a paragraph?" A logical way to proceed would be to think of a particular time you have gone through this process. For instance, if the general topic is "How to decorate economi-cally," you might think about a time you decorated your own apartment.

b   Write a topic sentence about the process you are going to describe. Your topic sentence should clearly reflect the narrowed-down topic you have chosen. If you chose the topic described in step *a*, for example, your topic sentence could be "I made my first apartment look nice without spending a fortune."

c   Make a list of as many different items as you can think of that concern your topic. Don't worry about repeating yourself, about putting the items in order, about whether details are major or minor, or about spelling. Simply make a list of everything about your topic that occurs to you. Here, for instance, is a list of items generated by the student writing about decorating her apartment on a budget:

Bought pretty towels and used them as wall hangings

Trimmed overgrown shrubs in front yard

Used old mayonnaise jars for vases to hold flowers picked in the yard

Found an old oriental rug at a yard sale

Painted mismatched kitchen chairs in bright colors

Kept dishes washed and put away

Bought a slipcover for a battered couch

Used pink lightbulbs

Hung pretty colored sheets over the windows

d   Next, decide what order you will present your items in and number them. (As in the example of "decorating an apartment," there may not be an order that the steps *must* be done in. If that is the case, you'll need to make a decision about a sequence that makes sense, or that you followed yourself.) As you number your items, strike out items that do not fit in the list and add others that you think of, like this:

6 Bought pretty towels and used them as wall hangings

~~Trimmed overgrown shrubs in front yard~~

7 Used old mayonnaise jars for vases to hold flowers picked in the yard

4 Found an old oriental rug at a yard sale

2 Painted mismatched kitchen chairs in bright colors

~~Kept dishes washed and put away~~

1 Bought a slipcover for a battered couch

8 Used pink lightbulbs

5 Hung pretty colored sheets over the windows

3 Built bookshelves out of cinder blocks and boards

e   Referring to your list of steps, write the first draft of your paper. Add additional steps as they occur to you.

Revising

If you can, put your first draft away for a day or so and then return to it. Read it out loud to yourself or, better yet, to a friend who will give you honest feedback.

Here are questions to ask yourself as you read over your first draft and the drafts to follow:

- Have I included a clear topic sentence that tells what process I will be describing?
- Have I included all the essential information so that anyone reading my paper could follow the same process?
- Have I made the sequence of steps easy to follow by using transitions like *first, second, then, next, during*, and *finally*?
- Can I answer "yes" to other questions about unity, support, and coherence found on the inside front cover of the book?
- Have I corrected sentence-skills mistakes, including spelling?

Continue revising your work until you can answer "yes" to all these questions.

WRITING ASSIGNMENT 3

Look at the poster headed "The Awesome Power of Reading" on page 208. It lists ways that regular reading can improve a person's life.

What are some steps that a person could take in order to make himself or herself a regular reader? Alternatively, what steps could a person take to encourage a child to read more? Write a process paragraph in which you describe a sequence of steps. If you write about how an adult might become a regular reader, for instance, you might talk about the first action to take, then a second, then a third. If you write about encouraging a child to read more, your goal here, too, should be to present a series of steps to follow to promote a child's love of reading.

Copyright ©2006 The McGraw-Hill Companies, Inc. All rights reserved.

THE POWER OF READING

Want power? Reading can give it to you. Research has
proven that regular reading makes you a better reader,
writer, speaker, listener, and thinker. Regular reading
boosts test scores, sharpens your mind, and leads to
school and job success.

Want power? If so, READ!

TP www.townsendpress.com

© All Rights Reserved.

WRITING ASSIGNMENT 4

Write a process paragraph on how to succeed at a job interview. Using strategies
described in Chapter 19 (pages 339–352), do some research on the topic. Your
reading will help you think about how to proceed with the paper.

Condense the material you have found into three, four, or five basic steps. Choose the steps, tips, and pointers that seem most important to you or that recur most often in the material. Remember that you are reading only to obtain background information for your paper. Do not copy material or repeat someone else's words or phrases in your own work.

WRITING ASSIGNMENT 5

Writing for a Specific Purpose and Audience

In this process paragraph, you will write with a specific purpose and for a specific audience. You have two options.

Option 1   Imagine that you have a part-time job helping out in a day-care center. The director, who is pleased with your work and wants to give you more responsibility, has put you in charge of a group activity (for example, an exercise session, an alphabet lesson, or a valentine-making project). But before you actually begin the activity, the director wants to see a summary of how you would go about it. What advance preparation would be needed, and what exactly would you be doing throughout the time of the project? Write a paragraph explaining the steps you would follow in conducting the activity.

Option 2   Alternatively, write an explanation you might give to one of the children of how to do a simple classroom task—serving juice and cookies, getting ready for nap time, watering a plant, putting toys or other classroom materials away, or any other task you choose. Explain each step of the task in a way that a child would understand.

Copyright ©2006 The McGraw-Hill Companies, Inc. All rights reserved.

10 Examining Cause and Effect

What caused Pat to drop out of school? Why are soap operas so popular? Why does our football team do so poorly each year? How has retirement affected Dad? What effects does divorce have on children? Every day we ask such questions and look for answers. We realize that situations have causes and also effects—good or bad. By examining causes and effects, we seek to understand and explain things.

In this section, you will be asked to do some detective work by examining the causes of something or the effects of something. First read the three paragraphs that follow and answer the questions about them. All three paragraphs support their opening points by explaining a series of causes or a series of effects.

Paragraphs to Consider

New Puppy in the House

¹Buying a new puppy can have significant effects on a household. ²For one thing, the puppy keeps the entire family awake for at least two solid weeks. ³Every night when the puppy is placed in its box, it begins to howl, yip, and whine. ⁴Even after the lights go out and the house quiets down, the puppy continues to moan. ⁵A second effect is that the puppy tortures the family by destroying material possessions. ⁶Every day something different is damaged. ⁷Family members find chewed belts and shoes, gnawed table legs, and ripped sofa cushions leaking stuffing. ⁸In addition, the puppy often misses the paper during the paper-training stage of life, thus making the house smell like the public restroom at a city bus station. ⁹Maybe the most serious problem, though, is that the puppy causes family arguments. ¹⁰Parents argue with children about who is supposed to feed and walk the dog. ¹¹Children argue about who gets to play with the puppy first. ¹²Everyone argues about who left socks and shoes around for the puppy to find. ¹³These continual arguments, along with the effects of sleeplessness and the loss of valued possessions, can really disrupt a household. ¹⁴Only when the puppy gets a bit older does the household settle back to normal.

My Car Accident

¹Several factors caused my recent car accident. ²First of all, because a heavy snow and freezing rain had fallen the day before, the road that I was driving on was hazardous. ³The road had been plowed but was dangerously icy in spots where dense clusters of trees kept the early-morning sun from hitting the road and melting the ice. ⁴Second, despite the slick patches, I was stupidly going along at about fifty miles an hour instead of driving more cautiously. ⁵I have a daredevil streak in my nature and sometimes feel I want to become a stock-car racer after I finish school, rather than an accountant as my parents want me to be. ⁶A third factor contributing to my accident was a dirty green Chevy van that suddenly pulled onto the road from a small intersecting street about fifty yards ahead of me. ⁷The road was a sheet of ice at that point, but I was forced to apply my brake and also swing my car into the next lane. ⁸Unfortunately, the fourth and final cause of my accident now came into play. ⁹The rear of my Honda Civic was heavy because I had a set of barbells in the backseat. ¹⁰I was selling this fairly new weight-lifting set to someone at school, since the weights had failed to build up my muscles immediately and I had gotten tired of practicing with them. ¹¹The result of all the weight in the rear was that after I passed the van, my car spun completely around on the slick road. ¹²For a few horrifying, helpless moments, I was sliding down the highway backward at fifty miles an hour, with no control whatsoever over the car. ¹³Then, abruptly, I slid off the road, thumping into a huge snowbank. ¹⁴I felt stunned for a moment but then also relieved. ¹⁵I saw a telephone pole about six feet to the right of me and realized that my accident could have been disastrous.

Why I Stopped Smoking

¹For one thing, I realized that my cigarette smoke bothered others, irritating people's eyes and causing them to cough and sneeze. ²They also had to put up with my stinking smoker's breath. ³Also, cigarettes are a messy habit. ⁴Our house was littered with ashtrays piled high with butts, matchsticks, and ashes, and the children were always knocking them over. ⁵Cigarettes are expensive, and I estimated that the carton a week that I was smoking cost me about $1,500 a year. ⁶Another reason I stopped was that the message about cigarettes being harmful to health finally got through to me. ⁷I'd known they could hurt the smoker—in fact, a heavy smoker I know from work is in Eagleville Hospital now with lung cancer. ⁸But when I realized what secondhand smoke could do to my wife and children, causing them bronchial problems and even increasing their risk of cancer, it really bothered me. ⁹Cigarettes were also inconvenient. ¹⁰Whenever I smoked, I

Copyright ©2006 The McGraw-Hill Companies, Inc. All rights reserved.

would have to drink something to wet my dry throat, and that meant I had to keep going to the bathroom all the time. [11]I sometimes seemed to spend whole weekends doing nothing but smoking, drinking, and going to the bathroom. [12]Most of all, I resolved to stop smoking because I felt exploited. [13]I hated the thought of wealthy, greedy corporations making money off my sweat and blood. [14]The rich may keep getting richer, but—at least as regards cigarettes—with no thanks to me.

■ Questions

About Unity

1. Which two sentences in "My Car Accident" do not support the opening idea and so should be omitted? (*Write the sentence numbers here.*)

_____   _____

2. Which of the above paragraphs lacks a topic sentence?

_____

About Support

3. How many separate causes are given in "Why I Stopped Smoking"?

_____ four _____ six _____ seven _____ eight

4. How many effects of bringing a new puppy into the house are given in "New Puppy in the House"?

_____ one _____ two _____ three _____ four

About Coherence

5. What transition words or phrases are used to introduce the four reasons listed in "My Car Accident"?

_____   _____   _____   _____

6. In "New Puppy in the House," what words signal the effect that the author feels may be the most important?

_____

Developing a Cause-and-Effect Paragraph

Development through Prewriting

In order to write a good cause-and-effect paragraph, you must clearly define an effect (*what* happened) and the contributing causes (*why* it happened). In addition, you will need to provide details that support the causes and effects you're writing about.

Jerome is the student author of "Why I Stopped Smoking." As soon as the topic occurred to him, he knew he had his *effect* (he had stopped smoking). His next task was to come up with a list of *causes* (reasons he had stopped). He decided to make a list of all the reasons for his quitting smoking that he could think of. This is what he came up with:

Annoyed others

Messy

Bad for health

Expensive

Taking his list, Jerome then jotted down details that supported each of those reasons:

Annoyed others

Bad breath

Irritates eyes

Makes other people cough

People hate the smell

Messy

Ashtrays, ashes, butts everywhere

Messes up my car interior

Bad for health

Marco in hospital with lung cancer

Secondhand smoke dangerous to family

My morning cough

Copyright ©2006 The McGraw-Hill Companies, Inc. All rights reserved.

Expensive

Carton a week costs more than $1,500 a year

Tobacco companies getting rich off me

Jerome then had an effect and four causes with details to support them. On the basis of this list, he wrote a first draft:

> My smoking annoyed other people, making them cough and burning their eyes. I bothered them with my smoker's breath. Nonsmokers usually hate the smell of cigarettes and I got embarrassed when nonsmokers visited my house. I saw them wrinkle their noses in disgust at the smell. It is a messy habit. My house was full of loaded ashtrays that the kids were always knocking over. My car was messy too. A guy from work, Marco, who has smoked for years, is in the hospital now with lung cancer. It doesn't look as though he's going to make it. Secondhand smoke is bad for people too and I worried it would hurt my wife and kids. Also I realized I was coughing once in a while. The price of cigarettes keeps going up and I was spending too much on smokes. When I see things in the paper about tobacco companies and their huge profits it made me mad.

Development through Revising

The next day, Jerome traded first drafts with his classmate Roger. This is what Roger had to say about Jerome's work:

> The biggest criticism I have is that you haven't used many transitions to tie your sentences together. Without them, the paragraph sounds like a list, not a unified piece of writing.
>
> Is one of your reasons more important than the others? If so, it would be good if you indicated that.
>
> You could add a little more detail in several places. For instance, how could secondhand smoke hurt your family? And how much were you spending on cigarettes?

As Jerome read his own paper, he realized he wanted to add one more reason to his paragraph: the inconvenience to himself. "Maybe it sounds silly to write about always getting drinks and going to the bathroom, but that's one of the ways that smoking takes over your life that you never think about when you start," he said. Using Roger's comments and his own new idea, he produced the paragraph that appears on page 211.

Writing a Cause-and-Effect Paragraph

Copyright ©2006 The McGraw-Hill Companies, Inc. All rights reserved.

WRITING ASSIGNMENT 1

Choose one of the three topic sentences and brief outlines below. Each is made up of three supporting points (causes or effects). Your task is to turn the topic sentence and outline into a cause or effect paragraph.

Option 1

Topic sentence: There are several reasons why some high school graduates are unable to read.

(1) Failure of parents (*cause*)

(2) Failure of schools (*cause*)

(3) Failure of students themselves (*cause*)

Option 2

Topic sentence: Attending college has changed my personality in positive ways.

(1) More confident (*effect*)

(2) More knowledgeable (*effect*)

(3) More adventurous (*effect*)

Option 3

Topic sentence: Living with roommates (or family) makes attending college difficult.

(1) Late-night hours (*cause*)

(2) More temptations to cut class (*cause*)

(3) More distractions from studying (*cause*)

Prewriting

a   After you've chosen the option that appeals to you most, jot down all the details you can think of that might go under each of the supporting points. Use separate paper for your lists. Don't worry yet about whether you can use all the items—your goal is to generate more material than you need. Here, for example, are some of the details generated by the author of "New Puppy in the House" to back up her supporting points:

Topic sentence: Having a new puppy disrupts a household.

1. Keeps family awake
    a. Whines at night
    b. Howls
    c. Loss of sleep
2. Destroys possessions
    a. Chews belts and shoes
    b. Chews furniture
    c. Tears up toys it's supposed to fetch
3. Has accidents in house
    a. Misses paper
    b. Disgusting cleanup
    c. Makes house smell bad
4. Causes arguments
    a. Arguments about walking dog
    b. Arguments about feeding dog
    c. Arguments about who gets to play with dog
    d. Arguments about vet bills

b   Now go through the details you have generated and decide which are most effective. Strike out the ones you decide are not worth using. Do other details occur to you? If so, jot them down as well.

c   Now you are ready to write your paragraph. Begin the paragraph with the topic sentence you chose. Make sure to develop each of the supporting points from the outline into a complete sentence, and then back it up with the best of the details you have generated.

Revising

Review your paragraph with these questions in mind:

- Have I begun the paragraph with the topic sentence provided?
- Is each supporting point stated in a complete sentence?
- Have I provided effective details to back up each supporting point?
- Have I used transitions such as *in addition, another thing,* and *also* to make the relationships between the sentences clear?
- Have I proofread the paragraph for sentence-skills errors, including spelling?

Revise your paragraph until you are sure the answer to each question is "yes."

Copyright ©2006 The McGraw-Hill Companies, Inc. All rights reserved

WRITING ASSIGNMENT 2

Most of us find it easy to criticize other people, but we may find it harder to give compliments. In this assignment, you will be asked to write a one-paragraph letter praising someone. The letter may be to a person you know (for instance, a parent, relative, or friend); to a public figure (an actor, politician, religious leader, sports star, and so on); or to a company or organization (for example, a newspaper, a government agency, a store where you shop, or the manufacturer of a product you own).

Prewriting

a   The fact that you are writing this letter indicates that its recipient has had an *effect* on you: you like, admire, or appreciate the person or organization. Your job will be to put into words the *causes,* or reasons, for this good feeling. Begin by making a list of reasons for your admiration. Here, for example, are a few reasons a person might praise an automobile manufacturer:

> My car is dependable.
>
> The price was reasonable.
>
> I received prompt action on a complaint.
>
> The car is well-designed.
>
> The car dealer was honest and friendly.
>
> The car has needed little maintenance.

Reasons for admiring a parent might include these:

> You are patient with me.
>
> You are fair.
>
> You have a great sense of humor.
>
> You encourage me in several ways.
>
> I know you have made sacrifices for me.

Develop your own list of reasons for admiring the person or organization you've chosen.

b   Now that you have a list of reasons, you need details to back up each reason. Jot down as many supporting details as you can for each reason. Here is what the writer of a letter to the car manufacturer might do:

> **My car is dependable.**
> Started during last winter's coldest days when neighbors' cars wouldn't start
> Has never stranded me anywhere

The price was reasonable.
Costs less than other cars in its class
Came standard with more options than other cars of the same price

I received prompt action on a complaint.
When I complained about rattle in door, manufacturer arranged for a part to be replaced at no charge

The car is well-designed.
Controls are easy to reach
Dashboard gauges are easy to read

The car dealer was honest and friendly.
No pressure, no fake "special deal only today"

The car has needed little maintenance.
Haven't done anything but regular tune-ups and oil changes

c   Next, select from your list the three or four reasons that you can best support with effective details. These will make up the body of your letter.

d   For your topic sentence, make the positive statement you wish to support. For example, the writer of the letter to the car manufacturer might begin like this: "I am a very satisfied owner of a 2006 Camry."

e   Now combine your topic sentence, reasons, and supporting details, and write a draft of your letter.

Revising

If possible, put your letter aside for a day. Then read it aloud to a friend. As you and he or she listen to your words, you should both keep these questions in mind:

- Is the topic sentence a positive statement that is supported by the details?
- Does the paragraph clearly state several different reasons for liking or admiring the person or organization?
- Is each of those reasons supported with specific evidence?
- Are the sentences linked together with transitional words and phrases?
- Is the letter free of sentence-skills mistakes, including spelling errors?

Continue revising your work until you and your reader can answer "yes" to all these questions.

WRITING ASSIGNMENT 3

The poster here suggests that people are chained or imprisoned by their addictions. It also seems to say that addictions can come in many forms, including drinking, smoking, and eating. And the woman's expression and clenched fists suggest how her addiction makes her feel about herself.

Write a paragraph about a particular addiction. You might write about someone you know who is addicted to smoking, drinking, shopping, watching TV, or surfing the Internet. In your paragraph, discuss several possible reasons for this addiction, or several effects on the person's life.

Here are some sample topic sentences for such a paragraph:

> My cousin is addicted to overeating, and her addiction is harming her in a number of ways.
>
> There were at least three reasons why I became addicted to cigarettes.
>
> Although shopping can be a pleasant activity, addictive shopping can be destructive for several reasons.

WRITING ASSIGNMENT 4

Investigate the reasons behind a current news event. For example, you may want to discover the causes of one of the following:

> A labor strike or some other protest
>
> A military action by our or some other government
>
> A murder or some other act of violence
>
> A tax increase
>
> A traffic accident, a fire, a plane crash, or some other disaster

Research the reasons for the event by reading current newspapers (especially big-city dailies that are covering the story in detail), reading weekly newsmagazines (such as *Time* and *Newsweek*), watching television shows and specials, or consulting an Internet news source.

Copyright ©2006 The McGraw-Hill Companies, Inc. All rights reserved.

Decide on the major cause or causes of the event and their specific effects. Then write a paragraph explaining in detail the causes and effects. Below is a sample topic sentence for this assignment.

The rape and murder that occurred recently on X Street have caused much fear and caution throughout the neighborhood.

Note how this topic sentence uses general words (*fear, caution*) that can summarize specific supporting details. Support for the word *caution,* for example, might include specific ways in which people in the neighborhood are doing a better job of protecting themselves.

WRITING ASSIGNMENT 5

Writing for a Specific Purpose and Audience

In this process paragraph, you will write with a specific purpose and for a specific audience. Choose one of the following options:

Option 1   Assume that there has been an alarming increase in drug abuse among the students at the high school you attended. What might be the causes of this increase? Spend some time thinking and freewriting about several possible causes. Then, as a concerned member of the community, write a letter to the high school guidance counselor explaining the reasons for the increased drug abuse. Your purpose is to provide information the counselor may be able to use in dealing with the problem.

Option 2   Your roommate has been complaining that it's impossible to succeed in Mr. X's class because the class is too stressful. You volunteer to attend the class and see for yourself. Afterward, you decide to write a letter to the instructor calling attention to the stressful conditions and suggesting concrete ways to deal with them. Write this letter, explaining in detail the causes and effects of stress in the class.

11 Comparing or Contrasting

Copyright ©2006 The McGraw-Hill Companies, Inc. All rights reserved.

Comparison and contrast are two everyday thought processes. When we *compare* two things, we show how they are similar; when we *contrast* two things, we show how they are different. We might compare or contrast two brand-name products (for example, Nike versus Adidas running shoes), two television shows, two instructors, two jobs, two friends, or two courses of action we could take in a given situation. The purpose of comparing or contrasting is to understand each of the two things more clearly and, at times, to make judgments about them.

In this chapter, you will be asked to write a paper of comparison or contrast. First, however, you must learn the two common methods of developing a comparison or contrast paragraph. Read the two paragraphs that follow and try to explain the difference in the two methods of development.

Paragraphs to Consider

My Senior Prom

¹My senior prom was nothing like what I expected it to be. ²From the start of my senior year, I had pictured putting on a sleek silvery slip dress that my aunt would make and that would cost $300 in any store. ³No one else would have a gown as attractive as mine. ⁴I imagined my boyfriend coming to the door with a lovely deep-red corsage, and I pictured myself happily inhaling its perfume all evening long. ⁵I saw us setting off for the evening in his brother's BMW convertible. ⁶We would make a flourish as we swept in and out of a series of parties before the prom. ⁷Our evening would be capped by a delicious shrimp dinner at the prom and by dancing close together into the early morning hours. ⁸The prom was held on May 15, 2005, at the Pony Club on Black Horse Pike. ⁹However, because of sickness in her family, my aunt had no time to finish my gown and I had to buy an ugly pink one off the discount rack at the last minute. ¹⁰My corsage of red roses looked terrible on my pink gown, and I do not remember its having any scent. ¹¹My boyfriend's brother was out of town, and I stepped outside and saw the stripped

down Chevy that he used at the races on weekends. [12]We went to one party where I drank a lot of wine that made me sleepy and upset my stomach. [13]After we arrived at the prom, I did not have much more to eat than a roll and some celery sticks. [14]Worst of all, we left early without dancing because my boyfriend and I had had a fight several days before, and at the time we did not really want to be with each other.

Day versus Evening Students

[1]As a part-time college student who has taken both day and evening courses, I have observed notable differences between day and evening students. [2]First of all, day and evening students differ greatly in age, styles, and interests. [3]The students in my daytime classes are all about the same age, with similar clothing styles and similar interests. [4]Most are in their late teens to early twenties, and whether male or female, they pretty much dress alike. [5]Their uniform consists of jeans, a T-shirt, running shoes, a baseball cap, and maybe a gold earring or two. [6]They use the same popular slang, talk about the same movies and TV shows, and know the same musical artists. [7]But students in my evening courses are much more diverse. [8]Some are in their late teens, but most range from young married people in their twenties and thirties to people my grandparents' age. [9]Generally, their clothing is more formal than the day students'. [10]They are dressed for the workplace, not for a typical college classroom. [11]Many of the women wear skirts or dresses; the men often wear dress shirts or sweaters. [12]And they are more comfortable talking about mortgages or work schedules or child care than about what was on TV last night. [13]Day and evening students also have very different responsibilities. [14]For day students, college and a part-time job are generally the only major responsibilities. [15]They have plenty of time to study and get assignments done. [16]However, evening students lead much more complicated lives than most day students. [17]They may come to campus after putting in a nine-to-five day at work. [18]Most have children to raise or grandchildren to baby-sit for. [19]When they miss a class or hand in an assignment late, it's usually because of a real problem, such as a sick child or an important deadline at work. [20]Finally, day and evening students definitely have different attitudes toward school. [21]Day students often seem more interested in the view out the window or the cute classmate in the next row than in what the instructor is saying. [22]They doze, draw cartoons, whisper, and write notes instead of paying attention. [23]In contrast, evening students sit up straight, listen hard, and ask the instructor lots of questions. [24]They obviously are there to learn, and they don't want their time wasted. [25]In short, day students and night students are as different as . . . day and night.

Complete this comment: The difference in the methods of contrast in the two paragraphs is that

_____

_____

_____

Compare your answer with the following explanation of the two methods of development used in comparison or contrast paragraphs.

Methods of Development

There are two common methods, or formats, of development in a comparison or contrast paper. One format presents the details *one side at a time*. The other presents the details *point by point*. Each format is explained below.

One Side at a Time

Look at the outline of "My Senior Prom":

Topic sentence: My senior prom was nothing like what I had expected it to be.

A. Expectations (first half of paper)
   1. Dress (expensive, silver)
   2. Corsage (deep red, fragrant)
   3. Car (BMW convertible)
   4. Parties (many)
   5. Dinner (shrimp)
   6. Dancing (all night)
B. Reality (second half of paper)
   1. Dress (cheap, pink)
   2. Corsage (wrong color, no scent)
   3. Car (stripped-down Chevy)
   4. Parties (only one)
   5. Dinner (roll and celery)
   6. Dancing (none because of quarrel)

Copyright ©2006 The McGraw-Hill Companies, Inc. All rights reserved.

When you use the one-side-at-a-time method, follow the same order of points of contrast or comparison for each side, as in the outline above. For example, both the first half of the paper and the second half begin with the same idea: what dress would be worn. Then both sides go on to the corsage, the car, and so on.

Point by Point

Now look at the outline of "Day versus Evening Students":

Topic sentence: There are notable differences between day and night students.

A. Age and related interests and tastes in clothing
   1. Youthful nature of day students
   2. Older nature of evening students
B. Amount of responsibilities
   1. Lighter responsibilities of day students
   2. Heavier responsibilities of evening students
C. Attitude toward school
   1. Casual attitude of day students
   2. Serious attitude of evening students

The outline shows how the two kinds of students are contrasted point by point. First, the writer contrasts the ages, clothing styles, and interests of the young daytime students and the older evening students. Next, the writer contrasts the limited responsibilities of the daytime students with the heavier responsibilities of the evening students. Finally, the writer contrasts the casual attitude toward school of the daytime students and the serious attitude of the evening students.

When you begin a comparison or contrast paper, you should decide right away which format you are going to use: one side at a time or point by point. An outline is an essential step in helping you decide which format will be more workable for your topic. Keep in mind, however, that an outline is just a guide, not a permanent commitment. If you later feel that you've chosen the wrong format, you can reshape your outline to the other format.

ACTIVITY

Complete the partial outlines provided for the two paragraphs that follow.

1.
How My Parents' Divorce Changed Me

In the three years since my parents' divorce, I have changed from a spoiled brat to a reasonably normal college student. Before the divorce, I expected my mother to wait on me. She did my laundry, cooked and cleaned up after meals, and even straightened up my room. My only response was to complain if the meat was too well done or if the sweater I wanted to wear was not clean. In addition, I expected money for anything I wanted. Whether it was a digital music player or my own cell phone, I expected Mom to hand over the money. If she refused, I would get it from Dad. However, he left when I was fifteen, and things changed. When Mom got a full-time job to support us, I was the one with the free time to do housework. Now, I did the laundry, started the dinner, and cleaned not only my own room but also the rest of the house. Also, I no longer asked her for money, since I knew there was none to spare. Instead, I got a part-time job on weekends to earn my own spending money. Today, I have my own car that I am paying for, and I am putting myself through college. Things have been hard sometimes, but I am glad not to be that spoiled kid any more.

Topic sentence: In the three years since my parents' divorce, I have changed from a spoiled brat to a reasonably normal college student.

   a.　Before the divorce

      (1) _____

      (2) _____

   b.　After the divorce

      (1) _____

      (2) _____

Complete the following statement: Paragraph 1 uses the _____ method of development.

2.
Good and Bad Horror Movies

A good horror movie is easily distinguishable from a bad one. A good horror movie, first of all, has both male and female victims. Both sexes suffer terrible fates at the hands of monsters and maniacs. Therefore,

Copyright ©2006 The McGraw-Hill Companies, Inc. All rights reserved.

everyone in the audience has a chance to identify with the victim. Bad horror movies, on the other hand, tend to concentrate on women, especially half-dressed ones. These movies are obviously prejudiced against half the human race. Second, a good horror movie inspires compassion for its characters. For example, the audience will feel sympathy for the victims in the horror classics about the Wolfman, played by Lon Chaney, Jr., and also for the Wolfman himself, who is shown to be a sad victim of fate. In contrast, a bad horror movie encourages feelings of aggression and violence in viewers. For instance, in the <u>Halloween</u> films, the murders are seen from the murderer's point of view. The effect is that the audience stalks the victims along with the killer and feels the same thrill he does. Finally, every good horror movie has a sense of humor. In <u>Alien</u>, as a crew member is coughing and choking just before the horrible thing bursts out of his chest, a colleague chides him, "The food ain't <u>that</u> bad, man." Humor provides relief from the horror and makes the characters more human. A bad horror movie, though, is humorless and boring. One murder is piled on top of another, and the characters are just cardboard figures. Bad horror movies may provide cheap thrills, but the good ones touch our emotions and live forever.

Topic sentence: A good horror movie is easily distinguished from a bad one.

    a. Kinds of victims

        (1) _____

        (2) _____

    b. Effect on audience

        (1) _____

        (2) _____

    c. Tone

        (1) _____

        (2) _____

Complete the following statement: Paragraph 1 uses the _____ method of development.

Additional Paragraphs to Consider

Read these additional paragraphs of comparison or contrast and then answer the questions that follow.

My Broken Dream

[1]When I became a police officer in my town, the job was not as I had dreamed it would be. [2]I began to dream about being a police officer at about age ten. [3]I could picture myself wearing a handsome blue uniform with an impressive-looking badge on my chest. [4]I could also picture myself driving a powerful patrol car through town and seeing everyone stare at me with envy. [5]But most of all, I dreamed of wearing a gun and using all the equipment that "TV cops" use. [6]I knew everyone would be proud of me. [7]I could almost hear the guys on the block saying, "Boy, Steve made it big. [8]Did you hear he's a cop?" [9]I dreamed of leading an exciting life, solving big crimes, and meeting lots of people. [10]I knew that if I became a cop, everyone in town would look up to me. [11]However, when I actually did become a police officer, I soon found out that the reality was different. [12]My first disappointment came when I was sworn in and handed a well-used, baggy uniform. [13]My disappointment continued when I was given a badge that looked like something pulled out of a Cracker Jack box. [14]I was assigned a beat-up old junker and told that it would be my patrol car. [15]It had a striking resemblance to a car that had lost in a demolition derby at a stock-car raceway. [16]Disappointment seemed to continue. [17]I soon found out that I was not the envy of all my friends. [18]When I drove through town, they acted as if they had not seen me, despite the gun and nightstick at my side. [19]I was told I was crazy doing this kind of job by people I thought would look up to me. [20]My job was not as exciting as I had dreamed it would be, either. [21]Instead of solving robberies and murders every day, I found that I spent a great deal of time comforting a local resident because a neighborhood dog had watered his favorite bush.

Two Views on Toys

[1]Children and adults have very different preferences. [2]First, there is the matter of taste. [3]Adults pride themselves on taste, while children ignore the matter of taste in favor of things that are fun. [4]Adults, especially grandparents, pick out tasteful toys that go unused, while children love the cheap playthings advertised on television. [5]Second, of course, there is the matter of money. [6]The new games on the market today are a case in point. [7]Have you ever tried to lure a child away from some expensive game in order

Copyright ©2006 The McGraw-Hill Companies, Inc. All rights reserved.

to get him or her to play with an old-fashioned game or toy? ^{8}Finally, there is a difference between an adult's and a child's idea of what is educational. ^{9}Adults, filled with memories of their own childhood, tend to be fond of the written word. ^{10}Today's children, on the other hand, concentrate on anything electronic. ^{11}These things mean much more to them than to adults. ^{12}Next holiday season, examine the toys that adults choose for children. ^{13}Then look at the toys the children prefer. ^{14}You will see the difference.

Mike and Helen

^{1}Like his wife, Helen, Mike has a good sense of humor. ^{2}Also, they are both short, dark-haired, and slightly pudgy. ^{3}Unlike Helen, Mike tends to hold a grudge. ^{4}He is slow to forget a cruel remark, a careless joke, or an unfriendly slight. ^{5}Mike enjoys swimming, camping, and tennis, but Helen is an indoor type. ^{6}Both Mike and Helen can be charming when they want to be, and they seem to handle small crises in a calm, cool way. ^{7}A problem such as an overflowing washer, a stalled car, or a sick child is not a cause for panic; they seem to take such events in stride. ^{8}In contrast to Helen, though, Mike tends to be disorganized. ^{9}He is late for appointments and unable to keep important documents—bank records, receipts, and insurance papers—where he can find them.

QUESTIONS

About Unity

1. Which paragraph lacks a topic sentence?

   _____

2. Which paragraph has a topic sentence that is too broad?

   _____

About Support

3. Which paragraph contains almost no specific details?

   _____

4. Which paragraph provides the most complete support?

   _____

Copyright ©2006 The McGraw-Hill Companies, Inc. All rights reserved.

About Coherence

5. What method of development (one side at a time or point by point) is used in "My Broken Dream"?

_____

In "Two Views in Toys"?

_____

6. Which paragraph offers specific details but lacks a clear, consistent method of development?

_____

Developing a Comparison or Contrast Paragraph

Development through Prewriting

Gayle, the author of "My Senior Prom," had little trouble thinking of a topic for her comparison or contrast paragraph.

"My instructor said, 'You might compare or contrast two individuals, jobs you've had, or places you've lived,'" Gayle said. "Then he added, 'Or you might compare or contrast your expectations of a situation with the reality.' I immediately thought of my prom—boy, were my expectations different from the reality! I had thought it would be the high point of my senior year, but instead it was a total disaster."

Because she is a person who likes to think visually, Gayle started her preparations for her paragraph by clustering. She found this a helpful way to "see" the relationships between the points she was developing. Her diagram is shown here:

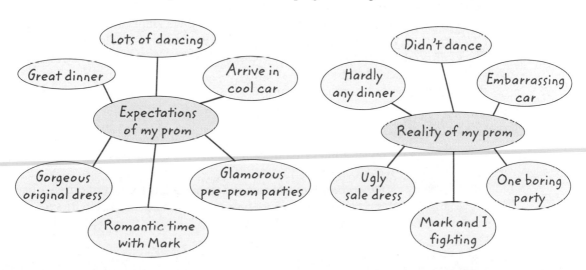

Taking a detail first from the "Expectations" part of the diagram, then one from the "Reality" portion, then another from "Expectations," and so on, Gayle began to write her paragraph using a point-by-point format:

My senior prom was nothing like what I expected. First of all, I expected to be wearing a beautiful dress that my aunt would make for me. But because she couldn't finish it in time, I had to buy an ugly one at the last minute. Second, I thought I'd have a wonderful romantic evening with my boyfriend. But we'd been fighting that week and by the time the prom came around we were barely speaking. I thought we'd have a great time stopping in at lots of parties before the prom, but we went to only one and I left with an upset stomach.

Gayle stopped here, because she wasn't satisfied with the way the paragraph was developing. "I wanted the reader to picture the way I had imagined my prom, and I didn't like interrupting that picture with the reality of the evening. So I decided to try the one-side-at-a-time approach instead." Here is Gayle's first draft:

My senior prom was nothing like what I expected. I imagined myself wearing a beautiful, expensive-looking dress that my aunt would make. I thought my boyfriend and I would have a wonderful romantic evening together. We'd dance all through the night and we would cruise around in my boyfriend's brother's hot car. We would stop in at a lot of fun pre-prom parties, I thought, and we'd have a delicious shrimp dinner at the prom itself. But instead my uncle had a gallbladder attack that the doctor thought might be a heart attack and my aunt went to the hospital with him instead of finishing my dress. I had to go to the mall at the last minute and buy an ugly dress that nobody else had wanted off the sale rack. Mark and I had been fighting all week. Because he's in track and has a part-time job too we don't have much time together and still he wants to go out on Saturdays with his guy friends. So by the night of the prom we were hardly speaking to each other. We went to only one party before the prom and I left it feeling sick. And the restaurant was so crowded and noisy that I hardly got anything to eat. Because we were angry at each other, we didn't dance at all. And instead of his brother's luxury car, we had to use a stripped-down racing car.

Development through Revising

Gayle's instructor reviewed her first draft. Here are his comments:

All this is very promising, but some of your details are out of order—for example, you mention the pre-prom parties after the dance itself. Be sure to follow the evening's sequence of events.

More descriptive details are needed! For instance, what was your "beautiful" dress supposed to look like, and what did the "ugly" one you ended up with look like?

You include some unnecessary information: for example, the details of your uncle's illness. Everything in your paragraph should support your topic sentence.

Following her instructor's suggestions (and remembering a few more details she wanted to include), Gayle wrote the version of her paragraph that appears on page 221.

Writing a Comparison or Contrast Paragraph

Copyright ©2006 The McGraw-Hill Companies, Inc. All rights reserved.

WRITING ASSIGNMENT 1

Write a comparison or contrast paragraph on one of the topics below:

Two holidays	Two characters in the same movie or TV show
Two instructors	
Two children	Two homes
Two kinds of eaters	Two neighborhoods
Two drivers	Two cartoon strips
Two coworkers	Two cars
Two members of a team (or two teams)	Two friends
Two singers or groups	Two crises
Two pets	Two bosses or supervisors
Two parties	Two magazines
Two jobs	

Prewriting

a   Choose your topic, the two subjects you will write about.

b   Decide whether your paragraph will *compare* the two subjects (discuss their similarities) or *contrast* them (discuss their differences). Students most often choose to write about differences. For example, you might write about how a musical group you enjoy differs from a musical group you dislike. You might discuss important differences between two employers you have had or between two neighborhoods you've lived in. You might contrast a job you've had in a car factory with a white-collar job you've had as a receptionist.

c   Write a direct topic sentence for your paragraph. Here's an example: "My job in a car-parts factory was very different from my job as a receptionist."

d   Come up with at least three strong points to support your topic sentence. If you are contrasting two jobs, for example, your points might be that they differed greatly (1) in their physical setting, (2) in the skills they required, and (3) in the people they brought you into contact with.

e   Use your topic sentence and supporting points to create a scratch outline for your paragraph. For the paragraph about jobs, the outline would look like this:

<u>Topic sentence:</u> My job in a car-parts factory was very different from my job as a receptionist.

1. The jobs differed in physical setting.
2. The jobs differed in the skills they required.
3. The jobs differed in the people they brought me into contact with.

f   Under each of your supporting points, jot down as many details as occur to you. Don't worry yet about whether the details all fit perfectly or whether you will be able to use them all. Your goal is to generate a wealth of material to draw on. An example:

<u>Topic sentence:</u> My job in a car-parts factory was very different from my job as a receptionist.

1. <u>The jobs differed in physical setting.</u>
    Factory loud and dirty
    Office clean and quiet
    Factory full of machines, hunks of metal, tools
    Office full of desks, files, computers
    Factory smelled of motor oil
    Office smelled of new carpet
    Windows in factory too high and grimy to look out of
    Office had clean windows onto street
2. <u>The jobs differed in the skills and behavior they required.</u>
    Factory required physical strength
    Office required mental activity
    Didn't need to be polite in factory
    Had to be polite in office

Didn't need to think much for self in factory

Constantly had to make decisions in office

3. <u>The jobs differed in the people they brought me into contact with.</u>

In factory, worked with same crew every day

In office, saw constant stream of new customers

Most coworkers in factory had high-school education or less

Many coworkers and clients in office well educated

Coworkers in factory spoke variety of languages

Rarely heard anything but English in office

g   Decide which format you will use to develop your paragraph: one side at a time or point by point. Either is acceptable; it is up to you to decide which you prefer. The important thing is to be consistent: whichever format you choose, be sure to use it throughout the entire paragraph.

h   Write the first draft of your paragraph.

Revising

Put your writing away for a day or so. You will return to it with a fresh perspective and a better ability to critique what you have done.

Reread your work with these questions in mind:

- Does my topic sentence make it clear what two things I am comparing or contrasting?
- Have I compared or contrasted the subjects in at least three important ways?
- Have I provided specific details that effectively back up my supporting points?
- If I have chosen the point-by-point format, have I consistently discussed a point about one subject, then immediately discussed the same point about the other subject before moving on to the next point?
- If I have chosen the one-side-at-a-time format, have I discussed every point about one of my subjects, then discussed the same points *in the same order* about the second subject?
- Have I used appropriate transitions, such as *first, in addition, also,* and *another way,* to help the reader follow my train of thought?
- Have I carefully proofread my paragraph, using the list on the inside front cover of the book, and corrected all sentence-skills mistakes, including spelling?

Continue revising your work until you can answer "yes" to all these questions.

Copyright ©2006 The McGraw-Hill Companies, Inc. All rights reserved.

WRITING ASSIGNMENT 2

Write a paragraph in which you compare or contrast your life in the real world with your life in an imagined "perfect world." Your paragraph may be humorous or serious.

Prewriting

a   As your "real life" and "ideal life" are too broad for a paragraph, choose three specific areas to focus on. You might select any of the areas below, or think of a specific area yourself.

Work	Friends
Money	Possessions
Romance	Housing
Physical location	Talents
Personal appearance	

b   Write the name of one of your three areas (for example, "Work"), across the top of a page. Divide the page into two columns. Label one column "real world" and the other "perfect world." Under "real world," write down as many details as you can think of describing your real-life work situation. Under "perfect world," write down details describing what your perfect work life would be like. Repeat the process on separate pages for your other two major areas.

c   Write a topic sentence for your paragraph. Here's an example: "In my perfect world, my life would be quite different in the areas of work, money, and housing."

d   Decide which approach you will take: one side at a time or point by point.

e   Write a scratch outline that reflects the format you have selected. The outline for a point-by-point format would look like this:

Topic sentence: In my perfect world, my life would be quite different in the areas of work, money, and housing.

1. Work
   a. Real-life work
   b. Perfect-world work

Copyright ©2005 The McGraw-Hill Companies, Inc. All rights reserved.

2. Money

    a. Real-life money

    b. Perfect-world money

3. Housing

    a. Real life housing

    b. Perfect-world housing

The outline for a one-side-at-a-time format would look like this:

<u>Topic sentence:</u> In my perfect world, my life would be quite different in the areas of work, money, and housing.

1. Real life

    a. Work

    b. Money

    c. Housing

2. Perfect world

    a. Work

    b. Money

    c. Housing

f   Drawing from the three pages of details you generated in step *b*, complete your outline by jotting down your strongest supporting details for each point.

g   Write the first draft of your paragraph.

Revising

Reread your paragraph, and then show it to a friend who will give you honest feedback. You should both review it with these questions in mind:

- Does the topic sentence make it clear what three areas of life are being compared or contrasted?

- Does the paragraph follow a consistent format: point by point or one side at a time?

- Does the paragraph provide specific details that describe both the "real life" situation and the "perfect world" situation?

- Does the paragraph include transitional words and phrases that make it easy to follow?
- Have all sentence-skills mistakes, including spelling, been corrected?

Continue revising your work until you and your reader can answer "yes" to all these questions.

WRITING ASSIGNMENT 3

Write a contrast paragraph on one of the topics below.

Neighborhood stores versus a shopping mall

Driving on an expressway versus driving on country roads

People versus *Us* (or any other two popular magazines)

Camping in a tent versus camping in a recreational vehicle

Working parents versus stay-at-home parents

Shopping at a department store versus shopping on the Internet

A used car versus a new one

Recorded music versus live music

PG-rated movies versus R-rated movies

News in a newspaper versus news on television or on the Internet

Yesterday's toys versus today's toys

Fresh food versus canned or frozen food

The locker room of a winning team after a game versus the locker room of a losing team

An ad on television versus an ad for the same product in a magazine

Amateur sports teams versus professional teams

Follow the directions for prewriting and rewriting given in Writing Assignment 2.

WRITING ASSIGNMENT 4

Use the cartoon shown here as the basis for a comparison-contrast paragraph. Assume that your audience has not seen the cartoon. It is your job, then, to compare and contrast elements in the cartoon so effectively that your readers will clearly understand both what the cartoon looks like and what it means. Before writing your paragraph, you might make a list for yourself of exactly how the two characters in the cartoon are the same and how they are different. When comparing, you may want to use transitions such as *just as, alike, likewise,* and *similarly.* When contrasting, you may want to use transitions such as *in contrast, on the other hand, differs from, unlike,* or *however.*

©1996 The Philadelphia Inquirer. Reprinted with permission of UNIVERSAL PRESS SYNDICATE. All rights reserved.

WRITING ASSIGNMENT 5

Writing for a Specific Purpose and Audience

In this comparison-contrast paragraph, you will write with a specific purpose and for a specific audience. Imagine that you are living in an apartment building in which new tenants are making life unpleasant for you. Write a letter of complaint to your landlord comparing and contrasting life before and after the tenants arrived. You might want to focus on one or more of the following:

Noise

Trash

Safety hazards

Parking situation

Copyright ©2005 The McGraw-Hill Companies, Inc. All rights reserved.

12 Defining a Term

In talking with other people, we sometimes offer informal definitions to explain just what we mean by a particular term. Suppose, for example, we say to a friend, "Karen can be so clingy." We might then expand on our idea of "clingy" by saying, "You know, a clingy person needs to be with someone every single minute. If Karen's best friend makes plans that don't include her, she becomes hurt. And when she dates someone, she calls him several times a day and gets upset if he even goes to the grocery store without her. She hangs on to people too tightly." In a written definition, we make clear in a more complete and formal way our own personal understanding of a term. Such a definition typically starts with one meaning of a term. The meaning is then illustrated with a series of examples or a story.

In this section, you will be asked to write a paragraph that begins with a one-sentence definition; that sentence will be the topic sentence. The three student papers below are all examples of definition paragraphs. Read them and then answer the questions that follow.

Paragraphs to Consider

Luck

[1]Luck is putting $1.75 into a vending machine and getting the money back with your snack. [2]It is an instructor's decision to give a retest on a test on which you first scored thirty. [3]Luck refers to moments of good fortune that happen in everyday life. [4]It is not going to the dentist for two years and then going and finding out that you do not have any cavities. [5]It is calling up a plumber to fix a leak on a day when the plumber has no other work to do. [6]Luck is finding a used car for sale at a good price at exactly the time when your car rolls its last mile. [7]Luck is driving into a traffic bottleneck and choosing the lane that winds up moving most rapidly. [8]Luck is being late for work on a day when your boss arrives later than you do. [9]It is having a new checkout aisle at the supermarket open up just as your cart arrives. [10]The best kind of luck is winning a new wide-screen TV on a chance for which you paid only a quarter.

Disillusionment

[1]Disillusionment is the feeling we have when one of our most cherished beliefs is stolen from us. [2]I learned about disillusionment firsthand the day Mr. Keller, our eighth-grade teacher, handed out the grades for our class biology projects. [3]I had worked hard to assemble what I thought was the best insect collection any school had ever seen. [4]For weeks, I had set up homemade traps around our house, in the woods, and in vacant lots. [5]At night, I would stretch a white sheet between two trees, shine a lantern on it, and collect the night-flying insects that gathered there. [6]With my own money, I had bought killing jars, insect pins, gummed labels, and display boxes. [7]I carefully arranged related insects together, with labels listing each scientific name and the place and date of capture. [8]Slowly and painfully, I wrote and typed the report that accompanied my project at the school science fair. [9]In contrast, my friend Eddie did almost nothing for his project. [10]He had his father, a psychologist, build an impressive maze complete with live rats and a sign that read, "You are the trainer." [11]A person could lift a little plastic door, send a rat running through the maze, and then hit a button to release a pellet of rat food as a reward. [12]This exhibit turned out to be the most popular one at the fair. [13]I felt sure that our teacher would know that Eddie could not have built it, and I was certain that my hard work would be recognized and rewarded. [14]Then the grades were finally handed out, and I was crushed. [15]Eddie had gotten an A-plus, but my grade was a B. [16]I suddenly realized that honesty and hard work don't always pay off in the end. [17]The idea that life is not fair, that sometimes it pays to cheat, hit me with such force that I felt sick. [18]I will never forget that moment.

A Mickey Mouse Course

[1]A Mickey Mouse course is any college course that is so easy that even Mickey Mouse could achieve an A. [2]A student who is taking a heavy schedule, or who does not want four or five especially difficult courses, will try to sandwich in a Mickey Mouse course. [3]A student can find out about such a course by consulting other students, since word of a genuine Mickey Mouse course spreads like wildfire. [4]Or a student can study the college master schedule for telltale course titles like The Art of Pressing Wildflowers, History of the Comic Book, or Watching Television Creatively. [5]In an advanced course such as microbiology, though, a student had better be prepared to spend a good deal of time during the semester on the course. [6]Students in a Mickey Mouse course can attend classes while half-asleep, hungover, or wearing Walkman earphones or a blindfold; they will still pass. [7]The course exams (if there are any) would not challenge a five-year-old. [8]The course lectures usually consist of information that anyone with common sense knows anyway. [9]Attendance may be required, but

Copyright ©2006 The McGraw-Hill Companies, Inc. All rights reserved.

participation or involvement in the class is not. [10]The main requirement for passing is that a student's body is there, warming a seat in the classroom. [11]There are no difficult labs or special projects, and term papers are never mentioned. [12]Once safely registered for such a course, all the students have to do is sit back and watch the credits accumulate on their transcripts.

QUESTIONS

About Unity

1. Which paragraph places its topic sentence within the paragraph rather than, more appropriately, at the beginning?

   _____

2. Which sentence in "A Mickey Mouse Course" should be omitted in the interest of paragraph unity? *(Write the sentence number here.)* _____

About Support

3. Which two paragraphs develop their definitions through a series of short examples?

   _____

   _____

4. Which paragraph develops its definition through a single extended example?

   _____

About Coherence

5. Which paragraph uses emphatic order, saving its best detail for last?

   _____

6. Which paragraph uses time order to organize its details?

   _____

Developing a Definition Paragraph

Development through Prewriting

When Harry, the author of "Disillusionment," started working on his assignment, he did not know what he wanted to write about. He looked around the house for inspiration. His two-year-old twins racing around the room made him think about defining "energy." The fat cat asleep on a sunny windowsill suggested that he might write about "laziness" or "relaxation." Still not sure of a topic, he looked over his notes from that day's class. His instructor had jotted a list of terms on the blackboard, saying, "Maybe you could focus on what one of these words has meant in your own life." Harry looked over the words he had copied down: *honesty, willpower, faith, betrayal, disillusionment*—"When I got to the word 'disillusionment,' the eighth-grade science fair flashed into my mind," Harry said. "That was a bitter experience that definitely taught me what disillusionment was all about."

Because the science fair had occurred many years before, Harry had to work to remember it well. He decided to try the technique of questioning himself to come up with the details of what had happened. Here are the questions Harry asked himself and the answers he wrote:

<u>When did I learn about disillusionment?</u>

When I was in eighth grade

<u>Where did it happen?</u>

At the school science fair

<u>Who was involved?</u>

Me, Eddie Loomis and his father, and Mr. Keller

<u>What happened?</u>

I had worked very hard on my insect collection. Eddie had done almost nothing but he had a rat maze that his father had built. I got a B on my project while Eddie got an A+.

<u>Why was the experience so disillusioning?</u>

I thought my hard work would be rewarded. I was sure Mr. Keller would recognize that I had put far more effort into my project than Eddie had. When Eddie won, I learned that cheating can pay off and that honest work isn't always rewarded.

<u>How did I react?</u>

I felt sick to my stomach. I wanted to confront Mr. Keller and Eddie and make them see how unfair the grades were. But I knew I'd just look like a poor loser, so I didn't do anything.

<u>On the basis of this experience, how would I define disillusionment?</u>

It's finding out that something you really believed in isn't true.

Copyright ©2006 The McGraw-Hill Companies, Inc. All rights reserved.

Drawing from the ideas generated by his self-questioning, Harry wrote the following draft of his paragraph:

> Disillusionment is finding out that one of your most important beliefs isn't true. I learned about disillusionment at my eighth-grade science fair. I had worked very hard on my project, an insect collection. I was sure it would get an A. I had worked so hard on it, even spending nights outside making sure it was very good. My friend Eddie also did a project, but he barely worked on his at all. Instead, he had his father build a maze for a rat to run through. The trainer lifted a little plastic door to let the rat into the maze, and if it completed the maze, the trainer could release a pellet of food for it to eat. It was a nice project, but the point is that Eddie hadn't made it. He just made things like the banner that hung over it. Mr. Keller was our science teacher. He gave Eddie an A+ and me just a B. So that really taught me about disillusionment.

Development through Revising

The next day, Harry's teacher divided the class into groups of three. The groups reviewed each member's paragraph. Harry was grouped with Curtis and Jocelyn. After reading through Harry's paper several times, the group had the following discussion:

"My first reaction is that I want to know more about your project," said Jocelyn. "You give details about Eddie's, but not many about your own. What was so good about it? You need to show us, not just tell us. Also, you said that you worked very hard, but you didn't show us how hard."

"Yeah," said Harry. "I remember my project clearly, but I guess the reader has to know what it was like and how much effort went into it."

Curtis said, "I like your topic sentence, but when I finished the paragraph I wasn't sure what 'important belief' you'd learned wasn't true. What would you say that belief was?"

Harry thought a minute. "I'd believed that honest hard work would always be rewarded. I found out that it doesn't always happen that way, and that cheating can actually win."

Curtis nodded. "I think you need to include that in your paper."

Jocelyn added, "I'd like to read how you felt or reacted after you saw your grade, too. If you don't explain that, the paragraph ends sort of abruptly."

Harry agreed with his classmates' suggestions. After he had gone through several revisions, he produced the version that appears on page 239.

Writing a Definition Paragraph

WRITING ASSIGNMENT 1

Write a paragraph that defines the term *TV addict*. Base your paragraph on the topic sentence and three supporting points provided below.

Topic sentence: Television addicts are people who will watch all the programs they can, for as long as they can, without doing anything else.

(1) TV addicts, first of all, will watch anything on the tube, no matter how bad it is. . . .

(2) In addition, addicts watch more hours of TV than normal people do. . . .

(3) Finally, addicts feel that TV is more important than other people or any other activities that might be going on. . . .

Prewriting

a Generate as many examples as you can for each of the three qualities of a TV addict. You can do this by asking yourself the following questions:

  • What are some truly awful shows that I (or TV addicts I know) watch just because the television is turned on?

  • What are some examples of the large amounts of time that I (or TV addicts I know) watch television?

  • What are some examples of ways that I (or TV addicts I know) neglect people or give up activities in order to watch TV?

Write down every answer you can think of for each question. At this point, don't worry about writing full sentences or even about grammar or spelling. Just get your thoughts down on paper.

b Look over the list of examples you have generated. Select the strongest examples you have thought of. You should have at least two or three for each quality. If not, ask yourself the questions in step *a* again.

c Write out the examples you will use, this time expressing them in full, grammatically correct sentences.

d Start with the topic sentence and three points provided in the assignment. Fill in the examples you've generated to support each point and write a first draft of your paragraph.

Copyright ©2005 The McGraw-Hill Companies, Inc. All rights reserved.

Revising

Put your first draft away for a day or so. When you come back to it, reread it critically, asking yourself these questions:

- Have I used the topic sentence and the three supporting points that were provided?
- Have I backed up each supporting point with at least two examples?
- Does each of my examples truly illustrate the point that it backs up?
- Have I used appropriate transitional language (*another, in addition, for example*) to tie my thoughts together?
- Have I proofread my paragraph and corrected any sentence-skills mistakes, including spelling?

Keep revising your paragraph until you can answer "yes" to each question.

WRITING ASSIGNMENT 2

Write a paragraph that defines one of the following terms. Each term refers to a certain kind of person.

Know-it-all	Clown	Workaholic
Charmer	Jellyfish	Showoff
Loser	Leader	Control freak
Lazybones	Nerd	Mother hen
Snob	Good neighbor	Toady
Con artist	Optimist	Fusspot
Fair-weather friend	Pessimist	
Good sport	Pack rat	

Prewriting

a   Write a topic sentence for your definition paragraph. This is a two-part process:

- *First,* place the term in a class, or category. For example, if you are writing about a certain kind of person, the general category is *person*. If you are describing a type of friend, the general category is *friend*.

- *Second,* describe what you consider the special feature or features that set your term apart from other members of its class. For instance, say what *kind* of person you are writing about or what *type* of friend.

In the following topic sentence, try to identify three things: the term being defined, the class it belongs to, and the special feature that sets the term apart from other members of the class.

A chocoholic is a person who craves chocolate.

The term being defined is *chocoholic.* The category it belongs to is *person.* The words that set *chocoholic* apart from any other person are *craves chocolate.*

Below is another example of a topic sentence for this assignment. It is a definition of *whiner.* The class, or category, is underlined: A whiner is a type of person. The words that set the term *whiner* apart from other members of the class are double-underlined.

A whiner is a <u>person</u> who <u><u>feels wronged by life.</u></u>

In the following sample topic sentences, underline the class and double-underline the special features.

A clotheshorse is a person who needs new clothes to be happy.

The class clown is a student who gets attention through silly behavior.

A worrywart is a person who sees danger everywhere.

b Develop your definition by using one of the following methods:

Examples. Give several examples that support your topic sentence.

Extended example. Use one longer example to support your topic sentence.

Contrast. Support your topic sentence by contrasting what your term *is* with what it is *not.* For instance, you may want to define a *fair-weather friend* by contrasting his or her actions with those of a true friend.

c Once you have created a topic sentence and decided how to develop your paragraph, make a scratch outline. If you are using a contrast method of development, remember to present the details one side at a time or point by point (see pages 223–224).

d Write a first draft of your paragraph.

Copyright ©2006 The McGraw-Hill Companies, Inc. All rights reserved.

Revising

As you revise your paragraph, keep these questions in mind:

- Does my topic sentence (1) place my term in a class and (2) name some special features that set it apart from its class?
- Have I made a clear choice to develop my topic sentence through either several examples, one extended example, or contrast?
- If I have chosen to illustrate my topic through contrast, have I consistently followed either a point-by-point or a one-side-at-a-time format?
- Have I used appropriate transitions (*another, in addition, in contrast, for example*) to tie my thoughts together?
- Is my paragraph free of sentence-skills errors and spelling errors?

Continue revising your work until you can answer "yes" to all these questions.

WRITING ASSIGNMENT 3

Write a paragraph that defines one of the abstract terms below.

Arrogance	Family	Persistence
Assertiveness	Fear	Practicality
Class	Freedom	Rebellion
Common sense	Gentleness	Responsibility
Conscience	Innocence	Self-control
Curiosity	Insecurity	Sense of humor
Danger	Jealousy	Shyness
Depression	Nostalgia	Violence
Escape	Obsession	

As a guide in writing your paper, use the suggestions for prewriting and rewriting in Writing Assignment 2. Remember to place your term in a class or category and to describe what *you* feel are the distinguishing features of that term.

After writing your topic sentence, check that it is complete and correct by doing the following:

- Single-underline the category of the term you're defining.
- Double-underline the term's distinguishing characteristic or characteristics.

Here are three sample topic sentences:

Laziness is the trait of resisting all worthwhile work as much as possible.

Jealousy is the feeling of wanting a possession or quality that someone else has.

A family is a group whose members are related to one another in some way.

WRITING ASSIGNMENT 4

Since stress affects all of us to some degree—in the workplace (as shown in the cartoon here), in school, in our families, and in our everyday lives—it is a useful term to explore. Write a paragraph defining *stress*. Organize your paragraph in one of these ways:

© 2005 David Sipress from cartoonbank.com. All Rights Reserved.

- Use a series of examples (see page 185) of stress.

- Use narration (see page 275) to provide one longer example of stress: Create a hypothetical person (or use a real person) and show how this person's typical morning or day illustrates your definition of *stress*.

Using strategies described in Chapter 19 (pages 341–352), do some research on stress. Your reading will help you think about how to proceed with the paper.

Hints   Do not simply write a series of general, abstract sentences that repeat and reword your definition. If you concentrate on providing specific support, you will avoid the common trap of getting lost in a maze of generalities.

Make sure your paper is set firmly on the four bases: unity, support, coherence, and sentence skills. Edit the next-to-final draft of the paragraph carefully for sentence-skills errors, including spelling.

Copyright ©2006 The McGraw-Hill Companies, Inc. All rights reserved.

WRITING ASSIGNMENT 5

Writing for a Specific Purpose and Audience

In this definition paragraph, you will write with a specific purpose and for a specific audience. Choose one of the following options.

Option 1   Imagine that at the place where you work, one employee has just quit, creating a new job opening. Since you have been working there for a while, your boss has asked you to write a description of the position. That description, a detailed definition of the job, will be sent to employment agencies. These agencies will be responsible for interviewing candidates. Choose any position you know about, and write a paragraph defining it. First state the purpose of the job, and then list its duties and responsibilities. Finally, describe the qualifications for the position. Below is a sample topic sentence for this assignment.

> Purchasing-department secretary is a position in which someone provides a variety of services to the purchasing-department managers.

In a paragraph with the topic sentence above, the writer would go on to list and explain the various services the secretary must provide.

Option 2   Alternatively, imagine that a new worker has been hired, and your boss has asked you to explain "team spirit" to him or her. The purpose of your explanation will be to give the newcomer an idea of the kind of teamwork that is expected in this workplace. Write a paragraph that defines in detail what your boss means by *team spirit*. Use examples or one extended example to illustrate each of your general points about team spirit.

13 Dividing and Classifying

If you were doing the laundry, you might begin by separating the clothing into piles. You would then put all the whites in one pile and all the colors in another. Or you might classify the laundry, not according to color, but according to fabric—putting all cottons in one pile, polyesters in another, and so on. *Classifying* is the process of taking many things and separating them into categories. We generally classify to better manage or understand many things. Librarians classify books into groups (novels, travel, health, etc.) to make them easier to find. A scientist sheds light on the world by classifying all living things into two main groups: animals and plants.

Dividing, in contrast, is taking one thing and breaking it down into parts. We often divide, or analyze, to better understand, teach, or evaluate something. For instance, a tinkerer might take apart a clock to see how it works; a science text might divide a tree into its parts to explain their functions. A music reviewer may analyze the elements of a band's performance—for example, the skill of the various players, rapport with the audience, selections, and so on.

In short, if you are classifying, you are sorting *numbers of things* into categories. If you are dividing, you are breaking *one thing* into parts. It all depends on your purpose—you might classify flowers into various types or divide a single flower into its parts.

In this section, you will be asked to write a paragraph in which you classify a group of things into categories according to a single principle. To prepare for this assignment, first read the paragraphs below, and then work through the questions and the activity that follow.

Paragraphs to Consider

Types of E-Mail

[1]As more and more people take advantage of e-mailing, three categories of e-mail have emerged. [2]One category of e-mail is junk mail. [3]When most people sign on to their computers, they are greeted with a flood of get-rich-quick schemes, invitations to pornographic Web sites, and ads for a variety of unwanted products. [4]E-mail users quickly become good at hitting the

Copyright ©2006 The McGraw-Hill Companies Inc. All rights reserved.

"delete" button to get rid of this garbage. [5]The second category that clogs most people's electronic mailbox is forwarded mail, most of which also gets deleted without being read. [6]The third and best category of e-mail is genuine personal e-mail from genuine personal friends. [7]Getting such real, thoughtful e-mail can almost make up for the irritation of the other two categories.

Studying for a Test

[1]Phase 1 of studying for a test, often called the "no problem" phase, runs from the day the test is announced to approximately forty-eight hours before the dreaded exam is passed out. [2]During phase 1, the student is carefree, smiling, and kind to helpless animals and small children. [3]When asked by classmates if he or she has studied for the test yet, the reply will be an assured "No problem." [4]During phase 1, no actual studying takes place. [5]Phase 2 is entered two days before the test. [6]For example, if the test is scheduled for 9 A.M. Friday, phase 2 begins at 9 A.M. Wednesday. [7]During phase 2, again, no actual studying takes place. [8]Phase 3, the final phase, is entered twelve hours before "zero hour." [9]This is the cram phase, characterized by sweaty palms, nervous twitches, and confused mental patterns. [10]For a test at nine o'clock on Friday morning, a student begins exhibiting these symptoms at approximately nine o'clock on Thursday night. [11]Phase 3 is also termed the "shock" phase, since the student is shocked to discover the imminence of the exam and the amount of material to be studied. [12]During this phase, the student will probably be unable to sleep and will mumble meaningless phrases like "$a^2 + c^2$." [13]This phase will not end until the exam is over. [14]If the cram session has worked, the student will fall gratefully asleep that night. [15]On waking up, he or she will be ready to go through the whole cycle again with the next test.

Three Kinds of Dogs

[1]A city walker will notice that most dogs fall into one of three categories. [2]First there are the big dogs, which are generally harmless and often downright friendly. [3]They walk along peacefully with their masters, their tongues hanging out and big goofy grins on their faces. [4]Apparently they know they're too big to have anything to worry about, so why not be nice? [5]Second are the spunky medium-sized dogs. [6]When they see a stranger approaching, they go on alert. [7]They prick up their ears, they raise their hackles, and they may growl a little deep in their throats. [8]"I could tear you up," they seem to be saying, "but I won't if you behave yourself." [9]Unless the walker leaps for their master's throat, these dogs usually won't do anything more than threaten. [10]The third

category is made up of the shivering neurotic little yappers whose shrill barks could shatter glass and whose needle-like little teeth are eager to sink into a friendly outstretched hand. [11]Walkers always wonder about these dogs—don't they know that people who really wanted to could squash them under their feet like bugs? [12]Apparently not, because of all the dogs a walker meets, these provide the most irritation. [13]Such dogs are only one of the potential hazards that the city walker encounters.

QUESTIONS

About Unity

1. Which paragraph lacks a topic sentence?

   _____

2. Which sentence in "Three Kinds of Dogs" should be eliminated in the interest of paragraph unity? *(Write the sentence number here.)* _____

About Support

3. Which of the three phases in "Studying for a Test" lacks specific details?

   _____

4. After which sentence in "Types of E-Mail" are supporting details needed? *(Write the sentence number here.)* _____

About Coherence

5. Which paragraph uses emphatic order to organize its details?

   _____

6. Which words in the emphatic-order paragraph signal the most important detail?

   _____

ACTIVITY

This activity will sharpen your sense of the classifying process. In each of the ten groups, cross out the one item that has not been classified on the same basis as the other three. Also, indicate in the space provided the single principle of classification used for the remaining three items. Note the examples.

Copyright ©2006 The McGraw-Hill Companies, Inc. All rights reserved

EXAMPLES   Water
   a. Cold
   ~~b. Lake~~
   c. Hot
   d. Lukewarm
   Unifying principle:
      Temperature

Household pests
~~a. Mice~~
b. Ants
c. Roaches
d. Flies
Unifying principle:
   Insects

1. Eyes
   a. Blue
   b. Nearsighted
   c. Brown
   d. Hazel
   Unifying principle:

   _____

2. Mattresses
   a. Double
   b. Twin
   c. Queen
   d. Firm
   Unifying principle:

   _____

3. Zoo animals
   a. Flamingo
   b. Peacock
   c. Polar bear
   d. Ostrich
   Unifying principle:

   _____

4. Vacation
   a. Summer
   b. Holiday
   c. Seashore
   d. Weekend
   Unifying principle:

   _____

5. Books
   a. Novels
   b. Biographies
   c. Boring
   d. Short stories
   Unifying principle:

   _____

6. Wallets
   a. Leather
   b. Plastic
   c. Stolen
   d. Fabric
   Unifying principle:

   _____

7. Newspaper
   a. Wrapping garbage
   b. Editorials
   c. Making paper planes
   d. Covering floor while painting
   Unifying principle:

   _____

8. Students
   a. First-year
   b. Transfer
   c. Junior
   d. Sophomore
   Unifying principle:

   _____

9. Exercise
   a. Running
   b. Swimming
   c. Gymnastics
   d. Fatigue
   Unifying principle:

10. Leftovers
    a. Cold chicken
    b. Feed to dog
    c. Reheat
    d. Use in a stew
    Unifying principle:

_____

_____

Developing a Division-Classification Paragraph

Development through Prewriting

Marcus walked home from campus to his apartment, thinking about the assignment to write a division-classification paragraph. As he strolled along his familiar route, his observations made him think of several possibilities. "First I thought of writing about the businesses in my neighborhood, dividing them into the ones run by Hispanics, Asians, and African-Americans," he said. "When I stopped in at my favorite coffee shop, I thought about dividing the people who hang out there. There is a group of old men who meet to drink coffee and play cards, and there are students like me, but there didn't seem to be a third category and I wasn't sure two was enough. As I continued walking home, though, I saw Mr. Enriquez and his big golden retriever, and a woman with two nervous little dogs that acted as if they wanted to eat me, and the newsstand guy with his mutt that's always guarding the place, and I thought 'Dogs! I can classify types of dogs.'"

But how would he classify them? Thinking further, Marcus realized that he thought of dogs as having certain personalities depending on their size. "I know there are exceptions, of course, but since this was going to be a lighthearted, even comical paragraph, I thought it would be OK if I exaggerated a bit." He wrote down his three categories:

Big dogs
Medium-sized dogs
Small dogs

Under each division, then, he wrote down as many characteristics as he could think of:

Big dogs
    calm
    friendly

Copyright ©2006 The McGraw-Hill Companies, Inc. All rights reserved.

good-natured

dumb

lazy

Medium-sized dogs

spunky

energetic

ready to fight

protective

friendly if they know you

Small dogs

nervous

trembling

noisy

yappy

snappy

annoying

Marcus then wrote a topic sentence: "Dogs seem to fall into three categories." Using that topic sentence and the scratch outline he'd just produced, he wrote the following paragraph:

Most dogs seem to fall into one of three categories. First there are the big dumb friendly dogs. They give the impression of being sweet but not real bright. One example of this kind of dog is Lucy. She's a golden retriever belonging to a man in my neighborhood. Lucy goes everywhere with Mr. Enriquez. She doesn't even need a leash but just follows him. Dogs like Lucy never bother anybody. She just lies at Mr. Enriquez's feet when he stops to talk to anyone. The guy who runs the corner newsstand I pass every day has a spunky medium-sized dog. Once the dog knows you he's friendly and even playful. But he's always on the lookout for a stranger who might mean trouble. For a dog who's not very big he can make himself look pretty fierce if he wants to. Then there are my least favorite kind of dogs. Little nervous yappy ones. My aunt used to have a Chihuahua like that. It knew me for nine years and still went crazy shaking and yipping at me every time we met. She loved that dog but I can't imagine why. If I had a dog it would definitely come from category 1 or 2.

Development through Revising

Marcus traded his first draft with a fellow student, Rachel, and asked her to give him feedback. Here are the comments Rachel wrote on his paper:

Copyright ©2006 The McGraw-Hill Companies, Inc. All rights reserved.

This is a change in point of view—you haven't been using "you" before.

Is this the beginning of a second category? That's not clear.

Not a complete sentence.

Another change in point of view—you've gone from writing in the third person to "you" to "me."

> Most dogs seem to fall into three categories. First there are the big dumb friendly dogs. They give the impression of being sweet but not real bright. One example of this kind of dog is Lucy, a golden retriever belonging to a man in my neighborhood. Lucy goes everywhere with Mr. Enriquez. She doesn't even need a leash but just follows him everywhere. Lucy never bothers you. She just lies at Mr. Enriquez's feet when he stops to talk to anyone. The guy who runs the corner newsstand I pass every day has a spunky medium-sized dog. Once the dog knows you he's friendly and even playful. But he's always on the lookout for a stranger who might mean trouble. For a dog who's not very big he can make himself look pretty fierce if he wants to scare you. Then there are my least favorite kind of dogs. Little nervous yappy ones. My aunt used to have a Chihuahua like that. It knew me for nine years and still went crazy shaking and yipping at me every time we met. She loved that dog but I can't imagine why. If I had a dog it would definitely come from category 1 or 2.

Marcus—I think you need to make your three categories clearer. Your first one is OK—"big dogs," which you say are friendly—but categories 2 and 3 aren't stated as clearly.

It's distracting to have your point of view change from third person to "you" to "me."

Since you're trying to divide and classify all dogs, I'm not sure it's a good idea to talk only about three individual dogs. This way it sounds as if you're just describing those three dogs instead of putting them into three groups.

When Marcus considered Rachel's comments and reread his paragraph, he agreed with what she had written. "I realized it was too much about three particular dogs and not enough about the categories of dogs," he said. "I decided to revise it and focus on the three classes of dogs."

Marcus then wrote the version that appears on page 250.

Writing a Division-Classification Paragraph

WRITING ASSIGNMENT 1

Below are four options to develop into a classification paragraph. Each one presents a topic to classify into three categories. Choose one option to develop into a paragraph.

Option 1

Supermarket shoppers

(1) Slow, careful shoppers

(2) Average shoppers

(3) Hurried shoppers

Option 3

Types of housekeepers

(1) Never clean

(2) Clean on a regular basis

(3) Clean constantly

Option 2

Eaters

(1) Very conservative eaters

(2) Typical eaters

(3) Adventurous eaters

Option 4

Attitudes toward money

(1) Tightfisted

(2) Reasonable

(3) Extravagant

Prewriting

a   Begin by doing some freewriting on the topic you have chosen. For five or ten minutes, simply write down everything that comes into your head when you think about "types of housekeepers, "attitudes toward money," or whichever option you choose. Don't worry about grammar, spelling, or organization—just write.

b   Now that you've "loosened up your brain" a little, try asking yourself questions about the topic and writing down your answers. If you are writing about supermarket shoppers, for instance, you might ask questions like these:

How do the three kinds of shoppers prepare for their shopping trip?

How many aisles will each kind of shopper visit?

Copyright ©2006 The McGraw-Hill Companies, Inc. All rights reserved.

What do the different kinds of shoppers bring along with them—lists, calculators, coupons, etc.?

How long does each type of shopper spend in the store?

Write down whatever answers occur to you for these and other questions. Again, do not worry at this stage about writing correctly. Instead, concentrate on getting down all the information you can think of that supports your three points.

c   Reread the material you have accumulated. If some of the details you have written make you think of even better ones, add them. Select the details that best support your three points. Number them in the order you will present them.

d   Restate your topic as a grammatically complete topic sentence. For example, if you're writing about eaters, your topic sentence might be "Eaters can be divided into three categories." Turn each of your three supporting points into a full sentence as well.

e   Using your topic sentence and three supporting sentences and adding the details you have generated, write the first draft of your paragraph.

Revising

Put away your work for a day or so. Then reread it with a critical eye, asking yourself these questions:

- Does my paragraph include a complete topic sentence and three supporting points?
- Have I backed up each supporting point with strong, specific details?
- Does my paragraph hang together in terms of unity, support, and coherence?
- Have I edited my paragraph and corrected sentence-skills mistakes, including spelling errors?

Continue revising your work until you can answer "yes" to all these questions.

WRITING ASSIGNMENT 2

Write a classification paragraph on one of the following topics:

Instructors	Drivers
Sports fans	Mothers or fathers
Restaurants	Women's or men's magazines

Attitudes toward life	Presents
Commercials	Neighbors
Employers	Rock, pop, rap, or country singers
Jobs	Houseguests
Bars	Baseball, basketball, football, or hockey players
Family get-togethers	Cars
First dates	

Prewriting

a   Classify members of the group you are considering writing about into three categories. Remember: *You must use a single principle of division when you create your three categories.* For example, if your topic is "school courses" and you classify them into easy, moderate, and challenging, your basis for classification is "degree of difficulty." It would not make sense to have as a fourth type "foreign language" (the basis of such a categorization would be "subject matter") or "early morning" (the basis of that classification would be "time of day the classes meet"). You *could* categorize school courses on the basis of subject matter or time of day they meet, for almost any subject can be classified in more than one way. In a single paper, however, you must choose *one* basis for classification and stick to it.

b   Once you have a satisfactory three-part division, spend at least five minutes freewriting about each of your three points. Don't be concerned yet with grammar, spelling, or organization. Just write whatever comes into your mind about each of the three points.

c   Expand your topic into a fully stated topic sentence.

d   At this point, you have all three elements of your paragraph: the topic sentence, the three main points, and the details needed to support each point. Now weave them all together in one paragraph.

Revising

Do not attempt to revise your paragraph right away. Put it away for a while, if possible until the next day. When you reread it, try to be as critical of it as you would be if someone else had written it. As you go over the work, ask yourself these questions:

- Have I divided my topic into three distinct parts?
- Is each of those three parts based on the same principle of division?

- Have I given each of the three parts approximately equal weight? In other words, have I spent about the same amount of time discussing each part?
- Have I provided effective details to back up each of my three points?
- Does my paragraph satisfy the requirements of unity, coherence, and support?
- Have I edited my paragraph for sentence-skills mistakes, including spelling?

Continue revising until you are sure the answer to each question is "yes."

WRITING ASSIGNMENT 3

There are many ways you could classify your fellow students. Pick out one of your courses and write a paragraph in which you classify the students in that class according to one underlying principle. You may wish to choose one of the classification principles below.

Attitude toward the class	Punctuality
Participation in the class	Attendance
Method of taking notes in class	Level of confidence
Performance during oral reports, speeches, presentations, lab sessions	

If you decide, for instance, to classify students according to their attitude toward class, you might come up with these three categories:

Students actually interested in learning the material

Students who know they need to learn the material, but don't want to overdo it

Students who find the class a good opportunity to catch up with lost sleep

Of course, you may use any other principle of classification that seems appropriate. Follow the steps listed under "Prewriting" and "Rewriting" for Writing Assignment 2.

WRITING ASSIGNMENT 4

When we go to a restaurant, we probably hope that the service will be helpful, the atmosphere will be pleasant, and the food will be tasty. But as the cartoon shown on the following page suggests, restaurants that are good in all three respects may be hard to find. Write a review of a restaurant, analyzing its (1) service, (2) atmosphere, and (3) food. Visit a restaurant for this assignment, or draw on an experience you have had recently. Freewrite or make a list of observations about such elements as:

Copyright ©2006 The McGraw-Hill Companies, Inc. All rights reserved.

© The New Yorker Collection 2002 Leo Cullum from cartoonbank.com. All Rights Reserved.

"The little sad faces next to some items mean they don't taste very good."

Quantity of food you receive	Attitude of the servers
Taste of the food	Efficiency of the servers
Temperature of the food	Decor
Freshness of the ingredients	Level of cleanliness
How the food is presented (garnishes, dishes, and so on)	Noise level and music, if any

Feel free to write about details other than those listed above. Just be sure each detail fits into one of your three categories: food, service, or atmosphere.

For your topic sentence, rate the restaurant by giving it from one to five stars, on the basis of your overall impression. Include the restaurant's name and location in your topic sentence. Here are some examples:

Guido's, an Italian restaurant downtown, deserves three stars.

The McDonald's on Route 70 merits a four-star rating.

The Circle Diner in Westfield barely earns a one-star rating.

WRITING ASSIGNMENT 5

Writing for a Specific Purpose and Audience

In this division-classification paragraph, you will write with a specific purpose and for a specific audience. Imagine that you are a travel agent and someone has asked you for suggestions about family vacations. Write a paragraph classifying vacations for families into three or more types—for example, vacations in theme parks, in national parks, in the city, or in the countryside. For each type, include an explanation with one or more examples (see page 185).

14 Describing a Scene or Person

When you describe something or someone, you give your readers a picture in words. To make this "word picture" as vivid and real as possible, you must observe and record specific details that appeal to your readers' senses (sight, hearing, taste, smell and touch). More than any other type of writing, a descriptive paragraph needs sharp, colorful details.

Here is a description in which only the sense of sight is used:

A rug covers the living-room floor.

In contrast, here is a description rich in sense impressions:

A thick, reddish-brown shag rug is laid wall to wall across the living-room floor. The long, curled fibers of the shag seem to whisper as you walk through them in your bare feet, and when you squeeze your toes into the deep covering, the soft fibers push back at you with a spongy resilience.

Sense impressions include sight (*thick, reddish-brown shag rug; laid wall to wall; walk through them in your bare feet; squeeze your toes into the deep covering; push back*), hearing (*whisper*), and touch (*bare feet, soft fibers, spongy resilience*). The sharp, vivid images provided by the sensory details give us a clear picture of the rug and enable us to share the writer's experience.

In this section, you will be asked to describe a person, place, or thing for your readers by using words rich in sensory details. To prepare for the assignment, first read the three paragraphs ahead and then answer the questions that follow.

Paragraphs to Consider

My Teenage Son's Room

¹I push open the door with difficulty. ²The doorknob is loose and has to be jiggled just right before the catch releases from the doorjamb. ³Furthermore, as I push at the door, it runs into a basketball shoe lying

Copyright ©2006 The McGraw-Hill Companies, Inc. All rights reserved.

on the floor. [4]I manage to squeeze in through the narrow opening. [5]I am immediately aware of a pungent odor in the room, most of which is coming from the closet, to my right. [6]That's the location of a white wicker clothes hamper, heaped with grass-stained jeans, sweat-stained T-shirts, and smelly socks. [7]But the half-eaten burrito, lying dried and unappetizing on the bedside table across the room, contributes a bit of aroma, as does the glass of curdled sour milk sitting on the sunny windowsill. [8]To my left, the small wire cage on Greg's desk is also fragrant, but pleasantly. [9]From its nest of sweet-smelling cedar chips, the gerbil peers out at me with its bright eyes, its tiny claws scratching against the cage wall. [10]The floor around the wastebasket that is next to the desk is surrounded by what appears to be a sprinkling of snowballs. [11]They're actually old wadded-up school papers, and I can picture Greg sitting on his bed, crushing them into balls and aiming them at the "basket"—the trash can. [12]I glance at the bed across from the desk and chuckle because pillows stuffed under the tangled nest of blankets make it look as if someone is still sleeping there, though I know Greg is in history class right now. [13]I step carefully through the room, trying to walk through the obstacle course of science-fiction paperbacks, a wristwatch, sports magazines, and a dust-covered computer on which my son stacks empty soda cans. [14]I leave everything as I find it, but tape a note to Greg's door saying, "Isn't it about time to clean up?"

A Depressing Place

[1]The pet shop in the mall is a depressing place. [2]A display window attracts passersby who stare at the prisoners penned inside. [3]In the right-hand side of the window, two puppies press their forepaws against the glass and attempt to lick the human hands that press from the outside. [4]A cardboard barrier separates the dogs from several black-and-white kittens piled together in the opposite end of the window. [5]Inside the shop, rows of wire cages line one wall from top to bottom. [6]At first, it is hard to tell whether a bird, hamster, gerbil, cat, or dog is locked inside each cage. [7]Only an occasional movement or a clawing, shuffling sound tells visitors that living creatures are inside. [8]Running down the center of the store is a line of large wooden perches that look like coatracks. [9]When customers pass by, the parrots and mynahs chained to these perches flutter their clipped wings in a useless attempt to escape. [10]At the end of this center aisle is a large plastic tub of dirty, stagnant-looking water containing a few motionless turtles. [11]The shelves against the left-hand wall are packed with all kinds of pet-related items. [12]The smell inside the entire shop is an unpleasant mixture of strong chemical deodorizers, urine-soaked newspapers, and musty sawdust. [13]Because so many animals are crammed together, the normally pleasant, slightly milky smell of the puppies and kittens is sour and strong. [14]The droppings inside the

uncleaned birdcages give off a dry, stinging odor. ¹⁵Visitors hurry out of the shop, anxious to feel fresh air and sunlight. ¹⁶The animals stay on.

Karla

¹Karla, my brother's new girlfriend, is a catlike creature. ²Framing her face is a layer of sleek black hair that always looks just-combed. ³Her face, with its wide forehead, sharp cheekbones, and narrow, pointed chin, resembles a triangle. ⁴Karla's skin is a soft, velvety brown. ⁵Her large brown eyes slant upward at the corners, and she emphasizes their angle with a sweep of maroon eye shadow. ⁶Karla's habit of looking sidelong out of the tail of her eye makes her appear cautious, as if she were expecting something to sneak up on her. ⁷Her nose is small and flat. ⁸The sharply outlined depression under it leads the observer's eye to a pair of red-tinted lips. ⁹With their slight upward tilt at the corners, Karla's lips make her seem self-satisfied and secretly pleased. ¹⁰One reason Karla may be happy is that she recently was asked to be in a local beauty contest. ¹¹Her long neck and slim body are perfectly in proportion with her face. ¹²Karla manages to look elegant and sleek no matter how she is standing or sitting, for her body seems to be made up of graceful angles. ¹³Her slender hands are tipped with long, polished nails. ¹⁴Her narrow feet are long, too, but they appear delicate even in flat-soled running shoes. ¹⁵Somehow, Karla would look perfect in a cat's jeweled collar.

QUESTIONS

About Unity

1. Which paragraph lacks a topic sentence?

   _____

2. Which sentence in the paragraph about Karla should be omitted in the interest of paragraph unity? (*Write the sentence number here.*) _____

About Support

3. Label as *sight*, *touch*, *hearing*, or *smell* all the sensory details in the following sentences taken from the three paragraphs. The first sentence is done for you as an example.

   a. *smell*
       From its nest of sweet-smelling cedar chips, the gerbil peers out at me
       sight   *sight*   *hearing*
       with its bright eyes, its tiny claws scratching against the cage wall.

Copyright ©2006 The McGraw-Hill Companies, Inc. All rights reserved.

b.   Because so many animals are crammed together, the normally pleasant, slightly milky smell of the puppies and kittens is sour and strong.

c.   Her slender hands are tipped with long, polished nails.

d.   That's the location of a white wicker clothes hamper, heaped with grass-stained jeans, sweat-stained T-shirts, and smelly socks.

4. After which sentence in "A Depressing Place" are specific details needed?

_____

About Coherence

5. Spatial signals (*above, next to, to the right*, and so on) are often used to help organize details in a descriptive paragraph. List four space signals that appear in "My Teenage Son's Room":

_____   _____   _____   _____

6. The writer of "Karla" organizes the details by observing Karla in an orderly way. Which of Karla's features is described first? _____ Which is described last? _____ Check the method of spatial organization that best describes the paragraph:

_____ Interior to exterior

_____ Near to far

_____ Top to bottom

Developing a Descriptive Paragraph

Development through Prewriting

When Victor was assigned a descriptive paragraph, he thought at first of describing his own office at work. He began by making a list of details he noticed while looking around the office:

adjustable black chair   computer

beige desk   pictures of Marie and kids on desk

piles of papers   desk calendar

But Victor quickly became bored. Here is how he describes what happened next:

> "As I wrote down what I saw in my office, I was thinking, 'What a drag.' I gave up and worked on something else. Later that evening I told my wife that I was going to write a boring paragraph about my boring office. She started laughing at me. I said 'What's so funny?' and she said, 'You're so certain that a writing assignment has to be boring that you deliberately chose a subject that bores you. How about writing about something you care about?' At first I was annoyed, but then I realized she was right. When I hear 'assignment' I automatically think 'pain in the neck' and just want to get it over with."

Victor's attitude is not uncommon. Many students who are not experienced writers don't take the time to find a topic that interests them. They grab the one closest at hand and force themselves to write about it just for the sake of completing the assignment. Like Victor, they ensure that they (and probably their instructors as well) will be bored with the task.

In Victor's case, he decided that this assignment would be different. That evening as he talked with his son, Mikey, he remembered a visit the two had made to a mall a few days earlier. Mikey had asked Victor to take him to the pet store. Victor had found the store a very unpleasant place. "As I remembered the store, I recalled a lot of descriptive details—sounds, smells, sights," Victor said. "I realized not only that would it be easier to describe a place like that than my bland, boring office, but that I would actually find it an interesting challenge to make a reader see it through my words. For me to realize writing could be enjoyable was a real shock!"

Now that Victor had his subject, he began making a list of details about the pet shop. Here is what he wrote:

Sawdust, animal droppings on floor

Unhappy-looking puppies and kittens

Dead fish floating in tanks

Screech of birds

Chained parrots

Tanks full of dirty water

Strong urine smell

No place for animals to play

Bored-looking clerks

Animals scratching cages for attention

Copyright ©2006 The McGraw-Hill Companies, Inc. All rights reserved.

As he looked over his list of details, the word that came to mind was "depressing." He decided his topic sentence would be "The pet store in the mall is depressing." He then wrote this first draft:

> The pet store in the mall is depressing. There are sawdust and animal droppings all over the floor. Sad-looking puppies and kittens scratch on their cages for attention. Dead fish and motionless turtles float in tanks of stagnant water. The loud screeching of birds is everywhere, and parrots with clipped wings try to escape when customers walk too near. Everywhere there is the smell of animal urine that has soaked the sawdust and newspapers. The clerks, who should be cleaning the cages, stand around talking to each other and ignoring the animals.

Development through Revising

The next day Victor's instructor asked to see the students' first drafts. This is what she wrote in response to Victor's:

> This is a very good beginning. You have provided some strong details that appeal to the reader's senses of smell, hearing, and sight.
>
> In your next draft, organize your paragraph by using spatial order. In other words, describe the room in some logical physical order—maybe from left to right, or from the front of the store to its back. Such an organization mirrors the way a visitor might move through the store.
>
> I encourage you to become even more specific in your details. For instance, in what way did the puppies and kittens seem sad? As you work on each sentence, ask yourself if you can add more descriptive details to paint a more vivid picture in words.

In response to his teacher's suggestion about a spatial order method of organization, Victor rewrote the paragraph, beginning with the display window that attracts visitors, then going on to the store's right-hand wall, the center aisle, and the left-hand wall. He ended the paragraph with a sentence that brought the reader back outside the shop. Thinking about the shop in this way enabled Victor to remember and add a number of new specific details as well. He then wrote the version of "A Depressing Place" that appears on page 262.

Writing a Descriptive Paragraph

WRITING ASSIGNMENT 1

Write a paragraph describing a certain person's room. Use as your topic sentence "I could tell by looking at the room that a _____ lived there." There are many kinds of people who could be the focus for such a paragraph. You can select any one of the following, or think of another type of person.

Copyright ©2006 The McGraw-Hill Companies, Inc. All rights reserved.

Photographer	Music lover	Carpenter
Cook	TV addict	Baby
Student	Camper	Cat or dog lover
Musician	Computer expert	World traveler
Hunter	Cheerleader	Drug addict
Slob	Football player	Little boy or girl
Outdoors person	Actor	Alcoholic
Doctor	Dancer	In-line skater

Prewriting

a   After choosing a topic, spend a few minutes making sure it will work. Prepare a list of all the details you can think of that support the topic. For example, a student who planned to describe a soccer player's room made this list:

soccer balls

shin guards

posters of professional soccer teams

soccer trophies

shirt printed with team name and number

autographed soccer ball

medals and ribbons

photos of player's own team

sports clippings

radio that looks like soccer ball

soccer socks

soccer shorts

If you don't have enough details, choose another type of person. Check your new choice by listing details before committing yourself to the topic.

b   You may want to use other prewriting techniques, such as freewriting or questioning, to develop more details for your topic. As you continue prewriting, keep the following in mind:

• Everything in the paragraph should support your point. For example, if you are writing about a soccer player's room, every detail should serve to show that the person who lives in that room plays and loves soccer. Other details—for example, the person's computer, tropical fish tank, or daily "to-do" list—should be omitted.

- Description depends on the use of specific rather than general descriptive words. For example:

General	Specific
Mess on the floor	The obstacle course of science-fiction paperbacks, a wristwatch, sports magazines, and a dust-covered computer on which my son stacks empty soda cans.
Ugly turtle tub	Large plastic tub of dirty, stagnant-looking water containing a few motionless turtles
Bad smell	Unpleasant mixture of strong chemical deodorizers, urine-soaked newspapers, and musty sawdust
Nice skin	Soft, velvety brown skin

Remember that you want your readers to experience the room vividly. Your words should be as detailed as a clear photograph, giving readers a real feel for the room. Appeal to as many senses as possible. Most of your description will involve the sense of sight, but you may be able to include details about touch, hearing, and smell as well.

- Spatial order is a good way to organize a descriptive paragraph. Move as a visitor's eye might move around the room, from right to left or from larger items to smaller ones. Here are a few transition words of the sort that show spatial relationships.

to the left	across from	on the opposite side
to the right	above	nearby
next to	below	

Such transitions will help prevent you—and your reader—from getting lost as the description proceeds.

c   Before you write, see if you can make a scratch outline based on your list. Here is one possible outline of the paragraph about the soccer player's room. Note that the details are organized according to spatial order—from the edges of the room in toward the center.

Copyright ©2006 The McGraw-Hill Companies, Inc. All rights reserved.

<u>Topic sentence:</u> I could tell by looking at the room that a soccer player lived there.

1.   Walls
2.   Bookcase
3.   Desk
4.   Chair
5.   Floor

d   Then proceed to write a first draft of your paragraph.

Revising

Read your descriptive paragraph slowly out loud to a friend. Ask the friend to close his or her eyes and try to picture the room as you read. Read it aloud a second time. Ask your friend to answer these questions:

- Does every detail in the paragraph support the topic sentence? Here's one way to find out: Ask your friend to imagine omitting the key word or words (in the case of our example, "soccer player") in your topic sentence. Would readers know what word should fit in that empty space?
- Are the details specific and vivid rather than general?
- Has the writer included details that appeal to as many senses as possible?
- Does the paragraph follow a logical spatial order?
- Has the writer used transitions (such as *on top of, beside, to the left of*) to help the reader follow that order?

Continue revising your work until you and your reader can answer "yes" to all these questions.

In the later drafts of your paragraph, edit carefully for sentence-skills mistakes, including spelling. Refer to the checklist of these skills on the inside front cover of this book.

WRITING ASSIGNMENT 2

Write a paragraph describing a specific person. Select a dominant impression of the person, and use only details that will convey that impression. You might want to write about someone who falls into one of these categories.

TV or movie personality	Coworker
Instructor	Clergyman or clergywoman

Employer	Police officer
Child	Store owner or manager
Older person	Bartender
Close friend	Joker
Enemy	Neighbor

Prewriting

a   Reread the paragraph about Karla that appears earlier in this chapter. Note the dominant impression that the writer wanted to convey: that Karla is a catlike person. Having decided to focus on that impression, the writer included only details that contributed to her point. Similarly, you should focus on one dominant aspect of your subject's appearance, personality, or behavior.

Once you have chosen the person you will write about and the impression you plan to portray, put that information into a topic sentence. Here are some examples of topic sentences that mention a particular person and the dominant impression of that person:

Kate gives the impression of being permanently nervous.

The old man was as faded and brittle as a dying leaf.

The child was an angelic little figure.

Our high school principal resembled a cartoon drawing.

The TV newscaster seems as synthetic as a piece of Styrofoam.

Our neighbor is a fussy person.

The rock singer seemed to be plugged into some special kind of energy source.

The drug addict looked as lifeless as a corpse.

My friend Jeffrey is a slow, deliberate person.

The owner of that grocery store seems burdened with troubles.

b   Make a list of the person's qualities that support your topic sentence. Write quickly; don't worry if you find yourself writing down something that doesn't quite fit. You can always edit the list later. For now, just write down all the details that occur to you that support the dominant impression you want to convey. Include details that involve as many senses as possible (sight, sound, hearing, touch, smell). For instance, here's a list one writer jotted down to support the sentence "The child was an angelic little figure":

Copyright ©2006 The McGraw-Hill Companies, Inc. All rights reserved.

soft brown ringlets of hair

pink cheeks

wide shining eyes

shrieking laugh

joyful smile

starched white dress

white flowers in hair

c   Edit your list, striking out details that don't support your topic sentence and adding others that do. The author of the paragraph on an angelic figure crossed out one detail from the original list and added a new one:

soft brown ringlets of hair

pink cheeks

wide shining eyes

~~shrieking laugh~~

joyful smile

starched white dress

white flowers in hair

sweet singing voice

d   Decide on a spatial order of organization. In the example above, the writer ultimately decided to describe the child from head to toe.

e   Make a scratch outline for your paragraph, based on the organization you have chosen.

f   Then proceed to write a first draft of your paragraph.

Revising

Put your paragraph away for a day or so if at all possible. When you read it and your later drafts, ask yourself these questions:

- Does my topic sentence clearly state my dominant impression of my subject?
- If I left out the key words in my topic sentence (the words that state my dominant impression), would a reader know what idea fits there?

- Does every detail support my topic sentence?
- Are the details I have included specific rather than vague and general?
- Have I used a logical spatial organization that helps my reader follow my description?
- Have I checked my paper for sentence skills, as listed on the inside front cover of the book?

Continue revising your work until you can answer "yes" to all these questions.

WRITING ASSIGNMENT 3

Write a paragraph describing the cartoon shown here so that a person who has never seen it will be able to visualize it and fully understand it.

In order to write such a complete description, you must notice and report *every detail* in the cartoon. The details include such things as the way the room is arranged; the objects present in the room; what the characters are doing with those objects; the expressions on the characters' faces; and any motions that are occurring. Remember as you are describing the cartoon to give special attention to the same elements that the cartoonist gives special attention to. Your goal should be this: someone who reads your description of the cartoon will understand it as fully as someone who saw the cartoon itself.

© 2004 Mike Twohy. Reprinted with the permission of Mike Twohy and the Washington Post Writers Group. All rights reserved.

WRITING ASSIGNMENT 3

Write a paragraph describing an animal you have spent some time with—a pet, a friend's pet, an animal you've seen in a park or zoo or even on television. Write a paragraph about how the animal looks and behaves. Select details that support a dominant impression of your subject. Once you decide on the impression you wish to convey, compose a topic sentence, such as either of those below, that summarizes the details you will use.

The appearance of a gorilla named Koko gives no hint of the animal's intelligence and gentleness.

A cute squirrel who has taken up residence in my backyard exhibits surprising agility and energy.

Remember to provide colorful, detailed descriptions to help your readers picture the features and behavior you are writing about. Note the contrast in the two items below.

Lacks rich descriptive details: The squirrel was gray and enjoyed our deck.

Includes rich descriptive details: On our deck, the young gray squirrel dug a hole in the dirt in a planter full of marigolds and then deposited an acorn in the hole, his fluffy tail bobbing enthusiastically all the while.

WRITING ASSIGNMENT 4

Visit a place you have never gone to before and write a paragraph describing it. You may want to visit:

A restaurant

A classroom, a laboratory, an office, a workroom, or some other room in your school

A kind of store you ordinarily don't visit: for example, a hardware store, toy store, record shop, gun shop, or sports shop, or a particular men's or women's clothing store

A bus terminal, train station, or airport

A place of worship

A park, vacant lot, or street corner

You may want to jot down details about the place while you are there or very soon after you leave. Again, decide on a dominant impression you want to convey of the place, and use only those details which will support that impression. Follow the notes on prewriting, writing, and revising for Writing Assignment 2.

WRITING ASSIGNMENT 5

Writing for a Specific Purpose and Audience

In this descriptive paragraph, you will write with a specific purpose and for a specific audience. Choose one of the following options.

Copyright ©2006 The McGraw-Hill Companies, Inc. All rights reserved.

Option 1   Imagine that you are an interior designer. A new dormitory is going to be built on campus, and you have been asked to create a sample dormitory room for two students. Write a paragraph describing your design of the room, telling what it would include and how it would be arranged. In your prewriting for this assignment, you might list all the relevant student needs you can think of, such as a good study space, storage space, and appropriate lighting and colors. Then put all the parts together so that they work well as a whole. Use a spatial order in your paragraph to help readers "see" your room. Begin with the following topic sentence or something like it:

> My design for a dormitory room offers both efficiency and comfort for two students.

Feel free to use a less-than-serious tone.

Option 2   Alternatively, write a paragraph describing your design of another type of room, including any of the following:

Child's bedroom	Kitchen
Schoolroom	Porch
Restaurant	Bakery

15 Narrating an Event

At times we make a statement clear by relating in detail something that has happened. In the story we tell, we present the details in the order in which they happened. A person might say, for example, "I was embarrassed yesterday," and then go on to illustrate the statement with the following narrative:

> [1]I was hurrying across campus to get to a class. It had rained heavily all morning, so I was hopscotching my way around puddles in the pathway. I called to two friends ahead to wait for me, and right before I caught up to them, I came to a large puddle that covered the entire path. I had to make a quick choice of either stepping into the puddle or trying to jump over it. I jumped, wanting to seem cool, since my friends were watching, but didn't clear the puddle. Water splashed everywhere, drenching my shoe, sock, and pants cuff, and spraying the pants of my friends as well. "Well done, Dave!" they said. My embarrassment was all the greater because I had tried to look so casual.

The speaker's details have made his moment of embarrassment vivid and real for us, and we can see and understand just why he felt as he did.

In this section, you will be asked to tell a story that illustrates or explains some point. The paragraphs below all present narrative experiences that support a point. Read them and then answer the questions that follow.

Paragraphs to Consider

Heartbreak

[1]Bonnie and I had gotten engaged in August, just before she left for college at Penn State. [2]A week before Thanksgiving, I drove up to see her as a surprise. [3]When I knocked on the door of her dorm room, she was indeed surprised, but not in a pleasant way. [4]She introduced me to her roommate, who looked uncomfortable and quickly left. [5]I asked Bonnie how classes were going, and at the same time I tugged on the sleeve of my heavy sweater in order to pull it off. [6]As I was slipping it over my head,

Copyright ©2006 The McGraw-Hill Companies, Inc. All rights reserved.

I noticed a large photo on the wall—of Bonnie and a tall guy laughing together. [7]It was decorated with paper flowers and a yellow ribbon, and on the ribbon was written "Bonnie and Blake." [8]"What's going on?" I said. [9]I stood there stunned and then felt anger that grew rapidly. [10]"Who is Blake?" I asked. [11]Bonnie laughed nervously and said, "What do you want to hear about—my classes or Blake?" [12]I don't really remember what she then told me, except that Blake was a sophomore math major. [13]I felt a terrible pain in the pit of my stomach, and I wanted to rest my head on someone's shoulder and cry. [14]I wanted to tear down the sign and run out, but I did nothing. [15]Clumsily I pulled on my sweater again. [16]My knees felt weak, and I barely had control of my body. [17]I opened the room door, and suddenly more than anything I wanted to slam the door shut so hard that the dorm walls would collapse. [18]Instead, I managed to close the door quietly. [19]I walked away understanding what was meant by a broken heart.

Losing My Father

[1]Although my father died ten years ago, I felt that he'd been lost to me four years earlier. [2]Dad had been diagnosed with Alzheimer's disease, an illness that destroys the memory. [3]He couldn't work any longer, but in his own home he got along pretty well. [4]I lived hundreds of miles away and wasn't able to see my parents often. [5]So when my first child was a few weeks old, I flew home with the baby to visit them. [6]After Mom met us at the airport, we picked up Dad and went to their favorite local restaurant. [7]Dad was quiet, but kind and gentle as always, and he seemed glad to see me and his new little grandson. [8]Everyone went to bed early. [9]In the morning, Mom left for work. [10]I puttered happily around in my old bedroom. [11]I heard Dad shuffling around in the kitchen, making coffee. [12]Eventually I realized that he was pacing back and forth at the foot of the stairs as if he were uneasy. [13]I called down to him, "Everything all right there? [14]I'll be down in a minute." [15]"Fine!" he called back, with forced-sounding cheerfulness. [16]Then he stopped pacing and called up to me, "I must be getting old and forgetful. [17]When did you get here?" [18]I was surprised, but made myself answer calmly. [19]"Yesterday afternoon. [20]Remember, Mom met us at the airport, and then we went to The Skillet for dinner." [21]"Oh, yes," he said. [22]"I had roast beef." [23]I began to relax. [24]But then he continued, hesitantly, "And . . . who are you?" [25]My breath stopped as if I'd been punched in the stomach. [26]When I could steady my voice, I answered, "I'm Laura; I'm your daughter. [27]I'm here with my baby son, Max." [28]"Oh," is all he said. [29]"Oh." [30]And he wandered into the living room and sat down. [31]In a few minutes I joined him and found him staring blankly out the window. [32]He was a polite host, asking if I wanted anything to eat, and if the room was too cold. [33]I answered with an aching heart, mourning for his loss and for mine.

A Frustrating Job

¹Working as a baby-sitter was the most frustrating job I ever had. ²I discovered this fact when my sister asked me to stay with her two sons for the evening. ³I figured I would get them dinner, let them watch a little TV, and then put them to bed early. ⁴The rest of the night I planned to watch TV and collect an easy twenty dollars. ⁵It turned out to be anything but easy. ⁶First, right before we were about to sit down for a pizza dinner, Rickie let the parakeet out of its cage. ⁷This bird is really intelligent and can repeat almost any phrase. ⁸The dog started chasing it around the house, so I decided to catch it before the dog did. ⁹Rickie and Jeff volunteered to help, following at my heels. ¹⁰We had the bird cornered by the fireplace when Rickie jumped for it and knocked over the hamster cage. ¹¹Then the bird escaped again, and the hamsters began scurrying around their cage like crazy creatures. ¹²The dog had disappeared by this point, so I decided to clean up the hamsters' cage and try to calm them down. ¹³While I was doing this, Rickie and Jeff caught the parakeet and put it back in its cage. ¹⁴It was time to return to the kitchen and eat cold pizza. ¹⁵But upon entering the kitchen, I discovered why the dog had lost interest in the bird chase. ¹⁶What was left of the pizza was lying on the floor, and tomato sauce was dripping from the dog's chin. ¹⁷I cleaned up the mess and then served chicken noodle soup and ice cream to the boys. ¹⁸Only at nine o'clock did I get the kids to bed. ¹⁹I then returned downstairs to find that the dog had thrown up pizza on the living-room rug. ²⁰When I finished cleaning the rug, my sister returned. ²¹I took the twenty dollars and told her that she should get someone else next time.

QUESTIONS

About Unity

1. Which paragraph lacks a topic sentence?

   _____

   Write a topic sentence for the paragraph.

   _____

   _____

2. Which sentence in "A Frustrating Job" should be omitted in the interest of paragraph unity? (Write the sentence number here.) _____

Copyright ©2006 The McGraw-Hill Companies, Inc. All rights reserved.

About Support

3. What is for you the best (most real and vivid) detail or image in the paragraph "Heartbreak"?

    _____

    _____

    What is the best detail or image in "Losing My Father"?

    _____

    _____

    What is the best detail or image in "A Frustrating Job"?

    _____

    _____

4. Which two paragraphs include the actual words spoken by the participants?

    _____

    _____

About Coherence

5. Do the three paragraphs use time order or emphatic order to organize details?

    _____

6. What are four transition words used in "A Frustrating Job"?

    _____   _____   _____   _____

Developing a Narrative Paragraph

Development through Prewriting

Gary's instructor was helping her students think of topics for their narrative paragraphs. "A narrative is simply a story that illustrates a point," she said. "That point is often about an emotion you felt. Looking at a list of emotions may help you think of a topic. Ask yourself what incident in your life has made you feel any of these emotions."

The instructor then jotted these feelings on the board:

Copyright ©2006 The McGraw-Hill Companies, nc. All rights reserved.

Anger	Thankfulness
Embarrassment	Loneliness
Jealousy	Sadness
Amusement	Terror
Confusion	Relief

As Gary looked over the list, he thought of several experiences in his life. "The word 'angry' made me think about a time when I was a kid. My brother took my skateboard without permission and left it in the park, where it got stolen. 'Amused' made me think of when I watched my roommate, who claimed he spoke Spanish, try to bargain with a street vendor in Mexico. He got so flustered that he ended up paying even more than the vendor had originally asked for. When I got to 'sad,' though, I thought about when I visited Bonnie and found out she was dating someone else. 'Sad' wasn't a strong enough word, though—I was heartbroken. So I decided to write about heartbreak."

Gary's first step was to do some freewriting. Without worrying about spelling or grammar, he simply wrote down everything that came into his mind concerning his visit to Bonnie. Here is what he came up with:

> I hadn't expected to see Bonnie until Christmas. We'd got engaged just before she went off to college. The drive to Penn State took ten hours each way and that seemed like to much driving for just a weekend visit. But I realized I had a long weekend over thanksgiving I decided to surprise her. I think down deep I knew something was wrong. She had sounded sort of cool on the phone and she hadn't been writing as often. I guess I wanted to convince myself that everything was OK. We'd been dating since we were 16 and I couldn't imagine not being with her. When I knocked at her dorm door I remember how she was smiling when she opened the door. Her expression changed to one of surprise. Not happy surprise. I hugged her and she sort of hugged me back but like you'd hug your brother. Another girl was in the room. Bonnie said, "This is Pam," and Pam shot out of the room like I had a disease. Everything seemed wrong and confused. I started taking off my sweater and then I saw it. On a bulletin board was this photo of Bonnie with Blake, the guy she had been messing around with. They broke up about a year later, but by then I never wanted to see Bonnie again. I couldn't believe Bonnie would start seeing somebody else when we were planning to get married. It had even been her idea to get engaged Before she left for college. Later on I realized that wasn't the first dishonest thing she'd done. I got out of there as quick as I could.

Development through Revising

Gary knew that the first, freewritten version of his paragraph needed work. Here are the comments he made after he reread it the following day:

"Although my point is supposed to be that my visit to Bonnie was heartbreaking, I didn't really get that across. I need to say more about how the experience felt.

"I've included some information that doesn't really support my point. For instance, what happened to Bonnie and Blake later isn't important here. Also, I think I spend too much time explaining the circumstances of the visit. I need to get more quickly to the point where I arrived at Bonnie's dorm.

"I think I should include more dialogue, too. That would make the reader feel more like a witness to what really happened."

With this self-critique in mind, Gary revised his paragraph until he had produced the version that appears on page 275.

Writing a Narrative Paragraph

WRITING ASSIGNMENT 1

Write a paragraph about an experience in which a certain emotion was predominant. The emotion might be fear, pride, satisfaction, embarrassment, or any of these:

Frustration	Sympathy	Shyness
Love	Bitterness	Disappointment
Sadness	Violence	Happiness
Terror	Surprise	Jealousy
Shock	Nostalgia	Anger
Relief	Loss	Hate
Envy	Silliness	Nervousness

The experience you write about should be limited in time. Note that the three paragraphs presented in this chapter all detail experiences that occurred within relatively short periods. One writer describes a heartbreaking surprise he received the day he visited his girlfriend; another describes the loss of her father; the third describes a frustrating night of baby-sitting.

Copyright ©2006 The McGraw-Hill Companies, Inc. All rights reserved.

A good way to bring an event to life for your readers is to include some dialogue, as the writers of two of the three paragraphs in this chapter have done. Words that you said, or that someone else said, help make a situation come alive. First, though, be sure to check the section on quotation marks on pages 481–488.

Prewriting

a   Begin by freewriting. Think of an experience or event that caused you to feel a certain emotion strongly. Then spend ten minutes writing freely about the experience. Do not worry at this point about such matters as spelling or grammar or putting things in the right order. Instead, just try to get down all the details you can think of that seem related to the experience.

b   This preliminary writing will help you decide whether your topic is promising enough to develop further. If it is not, choose another emotion and repeat step *a.* If it does seem promising, do two things:

- First, write your topic sentence, underlining the emotion you will focus on. For example, "My first day in kindergarten was one of the <u>scariest</u> days of my life."
- Second, make up a list of all the details involved in the experience. Then number these details according to the order in which they occurred.

c   Referring to your list of details, write a rough draft of your paragraph. Use time signals such as *first, then, after, next, while, during,* and *finally* to help connect details as you move from the beginning to the middle to the end of your narrative. Be sure to include not only what happened but also how you felt about what was going on.

Revising

Put your first draft away for a day or so. When you return to it, read it over, asking yourself these questions:

- Does my topic sentence clearly state what emotion the experience made me feel?
- Have I included some dialogue to make the experience come alive?
- Have I explained how I felt as the experience occurred?
- Have I used time order to narrate the experience from beginning to end?
- Have I used time signals to connect one detail to the next?
- Have I checked my paper for sentence skills, including spelling, as listed on the inside front cover of the book?

Continue revising your work until you can answer "yes" to all these questions.

WRITING ASSIGNMENT 2

Narrate a real-life event you have witnessed. Listed below are some places where interesting personal interactions often happen. Think of an event that you saw happen at one of these places, or visit one of them and take notes on an incident to write about.

The traffic court or small-claims court in your area

The dinner table at your or someone else's home

A waiting line at a supermarket, unemployment office, ticket counter, movie theater, or cafeteria

A doctor's office

An audience at a movie, concert, or sports event

A classroom

A restaurant

A student lounge

Prewriting

a   Decide what point you will make about the incident. What one word or phrase characterizes the scene you witnessed? Your narration of the incident will emphasize that characteristic.

b   Write your topic sentence. The topic sentence should state where the incident happened as well as your point about it. Here are some possibilities:

I witnessed a *heartwarming* incident at Taco Bell yesterday.

Two fans at last week's baseball game got into a *hilarious* argument.

The scene at our family dinner table Monday was one of complete *confusion*.

A *painful* dispute went on in Atlantic County small-claims court yesterday.

c   Use the questioning technique to remind yourself of details that will make your narrative come alive. Ask yourself questions like these and write down your answers:

Whom was I observing?

How were they dressed?

What were their facial expressions like?

What tones of voice did they use?

What did I hear them say?

d   Drawing details from the notes you have written, write the first draft of your paragraph. Remember to use time signals such as *then, after that, during, meanwhile,* and *finally* to connect one sentence to another.

Revising

After you have put your paragraph away for a day, read it to a friend who will give you honest feedback. You and your friend should consider these questions:

- Does the topic sentence make a general point about the incident?
- Do descriptions of the appearance, tone of voice, and expressions of the people involved paint a clear picture of the incident?
- Is the sequence of events made clear by transitional words such as *at first, later,* and *then*?

Continue revising your work until you and your reader can answer "yes" to all these questions. Then check to make sure your paragraph is free of sentence-skills mistakes, including spelling errors. Use the list on the inside front cover of this book.

WRITING ASSIGNMENT 3

PEANUTS: © United Feature Syndicate, Inc.

Copyright ©2006 The McGraw-Hill Companies, Inc. All rights reserved.

In a story, something happens. The *Peanuts* cartoon here, for example, is a little story about the would-be writer, Snoopy, who gets a rejection letter and loses his temper. For this assignment, tell a story about something that happened to you.

Make sure that your story has a point, expressed in the first sentence of the paragraph. If necessary, tailor your narrative to fit your purpose. Use time order to organize your details (*first* this happened; *then* this; *after* that, this; *next,* this; and so on). Concentrate on providing as many specific details as possible so that the reader can really share your experience. Try to make it as vivid for the reader as it was for you when you first experienced it.

Use one of the topics below or a topic of your own choosing. Whatever topic you choose, remember that your story must illustrate or support a point stated in the first sentence of your paper.

A time you lost your temper

A moment of great happiness or sadness

Your best or worst date

A time you took a foolish risk

An incident that changed your life

A time when you did or did not do the right thing

Your best or worst holiday or birthday, or some other day

A time you learned a lesson or taught a lesson to someone else

An occasion of triumph in sports or some other area

You may wish to refer to the suggestions for prewriting and rewriting in Writing Assignment 1.

WRITING ASSIGNMENT 4

Write a paragraph that shows, through some experience you have had, the truth or falsity of a popular belief. You might write about any one of the following statements or some other popular saying.

Every person has a price.

Haste makes waste.

Don't count your chickens before they're hatched.

A bird in the hand is worth two in the bush.

It isn't what you know, it's who you know.

Copyright ©2006 The McGraw-Hill Companies, Inc. All rights reserved.

Borrowing can get you into trouble.

What you don't know won't hurt you.

A promise is easier made than kept.

You never really know people until you see them in an emergency.

If you don't help yourself, nobody will.

An ounce of prevention is worth a pound of cure.

Hope for the best but expect the worst.

Never give advice to a friend.

You get what you pay for.

A stitch in time saves nine.

A fool and his money are soon parted.

There is an exception to every rule.

Nice guys finish last.

Begin your narrative paragraph with a topic sentence that expresses your agreement or disagreement with a popular saying or belief, for example:

"Never give advice to a friend" is not always good advice, as I learned after helping a friend reunite with her boyfriend.

My sister learned recently that it is easier to make a promise than to keep one.

Refer to the suggestions for prewriting and revising on page 281. Remember that the purpose of your story is to support your topic sentence. Omit details that don't support your topic sentence. Also, feel free to use made-up details that will strengthen your support.

WRITING ASSIGNMENT 5

Writing for a Specific Purpose and Audience

In this narrative paragraph, you will write with a specific purpose and for a specific audience. Imagine that a younger brother or sister, or a young friend, has to make a difficult decision of some kind. Perhaps he or she must decide how to prepare for a job interview, whether or not to get help with a difficult class, or what to do about a coworker who is taking money from the cash register. Narrate a story from your own experience (or the experience of someone you know) that will teach a younger person something about the decision he or she must make. In your paragraph, include a comment or two about the lesson your story teaches. Write about any decision young people often face, including any of those already mentioned or those listed below.

Should he or she save a little from a weekly paycheck?

Should he or she live at home or move to an apartment with some friends?

How should he or she deal with a group of friends who are involved with drugs, stealing, or both?

16 Arguing a Position

Most of us know someone who enjoys a good argument. Such a person usually challenges any sweeping statement we might make. "Why do you say that?" he or she will ask. "Give your reasons." Our questioner then listens carefully as we cite our reasons, waiting to see if we really do have solid evidence to support our point of view. In an argument such as the one going on in the cartoon, the two parties each present their supporting evidence. The goal is to determine who has the more solid evidence to support his or her point of view. A questioner may make us feel a bit nervous, but we may also appreciate the way he or she makes us think through our opinions.

REAL LIFE ADVENTURES © 2002 GarLanco. Reprinted with permission of Universal Press Syndicate

The ability to advance sound, compelling arguments is an important skill in everyday life. We can use argument to get an extension on a term paper, obtain a favor from a friend, or convince an employer that we are the right person for a job. Understanding persuasion based on clear, logical reasoning can also help us see through the sometimes faulty arguments advanced by advertisers, editors, politicians, and others who try to bring us over to their side.

In this section, you will be asked to argue a position and defend it with a series of solid reasons. In a general way, you are doing the same thing with all the paragraph assignments in the book: making a point and then supporting it. The difference here is that, in a more direct and formal manner, you will advance a point about which you feel strongly and seek to persuade others to agree with you.

Copyright ©2006 The McGraw-Hill Companies, Inc. All rights reserved.

Paragraphs to Consider

Let's Ban Proms

[1]While many students regard proms as peak events in high school life, I believe that high school proms should be banned. [2]One reason is that even before the prom takes place, it causes problems. [3]Teenagers are separated into "the ones who were asked" and "the ones who weren't." [4]Being one of those who weren't asked can be heartbreaking to a sensitive young person. [5]Another pre-prom problem is money. [6]The price of the various items needed can add up quickly to a lot of money. [7]The prom itself can be unpleasant and frustrating, too. [8]At the beginning of the evening, the girls enviously compare dresses while the boys sweat nervously inside their rented suits. [9]During the dance, the couples who have gotten together only to go to the prom have split up into miserable singles. [10]When the prom draws to a close, the popular teenagers drive off happily to other parties while the less popular ones head home, as usual. [11]Perhaps the main reason proms should be banned, however, is the drinking and driving that go on after the prom is over. [12]Teenagers pile into their cars on their way to "after-proms" and pull out the bottles and cans stashed under the seat. [13]By the time the big night is finally over, at 4 or 5 A.M., students are trying to weave home without encountering the police or a roadside tree. [14]Some of them do not make it, and prom night turns into tragedy. [15]For all these reasons, proms have no place in our schools.

Bashing Men

[1]Our culture now puts down men in ways that would be considered very offensive if the targets were women. [2]For instance, men are frequently portrayed in popular culture as bumbling fools. [3]The popular TV show The Simpsons, for instance, shows the father, Homer, as a total idiot, dishonest and childish. [4]His son, Bart, is equally foolish; but the mother, Marge, and the sister, Lisa, are levelheaded and responsible. [5]Little children love the "Berenstain Bears" books, which are supposed to teach lessons about subjects including honesty, bad habits, and going to the doctor. [6]In every book, while the mother bear gives her cubs good advice, the father bear acts stupidly and has to be taught a lesson along with the kids. [7]In addition, society teaches us to think of men as having no value in a family other than to contribute money. [8]Popular stars go on national TV and proclaim that because they are financially independent women, their babies don't need a father. [9]Families on welfare are denied benefits if the children's father stays in the home—apparently if he isn't bringing in money, the family is better

off without him. [10]The welfare system is deeply flawed in other ways as well. [11]And women tell each other men-bashing jokes that would be considered sexist and offensive if they were directed at women. [12]Here's one: "Question: A woman has a flat tire. [13]Santa Claus, Oprah Winfrey, and a decent man all stop to help her. [14]Who actually changes the tire?" [15]The answer: "Oprah, of course. [16]The other two are fictional characters." [17]Women deserve to be treated with respect, but that doesn't mean men should be put down.

Living Alone

[1]Living alone is quite an experience. [2]People who live alone, for one thing, have to learn to do all kinds of tasks by themselves. [3]They must learn—even if they have had no experience—to change fuses, put up curtains and shades, temporarily dam an overflowing toilet, cook a meal, and defrost a refrigerator. [4]When there is no father, husband, mother, or wife to depend on, a person can't fall back on the excuse, "I don't know how to do that." [5]Those who live alone also need the strength to deal with people. [6]Alone, singles must face noisy neighbors, unresponsive landlords, dishonest repair people, and aggressive bill collectors. [7]Because there are no buffers between themselves and the outside world, people living alone have to handle every visitor—friendly or unfriendly—alone. [8]Finally, singles need a large dose of courage to cope with occasional panic and unavoidable loneliness. [9]That weird thump in the night is even more terrifying when there is no one in the next bed or the next room. [10]Frightening weather or unexpected bad news is doubly bad when the worry can't be shared. [11]Even when life is going well, little moments of sudden loneliness can send shivers through the heart. [12]Struggling through such bad times taps into reserves of courage that people may not have known they possessed. [13]Facing everyday tasks, confronting all types of people, and handling panic and loneliness can shape singles into brave, resourceful, and more independent people.

QUESTIONS

About Unity

1. The topic sentence in "Living Alone" is too broad. Circle the topic sentence below that states accurately what the paragraph is about.

    a. Living alone can make one a better person.

    b. Living alone can create feelings of loneliness.

    c. Living alone should be avoided.

2. Which sentence in "Bashing Men" should be eliminated in the interest of paragraph unity? (*Write the sentence number here.*) _____

Copyright ©2006 The McGraw-Hill Companies, Inc. All rights reserved.

3. How many reasons are given to support the topic sentence in each paragraph?

   a. In "Let's Ban Proms" ____ one ____ two ____ three ____ four

   b. In "Bashing Men" ____ one ____ two ____ three ____ four

   c. In "Living Alone" ____ one ____ two ____ three ____ four

4. After which sentence in "Let's Ban Proms" are more specific details needed?

   _____

About Coherence

5. Which paragraph uses a combination of time and emphatic order to organize

   its details? _____

6. What are the three main transition words in "Living Alone"?

   _____   _____   _____

ACTIVITY

Complete the outline below of "Bashing Men." Summarize in a few words the supporting material that fits under the topic sentence: After *1, 2,* and *3*, write in the three main points of support for the topic sentence. In the spaces after the numbers, write in the examples used to support those three main points. Two items have been done for you as examples.

Topic sentence: It's become more and more acceptable to bash men, acting as though they are less deserving of respect than women.

1. _____

    a. _____
    b. Berenstain Bears

2. _____

    a. _____
    b. Welfare benefits cut off if father in home

3. _____

    a. _____

Developing an Argument Paragraph

Development through Prewriting

Yolanda is the student author of "Let's Ban Proms." She decided on her topic after visiting her parents' home one weekend and observing her younger brother's concern about his upcoming prom.

> "I really felt bad for Martin as I saw what he was going through," Yolanda said. "He's usually a happy kid who enjoys school. But this weekend he wasn't talking about his track meets or term papers or any of the things he's usually chatting about. Instead he was all tied up in knots about his prom. The girl he'd really wanted to go with had already been asked, and so friends had fixed him up with a girl he barely knew who didn't have a date either. Neither of them was excited about being together, but they felt that they just 'had' to go. And now he's worried about how to afford renting a tux, and how will he get a cool car to go in, and all that stuff. It's shaping up to be a really stressful, expensive evening. When I was in high school, I saw a lot of bad things associated with the prom, too. I hate to see young kids feeling pressured to attend an event that is fun for only a few."

Yolanda began prewriting by making a list of all the negative aspects of proms. This is what she came up with:

Drinking after prom

Car accidents (most important!)

Competition for dates

Preparation for prom cuts into school hours

Rejection of not being asked

Waste of school money

Going with someone you don't like

Separates popular from unpopular

Expensive

Bad-tempered chaperones

Next, Yolanda numbered the details in the order she was going to present them. She also struck out details she decided not to use:

Copyright ©2006 The McGraw-Hill Companies, Inc. All rights reserved.

6 Drinking after prom

7 Car accidents (most important!)

3 Competition for dates

~~Preparation for prom cuts into school hours~~

1 Rejection of not being asked

~~Waste of school money~~

4 Going with someone you don't like

5 Separates popular from unpopular

2 Expensive

~~Bad-tempered chaperones~~

Drawing from these notes, Yolanda wrote the following first draft of her paragraph:

> In my opinion, high school proms should be banned. First, they cause unhappiness by separating students into "the ones who were asked" and "the ones who weren't." Proms are also expensive, as anyone who has attended one knows. The competition for dates can damage previously strong friendships. Many couples get together only in order to have a date for the prom and do not enjoy each other's company. After the prom, too, the kids are separated into "more popular" and "less popular" groups, with the popular ones going to after-prom parties. The biggest reason to ban proms, though, is the prom-night drinking that commonly occurs. Teenagers hide liquor in their cars and then try to drive home drunk. Some of them do not make it. For all these reasons, proms should be banned.

Development through Revising

Yolanda's instructor reviewed her first draft and made these comments:

> The order of your paragraph could be made stronger. Although you make good use of emphatic order (by ending with "the biggest reason to ban proms"), it's less clear that the paragraph is also organized according to time—in other words, you move from before the prom starts to during the prom to after it. Better use of transitional language will make the organization more clear.
>
> Also, you could make the paragraph more alive by including concrete details and illustrations. Your main points would be stronger with such support.

With these comments in mind, Yolanda revised her paragraph until she produced the version that appears on page 288.

Writing an Argument Paragraph

E SINCE 1953

DISTINCTIVE SINCE

Copyright ©2006 The McGraw-Hill Companies, Inc. All rights reserved.

WRITING ASSIGNMENT 1

Develop an argument paragraph based on one of the following statements:

Condoms should (*or* should not) be made available in schools.

_____ (*name a specific athlete*) is the athlete most worthy of admiration in his *or* her sport.

Television is one of the best (*or* worst) inventions of this century.

_____ make the best (*or* worst) pets.

Cigarette and alcohol advertising should (*or* should not) be banned.

Teenagers make poor parents.

_____ is one public figure today who can be considered a hero.

This college needs a better _____ (cafeteria *or* library *or* student center *or* grading policy *or* attendance policy).

Prewriting

a   Make up brief outlines for any three of the statements above. Make sure you have three separate and distinct reasons for each statement. Below is an example of a brief outline for a paragraph making another point.

Large cities should outlaw passenger cars.
1. Cut down on smog and pollution
2. Cut down on noise
3. Make more room for pedestrians

b   Decide, perhaps through discussion with your instructor or classmates, which of your outlines is the most promising for development into a paragraph. Make sure your supporting points are logical by asking yourself in each case, "Does this item truly support my topic sentence?"

c   Do some prewriting. Prepare a list of all the details you can think of that might actually support your point. Don't limit yourself; include more details than you can actually use. Here, for example, are details generated by the writer of "Living Alone":

Deal with power failures	Noisy neighbors
Nasty landlords	Develop courage
Scary noises at night	Do all the cooking
Spiders	Home repairs
Bill collectors	Obscene phone calls
Frightening storms	Loneliness

d   Decide which details you will use to develop your paragraph. Number the details in the order in which you will present them. Because presenting the strongest reason last (emphatic order) is the most effective way to organize an argument paragraph, be sure to save your most powerful reason for last. Here is how the author of "Living Alone" made decisions about details:

1   Deal with power failures

4   Nasty landlords

7   Scary noises at night

    ~~Spiders~~

6   Bill collectors

8   Frightening storms

5   Noisy neighbors

10 Develop courage

2   Do all the cooking

3   Home repairs

    ~~Obscene phone calls~~

9   Loneliness

e   Write the first draft of your paragraph. As you write, develop each reason with specific details. For example, in "Living Alone," notice how the writer makes the experience of living alone come alive with phrases like "That weird thump in the night" or "little moments of sudden loneliness can send shivers through the heart."

Revising

- Put your paragraph away for a day or so. When you reread it, imagine that your audience is a jury that will ultimately render a verdict on your argument. Have you presented a convincing case? If you were on the jury, would you be favorably impressed with this argument?

- As you work on subsequent drafts of your paragraph, keep in mind unity, support, and coherence.

- Edit the next-to-final draft of your paper for sentence-skills mistakes, including spelling. Use the list on the inside front cover of this book.

WRITING ASSIGNMENT 2

Write a paragraph in which you take a stand on one of the controversial points below. Support the point with three reasons.

Students should not be required to attend high school.

All handguns should be banned.

The death penalty should exist for certain crimes.

Abortion should be legal.

Federal prisons should be coed, and prisoners should be allowed to marry.

Parents of girls under eighteen should be informed if their daughters receive birth-control aids.

The government should set up centers where sick or aged persons can go voluntarily to commit suicide.

Any woman on welfare who has more than two illegitimate children should be sterilized.

Parents should never hit their children.

Prostitution should be legalized.

Prewriting

a   As a useful exercise to help you begin developing your argument, your instructor might give class members a chance to "stand up" for what they believe in. One side of the front of the room should be designated *strong agreement* and the other side *strong disagreement,* with an imaginary line representing varying degrees of agreement or disagreement in between. As the class stands in front of the room, the instructor will read one value statement at a time from the list above, and students will move to the appropriate spot, depending on their degree of agreement or disagreement. Some time will be allowed for students, first, to discuss

Copyright ©2006 The McGraw-Hill Companies, Inc. All rights reserved.

with those near them the reasons they are standing where they are; and, second, to state to those at the other end of the scale the reasons for their position.

b   Begin your paragraph by writing a sentence that expresses your attitude toward one of the value statements above, for example, "I feel that prostitution should be legalized."

c   Outline the reason or reasons you hold the opinion that you do. Your support may be based on your own experience, the experience of someone you know, or logic. For example, an outline of a paragraph based on one student's logic looked like this:

I feel that prostitution should be legalized for the following reasons:
1. Prostitutes would then have to pay their fair share of income tax.
2. Government health centers would administer regular checkups. This would help prevent the spread of AIDS and venereal disease.
3. Prostitutes would be able to work openly and independently and would not be controlled by pimps and gangsters.
4. Most of all, prostitutes would be less looked down on—an attitude that is psychologically damaging to those who may already have emotional problems.

Another outline, based on experience, proceeded as follows:

The experiences of a former prostitute I know show that prostitution should not be legalized.
1. The attention Linda received as a prostitute prevented her from seeing and working on her personal problems.
2. She became bitter toward all men, suspecting them all of wanting to exploit her.
3. She developed a negative self-image and felt that no one could love her.

d   Write a first draft of your paragraph, providing specific details to back up each point in your outline.

Revising

Put your paragraph away for a while, ideally at least a day. Ask a friend whose judgment you trust to read and critique it. Your friend should consider each of these questions as he or she reads:

- Does the topic sentence clearly state the author's opinion on a controversial subject?
- Does the paragraph include at least three separate and distinct reasons that support the author's argument?

- Is each of the three reasons backed up by specific, relevant evidence?
- Has the author saved the most powerful reason for last?
- Is the paragraph free of spelling errors and the other sentence-skills mistakes listed on the inside front cover of the book?

Continue revising your work until you and your reader can answer "yes" to all these questions.

WRITING ASSIGNMENT 3

Where do you think it is best to bring up children—in the country, the suburbs, or the city? Write a paragraph in which you argue that one of those three environments is best for families with young children. Your argument should cover two types of reasons: (1) the advantages of living in the environment you've chosen and (2) the disadvantages of living in the other places. Use the following, or something much like it, for your topic sentence:

> For families with young children, (*the country, a suburb,* or *the city*) _____ is the best place to live.

For each reason you advance, include at least one persuasive example. For instance, if you argue that the cultural life in the city is one important reason to live there, you should explain in detail just how going to a science museum is interesting and helpful to children. After deciding on your points of support, arrange them in a brief outline, saving your strongest point for last. In your paragraph, introduce each of your reasons with an addition transition, such as *first of all, another, also,* and *finally.*

WRITING ASSIGNMENT 4

The poster shown here makes an effective visual argument that "Smoking Kills." Write a paper in which you use research findings to help support one of the points below.

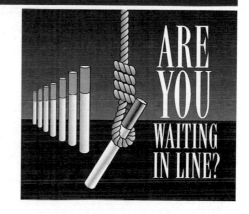

Cigarettes should be illegal.

Mandatory retirement ages should be abolished.

Any person convicted of drunken driving should be required to spend time in jail.

Copyright ©2006 The McGraw-Hill Companies, Inc. All rights reserved.

Drivers should not be permitted to use cell phones.

Everyone should own a pet.

High schools should (or should not) pass out birth control devices and information to students.

Homosexuals should (or should not) be allowed in the armed forces.

Schools should be open all year round.

Advertising should not be permitted on young children's TV shows.

Chapter 19, "A Quick Guide to Research" (pages 341–352), will show you how to use keywords and the Internet to think about your topic and do research. See if you can organize your paper in the form of three separate and distinct reasons that support the topic. Put these reasons into a scratch outline and use it as a guide in writing your paragraph.

WRITING ASSIGNMENT 5

Writing for a Specific Purpose and Audience

In this argument paragraph, you will write with a specific purpose and for a specific audience. Imagine that you have finally met Mr. or Ms. Right—but your parents don't approve of him or her. Specifically, they are against your doing one of the following:

Continuing to see this person

Seriously dating this person and no one else

Moving in together

Getting married at the end of the school year

Write a letter to your parents explaining in detail why you have made your choice. Do your best to convince them that it is a good choice.

Copyright ©2006 The McGraw-Hill Companies, Inc. All rights reserved.

PART THREE

Essay Development

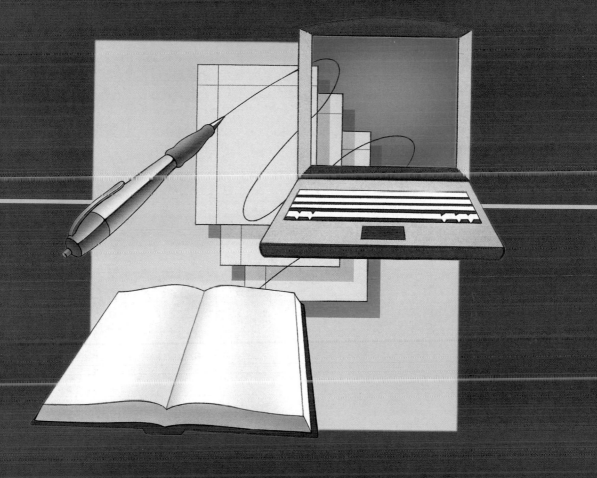

PREVIEW

Part Three moves from the single-paragraph paper to the several-paragraph essay. The differences between a paragraph and an essay are explained and then illustrated with a paragraph that has been expanded into an essay. You are shown how to begin an essay, how to tie its supporting paragraphs together, and how to conclude it. Three student essays are presented, along with questions to increase your understanding of the essay form. Finally, directions on how to plan an essay are followed by a series of essay writing assignments.

17 Additional Paragraph Assignments

This chapter contains a variety of paragraph writing assignments. The earlier assignments are especially suited for writing practice at the beginning of a course; the later ones can be used to measure progress at the end of the course. In general, more detailed instructions are provided with the earlier assignments; fewer guidelines appear for the later ones, so that writers must make more individual decisions about exactly how to proceed. In short, the section provides a wide range of writing assignments. Many choices are possible, depending on the needs and interests of students and the purposes of the instructor.

1 BEST OR WORST EXPERIENCE

Your instructor may pass out slips of paper and ask you to write, in the middle of the slip, your name; in the top left-hand corner, the best or worst job (or chore) you have ever had; in the top right-hand corner, the best or worst instructor you have ever had; in the lower left-hand corner, the best or worst place you have ever eaten in; in the lower right-hand corner, the best or worst thing that has happened to you in the past week. The instructor may also participate by writing on the board. Here is one student's paper.

```
Baby-sitting              B. O. Sullivan
for my sister             (tenth-grade
                          history teacher)


             Gail Battaglia


Fourth Street Diner       Trying to register
```

You should then get together with any person in the room whom you do not know, exchange papers, and talk for a bit about what you wrote. Then the two of you should join another pair, with members of the resulting group of four doing two things:

Copyright ©2006 The McGraw-Hill Companies Inc. All rights reserved.

- Mastering the first names of all the members of the group, so that, if asked, they could introduce the instructor to everyone in the group.

- Giving a "mini" speech to the group in which they talk with *as much specific detail as possible* about any one of the four responses on their slips of paper. During or after this speech, other members of the group should ask questions to get as full a sense as possible of why the experience described was "best" or "worst."

Finally, you should write a paper about any one of the best or worst experiences. The main purpose in writing this paper is to provide plenty of specific details that *show clearly* why your choice was "best" or "worst." The papers on pages 149–150 are examples of students' responses to this assignment.

2   WRITING UP AN INTERVIEW

Interview someone in the class. Take notes as you ask the person a series of questions.

How to Proceed

a   Begin by asking a series of factual questions about the person. You might ask such questions as:

Where is the person from? Where does he or she live now?

Does the person have brothers or sisters? Does the person live with other people, or alone?

What kinds of jobs (if any) has the person had? Where does he or she work now?

What are the person's school or career plans? What courses is he or she taking?

What are the person's favorite leisure activities?

Work at getting specific details rather than general ones. You do not want your introduction to include lines such as "Regina graduated from high school and worked for a year." You want to state specific places and dates: "Regina graduated from DeWitt Clinton High School in the Bronx in 2004. Within a week of graduation, she had gotten a job as a secretary for a branch of the Allstate Insurance Company located in Queens." Or if you are writing about a person's favorite activities, you do not want to simply say, "Regina enjoys watching TV in her few spare hours." Instead, go on and add details such as "Her favorite shows are *60 Minutes, Law & Order,* and *Dateline.*"

Copyright ©2006 The McGraw-Hill Companies, Inc. All rights reserved.

b   Then ask a series of questions about the person's attitudes and thoughts on various matters. You might ask the person's feeling about his or her

Writing ability

Parents

Boss (if any)

Courses

Past schooling

Strengths and talents

Areas for self-improvement

You might also ask what things make the person angry or sad or happy, and why.

c   After collecting all this information, use it in two paragraphs. Begin your introduction to the person with a line like "This is a short introduction to _____. Here is some factual information about him (her)." Then begin your second paragraph with the line, "New let's take a brief look at some of _____'s attitudes and beliefs."

3   KEEPING A JOURNAL

Keep a journal for one week, or for whatever time period your instructor indicates. At some point during each day—perhaps right before going to bed—write for fifteen minutes or more about some of the specific happenings, thoughts, and feelings of your day. You do not have to prepare what to write or be in the mood or worry about making mistakes; just write down whatever words come out. As a minimum, you should complete at least one page in each writing session.

Keeping a journal will help you develop the habits of thinking on paper and writing in terms of specific details. Also, the journal can serve as a sourcebook of ideas for possible papers.

A sample journal entry was given on page 17. It includes general ideas that the writer might develop into paragraphs; for example:

Working at a department store means that you have to deal with some irritating customers.

Certain preparations are advisable before you quit a job.

See if you can construct another general point from this journal entry that might be the basis for a detailed and interesting paragraph. Write the point in the space below.

_____

4   WRITING A DIALOGUE

Make up and write a *realistic* dialogue between two or more people. Don't have your characters talk like cardboard figures; have them talk the way people would in real life. Also, make sure their voices are consistent. (Do not have them suddenly talk out of character.)

The dialogue should deal with a lifelike situation. It may, for example, be a discussion or argument of some kind between two friends or acquaintances, a husband and wife, a parent and child, a brother and sister, a boyfriend and girlfriend, a clerk and customer, or other people. The conversation may or may not lead to a decision or action of some kind.

When writing dialogue, enclose your characters' exact words within quotation marks. (You should first review the material on quotation marks on pages 481–488.) Begin a new paragraph to mark each change in speaker. Also, include brief descriptions of whether your characters smile, sit down or stand up, or make other facial gestures or movements during the conversation. And be sure to include a title for your dialogue. The example that follows can serve as a guide.

A Supermarket Conversation

The supermarket checker rang up the total and said to the young woman in line, "That'll be $43.61."

The young woman fumbled with her pocketbook and then said in an embarrassed voice, "I don't think I have more than $40. How much did you say it was again?"

"It's $43.61," the checker said in a sharp, impatient tone.

As the young woman searched her pocketbook for the dollars she needed, the checker said loudly, "If you don't have enough money, you'll have to put something back."

A middle-aged man behind the young woman spoke up. "Look, Ma'am, I'll lend you a couple of dollars."

"No, I couldn't do that," said the young woman, "If . . . I don't think I need those sodas," she said hesitantly.

"Look lady, make up your mind. You're holding up the line," the checker snapped.

Copyright ©2006 The McGraw-Hill Companies, Inc. All rights reserved.

The man turned to the checker and said coldly, "Why don't you try being a little more courteous to people? If we weren't here buying things, you'd be out of a job."

5   ANNOYANCES IN EVERYDAY LIFE

Make up a list of things that bother you in everyday life. One student's list of "pet peeves" included the following items:

Drivers who suddenly slow down to turn without having signaled

The cold floor in my bathroom on a winter morning

Not having cable television to watch football and basketball games

The small napkin holder in my parents' home that is always running out of napkins

Not being able to fall asleep at night when I know I have to get up at 6:30 the next morning

Suggestions on How to Proceed

- Brainstorm a list of everyday annoyances by asking yourself questions: "What annoys me at home (or about my kitchen, bathroom, closets, and so on)?" "What annoys me about getting to school?" "What annoys me at school or work?" "What annoys me while I am driving or shopping?" You will probably be able to think of other questions.

- Decide which annoyances seem most promising to develop. Which are the most interesting or important? Which can be developed with specific, vivid details? Cross out the items you will not use. Next, number the annoyances you have listed in the order in which you will present them. You may want to group related items together (all those that are connected with shopping, for instance). Be sure to end with the item that annoys you the most.

- Now write a rough draft of the paragraph. Begin with a topic sentence that makes clear what your paragraph is about. Concentrate on providing plenty of details about each of the annoyances you are describing.

- In a second or third draft, add signal words (such as *one, also, another,* and *last*) to set off each annoyance.

- Use the checklist on the inside back cover to edit your paper for sentence-skills mistakes, including spelling.

6 GETTING COMFORTABLE

Getting comfortable is a quiet pleasure in life that we all share. Write a paper about the special way you make yourself comfortable, providing plenty of specific details so that the reader can really see and understand your method. Use transition words such as *first, next, then, in addition, also, finally,* and so on to guide readers through your paper. Transitions act like signposts on an unfamiliar route—they prevent your readers from getting lost.

A student paragraph on getting comfortable ("How I Relax") is on page 89.

7 A SPECIAL PERSON

Write in detail about a person who provided help at an important time in your life. State in the first sentence who the person is and the person's relationship to you (friend, father, cousin, etc.). For example, "My grandmother gave me a lot of direction during the difficult time when my parents were getting divorced." Then show through specific examples (the person's words and actions) why he or she was so special for you.

8 A FAVORITE CHILDHOOD PLACE

Describe a favorite childhood place that made you feel secure, safe, private, or in a world of your own. Here are some possibilities:

A closet

Under a piece of furniture

A grandparent's room

A basement or attic

The woods

A shed or barn

A tree

A bunk bed

Begin with a topic sentence something like this: "_____ was a place that made me feel _____ when I was a child." Keep the point of your topic sentence in mind as you describe this place. Include only details that will support the idea that your place was one of security, safety, privacy, or the like.

Copyright ©2006 The McGraw-Hill Companies, Inc. All rights reserved.

9   EXPRESSING UNIQUENESS

Write a paragraph providing examples of one quality or habit that helps make you unique. One student's response to this assignment appears below.

Floor-Cleaning Freak

The one habit that makes me unique is that I am a floor-cleaning freak. I use my Dustbuster to snap up crumbs seconds after they fall. When a rubber heel mark appears on my vinyl floor, I run for the steel wool. As I work in my kitchen preparing meals, I constantly scan the tiles, looking for spots where some liquid has been spilled or for a crumb that has somehow miraculously escaped my vision. After I scrub and wax my floors, I stand to one side of the room and try to catch the light in such a way as to reveal spots that have gone unwaxed. As I travel from one room to the other, my experienced eye is faithfully searching for lint that may have invaded my domain since my last passing. If I discover an offender, I discreetly tuck it into my pocket. The amount of lint I have gathered in the course of the day is the ultimate test of how diligently I am performing my task. I give my vacuum cleaner quite a workout, and I spend an excessive amount on replacement bags. My expenses for floor-cleaners and wax are alarmingly high, but somehow this does not stop me. Where my floors are concerned, money is not a consideration!

10   MAKING IT THROUGH THE DAY

Write about techniques you use to make it through a day of school or work. These may include:

Caffeine

A system of rewards

Humor

Food

Fantasizing

You might organize the paragraph by using time order. Show how you turn to your supports at various times during the day in order to cope with fatigue or boredom. For example, in the morning you might use coffee (with its dose of caffeine) to get started. Later in the day, you would go on to use other supports.

11 LIFE WITHOUT TV

Imagine that all the televisions in the United States go blank, starting tonight. What would you and your family do on a typical night without television? You may want to write about

What each individual would be doing

What the family could do together

Problems the lack of TV would cause

Benefits of family life without TV

Choose any of these approaches, or some other single approach, in writing about your family life without TV.

12 TEN TOPICS

Write a paper on one of the following topics. Begin with a clear, direct sentence that states exactly what your paper will be about. For example, if you choose the first topic, your opening sentence might be, "There were several delightful childhood games I played that occupied many of my summer days." An opening sentence for the second topic might be, "The work I had to do to secure my high school diploma is one of the special accomplishments of my life." Be sure to follow your opening sentence with plenty of specific supporting details that develop your topic.

A way you had fun as a child

A special accomplishment

A favorite holiday and why it is your favorite

Some problems a family member or friend is having

A superstition or fear

A disagreement you have had with someone

A debt you have repaid or have yet to repay

The sickest you've ever been

How your parents (or you and a special person in your life) met

Your father's or mother's attitude toward you

Copyright ©2006 The McGraw-Hill Companies, Inc. All rights reserved.

13   TEN MORE TOPICS

Write a paper on one of the topics below. Follow the instructions given for Assignment 12.

A wish or dream you have or had

Everyday pleasures

Ways you were punished by your parents as a child

Ways you were rewarded by your parents as a child

A difficult moment in your life

An experience you or someone you know has had with drugs

Your weaknesses as a student

Your strengths as a student

A time a prayer was answered

Something you would like to change

14   FIFTEEN TOPICS

Write a paper on one of the following topics:

Crime	Music	Books
Lies	Exercise	Transportation
Television	Debt	Exhaustion
Plants	Parking meters	Telephone
Comic books	Hunger	Drugs

Suggestions on How to Proceed

a   You might begin by writing several statements about your general topic. For example, suppose that you choose to do a paper on the subject "Neighborhood." Here are some statements you might write:

My neighborhood is fairly rural.

The neighborhood where I grew up was unique.

Many city neighborhoods have problems with crime.

My new neighborhood has no playgrounds for children.

Everyone in my neighborhood seems to mow the lawn almost daily.

My neighborhood became a community when it was faced with a hurricane last summer.

My neighborhood is a noisy place.

b   Choose (or revise) one of the statements that you could go on to develop in a paragraph. You should not select a narrow statement like "My new neighborhood has no playgrounds for children," for it is a simple factual sentence needing no support. Nor should you begin with a point such as "Many city neighborhoods have problems with crime," which is too broad for you to develop adequately in a single paragraph. (See also the information on topic sentences on pages 64–66.)

c   After you have chosen a promising sentence, make a scratch outline of supporting details that will develop the point of that sentence. For example, one student provided the following outline:

My neighborhood is a noisy place.
1. Businesses
   a. Tavern with loud music
   b. Twenty-four-hour drive-in burger restaurant
2. Children
   a. Skating and biking while carrying loud radios
   b. Street games
3. Traffic
   a. Truck route nearby
   b. Horn-blowing during frequent delays at intersection

d   While writing your paper, use the checklist on the inside front cover to make sure you can answer "yes" to the questions about unity, support, and coherence. Also, refer to the checklist when you edit the next-to-final draft of your paper for sentence-skills mistakes, including spelling.

15   FIFTEEN MORE TOPICS

Write a paper on one of the topics below. Follow the instructions given for Assignment 14.

Comics	Tryouts	Illness
Babies	Pens	Success
Vacation	Hospital	Failure
Red tape	Parties	Wisdom teeth
Dependability	Criticism	Home

18 Writing the Essay

What Is an Essay?

Differences between an Essay and a Paragraph

An essay is simply a paper of several paragraphs, rather than one paragraph, that supports a single point. In an essay, subjects can and should be treated more fully than they would be in a single-paragraph paper.

The main idea or point developed in an essay is called the *thesis statement* or *thesis sentence* (rather than, as in a paragraph, the *topic sentence*). The thesis statement appears in the introductory paragraph, and it is then developed in the supporting paragraphs that follow. A short concluding paragraph closes the essay.

The Form of an Essay

The diagram on the next page shows the form of an essay.

Copyright ©2006 The McGraw-Hill Companies, Inc. All rights reserved.

Introductory Paragraph

Introduction
Thesis statement
Plan of development:
Points 1, 2, 3

The *introduction* attracts the reader's interest.

The *thesis statement* (or *thesis sentence*) states the main idea advanced in the paper.

The *plan of development* is a list of points that support the thesis. The points are presented in the order in which they will be developed in the paper.

First Supporting Paragraph

Topic sentence (point 1)
Specific evidence

The *topic sentence* advances the first supporting point for the thesis, and the *specific evidence* in the rest of the paragraph develops that first point.

Second Supporting Paragraph

Topic sentence (point 2)
Specific evidence

The *topic sentence* advances the second supporting point for the thesis, and the *specific evidence* in the rest of the paragraph develops that second point.

Third Supporting Paragraph

Topic sentence (point 3)
Specific evidence

The *topic sentence* advances the third supporting point for the thesis, and the *specific evidence* in the rest of the paragraph develops that third point.

Concluding Paragraph

Summary, conclusion,
or both

A *summary* is a brief restatement of the thesis and its main points. A *conclusion* is a final thought or two stemming from the subject of the paper.

Copyright ©2006 The McGraw-Hill Companies, Inc. All rights reserved.

A Model Essay

Gene, the writer of the paragraph on working in an apple plant (page 7), later decided to develop his subject more fully. Here is the essay that resulted.

My Job in an Apple Plant

Introductory paragraph

[1]In the course of working my way through school, I have taken many jobs I would rather forget. [2]I have spent nine hours a day lifting heavy automobile and truck batteries off the end of an assembly belt. [3]I have risked the loss of eyes and fingers working a punch press in a textile factory. [4]I have served as a ward aide in a mental hospital, helping care for brain-damaged men who would break into violent fits at unexpected moments. [5]But none of these jobs was as dreadful as my job in an apple plant. [6]The work was physically hard; the pay was poor; and, most of all, the working conditions were dismal.

First supporting paragraph

[7]First, the job made enormous demands on my strength and energy. [8]For ten hours a night, I took cartons that rolled down a metal track and stacked them onto wooden skids in a tractor trailer. [9]Each carton contained twelve heavy bottles of apple juice. [10]A carton shot down the track about every fifteen seconds. [11]I once figured out that I was lifting an average of twelve tons of apple juice every night. [12]When a truck was almost filled, I or my partner had to drag fourteen bulky wooden skids into the empty trailer nearby and then set up added sections of the heavy metal track so that we could start routing cartons to the back of the empty van. [13]While one of us did that, the other performed the stacking work of two men.

Second supporting paragraph

[14]I would not have minded the difficulty of the work so much if the pay had not been so poor. [15]I was paid the minimum wage at that time, $3.65 an hour, plus just a quarter extra for working the night shift. [16]Because of the low salary, I felt compelled to get as much overtime pay as possible. [17]Everything over eight hours a night was time-and-a-half, so I typically worked twelve hours a night. [18]On Friday I would sometimes work straight through until Saturday at noon—eighteen hours. [19]I averaged over sixty hours a week but did not take home much more than $180.

Third supporting paragraph

[20]But even more than the low pay, what upset me about my apple plant job was the working conditions. [21]Our humorless supervisor cared only about his production record for each night and tried to keep the assembly line moving at breakneck pace. [22]During work I was limited to two ten-minute breaks and an unpaid half hour for lunch. [23]Most of my time was spent outside on the truck loading dock in near-zero-degree temperatures. [24]The steel floors of the trucks were like ice; the quickly penetrating cold made my feet feel like stone. [25]I had no shared interests with the man I loaded cartons with, and so I had to work without companionship on the job. [26]And after

the production line shut down and most people left, I had to spend two hours alone scrubbing clean the apple vats, which were coated with a sticky residue.

Concluding paragraph

²⁷I stayed on the job for five months, all the while hating the difficulty of the work, the poor money, and the conditions under which I worked. ²⁸By the time I quit, I was determined never to do such degrading work again.

Important Points about the Essay

Introductory Paragraph

An introductory paragraph has certain purposes or functions and can be constructed using various methods.

Purposes of the Introduction

An introductory paragraph should do three things:

1   Attract the reader's *interest*. Using one of the suggested methods of introduction described below can help draw the reader into your paper.

2   Present a *thesis sentence*—a clear, direct statement of the central idea that you will develop in your paper. The thesis statement, like a topic sentence, should have a keyword or keywords reflecting your attitude about the subject. For example, in the essay on the apple plant job, the keyword is *dreadful*.

3   Indicate a *plan of development*—a preview of the major points that will support your thesis statement, listed in the order in which they will be presented. In some cases, the thesis statement and plan of development may appear in the same sentence. In some cases, also, the plan of development may be omitted.

ACTIVITY

1.   In "My Job in an Apple Plant," which sentences are used to attract the reader's interest?

_____ sentences 1 to 3 _____ 1 to 4 _____ 1 to 5

2.   The thesis in "My Job in an Apple Plant" is presented in

_____ sentence 4 _____ sentence 5 _____ sentence 6

3. Is the thesis followed by a plan of development?

_____ Yes _____ No

4. Which words in the plan of development announce the three major supporting points in the essay? Write them below.

a. _____

b. _____

c. _____

Common Methods of Introduction

Here are some common methods of introduction. Use any one method, or a combination of methods, to introduce your subject in an interesting way.

1   **Broad statement.** Begin with a broad, general statement of your topic and narrow it down to your thesis statement. Broad, general statements ease the reader into your thesis statement by providing a background for it. In "My Job in an Apple Plant," Gene writes generally on the topic of his worst jobs and then narrows down to a specific worst job.

2   **Contrast.** Start with an idea or situation that is the opposite of the one you will develop. This approach works because your readers will be surprised, and then intrigued, by the contrast between the opening idea and the thesis that follows it. Here is an example of a "contrast" introduction:

> When I was a girl, I never argued with my parents about differences between their attitudes and mine. My father would deliver his judgment on an issue, and that was usually the end of the matter. Discussion seldom changed his mind, and disagreement was not tolerated. But the situation is different with today's parents and children. My husband and I have to contend with radical differences between what our children think about a given situation and what we think about it. We have had disagreements with all three of our daughters, Stephanie, Diana, and Giselle.

3   **"Relevance."** Explain the importance of your topic. If you can convince your readers that the subject applies to them in some way, or is something they should know more about, they will want to continue reading. The introductory paragraph of "Sports-Crazy America" (page 319) provides an example of a "relevance" introduction.

Copyright ©2006 The McGraw-Hill Companies, Inc. All rights reserved.

4   *Anecdote.* Use an incident or brief story. Stories are naturally interesting. They appeal to a reader's curiosity. In your introduction, an anecdote will grab the reader's attention right away. The story should be brief and should be related to your central idea. The incident in the story can be something that happened to you, something that you may have heard about, or something that you have read about in a newspaper or magazine. Here is an example of a paragraph that begins with a story:

> The husky man pushes open the door of the bedroom and grins as he pulls out a .38 revolver. An elderly man wearing thin pajamas looks at him and whimpers. In a feeble effort at escape, the old man slides out of his bed and moves to the door of the room. The husky man, still grinning, blocks his way. With the face of a small, frightened animal, the old man looks up and whispers, "Oh, God, please don't hurt me." The grinning man then fires four times. The television movie cuts now to a soap commercial, but the little boy who has been watching the set has begun to cry. Such scenes of direct violence on television must surely be harmful to children for a number of psychological reasons.

5   *Questions.* Ask your readers one or more questions. These questions catch the readers' interest and make them want to read on. Here is an example of a paragraph that begins with questions:

> What would happen if we were totally honest with ourselves? Would we be able to stand the pain of giving up self-deception? Would the complete truth be too much for us to bear? Such questions will probably never be answered, for in everyday life we protect ourselves from the onslaught of too much reality. All of us cultivate defense mechanisms that prevent us from seeing, hearing, or feeling too much. Included among such defense mechanisms are rationalization, reaction formation, and substitution.

Note, however, that the thesis itself must not be a question.

6   *Quotation.* A quotation can be something you have read in a book or an article. It can also be something that you have heard: a popular saying or proverb ("Never give advice to a friend"); a current or recent advertising slogan ("Just do it"); a favorite expression used by your friends or family ("My father always says . . ."). Using a quotation in your introductory paragraph lets you add someone else's voice to your own. Here is an example of a paragraph that begins with a quotation:

Copyright ©2006 The McGraw-Hill Companies, Inc. All rights reserved.

"Evil," wrote Martin Buber, "is lack of direction." In my school days as a fatherless boy, with a mother too confused by her own life to really care for me, I strayed down a number of dangerous paths. Before my eighteenth birthday, I had been a car thief, a burglar, and a drug dealer.

Supporting Paragraphs

Most essays have three supporting points, developed in three separate paragraphs. (Some essays will have two supporting points; others, four or more.) Each of the supporting paragraphs should begin with a topic sentence that states the point to be detailed in that paragraph. Just as the thesis provides a focus for the entire essay, the topic sentence provides a focus for each supporting paragraph.

ACTIVITY

1. What is the topic sentence for the first supporting paragraph of "My Job in an Apple Plant"? (*Write the sentence number here.*) _____

2. What is the topic sentence for the second supporting paragraph? _____

3. What is the topic sentence for the third supporting paragraph? _____

Transitional Sentences

In paragraphs, transitions and other connective devices (pages 90–98) are used to help link sentences. Similarly, in an essay *transitional sentences* are used to help tie the supporting paragraphs together. Such transitional sentences usually occur near the end of one paragraph or the beginning of the next.

In "My Job in an Apple Plant," the first transitional sentence is:

I would not have minded the difficulty of the work so much if the pay had not been so poor.

In this sentence, the keyword *difficulty* reminds us of the point of the first supporting paragraph, while *pay* tells us the point to be developed in the second supporting paragraph.

ACTIVITY

Here is the other transitional sentence in "My Job in an Apple Plant":

> But even more than the low pay, what upset me about my apple plant job was the working conditions.

Complete the following statement: In the sentence above, the keywords _____ echo the point of the second supporting paragraph, and the keywords _____ announce the topic of the third supporting paragraph.

Concluding Paragraph

The concluding paragraph often summarizes the essay by briefly restating the thesis and, at times, the main supporting points. Also, the conclusion brings the paper to a natural and graceful end, sometimes leaving the reader with a final thought on the subject.

ACTIVITY

1. Which sentence in the concluding paragraph of "My Job in an Apple Plant" restates the thesis and supporting points of the essay? _____

2. Which sentence contains the concluding thought of the essay? _____

Essays to Consider

Read the three student essays below and then answer the questions that follow.

Giving Up a Baby

[1]As I awoke, I overheard a nurse say, "It's a lovely baby boy. [2]How could a mother give him up?" [3]"Be quiet," another voice said. [4]"She's going to wake up soon." [5]Then I heard the baby cry, but I never heard him again. [6]Three years ago, I gave up my child to two strangers, people who wanted a baby but could not have one. [7]I was in pain over my decision, and I can still hear the voices of people who said I was selfish or crazy. [8]But the reasons I gave up my child were important ones, at least to me.

Copyright ©2006 The McGraw-Hill Companies, Inc. All rights reserved.

⁹I gave up my baby, first of all, because I was very young. ¹⁰I was only seventeen, and I was unmarried. ¹¹Because I was so young, I did not yet feel the desire to have and raise a baby. ¹²I knew that I would be a child raising a child and that, when I had to stay home to care for the baby, I would resent the loss of my freedom. ¹³I might also blame the baby for that loss. ¹⁴In addition, I had not had the experiences in life that would make me a responsible, giving parent. ¹⁵What could I teach my child, when I barely knew what life was all about myself?

¹⁶Besides my age, another factor in my decision was the problems my parents would have. ¹⁷I had dropped out of high school before graduation, and I did not have a job or even the chance of a job, at least for a while. ¹⁸My parents would have to support my child and me, possibly for years. ¹⁹My mom and dad had already struggled to raise their family and were not well off financially. ²⁰I knew I could not burden them with an unemployed teenager and her baby. ²¹Even if I eventually got a job, my parents would have to help raise my child. ²²They would have to be full-time babysitters while I tried to make a life of my own. ²³Because my parents are good people, they would have done all this for me. ²⁴But I felt I could not ask for such a big sacrifice from them.

²⁵The most important factor in my decision was, I suppose, a selfish one. ²⁶I was worried about my own future. ²⁷I didn't want to marry the baby's father. ²⁸I realized during the time I was pregnant that we didn't love each other. ²⁹My future as an unmarried mother with no education or skills would certainly have been limited. ³⁰I would be struggling to survive, and I would have to give up for years my dreams of getting a job and my own car and apartment. ³¹It is hard to admit, but I also considered the fact that, with a baby, I would not have the social life most young people have. ³²I would not be able to stay out late, go to parties, or feel carefree and irresponsible, for I would always have an enormous responsibility waiting for me at home. ³³With a baby, the future looked limited and insecure.

³⁴In summary, thinking about my age, my responsibility to my parents, and my own future made me decide to give up my baby. ³⁵As I look back today at my decision, I know that it was the right one for me at the time.

Sports-Crazy America

¹Almost all Americans are involved with sports in some way. ²They may play basketball or volleyball or go swimming or skiing. ³They may watch football or basketball games on the high school, college, or professional level. ⁴Sports may seem like an innocent pleasure, but it is important to look under the surface. ⁵In reality, sports have reached a point where they play too large a part in daily life. ⁶They take up too much media time, play too large a role in the raising of children, and give too much power and prestige to athletes.

[7]The overemphasis on sports can be seen most obviously in the vast media coverage of athletic events. [8]It seems as if every bowl game play-off, tournament, trial, bout, race, meet, or match is shown on one television channel or another. [9]On Saturday and Sunday, a check of TV Guide will show countless forty sports programs on network television alone, and countless more on cable stations. [10]In addition, sports make up about 30 percent of local news at six and eleven o'clock, and network world news shows often devote several minutes to major American sports events. [11]Radio offers a full roster of games and a wide assortment of sports talk shows. [12]Furthermore, many daily newspapers such as USA Today are devoting more and more space to sports coverage, often in an attempt to improve circulation. [13]The newspaper with the biggest sports section is the one people will buy.

[14]The way we raise and educate our children also illustrates our sports mania. [15]As early as age six or seven, kids are placed in little leagues, often to play under screaming coaches and pressuring parents. [16]Later, in high school, students who are singled out by the school and by the community are not those who are best academically but those who are best athletically. [17]And college sometimes seems to be more about sports than about learning. [18]The United States may be the only country in the world where people often think of their colleges as teams first and schools second. [19]The names Penn State, Notre Dame, and Southern Cal mean "sports" to the public.

[20]Our sports craziness is especially evident in the prestige given to athletes in the United States. [21]For one thing, we reward them with enormous salaries. [22]In 2003, for example, baseball players averaged over $2.5 million a year; the average annual salary in the United States is $36,800. [23]Besides their huge salaries, athletes receive the awe, the admiration, and sometimes the votes of the public. [24]Kids look up to someone like LeBron James or Tom Brady as a true hero; adults wear the jerseys and jackets of their favorite teams. [25]Former players become senators and congressmen. [26]And a famous athlete like Mia Hamm or Tiger Woods needs to make only one commercial for advertisers to see the sales of a product boom.

[27]Americans are truly mad about sports. [28]Perhaps we like to see the competitiveness we experience in our daily lives acted out on playing fields. [29]Perhaps we need heroes who can achieve clear-cut victories in a short time, of only an hour or two. [30]Whatever the reason, the sports scene in this country is more popular than ever.

An Interpretation of Lord of the Flies

[1]Modern history has shown us the evil that exists in human beings. [2]Assassinations are common, governments use torture to discourage dissent, and six million Jews were exterminated during World War II. [3]In Lord of the

Copyright ©2006 The McGraw-Hill Companies, Inc. All rights reserved.

Flies, William Golding describes a group of schoolboys shipwrecked on an island with no authority figures to control their behavior. [4]One of the boys soon yields to dark forces within himself, and his corruption symbolizes the evil in all of us. [5]First, Jack Merridew kills a living creature; then, he rebels against the group leader; and finally, he seizes power and sets up his own murderous society.

[6]The first stage in Jack's downfall is his killing of a living creature. [7]In Chapter 1, Jack aims at a pig but is unable to kill. [8]His upraised arm pauses "because of the enormity of the knife descending and cutting into living flesh, because of the unbearable blood," and the pig escapes. [9]Three chapters later, however, Jack leads some boys on a successful hunt. [10]He returns triumphantly with a freshly killed pig and reports excitedly to the others, "I cut the pig's throat." [11]Yet Jack twitches as he says this, and he wipes his bloody hands on his shorts as if eager to remove the stains. [12]There is still some civilization left in him.

[13]After the initial act of killing the pig, Jack's refusal to cooperate with Ralph shows us that this civilized part is rapidly disappearing. [14]With no adults around, Ralph has made some rules. [15]One is that a signal fire must be kept burning. [16]But Jack tempts the boys watching the fire to go hunting, and the fire goes out. [17]Another rule is that at a meeting, only the person holding a special seashell has the right to speak. [18]In Chapter 5, another boy is speaking when Jack rudely tells him to shut up. [19]Ralph accuses Jack of breaking the rules. [20]Jack shouts: "Bollocks to the rules! We're strong—we hunt! If there's a beast, we'll hunt it down! We'll close in and beat and beat and beat—!" [21]He gives a "wild whoop" and leaps off the platform, throwing the meeting into chaos. [22]Jack is now much more savage than civilized.

[23]The most obvious proof of Jack's corruption comes in Chapter 8, when he establishes his own murderous society. [24]Insisting that Ralph is not a "proper chief" because he does not hunt, Jack asks for a new election. [25]After he again loses, Jack announces, "I'm going off by myself. . . . Anyone who wants to hunt when I do can come too." [26]Eventually, nearly all the boys join Jack's "tribe." [27]Following his example, they paint their faces like savages, sacrifice to "the beast," brutally murder two of their schoolmates, and nearly succeed in killing Ralph as well. [28]Jack has now become completely savage—and so have the others.

[29]Through Jack Merridew, then, Golding shows how easily moral laws can be forgotten. [30]Freed from grown-ups and their rules, Jack learns to kill living things, defy authority, and lead a tribe of murdering savages. [31]Jack's example is a frightening reminder of humanity's potential for evil. [32]The "beast" the boys try to hunt and kill is actually within every human being.

QUESTIONS

1. In which essay does the thesis statement appear in the last sentence of the introductory paragraph?

   _____

2. In the essay on *Lord of the Flies*, which sentence of the introductory paragraph contains the plan of development? _____

3. Which method of introduction is used in "Giving Up a Baby"?

   a. General to narrow   c. Incident or story

   b. Stating importance of topic   d. Questions

4. Complete the following brief outline of "Giving Up a Baby":
   I gave up my baby for three reasons:

   a. _____

   b. _____

   c. _____

5. Which *two* essays use a transitional sentence between the first and second supporting paragraphs?

   _____

6. *Complete the following statement:* Emphatic order is shown in the last supporting paragraph of "Giving Up a Baby" with the words *most important* factor; in the last supporting paragraph of "Sports-Crazy America" with the words _____; and in the last supporting paragraph of "An Interpretation of *Lord of the Flies*" with the words _____.

7. Which essay uses time order as well as emphatic order to organize its three supporting paragraphs? _____

8. List four major transitions used in the supporting paragraphs of "An Interpretation of *Lord of the Flies*."

   a. _____   c. _____

   b. _____   d. _____

9. Which *two* essays include a sentence in the concluding paragraph that summarizes the three supporting points?

_____

_____

10. Which essay includes two final thoughts in its concluding paragraph?

_____

Copyright ©2006 The McGraw-Hill Companies, Inc. All rights reserved.

Planning the Essay

Outlining the Essay

When you write an essay, planning is crucial for success. You should plan your essay by outlining in two ways:

1   Prepare a scratch outline. This should consist of a short statement of the thesis followed by the main supporting points for the thesis. Here is Gene's scratch outline for his essay on the apple plant:

Working at an apple plant was my worst job.
1.   Hard work
2.   Poor pay
3.   Bad working conditions

Do not underestimate the value of this initial outline—or the work involved in achieving it. Be prepared to do a good deal of plain hard thinking at this first and most important stage of your paper.

2   Prepare a more detailed outline. The outline form that follows will serve as a guide. Your instructor may ask you to submit a copy of this form either before you actually write an essay or along with your finished essay.

Form for Planning an Essay

To write an effective essay, use a form like the one that follows.

Introduction

Opening remarks

Thesis statement _____

_____

Plan of development

Body

Topic sentence 1 _____

_____

Specific supporting evidence

Topic sentence 2 _____

_____

Specific supporting evidence

Topic sentence 3 _____

_____

Specific supporting evidence

Conclusion

Summary, closing remarks, or both

Practice in Writing the Essay

In this section, you will expand and strengthen your understanding of the essay form as you work through the following activities.

1 Understanding the Two Parts of a Thesis Statement

In the chapter, you learned that effective essays center on a thesis, or main point, that a writer wishes to express. This central idea is usually presented as a *thesis statement* in an essay's introductory paragraph.

A good thesis statement does two things. First, it tells readers an essay's *topic*. Second, it presents the *writer's attitude, opinion, idea,* or *point* about that topic. For example, look at the following thesis statement:

Celebrities are often poor role models.

In this thesis statement, the topic is *celebrities;* the writer's main point is celebrities are *often poor role models.*

ACTIVITY

For each thesis statement below, single-underline the topic and double-underline the main point that the writer wishes to express about the topic.

1. Several teachers have played important roles in my life.

2. A period of loneliness in life can actually have certain benefits.

3. Owning an old car has its own special rewards.

4. Learning to write takes work, patience, and a sense of humor.

5. Advertisers use several clever sales techniques to promote their message.

6. Anger in everyday life often results from a lack of time, a frustration with technology, and a buildup of stress.

7. The sale of handguns in this country should be sharply limited for several reasons.

8. My study habits in college benefited greatly from a course on note-taking, textbook study, and test-taking skills.

Copyright ©2006 The McGraw-Hill Companies, Inc. All rights reserved.

9. Retired people must cope with the mental, emotional, and physical stresses of being "old."

10. Parents should take certain steps to encourage their children to enjoy reading.

2 Supporting the Thesis with Specific Evidence

The first essential step in writing a successful essay is to form a clearly stated thesis. The second basic step is to support the thesis with specific reasons or details.

To ensure that your essay will have adequate support, you may find an informal outline very helpful. Write down a brief version of your thesis idea, and then work out and jot down the three points that will support your thesis.

Here is the scratch outline that was prepared for one essay:

The college cafeteria is poorly managed.

The checkout lines are always long.

The floor and tables are often dirty.

Food choices are often limited.

A scratch outline like the one above looks simple, but developing it often requires a good deal of careful thinking. The time spent on developing a logical outline is invaluable, though. Once you have planned the steps that logically support your thesis, you will be in an excellent position to go on to write an effective essay.

ACTIVITY

Following are five informal outlines in which two points (*a* and *b*) are already provided. Complete each outline by adding a third logical supporting point (*c*).

1. Poor grades in school can have various causes.
   a. Family problems
   b. Study problems

   c. _____

2. My landlord adds to the stress in my life.
   a. Keeps raising the rent
   b. Expects me to help maintain the apartment

   c. _____

3. My mother (*or some other adult*) has three qualities I admire.

    a. Sense of humor

    b. Patience

    c. _____

4. The first day in college was nerve-racking.

    a. Meeting new people

    b. Dealing with the bookstore

    c. _____

5. Getting married at nineteen was a mistake.

    a. Not finished with my education

    b. Not ready to have children

    c. _____

3 Identifying Introductions

The box lists six common methods for introducing an essay, discussed in this chapter.

1.	Broad statement	4.	Incident or story
2.	Contrast	5.	Question
3.	Relevance	6.	Quotation

ACTIVITY

After reviewing the six methods of introduction on pages 315–317, refer to the box above and read the following six introductory paragraphs. Then, in the space provided, write the number of the kind of introduction used in each paragraph. Each kind of introduction is used once.

Paragraph A

_____   Is bullying a natural, unavoidable part of growing up? Is it something that everyone has to either endure as a victim, practice as a bully, or tolerate as a bystander? Does bullying leave deep scars on its victims, or is it fairly harmless? Does being a bully indicate some deep-rooted problems, or is it not a big deal? These and other questions need to be looked at as we consider the three forms of bullying: physical, verbal, and social.

Copyright ©2006 The McGraw-Hill Companies, Inc. All rights reserved.

Paragraph B

_____   In a perfect school, students would treat each other with affection and respect. Differences would be tolerated, and even welcomed. Kids would become more popular by being kind and supportive. Students would go out of their way to make sure one another felt happy and comfortable. But most schools are not perfect. Instead of being places of respect and tolerance, they are places where the hateful act of bullying is widespread.

Paragraph C

_____   Students have to deal with all kinds of problems in schools. There are the problems created by difficult classes, by too much homework, or by personality conflicts with teachers. There are problems with scheduling the classes you need and still getting some of the ones you want. There are problems with bad cafeteria food, grouchy principals, or overcrowded classrooms. But one of the most difficult problems of all has to do with a terrible situation that exists in most schools: bullying.

Paragraph D

_____   Eric, a new boy at school, was shy and physically small. He quickly became a victim of bullies. Kids would wait after school, pull out his shirt, and punch and shove him around. He was called such names as "Mouse Boy" and "Jerk Boy." When he sat down during lunch hour, others would leave his table. In gym games he was never thrown the ball, as if he didn't exist. Then one day he came to school with a gun. When the police were called, he told them he just couldn't take it anymore. Bullying had hurt him badly, just as it hurts many other students. Every member of a school community should be aware of bullying and the three hateful forms that it takes: physical, verbal, and social bullying.

Paragraph E

_____   A British prime minister once said, "Courage is fire, and bullying is smoke." If that is true, there is a lot of "smoke" present in most schools today. Bullying in schools is a huge problem that hurts both its victims and the people who practice it. Physical, verbal, and social bullying are all harmful in their own ways.

Paragraph F

_____   A pair of students bring guns and homemade bombs to school, killing a number of their fellow students and teachers before taking their own lives. A young man hangs himself on Sunday evening rather than attend school the following morning. A junior high school girl is admitted to the emergency room after cutting her wrists. What do all these horrible reports have to do with each other? All were reportedly caused by a terrible practice that is common in schools: bullying.

Copyright ©2006 The McGraw-Hill Companies. Inc. All rights reserved.

4 Revising an Essay for All Four Bases: Unity, Support, Coherence, and Sentence Skills

You know from your work on paragraphs that there are four "bases" a paper must cover to be effective. In the following activity, you will evaluate and revise an essay in terms of all four bases: *unity, support, coherence,* and *sentence skills.*

ACTIVITY

Comments follow each supporting paragraph and the concluding paragraph. Circle the letter of the *one* statement that applies in each case.

A Hateful Activity: Bullying

Paragraph 1: Introduction

Eric, a new boy at school, was shy and physically small. He quickly became a victim of bullies. Kids would wait after school, pull out his shirt, and punch and shove him around. He was called such names as "Mouse Boy" and "Jerk Boy." When he sat down during lunch hour, others would leave his table. In gym games he was never thrown the ball, as if he didn't exist. Then one day he came to school with a gun. When the police were called, he told them he just couldn't take it anymore. Bullying had hurt him badly, just as it hurts many other students. Every member of a school community should be aware of bullying and the three hateful forms that it takes: physical, verbal, and social bullying.

Paragraph 2: First Supporting Paragraph

Bigger or meaner kids try to hurt kids who are smaller or unsure of themselves. They'll push kids into their lockers, knock books out of their hands, or shoulder them out of the cafeteria line. In gym class, a bully often likes to kick kids' legs out from under them while they are running. In the classroom, bullies might kick the back of the chair or step on the foot of the kids they want to intimidate. Bullies will corner a kid in a bathroom. There the victim will be slapped around, will have his or her clothes half pulled off, and might even be shoved into a trash can. Bullies will wait for kids after school and bump or wrestle them around, often while others are looking on. The goal is to frighten kids as much as possible and try to make them cry. Physical bullying is more common among boys, but it is not unknown for girls to be physical bullies as well. The victims are left bruised and hurting, but often in even more pain emotionally than bodily.

a. Paragraph 2 contains an irrelevant sentence.

b. Paragraph 2 lacks transition words.

c. Paragraph 2 lacks supporting details at one key spot.

d. Paragraph 2 contains a fragment and a run-on.

Paragraph 3: Second Supporting Paragraph

Perhaps even worse than physical attack is verbal bullying, which uses words, rather than hands or fists, as weapons. We may be told that "sticks and stones may break my bones, but words can never harm me," but few of us are immune to the pain of a verbal attack. Like physical bullies, verbal bullies tend to single out certain targets. From that moment on, the victim is subject to a hail of insults and put-downs. These are usually delivered in public, so the victim's humiliation will be greatest: "Oh, no; here comes the nerd!" "Why don't you lose some weight, blubber boy?" "You smell as bad as you look!" "Weirdo." "Fairy." "Creep." " Dork." "Slut." "Loser." Verbal bullying is an equal-opportunity activity, with girls as likely to be verbal bullies as boys. If parents don't want their children to be bullies like this, they shouldn't be abusive themselves. Meanwhile, the victim retreats farther and farther into his or her shell, hoping to escape further notice.

a. Paragraph 3 contains an irrelevant sentence.

b. Paragraph 3 lacks transition words.

c. Paragraph 3 lacks supporting details at one key spot.

d. Paragraph 2 contains a fragment and a run-on.

Paragraph 4: Third Supporting Paragraph

As bad as verbal bullying is, many would agree that the most painful type of bullying of all is social bullying. Many students have a strong need for the comfort of being part of a group. For social bullies, the pleasure of belonging to a group is increased by the sight of someone who is refused entry into that group. So, like wolves targeting the weakest sheep in a herd, the bullies lead the pack in isolating people who they decide are different. Bullies do everything they can to make those people feel sad and lonely. In class and out of it, the bullies make it clear that the victims are ignored and unwanted. As the victims sink farther into isolation and depression, the social bullies—who seem to be female more often than male—feel all the more puffed up by their own popularity.

a. Paragraph 4 contains an irrelevant sentence.

b. Paragraph 4 lacks transition words.

c. Paragraph 4 lacks supporting details at one key spot.

d. Paragraph 2 contains a fragment and a run-on.

Paragraph 5: Concluding Paragraph

Whether bullying is physical, verbal, or social, it can leave deep and lasting scars. If parents, teachers, and other adults were more aware of the types of bullying, they might help by stepping in. Before the situation becomes too extreme. If students were more aware of the terrible pain that bullying causes, they might think twice about being bullies themselves, their awareness could make the world a kinder place.

a. Paragraph 5 contains an irrelevant sentence.

b. Paragraph 5 lacks transition words.

c. Paragraph 5 lacks supporting details at one key spot.

d. Paragraph 2 contains a fragment and a run-on.

Essay Assignments

Hints   Keep the points below in mind when writing an essay on any of the topics that follow.

1   Your first step must be to plan your essay. Prepare both a scratch outline and a more detailed outline, as explained on the preceding pages.

2   While writing your essay, use the checklist below to make sure that your essay touches all four bases of effective writing.

Base 1: Unity

_____ Clearly stated thesis in the introductory paragraph of your paper

_____ All the supporting paragraphs on target in backing up your thesis

Base 2: Support

_____ Three separate supporting points for your thesis

_____ *Specific* evidence for each of the three supporting points

_____ *Plenty* of specific evidence for each supporting point

Copyright ©2006 The McGraw-Hill Companies, Inc. All rights reserved.

Base 3: Coherence

_____ Clear method of organization

_____ Transitions and other connecting words

_____ Effective introduction and conclusion

Base 4: Sentence Skills

_____ Clear, error-free sentences (use the checklist on the inside front cover of this book)

1 YOUR HOUSE OR APARTMENT

Write an essay on the advantages *or* disadvantages (not both) of the house or apartment where you live. In your introductory paragraph, describe briefly the place you plan to write about. End the paragraph with your thesis statement and a plan of development. Here are some suggestions for thesis statements:

> The best features of my apartment are its large windows, roomy closets, and great location.
>
> The drawbacks of my house are its unreliable oil burner, tiny kitchen, and old-fashioned bathroom.
>
> An inquisitive landlord, sloppy neighbors, and platoons of cockroaches came along with our rented house.
>
> My apartment has several advantages, including friendly neighbors, lots of storage space, and a good security system.

2 A BIG MISTAKE

Write an essay about the biggest mistake you made within the past year. Describe the mistake and show how its effects have convinced you that it was the wrong thing to do. For instance, if you write about "taking a full-time job while going to school" as your biggest mistake, show the problems it caused. (You might discuss such matters as low grades, constant exhaustion, and poor performance at work.)

To get started, make a list of all the things you did last year that, with hindsight, now seem to be mistakes. Then pick out the action that has had the most serious consequences for you. Make a brief outline to guide you as you write, as in the examples below.

Thesis: Separating from my husband was the worst mistake I made last year.
1.   Children have suffered
2.   Financial troubles
3.   Loneliness

Thesis: Buying a used car to commute to school was the worst mistake of last year.
1.   Unreliable—late for class or missed class
2.   Expenses for insurance, repairs
3.   Led to an accident

3 A VALUED POSSESSION

Write an essay about a valued material possession. Here are some suggestions:

Car	Appliance
Computer	Cell phone
TV set	Photograph album
Piece of furniture	Piece of clothing
Piece of jewelry	Stereo system (car or home)
Camera	Piece of hobby equipment

In your introductory paragraph, describe the possession: tell what it is, when and where you got it, and how long you have owned it. Your thesis statement should center on the idea that there are several reasons this possession is so important to you. In each of your supporting paragraphs, provide details to back up one of the reasons.

For example, here is a brief outline of an essay written about a leather jacket:

1.   It is comfortable.
2.   It wears well.
3.   It makes me look and feel good.

4 SINGLE LIFE

Write an essay on the advantages or drawbacks of single life. To get started, make a list of all the advantages and drawbacks you can think of. Advantages might include:

Fewer expenses

Fewer responsibilities

More personal freedom

More opportunities to move or travel

Copyright ©2006 The McGraw-Hill Companies, Inc. All rights reserved.

Drawbacks might include:

> Parental disapproval
>
> Being alone at social events
>
> No companion for shopping, movies, and so on
>
> Sadness at holiday time

After you make up two lists, select the thesis for which you feel you have more supporting material. Then organize your material into a scratch outline. Be sure to include an introduction, a clear topic sentence for each supporting paragraph, and a conclusion.

Alternatively, write an essay on the advantages or drawbacks of married life. Follow the directions given above.

5 INFLUENCES ON YOUR WRITING

Are you as good a writer as you want to be? Write an essay analyzing the reasons you have become a good writer or explaining why you are not as good as you'd like to be. Begin by considering some factors that may have influenced your writing ability.

> *Your family background:* Did you see people writing at home? Did your parents respect and value the ability to write?
>
> *Your school experience:* Did you have good writing teachers? Did you have a history of failure or success with writing? Was writing fun, or was it a chore? Did your school emphasize writing?
>
> *Social influences:* How did your school friends do at writing? What were your friends' attitudes toward writing? What feelings about writing did you pick up from TV or the movies?

You might want to organize your essay by describing the three greatest influences on your skill (or your lack of skill) as a writer. Show how each of these has contributed to the present state of your writing.

6 A MAJOR DECISION

All of us come to various crossroads in our lives—times when we must make an important decision about which course of action to follow. Think about a major decision you had to make (or one you are planning to make). Then write an essay on the reasons for your decision. In your introduction, describe the decision you have reached. Each of the body paragraphs that follow should fully explain one of the reasons for your decision. Here are some examples of major decisions that often confront people:

Copyright ©2006 The McGraw-Hill Companies, Inc. All rights reserved.

Enrolling in or dropping out of college

Accepting or quitting a job

Getting married or divorced

Breaking up with a boyfriend or girlfriend

Having a baby

Moving away from home

Student papers on this topic include the essay on page 318 and the paragraphs on pages 54–55.

7 REVIEWING A TV SHOW OR MOVIE

Write an essay about a television show or movie you have seen very recently. The thesis of your essay will be that the show (or movie) has both good and bad features. (If you are writing about a TV series, be sure that you evaluate only one episode.)

In your first supporting paragraph, briefly summarize the show or movie. Don't get bogged down in small details here; just describe the major characters briefly and give the highlights of the action.

In your second supporting paragraph, explain what you feel are the best features of the show or movie. Listed below are some examples of good features you might write about:

Suspenseful, ingenious, or realistic plot

Good acting

Good scenery or special effects

Surprise ending

Good music

Believable characters

In your third supporting paragraph, explain what you feel are the worst features of the show or movie. Here are some possibilities:

Far-fetched, confusing, or dull plot

Poor special effects

Bad acting

Cardboard characters

Unrealistic dialogue

Remember to cover only a few features in each paragraph; do not try to include everything.

8 YOUR HIGH SCHOOL

Imagine that you are an outside consultant called in as a neutral observer to examine the high school you attended. After your visit, you must send the school board a five-paragraph letter in which you describe the most striking features (good, bad, or a combination of both) of the school and the evidence for each of these features.

In order to write the letter, you may want to think about the following features of your high school:

Attitude of the teachers, student body, or administration

Condition of the buildings, classrooms, recreational areas, and so on

Curriculum

How classes are conducted

Extracurricular activities

Crowded or uncrowded conditions

Be sure to include an introduction, a clear topic sentence for each supporting paragraph, and a conclusion.

9 BEING ONE'S OWN WORST ENEMY

"A lot of people are their own worst enemies" is a familiar saying. We all know people who find ways to hurt themselves. Write an essay describing someone you know who is his or her own worst enemy. In your paper, introduce the person and explain his or her self-destructive behaviors. A useful way to gather ideas for this paper is to combine two prewriting techniques—outlining and listing. Begin with an outline of the general areas you expect to cover. Here's an outline that may work:

Introduce the person in the first paragraph.

Describe the self-destructive behavior in two or more supporting paragraphs.

Suggest changes in the concluding paragraph.

Once you have a workable outline, make a list to produce specific details for each point in the outline. For example, here are one student's lists for the points in the outline:

Person

    Vanessa

    Just graduated from high school

    Works at a department store

    Wants to go to college, but needs money

Hurtful behaviors

    Just moved into own apartment, which costs much more than living at home

    Spends a lot of money on clothing

    Makes no effort to find financial aid to continue her schooling

Changes

    Stop spending so much and start saving

    Get information from school financial aid offices

10 PARENTS AND CHILDREN

It has been said that the older we get, the more we see our parents in ourselves. Indeed, our temperament and many of our habits (good and bad) and beliefs can often be traced to one of our parents.

Write a paragraph in which you describe three characteristics you have "inherited" from a parent. You might want to think about your topic by asking yourself a series of questions: "How am I like my mother (or father)?" "When and where am I like her (or him)?" "Why am I like her (or him)?"

One student who wrote such a paper used the following thesis statement: "Although I hate to admit it, I know that in several ways I'm just like my mom." She then went on to describe how she works too hard, worries too much, and judges other people too harshly. Another student wrote, "I resemble my father in my love of TV sports, my habit of putting things off, and my reluctance to show my feelings." Be sure to include examples for each of the characteristics you mention.

11 INFLUENTIAL PEOPLE

Who are the three people who have been the most important influences in your life? Write an essay describing each of these people and explaining how each of them has helped you. For example:

It was my aunt who first impressed upon me the importance of a college education.

If it weren't for my father, I wouldn't be in college today.

My best friend has helped me with my college education in several ways.

Copyright ©2006 The McGraw-Hill Companies, Inc. All rights reserved.

To develop support for this paper, make a list of all the ways each person helped you get your bearings and focus on a college path. Alternatively, you could do some freewriting about each person you're writing about. These prewriting techniques—listing and freewriting—are both helpful ways of getting started with a paper and thinking about it on paper.

12 HEROES FOR THE HUMAN RACE

Many people would agree that three men who died in recent years were a credit to the human race. Christopher Reeve played Superman in the movies but became one in real life by fighting a spinal-cord injury. Charles Schultz was the creator of the world-famous comic strip *Peanuts,* whose characters dealt with anxieties we could all understand. Fred Rogers starred in the well-known television show *Mr. Rogers' Neighborhood,* which children and adults still watch today. Write an essay in which three separate supporting paragraphs explain in detail why each of these men can be regarded as a hero for humanity. Chapter 19, "A Quick Guide to Research" (pages 341–352), will show you how to do the necessary research.

Copyright ©2006 The McGraw-Hill Companies Inc. All rights reserved.

PART FOUR

A Quick Guide to Research

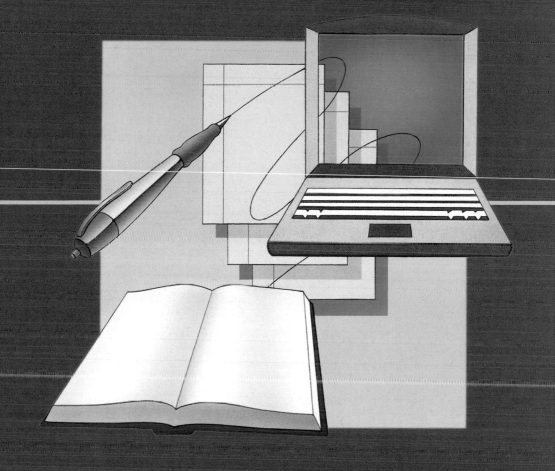

PREVIEW

The purpose of Part Four is to show you, in a clear, quick, and practical way, how to find information on almost any topic. With the help of a computer, research can be done more easily than ever before. When you have learned (1) how to use a computer search engine and (2) how to search for books online and in your library, you should be well-equipped to write the papers and reports required in your courses.

19 A Quick Guide to Research

Research on almost any subject can often be done in two simple steps:

1   Use a computer that connects you to the Internet.

2   Take advantage of the free search engine Google.

Copyright ©2006 The McGraw-Hill Companies, Inc. All rights reserved.

Using the Internet

Before we look at the wonders of Google, let's review briefly how the Internet works. The Internet is a giant network that connects computers at tens of thousands of educational, scientific, government, and commercial organizations around the world. All the individual Web sites in this global information system are linked together, forming a kind of web, and the Internet is sometimes called the World Wide Web.

To use the Internet, you need a personal computer with a *modem*—a device that sends or receives electronic data over a telephone or cable line. You also need software (such as AOL or Explorer) that will enable your computer to visit Web sites. And if you have a printer for your computer, you can do a good deal of your research at home, for you can simply print out information that you find. Alternatively, you can use a computer and printer available at your school library.

Once you are online, open up a search engine such as Google. A search engine, as its name suggests, and as the cartoon here humorously implies, is a powerful search tool. In a matter of seconds, it will help you go through a vast amount of information on the Web to find articles about almost any topic.

"Go ask your search engine."

© The New Yorker Collection 2000 John Caldwell from cartoonbank.com
All Rights Reserved.

Using Google

Open up Google by typing:

www.google.com

You'll then get a screen similar to the illustration here. As you can see, a box appears in which you can type one or more keywords—after which you then click "Google Search."

Examples of Google Searches

Here are ten examples of Google searches. As you read them, you should get a good sense of just how Google may be helpful in your research and school work.

Example 1   Your sociology instructor asks you to prepare a paper on gay marriage.

After typing in "gay marriage" and clicking "Google Search," Ryan got—in less than one second—a list of over 4 million "hits," with each item a link to individual articles, reports, stories, opinion papers, research studies, or even entire Web sites about gay marriage. Of course, 4 million items cannot be shown on one screen; Ryan would have to keep scrolling for many days to look at each item—let alone clicking, opening up, and reading each one! Fortunately, Ryan didn't have to do this, for Google does a good job of listing first what other people have found to be the most helpful items.

Ryan then decided to have Google help narrow his search. He typed in "drawbacks of gay marriage." The result was more than 17,000 items providing

Copyright ©2006 The McGraw-Hill Companies, Inc All rights reserved.

information about drawbacks of gay marriage. If that was the direction Ryan chose to take in a paper, he had plenty of material to choose from.

Example 2   Your psychology instructor asks you to prepare a report on Fred Rogers, of *Mr. Rogers' Neighborhood.*

After typing in "Fred Rogers" and clicking "Google Search," Michelle got, in less than one second, a list of over 1 million items. She then decided to have Google help narrow her search. She typed in "contribution of Fred Rogers to children" and got 27,000 items. Within the first 10 items she found all the information she needed for her report.

Michelle then decided she wanted to include a photograph of Fred Rogers in her report, so she went to Google again and clicked "Images" (which, as you'll see in the illustration on page 342, appears to the right of the word "Web"). A search box appeared, she typed in "Fred Rogers, " and she immediately got more than 2,000 photographs and illustrations of Fred Rogers to choose from.

Example 3   Your business instructor asks you to prepare a paper on the decline and fall of Enron Corporation.

Fred typed in "Enron," which yielded more than a 1.5 million items. He then narrowed his search by typing "what happened to Enron" and got almost 150,000 responses. He then decided to focus on the role of Enron's president, Ken Lay. He typed in "Ken Lay's role in what happened to Enron" and got more than 300 responses—more than enough for him to do the research needed for his paper.

Example 4   Your English instructor wants you to prepare a paper on Edgar Allan Poe's famous short story "The Tell-Tale Heart."

Lisa typed in "Poe's The Tell-Tale Heart" and got more than 7,000 hits. She then narrowed her search by typing "interpretations of Poe's The Tell-Tale Heart" and got 500 responses   more than enough for her to do the necessary research.

Example 5   You want to get current news.

Go to Google and click on "News" (which, as you'll see in the illustration on page 342, appears three items to the right of "Web"). When the news of the day comes up, you can type in the search box any current topic you want to investigate. For example, typing in "stem cell research" brought up 10,000 items.

Example 6   You want to find out what books are available online.

Go to Google and type "books online." You'll find enough books online, including many classics which are now out of copyright, for a lifetime of reading. If you are researching a particular topic, such as animal rights, type in "books online about animal rights" to find any books on your topic available online.

Example 7   You want to find other search engines.

Go to Google and type "other search engines." You'll find the names of plenty of other engines you could use to search the Web. As of this writing, however, Google is regarded as one of the best.

Example 8   You want to check the spelling of "accommodate."

Go to Google and type "spelling of acomodate." Google will respond "Did you mean: spelling of *accommodate*." It will do the same for many words you are unsure of how to spell.

Example 9   You want to review run-on sentences, which your English instructor has flagged in your writing.

Go to Google and type "run-on sentences." You'll find explanations and examples.

Example 10   You want to look up the meaning of a word.

Go to Google and type "meaning of cogent" or "meaning of surmise" or whatever word you need defined. You'll get an instant response.

I could go on and on with more examples, but you get the point: Use a first-rate Internet search engine such as Google to help you find information fast. Very often with searches, your challenge will be getting too much information rather than too little. Always be prepared, then, to experiment with keywords to narrow your topic.

Here are five topics along with narrowed versions of those topics. A rounded-off number of hits for each keyword is shown at the right. Note that very often when you type in a general topic like "date rape," the items that come up will give you ideas about how to narrow and focus your topic.

Date rape	2.5 million
How to stop date rape	600,000
How schools can stop date rape	170,000
Organ donation	500,000
How to donate organs	100,000
False ideas about organ donation	50,000
Prison reform	900,000
History of prison reform	400,000
Drawbacks to prison reform	6,000

Job prospects	2 million
Best job prospects	1 million
Best job prospects next ten years	400,000
Heroes	8 million
Absence of heroes today	115,000
Absence of sports heroes today	33,000

ACTIVITY

Do a search for the three items below. Suggest two ways of narrowing each search, as in the examples above.

1. Home schooling

   _____

   _____

2. Child abuse

   _____

   _____

3. Road rage

   _____

   _____

Copyright ©2006 The McGraw-Hill Companies, Inc. All rights reserved.

Finding Books

To find books on a topic you are researching, you can do two things:

1   Visit booksellers online.

2   Visit your library.

Books Online

To find books on your topic, go online and type in the Web address of one of the large commercial online booksellers:

Amazon at *www.amazon.com*

Barnes and Noble at *www.bn.com*

The easy-to-use search functions of both Amazon and Barnes and Noble are free, and you are under no obligation to buy books from them.

After you arrive at a bookstore Web site, go to the search box and type in keywords for the topic you would like to research. For example, I typed "drug abuse among teenagers" in the Amazon search box and got 37,000 book titles as a result. I then had the option of having the books shown in a list with the bestselling ones first. I clicked one of these books—*Drugs, Lies, and Teenagers*—and was able to browse the table of contents and an excerpt from the book.

Here's the point: Use an online bookstore site to get information quickly about books that might be of value in your research. Just the titles of books can help you decide on ways to narrow your focus for your research project. You can then go to your library to get a copy of books you want. Alternatively, you may be able to order used copies of books inexpensively online.

Books in Your Library

To get a book in your library, you need to know how to use your library. If you don't know, and time is short, you can say to someone at the library front desk, "I need such-and-such a book. Can you help me see if the library has it? If so, can you find it for me so I can check it out? I would really appreciate your help." In many cases, a library staff person will be able to help you.

Of course, in the long run you should know how to use your library. Following are guidelines that will help.

Main Desk   The main desk is usually located in a central spot. Find it and ask for a handout or map that describes the layout and services of the library. Or ask if someone can give you a tour.

ACTIVITY

Make up a floor plan of your college library. Label the main desk, card file, book stacks, magazine file, and magazine storage area.

Catalog   The *catalog* will be your starting point for almost any research project. The catalog is a list of all the books in the library. It may be an actual card catalog: a file of cards alphabetically arranged in drawers. More likely, the catalog is computerized and can be accessed on computer terminals located at different spots in the library. And increasingly, local and college libraries can be accessed online, so you may be able to check their book holdings on your home computer.

Copyright ©2006 The McGraw-Hill Companies, Inc. All rights reserved.

Finding a Book: Author, Title, and Subject   There are three ways to look up a book: according to *author, title,* or *subject.* For example, suppose you wanted to see if the library has the book *Amazing Grace* by Jonathan Kozol. You could check for the book in any of the following ways:

1   You could go to the *author* section of the catalog and look it up there under *K*. An author is always listed under his or her last name.

2   You could go to the *title* section of the catalog and look it up there under "Amazing." Note that you always look up a book under the first word in the title, excluding the words *A, An,* or *The*.

3   If you know the subject that the book deals with—in this case, "poor children"—you could go to the *subject* section of the catalog and look it up under *Poor*.

Here is the author entry in a computerized card catalog for Kozol's book *Amazing Grace:*

Author:	Kozol, Jonathan
Title:	Amazing Grace
Publisher:	Crown, 1995
LC Subjects:	1. Poor children—New York (N.Y.) 2. Racism and racial segregation—New York (N.Y.) 3. Children of minorities—New York (N.Y.) 4. AIDS, asthma, illnesses of children.
Call Number:	362.709 Koz
Material:	Book
Location:	Cherry Hill
Status:	Available

Note that in addition to giving you the publisher (Crown) and year of publication (1995), the entry also tells you the *call number*—where to find the book in the library. If the computerized catalog is part of a network of libraries, you may also learn at what branch or location the book is available. If the book is not at your library, you can probably arrange for an interlibrary loan.

Using Subject Headings to Research a Topic   Generally if you are looking for a particular book, it is easier to use the *author* or *title* section of the catalog. On the other hand, if you are researching a topic, then the *subject* section is where you should look.

The subject section performs three valuable functions:

- It will give you a list of books on a given topic.

- It will often provide related topics that might have information on your subject.

- It will suggest more limited topics, helping you narrow your general topic.

Chances are you will be asked to do a research paper of about five to fifteen pages. You do not want to choose a topic so broad that it could be covered only by an entire book or more. Instead, you want to come up with a limited topic that can be adequately supported in a relatively short paper. As you search the subject section, take advantage of ideas that it might offer on how you can narrow your topic.

ACTIVITY

Answer the following questions about the card catalog.

1. Is your library's book catalog an actual file of cards in drawers, or is it computerized? _____

2. Which section of the catalog will help you research and limit a topic?

   _____

Book Stacks   The *book stacks* are the library shelves where books are arranged according to their call numbers. The *call number,* as distinctive as a social security number, always appears on a call file for any book. It is also printed on the spine of every book in the library.

If your library has open stacks (ones that you are permitted to enter), here is how to find a book. Suppose you are looking for *Amazing Grace,* which has the call number HV875 / N48 / K69 in the Library of Congress system. (Libraries using the Dewey decimal system have call letters made up entirely of numbers rather than letters and numbers. However, you use the same basic method to locate a book.) First, you go to the section of the stacks that holds the H's. After you locate the H's, you look for the HV's. After that, you look for the HV875. Finally, you look for HV875 / N48 /K69, and you have the book.

If your library has *closed stacks* (ones you are not permitted to enter), you will have to write down the title, author, and call number on a slip of paper. (Such slips

Copyright ©2006 The McGraw-Hill Companies, Inc. All rights reserved.

of paper will be available near the card catalog or computer terminals.) You'll then give the slip to a library staff person, who will locate the book and bring it to you.

ACTIVITY

Which system of classifying books is used by your library: the Library of Congress system or the Dewey decimal system? _____

Notes on Writing a Research-Based Paper

Develop a Limited Topic

The paper should be narrow and deep rather than broad and shallow. Therefore, as you search on the Internet, look for ways to limit a general topic.

Do not expect to limit your topic and make your purpose clear all at once. Gradually, through trial and error, you can work out a limited focus for your paper. Note that many research-based papers have one of two purposes:

1   Your purpose might be to make and defend a point of some kind. For example, your purpose might be to provide evidence that gambling should be legalized in your state.

2   Depending on the course and the instructor, your purpose might be simply to present information about a particular subject. For instance, you might be asked to write a paper that describes the most recent scientific findings about what happens when we dream.

Prepare a Scratch Outline

As you read through material you are gathering, think constantly about the content and organization of your paper. Begin making decisions about exactly what information you will present and how you will arrange it. Prepare a scratch outline for your paper that shows both its thesis and the areas of support for the thesis. Try to plan at least three areas of support.

Thesis: _____

Support: (1) _____

(2) _____

(3) _____

Here, for example, is the brief outline that one student prepared for a paper on divorce mediation.

Thesis: Divorce mediation is an alternative to the painful, expensive process of a traditional divorce.

Support: 1. Saves time and money.

2. Produces less hostility.

3. Produces more acceptable agreement between former spouses.

Take Care Not to Plagiarize

If you fail to document information that is not your own, you will be stealing. The formal term is *plagiarizing*—using someone else's work as your own, whether you borrow a single idea, a sentence, or an entire essay.

One example of plagiarism is turning in a friend's paper as if it is one's own. Another example is copying an article found in a source on the Internet and turning it in as one's own. By copying someone else's work, you may risk being failed or even expelled. Equally, plagiarism deprives you of what can be a very helpful learning and organizational experience—researching and writing about a selected topic in detail.

Keep in mind, too, that while the Internet has made it easier for students to plagiarize, it has also made plagiarism riskier. Teachers can discover that a student has taken material from an Internet source by typing a sentence or two from the student's paper into a powerful search engine like Google; the source is then often quickly identified.

Be Careful about your Internet Sources

Keep in mind that the quality and reliability of information you find on the Internet may vary widely. Anyone with a bit of computer know-how can create a Web site and post information there. That person may be a Nobel Prize winner, a leading authority in a specialized field, a high school student, or a crackpot. Be careful, then, to look closely at your electronic source in the following ways:

a.   *Internet address.* Who is sponsoring the website? Look first at the address's extension—the part that follows the "dot." If the extension is *edu* (which indicates an educational institution), *gov* (which indicates a government source), or *org* (which indicates a nonprofit organization), it is probably a reliable source.

If the extension is *com* or *net* (which indicates a commercial or business or private individual source), reliability may vary.

b. *Author.* What credentials does the author have (if any)? Has the author published other material on the topic?

c. *Internal evidence.* Does the author produce solid, adequate support for his or her views?

d. *Date.* Is the information up-to-date? Check at the top or bottom of the document for copyright, publication, or revision dates. Knowing such dates will help you decide whether the material is current enough for your purposes.

Document Your Sources

When you take material from a source and use it in your paper, document that source. Here is an example from a paper on divorce mediation:

> Divorce is never easy. Even if two people both want to break up, ending a marriage is a painful experience. In order to become divorced, most people go through a process that increases this pain. Starting with the lawsuit that one partner files against the other, the two take on the roles of enemies. As one author describes it, "You will each hire lawyers who will fight on your behalf like ancient knights, charging each other with lances. But the wounds inflicted don't appear on the other warrior: they appear on you, your spouse, and your children" (James 3).

Within your paper, use only brief citations such as "James 3" above, in which "James" is the author's last name and "3" is the page number where the information was found. Then, at the end of your paper, include a page with the heading "Works Cited." On this page, list in full each source you drew on. Here is the full source for the quotation from James:

James, Paula. The Divorce Mediation Handbook. San
    Francisco: Jossey-Bass, 1997.

To get more information about documenting sources and to see a model research paper, visit www.mhhe.com/langan/es and click on **Ch. 19: Research Paper.**

Copyright ©2006 The McGraw-Hill Companies, Inc. All rights reserved.

ACTIVITY

1. By using Google and Amazon on the Internet, find the titles of three books and three Internet articles about teenage fathers *or* about adoption.

    Three books:

    _____

    _____

    _____

    Three Internet articles:

    _____

    _____

    _____

2. By using Google and Amazon on the Internet, find the titles of three books and three Internet articles about road rage *or* about noise pollution.

    Three books:

    _____

    _____

    _____

    Three Internet articles:

    _____

    _____

    _____

Copyright ©2006 The McGraw-Hill Companies, Inc. All rights reserved.

PART FIVE

Handbook of Sentence Skills

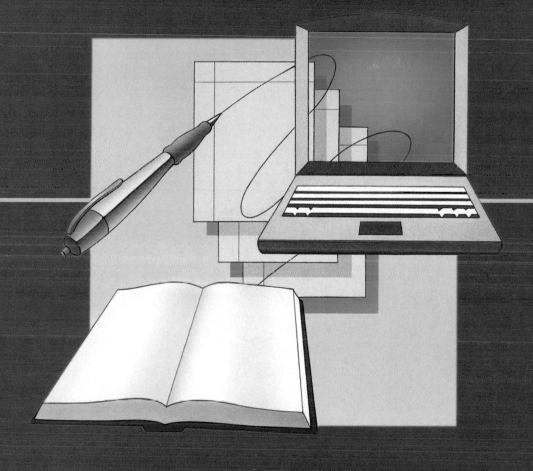

PREVIEW

As explained in Part One, there are four steps, or bases, in effective writing. Part Five is concerned with the fourth step: the ability to write clear, error-free sentences. First a diagnostic test is provided so that you can check your present understanding of important sentence skills. Then the skills themselves appear under the general headings "Grammar," "Mechanics," "Punctuation," and "Word Use." Then there is a chapter that presents pointers and brief activities for ESL students. Next come mastery tests and then editing tests that reinforce many basic writing skills and give you practice in editing and proofreading. Closing Part Five is an achievement test that helps you measure your improvement in important sentence skills.

Sentence-Skills Diagnostic Test

Part 1

This test will help you check your knowledge of important sentence skills. Certain parts of the following word groups are underlined. Write X in the answer space if you think a mistake appears at the underlined part. Write C in the answer space if you think the underlined part is correct.

A series of headings ("Fragments," "Run-Ons," and so on) will give you clues to the mistakes to look for. However, you do not have to understand the label to find a mistake. What you are checking is your own sense of effective written English.

Fragments

_____ 1. Until his mother called him twice. Barry did not get out of bed. He had stayed up too late the night before.

_____ 2. After I slid my aching bones into the hot water of the tub, I realized there was no soap. I didn't want to get out again.

_____ 3. Mother elephants devote much of their time to child care. Nursing their babies up to eight years.

_____ 4. Sweating under his heavy load. Brian staggered up the stairs to his apartment. He felt as though his legs were crumbling beneath him.

_____ 5. I love to eat and cook Italian food, especially lasagna and ravioli. I make everything from scratch.

_____ 6. One of my greatest joys in life is eating desserts. Such as blueberry cheesecake and vanilla cream puffs. Almond fudge cake makes me want to dance.

Run-Ons

_____ 7. He decided to stop smoking, for he didn't want to die of lung cancer.

_____ 8. The window shade snapped up like a gunshot her cat leaped four feet off the floor.

Copyright ©2006 The McGraw-Hill Companies, Inc. All rights reserved.

_____ 9. Billy is the meanest little kid on his block, he eats only the heads of animal crackers.

_____ 10. He knew he had flunked the driver's exam, he ran over a stop sign.

_____ 11. My first boyfriend was five years old. We met every day in the playground sandbox.

_____ 12. The store owner watched the shopper carefully, she suspected him of stealing from her before.

Standard English Verbs

_____ 13. Jed tows cars away for a living and is ashamed of his job.

_____ 14. You snored like a chain saw last night.

_____ 15. When I was about to finish work last night, a man walk into the restaurant and ordered two dozen hamburgers.

_____ 16. Charlotte react badly whenever she gets caught in a traffic jam.

Irregular Verbs

_____ 17. I gave a twenty-dollar bill to the cashier and waited for my change.

_____ 18. I had eaten so much food at the buffet dinner that I went into the bathroom just to loosen my belt.

_____ 19. When the mud slide started, the whole neighborhood began going downhill.

_____ 20. Juan has rode the bus to school for two years while saving for a car.

Subject-Verb Agreement

_____ 21. There is long lines at the checkout counter.

_____ 22. The little girl have a painful ear infection.

_____ 23. One of the crooked politicians was jailed for a month.

_____ 24. The cockroaches behind my stove gets high on Raid.

Consistent Verb Tense

_____ 25. My brother and I played video games for an hour before we start to do homework.

Copyright © 2006 The McGraw-Hill Companies, Inc. All rights reserved.

_____ 26. The first thing Jerry does every day is weigh himself. The scale informs him what kind of meals he can eat that day.

_____ 27. Sandy eats a nutritional breakfast, skips lunch, and then enjoys a big dinner.

_____ 28. His parents stayed together for his sake; only after he graduates from college were they divorced.

Pronoun Agreement, Reference, and Point of View

_____ 29. I get my hair cut by a barber who talks to you constantly.

_____ 30. I enjoy movies, like *The Return of the Vampire,* that frighten me.

_____ 31. Every guest at the party dressed like their favorite cartoon character.

_____ 32. Persons camping in those woods should watch their step because of wild dogs.

_____ 33. Angry because he had struck out, Tony hurled the baseball bat at the fence and broke it.

_____ 34. I love hot peppers, but they do not always agree with me.

Pronoun Types

_____ 35. Alfonso and me take turns driving to work.

_____ 36. No one is a better cook than she.

Adjectives and Adverbs

_____ 37. Bonnie ran quick up the steps, taking them two at a time.

_____ 38. Larry is more better than I am at darts.

Misplaced Modifiers

_____ 39. He swatted the wasp that stung him with a newspaper.

_____ 40. Charlotte returned the hamburger that was spoiled to the supermarket.

_____ 41. Jamal test-drove a car at the dealership with power windows and a sunroof.

_____ 42. I adopted a dog from a junkyard which is very close to my heart.

Dangling Modifiers

_____ 43. Tapping a pencil on the table, Ms. Garcia asked for the students' attention.

_____   44. Flunking out of school, my parents demanded that I get a job.

_____   45. While I was waiting for the bus, rain began to fall.

_____   46. Braking the car suddenly, the shopping bags tumbled onto the floor.

Faulty Parallelism

_____   47. Jeff enjoys hunting for rabbits, socializing with friends, and to read the comics.

_____   48. The recipe instructed me to chop onions, to peel carrots, and to boil a pot of water.

_____   49. When I saw my roommate with my girlfriend, I felt worried, angry, and embarrassment as well.

_____   50. Jackie enjoys shopping for new clothes, surfing the Internet, and walking her dog.

Capital Letters

_____   51. After being out in a cold drizzling rain, I looked forward to a bowl of campbell's soup for lunch.

_____   52. During july, Frank's company works a four-day week.

_____   53. A woman screamed, "He's stolen my purse!"

_____   54. On Summer days I will drink glass after glass of lemonade.

Apostrophe

_____   55. The Wolfman's bite is worse than his bark.

_____   56. Clydes quick hands reached out to break his son's fall.

_____   57. I'll be with you shortly if youll just wait a minute.

_____   58. We didn't leave the rude waiter any tip.

Quotation Marks

_____   59. Mark Twain once said, "The more I know about human beings, the more I like my dog."

_____   60. Say something tender to me, "whispered Tony to Lola."

_____   61. "I hate that commercial, he muttered."

_____   62. "If you don't leave soon," he warned, "you'll be late for work."

Comma

_____ 63. My favorite sandwich includes turkey tomatoes lettuce and mayonnaise on whole-wheat bread.

_____ 64. Although I have a black belt in karate I decided to go easy on the demented bully who had kicked sand in my face.

_____ 65. All the tree branches, which were covered with ice, glittered like diamonds.

_____ 66. We could always tell when our instructor felt disorganized for his shirt would not be tucked into his pants.

_____ 67. Dogs, according to most cat lovers, are inferior pets.

_____ 68. His father shouted "Why don't you go out and get a job?"

Commonly Confused Words

_____ 69. The best way to prevent colds and flu is to wash you're hands several times a day.

_____ 70. Since he's lost weight, most of Max's clothes are to big for him.

_____ 71. They're planning to trade in their old car.

_____ 72. Its important to get this job done properly.

_____ 73. Will you except this job if it's offered to you, or keep looking for something better?

_____ 74. Who's the culprit who left the paint can on the table?

Effective Word Choice

_____ 75. Because the school was flooded, the dance had to be postponed until a later date.

_____ 76. The movie was a real bomb, so we left early.

_____ 77. The victims of the car accident were shaken but none the worse for wear.

_____ 78. Anne is of the opinion that the death penalty should be abolished.

Answers are on page 739.

Copyright ©2006 The McGraw-Hill Companies, Inc. All rights reserved.

Part 2 (Optional)

Do Part 2 at your instructor's request. This second part of the test will provide more detailed information about skills you need to know. On separate paper, number and correct all the items you have marked with an X. For example, suppose you had marked the following word groups with an X. (Note that these examples are not taken from the test.)

4. <u>If football games disappeared entirely from television.</u> I would not even miss them. Other people in my family would perish.

7. The kitten suddenly saw her reflection in the <u>mirror, she</u> jumped back in surprise.

15. I wanted to get close enough to see the tag on the stray <u>dogs</u> collar.

29. When we go out to a <u>restaurant we</u> always order something we would not cook for ourselves.

Here is how you should write your corrections on a separate sheet of paper.

4. television, I

7. mirror, and

15. dog's

29. restaurant, we

There are more than forty corrections to make in all.

Copyright ©2005 The McGraw-Hill Companies, Inc. All rights reserved.

Grammar

20 Subjects and Verbs

The basic building blocks of English sentences are subjects and verbs. Understanding them is an important first step toward mastering a number of sentence skills.

Every sentence has a subject and a verb. Who or what the sentence speaks about is called the subject; what the sentence says about the subject is called the verb.

> The children laughed.
>
> Several branches fell.
>
> Most students passed the test.
>
> That man is a hero.

A Simple Way to Find a Subject

To find a subject, ask *who* or *what* the sentence is about. As shown below, your answer is the subject.

> *Who* is the first sentence about? Children
>
> *What* is the second sentence about? Several branches
>
> *Who* is the third sentence about? Most students
>
> *Who* is the fourth sentence about? That man

A Simple Way to Find a Verb

To find a verb, ask what the sentence *says about* the subject. As shown below, your answer is the verb.

> What does the first sentence *say about* the children? They laughed.
>
> What does the second sentence *say about* the branches? They fell.

What does the third sentence *say about* the students? They <u>passed</u>.

What does the fourth sentence *say about* that man? He <u>is</u> (a hero).

A second way to find the verb is to put *I, you, we, he, she, it,* or *they* (whichever form is appropriate) in front of the word you think is a verb. If the result makes sense, you have a verb. For example, you could put *they* in front of *laughed* in the first sentence above, with the result, *they laughed,* making sense. Therefore you know that *laughed* is a verb. You could use *they* or *he,* for instance, to test the other verbs as well.

Finally, it helps to remember that most verbs show action. In the sentences already considered, the three action verbs are *laughed, fell,* and *passed.* Certain other verbs, known as *linking verbs,* do not show action. They do, however, give information about the subject. In "That man is a hero," the linking verb *is* tells us that the man is a hero. Other common linking verbs include *am, are, was, were, feel, appear, look, become,* and *seem.*

ACTIVITY

In each of the following sentences, draw one line under the subject and two lines under the verb.

1. A sudden thunderstorm ended the baseball game.

2. The curious child stared silently at the shopping mall Santa.

3. The test directions confused the students.

4. Cotton shirts feel softer than polyester ones.

5. The fog rolled into the cemetery.

6. Yoko invited her friends to dinner.

7. A green fly stung her on the ankle.

8. Every other night, garbage trucks rumble down my street on their way to the river.

9. The elderly man sat for a few minutes on the park bench.

10. With their fingers, the children drew pictures on the steamed window.

More about Subjects and Verbs

1   A pronoun (a word like *he, she, it, we, you,* or *they* used in place of a noun) can serve as the subject of a sentence. For example:

> <u>He</u> <u>seems</u> like a lonely person.
> <u>They</u> both <u>like</u> to gamble.

Without a surrounding context (so that we know who *He* or *They* refers to), such sentences may not seem clear, but they *are* complete.

2   A sentence may have more than one verb, more than one subject, or several subjects and verbs:

> My <u>heart</u> <u>skipped</u> and <u>pounded</u>.
> The <u>money</u> and <u>credit cards</u> <u>were stolen</u> from the wallet.
> <u>Dave</u> and <u>Ellen</u> <u>prepared</u> the report together and <u>presented</u> it to the class.

3   The subject of a sentence never appears within a prepositional phrase. A *prepositional phrase* is simply a group of words that begins with a preposition. Following is a list of common prepositions:

about	before	by	inside	over
above	behind	during	into	through
across	below	except	of	to
among	beneath	for	off	toward
around	beside	from	on	under
at	between	in	onto	with

Cross out prepositional phrases when you are looking for the subject of a sentence.

> ~~Under my pillow~~ I found a quarter left by the tooth fairy.
> One ~~of the yellow lights at the school crossing~~ began flashing.
> The comics pages ~~of the newspaper~~ have disappeared.
> ~~In spite of my efforts~~, Bob dropped out of school.
> ~~During a rainstorm~~, I sat in my car reading magazines.

Copyright ©2006 The McGraw-Hill Companies, Inc. All rights reserved.

4   Many verbs consist of more than one word. Here, for example, are some of the many forms of the verb *smile*.

smile	smiled	should smile
smiles	were smiling	will be smiling
does smile	have smiled	can smile
is smiling	had smiled	could be smiling
are smiling	had been smiling	must have smiled

Notes

a   Words like *not, just, never, only,* and *always* are not part of the verb, although they may appear within the verb.

Larry <u>did</u> not <u>finish</u> the paper before class.

The road <u>was</u> just <u>completed</u> last week.

b   No verb preceded by *to* is ever the verb of a sentence.

My car suddenly <u>began</u> to sputter on the freeway.

I <u>swerved</u> to avoid a squirrel on the road.

c   No *-ing* word by itself is ever the verb of a sentence. (It may be part of the verb, but it must have a helping verb in front of it.)

They <u>leaving</u> early for the game. (not a sentence, because the verb is not complete)

They <u>are leaving</u> early for the game. (a sentence)

ACTIVITY

Draw a single line under the subjects and a double line under the verbs in the following sentences. Be sure to include all parts of the verb.

1. A burning odor from the wood saw filled the room.

2. At first, sticks of gum always feel powdery on your tongue.

3. Vampires and werewolves are repelled by garlic.

4. Three people in the long bank line looked impatiently at their watches.

5. The driving rain had pasted wet leaves all over the car.

6. She has decided to find a new apartment.

7. The trees in the mall were glittering with tiny white lights.

8. The puppies slipped and tumbled on the vinyl kitchen floor.

9. Tony and Lola ate at Pizza Hut and then went to a movie.

10. We have not met our new neighbors in the apartment building.

REVIEW TEST

Draw a single line under subjects and a double line under verbs. Crossing out prepositional phrases may help you to find the subjects.

1. A cloud of fruit flies hovered over the bananas.

2. Candle wax dripped onto the table and hardened into pools.

3. Nick and Fran are both excellent poker players.

4. The leaves of my dying rubber plant resembled limp brown rags.

5. During the first week of vacation, Ken slept until noon every day.

6. They have just decided to go on a diet together.

7. Psychology and graphic design are my favorite subjects.

8. The sofa in the living room has not been cleaned for over a year.

9. The water stains on her suede shoes did not disappear with brushing.

10. Fred was caught in traffic and, as a result, arrived late for work.

Copyright ©2006 The McGraw-Hill Companies, Inc. All rights reserved.

21 Sentence Sense

What Is Sentence Sense?

As a speaker of English, you already possess the most important of all sentence skills. You have *sentence sense*—an instinctive feel for where a sentence begins, where it ends, and how it can be developed. You learned sentence sense automatically and naturally, as part of learning the English language, and you have practiced it through all the years that you have been speaking English. It is as much a part of you as your ability to speak and understand English is a part of you.

Sentence sense can help you recognize and avoid fragments and run-ons, two of the most common and most serious sentence-skills mistakes in written English. Sentence sense will also help you to place commas, spot awkward and unclear phrasing, and add variety to your sentences.

You may ask, "If I already have this 'sentence sense,' why do I still make mistakes in punctuating sentences?" One answer could be that your past school experiences in writing were unrewarding or unpleasant. English courses may have been a series of dry writing topics and heavy doses of "correct" grammar and usage, or they may have given no attention at all to sentence skills. For any of these reasons, or perhaps for other reasons, the instinctive sentence skills you practice while *speaking* may turn off when you start *writing*. The very act of picking up a pen may shut down your natural system of language abilities and skills.

Turning On Your Sentence Sense

Chances are that you don't *read a paper aloud* after you write it, or you don't do the next best thing: read it "aloud" in your head. But reading aloud is essential to turn on the natural language system within you. By reading aloud, you will be able to hear the points where your sentences begin and end. In addition, you will be able to pick up any trouble spots where your thoughts are not communicated clearly and well.

The activities that follow will help you turn on and rediscover the enormous language power within you. You will be able to see how your built-in sentence sense can guide your writing just as it guides your speaking.

Copyright ©2C06 The McGraw-Hill Companies, Inc. All rights reserved.

ACTIVITY

Each item that follows lacks basic punctuation. There is no period to mark the end of one sentence and no capital letter to mark the start of the next. Read each item aloud (or in your head) so that you "hear" where each sentence begins and ends. Your voice will tend to drop and pause at the point of each sentence break. Draw a light slash mark (/) at every point where you hear a break. Then go back and read the item a second time. If you are now sure of each place where a split occurs, insert a period and change the first small letter after it to a capital. Minor pauses are often marked in English by commas; these are already inserted. Part of item 1 is done for you as an example.

1. I take my dog for a walk on Saturdays in the big park by the lake I do this very early in the morning before children come to the park that way I can let my dog run freely. *H*he jumps out the minute I open the car door and soon sees the first innocent squirrel. *T*then he is off like a shot and doesn't stop running for at least half an hour.

2. Lola hates huge tractor trailers that sometimes tailgate her Honda Civic the enormous smoke-belching machines seem ready to swallow her small car she shakes her fist at the drivers, and she rips out a lot of angry words recently she had a very satisfying dream she broke into an army supply depot and stole at bazooka she then became the first person in history to murder a truck.

3. When I sit down to write, my mind is blank all I can think of is my name, which seems to me the most boring name in the world often I get sleepy and tell myself I should take a short nap other times I start daydreaming about things I want to buy sometimes I decide I should make a telephone call to someone I know the piece of paper in front of me is usually still blank when I leave to watch my favorite television show.

4. One of the biggest regrets of my life is that I never told my father I loved him I resented the fact that he had never been able to say the words "I love you" to his children even during the long period of my father's illness, I remained silent and unforgiving then one morning he was dead, with my words left unspoken a guilt I shall never forget tore a hole in my heart I determined not to hold in my feelings with my daughters they know they are loved, because I both show and tell them this all people, no matter who they are, want to be told that they are loved.

5. Two days ago, Greg killed seven flying ants in his bedroom he also sprayed a column of ants forming a colony along the kitchen baseboard yesterday he picked the newspaper off the porch and two black army ants scurried onto his hand this morning, he found an ant crawling on a lollipop he had left in his shirt pocket if any more insects appear, he is going to call Orkin Pest Control he feels like the victim in a new horror movie called *The Ants* he is half afraid to sleep the darkness may be full of tiny squirming things waiting to crawl all over him.

Summary: Using Sentence Sense

You probably did well in locating the end stops in these selections—proving to yourself that you *do* have sentence sense. This instinctive sense will help you deal with fragments and run-ons, perhaps the two most common sentence-skills mistakes.

Remember the importance of *reading your paper aloud*. By reading aloud, you turn on the natural language skills that come from all your experience of speaking English. The same sentence sense that helps you communicate effectively in speaking will help you communicate effectively in writing.

22 Fragments

Copyright ©2006 The McGraw-Hill Companies, Inc. All rights reserved.

Introductory Project

Every sentence must have a subject and a verb and must express a complete thought. A word group that lacks a subject or a verb and that does not express a complete thought is a fragment. Underline the statement in each numbered item that you think is *not* a complete sentence.

1. Because I could not sleep. I turned on my light and read.

2. Calling his dog's name. Todd walked up and down the street.

3. My little sister will eat anything. Except meat, vegetables, and fruit.

4. The reporter turned on her laptop computer. Then began to type quickly.

Understanding the answers: Read and complete each explanation.

1. *Because I could not sleep* is not a complete sentence. The writer does not complete

   the _____ by telling us what happened because he could not sleep. Correct the fragment by joining it to the sentence that follows it:

   Because I could not sleep, I turned on my light and read.

2. *Calling his dog's name* is not a complete sentence. This word group has no

   _____ and no verb, and it does not express a complete thought. Correct the fragment by adding it to the sentence that follows it:

   Calling his dog's name, Todd walked up and down the street.

3. *Except meat, vegetables, and fruit* is not a complete sentence. Again, the word group

   has no subject and no _____, and it does not express a complete thought. Correct the fragment by adding it to the sentence that comes before it:

   My little sister will eat anything except meat, vegetables, and fruit.

4. *Then began to type quickly* is not a complete sentence. This word group has no

   _____. One way to correct the fragment is to add the subject *she:*

   Then she began to type quickly.

Answers are on page 740.

What Are Fragments?

Every sentence must have a subject and a verb and must express a complete thought. A word group that lacks a subject or a verb and does not express a complete thought is a *fragment*. The most common types of fragments are:

1   Dependent-word fragments

2   *-ing* and *to* fragments

3   Added-detail fragments

4   Missing-subject fragments

Once you understand what specific kinds of fragments you write, you should be able to eliminate them from your writing. The following pages explain all four types of fragments.

Dependent-Word Fragments

Some word groups that begin with a dependent word are fragments. Here is a list of common dependent words:

Dependent Words		
after	if, even if	when, whenever
although, though	in order that	where, wherever
as	since	whether
because	that, so that	which, whichever
before	unless	while
even though	until	who, whoever
how	what, whatever	whose

Whenever you start a sentence with one of these words, you must be careful that a fragment does not result.

Copyright ©2006 The McGraw-Hill Companies, Inc. All rights reserved.

The word group beginning with the dependent word *After* in the example below is a fragment.

After I learned the price of new cars. I decided to keep my old pickup.

A *dependent statement*—one starting with a dependent word like *After*—cannot stand alone. It depends on another statement to complete the thought. "After I learned the price of new cars" is a dependent statement. It leaves us hanging. We expect to find out—in the same sentence—*what happened after* the writer learned the price of new cars. When a writer does not follow through and complete a thought, a fragment results.

To correct the fragment, simply follow through and complete the thought:

After I learned the price of new cars, I decided to keep my old pickup.

Remember, then, that *dependent statements by themselves are fragments.* They must be attached to a statement that makes sense standing alone.

Here are two other examples of dependent-word fragments:

My daughter refused to stop smoking. Unless I quit also.

Tommy made an appointment. Which he did not intend to keep.

"Unless I quit also" is a fragment; it does not make sense standing by itself. We want to know—in the same statement—*what would not happen unless* the writer quit also. The writer must complete the thought. Likewise, "Which he did not intend to keep" is not in itself a complete thought. We want to know in the same statement what *which* refers to.

Correcting a Dependent-Word Fragment

In most cases you can correct a dependent-word fragment by attaching it to the sentence that comes after it or the sentence that comes before it:

After I learned the price of new cars, I decided to keep my old pickup.
(*The fragment has been attached to the sentence that comes after it.*)

My daughter refused to quit smoking unless I quit also.
(*The fragment has been attached to the sentence that comes before it.*)

Tommy made an appointment which he did not intend to keep.
(*The fragment has been attached to the sentence that comes before it.*)

Another way of connecting a dependent-word fragment is simply to eliminate the dependent word by rewriting the sentence:

I learned the price of new cars and decided to keep my old pickup.

She wanted me to quit also.

He did not intend to keep it.

Do not use this method of correction too frequently, however, for it may cut down on interest and variety in your writing style.

Notes

1   Use a comma if a dependent-word group comes at the beginning of a sentence (see also page 491):

   After I learned the price of new cars, I decided to keep my old pickup.

   However, do not generally use a comma if the dependent-word group comes at the end of a sentence:

   My daughter refused to stop smoking unless I quit also.

   Tommy made an appointment which he did not intend to keep.

2   Sometimes the dependent words *who, that, which,* or *where* appear not at the very start, but near the start, of a word group. A fragment often results:

   The town council decided to put more lights on South Street. A place where several people have been mugged.

   "A place where several people have been mugged" is not in itself a complete thought. We want to know in the same statement *where the place was* that several people were mugged. The fragment can be corrected by attaching it to the sentence that comes before it:

   The town council decided to put more lights on South Street, a place where several people have been mugged.

ACTIVITY 1

Turn each of the following dependent-word groups into a sentence by adding a complete thought. Put a comma after the dependent-word group if a dependent word starts the sentence.

EXAMPLES   Although I arrived in class late

Although I arrived in class late, I still did well on the test.

_____

The little boy who plays with our daughter

The little boy who plays with our daughter just came down with

German measles.

_____

1. Because the weather is bad

    _____

    _____

2. If I lend you twenty dollars

    _____

    _____

3. The car that we bought

    _____

    _____

4. Since I was tired

    _____

    _____

5. Before the instructor entered the room

    _____

    _____

ACTIVITY 2

Underline the dependent-word fragment or fragments in each item. Then correct
each fragment by attaching it to the sentence that comes before or the sentence that
comes after it—whichever sounds more natural. Put a comma after the dependent-
word group if it starts the sentence.

Copyright ©2003 The McGraw-Hill Companies, inc. All rights reserved.

1. When a flock of birds is resting in the trees. One always acts as a lookout. It will warn the others of possible danger.

   _____

   _____

   _____

2. Bill always turns on the radio in the morning to hear the news. He wants to get an update on world events. Before he gets on with his day.

   _____

   _____

   _____

3. Although Mr. Simon is over eighty years old. He walks briskly to work every day. He seems like a much younger man. Since he is so active and involved in life.

   _____

   _____

   _____

4. My dog ran in joyous circles on the wide beach. Until she found a dead fish. Before I had a chance to drag her away. She began sniffing and nudging the smelly remains.

   _____

   _____

   _____

5. When the air conditioner broke down. The temperature was over ninety degrees. I then found an old fan. Which turned out to be broken also.

   _____

   _____

   _____

-ing and *to* Fragments

When an *-ing* word appears at or near the start of a word group, a fragment may result. Such fragments often lack a subject and part of the verb. Underline the word groups in the examples below that contain *-ing* words. Each is a fragment.

Example 1

I spent almost two hours on the phone yesterday. Trying to find a garage to repair my car. Eventually I had to have it towed to a garage in another town.

Example 2

Maggie was at first happy with the used SUV she bought from a neighbor. Not realizing until a week later that the vehicle averaged just nine miles per gallon of gas.

Example 3

He looked forward to the study period at school. It being the only time he could sit unbothered and dream about his future. He imagined himself as a lawyer with lots of money and women to spend it on.

People sometimes write *-ing* fragments because they think the subject in one sentence will work for the next word group as well. Thus, in the first example, the writer thinks that the subject *I* in the opening sentence will also serve as the subject for "Trying to find a garage to repair my car." But the subject must actually be *in* the sentence.

Correcting *-ing* Fragments

1   Attach the *-ing* fragment to the sentence that comes before it or the sentence that comes after it, whichever makes sense. Example 1 could read: "I spent almost two hours on the phone yesterday, trying to find a garage to repair my car."

2   Add a subject and change the *-ing* verb part to the correct form of the verb. Example 2 could read: "She did not realize until a week later that the vehicle averaged nine miles per gallon of gas."

3   Change *being* to the correct form of the verb *be (am, are, is, was, were)*. Example 3 could read: "It was the only time he could sit unbothered and dream about his future."

Correcting *to* Fragments

When *to* appears at or near the start of a word group, a fragment sometimes results:

I plan on working overtime. To get this job finished. Otherwise, my boss may get angry at me.

Copyright ©2006 The McGraw-Hill Companies, Inc. All rights reserved.

The second word group is a fragment and can be corrected by adding it to the preceding sentence:

I plan on working overtime to get this job finished.

ACTIVITY 1

Underline the -*ing* fragment in each of the items that follow. Then make it a sentence by rewriting it, using the method described in parentheses.

EXAMPLE   A thunderstorm was brewing. A sudden breeze shot through the windows. <u>Driving the stuffiness out of the room.</u>
(Add the fragment to the preceding sentence.)

A sudden breeze shot through the windows, driving the stuffiness out of the room.

(In the example, a comma is used to set off "driving the stuffiness out of the room," which is extra material placed at the end of the sentence.)

1. Sweating under his heavy load. Brian staggered up the stairs to his apartment. He felt as though his legs were crumbling beneath him.
   (Add the fragment to the sentence that comes after it.)

   _____

   _____

2. He works 10 hours a day. Then going to class for 2½ hours. It is no wonder he writes fragments.
   (Connect the fragment by adding the subject *he* and changing *going* to the proper form of the verb, *goes.*)

   _____

   _____

3. Charlotte loved the classic movie *Gone with the Wind,* but Clyde hated it. His chief objection being that it lasted four hours.
   (Correct the fragment by changing *being* to the proper verb form, *was.*)

   _____

   _____

Copyright ©2006 The McGraw-Hill Companies, Inc. All rights reserved.

ACTIVITY 2

Underline the *-ing* or *to* fragment or fragments in each item. Then rewrite each item, using one of the methods of correction described on pages 374–376.

1. A mysterious package arrived on my porch yesterday. Bearing no return address. I half expected to find a bomb inside.

   _____

   _____

   _____

2. Jack bundled up and went outside on the bitterly cold day. To saw wood for his fireplace. He returned half frozen with only two logs.

   _____

   _____

   _____

3. Looking tired and drawn. The little girl's parents sat in the waiting room. The operation would be over in a few minutes.

   _____

   _____

   _____

4. Sighing with resignation. Jill set aside her credit card bill. She decided simply to not worry about the bill. It being the holiday season.

   _____

   _____

   _____

5. Jabbing the ice with a screwdriver. Luis attempted to speed up the defrosting process in his freezer. However, he used too much force. The result being a freezer compartment riddled with holes.

   _____

   _____

   _____

Added-Detail Fragments

Added-detail fragments lack a subject and a verb. They often begin with one of the following words:

also	except	including
especially	for example	such as

See if you can locate and underline the one added-detail fragment in each of the examples that follow:

Example 1

I love to cook and eat Italian food. Especially spaghetti and lasagna. I make everything from scratch.

Example 2

The class often starts late. For example, yesterday at a quarter after nine instead of at nine sharp. Today the class started at five after nine.

Example 3

He failed a number of courses before he earned his degree. Among them, English I, Economics, and General Biology.

People often write added-detail fragments for much the same reason they write -*ing* fragments. They think the subject and verb in one sentence will serve for the next word group as well. But the subject and verb must be in *each* word group.

Correcting Added-Detail Fragments

1   Attach the fragment to the complete thought that precedes it. Example 1 could read: "I love to cook and eat Italian food, especially spaghetti and lasagna."

2   Add a subject and a verb to the fragment to make it a complete sentence. Example 2 could read: "The class often starts late. For example, yesterday it began at a quarter after nine instead of at nine sharp."

3   Change words as necessary to make the fragment part of the preceding sentence. Example 3 could read: "Among the courses he failed before he earned his degree were English I, Economics, and General Biology."

Copyright ©2006 The McGraw-Hill Companies, Inc. All rights reserved.

ACTIVITY 1

Underline the fragment in each of the items below. Then make it a sentence by rewriting it, using the method described in parentheses.

EXAMPLE   I am always short of pocket money. <u>Especially for everyday items like magazines and sodas.</u> Luckily my friends often have change.
(Add the fragment to the preceding sentence.)

I am always short of pocket money, especially for everyday items like magazines and sodas.

1. There are many little things wrong with this apartment. For example, defective lights and leaking faucets. The landlord is not good about making repairs.
(Correct the fragment by adding the subject and verb *it has*.)

_____

_____

2. I could feel Bill's anger building. Like a land mine ready to explode. I was silent because I didn't want to be the one to set it off.
(Add the fragment to the preceding sentence.)

_____

_____

3. We went on vacation without several essential items. Among other things, our cell phones and rain jackets.
(Correct the fragment by adding the subject and verb *we forgot*.)

_____

_____

ACTIVITY 2

Underline the added-detail fragment in each item. Then rewrite that part of the item needed to correct the fragment. Use one of the three methods of correction described above.

1. It's always hard for me to get up for work. Especially on Monday after a holiday weekend. However, I always wake up early on free days.

_____

_____

2. Tony has enormous endurance. For example, the ability to run five miles in the morning and then play basketball all afternoon.

_____

_____

_____

3. A counselor gives you a chance to talk about your problems. With your family or the boss at work. You learn how to cope better with life.

_____

_____

_____

4. Fred and Martha do much of their gift shopping over the Internet. Especially at Amazon.com.

_____

_____

_____

5. One of my greatest joys in life is eating desserts. Such as cherry cheesecake and vanilla cream puffs. Almond fudge cake makes me want to dance.

_____

_____

_____

Missing-Subject Fragments

In each example below, underline the word group in which the subject is missing.

Example 1

The truck skidded on the rain-slick highway. But missed a telephone pole on the side of the road.

Example 2

Michelle tried each of the appetizers on the table. And then found that, when the dinner arrived, her appetite was gone.

Copyright ©2006 The McGraw-Hill Companies, Inc. All rights reserved.

People write missing-subject fragments because they think the subject in one sentence will apply to the next word group as well. But the subject, as well as the verb, must be in *each* word group to make it a sentence.

Correcting Missing-Subject Fragments

1   Attach the fragment to the preceding sentence. Example 1 could read: "The truck skidded on the rain-slick highway but missed a telephone pole on the side of the road."

2   Add a subject (which can often be a pronoun standing for the subject in the preceding sentence). Example 2 could read: "She then found that, when the dinner arrived, her appetite was gone."

ACTIVITY

Underline the missing-subject fragment in each item. Then rewrite that part of the item needed to correct the fragment. Use one of the two methods of correction described above.

1. I tried on an old suit hanging in our basement closet. And discovered, to my surprise, that it was too tight to button.

    _____

    _____

    _____

2. When Mary had a sore throat, friends told her to gargle with salt water. Or suck on an ice cube. The worst advice she got was to avoid swallowing.

    _____

    _____

    _____

3. One of my grade-school teachers abused us verbally. Also, seated us in rows from the brightest student to the dumbest. I can imagine the pain the student in the last seat must have felt.

    _____

    _____

    _____

> ### A Review: How to Check for Fragments
>
> 1   Read your paper aloud from the *last* sentence to the *first.* You will be better able to see and hear whether each word group you read is a complete thought.
>
> 2   If you think a word group is a fragment, ask yourself: Does this contain a subject and a verb and express a complete thought?
>
> 3   More specifically, be on the lookout for the most common fragments:
>
> - Dependent-word fragments (starting with words like *after, because, since, when,* and *before*)
> - *-ing* and *to* fragments (*-ing* or *to* at or near the start of a word group)
> - Added-detail fragments (starting with words like *for example, such as, also,* and *especially*)
> - Missing-subject fragments (a verb is present but not the subject)

REVIEW TEST 1

Turn each of the following word groups into a complete sentence. Use the spaces provided.

EXAMPLE   With sweaty palms

        With sweaty palms, I walked in for the job interview.

        Even when it rains

        The football teams practice even when it rains.

1. When the alarm sounded

2. In order to save some money

Copyright ©2006 The McGraw-Hill Companies, Inc. All rights reserved.

3. Were having a party

_____

_____

4. To pass the course

_____

_____

5. Geraldo, who is very impatient

_____

_____

6. During the holiday season

_____

_____

7. The store where I worked

_____

_____

8. Before the movie started

_____

_____

9. Down in the basement

_____

_____

10. Feeling very confident

_____

_____

REVIEW TEST 2

Each word group in the student paragraph below is numbered. In the space provided, write C if a word group is a *complete sentence;* write F if it is a *fragment.* You will find seven fragments in the paragraph.

1. _____
2. _____
3. _____
4. _____
5. _____
6. _____
7. _____
8. _____
9. _____
10. _____
11. _____
12. _____
13. _____
14. _____
15. _____
16. _____
17. _____
18. _____
19. _____
20. _____

A Disastrous First Date

¹My first date with Donna was a disaster. ²I decided to take her to a small Italian restaurant. ³That my friends told me had reasonable prices. ⁴I looked over the menu and realized I could not pronounce the names of the dishes. ⁵Such as "veal piccata" and "fettucini Alfredo." ⁶Then, I noticed a burning smell. ⁷The candle on the table was starting to blacken. ⁸And scorch the back of my menu. ⁹Trying to be casual, I quickly poured half my glass of water onto the menu. ¹⁰When the waiter returned to our table. ¹¹He asked me if I wanted to order some wine. ¹²I ordered a bottle of Blue Nun. ¹³The only wine that I had heard of and could pronounce. ¹⁴The waiter brought the wine, poured a small amount into my glass, and waited. ¹⁵I said, "You don't have to stand there. We can pour the wine ourselves." ¹⁶After the waiter put down the wine bottle and left. ¹⁷Donna told me I was supposed to taste the wine. ¹⁸Feeling like a complete fool. ¹⁹I managed to get through the dinner. ²⁰However, for weeks afterward, I felt like jumping out of a tenth-story window.

On separate paper, correct the fragments you have found. Attach each fragment to the sentence that comes before or after it, or make whatever other change is needed to turn the fragment into a sentence.

REVIEW TEST 3

Underline the two fragments in each item. Then rewrite the item in the space provided, making the changes needed to correct the fragments.

EXAMPLE   The people at the sandwich shop save money. By watering down the coffee. Also, using the cheapest grade of hamburger. Few people go there anymore.

The people at the sandwich shop save money by watering down the

coffee. Also, they use the cheapest grade of hamburger. . . .

1. Gathering speed with enormous force. The plane was suddenly in the air. Then it began to climb sharply. And several minutes later leveled off.

    _____

    _____

    _____

Copyright ©2006 The McGraw-Hill Companies, Inc. All rights reserved.

2. Before my neighbors went on vacation. They asked me to watch their house. I agreed to check the premises once a day. Also, to take in their mail.

_____

_____

_____

3. Running untouched into the end zone. The halfback raised his arms in triumph. Then he slammed the football to the ground. And did a little victory dance.

_____

_____

_____

4. It's hard to keep up with bills. Such as the telephone, gas, and electricity. After you finally mail the checks. New bills seem to arrive a day or two later.

_____

_____

_____

5. While a woman ordered twenty pounds of sliced turkey. Customers at the deli counter waited impatiently. The woman explained that she was in charge of a school picnic. And apologized for taking up so much time.

_____

_____

_____

REVIEW TEST 4

Write quickly for five minutes about what you like to do in your leisure time. Don't worry about spelling, punctuation, finding exact words, or organizing your thoughts. Just focus on writing as many words as you can without stopping.

After you have finished, go back and make whatever changes are needed to correct any fragments in your writing.

23 Run-Ons

Introductory Project

A run-on occurs when two sentences are run together with no adequate sign given to mark the break between them. Shown below are four run-ons and four correctly marked sentences. See if you can complete the statement that explains how each run-on is corrected.

1. He is the meanest little kid on his block he eats only the heads of animal crackers. *Run-on*

   He is the meanest little kid on his block. He eats only the heads of animal crackers. *Correct*

   The run-on has been corrected by using a _____ and a capital letter to separate the two complete thoughts.

2. Fred Grencher likes to gossip about other people, he doesn't like them to gossip about him. *Run-on*

   Fred Grencher likes to gossip about other people, but he doesn't like them to gossip about him. *Correct*

   The run-on has been corrected by using a joining word, _____, to connect the two complete thoughts.

3. The chain on my bike likes to chew up my pants, it leaves grease marks on my ankle as well. *Run-on*

   The chain on my bike likes to chew up my pants; it leaves grease marks on my ankles as well. *Correct*

   The run-on has been corrected by using a _____ to connect the two closely related thoughts.

4. The window shade snapped up like a gunshot, her cat leaped four feet off the floor. *Run-on*

   When the window shade snapped up like a gunshot, her cat leaped four feet off the floor. *Correct*

   The run-on has been corrected by using the subordinating word _____ to connect the two closely related thoughts.

   Answers are on page 740.

What Are Run-Ons?

A *run-on* is two complete thoughts that are run together with no adequate sign given to mark the break between them.* Some run-ons have no punctuation at all to mark the break between the thoughts. Such run-ons are known as *fused sentences:* they are fused, or joined together, as if they were only one thought.

Fused Sentences

My grades are very good this semester my social life rates only a C.

Our father was a madman in his youth he would do anything on a dare.

In other run-ons, known as *comma splices,* a comma is used to connect, or "splice" together, the two complete thoughts. However, a comma alone is *not enough* to connect two complete thoughts. Some stronger connection than a comma alone is needed.

Comma Splices

My grades are very good this semester, my social life rates only a C.

Our father was a madman in his youth, he would do anything on a dare.

Comma splices are the most common kind of run-on. Students sense that some kind of connection is needed between two thoughts and so put a comma at the dividing point. But the comma alone is not sufficient: a stronger, clearer mark is needed between the two thoughts.

A Warning about Words That Can Lead to Run-Ons   People often write run-ons when the second complete thought begins with one of the following words:

I	we	there	now
you	they	this	then
he, she, it		that	next

Remember to be on the alert for run-ons whenever you use one of these words in writing a paper.

*Notes:

1 Some instructors feel that the term *run-ons* should be applied only to fused sentences, not to comma splices. But for many other instructors, and for our purposes in this book, the term *run-on* applies equally to fused sentences and comma splices. The point is that you do not want either fused sentences or comma splices in your writing.

2 Some instructors refer to each complete thought in a run-on as an *independent clause.* A *clause* is simply a group of words having a subject and a verb. A clause may be *independent* (expressing a complete thought and able to stand alone) or *dependent* (not expressing a complete thought and not able to stand alone). A run-on is two independent clauses that are run together with no adequate sign given to mark the break between them.

Copyright ©2006 The McGraw-Hill Companies, Inc. All rights reserved.

Correcting Run-Ons

Here are four common methods of correcting a run-on:

1   Use a period and a capital letter to break the two complete thoughts into separate sentences.

> My grades are very good this semester. My social life rates only a C.
>
> Our father was a madman in his youth. He would do anything on a dare.

2   Use a comma plus a joining word (*and, but, for, or, nor, so, yet*) to connect the two complete thoughts.

> My grades are very good this semester, but my social life rates only a C.
>
> Our father was a madman in his youth, for he would do anything on a dare.

3   Use a semicolon to connect the two complete thoughts.

> My grades are very good this semester; my social life rates only a C.
>
> Our father was a madman in his youth; he would do anything on a dare.

4   Use subordination.

> Although my grades are very good this semester, my social life rates only a C.
>
> Because my father was a madman in his youth, he would do anything on a dare.

The following pages will give you practice in all four methods of correcting a run-on. The use of subordination is explained on pages 123–124.

Method 1: Period and a Capital Letter

One way of correcting a run-on is to use a period and a capital letter at the break between the two complete thoughts. Use this method especially if the thoughts are not closely related or if another method would make the sentence too long.

ACTIVITY 1

Locate the split in each of the following run-ons. Each is a *fused sentence*—that is, each consists of two sentences that are fused, or joined together, with no punctuation at all between them. Reading each fused sentence aloud will help you "hear" where a major break or split in the thought occurs. At such a point, your voice will probably drop and pause.

Correct the run-on by putting a period at the end of the first thought and a capital letter at the start of the next thought.

EXAMPLE   Martha Grencher shuffled around the apartment in her slippers. H̶er husband couldn't stand their slapping sound on the floor.

1. A felt-tip pen is easy to ruin just leave it lying around without its cap.

2. Phil cringed at the sound of the dentist's drill it buzzed like a fifty-pound mosquito.

3. Last summer no one swam in the lake a little boy had dropped his pet piranhas into the water.

4. A horse's teeth never stop growing they will eventually grow outside the horse's mouth.

5. Sue's doctor told her he was an astrology nut she did not feel good about learning that.

6. Ice water is the best remedy for a burn using butter is like adding fat to a flame.

7. In the apartment the air was so dry that her skin felt parched the heat was up to eighty degrees.

8. Thousands of people are waiting for organ transplants my sister is one of them.

9. Lobsters are cannibalistic this is one reason they are hard to raise in captivity.

10. Last week a student brought a gun to school the principal has now decided to install metal detectors at the school's entrance.

Copyright ©2006 The McGraw-Hill Companies, Inc. All rights reserved.

ACTIVITY 2

Locate the split in each of the following run-ons. Some of the run-ons are fused sentences, and some are *comma splices*—run-ons spliced, or joined together, with only a comma. Correct each run-on by putting a period at the end of the first thought and a capital letter at the start of the next thought.

1. A bird got into the house through the chimney we had to catch it before our cat did.

2. Some so-called health foods are not so healthy, many are made with oils that raise cholesterol levels.

3. We sat only ten feet from the magician, we still couldn't see where all the birds came from.

4. Jerome needs only five hours of sleep each night his wife needs at least seven.

5. Our image of dentistry will soon change dentists will use lasers instead of drills.

6. Gale entered her apartment and jumped with fright someone was leaving through her bedroom window.

7. There were several unusual hairstyles at the party one woman had bright green braids.

8. Todd saves all his magazines, once a month, he takes them to a nearby nursing home.

9. The doctor seemed to be in a rush, I still took time to ask all the questions that were on my mind.

10. When I was little, my brother tried to feed me flies, he told me they were raisins.

Copyright ©2006 The McGraw-Hill Companies, Inc. All rights reserved.

ACTIVITY 3

Write a second sentence to go with each of the sentences that follow. Start the second sentence with the word given at the left. Your sentences can be serious or playful.

EXAMPLE She   Jackie works for the phone company. *She climbs telephone poles in all kinds of weather.*

It   1. The alarm clock is unreliable. _____

He   2. My uncle has a peculiar habit. _____

Then 3. Lola studied for the math test for two hours. _____

It   4. I could not understand why the car would not start. _____

There 5. We saw all kinds of litter on the highway. _____

Method 2: Comma and a Joining Word

A second way of correcting a run-on is to use a comma plus a joining word to connect the two complete thoughts. Joining words (also called *conjunctions*) include *and, but, for, or, nor, so,* and *yet.* Here is what the four most common joining words mean:

and   in addition to, along with

His feet hurt from the long hike, and his stomach was growling.

(*And* means "in addition": His feet hurt from the long hike; *in addition,* his stomach was growling.)

but   however, except, on the other hand, just the opposite

I remembered to get the cocoa, but I forgot the marshmallows.

(*But* means "however": I remembered to get the cocoa; *however,* I forgot the marshmallows.)

for   because, the reason why, the cause of something

> She was afraid of not doing well in the course, for she had always had bad luck with English before.

(*For* means "because" or "the reason why": She was afraid of not doing well in the course; *the reason why* was that she had always had bad luck with English before.)

Note   If you are not comfortable using *for*, you may want to use *because* instead of *for* in the activities that follow. If you do use *because*, omit the comma before it.

so   as a result, therefore

> The windshield wiper was broken, so she was in trouble when the rain started.

(*So* means "as a result": The windshield wiper was broken; *as a result*, she was in trouble when the rain started.)

ACTIVITY 1

Insert the joining word *(and, but, for, so)* that logically connects the two thoughts in each sentence.

1. The couple wanted desperately to buy the house, _____ they did not qualify for a mortgage.

2. The hurricane caused record flooding across the state, _____ it also knocked out power for millions.

3. Clyde asked his wife if she had any bandages, _____ he had just sliced his finger with a paring knife.

4. A group of teens talked and giggled loudly during the movie, _____ the ushers asked them to leave.

5. The restaurant was beautiful, _____ the food was overpriced.

ACTIVITY 2

Add a complete, closely related thought to go with each of the following statements. Use a comma plus the joining word at the left when you write the second thought.

EXAMPLE   for   Lola spent the day walking barefoot, *for the heel of one of her shoes had come off.*

but   1.   She wanted to go to the party _____

_____

and   2.   Tony washed his car in the morning _____

_____

so   3.   The day was dark and rainy _____

_____

for   4.   I'm not going to eat in the school cafeteria anymore _____

_____

but   5.   I asked my brother to get off the telephone _____

_____

Method 3: Semicolon

A third method of correcting a run-on is to use a semicolon to mark the break between two thoughts. A *semicolon* (;) is made up of a period above a comma and is sometimes called a *strong comma*. The semicolon signals more of a pause than a comma alone but not quite the full pause of a period.

Semicolon Alone   Here are some earlier sentences that were connected with a comma plus a joining word. Notice that a semicolon alone, unlike a comma alone, can be used to connect the two complete thoughts in each sentence:

The hurricane caused record flooding across the state; it also knocked out power for millions.

She was afraid of not doing well in the course; she had always had bad luck with English before.

The restaurant was beautiful; the food was overpriced.

The semicolon can add to sentence variety. For some people, however, the semicolon is a confusing mark of punctuation. Keep in mind that if you are not comfortable using it, you can and should use one of the first two methods of correcting a run-on.

Copyright ©2006 The McGraw-Hill Companies, Inc. All rights reserved.

ACTIVITY

Insert a semicolon where the break occurs between the two complete thoughts in each of the following run-ons.

EXAMPLE   I missed the bus by seconds; there would not be another for half an hour.

1. I spend eight hours a day in a windowless office it's a relief to get out into the open air after work.

2. The audience howled with laughter the comedian enjoyed a moment of triumph.

3. It rained all week parts of the highway were flooded.

4. Tony never goes to a certain gas station anymore he found out that the service manager overcharged him for a valve job.

5. The washer shook and banged with its unbalanced load then it began to walk across the floor.

Semicolon with a Transitional Word   A semicolon is sometimes used with a transitional word and a comma to join two complete thoughts.

> We were short of money; therefore, we decided not to eat out that weekend.
>
> The roots of a geranium have to be crowded into a small pot; otherwise, the plants may not flower.
>
> I had a paper to write; however, my brain had stopped working for the night.

Following is a list of common transitional words (also known as *adverbial conjunctions*). Brief meanings are given for the words.

Transitional Word	Meaning
however	but
nevertheless	but
on the other hand	but
instead	as a substitute
meanwhile	in the intervening time
otherwise	under other conditions

Copyright ©2006 The McGraw-Hill Companies, Inc. All rights reserved.

indeed	in fact
in addition	and
also	and
moreover	and
furthermore	and
as a result	in consequence
thus	as a result
consequently	as a result
therefore	as a result

ACTIVITY 1

Choose a logical transitional word from the list in the box and write it in the space provided. Put a semicolon *before* the connector and a comma *after* it.

EXAMPLE Exams are over _____*; however,*_____ I still feel tense and nervous.

1. I did not understand her point _____ I asked her to repeat it.

2. Janis spent several minutes trying to pry open the case of her new CD _____ she didn't succeed until she attacked it with a hammer.

3. Post offices are closed for today's holiday _____ no mail will be delivered.

4. Mac and Alana didn't have a fancy wedding _____ they used their money for a nice honeymoon.

5. I had to skip lunch _____ I would have been late for class.

ACTIVITY 2

Punctuate each sentence by using a semicolon and a comma.

EXAMPLE My brother's asthma was worsening; as a result, he quit the soccer team.

1. My brother ate an entire pizza for supper in addition he had a big chunk of pound cake for dessert.

2. The man leaned against the building in obvious pain however no one stopped to help him.

3. Our instructor was absent therefore the test was postponed.

4. I had no time to type up the paper instead I printed it out neatly in black ink.

5. Lola loves the velvety texture of cherry Jell-O moreover she loves to squish it between her teeth.

Method 4: Subordination

A fourth method of joining related thoughts is to use subordination. *Subordination* is a way of showing that one thought in a sentence is not as important as another thought.

Here are three earlier sentences that have been recast so that one idea is subordinated to (made less important than) the other idea:

When the window shade snapped up like a gunshot, her cat leaped four feet off the floor.

Because it rained all week, parts of the highway were flooded.

Although my grades are very good this year, my social life rates only a C.

Notice that when we subordinate, we use dependent words like *when, because,* and *although.* Here is a brief list of common dependent words:

Common Dependent Words		
after	before	unless
although	even though	until
as	if	when
because	since	while

Subordination is explained on pages 123–124.

ACTIVITY

Choose a logical dependent word from the box above and write it in the space provided.

EXAMPLE   _____*Because*_____ I had so much to do, I never even turned on the TV last night.

1. _____ we emerged from the darkened theater, it took several minutes for our eyes to adjust to the light.

2. _____ "All Natural" was printed in large letters on the yogurt carton, the fine print listing the ingredients told a different story.

3. I can't study for the test this weekend _____ my boss wants me to work overtime.

4. _____ the vampire movie was over, my children were afraid to go to bed.

5. _____ you have a driver's license and two major credit cards, that store will not accept your check.

A Review: How to Check for Run-Ons

1   To see if a sentence is a run-on, read it aloud and listen for a break marking two complete thoughts. Your voice will probably drop and pause at the break.

2   To check an entire paper, read it aloud from the *last* sentence to the *first*. Doing so will help you hear and see each complete thought.

3   Be on the lookout for words that can lead to run-on sentences:

| I | he, she, it | they | this | next |
| you | we | there | that | then |

4   Correct run-on sentences by using one of the following methods:
- Period and capital letter
- Comma and joining word (*and, but, for, or, nor, so, yet*)
- Semicolon
- Subordination

Copyright ©2006 The McGraw-Hill Companies, Inc. All rights reserved.

REVIEW TEST 1

Some of the run-ons that follow are fused sentences, having no punctuation between the two complete thoughts; others are comma splices, having only a comma between the two complete thoughts. Correct the run-ons by using one of the following three methods:

- Period and capital letter
- Comma and joining word
- Semicolon

Do not use the same method of correction for every sentence.

EXAMPLE   Three people did the job, *but* I could have done it alone.

1. The impatient driver tried to get a jump on the green light he kept edging his car into the intersection.

2. The course on the history of UFOs sounded interesting, it turned out to be very dull.

3. That clothing store is a strange place to visit you keep walking up to dummies that look like real people.

4. Everything on the menu of the Pancake House sounded delicious they wanted to order the entire menu.

5. Chung pressed a cold washcloth against his eyes, it helped relieve his headache.

6. Marc used to be a fast-food junkie now he eats only vegetables and sunflower seeds.

7. I knew my term paper was not very good, I placed it in a shiny plastic cover to make it look better.

8. The boy smiled joyously, his silver braces flashed in the sun.

Copyright ©2006 The McGraw-Hill Companies, Inc. All rights reserved.

9. My boss does not know what he is doing half the time then he tries to tell me what to do.

10. In the next minute, 100 people will die, over 240 babies will be born.

REVIEW TEST 2

Correct each run-on by using subordination. Choose from among the following dependent words:

after	before	unless
although	even though	until
as	if	when
because	since	while

EXAMPLE My eyes have been watering all day, I can tell the pollen count is high.

Because my eyes have been watering all day, I can tell the pollen count is high.

1. There are a number of suits and jackets on sale, they all have very noticeable flaws.

_____

_____

2. Rust has eaten a hole in the muffler, my car sounds like a motorcycle.

_____

_____

3. I finished my household chores, I decided to do some shopping.

_____

_____

4. The power went off for an hour during the night, all the clocks in the house must be reset.

   _____

   _____

5. Gas-saving hybrid vehicles are now available, they make up only a fraction of the new car market.

   _____

   _____

REVIEW TEST 3

There are two run-ons in each passage. Correct them by using the following methods.

- Period and capital letter
- Comma and one of these joining words: *and, but,* or *so*
- One of these dependent words: *although, because,* or *when*

1. The dog raced into the house it was happy to be among people. Its owner bent down to pet it he drew back in disgust. The dog had rolled in something with a horrible smell.

   _____

   _____

   _____

2. Small feet were admired in ancient China, some female infants had their feet tightly bound. The feet then grew into a tiny, deformed shape. The women could barely walk their feet were crippled for life.

   _____

   _____

   _____

3. Kanye insisted on dressing himself for nursery school. It was a cold winter day, he put on shorts and a tank top. He also put on cowboy boots over his bare feet. He liked his image in the mirror his mother made him change.

_____

_____

_____

4. A stimulating scent such as peppermint can help people concentrate better. The idea has practical applications, studies have shown that students do better on tests when peppermint is in the air. Maybe scented air could improve students' performance, it might help office workers be more alert, too.

_____

_____

_____

REVIEW TEST 4

Write quickly for five minutes about what you did this past weekend. Don't worry about spelling, punctuation, finding exact words, or organizing your thoughts. Just focus on writing as many words as you can without stopping.

After you have finished, go back and make whatever changes are needed to correct any run-ons in your writing.

Copyright ©2006 The McGraw-Hill Companies, Inc. All rights reserved.

24 Standard English Verbs

Introductory Project

Underline what you think is the correct form of the verb in each of the sentences below:

> As a boy, he (enjoy, enjoyed) watching nature shows on television.
>
> He still (enjoy, enjoys) watching such shows today as an adult.
>
> When my car was new, it always (start, started) in the morning.
>
> Now it (start, starts) only sometimes.
>
> A couple of years ago, when Maya (cook, cooked) dinner, you needed an antacid tablet.
>
> Now, when she (cook, cooks), neighbors invite themselves over to eat with us.

On the basis of the above examples, see if you can complete the following statements:

1. The first example in each pair refers to a (past, present) action, and the regular verb ends in _____.

2. The second example in each pair refers to a (past, present) action, and the regular verb ends in _____.

Answers are on page 740.

Copyright ©2006 The McGraw-Hill Companies, Inc. All rights reserved.

Many people have grown up in communities where nonstandard verb forms are used in everyday life. Such forms include *I thinks, he talk, it done, we has, you was,* and *she don't*. Community dialects have richness and power but are a drawback in college and the world at large, where standard English verb forms must be used. Standard English helps ensure clear communication among English-speaking people everywhere, and it is especially important in the world of work.

This chapter compares community dialect and standard English forms of one regular verb and three common irregular verbs.

Regular Verbs: Dialect and Standard Forms

The chart below compares community dialect (nonstandard) and standard English forms of the regular verb *smile*.

Smile

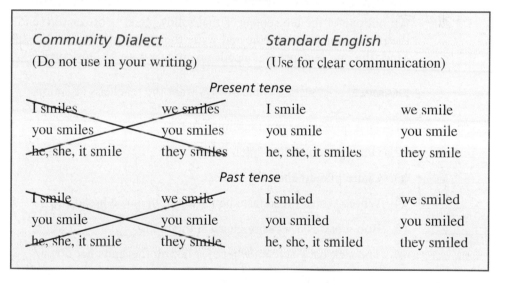

Community Dialect		Standard English	
(Do not use in your writing)		(Use for clear communication)	
Present tense			
I smiles	we smiles	I smile	we smile
you smiles	you smiles	you smile	you smile
he, she, it smile	they smiles	he, she, it smiles	they smile
Past tense			
I smile	we smile	I smiled	we smiled
you smile	you smile	you smiled	you smiled
he, she, it smile	they smile	he, she, it smiled	they smiled

One of the most common nonstandard forms results from dropping the endings of regular verbs. For example, people might say, "David never *smile* anymore" instead of "David never *smiles* anymore." Or they will say, "Before he lost his job, David *smile* a lot," instead of, "Before he lost his job, David *smiled* a lot." To avoid such nonstandard usage, memorize the forms shown above for the regular verb *smile*. Then use the activities that follow to help make a habit of including verb endings when you write.

Present Tense Endings

The verb ending -s or -es is needed with a regular verb in the present tense when the subject is *he, she, it,* or any *one person* or *thing.* Consider the following examples of present tense endings.

He	He yell*s.*
She	She throw*s* things.
It	It really anger*s* me.
One person	Their son storm*s* out of the house.
One person	Their frightened daughter crouch*es* behind the bed.
One thing	At night the house shake*s.*

ACTIVITY 1

All but one of the ten sentences that follow need -s or -es verb endings. Cross out the nonstandard verb forms and write the standard forms in the spaces provided. Mark the one sentence that needs no change with a *C* for *correct.*

EXAMPLE ___wants___ Dana always ~~want~~ the teacher's attention.

_____   1. That newspaper print nothing but bad news.

_____   2. Don't eat a fish that smell funny.

_____   3. Claire plan to enter the contest.

_____   4. Whole-wheat bread taste better to me than rye bread.

_____   5. Bob work as a security guard at the mall.

_____   6. The sick baby scream whenever her mother puts her down.

_____   7. You make me angry sometimes.

_____   8. Troy run faster than anybody else on the track team.

_____   9. She live in a rough section of town.

_____ 10. Martha like mystery novels better than romances.

ACTIVITY 2

Rewrite the short passage below, adding present *-s* or *-es* verb endings wherever needed.

Terri work in a big office downtown. Her cubicle sit right next to another worker's. This worker drive Terri crazy. He make more noise than you can imagine. Every day he bring a bag of raw carrots to work. The crunching noise fill the air. After he eat the carrots, he chew gum. He pop it so loud it sound like gunfire.

_____

_____

_____

_____

_____

Past Tense Endings

The verb ending *-d* or *-ed* is needed with a regular verb in the past tense.

A midwife deliver*ed* my baby.

The visitor puzz*led* over the campus map.

The children watch*ed* cartoons all morning.

ACTIVITY 1

All but one of the ten sentences that follow need *-d* or *-ed* verb endings. Cross out the nonstandard verb forms and write the standard forms in the spaces provided. Mark the one sentence that needs no change with a *C*.

EXAMPLE ____*failed*____ Yesterday I ~~fail~~ a chemistry quiz.

_____   1. Lily carefully color her lips with red lipstick.

_____   2. The Vietnamese student struggle with the new language.

_____   3. The sick little boy start to whimper again.

_____   4. The tired mother turned on the TV for him.

_____   5. I miss quite a few days of class early in the semester.

Copyright ©2006 The McGraw-Hill Companies, Inc. All rights reserved.

_____   6. The weather forecaster promise blue skies, but rain began early this morning.

_____   7. Sam attempt to put out the candle flame with his finger.

_____   8. However, he end up burning himself.

_____   9. On the bus, Yolanda listen to music through the headphones of her Walkman.

_____   10. As the photographer was about to take a picture of the smiling baby, a sudden noise frighten the child and made her cry.

ACTIVITY 2

Rewrite the following short passage, adding past tense -*d* or -*ed* verb endings wherever needed.

> I smoke for two years and during that time suffer no real side effects. Then my body attack me. I start to have trouble falling asleep, and I awaken early every morning. My stomach digest food very slowly, so that at lunchtime I seem to be still full with breakfast. My lips and mouth turn dry, and I swallow water constantly. Also, mucus fill my lungs and I cough a lot. I decide to stop smoking when my wife insist I take out more life insurance for our family.

_____

_____

_____

_____

_____

_____

_____

Three Common Irregular Verbs: Dialect and Standard Forms

The following charts compare community dialect and standard English forms of the common irregular verbs *be, have,* and *do.* (For more on irregular verbs, see pages 412–419.)

Copyright: ©2006 The McGraw-Hill Companies, Inc. All rights reserved.

Be

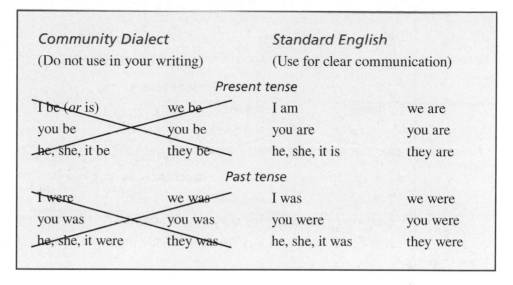

Community Dialect
(Do not use in your writing)

Standard English
(Use for clear communication)

Present tense

I be (or is)	we be	I am	we are
you be	you be	you are	you are
he, she, it be	they be	he, she, it is	they are

Past tense

I were	we was	I was	we were
you was	you was	you were	you were
he, she, it were	they was	he, she, it was	they were

Have

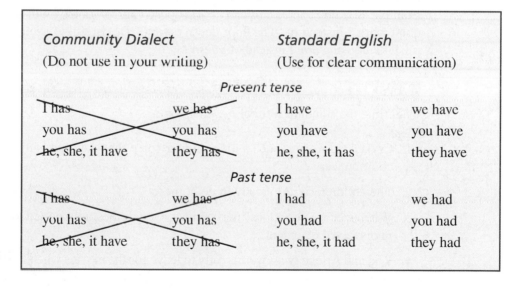

Community Dialect
(Do not use in your writing)

Standard English
(Use for clear communication)

Present tense

I has	we has	I have	we have
you has	you has	you have	you have
he, she, it have	they has	he, she, it has	they have

Past tense

I has	we has	I had	we had
you has	you has	you had	you had
he, she, it have	they has	he, she, it had	they had

Do

Community Dialect		Standard English	
(Do not use in your writing)		(Use for clear communication)	
Present tense			
I does	we does	I do	we do
you does	you does	you do	you do
he, she, it do	they does	he, she, it does	they do
Past tense			
I done	we done	I did	we did
you done	you done	you did	you did
he, she, it done	they done	he, she, it did	they did

Note   Many people have trouble with one negative form of *do*. They will say, for example, "He don't agree" instead of "He doesn't agree," or they will say, "The door don't work," instead of "The door doesn't work." Be careful to avoid the common mistake of using *don't* instead of *doesn't*.

ACTIVITY 1

Underline the standard form of *be, have,* or *do.*

1. Crystal (have, has) such a nice singing voice that she often sings solos at our choir concerts.

2. The children (is, are) ready to go home.

3. Whenever we (do, does) the laundry, our clothes are spotted with blobs of undissolved detergent.

4. Rod and Arlene (was, were) ready to leave for the movies when the baby began to wail.

5. Our art class (done, did) the mural on the wall of the cafeteria.

6. If I (have, has) the time later, I will help you set up your new laser printer.

7. Jesse (be, is) the best basketball player at our school.

Copyright ©2006 The McGraw-Hill Companies, Inc. All rights reserved.

8. My mom always goes to the same hairstylist because she (do, does) Mom's hair just the way mom likes.

9. The mice in our attic (have, has) chewed several holes in our ceiling.

10. The science instructor said that the state of California (be, is) likely to have a major earthquake any day.

ACTIVITY 2

Fill in each blank with the standard form of *be, have,* or *do.*

1. My car _____ a real personality.

2. I think it _____ almost human.

3. On cold mornings, it _____ not want to start.

4. Like me, the car _____ a problem dealing with freezing weather.

5. I don't want to get out of bed, and my car _____ not like leaving the garage.

6. Also, we _____ the same feeling about rainstorms.

7. I hate driving to school in a downpour, and so _____ the car.

8. When the car _____ stopped at a light, it stalls.

9. The habits my car _____ may be annoying.

10. But they _____ understandable.

REVIEW TEST 1

Underline the standard verb form.

1. Alex (argue, argues) just to hear himself talk.

2. Manuel and Yvonne (do, does) their grocery shopping first thing in the morning when the store is nearly empty.

3. The cheap ballpoint pen (leak, leaked) all over the lining of my pocketbook.

4. Dan (climb, climbed) up on the roof to see where the water was coming in.

5. If you (has, have) any trouble with the assignment, give me a call.

6. As soon as she gets home from work, Missy (boil, boils) some water to make tea.

7. My daughter often (watch, watches) TV after the rest of the family is in bed.

8. Two of the players (was, were) suspended from the league for ten games for using drugs.

9. Jeannie (has, have) just one contact lens; she lost the other one in the bathroom sink.

10. I remember how my wet mittens (use, used) to steam on the hot school radiator.

REVIEW TEST 2

Cross out the two nonstandard verb forms in each sentence below. Then write the standard English verbs in the spaces provided.

EXAMPLE ___is___ When our teacher ~~be~~ angry, his eyelid ~~begin~~ to twitch.
___begins___

_____   1. My mother work for the local newspaper; she take classified ads over the
_____   phone.

_____   2. Last week the city tow away my car; this morning I paid sixty dollars and pick
_____   it up from the towing company.

_____   3. When my wife be late for work, she rush around the house like a speeded-up
_____   cartoon character.

_____   4. Henry love to go camping until two thieves in the campground remove his
_____   cooler, stove, and sleeping bag from his tent.

_____   5. If the baby have a bad cold, I takes her into a steamy bathroom for a while to
_____   ease her breathing.

_____   6. Although my little girls knows they shouldn't tease the cat, they often dresses
_____   up the animal in doll clothes.

_____   7. Whenever my brothers watches *Monday Night Football,* they screams at the TV
_____   as if they are actually at the game.

_____   8. The hot, sweaty children jumps into the cool water of the pool and splashes
_____   around like a couple of happy seals.

_____   9. I show the receipt to the manager to prove that the clerk had accidentally
_____   overcharge me.

_____   10. As far as our son be concerned, oatmeal taste like soggy cardboard.

_____

Copyright ©2006 The McGraw-Hill Companies, Inc. All rights reserved.

25 Irregular Verbs

Introductory Project

You may already have a sense of which common English verbs are regular and which are not. To test yourself, fill in the past tense and past participle of the verbs below. Five are regular verbs and so take *-d* or *-ed* in the past tense and past participle. (The item at the top is an example.) Five are irregular verbs and will probably not sound right when you try to add *-d* or *-ed*. Write *I* for *irregular* in front of these verbs. Also, see if you can write in their irregular verb forms.

Present	Past	Past Participle
shout	*shouted*	*shouted*
1. crawl		
2. bring		
3. use		
4. do		
5. give		
6. laugh		
7. go		
8. scare		
9. dress		
10. see		

Answers are on page 740.

A Brief Review of Regular Verbs

Every verb has four principal parts: present, past, past participle, and present participle. These parts can be used to build all the verb tenses (the times shown by a verb).

The past and past participle of a regular verb are formed by adding *-d* or *-ed* to the present. The *past participle* is the form of the verb used with the helping verbs *have, has,* or *had* (or some form of *be* with passive verbs). The *present participle* is formed by adding *-ing* to the present. Here are the principal forms of some regular verbs:

Present	Past	Past Participle	Present Participle
crash	crashed	crashed	crashing
shiver	shivered	shivered	shivering
kiss	kissed	kissed	kissing
apologize	apologized	apologized	apologizing
tease	teased	teased	teasing

Most verbs in English are regular.

List of Irregular Verbs

Irregular verbs have irregular forms in the past tense and past participle. For example, the past tense of the irregular verb *know* is *knew;* the past participle is *known.*

Almost everyone has some degree of trouble with irregular verbs. When you are unsure about the form of a verb, you can check the following list of irregular verbs. (The present participle is not shown on this list, because it is formed simply by adding *-ing* to the base form of the verb.) Or you can check a dictionary, which gives the principal parts of irregular verbs.

Present	Past	Past Participle
arise	arose	arisen
awake	awoke *or* awaked	awoken *or* awaked
be (am, are, is)	was (were)	been
become	became	become
begin	began	begun
bend	bent	bent

Copyright ©2006 The McGraw-Hill Companies, Inc. All rights reserved.

Present	Past	Past Participle
bite	bit	bitten
blow	blew	blown
break	broke	broken
bring	brought	brought
build	built	built
burst	burst	burst
buy	bought	bought
catch	caught	caught
choose	chose	chosen
come	came	come
cost	cost	cost
cut	cut	cut
do (does)	did	done
draw	drew	drawn
drink	drank	drunk
drive	drove	driven
eat	ate	eaten
fall	fell	fallen
feed	fed	fed
feel	felt	felt
fight	fought	fought
find	found	found
fly	flew	flown
forget	forgot	forgotten
freeze	froze	frozen
get	got	got *or* gotten
give	gave	given
go (goes)	went	gone
grow	grew	grown
have (has)	had	had
hear	heard	heard
hide	hid	hidden
hold	held	held
hurt	hurt	hurt
keep	kept	kept
know	knew	known
lay	laid	laid
lead	led	led
leave	left	left

Copyright ©2005 The McGraw-Hill Companies, Inc. All rights reserved.

Present	Past	Past Participle
lend	lent	lent
let	let	let
lie	lay	lain
lose	lost	lost
make	made	made
meet	met	met
pay	paid	paid
ride	rode	ridden
ring	rang	rung
rise	rose	risen
run	ran	run
say	said	said
see	saw	seen
sell	sold	sold
send	sent	sent
shake	shook	shaken
shrink	shrank	shrunk
shut	shut	shut
sing	sang	sung
sit	sat	sat
sleep	slept	slept
speak	spoke	spoken
spend	spent	spent
stand	stood	stood
steal	stole	stolen
stick	stuck	stuck
sting	stung	stung
swear	swore	sworn
swim	swam	swum
take	took	taken
teach	taught	taught
tear	tore	torn
tell	told	told
think	thought	thought
throw	threw	thrown
wake	woke *or* waked	woken *or* waked
wear	wore	worn
win	won	won
write	wrote	written

ACTIVITY 1

Cross out the incorrect verb form in each of the following sentences. Then write the correct form of the verb in the space provided.

EXAMPLE ___drew___ The little boy ~~drawed~~ on the marble table with permanent ink.

_____ 1. Tomatoes were once thought to be poisonous, and they were growed only as ornamental shrubs.

_____ 2. On the last day of swim class, every student swimmed the whole length of the pool.

_____ 3. My cats have tore little holes in all my good wool sweaters.

_____ 4. The pipes in the bathroom freezed last winter, and they burst when they thawed.

_____ 5 Every time my telephone has rang today, there has been bad news on the line.

_____ 6. Only seven people have ever knowed the formula for Coca-Cola.

_____ 7. Amy blowed up animal-shaped balloons for her son's birthday party.

_____ 8. I shaked the bottle of medicine before I took a teaspoonful of it.

_____ 9. While waiting for the doctor to arrive, I sitted in a plastic chair for over two hours.

_____ 10. The pile of bones on the plate showed how much chicken the family had ate.

ACTIVITY 2

For each of the italicized verbs, fill in the three missing forms in the following order:

> **a** Present tense, which takes an -*s* ending when the subject is *he, she, it,* or any *one person* or *thing* (see pages 403–404)
>
> **b** Past tense
>
> **c** Past participle—the form that goes with the helping verb *have, has,* or *had*

EXAMPLE My uncle likes to give away certain things. He (a) ___gives___ old, threadbare clothes to the Salvation Army. Last year he (b) ___gave___ me a worthless television set whose picture tube was burned out. He has (c) ___given___ away stuff that a junk dealer would reject.

1. I like to *freeze* Hershey bars. A Hershey bar *(a)* _____ in half an hour. Once I *(b)* _____ a bottle of Pepsi. I put it in the freezer to chill and then forgot about it. Later I opened the freezer and discovered that it had *(c)* _____ and exploded.

2. Natalie *speaks* French. She *(a)* _____ German too. Her grand-mother *(b)* _____ both languages and taught them to her. Since she was a baby, Natalie has *(c)* _____ them both as well as she speaks English.

3. An acquaintance of mine is a shoplifter, although he knows it's wrong to *steal*. He *(a)* _____ candy bars from supermarkets. Last month he *(b)* _____ a digital camera and was caught by a store detective. He has *(c)* _____ pants and shirts by wearing several layers of clothes out of a store.

4. I *go* to parties a lot. Often Camille *(a)* _____ with me. She *(b)* _____ with me just last week. I have *(c)* _____ to parties every Friday for the past month.

5. My brother likes to *throw* things. Sometimes he *(a)* _____ socks into his bureau drawer. In high school he *(b)* _____ footballs while quarterbacking the team. And he has *(c)* _____ Frisbees in our backyard for as long as I can remember.

6. I would like to *see* a UFO. I spend hours looking at the night sky, hoping to *(a)* _____ one. A neighbor of ours claims he *(b)* _____ one last month. But he says he has *(c)* _____ the Abominable Snowman, too.

7. I often *lie* down for a few minutes after a hard day's work. Sometimes my cat *(a)* _____ down near me. Yesterday was Saturday, so I *(b)* _____ in bed all morning. I probably would have *(c)* _____ in bed all afternoon, but I wanted to get some planting done in my vegetable garden.

Copyright ©2006 The McGraw-Hill Companies, Inc. All rights reserved.

8   I *do* not understand the assignment. It simply *(a)* _____ not make

sense to me. I was surprised to learn that Shirley *(b)* _____ understand

it. In fact, she had already *(c)* _____ the assignment.

9.   I often find it hard to *begin* writing a paper. The assignment that I must do

(a) _____ to worry me while I'm watching television, but
I seldom turn off the set. Once I waited until the late movie had ended before

I *(b)* _____ to write. If I had *(c)* _____ earlier,
I would have gotten a decent night's sleep.

10.   Martha likes to *eat*. She *(a)* _____ as continuously as some

people smoke. Once she *(b)* _____ a large pack of cookies in

half an hour. Even if she has *(c)* _____ a heavy meal, she often
starts munching snacks right afterward.

REVIEW TEST 1

Underline the correct verb in the parentheses.

1.   As I began my speech, my hands (shaked, shook) so badly I nearly dropped
     my notes.

2.   Oscar came into the gym and (began, begun) to practice on the parallel bars.

3.   Over half the class has (taken, took) this course on a pass-fail basis.

4.   Even though my father (teached, taught) me how to play baseball, I never
     enjoyed any part of the game.

5.   Because I had (lended, lent) him money, I had a natural concern about what he
     did with it.

6.   The drugstore clerk (gave, gived) him the wrong change.

7.   Lola (brang, brought) a sweatshirt with her, for she knew the mountains got
     cold at night.

8.   My sister (was, be) at school when a stranger came asking for her at our home.

9.   The mechanic (did, done) an expensive valve job on my engine without getting
     my permission.

10.   The basketball team has (broke, broken) the school record for most losses in
      one year.

11.   Someone (leaved, left) his or her books in the classroom.

12. Fran's muscle was (tore, torn) when she slipped on the wet pavement.

13. If I hadn't (threw, thrown) away the receipt, I could have gotten my money back.

14. I would have (become, became) very angry if you had not intervened.

15. As the flowerpot (fell, falled) from the windowsill, the little boy yelled, "Bombs away!"

REVIEW TEST 2

Write short sentences that use the form indicated for the following irregular verbs.

EXAMPLE Past of *grow* _I grew eight inches in one year._

1. Past of *know* _____

_____

2. Past participle of *take* _____

_____

3. Past of *give* _____

_____

4. Past participle of *write* _____

_____

5. Past of *bring* _____

_____

6. Past participle of *speak* _____

_____

7. Past of *begin* _____

_____

8. Past of *go* _____

_____

9. Past participle of *see* _____

_____

10. Past of *drive* _____

_____

Copyright ©2006 The McGraw-Hill Companies, Inc. All rights reserved.

26 Subject-Verb Agreement

Introductory Project

As you read each pair of sentences below, write a check mark beside the sentence that you think uses the underlined word correctly.

There was too many people talking at once. _____

There were too many people talking at once. _____

The onions in that spaghetti sauce gives me heartburn. _____

The onions in that spaghetti sauce give me heartburn. _____

The mayor and her husband attends our church. _____

The mayor and her husband attend our church. _____

Everything seem to slow me down when I'm in a hurry. _____

Everything seems to slow me down when I'm in a hurry. _____

Answers are on page 740.

Copyright ©2006 The McGraw-Hill Companies, Inc. All rights reserved.

A verb must agree with its subject in number. A *singular subject* (one person or thing) takes a singular verb. A *plural subject* (more than one person or thing) takes a plural verb. Mistakes in subject-verb agreement are sometimes made in the situations listed below (each situation is explained on the following pages):

1   When words come between the subject and the verb

2   When a verb comes before the subject

3   With compound subjects

4   With indefinite pronouns

Words between Subject and Verb

Words that come between the subject and the verb do not change subject-verb agreement. In the sentence

The tomatoes in this salad are brown and mushy.

the subject (tomatoes) is plural, and so the verb (are) is plural. The words *in this salad* that come between the subject and the verb do not affect subject-verb agreement.

To help find the subject of certain sentences, you should cross out prepositional phrases (see page 363):

Nell, ~~with her three dogs close behind,~~ runs around the park every day.

The seams ~~in my new coat~~ have split after only two wearings.

ACTIVITY

Underline the correct verb form in the parentheses.

1. The decisions of the judge (seem, seems) questionable.

2. The flakes in this cereal (taste, tastes) like sawdust.

3. The woman with the dark sunglasses (is, are) our mayor.

4. Many people in Europe (speak, speaks) several languages.

5. A hamburger with a large order of french fries (is, are) my usual lunch.

6. That silk flower by the candles (look, looks) real.

7. One of my son's worst habits (is, are) leaving an assortment of dirty plates on the kitchen counter.

8. The rust spots on the back of Emily's car (need, needs) to be cleaned with a special polish.

9. The collection of medicine bottles in my parents' bathroom (overflow, overflows) the cabinet shelves.

10. A tired-looking student in my classes often (sleep, sleeps) through most of the lectures.

Verb before Subject

A verb agrees with its subject even when the verb comes *before* the subject. Words that may precede the subject include *there, here,* and, in questions, *who, which, what,* and *where.*

On Glen's doorstep were two police officers.

There are many pizza places in our town.

Here is your receipt.

Where are they going to sleep?

If you are unsure about the subject, look at the verb and ask *who* or *what.* With the first example above, you might ask, "*Who* were on the doorstep?" The answer, *police officers,* is the subject.

ACTIVITY

Write the correct form of the verb in the space provided.

is, are 1. What _____ your middle name?

was, were 2. Among the guests _____ a private detective.

do, does 3. Where _____ you go when you want to be alone?

is, are 4. There _____ many hungry people in American cities.

rest, rests 5. In that grave _____ the bones of my great-grandfather.

was, were 6. There _____ too many people in the room for me to feel comfortable.

is, are 7. Why _____ the lights turned off?

stand, stands 8. Across the street _____ the post office.

Copyright ©2006 The McGraw-Hill Companies, Inc. All rights reserved.

is, are   9. Here _____ the tickets for tonight's game.

was, were   10. Stuffed into the mailbox _____ ten pieces of junk mail and three ripped magazines.

Compound Subjects

Subjects joined by *and* generally take a plural verb.

> Maple syrup and sweet butter taste delicious on pancakes.
>
> Fear and ignorance have a lot to do with hatred.

When subjects are joined by *either . . . or, neither . . . nor, not only . . . but also,* the verb agrees with the subject closer to the verb.

> Neither TV shows nor the Internet is as enjoyable to me as spending time with my friends.

The nearer subject, *Internet,* is singular, and so the verb is singular.

ACTIVITY

Write the correct form of the verb in the space provided.

stays, stay   1. Our cats and dog _____ at a neighbor's house when we go on vacation.

Is, Are   2. _____ the birthday cake and ice cream ready to be served?

holds, hold   3. Staples and Scotch tape _____ all our old photo albums together.

was, were   4. Rent and car insurance _____ my biggest expenses last month.

wants,   5. Neither the students nor the instructor _____ to postpone the final exam
want   till after the holidays.

is, are   6. An egg and a banana _____ required for the recipe.

was, were   7. Owning a car and having money in my pocket _____ the chief ambitions
                  of my adolescence.

visits, visit 8. My aunt and uncle from Ireland _____ us every other summer.

was, were   9. Before they saw a marriage therapist, Peter and Jenny _____ planning to
                  get divorced.

acts, act   10. Not only the landlady but also her children _____ unfriendly to us.

Indefinite Pronouns

The following words, known as *indefinite pronouns,* always take singular verbs:

(-one *words*)	(-body *words*)	(-thing *words*)	
one	nobody	nothing	each
anyone	anybody	anything	either
everyone	everybody	everything	neither
someone	somebody	something	

Note   *Both* always takes a plural verb.

ACTIVITY

Write the correct form of the verb in the space provided.

is, are   1. Everybody at my new school _____ friendly.

feel, feels   2. Neither of those mattresses _____ comfortable.

knows,   3. Nobody in my family _____ how to swim.
know

needs,   4. Each of the children _____ some attention.
need

sounds,   5. Something about Robbie's story _____ suspicious.
sound

pitches,   6. If each of us _____ in, we can finish this job in an hour.
pitch

was, were   7. Everybody in the theater _____ getting up and leaving before the movie
                     ended.

provides,   8. Neither of the restaurants _____ facilities for the handicapped.
provide

likes, like   9. No one in our family _____ housecleaning, but we all take a turn at it.

steals,   10. Someone in our neighborhood _____ vegetables from people's gardens.
steal

Copyright ©2006 The McGraw-Hill Companies, Inc. All rights reserved.

REVIEW TEST 1

Underline the correct verb in parentheses.

1. Lettuce in most of the stores in our area now (costs, cost) almost three dollars a head.

2. Nobody in the class of fifty students (understands, understand) how to solve the equation on the blackboard.

3. The packages in the shopping bag (was, were) a wonderful mystery to the children.

4. My exercise class of five students (meets, meet) every Thursday afternoon.

5. Anyone who (steals, steal) my purse won't find much inside it.

6. Business contacts and financial backing (is, are) all that I need to establish my career as a dress designer.

7. Each of those breakfast cereals (contains, contain) a high proportion of sugar.

8. The serious look in that young girl's eyes (worries, worry) me.

9. All the cars on my block (has, have) to be moved one day a month for street cleaning.

10. Some people (know, knows) more about their favorite TV characters than they do about the members of their own family.

REVIEW TEST 2

Each of the following passages contains *two* mistakes in subject-verb agreement. Find these two mistakes and cross them out. Then write the correct form of each verb in the space provided.

1. Few people recalls seeing baby pigeons. The reason is simple. Baby pigeons in the nest eats a huge amount of food each day. Upon leaving the nest, they are close to the size of their parents.

   a. _____

   b. _____

2. Everything in the mall stores are on sale today. Customers from all over are crowding the aisles. There is terrific bargains in many departments.

   a. _____

   b. _____

3. All the neighbors meets once a year for a block party. Everyone talks and dances far into the night. Huge bowls of delicious food sits on picnic tables. Afterward, everyone goes home and sleeps all day.

   a. _____

   b. _____

4. The members of the swimming team paces nervously beside the pool. Finally, an official blows a whistle. Into the pool dive a swimmer with thick, tan arms. He paddles quickly through the water.

   a. _____

   b. _____

5. When Lin Soo comes home from school each day, her work is just beginning. The members of her family all works in their small restaurant. Nobody rest until the last customer is served. Only then do Lin Soo and her brother start their homework.

   a. _____

   b. _____

27 Pronoun Agreement and Reference

Copyright ©2006 The McGraw-Hill Companies, Inc. All rights reserved.

Introductory Project

Read each pair of sentences below. Then write a check mark beside the sentence that you think uses the underlined word or words correctly.

Someone in my neighborhood lets their dog run loose. _____

Someone in my neighborhood lets his or her dog run loose. _____

After Tony reviewed his notes with Bob, he passed the exam with ease.

_____

After reviewing his notes with Bob, Tony passed the exam with ease.

_____

Answers are on page 740.

Pronouns are words that take the place of nouns (persons, places, or things). In fact, the word *pronoun* means "for a noun." Pronouns are shortcuts that keep you from unnecessarily repeating words in writing. Here are some examples of pronouns:

> Shirley had not finished *her* paper. (*Her* is a pronoun that takes the place of *Shirley's*.)
>
> Tony swung so heavily on the tree branch that *it* snapped. (*It* replaces *branch*.)
>
> When the three little pigs saw the wolf, *they* pulled out cans of Mace. (*They* is a pronoun that takes the place of *pigs*.)

This section presents rules that will help you avoid two common mistakes people make with pronouns. The rules are as follows:

1   A pronoun must agree in number with the word or words it replaces.

2   A pronoun must refer clearly to the word it replaces.

Pronoun Agreement

A pronoun must agree in number with the word or words it replaces. If the word a pronoun refers to is singular, the pronoun must be singular; if that word is plural, the pronoun must be plural. (Note that the word a pronoun refers to is also known as the *antecedent*.)

> Barbara agreed to lend me her Ray Charles CDs.
>
> People walking the trail must watch their step because of snakes.

In the first example, the pronoun *her* refers to the singular word *Barbara*; in the second example, the pronoun *their* refers to the plural word *People*.

ACTIVITY

Write the appropriate pronoun (*their, they, them, it*) in the blank space in each of the following sentences.

EXAMPLE   I lifted the pot of hot potatoes carefully, but ___*it*___ slipped out of my hand.

1. People should try to go into a new situation with ＿＿＿＿＿＿ minds open, not with opinions already firmly formed.

2. Fred never misses his daily workout; he believes ＿＿＿＿＿＿ keeps him healthy.

3. Sometimes, in marriage, partners expect too much from ＿＿＿＿＿＿ mates.

4. For some students, college is often their first experience with an unsupervised learning situation, and ＿＿＿＿＿＿ are not always ready to accept the responsibility.

5. Our new neighbors moved in three months ago, but I have yet to meet ＿＿＿＿＿＿.

Indefinite Pronouns

The following words, known as *indefinite pronouns,* are always singular.

(-one words)	(-body words)	
one	nobody	each
anyone	anybody	either
everyone	everybody	neither
someone	somebody	

If a pronoun in a sentence refers to one of the above singular words, the pronoun should be singular.

Each father felt that (his) child should have won the contest.

One of the women could not find (her) purse.

Everyone must be in (his) seat before the instructor takes attendance.

In each example, the circled pronoun is singular because it refers to one of the special singular words.

Copyright ©2006 The McGraw-Hill Companies, Inc. All rights reserved.

Note   The last example is correct if everyone in the class is a man. If everyone in the class is a woman, the pronoun would be *her*. If the class has both women and men, the pronoun form would be *his or her:*

Everyone must be in his or her seat before the instructor takes attendance.

Some writers follow the traditional practice of using *his* to refer to both women and men. Many now use *his or her* to avoid an implied sexual bias. To avoid using *his* or the somewhat awkward *his or her,* a sentence can often be rewritten in the plural:

Students must be in their seats before the instructor takes attendance.

ACTIVITY

Underline the correct pronoun.

1. Some young man has blocked the parking lot exit with (his, their) sports car.

2. Everyone in the women's group has volunteered some of (her, their) time for the voting drive.

3. Neither of the men arrested as terrorists would reveal (his, their) real name.

4. Not one of the women coaches will be returning to (her, their) job next year.

5. Each of the president's female advisers offered (her, their) opinion about the abortion bill.

Pronoun Reference

A sentence may be confusing and unclear if a pronoun appears to refer to more than one word, or if the pronoun does not refer to any specific word. Look at this sentence:

Joe almost dropped out of high school, for he felt *they* emphasized discipline too much.

Who emphasized discipline too much? There is no specific word that *they* refers to. Be clear:

Joe almost dropped out of high school, for he felt *the teachers* emphasized discipline too much.

Copyright ©2006 The McGraw-Hill Companies, Inc. All rights reserved.

Here are sentences with other kinds of faulty pronoun reference. Read the explanations of why they are faulty and look carefully at how they are corrected.

Faulty	Clear
June told Margie that *she* lacked self-confidence. (*Who* lacked self-confidence: June or Margie? Be clear.)	June told Margie, "You lack self-confidence." (Quotation marks, which can sometimes be used to correct an unclear reference, are explained on pages 481–488.)
Nancy's mother is a hairdresser, but Nancy is not interested in *it*. (There is no specific word that *it* refers to. It would not make sense to say, "Nancy is not interested in hairdresser.")	Nancy's mother is a hairdresser, but Nancy is not interested in becoming one.
Ron blamed the police officer for the ticket, *which* was foolish. (Does *which* mean that the ticket was foolish, or that Ron's blaming the officer was foolish? Be clear.)	Foolishly, Ron blamed the police officer for the ticket.

ACTIVITY

Rewrite each of the following sentences to make the vague pronoun reference clear. Add, change, or omit words as necessary.

EXAMPLE   Our cat was friends with our hamster until he bit him.

Until the cat bit the hamster, the two were friends.

1. Maria's mother let her wear her new earrings to school.

2. When I asked why I failed my driver's test, he said I drove too slowly.

3. Dad ordered my brother to paint the garage because he didn't want to do it.

4. Herb dropped his psychology courses because he thought they assigned too much reading.

_____

5. I love Parmesan cheese on veal, but it does not always digest well.

_____

REVIEW TEST 1

Cross out the pronoun error in each sentence and write the correction in the space provided at the left. Then circle the letter that correctly describes the type of error that was made.

EXAMPLES

his (or her)   Each player took ~~their~~ position on the court.

    Mistake in: (a.) pronoun agreement.   b. pronoun reference.

the store   I was angry when ~~they~~ wouldn't give me cash back when I returned the sweater I had bought.

    Mistake in: a. pronoun agreement.   (b.) pronoun reference.

_____   1. Dan asked Mr. Sanchez if he could stay an extra hour at work today.

    Mistake in: a. pronoun agreement.   b. pronoun reference.

_____   2. Both the front door and the back door of the abandoned house had fallen off its hinges.

    Mistake in: a. pronoun agreement.   b. pronoun reference.

_____   3. I've been taking cold medicine, and now it is better.

    Mistake in: a. pronoun agreement.   b. pronoun reference.

_____   4. Norm was angry when they raised the state tax on cigarettes.

    Mistake in: a. pronoun agreement.   b. pronoun reference.

_____   5. Every one of those musicians who played for two hours in the rain truly earned their money last night.

    Mistake in: a. pronoun agreement.   b. pronoun reference.

_____   6. An annual flu shot is a good idea; they will help children and older people stay healthy.

    Mistake in: a. pronoun agreement.   b. pronoun reference.

Copyright ©2006 The McGraw-Hill Companies, Inc. All rights reserved.

7. Each of the candidates is asked a thought-provoking question and then judged on their answer.

    Mistake in: a. pronoun agreement.   b. pronoun reference.

8. Indira could not believe that they had changed the immigration laws again.

    Mistake in: a. pronoun agreement.   b. pronoun reference.

9. At the dental office, I asked him if it was really necessary to take X rays of my mouth again.

    Mistake in: a. pronoun agreement.   b. pronoun reference.

10. Every ant in the bustling anthill has their own job to do that helps support the entire community.

    Mistake in: a. pronoun agreement.   b. pronoun reference.

REVIEW TEST 2

Underline the correct word in parentheses.

1. Cindy is the kind of woman who will always do (their, her) best.

2. Hoping to be first in line when (they, the ushers) opened the doors, we arrived two hours early for the concert.

3. If a person really wants to appreciate good coffee, (he or she, they) should drink it black.

4. My children are hooked on science fiction stories because (they, the stories) allow readers to escape to other worlds.

5. Lois often visits the reading center in school, for she finds that (they, the tutors) give her helpful instruction.

6. Nobody in our house can express (his or her, their) opinion without starting an argument.

7. As the room got colder, everybody wished for (his or her, their) coat.

8. Each of my brothers has had (his, their) apartment broken into.

9. If someone is going to write a composition, (he or she, they) should prepare at least one rough draft.

10. My wife and I both need thick glasses, so I imagine our children won't escape (it, needing glasses).

28 Pronoun Types

This chapter describes some common types of pronouns: subject and object pronouns, possessive pronouns, and demonstrative pronouns.

Subject and Object Pronouns

Pronouns change their form depending on the purpose they serve in a sentence. In the box that follows is a list of subject and object pronouns.

Subject Pronouns	Object Pronouns
I	me
you	you *(no change)*
he	him
she	her
it	it *(no change)*
we	us
they	them

Subject Pronouns

Subject pronouns are subjects of verbs.

She is wearing blue nail polish on her toes. (*She* is the subject of the verb *is wearing*)

They ran up three flights of steps. (*They* is the subject of the verb *ran*).

We children should have some privacy too. (*We* is the subject of the verb *should have*.)

Copyright ©2006 The McGraw-Hill Companies, Inc. All rights reserved.

Rules for using subject pronouns, and several kinds of mistakes people sometimes make with subject pronouns, are explained below.

Rule 1   Use a subject pronoun in spots where you have a compound (more than one) subject.

Incorrect	Correct
Sally and *me* are exactly the same size.	Sally and *I* are exactly the same size.
Her and *me* share our wardrobes with each other.	*She* and *I* share our wardrobes with each other.

Hint   If you are not sure what pronoun to use, try each pronoun by itself in the sentence. The correct pronoun will be the one that sounds right. For example, "her shares her wardrobe" does not sound right. "She shares her wardrobe" does.

Rule 2   Use a subject pronoun after forms of the verb *be*. Forms of *be* include *am, are, is, was, were, has been,* and *have been.*

It was *I* who called you a minute ago and then hung up.

It may be *they* entering the diner.

It was *he* who put the white tablecloth into the washing machine with a red sock.

The sentences above may sound strange and stilted to you because they are seldom used in conversation. When we speak with one another, forms such as "It was me," "It may be them," and "It is her" are widely accepted. In formal writing, however, the grammatically correct forms are still preferred.

Hint   To avoid having to use the subject pronoun form after *be,* you can simply reword a sentence. Here is how the preceding examples could be reworded:

I was the one who called you a minute ago and then hung up.

They may be the ones entering the diner.

He put the white tablecloth into the washing machine with a red sock.

Rule 3   Use subject pronouns after *than* or *as.* The subject pronoun is used because a verb is understood after the pronoun.

Mark can hold his breath longer than *I* (can). (The verb *can* is understood after *I*.)

Her thirteen-year-old daughter is as tall as *she* (is). (The verb *is* is understood after *she*.)

You drive much better than *he* (drives). (The verb *drives* is understood after *he*.)

Hint   Avoid mistakes by mentally adding the "missing" verb at the end of the sentence.

Object Pronouns

Object pronouns *(me, him, her, us, them)* are the objects of verbs or prepositions. (*Prepositions* are connecting words like *for, at, about, to, before, by, with,* and *of.* See also page 363.)

Lee pushed *me*. (*Me* is the object of the verb *pushed*.)

We dragged *them* all the way home. (*Them* is the object of the verb *dragged*.)

She wrote all about *us* in her diary. (*Us* is the object of the preposition *about*.)

Vera passed a note to *him* as she walked to the pencil sharpener. (*Him* is the object of the preposition *to*.)

People are sometimes uncertain about which pronoun to use when two objects follow the verb.

Incorrect	Correct
I argued with his sister and *he*.	I argued with his sister and *him*.
The cashier cheated Rick and *I*.	The cashier cheated Rick and *me*.

Hint   If you are not sure which pronoun to use, try each pronoun by itself in the sentence. The correct pronoun will be the one that sounds right. For example, "I argued with he" does not sound right; "I argued with him" does.

ACTIVITY

Underline the correct subject or object pronoun in each of the following sentences. Then show whether your answer is a subject or an object pronoun by circling S or O in the margin. The first one is done for you as an example.

Ⓢ   O   1. Darcy and (<u>she</u>, her) kept dancing even after the band stopped playing.

S   O   2   The letters Mom writes to my brother and (I, me) are always typed in red.

S   O   3. Dawn is good at bowling, but her little sister is even better than (she, her).

S   O   4. Their track team won because they practiced more than (we, us).

S   O   5. (We, Us) choir members get to perform for the governor.

S   O   6. The rest of (they, them) came to the wedding by train.

S   O   7. (She, Her) and Sammy got divorced and then remarried.

S   O   8. Since we were both taking a tough statistics course, it was a long, hard semester for my best friend and (me, I).

S   O   9. Tony and (he, him) look a lot alike, but they're not even related.

S   O   10. Our neighbors asked Rosa and (I, me) to help with their parents' surprise party.

Possessive Pronouns

Possessive pronouns show ownership or possession.

> Using a small branch, Stu wrote *his* initials in the wet cement.
>
> The furniture is *mine,* but the car is *hers.*

Here is a list of possessive pronouns:

my, mine	our, ours
your, yours	your, yours
his	their, theirs
her, hers	
its	

Note   A possessive pronoun *never* uses an apostrophe. (See also page 476.)

Incorrect	**Correct**
That earring is *her's.*	That earring is *hers.*
The orange cat is *theirs'.*	The orange cat is *theirs.*

Copyright ©2006 The McGraw-Hill Companies, Inc. All rights reserved.

ACTIVITY

Cross out the incorrect pronoun form in each of the sentences below. Write the correct form in the space at the left.

EXAMPLE   _____ours_____   The house with the maroon shutters is ~~ours'~~.

_____   1. A porcupine has no quills on it's belly.

_____   2. The laptop computer on that table is theirs'.

_____   3. You can easily tell which team is ours' by when we cheer.

_____   4. My dog does not get along with her's.

_____   5. Grandma's silverware and dishes will be yours' when you get married.

Demonstrative Pronouns

Demonstrative pronouns point to or single out a person or thing. There are four demonstrative pronouns:

this	these
that	those

Generally speaking, *this* and *these* refer to things close at hand; *that* and *those* refer to things farther away. These four pronouns are commonly used in the role of demonstrative adjectives as well.

This milk has gone sour.

My son insists on saving all *these* hot rod magazines.

I almost tripped on *that* roller skate at the bottom of the steps.

Those plants in the corner don't get enough light.

Note   Do not use *them, this here, that there, these here,* or *those there* to point out. Use only *this, that, these,* or *those.*

PRO

ACTIVITY

Cross out the incorrect form of the demonstrative pronoun and write the correct form in the space provided.

EXAMPLE ___*Those*___ ~~Those there~~ tires look worn.

_____ 1. This here child has a high fever.

_____ 2. These here pants I'm wearing are so tight I can hardly breathe.

_____ 3. Them kids have been playing in the alley all morning.

_____ 4. That there umpire won't stand for any temper tantrums.

_____ 5. I am saving them old baby clothes for my daughter's dolls.

REVIEW TEST

Underline the correct word in the parentheses.

1. If I left dinner up to (he, him), we'd have pizza every night.

2. The vase on my dresser belonged to my grandmother, and the candlesticks on the windowsill were (hers', hers) as well.

3. My boyfriend offered to drive his mother and (I, me) to the mall to shop for his birthday present.

4. (Them, Those) little marks on the floor are scratches, not crumbs.

5. I took a picture of my brother and (I, me) looking into the hallway mirror.

6. When Lin and (she, her) drove back from the airport, they talked so much that they missed their exit.

7. (That there, That) orange juice box says "Fresh," but the juice is made from concentrate.

8. Eliot swears that he dreamed about (she, her) and a speeding car the night before Irina was injured in a car accident.

9. The waitress brought our food to the people at the next table and gave (theirs, theirs') to us.

10. Since it was so hot out, Lana and (he, him) felt they had a good excuse to study at the beach.

Copyright: ©2006 The McGraw-Hill Companies, Inc. All rights reserved.

29 Adjectives and Adverbs

Adjectives

What Are Adjectives?

Adjectives describe nouns (names of persons, places, or things) or pronouns.

> Ernie is a *rich* man. (The adjective *rich* describes the noun *man*.)
>
> He is also *generous*. (The adjective *generous* describes the pronoun *he*.)
>
> Our *gray* cat sleeps a lot. (The adjective *gray* describes the noun *cat*.)
>
> She is *old*. (The adjective *old* describes the pronoun *she*.)

Adjectives usually come before the word they describe (as in *rich man* and *gray cat*). But they also come after forms of the verb *be* (*is, are, was, were,* and so on). They also follow verbs such as *look, appear, seem, become, sound, taste,* and *smell*.

> That speaker was *boring*. (The adjective *boring* describes the speaker.)
>
> The Petersons are *homeless*. *(*The adjective *homeless* describes the Petersons.)
>
> The soup looked *good*. (The adjective *good* describes the soup.)
>
> But it tasted *salty*. (The adjective *salty* describes the pronoun *it*.)

Using Adjectives to Compare

For nearly all one-syllable adjectives and some two-syllable adjectives, add *-er* when comparing two things and *-est* when comparing three or more things.

> My sister's handwriting is *neater* than mine, but Mother's is the *neatest*.
>
> Canned juice is sometimes *cheaper* than fresh juice, but frozen juice is often the *cheapest*.

Copyright ©2006 The McGraw-Hill Companies, Inc All rights reserved.

For some two-syllable adjectives and all longer adjectives, add *more* when comparing two things and *most* when comparing three or more things.

> In general, scorpion venom is *more poisonous* than bee venom, but the *most poisonous* venom comes from snakes.

> Basketball is *more exciting* than baseball, but football is the *most exciting* sport of all.

You can usually tell when to use *more* and *most* by the sound of a word. For example, you can probably tell by its sound that "carefuller" would be too awkward to say and that *more careful* is thus correct. In addition, there are many words for which both *-er* or *-est* and *more* or *most* are equally correct. For instance, either "a more fair rule" or "a fairer rule" is correct.

To form negative comparisons, use *less* and *least*.

> When kids called me "Dum-dum," I tried to look *less* hurt than I felt.

> They say men gossip *less* than women do, but I don't believe it.

> Suzanne is the most self-centered, *least* thoughtful person I know.

Points to Remember about Comparing

Point 1 Use only one form of comparison at a time. In other words, do not use both an *-er* ending and *more* or both an *-est* ending and *most*.

Incorrect	**Correct**
My southern accent is always *more stronger* after I visit my family in Georgia.	My southern accent is always *stronger* after I visit my family in Georgia.
My *most luckiest* day was the day I met my wife.	My *luckiest* day was the day I met my wife.

Point 2 Learn the irregular forms of the following words.

	Comparative (for Comparing Two Things)	Superlative (for Comparing Three or More Things)
bad	worse	worst
good, well	better	best
little (in amount)	less	least
much, many	more	most

Do not use both *more* and an irregular comparative or *most* and an irregular superlative.

Incorrect

It is *more better* to stay healthy than to have to get healthy.

Yesterday I went on the *most best* date of my life—and all we did was go on a picnic.

Correct

It is *better* to stay healthy than to have to get healthy.

Yesterday I went on the *best* date of my life—and all we did was go on a picnic.

ACTIVITY

Add to each sentence the correct form of the word in the margin.

EXAMPLES   bad   The _____worst_____ scare I ever had was the time when I thought my son was on an airplane that had crashed.

wonderful   The day of my divorce was even _more wonderful_ than the day of my wedding.

good
1. The Grammy awards are given to the _____ recording artists of each year.

popular
2. Vanilla ice cream is even _____ than chocolate ice cream.

bad
3. One of the _____ things you can do to people is ignore them.

light
4. A pound of feathers is no _____ than a pound of stones.

little
5. The _____ expensive way to accumulate a wardrobe is to buy used clothing whenever possible.

Adverbs

What Are Adverbs?

Adverbs—which usually end in *-ly*—describe verbs, adjectives, or other adverbs.

The referee *suddenly* stopped the fight. (The adverb *suddenly* describes the verb *stopped*.)

Her yellow rosebushes are *absolutely* beautiful. (The adverb *absolutely* describes the adjective *beautiful*.)

The auctioneer spoke so *terribly* fast that I couldn't understand him. (The adverb *terribly* describes the adverb *fast*.)

A Common Mistake with Adverbs and Adjectives

People often mistakenly use an adjective instead of an adverb after a verb.

Incorrect	**Correct**
I jog *slow*.	I jog *slowly*.
The nervous witness spoke *quiet*.	The nervous witness spoke *quietly*.
The first night I quit smoking, I wanted a cigarette *bad*.	The first night I quit smoking, I wanted a cigarette *badly*.

ACTIVITY

Underline the adjective or adverb needed. (Remember that adjectives describe nouns, and adverbs describe verbs, adjectives, or other adverbs.)

1. During a quiet moment in class, my stomach rumbled (loud, loudly).

2. I'm a (slow, slowly) reader, so I have to put aside more time to study than some of my friends.

3. Thinking no one was looking, my daughter (quick, quickly) peeked into the bag to see what we had bought for her.

4. The kitchen cockroaches wait (patient, patiently) in the shadows; at night they'll have the place to themselves.

5. I hang up the phone (immediate, immediately) whenever the speaker is a recorded message.

Copyright ©2006 The McGraw-Hill Companies, Inc. All rights reserved.

Well and *Good*

Two words that are often confused are *well* and *good*. *Good* is an adjective; it describes nouns. *Well* is usually an adverb; it describes verbs. *Well* (rather than *good*) is also used to refer to a person's health.

ACTIVITY

Write *well* or *good* in each of the sentences that follow.

1. I could tell by the broad grin on Della's face that the news was _____.

2. They say my grandfather sang so _____ that even the wind stopped to listen.

3. The food at the salad bar must not have been too fresh, because I didn't feel _____ after dinner.

4. When I want to do a really _____ job of washing the floor, I do it on my hands and knees.

5. The best way to get along _____ with our boss is to stay out of his way.

REVIEW TEST

Underline the correct word in the parentheses.

1. In Egypt, silver was once (more valued, most valued) than gold.

2. The doctor predicted that Ben would soon be (good, well) enough to go home.

3. The (little, less) coffee I drink, the better I feel.

4. Light walls make a room look (more large, larger) than dark walls do.

5. One of the (unfortunatest, most unfortunate) men I know is a millionaire.

6. The moth (continuous, continuously) thumped against the screen.

7. The Amish manage (good, well) without radios, telephones, or television.

8. When the store owner caught the little boys stealing, he scolded them (bad, badly) and called their parents.

9. It is (good, better) to teach people to fish than to give them fish.

10. Today computers can send a letter around the world more (quick, quickly) than you can write your name on a sheet of paper.

30 Misplaced Modifiers

Copyright ©2006 The McGraw-Hill Companies, Inc. All rights reserved.

Introductory Project

Because of misplaced words, each of the sentences below has more than one possible meaning. In each case, see if you can explain the intended meaning and the unintended meaning. Also, circle the words that you think create the confusion because they are misplaced.

1. The sign in the restaurant window reads, "Wanted: Young Man—To Open Oysters with References."

   Intended meaning: _____

   _____

   Unintended meaning: _____

   _____

2. Clyde and Charlotte decided to have two children on their wedding day.

   Intended meaning: _____

   _____

   Unintended meaning: _____

   _____

3. The students no longer like the math instructor who failed the test.

   Intended meaning: _____

   _____

   Unintended meaning: _____

   _____

Answers are on page 740.

What Misplaced Modifiers Are and How to Correct Them

Modifiers are descriptive words. *Misplaced modifiers* are words that, because of awkward placement, do not describe the words the writer intended them to describe. Misplaced modifiers often obscure the meaning of a sentence. To avoid them, place words as close as possible to what they describe.

Misplaced Words	Correctly Placed Words
Tony bought an old car from a crooked dealer *with a faulty transmission.* (The *dealer* had a faulty transmission?)	Tony bought an old car with a faulty transmission from a crooked dealer. (The words describing the old car are now placed next to "car.")
I *nearly* earned two hundred dollars last week. (You just missed earning two hundred dollars, but in fact earned nothing?)	I earned nearly two hundred dollars last week. (The meaning—that you earned a little under two hundred dollars—is now clear.)
Bill yelled at the howling dog *in his underwear.* (The *dog* wore underwear?)	Bill, in his underwear, yelled at the howling dog. (The words describing Bill are placed next to "Bill.")

ACTIVITY

Underline the misplaced word or words in each sentence. Then rewrite the sentence, placing related words together and thereby making the meaning clear.

EXAMPLES   The suburbs <u>nearly</u> had five inches of rain.
The suburbs had nearly five inches of rain.
_____

We could see the football stadium <u>driving</u> across the bridge.
Driving across the bridge, we could see the football stadium.
_____

1. I saw mountains of uncollected trash walking along the city streets.

_____

2. I almost had a dozen job interviews after I sent out my résumé.

   _____

3. The child stared at the movie monster with huge, innocent eyes.

   _____

4. Joanne decided to live with her grandparents while she attended college to save money.

   _____

5. Charlotte returned the hamburger to the supermarket that was spoiled.

   _____

6. Roger visited the old house still weak with the flu.

   _____

7. The phone almost rang fifteen times last night.

   _____

8. My uncle saw a kangaroo at the window under the influence of whiskey.

   _____

9. We decided to send our daughter to college on the day she was born.

   _____

10. Fred always opens the bills that arrive in the mailbox with a sigh.

   _____

REVIEW TEST

Underline the misplaced word or words in each sentence. Write *M* for *misplaced modifier* or *C* for *correct* in front of each sentence.

_____ 1. Rita found it difficult to mount the horse wearing tight jeans.

_____ 2. Rita, wearing tight jeans, found it difficult to mount the horse.

_____ 3. I noticed a crack in the window walking into the delicatessen.

_____ 4. Walking into the delicatessen, I noticed a crack in the window.

_____ 5. The biology teacher told us there would be a pop quiz with an evil grin.

Copyright ©2006 The McGraw-Hill Companies, Inc. All rights reserved.

_____ 6. With an evil grin, the biology teacher told us there would be a pop quiz.

_____ 7. I almost caught a hundred lightning bugs.

_____ 8. I caught almost a hundred lightning bugs.

_____ 9. In a secondhand store, Willie found a television set that had been stolen from me last month.

_____ 10. Willie found a television set in a secondhand store that had been stolen from me last month.

_____ 11. Willie found, in a secondhand store, a television set that had been stolen from me last month.

_____ 12. In his shrillest voice, the reporter yelled a question at the departing mayor.

_____ 13. The reporter yelled a question at the departing mayor in his shrillest voice.

_____ 14. The president was quoted on the _NBC Evening News_ as saying that the recession was about to end.

_____ 15. The president was quoted as saying that the recession was about to end on the _NBC Evening News_.

31 Dangling Modifiers

Copyright ©2006 The McGraw-Hill Companies, Inc. All rights reserved.

Introductory Project

Because of dangling words, each of the sentences below has more than one possible meaning. In each case, see if you can explain the intended meaning and the unintended meaning.

1. While smoking a pipe, my dog sat with me by the crackling fire.

   Intended meaning: _____

   Unintended meaning: _____

2. Busy talking on a cell phone, his car went through a red light.

   Intended meaning: _____

   Unintended meaning: _____

3. After baking for several hours, Grandmother removed the beef pie from the oven.

   Intended meaning: _____

   Unintended meaning: _____

Answers are on page 740.

What Dangling Modifiers Are and How to Correct Them

A modifier that opens a sentence must be followed immediately by the word it is meant to describe. Otherwise, the modifier is said to be *dangling*, and the sentence takes on an unintended meaning. For example, in the sentence

While smoking a pipe, my dog sat with me by the crackling fire.

the unintended meaning is that the *dog* was smoking the pipe. What the writer meant, of course, was that *he,* the writer, was smoking the pipe. The dangling modifier could be corrected by placing *I,* the word being described, directly after the opening modifier and revising as necessary:

While smoking a pipe, *I sat with* my dog by the crackling fire.

The dangling modifier could also be corrected by placing the subject within the opening word group:

While *I was* smoking my pipe, my dog sat with me by the crackling fire.

Here are other sentences with dangling modifiers. Read the explanations of why they are dangling and look carefully at how they are corrected.

Dangling	Correct
Swimming at the lake, a rock cut Sue's foot. (*Who* was swimming at the lake? The answer is not *rock* but *Sue.* The subject *Sue* must be added.)	Swimming at the lake, Sue cut her foot on a rock. *Or:* When Sue was swimming at the lake, she cut her foot on a rock.
While eating my sandwich, five mosquitoes bit me. (*Who* is eating the sandwich? The answer is not *five mosquitoes,* as it unintentionally seems to be, but *I.* The subject *I* must be added.)	While *I* was eating my sandwich, five mosquitoes bit me. *Or:* While eating my sandwich, *I* was bitten by five mosquitoes.

Copyright ©2006 The McGraw-Hill Companies, Inc. All rights reserved.

Dangling	**Correct**
Getting out of bed, the tile floor was so cold that Yoko shivered all over. (*Who* got out of bed? The answer is not *tile floor* but *Yoko*. The subject *Yoko* must be added.)	Getting out of bed, *Yoko* found the tile floor so cold that she shivered all over. *Or:* When *Yoko* got out of bed, the tile floor was so cold that she shivered all over.
To join the team, a C average or better is necessary. (*Who* is to join the team? The answer is not *C average* but *you*. The subject *you* must be added.)	To join the team, *you* must have a C average or better. *Or:* For *you* to join the team, a C average or better is necessary.

The preceding examples make clear the two ways of correcting a dangling modifier. Decide on a logical subject and do one of the following:

1   Place the subject *within* the opening word group.

> When Sue was swimming at the lake, she cut her foot on a rock.

Note   In some cases an appropriate subordinating word such as *When* must be added, and the verb may have to be changed slightly as well.

2   Place the subject right *after* the opening word group.

> Swimming at the lake, Sue cut her foot on a rock.

ACTIVITY

Ask *Who?* as you look at the opening words in each sentence. The subject that answers the question should be nearby in the sentence. If it is not, provide the logical subject by using either method of correction described above.

EXAMPLE   While sleeping at the campsite, a football hit Derek on the head.

> *While Derek was sleeping at the campsite, a football hit him on the head.*

or   *While sleeping at the campsite, Derek was hit on the head by a football.*

1. Watching the horror movie, goose bumps covered my spine.

_____

2. After putting on a wool sweater, the room didn't seem as cold.

    _____

    _____

3. Flunking out of school, my parents demanded that I get a job.

    _____

    _____

4. Covered with food stains, my mother decided to wash the tablecloth.

    _____

    _____

5. Joining several college clubs, Antonio's social life became more active.

    _____

    _____

6. While visiting the Jungle Park Safari, a baboon scrambled onto the hood of their car.

    _____

    _____

7. Under attack by beetles, Charlotte sprayed her roses with insecticide.

    _____

    _____

8. Standing at the ocean's edge, the wind coated my glasses with a salty film.

    _____

    _____

9. Braking the car suddenly, my shopping bags tumbled off the seat.

    _____

    _____

10. Using binoculars, the hawk was clearly seen following its prey.

    _____

    _____

REVIEW TEST

Write *D* for *dangling* or *C* for *correct* in the blank next to each sentence. Remember that the opening words are a dangling modifier if they have no nearby logical subject to modify.

1. Advertising in the paper, Ian's car was quickly sold.

2. By advertising in the paper, Ian quickly sold his car.

3. After painting the downstairs, the house needed airing to clear out the fumes.

4. After we painted the downstairs, the house needed airing to clear out the fumes.

5. Frustrated by piles of homework, Wanda was tempted to watch television.

6. Frustrated by piles of homework, Wanda's temptation was to watch television.

7. After I waited patiently in the bank line, the teller told me I had filled out the wrong form.

8. After waiting patiently in the bank line, the teller told me I had filled out the wrong form.

9. When dieting, desserts are especially tempting.

10. When dieting, I find desserts especially tempting.

11. Looking through the telescope, I saw a brightly lit object come into view.

12. As I was looking through the telescope, a brightly lit object came into view.

13. Looking through the telescope, a brightly lit object came into my view.

14. Tossed carelessly over the arm of a chair, Teresa saw her new raincoat slide onto the floor.

15. Teresa saw her new raincoat, which had been tossed carelessly over the arm of a chair, slide onto the floor.

Copyright ©2006 The McGraw-Hill Companies, Inc. All rights reserved.

32 Paper Format

When you hand in a paper for any of your courses, probably the first thing you will be judged on is its format. It is important, then, that you do certain things to make your papers look attractive, neat, and easy to read.

Here are guidelines to follow in preparing a paper for an instructor:

1 Use full-size theme or typewriter paper, 8½ by 11 inches.

2 Leave wide margins (1 to 1½ inches) on all four sides of each page. In particular, do not crowd the right-hand or bottom margin. The white space makes your paper more readable; also, the instructor has room for comments.

3 If you write by hand:

   a Use a pen with blue or black ink (*not* a pencil).

   b Do not overlap letters. Do not make decorative loops on letters. On narrow-ruled paper, write only on every other line.

   c Make all your letters distinct. Pay special attention to *a, e, i, o,* and *u*—five letters that people sometimes write illegibly.

   d Keep your capital letters clearly distinct from small letters. You may even want to print all the capital letters.

   e Make commas, periods, and other punctuation marks firm and clear. Leave a slight space after each period.

4 Center the title of your paper on the first line of page 1. Do *not* put quotation marks around the title, do not underline it, and do not put a period after it. Capitalize all the major words in a title, including the first word. Short connecting words within a title like *of, for, the, in,* and *to* are not capitalized. Skip a line between the title and the first line of your text.

5 Indent the first line of each paragraph about five spaces (half an inch) from the left-hand margin.

6 When you keyboard, use double-spacing between lines. Also double-space after a period.

7 Whenever possible, avoid breaking (hyphenating) words at the end of lines. If you must break a word, break only between syllables (see page 502). Do not break words of one syllable.

8 Write your name, the date, and the course number where your instructor asks for them.

Also keep in mind these important points about the *title* and *first sentence* of your paper:

9 The title should simply be several words that tell what the paper is about. It should usually *not* be a complete sentence. For example, if you are writing a paper about one of the most frustrating jobs you have ever had, the title could be just "A Frustrating Job."

10 Do not rely on the title to help explain the first sentence of your paper. The first sentence must be independent of the title. For instance, if the title of your paper is "A Frustrating Job," the first sentence should *not* be "It was working as a babysitter." Rather, the first sentence might be "Working as a babysitter was the most frustrating job I ever had."

ACTIVITY 1

Identify the mistakes in format in the following lines from a student theme. Explain the corrections in the spaces provided. One correction is provided as an example.

	"an unpleasant dining companion"
	My little brother is often an unpleasant dining companion. Last
	night was typical. For one thing, his appearance was disgusting.
	His shoes were not tied, and his shirt was unbuttoned and han-
	ging out of his pants, which he had forgotten to zip up. Traces
	of his afternoon snack of grape juice and chocolate cookies were

1. _Hyphenate only between syllables._

2. _____

3. _____

4. _____

5. _____

6. _____

Copyright ©2006 The McGraw-Hill Companies, Inc. All rights reserved.

ACTIVITY 2

As already stated, a title should tell in several words (but *not* a complete sentence) what a paper is about. Often a title can be based on the topic sentence—the sentence that expresses the main idea of the paper. Following are five topic sentences from student papers. Write a suitable and specific title for each paper, basing the title on the topic sentence. (Note the example.)

EXAMPLE   *Compromise in a Relationship*

Learning how to compromise is essential to a good relationship.

1. *Title:* _____
   Some houseplants are dangerous to children and pets.

2. *Title:* _____
   A number of fears haunted me when I was a child.

3. *Title:* _____
   You don't have to be a professional to take good photographs if you keep a few guidelines in mind.

4. *Title:* _____
   My husband is compulsively neat.

5. *Title:* _____
   There are a number of drawbacks to having a roommate.

ACTIVITY 3

As has already been stated, you must *not* rely on the title to help explain your first sentence. In four of the five sentences that follow, the writer has, inappropriately, used the title to help explain the first sentence.

Rewrite these four sentences so that they stand independent of the title. Write *Correct* under the one sentence that is independent of the title.

EXAMPLE   *Title:* My Career Plans
           First sentence: They have changed in the last six months.

           Rewritten: *My career plans have changed in the last six months.*

1. *Title:* Contending with Dogs
   First sentence: This is the main problem in my work as a mail carrier.

   Rewritten : _____

   _____

Copyright ©2006 The McGraw-Hill Companies, Inc. All rights reserved.

2. *Title:* Study Skills
   First sentence: They are necessary if a person is to do well in college.

   Rewritten : _____

   _____

3. *Title:* Summer Vacation
   First sentence: Contrary to popular belief, a summer vacation can be the most miserable experience of the year.

   Rewritten : _____

   _____

4. *Title:* My Wife and the Sunday Newspaper
   First sentence: My wife has a peculiar way of reading it.

   Rewritten : _____

   _____

5. *Title:* Cell Phones
   First sentence: Many motorists have learned the hard way just how dangerous these handy tools can be.

   Rewritten : _____

   _____

REVIEW TEST

In the space provided, rewrite the following sentences from a student paper. Correct the mistakes in format.

	"disciplining our children"
	My husband and I are becoming experts in disciplining our child-
	ren. We have certain rules that we insist upon, and if there are
	any violations, we are swift to act. When our son simply doesn't
	do what he is told to do, he must write that particular action
	twenty times. For example, if he doesn't brush his teeth, he
	writes, "I must brush my teeth." If a child gets home after the

33 Capital Letters

Copyright ©2006 The McGraw-Hill Companies, Inc. All rights reserved.

Introductory Project

Items 1–13   You probably know a good deal about the uses of capital letters. Answering the questions below will help you check your knowledge.

1. Write the full name of a person you know: _____
2. In what city and state were you born? _____
3. What is your present street address? _____
4. Name a country where you would like to travel: _____
5. Name a school that you attended: _____
6. Give the name of a store where you buy food: _____
7. Name a company where someone you know works: _____
8. What day of the week gives you the best chance to relax? _____
9. What holiday is your favorite? _____
10. What brand of toothpaste do you use? _____
11. Write the brand name of a candy or gum you like: _____
12. Name a song or a television show you enjoy: _____
13. Write the title of a magazine you read: _____

Items 14–16   Three capital letters are needed in the lines below. Underline the words that you think should be capitalized. Then write them, capitalized, in the spaces provided.

the masked man reared his silvery-white horse, waved good-bye, and rode out of town. My heart thrilled when i heard someone say, "that was the Lone Ranger. You don't see his kind much, anymore."

14. _____   15. _____   16. _____

Answers are on page 740.

Main Uses of Capital Letters

Capital letters are used with:

1   The first word in a sentence or direct quotation

2   Names of persons and the word *I*

3   Names of particular places

4   Names of days of the week, months, and holidays

5   Names of commercial products

6   Names of organizations such as religious and political groups, associations, companies, unions, and clubs

7   Titles of books, magazines, newspapers, articles, stories, poems, films, television shows, songs, papers that you write, and the like

Each use is illustrated on the pages that follow.

First Word in a Sentence or Direct Quotation

The panhandler touched me and asked, "Do you have any change?"

(Capitalize the first word in the sentence.)

(Capitalize the first word in the direct quotation.)

"If you want a ride," said Tawana, "get ready now. Otherwise, I'm going alone."

(*If* and *Otherwise* are capitalized because they are the first words of sentences within a direct quotation. But *get* is not capitalized, because it is part of the first sentence within the quotation.)

Names of Persons and the Word *I*

Last night I ran into Tony Curry and Lola Morrison.

Names of Particular Places

Charlotte graduated from Fargone High School in Orlando, Florida. She then moved with her parents to Bakersfield, California, and worked for a time there at Alexander's Gift House. Eventually she married and moved with her husband to the Naval Reserve Center in Atlantic County, New Jersey. She takes courses two nights a week at Stockton State College. On weekends she and her family often visit the nearby Wharton State Park and go canoeing on the Mullica River. She does volunteer work at Atlantic City Hospital in connection with the First Christian Church. In addition, she works during the summer as a hostess at Convention Hall and the Holiday Inn.

But   Use small letters if the specific name of a place is not given.

Charlotte sometimes remembers her unhappy days in high school and at the gift shop where she worked after graduation. She did not imagine then that she would one day be going to college and doing volunteer work for a church and a hospital in the community where she and her husband live.

Names of Days of the Week, Months, and Holidays

I was angry at myself for forgetting that Sunday was Mother's Day.

During July and August, Fred works a four-day week, and he has Mondays off.

Bill still has a scar on his ankle from a cherry bomb that exploded near him on a Fourth of July and a scar on his arm where he stabbed himself with a fishhook on a Labor Day weekend.

But   Use small letters for the seasons—summer, fall, winter, spring.

Names of Commercial Products

After brushing with Colgate toothpaste in the morning, Clyde typically has a glass of Tropicana orange juice and Total cereal with milk, followed by a Marlboro cigarette.

My sister likes to play Monopoly and Sorry; I like chess and poker; my brother likes Scrabble, baseball, and table tennis.

But   Use small letters for the *type* of product (toothpaste, orange juice, cereal, cigarette, and so on).

Names of Organizations Such as Religious and Political Groups, Associations, Companies, Unions, and Clubs

Fred Grencher was a Lutheran for many years but converted to Catholicism when he married. Both he and his wife, Martha, are members of the Democratic

Copyright ©2006 The McGraw-Hill Companies, Inc. All rights reserved.

Party. Both belong to the American Automobile Association. Martha works part time as a refrigerator salesperson at Sears. Fred is a mail carrier and belongs to the Postal Clerks' Union.

Tony met Lola when he was a Boy Scout and she was a Campfire Girl; she asked him to light her fire.

Titles of Books, Magazines, Newspapers, Articles, Stories, Poems, Films, Television Shows, Songs, Papers That You Write, and the Like

On Sunday Lola read the first chapter of *I Know Why the Caged Bird Sings*, a book required for her writing course. She looked through her parents' copy of the *New York Times*. She then read an article titled "Thinking about a Change in Your Career" and a poem titled "Some Moments Alone" in *Cosmopolitan* magazine. At the same time she played an old Beatles album, *Abbey Road*. In the evening she watched *60 Minutes* on television and an old movie, *High Noon*, starring Gary Cooper. Then from 11 P.M. to midnight she worked on a paper titled "Uses of Leisure Time in Today's Culture" for her sociology class.

ACTIVITY

Cross out the words that need capitals in the following sentences. Then write the capitalized forms of the words in the spaces provided. The number of spaces tells you how many corrections to make in each case.

EXAMPLE   I brush with ~~Crest~~ toothpaste but get cavities all the time. _____*Crest*_____

1. A spokesperson for general motors announced that the prices of all chevrolets will rise next year.

   _____   _____   _____

2. In may 2005 mario's family moved here from brownsville, Texas.

   _____   _____   _____

3. The mild-mannered reporter named clark kent said to the Wolfman, "you'd better think twice before you mess with me, Buddy."

   _____   _____   _____

4. While watching television, Spencer drank four pepsis, ate an entire package of ritz crackers, and finished a bag of oreo cookies.

   _____   _____   _____

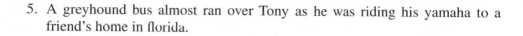
5. A greyhound bus almost ran over Tony as he was riding his yamaha to a friend's home in florida.

_____   _____   _____

6. Before I lent my nikon camera to Janet, I warned her, "be sure to return it by friday."

_____   _____   _____

7. Before christmas George took his entire paycheck, went to sears, and bought a twenty-inch zenith color television.

_____   _____   _____

8. On their first trip to New York City, Fred and Martha visited the empire State Building and Times square. They also saw the New York mets play at Shea Stadium.

_____   _____   _____

9. Clyde was listening to Ray Charles's recording of "America the beautiful," Charlotte was reading an article in *Reader's digest* titled "let's Stop Peddling Sex," and their son was watching *sesame Street.*

_____   _____   _____

10. When a sign for a burger king rest stop appeared on the highway, anita said, "let's stop here. I'm exhausted."

_____   _____   _____

Copyright ©2006 The McGraw-Hill Companies, Inc. All rights reserved.

Other Uses of Capital Letters

Capital letters are also used with:

1   Names that show family relationships

2   Titles of persons when used with their names

3   Specific school courses

4   Languages

5   Geographic locations

6   Historical periods and events

7   Races, nations, and nationalities

8   Opening and closing of a letter

Each use is illustrated on the pages that follow.

Names That Show Family Relationships

I got Mother to babysit for me.

I went with Grandfather to the church service.

Uncle Carl and Aunt Lucy always enclose twenty dollars with birthday cards.

But   Do not capitalize words like *mother, father, grandmother, aunt,* and so on, when they are preceded by a possessive word (*my, your, his, her, our, their*).

I got my mother to babysit for me.

I went with my grandfather to the church service.

My uncle and aunt always enclose twenty dollars with birthday cards.

Titles of Persons When Used with Their Names

I wrote to Senator Grabble and Congresswoman Punchie.

Professor Snorrel sent me to Chairperson Ruck, who sent me to Dean Rappers.

He drove to Dr. Helen Thompson's office after the cat bit him.

But   Use small letters when titles appear by themselves, without specific names.

I wrote to my senator and my congresswoman.

The professor sent me to the chairperson, who sent me to the dean.

He drove to the doctor's office after the cat bit him.

Specific School Courses

I got an A in both Accounting and Small Business Management, but I got a C in Human Behavior.

But   Use small letters for general subject areas.

I enjoyed my business courses but not my psychology or language courses.

Languages

She knows German and Spanish, but she speaks mostly American slang.

Geographic Locations

I grew up in the Midwest. I worked in the East for a number of years and then moved to the West Coast.

But   Use small letters for directions.

A new high school is being built at the south end of town.

Because I have a compass in my car, I know that I won't be going east or west when I want to go north.

Historical Periods and Events

Hector did well answering an essay question about the Second World War, but he lost points on a question about the Great Depression.

Races, Nations, and Nationalities

The research study centered on African Americans and Hispanics.

They have German knives and Danish glassware in the kitchen, an Indian wood carving in the bedroom, Mexican sculptures in the study, and a Turkish rug in the living room.

Opening and Closing of a Letter

Dear Sir:

Dear Madam:

Sincerely yours,

Truly yours,

Note   Capitalize only the first word in a closing.

ACTIVITY

Cross out the words that need capitals in the following sentences. Then write the capitalized forms of the words in the spaces provided. The number of spaces tells you how many corrections to make in each case.

1. Although my grandfather spoke german and polish, my mother never learned either language.

   _____   _____

Copyright ©2006 The McGraw-Hill Companies, Inc. All rights reserved.

2. The e-mail letter began, "dear friend—You must send twenty copies of this message if you want good luck."

_____   _____

3. Tomorrow in our history class, dr. connalley will start lecturing on the civil war.

_____   _____   _____   _____

4. aunt Sarah and uncle Hal, who are mormons, took us to their church services when we visited them in the midwest.

_____   _____   _____   _____

5. While visiting san francisco, Liza stopped in at a buddhist temple and talked to a chinese nun there.

_____   _____   _____   _____

Unnecessary Use of Capitals

Many errors in capitalization are caused by using capitals where they are not needed.

ACTIVITY

Cross out the incorrectly capitalized words in the following sentences. Then write the correct forms of the words in the spaces provided. The number of spaces tells you how many corrections to make in each sentence.

1. The old man told the Cabdriver, "I want to go out to the Airport, and don't try to cheat me."

_____   _____

2. When I see Nike Ads that say, "Just do it," I always think, "Why should a Sneaker tell Me what to do?"

_____   _____   _____

3. A front-page Newspaper story about the crash of a commercial Jet has made me nervous about my Overseas trip.

_____   _____   _____

Copyright: ©2006 The McGraw-Hill Companies, Inc. All rights reserved.

4. During a Terrible Blizzard in 1888, People froze to Death on the streets of New York.

_____   _____   _____   _____

5. I asked the Bank Officer at Citibank, "How do I get a Card to use the automatic teller machines?"

_____   _____   _____

REVIEW TEST 1

Cross out the words that need capitals in the following sentences. Then write the capitalized forms of the words in the spaces provided. The number of spaces tells you how many corrections to make in each sentence.

1. wanda and i agreed to meet on saturday before the football game.

_____   _____   _____

2. Between Long island and the atlantic Ocean lies a long, thin sandbar called fire island.

_____   _____   _____   _____

3. When I'm in the supermarket checkout line, it seems as if every magazine on display has an article called "how You Can Lose Twenty pounds in two weeks."

_____   _____   _____   _____

4. At the bookstore, each student received a free sample pack of bayer aspirin, arrid deodorant, and pert shampoo.

_____   _____   _____

5. "can't you be quiet?" I pleaded. "do you always have to talk while I'm watching *general hospital* on television?"

_____   _____   _____   _____

6. On father's day, the children drove home and took their parents out to dinner at the olive garden.

_____   _____   _____   _____

7. I will work at the holly Day School on mondays and fridays for the rest of september.

_____   _____   _____   _____

8. glendale bank, where my sister Amber works, is paying for her night course, business accounting I.

   _____   _____   _____   _____

9. I subscribe to one newspaper, the *daily news;* and two magazines, *people* and *glamour.*

   _____   _____   _____   _____

10. On thanksgiving my brother said, "let's hurry and eat so i can go watch the football game on our new sony TV."

    _____   _____   _____   _____

REVIEW TEST 2

On separate paper,

1. Write seven sentences demonstrating the seven main uses of capital letters.

2. Write eight sentences demonstrating the eight additional uses of capital letters.

34 Numbers and Abbreviations

Copyright ©2006 The McGraw-Hill Companies, Inc. All rights reserved.

Numbers

1 Spell out numbers that can be expressed in one or two words. Otherwise, use numerals—the numbers themselves.

> During the past five years, over twenty-five barracuda have been caught in the lake.
>
> The parking fine was ten dollars.
>
> In my grandmother's attic are eighty-four pairs of old shoes.

> *But*
>
> Each year about 250 baby trout are added to the lake.
>
> My costs after contesting a parking fine in court were $135.
>
> Grandmother has 382 back copies of *Reader's Digest* in her attic.

2 Be consistent when you use a series of numbers. If some numbers in a sentence or paragraph require more than two words, then use numerals throughout the selection:

> During his election campaign, State Senator Mel Grabble went to 3 county fairs, 16 parades, 45 cookouts, and 112 club dinners, and delivered the same speech 176 times.

3 Use numerals for dates, times, addresses, percentages, and parts of a book.

> The letter was dated April 3, 1872.
>
> My appointment was at 6:15. (*But:* Spell out numbers before *o'clock*. For example: The doctor didn't see me until seven o'clock.)
>
> He lives at 212 West 19th Street.
>
> About 20 percent of our class dropped out of school.
>
> Turn to page 179 in Chapter 8 and answer questions 1–10.

ACTIVITY

Cross out the mistakes in numbers and write the corrections in the spaces provided.

1. Pearl Harbor was attacked on December the seventh, nineteen forty-one.

    _____

    _____

2. When the 2 children failed to return from school, more than 50 people volunteered to search for them.

    _____

    _____

3. At 1 o'clock in the afternoon last Thursday, an earthquake destroyed at least 20 buildings in the town.

    _____

    _____

Abbreviations

While abbreviations are a helpful time-saver in note-taking, you should avoid most abbreviations in formal writing. Listed below are some of the few abbreviations that can be used acceptably in compositions. Note that a period is used after most abbreviations.

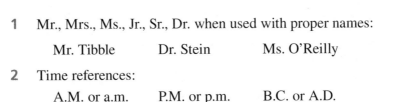

1   Mr., Mrs., Ms., Jr., Sr., Dr. when used with proper names:

    Mr. Tibble   Dr. Stein   Ms. O'Reilly

2   Time references:

    A.M. or a.m.   P.M. or p.m.   B.C. or A.D.

3   First or middle name in a signature:

    R. Anthony Curry   Otis T. Redding   J. Alfred Prufrock

4   Organizations and common terms known primarily by their initials:

    FBI   UN   CBS   FM   DVD

Copyright ©2006 The McGraw-Hill Companies, Inc. All rights reserved.

ACTIVITY

Cross out the words that should not be abbreviated and correct them in the spaces provided.

1. On a Sat. morning I will never forget, Jan. 15, 2004, at ten min. after eight o'clock, I came downstairs and discovered that I had been robbed.

   _____   _____   _____

2. For six years I lived at First Ave. and Gordon St. right next to Shore Memorial Hosp., in San Fran., Calif.

   _____   _____   _____   _____   _____

3. Before her biol. and Eng. exams, Linda was so nervous that her doc. gave her a tranq.

   _____   _____   _____   _____

REVIEW TEST

Cross out the mistakes in numbers and abbreviations and correct them in the spaces provided.

1. At three-fifteen P.M., an angry caller said a bomb was planted in a bus stat. locker.

   _____   _____

2. Page eighty-two is missing from my chem. book.

   _____   _____

3. Martha has over 200 copies of *People* mag.; she thinks they may be worth money someday.

   _____   _____

4. When I was eight yrs. old, I owned three cats, two dogs, and 4 rabbits.

   _____   _____

5. Approx. half the striking workers returned to work on Nov. third, two thousand four.

   _____   _____   _____   _____

Punctuation

35 Apostrophe

> **Introductory Project**
>
> 1. Larry's motorcycle
>   my sister's boyfriend
>   Grandmother's shotgun
>   the men's room
>
>   What is the purpose of the *'s* in the examples above?
>
>   _____
>
> 2. They didn't mind when their dog bit people, but now they're leashing him because he's eating all their garden vegetables.
>
>   What is the purpose of the apostrophe in *didn't, they're,* and *he's?*
>
>   _____
>
> 3. I used to believe that vampires lived in the old coal bin of my cellar.
>   The vampire's whole body recoiled when he saw the crucifix.
>   Fred ate two baked potatoes.
>   One baked potato's center was still hard.
>
>   In each of the sentence pairs above, why is the *'s* used in the second sentence but not in the first?
>
>   _____
>
>   _____
>
> Answers are on page 741.

Copyright ©2006 The McGraw-Hill Companies, Inc. All rights reserved.

The two main uses of the apostrophe are:

1 To show the omission of one or more letters in a contraction

2 To show ownership or possession

Each use is explained on the pages that follow.

Apostrophe in Contractions

A *contraction* is formed when two words are combined to make one word. An apostrophe is used to show where letters are omitted in forming the contraction. Here are two contractions:

have + not = haven't (*o* in *not* has been omitted)

I + will = I'll (*wi* in *will* has been omitted)

The following are some other common contractions:

I	+ am	= I'm	it	+ is	= it's
I	+ have	= I've	it	+ has	= it's
I	+ had	= I'd	is	+ not	= isn't
who	+ is	= who's	could	+ not	= couldn't
do	+ not	= don't	I	+ would	= I'd
did	+ not	= didn't	they	+ are	= they're

Note Will + not has an unusual contraction, won't.

ACTIVITY 1

Combine the following words into contractions. One is done for you.

1. we + are = *we're*

2. are + not = _____

3. you + are = _____

4. they + have = _____

5. would + not = _____

6. you + have = _____

7. has + not = _____

8. who + is = _____

9. does + not = _____

10. there + is = _____

ACTIVITY 2

Write the contractions for the words in parentheses. One is done for you.

1. (Are not) _____*Aren't*_____ you coming with us to the concert?

2. (I am) _____ going to take the car if (it is) _____ all right with you.

3. (There is) _____ an extra bed upstairs if (you would) _____ like to stay here for the night.

4. (I will) _____ give you the name of the personnel director, but there (is not) _____ much chance that (he will) _____ speak to you.

5. Denise (should not) _____ complain about the cost of food if (she is) _____ not willing to grow her own by planting a backyard garden.

Note   Even though contractions are common in everyday speech and in written dialogue, it is usually best to avoid them in formal writing.

Apostrophe to Show Ownership or Possession

To show ownership or possession, we can use such words as *belongs to, possessed by, owned by,* or (most commonly) *of.*

the jacket that *belongs to* Tony
the grades *possessed by* James
the gas station *owned by* our cousin
the footprints *of* the animal

But often the quickest and easiest way to show possession is to use an apostrophe plus *s* (if the word is not a plural ending in *-s*). Thus we can say:

Tony's jacket
James's grades
our cousin's gas station
the animal's footprints

Points to Remember

1   The *'s* goes with the owner or possessor (in the examples given, *Tony, James, cousin, the animal).* What follows is the person or thing possessed (in the examples given, *the jacket, grades, gas station, footprints).*

2   When *'s* is handwritten, there should always be a break between the word and the *'s*.

    Tony's   not   *Tony's*
    Yes   No

3   A singular word ending in *-s* (such as *James* in the earlier example) also shows possession by adding an apostrophe plus *s (James's).*

ACTIVITY 1

Rewrite the italicized part of each of the sentences below, using *'s* to show possession. Remember that the *'s* goes with the owner or possessor.

EXAMPLE   *The toys belonging to the children* filled an entire room.

          The children's toys

1. *The new sunglasses belonging to Elena* have been stolen.

    _____

2. *The visit of my cousin* lasted longer than I wanted it to.

    _____

3. *The owner of the pit bull* was arrested after the dog attacked a child.

    _____

4. *A prescription of a doctor* is needed for the pills.

    _____

5. *The jeep owned by Dennis* was recalled because of an engine defect.

    _____

6. Is this *the hat of somebody?*

    _____

7. You will probably hate *the surprise ending of the movie.*

    _____

Copyright ©2006 The McGraw-Hill Companies, Inc. All rights reserved.

8. *The cords coming from the computer* were so tangled they looked like spaghetti.

_____

9. *The energy level possessed by the little boy* is much higher than hers.

_____

10. *The foundation of the house* is crumbling.

_____

ACTIVITY 2

Add *'s* to each of the following words to make them the possessors or owners of something. Then write sentences using the words. Your sentences can be serious or playful. One is done for you.

1. *parakeet* ___parakeet's___   ___The parakeet's cage needs cleaning.___

_____

2. instructor _____   _____

_____

3. Lola _____   _____

_____

4. store _____   _____

_____

5. mother _____   _____

_____

Apostrophe versus Possessive Pronouns

Do not use an apostrophe with possessive pronouns. They already show ownership. Possessive pronouns include *his, hers, its, yours, ours,* and *theirs.*

Incorrect	Correct
The bookstore lost its' lease.	The bookstore lost its lease.
The racing bikes were theirs'.	The racing bikes were theirs.
The change is your's.	The change is yours.
His' problems are ours', too.	His problems are ours, too.
His' skin is more sunburned than her's.	His skin is more sunburned than hers.

Apostrophe versus Simple Plurals

When you want to make a word plural, just add -*s* at the end of the word. Do *not* add an apostrophe. For example, the plural of the word *movie* is *movies,* not *movie's* or *movies'.* Look at this sentence:

Lola adores Tony's broad shoulders, rippling muscles, and warm eyes.

The words *shoulders, muscles,* and *eyes* are simple plurals, meaning *more than one shoulder, more than one muscle, more than one eye.* The plural is shown by adding only -*s*. On the other hand, the *'s* after *Tony* shows possession—that Tony owns the shoulders, muscles, and eyes.

ACTIVITY

In the space provided under each sentence, add the one apostrophe needed and explain why the other word or words ending in *s* are simple plurals.

EXAMPLE Karens tomato plants are almost six feet tall.

Karens: *Karen's, meaning "belonging to Karen"*

plants: *simple plural meaning "more than one plant"*

1. The restaurants reputation brought hungry diners from miles around.

   restaurants: _____

   diners: _____

2. Phils job—slaughtering pigs—was enough to make him a vegetarian.

   Phils: _____

   pigs: _____

3. As Tinas skill at studying increased, her grades improved.

   Tinas: _____

   grades: _____

4. When I walked into my doctors office, there were six people waiting who also had appointments.

   doctors: _____

   appointments: _____

Copyright ©2006 The McGraw-Hill Companies, Inc. All rights reserved.

5. I bought two magazines and a copy of Stephen Kings latest novel at the bookstore.

   magazines: _____

   Kings: _____

6. After six weeks without rain, the nearby streams started drying up, and the lakes water level fell sharply.

   weeks: _____

   streams: _____

   lakes: _____

7. Rebeccas hooded red cloak makes her look like a fairy-tale character, but her heavy black boots spoil the effect.

   Rebeccas: _____

   boots: _____

8. When the brakes failed on Eriks truck, he narrowly avoided hitting several parked cars and two trees.

   brakes: _____

   Eriks: _____

   cars: _____

   trees: _____

9. My familys favorite breakfast is bacon, eggs, and home-fried potatoes.

   familys: _____

   eggs: _____

   potatoes: _____

10. My parents like Floridas winters, but they prefer to spend their summers back home in Maine.

    Floridas: _____

    winters: _____

    summers: _____

Apostrophe with Plural Words Ending in -s

Plurals that end in -s show possession simply by adding the apostrophe (rather than an apostrophe plus s):

My *parents'* station wagon is ten years old.

The *students'* many complaints were ignored by the high school principal.

All the *Boy Scouts'* tents were damaged by the hailstorm.

ACTIVITY

In each sentence, cross out the one plural word that needs an apostrophe. Then write the word correctly, with the apostrophe, in the space provided.

EXAMPLE ___soldiers'___ All the ~~soldiers~~ rifles were cleaned for inspection.

1. My parents car was stolen last night.

   _____

2. The transit workers strike has just ended.

   _____

3. Two of our neighbors homes are up for sale.

   _____

4. The door to the ladies room is locked.

   _____

5. When students gripes about the cafeteria were ignored, many started to bring their own lunches.

   _____

REVIEW TEST 1

In each sentence, cross out the two words that need apostrophes. Then write the words correctly in the spaces provided.

1. The contestants face fell when she learned that all she had won was a years supply of Ajax cleanser.

   _____   _____

Copyright ©2006 The McGraw-Hill Companies, Inc All rights reserved.

2. Weve been trying for weeks to see that movie, but theres always a long line.

   _____   _____

3. Freds car wouldnt start until the baby-faced mechanic replaced its spark plugs and points.

   _____   _____

4. The citys budget director has trouble balancing his own familys checkbook.

   _____   _____

5. Taking Dianes elderly parents to church every week is one example of Pauls generous behavior.

   _____   _____

6. Heres a checklist of points to follow when youre writing your class reports.

   _____   _____

7. The curious child dropped his sisters makeup into the bedrooms hot-air vent.

   _____   _____

8. The cats babies are under my chair again; I cant find a way to keep her from bringing them near me.

   _____   _____

9. Because of a family feud, Julie wasnt invited to a barbecue at her only cousins house.

   _____   _____

10. Phyllis grade was the highest in the class, and Kevin grade was the lowest.

   _____   _____

REVIEW TEST 2

Make the following words possessive and then use at least five of them in a not-so-serious paragraph that tells a story. In addition, use at least three contractions in the paragraph.

mugger	restaurant	Tony	student
New York	sister	children	vampire
skunk	Jay Leno	boss	Oprah Winfrey
customer	bartender	police car	yesterday
instructor	someone	mob	Chicago

36 Quotation Marks

Copyright ©2006 The McGraw-Hill Companies, Inc. All rights reserved.

Introductory Project

Read the following scene and underline all the words enclosed within quotation marks. Your instructor may also have you dramatize the scene, with one person reading the narration and two persons acting the two speaking parts—the young man and the old woman. The two speakers should imagine the scene as part of a stage play and try to make their words seem as real and true-to-life as possible.

An old woman in a Rolls-Royce was preparing to back into a parking space. Suddenly a small sports car appeared and pulled into the space. "That's what you can do when you're young and fast," the young man in the car yelled to the old woman. As he strolled away, laughing, he heard a terrible crunching sound. "What's that noise?" he said. Turning around, he saw the old woman backing repeatedly into his small car and crushing it. "You can't do that, old lady!" he yelled.

"What do you mean, I can't?" she chuckled, as metal grated against metal. "This is what you can do when you're old and rich."

1. On the basis of the above passage, what is the purpose of quotation marks?

   _____

2. Do commas and periods that come after a quotation go inside or outside the quotation marks?

   _____

Answers are on page 741.

The two main uses of quotation marks are:

1   To set off the exact words of a speaker or a writer

2   To set off the titles of short works

Each use is explained on the pages that follow.

Quotation Marks to Set Off Exact Words of a Speaker or Writer

Use quotation marks when you want to show the exact words of a speaker or a writer.

"Say something tender to me," whispered Lola to Tony.
(Quotation marks set off the exact words that Lola spoke to Tony.)

Mark Twain once wrote, "The more I know about human beings, the more I like my dog."
(Quotation marks set off the exact words that Mark Twain wrote.)

"The only dumb question," the instructor said, "is the one you don't ask."
(Two pairs of quotation marks are used to enclose the instructor's exact words.)

Sharon complained, "I worked so hard on this paper. I spent two days getting information in the library and two days writing it. Guess what grade I got on it."
(Note that the end quotation marks do not come until the end of Sharon's speech. Place quotation marks before the first quoted word of a speech and after the last quoted word. As long as no interruption occurs in the speech, do not use quotation marks for each new sentence.)

Punctuation Hint   In the four examples above, notice that a comma sets off the quoted part from the rest of the sentence. Also observe that commas and periods at the end of a quotation always go *inside* quotation marks.

Complete the following statements explaining how capital letters, commas, and periods are used in quotations. Refer to the four examples as guides.

1. Every quotation begins with a _____ letter.

2. When a quotation is split (as in the sentence above about dumb questions), the

   second part does not begin with a capital letter unless it is a _____
   sentence.

3. _____ are used to separate the quoted part of a sentence from the
   rest of the sentence.

4. Commas and periods that come at the end of a quotation should go _____ the quotation marks.

The answers are *capital, new, Commas,* and *inside.*

ACTIVITY 1

Place quotation marks around the exact words of a speaker or writer in the sentences that follow.

1. The health-food store clerk said, Sucking on zinc lozenges can help you get over a cold.

2. How are you doing in school? my uncle always asks me.

3. An epitaph on a tombstone in Georgia reads, I told you I was sick!

4. Dave said, Let's walk faster. I think the game has already started.

5. Mark Twain once said, The man who doesn't read good books has no advantage over the man who can't.

6. Thelma said, My brother is so lazy that if opportunity knocked, he'd resent the noise.

7. It's extremely dangerous to mix alcohol and pills, Dr. Wilson reminded us. The combination could kill you.

8. Ice-cold drinks! shouted the vendor selling lukewarm drinks.

9. Be careful not to touch the fence, the guard warned. It's electrified.

10. Just because I'm deaf, Lynn said, many people treat me as if I were stupid.

ACTIVITY 2

1. Write a sentence in which you quote a favorite expression of someone you know. Identify the relationship of the person to you.

    EXAMPLE *One of my father's favorite expressions is, "Don't sweat the small stuff."*

    _____

    _____

    _____

    _____

Copyright ©2006 The McGraw-Hill Companies, Inc. All rights reserved.

2. Write a quotation that contains the words *Tony asked Lola.* Write a second quotation that includes the words *Lola replied.*

_____

_____

_____

_____

_____

3. Copy a sentence or two that interest you from a book or magazine. Identify the title and author of the work.

EXAMPLE   In *Night Shift*, Stephen King writes, "I don't like to sleep with one leg sticking out. Because if a cool hand ever reached out from under the bed and grasped my ankle, I might scream."

_____

_____

_____

Indirect Quotations

An indirect quotation is a rewording of someone else's comments, rather than a word-for-word direct quotation. The word *that* often signals an indirect quotation. Quotation marks are *not* used with indirect quotations.

Direct Quotation	**Indirect Quotation**
Fred said, "The distributor cap on my car is cracked." (Fred's exact spoken words are given, so quotation marks are used.)	Fred said that the distributor cap on his car was cracked. (We learn Fred's words indirectly, so no quotation marks are used.)
Sally's note to Jay read, "I'll be working late. Don't wait up for me." (The exact words that Sally wrote in the note are given, so quotation marks are used.)	Sally left a note for Jay saying she would be working late and he should not wait up for her. (We learn Sally's words indirectly, so no quotation marks are used.)

Copyright ©2006 The McGraw-Hill Companies, Inc. All rights reserved.

ACTIVITY

Rewrite the following sentences, changing words as necessary to convert the sentences into direct quotations. The first one is done for you as an example.

1. The instructor told everyone to take out a pen and sheet of paper.

   The instructor said, "Take out a pen and sheet of paper."

2. A student in the front row asked if this was a test.

   _____

3. The instructor replied that it was more of a pop quiz.

   _____

4. She added that anyone who did the homework would find it easy.

   _____

5. The student groaned that he was a dead man.

   _____

Quotation Marks to Set Off Titles of Short Works

Titles of short works are usually set off by quotation marks, while titles of long works are underlined. Use quotation marks to set off the titles of such short works as articles in books, newspapers, or magazines; chapters in a book; short stories; poems; and songs.

On the other hand, you should underline the titles of books, newspapers, magazines, plays, movies, record albums, and television shows.

Quotation Marks	**Underlines**
the article "The Mystique of Lawyers"	in the book Verdicts on Lawyers
the article "Getting a Fix on Repairs"	in the newspaper the New York Times
the article "Animal Facts and Fallacies"	in the magazine Reader's Digest
the chapter "Why Do Men Marry?"	in the book Passages
the story "The Night the Bed Fell"	in the book A Thurber Carnival

Quotation Marks	**Underlines**
the poem "A Prayer for My Daughter"	in the book <u>Poems of W.B. Yeats</u>
the song "Jeremy"	in the album <u>Ten</u>
	the television show <u>Dateline NBC</u>
	the movie <u>Gone with the Wind</u>

Note   In printed works, titles of books, newspapers, and so on are set off by italics—slanted type that looks *like this*—instead of being underlined.

ACTIVITY

Use quotation marks or underlines as needed.

1. Whenever Gina sees the movie The Sound of Music, the song near the end, Climb Every Mountain, makes her cry.

2. No advertising is permitted in Consumer Reports, a nonprofit consumer magazine.

3. I printed out an article titled Too Much Homework? from the online version of Time to use in my sociology report.

4. Eliza's favorite television show is Law and Order, and her favorite movie is Breakfast at Tiffany's.

5. Our instructor gave us a week to buy the textbook titled Personal Finance and to read the first chapter, Work and Income.

6. Every holiday season, our family watches the movie A Christmas Carol on television.

7. Looking around to make sure no one he knew saw him, Bob bought the newest National Enquirer in order to read the story called Man Explodes on Operating Table.

8. Edgar Allan Poe's short story The Murders in the Rue Morgue and his poem The Raven are in a paperback titled Great Tales and Poems of Edgar Allan Poe.

9. When Ling got her TV Guide, she read an article called Who Will Oscar Smile Upon? and thumbed through the listings to read the preview for The Sopranos.

10. The night before his exam, he discovered with horror that the chapter Becoming Mature was missing from Childhood and Adolescence, the psychology text that he had bought secondhand.

Other Uses of Quotation Marks

1   Quotation marks are used to set off special words or phrases from the rest of a sentence:

> Many people spell the words "a lot" as *one* word, "alot," instead of correctly spelling them as two words.
>
> I have trouble telling the difference between "their" and "there."

Note   In printed works, *italics* are often used to set off special words or phrases. That is usually done in this book, for example.

2   Single quotation marks are used to mark off a quotation within a quotation.

> The instructor said, "Know the chapter titled 'Status Symbols' in *Adolescent Development* if you expect to pass the test."
>
> Lola said, "One of my favorite Mae West lines is 'I used to be Snow White, but I drifted.' "

REVIEW TEST 1

Insert quotation marks or underlines where needed in the sentences that follow.

1. Don't you ever wash your car? Lola asked Tony.

2. When the washer tilted and began to buzz, Martha shouted, Let's get rid of that stupid machine!

3. Take all you want, read the sign above the cafeteria salad bar, but please eat all you take.

4. After scrawling formulas all over the board with lightning speed, my math instructor was fond of asking, Any questions now?

5. Move that heap! the truck driver yelled. I'm trying to make a living here.

6. I did a summary of an article titled Aspirin and Heart Attacks in the latest issue of Time.

7. Writer's block is something that happens to everyone at times, the instructor explained. You simply have to keep writing to break out of it.

8. A passenger in the car ahead of Clyde threw food wrappers and empty cups out the window. That man, said Clyde to his son, is a human pig.

Copyright ©2006 The McGraw-Hill Companies, Inc. All rights reserved.

9. If you are working during the day, said the counselor, the best way to start college is with a night course or two.

10. I told the dentist that I wanted Novocain. Don't be a sissy, he said. A little pain won't hurt. I told him that a little pain wouldn't hurt him, but it would bother me.

REVIEW TEST 2

Go through the comics section of a newspaper to find a comic strip that amuses you. Be sure to choose a strip in which two or more characters are speaking to each other. Write a full description that will enable people who have not read the comic strip to visualize it clearly and appreciate its humor. Describe the setting and action in each panel, and enclose the words of the speakers in quotation marks.

37 Comma

Copyright ©2006 The McGraw-Hill Companies, Inc. All rights reserved.

Introductory Project

Commas often (though not always) signal a minor break, or pause, in a sentence. Each of the six pairs of sentences below illustrates one of the six main uses of the comma. Read each pair of sentences aloud and place a comma wherever you feel a slight pause occurs.

1. a. Frank's interests are Maria television and sports.
   b. My mother put her feet up sipped some iced tea and opened the newspaper.

2. a. Although they are tiny insects ants are among the strongest creatures on earth.
   b. To remove the cap of the aspirin bottle you must first press down on it.

3. a. Kitty Litter and Dredge Rivers Hollywood's leading romantic stars have made several movies together.
   b. Sarah who is my next-door neighbor just entered the hospital with an intestinal infection.

4. a. The wedding was scheduled for four o'clock but the bride changed her mind at two.
   b. Verna took three coffee breaks before lunch and then she went on a two-hour lunch break.

5. a. Lola's mother asked her "What time do you expect to get home?"
   b. "Don't bend over to pat the dog" I warned "or he'll bite you."

6. a. Roy ate seventeen hamburgers on July 29 2003 and lived to tell about it.
   b. Roy lives at 817 Cresson Street Detroit Michigan.

Answers are on page 741.

Six Main Uses of the Comma

Commas are used mainly as follows:

1   To separate items in a series

2   To set off introductory material

3   Before and after words that interrupt the flow of thought in a sentence

4   Before two complete thoughts connected by *and, but, for, or, nor, so, yet*

5   To set off a direct quotation from the rest of a sentence

6   For certain everyday material

Each use is explained on the pages that follow.

You may find it helpful to remember that the comma often marks a slight pause, or break, in a sentence. Read aloud the sentence examples given for each use, and listen for the minor pauses, or breaks, that are signaled by commas.

Comma between Items in a Series

Use commas to separate items in a series.

Do you drink tea with milk, lemon, or honey?

Today the dishwasher stopped working, the garbage bag split, and the refrigerator turned into an icebox.

The television talk shows enraged him so much he did not know whether to laugh, cry, or throw up.

Reiko awoke from a restless, nightmare-filled sleep.

Notes

a   The final comma in a series is optional, but it is often used.

b   A comma is used between two descriptive words in a series only if *and* inserted between the words sounds natural. You could say:

Reiko awoke from a restless *and* nightmare-filled sleep.

But notice in the following sentence that the descriptive words do not sound natural when *and* is inserted between them. In such cases, no comma is used.

Wanda drove a shiny blue Corvette. (A shiny *and* blue Corvette doesn't sound right, so no comma is used.)

Copyright ©2006 The McGraw-Hill Companies, Inc. All rights reserved.

ACTIVITY

Place commas between items in a series.

1. Superman believes in truth justice and the American way.

2. Jerry opened his textbook made sure his pencil was sharpened and fell asleep with his head on the desk.

3. Felipe added white wine mushrooms salt pepper and oregano to his spaghetti sauce.

4. Baggy threadbare jeans feel more comfortable than pajamas to me.

5. Carmen grabbed a tiny towel bolted out of the bathroom and ran toward the ringing phone.

Comma after Introductory Material

Use a comma to set off introductory material.

After punching the alarm clock with his fist, Bill turned over and went back to sleep.

Looking up at the sky, I saw a man who was flying faster than a speeding bullet.

Holding a baited trap, Clyde cautiously approached the gigantic mousehole.

In addition, he held a broom in his hand.

Also, he wore a football helmet in case a creature should leap out at his head.

Notes

a   If the introductory material is brief, the comma is sometimes omitted. In the activities here, you should use the comma.

b   A comma is also used to set off extra material at the end of a sentence. Here are two sentences where this comma rule applies:

A sudden breeze shot through the windows, driving the stuffiness out of the room.

I love to cook and eat Italian food, especially spaghetti and lasagna.

ACTIVITY

Place commas after introductory material.

1. When the president entered the room became hushed.

2. Feeling brave and silly at the same time Tony volunteered to go onstage and help the magician.

3. While I was eating my tuna sandwich the cats circled my chair like hungry sharks.

4. Because my parents died when I was young I have learned to look after myself. Even though I am now independent I still carry a special loneliness within me.

5. At first putting extra hot pepper flakes on the pizza seemed like a good idea. However I felt otherwise when flames seemed about to shoot out of my mouth.

Comma around Words Interrupting the Flow of Thought

Use commas before and after words or phrases that interrupt the flow of thought in a sentence.

My brother, a sports nut, owns over five thousand baseball cards.

That game show, at long last, has been canceled.

The children used the old Buick, rusted from disuse, as a backyard clubhouse.

Usually you can "hear" words that interrupt the flow of thought in a sentence. However, if you are not sure that certain words are interrupters, remove them from the sentence. If it still makes sense without the words, you know that the words are interrupters and the information they give is nonessential. Such nonessential information is set off with commas. In the sentence

Dody Thompson, who lives next door, won the javelin-throwing competition.

the words *who lives next door* are extra information, not needed to identify the subject of the sentence, *Dody Thompson*. Put commas around such nonessential information. On the other hand, in the sentence

The woman who lives next door won the javelin-throwing competition.

the words *who lives next door* supply essential information—information needed for us to identify the woman being spoken of. If the words were removed from the sentence, we would no longer know who won the competition. Commas are *not* used around such essential information.

Here is another example:

Wilson Hall, which the tornado destroyed, was ninety years old.

Here the words *which the tornado destroyed* are extra information, not needed to identify the subject of the sentence, *Wilson Hall*. Commas go around such nonessential information. On the other hand, in the sentence

The building which the tornado destroyed was ninety years old.

the words *which the tornado destroyed* are needed to identify the building. Commas are *not* used around such essential information.

As noted above, however, most of the time you will be able to "hear" words that interrupt the flow of thought in a sentence and will not have to think about whether the words are essential or nonessential.

ACTIVITY

Use commas to set off interrupting words.

1. On Friday my day off I went to get a haircut.

2. Dracula who had a way with women is Tony's favorite movie hero. He feels that the Wolfman on the other hand showed no class in handling women.

3. Many people forget that Franklin Roosevelt one of our most effective presidents was disabled.

4. Mowing the grass especially when it is six inches high is my least favorite job.

5. A jar of chicken noodle soup which was all there was in the refrigerator did not make a very satisfying meal.

Comma between Complete Thoughts

Use a comma between two complete thoughts connected by *and, but, for, or, nor, so, yet.*

The wedding was scheduled for four o'clock, but the bride changed her mind at two.

We could always tell when our instructor felt disorganized, for his shirt would not be tucked in.

Rich has to work on Monday nights, so he always remembers to record the TV football game.

Copyright ©2006 The McGraw-Hill Companies, Inc. All rights reserved.

Notes

a   The comma is optional when the complete thoughts are short.

Grace has a headache and Mark has a fever.

Her soda was watery but she drank it anyway.

The day was overcast so they didn't go swimming.

b   Be careful not to use a comma in sentences having *one* subject and a *double* verb. The comma is used only in sentences made up of two complete thoughts (two subjects and two verbs). In the following sentence, there is only one subject (*Kevin*) with a double verb (*will go* and *forget*). Therefore, no comma is needed:

Kevin will go partying tonight and forget all about tomorrow's exam.

Likewise, the following sentence has only one subject (*Rita*) and a double verb (*was* and *will work*); therefore, no comma is needed:

Rita was a waitress at the Red Lobster last summer and probably will work there this summer.

ACTIVITY

Place a comma before a joining word that connects two complete thoughts (two subject-verb combinations). Remember, do *not* place a comma within sentences that have only one subject and a double verb.

1. The oranges in the refrigerator were covered with blue mold and the potatoes in the cupboard felt like sponges.

2. All the pants in the shop were on sale but not a single pair was my size.

3. Martha often window-shops in the malls for hours and comes home without buying anything.

4. Tony left the dentist's office with his mouth still numb from Novocain and he talked with a lisp for two hours.

5. The whole family searched the yard inch by inch but never found Mom's missing wedding ring.

6. The car squealed down the entrance ramp and sped recklessly out onto the freeway.

7. No one volunteered to read his or her paper out loud so the instructor called on Amber.

8. The aliens in the science fiction film visited our planet in peace but we greeted them with violence.

9. I felt like shouting at the gang of boys but didn't dare open my mouth.

10. Lenny claims that he wants to succeed in college but he has missed classes all semester.

Comma with Direct Quotations

Use a comma to set off a direct quotation from the rest of a sentence.

His father shouted, "Why don't you go out and get a job?"

"Our modern world has lost a sense of the sacredness of life," the speaker said.

"No," said Celia to Jerry. "I won't write your paper for you."

"Can anyone remember," wrote Emerson, "when the times were not hard and money not scarce?"

Note   Commas and periods at the end of a quotation go inside quotation marks. See also page 482.

ACTIVITY

Use commas to set off quotations from the rest of the sentence.

1. Hassan came to the door and called out "Welcome to my home!"

2. My partner on the dance floor said "Don't be so stiff. You look as if you swallowed an umbrella."

3. The question on the anatomy test read "What human organ grows faster than any other, never stops growing, and always remains the same size?"

4. The student behind me whispered "The skin."

5. "My stomach hurts" Bruce said "and I don't know whether it was the hamburger or the math test."

Comma with Everyday Material

Use a comma with certain everyday material.

Copyright ©2006 The McGraw-Hill Companies, Inc. All rights reserved.

Persons Spoken To

Tina, go to bed if you're not feeling well.

Cindy, where did you put my shoes?

Are you coming with us, Owen?

Dates

March 4, 2005, is when Martha buried her third husband.

Addresses

Tony's grandparents live at 183 Roxborough Avenue, Cleveland, Ohio 44112.

Note   No comma is used to mark off the zip code.

Openings and Closings of Letters

Dear Santa,

Dear Larry,

Sincerely yours,

Truly yours,

Note   In formal letters, a colon is used after the opening: Dear Sir: *or* Dear Madam:

Numbers

The dishonest dealer turned the used car's odometer from 98,170 miles to 39,170 miles.

ACTIVITY

Place commas where needed.

1. I expected you to set a better example for the others Mike.

2. Janet with your help I passed the test.

3. The movie stars Kitty Litter and Dredge Rivers were married on September 12 2004 and lived at 3865 Sunset Boulevard Los Angeles California for one month.

4. They received 75000 congratulatory fan letters and were given picture contracts worth $3000000 in the first week of their marriage.

5. Kitty left Dredge on October 12 2004 and ran off with their marriage counselor.

Copyright ©2006 The McGraw-Hill Companies, Inc. All rights reserved.

REVIEW TEST 1

Insert commas where needed. In the space provided below each sentence, summarize briefly the rule that explains the use of the comma or commas.

1. The best features of my new apartment are its large kitchen its bay windows and its low rent.

   _____

2. Because we got in line at dawn we were among the first to get tickets for the concert.

   _____

3. "When will someone invent a telephone" Lola asked "that will ring only at convenient moments?"

   _____

4. Without opening his eyes Simon stumbled out of bed and opened the door for the whining dog.

   _____

5. I think Roger that you had better ask someone else for your $2500 loan.

   _____

6. Hot dogs are the most common cause of choking deaths in children for a bite-size piece can easily plug up a toddler's throat.

   _____

7. Tax forms though shortened and revised every year never seem to get any simpler.

   _____

8. Sandra may decide to go to college full-time or she may start by enrolling in a couple of evening courses.

   _____

9. I remember how with the terrible cruelty of children we used to make fun of the shy girl who lived on our street.

   _____

10. Although that old man on the corner looks like a Skid Row bum he is said to have a Swiss bank account.

    _____

REVIEW TEST 2

Insert commas where needed.

1. My dog who is afraid of the dark sleeps with a night-light.

2. "Although men have more upper-body strength" said the lecturer "women are more resistant to fatigue."

3. The hot dogs at the ball park tasted delicious but they reacted later like delayed time bombs.

4. Janice attended class for four hours worked at the hospital for three hours and studied at home for two hours.

5. The patient as he gasped for air tried to assure the hospital clerk that he had an insurance card somewhere.

6. George and Ida sat down to watch the football game with crackers sharp cheese salty pretzels and two frosty bottles of beer.

7. Although I knew exactly what was happening the solar eclipse gave me a strong feeling of anxiety.

8. The company agreed to raise a senior bus driver's salary to $42000 by January 1 2007.

9. Even though King Kong was holding her at the very top of the Empire State Building Fay Wray kept yelling at him "Let me go!"

10. Navel oranges which Margery as a little girl called belly-button oranges are her favorite fruit.

REVIEW TEST 3

On separate paper, write six sentences, each demonstrating one of the six main comma rules.

38 Other Punctuation Marks

Copyright ©2006 The McGraw-Hill Companies, Inc. All rights reserved.

Introductory Project

Each of the sentences below needs one of the following punctuation marks:

     ;   **—**   **-**   **( )**   **:**

See if you can insert the correct mark in each sentence. Each mark should be used once.

1. The following holiday plants are poisonous and should be kept away from children and pets holly, mistletoe, and poinsettias.

2. The freeze dried remains of Annie's canary were in the clear bottle on her bookcase.

3. William Shakespeare 1564–1616 married a woman eight years his senior when he was eighteen.

4. Grooming in space is more difficult than on Earth no matter how much astronauts comb their hair, for instance, it still tends to float loosely around their heads.

5. I opened the front door, and our cat walked in proudly with a live bunny hanging from his mouth.

Answers are on page 741.

499

Colon (:)

Use the colon at the end of a complete statement to introduce a list, a long quotation, or an explanation.

List

The following were my worst jobs: truck loader in an apple plant, assembler in a battery factory, and attendant in a state mental hospital.

Long Quotation

Thoreau explains in *Walden:* "I went to the woods because I wished to live deliberately, to front only the essential facts of life, and see if I could not learn what it had to teach, and not, when I came to die, discover that I had not lived."

Explanation

There are two softball leagues in our town: the fast-pitch league and the lob-pitch league.

ACTIVITY

Place colons where needed.

1. Foods that are high in cholesterol include the following eggs, butter, milk, cheese, shrimp, and red meats.

2. All the signs of the flu were present hot and cold spells, heavy drainage from the sinuses, a bad cough, and an ache through the entire body.

3. In his book *Illiterate America,* Jonathan Kozol has written "Twenty-five million American adults cannot read the poison warnings on a can of pesticide, a letter from their child's teacher, or the front page of a daily paper. An additional 35 million read only at a level which is less than equal to the full survival needs of our society. Together, these 60 million people represent more than one-third of the entire adult population."

Semicolon (;)

The main use of the semicolon is to mark a break between two complete thoughts, as explained on page 393. Another use of the semicolon is to mark off items in a series when the items themselves contain commas. Here are some examples:

Winning prizes at the national flower show were Roberta Collins, Alabama, azaleas; Sally Hunt, Kentucky, roses; and James Weber, California, Shasta daisies.

The following books must be read for the course: *The Color Purple,* by Alice Walker; *In Our Time,* by Ernest Hemingway; and *Man's Search for Meaning,* by Victor Frankl.

ACTIVITY

Place semicolons where needed.

1. The specials at the restaurant today are eggplant Parmesan, for $6.95 black beans and rice, for $5.95 and chicken potpie, for $7.95.

2. The top of the hill offered an awesome view of the military cemetery thousands of headstones were arranged in perfect rows.

3. Lola's favorite old movies are *To Catch a Thief,* starring Cary Grant and Grace Kelly *Animal Crackers,* a Marx Brothers comedy and *The Wizard of Oz,* with Judy Garland.

Dash (—)

A dash signals a pause longer than a comma but not as complete as a period. Use a dash to set off words for dramatic effect:

I didn't go out with him a second time—once was more than enough.

Some of you—I won't mention you by name—cheated on the test.

It was so windy that the VW passed him on the highway—overhead.

Notes

a   The dash can be formed on a keyboard by striking the hyphen twice (--). In handwriting, the dash is as long as two letters would be.

b   Be careful not to overuse dashes.

ACTIVITY

Place dashes where needed.

1. Riding my bike, I get plenty of exercise especially when dogs chase me.

Copyright ©2006 The McGraw-Hill Companies, Inc. All rights reserved.

2. I'm advising you in fact, I'm telling you not to bother me again.

3. The package finally arrived badly damaged.

Hyphen (-)

1   Use a hyphen with two or more words that act as a single unit describing a noun.

> When Jeff removed his mud-covered boots, he discovered a thumb-size hole in his sock.
>
> I both admire and envy her well-rounded personality.
>
> When the dude removed his blue-tinted shades, Lonnell saw the spaced-out look in his eyes.

2   Use a hyphen to divide a word at the end of a line of writing. When you need to divide a word at the end of a line, divide it between syllables. Use your dictionary to be sure of correct syllable divisions (see also page 508).

> When Josh lifted up the hood of his Toyota, he realized that one of the radi-ator hoses had broken.

Notes
a   Do not divide words of one syllable.

b   Do not divide a word if you can avoid doing so.

ACTIVITY

Place hyphens where needed.

1. High flying jets and gear grinding trucks are constant sources of noise pollution in our neighborhood.

2. When Linda turned on the porch light, ten legged creatures scurried every where over the crumb filled floor.

3. Fred had ninety two dollars in his pocket when he left for the supermarket, and he had twenty two dollars when he got back.

Parentheses ( )

Parentheses are used to set off extra or incidental information from the rest of a sentence:

> The section of that book on the medical dangers of abortion (pages 35 to 72) is outdated.

> Yesterday at Hamburger House (my favorite place to eat), the guy who makes french fries asked me to go out with him.

Note   Do not use parentheses too often in your writing.

ACTIVITY

Add parentheses where needed.

1. Certain sections of the novel especially Chapter 5 made my heart race with suspense.

2. Did you hear that George Linda's first husband just got remarried?

3. Sigmund Freud 1856–1939 was the founder of psychoanalysis.

REVIEW TEST

At the appropriate spot, place the punctuation mark shown in the margin.

;

1. Efra's savings have dwindled to nothing she's been borrowing from me to pay her rent.

—

2. There's the idiot I'd know him anywhere who dumped trash on our front lawn.

-

3. Today's two career couples spend more money on eating out than their parents did.

:

4. Ben Franklin said "If a man empties his purse into his head, no man can take it away from him. An investment in knowledge always pays the best interest."

( )

5. One-fifth of our textbook pages 401–498 consists of footnotes and a bibliography.

Copyright ©2006 The McGraw-Hill Companies, Inc. All rights reserved.

Word Use

39 Using the Dictionary

The dictionary is a valuable tool. To help you use it, this chapter explains essential information about dictionaries and the information they provide.

Owning Your Own Dictionaries

You can benefit greatly by owning two dictionaries. First, you should own a paperback dictionary that you can carry with you. Any of the following would be an excellent choice:

The American Heritage Dictionary, Paperback Edition

The Random House Dictionary, Paperback Edition

Webster's New World Dictionary, Paperback Edition

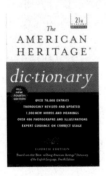
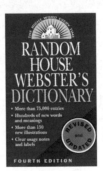

Second, you should own a desk-size, hardcover dictionary that you keep in the room where you study. All the above dictionaries come in hardbound versions.

Copyright ©2006 The McGraw-Hill Companies, Inc. All rights reserved.

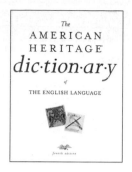 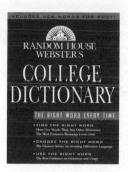 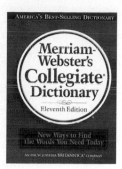

Hardbound dictionaries contain a good deal more information than the paperback editions. For instance, a desk-size dictionary defines far more words than a paperback dictionary. And there are more definitions per word, as well. Although desk-size dictionaries cost more, they are worth the investment, because they are valuable study aids.

Dictionaries are often updated to reflect changes which occur in the language. New words come into use, and old words take on new meanings. So you should not use a dictionary which has been lying around the house for a number of years. Instead, buy yourself a new dictionary. It is easily among the best investments you will ever make.

Dictionaries on Your Computer

If you use a computer, you may have two additional ways to look up a word: online dictionaries and a dictionary that may come with your computer software.

Online Dictionaries

If your computer is connected to the Internet, you may find it easy to check words online. Here are three sites with online dictionaries:

www.merriam-webster.com

www.dictionary.com

www.yourdictionary.com

For example, if you go online to www.merriam-webster.com and type in the word *murder,* you may see the page shown in the illustration.

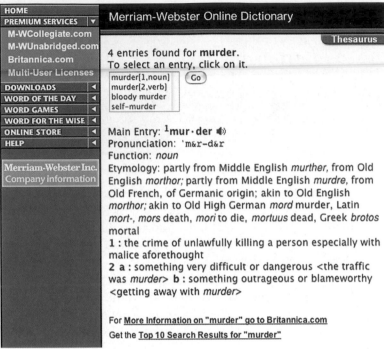

By permission. From Merriam-Webster Online ©2004 at www.Merriam-Webster.com

Notice the speaker icon next to the word *murder*. If you click on this icon, the word will be pronounced for you.

Often, you will also get information on *synonyms* (words with meanings similar to the word you have looked up) and *antonyms* (words with meanings opposite to the word you have looked up).

Software Dictionaries

Some word-processing programs come with a built-in dictionary. For example, if you use Microsoft Word on a Macintosh, just click "Tools" and then choose "Dictionary."

Understanding a Dictionary Entry

Look at the information provided for the word *murder* in the following entry from *Random House Webster's College Dictionary:*

Spelling and syllabication

Pronunciation

Parts of speech

mur•der (mûr′dər), *n.*, *v.*, **-dered. -der•ing.** —*n.* **1.** the unlawful killing of a person, esp. when done with deliberation or premeditation or
occurring during the commission of another seriuos crime **(first-
degree murder)** or with intent but without deliberation or premeditation **(second-degree murder). 2.** something injurious, immoral, or
otherwise censurable: *to get away with murder.* **3.** something extremely difficult or unpleasant: *That exam was murder!* —*v.t.* **4.** to
kill by an act constituting murder. **5.** to kill or slaughter barbarously.
6. to spoil or mar through incompetence: *The singer murdered the
aria.* **7.** *Informal.* to defeat thoroughly.

Meanings

Spelling

The first bit of information, in the boldface (heavy-type) entry itself, is the spelling
of *murder.* You probably already know the spelling of *murder,* but if you didn't, you
could find it by pronouncing the syllables in the word carefully and then looking
it up in the dictionary.

   Use your dictionary to correct the spelling of the following words:

compatable _____	insite _____
althogh _____	troble _____
aksident _____	untill _____
embelish _____	easyer _____
systimatise _____	prepostrous _____
shedule _____	comotion _____
attenshun _____	Vasaline _____
wierd _____	fatel _____
hurryed _____	busines _____
alright _____	jenocide _____
fony _____	poluted _____
kriterion _____	perpose _____
hetirosexual _____	chalange _____

Copyright ©2006 The McGraw-Hill Companies, Inc. All rights reserved.

Syllabication

The second bit of information that the dictionary gives, also in the boldface entry, is the syllabication of *murder*. Note that a dot separates the syllables.

Use your dictionary to mark the syllable divisions in the following words. Also indicate how many syllables are in each word.

j i t t e r   (_____ syllables)

m o t i v a t e   (_____ syllables)

o r a n g u t a n   (_____ syllables)

i n c o n t r o v e r t i b l e   (_____ syllables)

Noting syllable divisions will enable you to *hyphenate* a word: divide it at the end of one line of writing and complete it at the beginning of the next line. You can correctly hyphenate a word only at a syllable division, and you may have to check your dictionary to make sure of the syllable divisions.

Pronunciation

The third bit of information in the dictionary entry is the pronunciation of *murder:* (*mûr′dər*). You already know how to pronounce *murder,* but if you didn't, the information within the parentheses would serve as your guide. Use your dictionary to complete the following exercises that relate to pronunciation.

Vowel Sounds   You will probably use the pronunciation key in your dictionary mainly as a guide to pronouncing vowel sounds (vowels are the letters *a, e, i, o,* and *u*). Here is a part of the pronunciation key in *Random House Webster's College Dictionary:*

a   bat   ā   say   e   set   ē   bee   i   big

The key tells you, for example, that the sound of the short *a* is like the *a* in *bat,* the sound of the long *a* is like the *a* in *say,* and the sound of the short *e* is like the *e* in *set.*

Now look at the pronunciation key in your own dictionary. The key is probably located in the front of the dictionary or at the bottom of alternate pages. What common word in the key tells you how to pronounce each of the following sounds?

ī _____   ŭ _____

ŏ _____   o͞o _____

ō _____   o͞o _____

(Note that a long vowel always has the sound of its own name.)

The Schwa (ə)   The symbol ə looks like an upside-down *e*. It is called a *schwa*, and it stands for the unaccented sound in such words as *ago, item, easily, gallop,* and *circus.* More approximately, it stands for the sound *uh*—like the *uh* that speakers sometimes make when they hesitate. Perhaps it would help to remember that *uh*, as well as ə, could be used to represent the schwa sound.

Here are some of the many words in which the schwa sound appears: *imitation (im-uh-tā'shuhn or im-ə-tā'shən)*; *elevate (el'uh-vāt or el'ə-vāt)*; *horizon (huh-rī'zuhn or hə-rī'zən)*. Open your dictionary to any page, and you will almost surely be able to find three words that make use of the schwa in the pronunciation in parentheses after the main entry.

In the spaces below, write three words that make use of the schwa, and their pronunciations.

1. _____   (_____)

2. _____   (_____)

3. _____   (_____)

Accent Marks   Some words contain both a primary accent, shown by a heavy stroke ('), and a secondary accent, shown by a lighter stroke ('). For example, in the word *controversy (kon'trə vûr'se)*, the stress, or accent, goes chiefly on the first syllable *(kon')*, and, to a lesser extent, on the third syllable *(vûr')*.

Use your dictionary to add stress marks to the following words:

preclude (pri klo͞od)

atrophy (at rə fē)

inveigle (in vā gəl)

ubiquitous (yo͞o bik wi təs)

prognosticate (prog nos ti kāt)

Full Pronunciation   Use your dictionary to write the full pronunciation (the information given in parentheses) for each of the following words.

1. inveigh _____   11. penchant _____

2. diatribe _____   12. antipathy _____

3. raconteur _____   13. capricious _____

Copyright ©2006 The McGraw-Hill Companies, Inc. All rights reserved.

4. panacea _____   14. schizophrenia _____

5. esophagus _____   15. euphemism _____

6. cesarean _____   16. internecine _____

7. clandestine _____   17. amalgamate _____

8. vicarious _____   18. quixotic _____

9. quiescent _____   19. laissez-faire _____

10. parsimony _____

20. antidisestablishmentarianism (This word is probably not in a paperback dictionary, but if you can say *establish* and if you break the rest of the word into individual syllables, you should be able to pronounce it.)

_____

Now practice pronouncing each word. Use the pronunciation key in your dictionary as an aid to sounding out each syllable. Do *not* try to pronounce a word all at once; instead, work on mastering *one syllable at a time*. When you can pronounce each of the syllables in a word successfully, then say them in sequence, add the accent, and pronounce the entire word.

Parts of Speech

The next bit of information that the dictionary gives about *murder* is *n*. This abbreviation means that the meanings of *murder* as a noun will follow.

Use your dictionary if necessary to fill in the meanings of the following abbreviations:

v. = _____   sing. = _____

adj. = _____   pl. = _____

Principal Parts of Irregular Verbs

Murder is a regular verb and forms its principal parts by adding *-ed, -ed,* and *-ing* to the stem of the verb. When a verb is irregular, the dictionary lists its principal parts. For example, with *give* the present tense comes first (the entry itself, *give*). Next comes the past tense (*gave*), and then the past participle (*given*)—the form of the verb used with such helping words as *have, had,* and *was*. Then comes the present participle (*giving*)—the *-ing* form of the verb.

Copyright ©2006 The McGraw-Hill Companies, Inc. All rights reserved.

Look up the principal parts of the following irregular verbs and write them in the spaces provided. The first one has been done for you.

Present	Past	Past Participle	Present Participle
tear	_____	_____	_____
go	_____	_____	_____
know	_____	_____	_____
steal	_____	_____	_____

Plural Forms of Irregular Nouns

The dictionary supplies the plural forms of all irregular nouns. (Regular nouns like *murder* form the plural by adding -*s* or -*es*). Give the plurals of the following nouns. If two forms are shown, write down both.

analysis _____

dictionary _____

criterion _____

activity _____

thesis _____

Meanings

When a word has more than one meaning, the meanings are numbered in the dictionary, as with the verb *murder*. In many dictionaries, the most common meanings of a word are presented first. The introductory pages of your dictionary will explain the order in which meanings are presented.

Use the sentence context to try to explain the meaning of the underlined word in each of the following sentences. Write your definition in the space provided. Then look up and record the dictionary meaning of the word. Be sure to select the meaning that fits the word as it is used in the sentence.

1. I spend an <u>inordinate</u> amount of time watching television.

   Your definition: _____

   Dictionary definition: _____

2. I appreciated her <u>candid</u> remark that my pants were so baggy they made me look like a clown.

Your definition: _____

Dictionary definition: _____

3. The FBI <u>squelched</u> the terrorists' plan to plant a bomb in the White House.

Your definition: _____

Dictionary definition: _____

4. One of the <u>cardinal</u> rules in our house was, "Respect other people's privacy."

Your definition: _____

Dictionary definition: _____

5. A special <u>governor</u> prevents the school bus from traveling more than fifty-five miles an hour.

Your definition: _____

Dictionary definition: _____

Usage Labels

As a general rule, use only standard English words in your writing. If a word is not standard English (as is the case, for example, with the fourth meaning of *murder* as a verb), your dictionary will probably give it a usage label like one of the following: *informal, nonstandard, slang, vulgar, obsolete, archaic, rare.*

Look up the following words and record how your dictionary labels them. Remember that a recent hardbound desk dictionary will always be the best source of information about usage.

flunk _____

tough (meaning "unfortunate, too bad") _____

creep (meaning "an annoying person") _____

ain't _____

scam _____

SP

Synonyms

A *synonym* is a word that is close in meaning to another word. Using synonyms helps you avoid unnecessary repetition of the same word in a paper. A paperback dictionary is not likely to give you synonyms for words, but a good desk dictionary or an online dictionary will. You might also want to own a *thesaurus,* a book that lists synonyms and *antonyms* (words approximately opposite in meaning to another word). You can also find a thesaurus online—for example, www.merriam-webster. com will give you access to a thesaurus as well as a dictionary.

Consult a desk dictionary that gives synonyms for the following words, and write the synonyms in the spaces provided.

heavy _____

escape _____

necessary _____

Copyright ©2006 The McGraw-Hill Companies, Inc. All rights reserved.

40 Improving Spelling

Poor spelling often results from bad habits developed in early school years. With work, you can correct such habits. If you can write your name without misspelling it, there is no reason why you can't do the same with almost any word in the English language. Following are five steps you can take to improve your spelling.

Step 1: Use the Dictionary

Get into the habit of using the dictionary (see pages 504–513). When you write a paper, allow yourself time to look up the spelling of all those words you are unsure about. Do not overlook the value of this step just because it is such a simple one. By using the dictionary, you can probably make yourself a 95 percent better speller.

Step 2: Keep a Personal Spelling List

Keep a list of words you misspell, and study these words regularly. Use the chart on pages 517–520 as a starter. When you accumulate additional words, write them on the back page of a frequently used notebook or keep a computer file titled "Personal Spelling List."

To master the words on your list, do the following:

1   Write down any hint that will help you remember the spelling of a word. For example, you might want to note that *occasion* is spelled with two *c's* and one *s,* or that *all right* is two words, not one word.

2   Study a word by looking at it, saying it, and spelling it. You may also want to write out the word one or more times, or "air-write" it with your finger in large, exaggerated motions.

3   When you have trouble spelling a long word, try to break the word into syllables and see whether you can spell the syllables. For example, *inadvertent* can be spelled easily if you can hear and spell in turn its four syllables: *in ad ver tent.*

Copyright ©2006 The McGraw-Hill Companies, Inc. All rights reserved.

And *consternation* can be spelled easily if you hear and spell in turn its four syllables: *con ster na tion*. Remember, then: try to see, hear, and spell long words syllable by syllable.

4   Keep in mind that review and repeated self-testing are the keys to effective learning. When you are learning a series of words, go back after studying each new word and review all the preceding ones.

Step 3: Master Commonly Confused Words

Master the meanings and spellings of the commonly confused words on pages 526–534. Your instructor may assign twenty words at a time for you to study and may give you a series of quizzes until you have mastered the words.

Step 4: Understand Basic Spelling Rules

Explained briefly here are three rules that may improve your spelling. While exceptions sometimes occur, the rules hold true most of the time.

Rule 1: *Changing y to i*   When a word ends in a consonant plus *y*, change *y* to *i* when you add an ending (but keep the *y* before *-ing*).

try + ed = tried	easy + er = easier
defy + es = defies	carry + ed = carried
ready + ness = readiness	penny + less = penniless

Rule 2: *Final Silent e*   Drop a final *e* before an ending that starts with a vowel (the vowels are *a, e, i, o,* and *u*).

create + ive = creative	believe + able = believable
nerve + ous = nervous	share + ing = sharing

Keep the final *e* before an ending that starts with a consonant.

extreme + ly = extremely	life + less = lifeless
hope + ful = hopeful	excite + ment = excitement

Rule 3: *Doubling a Final Consonant*   Double the final consonant of a word when all three of the following are true:

a   The word is one syllable or is accented on the last syllable.
b   The word ends in a single consonant preceded by a single vowel.
c   The ending you are adding starts with a vowel.

shop	+ er	= shopper	thin	+ est = thinnest
equip	+ ed	= equipped	submit	+ ed = submitted
swim	+ ing	= swimming	drag	+ ed = dragged

ACTIVITY

Combine the following words and endings by applying the three rules above.

1. worry   + ed   = _____
2. write   + ing   = _____
3. marry   + es   = _____
4. run   + ing   = _____
5. terrify + ed   = _____
6. dry   + es   = _____
7. forget   + ing   = _____
8. care   + ful   = _____
9. control + ed   = _____
10. debate   + able = _____

Step 5: Study a Basic Word List

Study the spellings of the words in the following list. They are five hundred of the words most often used in English. Your instructor may assign twenty-five or fifty words for you to study at a time and give you a series of quizzes until you have mastered the list.

Five Hundred Basic Words

ability	approve	breast	college
absent	argue	breathe	color
accept	around	brilliant	come
accident	arrange	brother	comfortable **100**
ache	attempt	building	company
across	attention	bulletin	condition
address	August	bureau	conversation
advertise	automobile	business	copy
advice	autumn	came	daily
after	avenue	can't	danger
again	awful	careful **75**	daughter
against	awkward	careless	daybreak
agree	back	cereal	dear
all right	balance	certain	death
almost	bargain	chair	December
a lot	beautiful	change	decide
already	because	charity	deed
also	become **50**	cheap	dentist
although	been	cheat	deposit
always	before	cheek	describe
amateur	begin	chicken	did
American	being	chief	died
among	believe	children	different
amount	between	choose	dinner
angry **25**	bicycle	church	direction
animal	black	cigarette	discover
another	blue	citizen	disease
answer	board	city	distance
anxious	borrow	close	doctor **125**
appetite	bottle	clothing	does
apply	bottom	coffee	dollar
approach	brake	collect	don't

Copyright: ©2006 The McGraw-Hill Companies, Inc. All rights reserved.

doubt	forty	however	light
down	forward	hundred	listen
dozen	found	hungry	little
during	fourteen	husband	loaf
each	Friday	instead	loneliness
early	friend	intelligence **200**	long
earth	from	interest	lose
easy	gallon	interfere	made
education	garden	interrupt	making
eight	general	into	many
either	get	iron	March
empty	good	itself	marry
English	grammar	January	match
enough	great **175**	July	matter
entrance	grocery	June	may
evening	grow	just	measure
everything	guess	kindergarten	medicine
examine	half	kitchen	men
except	hammer	knock	middle
exercise	hand	knowledge	might
exit	handkerchief	labor	million
expect **150**	happy	laid	minute
fact	having	language	mistake **250**
factory	head	last	Monday
family	heard	laugh	money
far	heavy	learn	month
February	high	led	more
few	himself	left	morning
fifteen	hoarse	leisure	mother
fight	holiday	length	mountain
flower	home	lesson **225**	mouth
forehead	hospital	letter	much
foreign	house	life	must

Copyright ©2006 The McGraw-Hill Companies, Inc. All rights reserved.

nail	ounce	put	sentence
near	overcoat	quart	September
needle	pain	quarter	service
neither	paper	quick	seventeen
never	part	quiet	several
newspaper	peace	quit	shoes
nickel	pear **300**	quite	should
niece	pencil	quiz	sight
night	penny	raise	since
ninety	people	read	sister
noise	perfect	ready	sixteenth
none	period	really	sleep
not	person	reason	smoke
nothing	picture	receive	soap
November **275**	piece	recognize	soldier
now	pillow	refer	something **375**
number	place	religion	sometimes
ocean	plain	remember	soul
o'clock	please	repeat	soup
October	pocket	resource	south
offer	policeman	restaurant	stamp
often	possible	ribbon	state
old	post office	ridiculous	still
omit	potato	right **350**	stockings
once	power	said	straight
one	prescription	same	street
only	president	sandwich	strong
operate	pretty	Saturday	student
opinion	probably	say	studying
opportunity	promise	school	such
optimist	psychology	scissors	suffer
original	public **325**	season	sugar
ought	pursue	see	suit

summer	Thursday	vegetable	what
Sunday	ticket	very	whether **475**
supper	time	view	which
sure	tired	villain **450**	while
sweet	today	visitor	white
take	together **425**	voice	whole
teach	tomorrow	vote	whose
tear **400**	tongue	wage	wife
telegram	tonight	wagon	window
telephone	touch	waist	winter
tenant	toward	wait	without
tenth	travel	wake	woman
than	trouble	walk	wonder
Thanksgiving	trousers	warm	won't
that	truly	warning	work
theater	twelve	Washington	world
them	uncle	watch	worth
there	under	water	would
they	understand	wear	writing
thing	United States	weather	written
thirteen	until	Wednesday	wrong
this	upon	week	year
though	used	weigh	yesterday
thousand	usual	welcome	yet
thread	valley	well	young
three	value	went	your
through	variety	were	you're **500**

Note   Two spelling mistakes that students often make are to write *a lot* as one word (*alot*) and to write *all right* as one word (*alright*). Do not write either *a lot* or *all right* as one word.

41 Vocabulary Development

Copyright ©2006 The McGraw-Hill Companies, Inc. All rights reserved.

A good vocabulary is a vital part of effective communication. A command of many words will make you a better writer, speaker, listener, and reader. Studies have shown that students with a strong vocabulary, and students who work to improve a limited vocabulary, are more successful in school. And one research study found that *a good vocabulary, more than any other factor, was common to people enjoying successful careers.* This section will describe three ways of developing your word power: (1) regular reading, (2) vocabulary wordsheets, and (3) vocabulary study books. You should keep in mind from the start, however, that none of the approaches will help unless you truly decide that vocabulary development is an important goal. Only when you have this attitude can you begin doing the sustained work needed to improve your word power.

Regular Reading

Through reading a good deal, you will learn words by encountering them a number of times in a variety of sentences. Repeated exposure to a word in context will eventually make it a part of your working language.

You should develop the habit of reading a daily newspaper and one or more weekly magazines like *Time, Newsweek,* or even *People,* as well as monthly magazines suited to your interests. In addition, you should try to read some books for pleasure. This may be especially difficult at times when you also have textbook reading to do. Try, however, to redirect a regular half hour to one hour of your recreational time to reading books, rather than watching television, listening to music, or the like. Doing so, you may eventually reap the rewards of an improved vocabulary *and* discover that reading can be truly enjoyable. If you would like some recommendations, ask your instructor for a copy of the "List of Interesting Books" in the Instructor's Manual that accompanies *English Skills with Readings.*

Vocabulary Wordsheets

Vocabulary wordsheets are another means of vocabulary development. Whenever you read, you should mark off words that you want to learn. After you have accumulated a number of words, sit down with a dictionary and look up basic information about each of them. Put this information on a wordsheet like the one shown below. Be sure also to write down a sentence in which each word appears. A word is always best learned not in a vacuum but in the context of surrounding words.

Study each word as follows. To begin with, make sure you can correctly pronounce the word and its derivations. (Page 508 explains the dictionary pronunciation key that will help you pronounce each word properly.) Next, study the main meanings of the word until you can say them without looking at them. Finally, spend a moment looking at the example of the word in context. Follow the same process with the second word. Then, after testing yourself on the first and the second words, go on to the third word. After you learn each new word, remember to continue to test yourself on all the words you have studied. Repeated self-testing is a key to effective learning.

ACTIVITY

In your reading, locate four words that you would like to master. Enter them in the spaces on the vocabulary wordsheet below and fill in all the needed information. Your instructor may then check your wordsheet and perhaps give you a quick oral quiz on selected words.

You may receive a standing assignment to add five words a week to a wordsheet and to study the words. Note that you can create your own wordsheets using a notebook or a computer file, or your instructor may give you copies of the wordsheet that appears below.

Vocabulary Wordsheet

1. Word: _____formidable_____ Pronunciation: __(fôr´mi də bəl)__

   Meanings: ___1. feared or dreaded___

   _____ 2. extremely difficult _____

   Other forms of the word: _formidably   formidability_

   Use of the word in context: _Several formidable obstacles stand between Matt and his goal._

2. Word: _____   Pronunciation: _____

    Meanings: _____

    _____

    Other forms of the word: _____

    Use of the word in context: _____

    _____

3. Word: _____   Pronunciation: _____

    Meanings: _____

    _____

    Other forms of the word: _____

    Use of the word in context: _____

    _____

4. Word: _____   Pronunciation: _____

    Meanings: _____

    _____

    Other forms of the word: _____

    Use of the word in context: _____

    _____

5. Word: _____   Pronunciation: _____

    Meanings: _____

    _____

    Other forms of the word: _____

    Use of the word in context: _____

    _____

Copyright ©2006 The McGraw-Hill Companies, Inc. All rights reserved.

Vocabulary Study Books

A third way to increase your word power is to use vocabulary study books. Many vocabulary books and programs are available. The best are those that present words in one or more contexts and then provide several reinforcement activities for each word. These books will help you increase your vocabulary if you have the determination required to work with them on a regular basis.

42 Commonly Confused Words

Introductory Project

Circle the five words that are misspelled in the following passage. Then see if you can write the correct spellings in the spaces provided.

You're mind and body are not as separate as you might think. Their is a lot of evidence, for instance, that if you believe a placebo (a substance with no medicine) will help you, than it will. One man is said too have recovered rapidly from an advanced case of cancer after only one dose of a drug that he believed was highly effective. Its not clear just how placebos work, but they do show how closely the mind and body are related.

1. _____
2. _____
3. _____
4. _____
5. _____

Answers are on page 741.

Copyright ©2006 The McGraw-Hill Companies, Inc. All rights reserved.

Homonyms

The commonly confused words on the following pages have the same sounds but different meanings and spellings; such words are known as *homonyms*. Complete the activity for each set of homonyms, and check off and study the words that give you trouble.

all ready   completely prepared
already   previously; before

> We were *all ready* to start the play, but the audience was still being seated.
> I have *already* called the police.

Fill in the blanks: I am _____ for the economics examination because

I have _____ studied the chapter three times.

brake   stop; the stopping device in a vehicle
break   come apart

> His car bumper has a sticker reading, "I *brake* for animals."
> "I am going to *break* up with Bill if he keeps seeing other women," said Rita.

Fill in the blanks: When my car's emergency _____ slipped, the car

rolled back and demolished my neighbor's rose garden, causing a _____
in our good relations with each other.

coarse   rough
course   part of a meal; a school subject; direction; certainly (as in *of course*).

> By the time the waitress served the customers the second *course* of the meal, she was aware of their *coarse* eating habits.

Fill in the blanks: Ted felt that the health instructor's humor was too

_____ for his taste and was glad when he finished the

_____.

Copyright ©2006 The McGraw-Hill Companies, Inc. All rights reserved.

hear   perceive with the ear
here   in this place

> "The salespeople act as though they don't see or *hear* me, even though I've been standing *here* for fifteen minutes," the woman complained.

Fill in the blanks: "Did you _____ about the distinguished visitor who just came into town and is staying _____ at this very hotel?"

hole   an empty spot
whole   entire

> "I can't believe I ate the *whole* pizza," moaned Ralph. "I think it's going to make a *hole* in my stomach lining."

Fill in the blanks: The _____ time I was at the party I tried to conceal the _____ I had in my pants.

its   belonging to it
it's   shortened form of *it is* or *it has*

> The car blew *its* transmission (the transmission belonging to it, the car).
> *It's* (it has) been raining all week and *it's* (it is) raining now.

Fill in the blanks: _____ hot and unsanitary in the restaurant kitchen I work in, and I don't think the restaurant deserves _____ good reputation.

knew   past form of *know*
new   not old

> "I had *new* wallpaper put up," said Sarah.
> "I *knew* there was some reason the place looked better," said Bill.

Fill in the blanks: Lola _____ that getting her hair cut would give her face a _____ look.

know   to understand
no   a negative

"I don't *know* why my dog Fang likes to attack certain people," said Martha. "There's *no* one thing the people have in common."

Fill in the blanks: I _____ of _____ way to tell whether that politician is honest or not.

pair   set of two
pear   fruit

"What a great *pair* of legs Tony has," said Lola to Vonnie. Tony didn't hear her, for he was feeling very sick after munching on a green *pear*.

Fill in the blanks: In his lunch box was a _____ of _____s.

passed   went by; succeeded in; handed to
past   time before the present; beyond, as in "We worked past closing time."

Someone *passed* him a wine bottle; it was the way he chose to forget his unhappy *past*.

Fill in the blanks: I walked _____ the instructor's office but was afraid to ask her whether or not I had _____ the test.

peace   calm
piece   part

Nations often risk world *peace* by fighting over a *piece* of land.

Fill in the blanks: Martha did not have any _____ until she gave her dog a _____ of meat loaf.

plain   simple
plane   aircraft

The movie star dressed in *plain* clothes and with no makeup so she would not stand out on the *plane*.

Copyright ©2006 The McGraw-Hill Companies, Inc. All rights reserved.

Fill in the blanks: The game-show contestant opened the small box wrapped in _____ brown paper and found inside the keys to his own jet

_____.

principal   main; a person in charge of a school
principle   law, standard, or rule

> Pete's high school *principal* had one *principal* problem: Pete. This was because there were only two *principles* in Pete's life: rest and relaxation.

Fill in the blanks: The _____ reason she dropped out of school was that she believed in the _____ of complete freedom of choice.

Note   It might help to remember that the *e* in *principle* is also in *rule*—the meaning of *principle.*

right   correct; opposite of *left*
write   put words on paper

> If you have the *right* course card, I'll *write* your name on the class roster.

Fill in the blanks: Eddie thinks I'm weird because I _____ with both my _____ and my left hand.

than   used in comparisons
then   at that time

> When we were kids, my friend Elaine had prettier clothes *than* I did. I really envied her *then.*

Fill in the blanks: Marge thought she was better _____ the rest of us, but _____ she got the lowest grade on the history test.

Note   It might help to remember that the*n* (with an *e*) is also a tim*e* signal.

their   belonging to them
there   at that place; neutral word used with verbs like *is, are, was, were, have,* and *had*
they're shortened form of *they are*

Two people own that van over *there* (at that place). *They're* (they are) going to move out of *their* apartment (the apartment belonging to them) and into the van, in order to save money.

Fill in the blanks: _____ not going to invite us to _____ table

because _____ is no room for us to sit down.

threw   past form of *throw*
through   from one side to the other; finished

The fans *threw* so much litter onto the field that the teams could not go *through* with the game.

Fill in the blanks: When Mr. Jefferson was _____ screaming about the

violence on television, he _____ the newspaper at his dog.

to   verb part, as in *to smile;* toward, as in "I'm going *to* heaven"
too   overly, as in "The pizza was *too* hot"; also, as in "The coffee was hot, *too.*"
two   the number 2

Tony drove *to* the park *to* be alone with Lola. (The first *to* means "toward"; the second *to* is a verb part that goes with *be.)*

Tony's shirt is *too* tight, *too.* (The first *too* means "overly"; the second *too* means "also.")

You need *two* hands (2 hands) to handle a Whopper.

Fill in the blanks: _____ times tonight, you have been _____

ready _____ make assumptions without asking questions first.

wear   to have on
where   in what place

Fred wanted to *wear* his light pants on the hot day, but he didn't know *where* he had put them.

Fill in the blanks: Exactly _____ on my leg should I _____
this elastic bandage?

weather   atmospheric conditions
whether   if it happens that; in case; if

Some people go on vacations *whether* or not the *weather* is good.

Fill in the blanks: I always ask Bill _____ or not we're going to have a
storm, for his bad knee can feel rainy _____ approaching.

whose   belonging to whom
who's   shortened form of *who is* and *who has*

Who's the instructor *whose* students are complaining?

Fill in the blanks: _____ the guy _____ car I saw you in?

your   belonging to you
you're   shortened form of *you are*

You're (meaning "you are") not going to the fair unless *your* brother (the
brother belonging to you) goes with you.

Fill in the blanks: _____ going to have to put aside individual differences
and play together for the sake of _____ team.

Other Words Frequently Confused

Following is a list of other words that people frequently confuse. Complete the activities
for each set of words, and check off and study the words that give you trouble.

a, an   Both *a* and *an* are used before other words to mean, approximately, "one."

Generally you should use *an* before words starting with a vowel (*a, e, i, o, u*):

    an ache   an experiment   an elephant   an idiot   an ox

Generally you should use *a* before words starting with a consonant (all other letters):

    a Coke   a brain   a cheat   a television   a gambler

Copyright ©2006 The McGraw-Hill Companies, Inc. All rights reserved.

Fill in the blanks: The girls had _____ argument over _____ former boyfriend.

accept (ăk sĕpt′)   receive; agree to
except (ĕk sĕpt′)   exclude; but

> "I would *accept* your loan," said Bill to the bartender, "*except* that I'm not ready to pay 25 percent interest."

Fill in the blanks: _____ for the fact that she can't _____ any criticism, Lori is a good friend.

advice (ăd vīs′)   noun meaning "an opinion"
advise (ăd vīz′)   verb meaning "to counsel, to give advice"

> I *advise* you to take the *advice* of your friends and stop working so hard.

Fill in the blanks: I _____ you to listen carefully to any _____ you get from your boss.

affect (uh fĕkt′)   verb meaning "to influence"
effect (i fĕkt′)   verb meaning "to bring about something"; noun meaning "result"

> The full *effects* of marijuana and alcohol on the body are only partly known; however, both drugs clearly *affect* the brain in various ways.

Fill in the blanks: The new tax laws go into _____ next month, and they are going to _____ your income tax deductions.

among   implies three or more
between   implies only two

> We had to choose from *among* fifty shades of paint but *between* only two fabrics.

Fill in the blanks: The layoff notices distributed _____ the unhappy workers gave them a choice _____ working for another month at full pay and leaving immediately with two weeks' pay.

Copyright ©2006 The McGraw-Hill Companies, Inc. All rights reserved.

beside   along the side of
besides   in addition to

   I was lucky I wasn't standing *beside* the car when it was hit.
   Besides being unattractive, these uniforms are impractical.

Fill in the blanks: _____ the alarm system hooked up to the door, our

neighbors keep a gun _____ their beds.

desert (děz′ərt)   stretch of dry land; (dĭ zûrt′) to abandon one's post or duty
dessert (dĭ zûrt′)   last part of a meal

   Sweltering in the *desert,* I was tormented by the thought of an icy *dessert.*

Fill in the blanks: After their meal, they carried their _____ into the

living room so that they would not miss the start of the old _____ movie
about Lawrence of Arabia.

fewer   used with things that can be counted
less   refers to amount, value, or degree

   There were *fewer* than seven people in all my classes today.
   I seem to feel *less* tired when I exercise regularly.

Fill in the blanks: With _____ people able to stay home with children,

today's families spend _____ time together than in the past.

loose (lōōs)   not fastened; not tight-fitting
lose (lōōz)   misplace; fail to win

   Phil's belt is so *loose* that he always looks ready to *lose* his pants.

Fill in the blanks: At least once a week our neighbors _____ their dog;

it's because they let him run _____.

quiet (kwī′ ĭt)   peaceful
quite (kwīt)   entirely; really; rather

   After a busy day, the children are now *quiet,* and their parents are *quite* tired.

Fill in the blanks: The _____ halls of the church become _____ lively during square-dance evenings.

though (thō)   despite the fact that
thought (thôt)   past form of *think*

Even *though* she worked, she *thought* she would have time to go to school.

Fill in the blanks: Yoshiko _____ she would like the job, but even _____ the pay was good, she hated the traveling involved.

REVIEW TEST 1

Underline the correct word in the parentheses. Don't try to guess. If necessary, look back at the explanations of the words.

1. Please take my (advice, advise) and (where, wear) something warm and practical, rather (than, then) something fashionable and flimsy.

2. Glen felt that if he could (loose, lose) twenty pounds, the (affect, effect) on his social life might be dramatic.

3. (Their, There, They're) going to show seven horror films at (their, there, they're) Halloween festival; I hope you'll be (their, there, they're).

4. (Your, You're) going to have to do (a, an) better job on (your, you're) final exam if you expect to pass the (coarse, course).

5. Those (to, too, two) issues are (to, too, two) hot for any politician (to, too, two) handle.

6. Even (though, thought) the (brakes, breaks) on my car were worn, I did not have (quiet, quite) enough money to get them replaced (right, write) away.

7. (Accept, Except) for the fact that my neighbor receives most of his mail in (plain, plane) brown wrappers, he is (know, no) stranger (than, then) anyone else in this rooming house.

8. Because the Randalls are so neat and fussy, (its, it's) hard (to, too, two) feel comfortable when (your, you're) in (their, there, they're) house.

9. (Whose, Who's) the culprit who left the paint can on the table? The paint has ruined a (knew, new) tablecloth, and (its, it's) soaked (threw, through) the linen and (affected, effected) the varnish.

SP

10. I would have been angry at the car that (passed, past) me at ninety miles an hour on the highway, (accept, except) that I (knew, new) it would not get (passed, past) the speed trap (to, too, two) miles down the road.

REVIEW TEST 2

On a separate paper, write short sentences using the ten words shown below.

their	principal
its	except
you're	past
too	through
then	who's

Copyright ©2006 The McGraw-Hill Companies, Inc. All rights reserved.

43 Effective Word Choice

Introductory Project

Write a check mark beside the sentence in each pair that makes more effective use of words.

1. I flipped out when Faye broke our date. _____

   I got very angry when Faye broke our date. _____

2. Doctors as dedicated as Dr. Curtin are few and far between. _____

   Doctors as dedicated as Dr. Curtin are rare. _____

3. Yesterday I ascertained that Elena and Wes broke up. _____

   Yesterday I found out that Elena and Wes broke up. _____

Now see if you can circle the correct number in each case:

Pair (1, 2, 3) contains a sentence with slang.

Pair (1, 2, 3) contains a sentence with a cliché.

Pair (1, 2, 3) contains a sentence with a pretentious word.

Answers are on page 741.

Choose your words carefully when you write. Always take the time to think about your word choices rather than simply using the first word that comes to mind. You want to develop the habit of selecting words that are appropriate and exact for your purposes. One way you can show sensitivity to language is by avoiding slang, clichés, and pretentious words.

Slang

Copyright ©2006 The McGraw-Hill Companies, Inc. All rights reserved.

We often use slang expressions when we talk because they are so vivid and colorful. However, slang is usually out of place in formal writing. Here are some examples of slang expressions:

My girlfriend *got straight* with me by saying she wanted to see other men.

Rick spent all Saturday *messing around* with his car stereo.

My boss *keeps getting on my case* for coming to work late.

My sister *cracked up* when she saw me slip on the wet grass.

The crowd was *psyched up* when the game began.

Slang expressions have a number of drawbacks: they go out of date quickly, they become tiresome if used excessively in writing, and they may communicate clearly to some readers but not to others. Also, the use of slang can be a way of evading the specific details that are often needed to make one's meaning clear in writing. For example, in "The tires on the Corvette make the car look like something else," the writer has not provided the specific details about the tires necessary for us to understand the statement clearly. In general, then, you should avoid slang in your writing. If you are in doubt about whether an expression is slang, it may help to check a recently published hardbound dictionary.

ACTIVITY

Rewrite the following sentences, replacing the italicized slang words with more formal ones.

EXAMPLE The movie was *a real bomb*, so we cut out early.

The movie was terrible, so we left early.

1. My roommate told me he was going to quit school and *hit the road*, but later he admitted he was just *messing with me*.

2. The car was a *steal* until the owner *jacked up* the price.

   _____

   _____

3. If the instructor stops *hassling* me, I am going to *get my act together* in the course.

   _____

   _____

Clichés

A *cliché* is an expression that has been worn out through constant use. Some typical clichés are listed below:

Clichés

all work and no play	saw the light
at a loss for words	short but sweet
better late than never	sigh of relief
drop in the bucket	singing the blues
easier said than done	taking a big chance
had a hard time of it	time and time again
in the nick of time	too close for comfort
in this day and age	too little, too late
it dawned on me	took a turn for the worse
it goes without saying	under the weather
last but not least	where he (she) is coming from
make ends meet	word to the wise
on top of the world	work like a dog
sad but true	

Clichés are common in speech but make your writing seem tired and stale. Also, clichés—like slang—are often a way of evading the specific details that you must work to provide in your writing. You should, then, avoid clichés and try to express your meaning in fresh, original ways.

Copyright ©2c06 The McGraw-Hill Companies, Inc. All rights reserved.

ACTIVITY

Underline the cliché in each of the following sentences. Then substitute specific, fresh words for the trite expression.

EXAMPLE I passed the test by the skin of my teeth.
   I barely passed the test.

1. Hal decided not to eat anything because he was feeling under the weather.

   _____

2. Judy doesn't make any bones about her ambition.

   _____

3. I met with my instructor to try to iron out the problems in my paper.

   _____

Pretentious Words

Some people feel they can improve their writing by using fancy, elevated words rather than simple, natural words. They use artificial and stilted language that more often obscures their meaning than communicates it clearly.

Here are some unnatural-sounding sentences:

I comprehended her statement.

While partaking of our morning meal, we engaged in an animated conversation.

I am a stranger to excessive financial sums.

Law enforcement officers directed traffic when the lights malfunctioned.

The same thoughts can be expressed more clearly and effectively by using plain, natural language, as below:

I understood what she said.

While eating breakfast, we had a lively talk.

I have never had much money.

Police officers directed traffic when the lights stopped working.

ACTIVITY

Cross out the pretentious words in each sentence. Then substitute clear, simple language for the artificial words.

EXAMPLE   The manager ~~reproached~~ me for my ~~tardiness~~.

The manager criticized me for being late.

1. One of Colleen's objectives in life is to accomplish a large family.

   _____

   _____

2. Upon entering our residence, we detected smoke in the atmosphere.

   _____

   _____

3. I am not apprehensive about the test, which encompasses five chapters of the book.

   _____

   _____

REVIEW TEST

Certain words are italicized in the following sentences. In the space provided, identify the words as *slang* (S), *clichés* (C), or *pretentious words* (PW). Then rewrite the sentences, replacing the words with more effective diction.

_____   1. We're *psyched* for tonight's concert, which is going to be *totally awesome*.

   _____

   _____

_____   2. Getting good grades in college is sometimes *easier said than done*.

   _____

   _____

_____   3. I *availed myself* of the chance to *participate in* the computer course.

   _____

   _____

4. The victims of the car accident were shaken but *none the worse for wear.*

_____

_____

5. After *pulling an all-nighter,* my roommate *crashed* on the couch.

_____

_____

6. Be sure to *deposit* your trash in the appropriate *receptacle.*

_____

_____

7. Fred has to *work like a dog* in his advanced math class.

_____

_____

8. My sister's constant criticism *drives me up the wall.*

_____

_____

9. Everyone in our family *congregates* at Miriam's house for the annual Thanksgiving *repast.*

_____

_____

10. Carlos *totally lost it* when the clerk told him that she didn't have any blue shirts in his size.

_____

_____

Copyright ©2006 The McGraw-Hill Companies, Inc. All rights reserved.

44 ESL Pointers

This section covers rules that most native speakers of English take for granted but that are useful for speakers of English as a second language (ESL).

Articles

An *article* is a noun marker—it signals that a noun will follow. There are two kinds of articles: indefinite and definite. The indefinite articles are *a* and *an*. Use *a* before a word that begins with a consonant sound:

> **a c**arrot, **a p**ig, **a u**niform
>
> (*A* is used before *uniform* because the *u* in that word sounds like the consonant *y* plus *u*, not a vowel sound.)

Use *an* before a word beginning with a vowel sound:

> **an e**xcuse, **an o**nion, **an h**onor
>
> (*Honor* begins with a vowel because the *h* is silent.)

The definite article is *the*.

> **the** lemon, **the** fan

An article may come right before a noun:

> **a** circle, **the** summer

Or an article may be separated from the noun by words that describe the noun:

> **a** large circle, **the** long hot summer.

Note There are various other noun markers, including quantity words (*a few, many, a lot of*), numerals (*one, ten, 120*), demonstrative adjectives (*this, these*), adjectives (*my, your, our*), and possessive nouns (*Vinh's, the school's*).

Articles with Count and Noncount Nouns

To know whether to use an article with a noun and which article to use, you must recognize count and noncount nouns. (A *noun* is a word used to name something—a person, place, thing, or idea.)

Count nouns name people, places, things, or ideas that can be counted and made into plurals, such as *window, table,* and *principal* (*one window, two tables, three principals*).

Noncount nouns refer to things or ideas that cannot be counted and therefore cannot be made into plurals, such as *weather, anger,* and *happiness.* The box below lists and illustrates common types of noncount nouns.

Copyright ©2006 The McGraw-Hill Companies, Inc. All rights reserved.

Common Noncount Nouns

Abstractions and emotions: joy, humor, patience, mercy, curiosity

Activities: soccer, gardening, reading, writing, searching

Foods: sugar, spaghetti, fudge, chicken, lettuce

Gases and vapors: air, nitrogen, oxygen, smoke, steam

Languages and areas of study: Laotian, German, social studies, calculus, biology

Liquids: coffee, gasoline, soda, milk, water

Materials that come in bulk or mass form: lumber, soil, dust, detergent, hay

Natural occurrences: gravity, hail, snow, thunder, rust

Other things that cannot be counted: clothing, furniture, homework, machinery, money, news, transportation, vocabulary, work

---

The quantity of a noncount noun can be expressed with a word or words called a *qualifier,* such as *some, more, a unit of,* and so on. In the following two examples, the qualifiers are shown in *italic* type, and the noncount nouns are shown in **boldface** type.

I hear *a little* **anger** in your voice.

The pea soup had gotten thick overnight, so Kala added *more* **water** to it.

Some words can be either count or noncount nouns, depending on whether they refer to one or more individual items or to something in general:

The yearly **rains** in India are called monsoons.

(This sentence refers to individual rains; *rains* in this case is a count noun.)

Rain is something that farmers cannot live without.

(This sentence refers to rain in general; in this case, *rain* is a noncount noun.)

Using *a* or *an* with Nonspecific Singular Count Nouns   Use *a* or *an* with singular nouns that are nonspecific. A noun is nonspecific when the reader doesn't know its specific identity.

A penguin cannot fly; it uses its "wings" to "fly" through the water.

(The sentence refers to any penguin, not a specific one.)

There was **a** fire today in our neighborhood.

(The reader isn't familiar with the fire. This is the first time it is mentioned.)

Using *the* with Specific Nouns   In general, use *the* with all specific nouns—specific singular, plural, and noncount nouns. A noun is specific—and therefore requires the article *the*—in the following cases:

- When it has already been mentioned once

   There was a fire today in our neighborhood. **The** fire destroyed the Smiths' garage.

   (*The* is used with the second mention of *fire*.)

- When it is identified by a word or phrase in the sentence

   The lights in the bathroom do not work.

   (*Lights* is identified by the words *in the bathroom*.)

- When its identity is suggested by the general context

   The coffee at Billy's Diner always tastes a week old.

   (*Coffee* is identified by the words *at Billy's Diner*.)

- When it is unique

   Scientists warn that there is a growing hole in **the** ozone layer.

   (Earth has only one ozone layer.)

- When it comes after a superlative adjective (*best, biggest, wisest*)

   Many of **the** best distance runners come from East Africa.

Copyright ©2006 The McGraw-Hill Companies, Irc. All rights reserved.

Omitting Articles   Omit articles with nonspecific plurals and nonspecific noncount nouns. Plurals and noncount nouns are nonspecific when they refer to something in general.

> **Lights** were on all over the empty house.
>
> **Coffee** should be stored in the refrigerator or freezer if possible.
>
> **Runners** from Kenya, Ethiopia, and Tanzania often win world-class races.

Using *the* with Proper Nouns

Proper nouns name particular people, places, things, or ideas and are always capitalized. Most proper nouns do not require articles; those that do, however, require *the*. Following are general guidelines about when and when not to use *the*.

Do not use *the* for most singular proper nouns, including names of the following:

- *People and animals* (Rosa Parks, Skipper)

- *Continents, states, cities, streets, and parks* (Asia, North Dakota, San Diego, Rodeo Boulevard, Fairmount Park)

- *Most countries* (Thailand, Argentina, England)

- *Individual bodies of water, islands, and mountains* (Lake Tahoe, Prince Edward Island, Mount Saint Helens)

Use *the* for the following types of proper nouns:

- *Plural proper nouns* (the Jacksons, the United Arab Emirates, the Great Lakes, the Appalachian Mountains)

- *Names of large geographic areas, deserts, oceans, seas, and rivers* (the Northeast, the Gobi Desert, the Indian Ocean, the Mediterranean Sea, the Thames River)

- *Names with the format* "the _____ of _____" (the king of Sweden, the Gulf of Aden, the University of New Hampshire)

ACTIVITY

Underline the correct form of the noun in parentheses.

1. (A telephone, Telephone) is found in almost every American home.

2. Today Kim bought (a used car, the used car).

3. (The car, A car) Kim bought is four years old but in very good condition.

4. Thick (fog, fogs) blocked the plane's approach to the airport.

5. My grandparents and cousins all live in (New Jersey, the New Jersey).

6. Adults should have (patience, the patience) when dealing with children.

7. (Indian Ocean, The Indian Ocean) lies between the east coast of Africa and the west coast of Australia.

8. Cats are known for having a great deal of (curiosity, the curiosity).

9. Through the ages, (wine, the wine) has been made out of many fruits other than grapes, such as apples and blueberries.

10. (Water, The water) in the barrel outside is for watering the vegetable garden.

Subjects and Verbs

Avoiding Repeated Subjects

In English, a particular subject can be used only once in a word group with a subject and a verb. Don't repeat a subject in the same word group by following a noun with a pronoun.

> Incorrect: My *friend she* is a wonderful cook.
> Correct: My **friend** is a wonderful cook.
> Correct: **She** is a wonderful cook.

Even when the subject and verb are separated by several words, the subject cannot be repeated in the same word group.

> Incorrect: The *flowers* that are blooming in the yard *they* are called snapdragons.
> Correct: The **flowers** that are blooming in the yard **are called** snapdragons.

Including Pronoun Subjects and Linking Verbs

Some languages may omit a pronoun as a subject, but in English, every sentence other than a command must have a subject. (In a command, the subject *you* is understood: [**You**] Hand in your papers now.)

Incorrect: The party was a success. *Was* lots of fun.

Correct: The party was a success. **It was** lots of fun.

Every English sentence must also have a verb, even when the meaning of the sentence is clear without the verb.

Incorrect: Rosa's handwriting very neat.

Correct: Rosa's handwriting **is** very neat.

Including *There* and *Here* at the Beginning of Sentences

Some English sentences begin with *there* or *here* plus a linking verb (usually a form of *to be: is, are,* and so on). In such sentences, the verb comes before the subject.

There are oranges in the refrigerator.

(The subject is the plural noun *oranges*, so the plural verb *are* is used.)

Here is the book you wanted.

(The subject is the singular noun *book*, so the singular verb *is* is used.)

In sentences like those above, remember not to omit *there* or *here*.

Incorrect: *Are* many good reasons to quit smoking.

Correct: **There are** many good reasons to quit smoking.

Not Using the Progressive Tense of Certain Verbs

The progressive tenses are made up of forms of *be* plus the *-ing* form of the main verb. They express actions or conditions still in progress at a particular time.

Iris **will be running** for student-body president this year.

However, verbs for mental states, the senses, possession, and inclusion are normally not used in the progressive tense.

Incorrect: I **am loving** chocolate.

Correct: I **love** chocolate.

Incorrect: Sonia **is having** a lovely singing voice.

Correct: Sonia **has** a lovely singing voice.

Copyright ©2006 The McGraw-Hill Companies Inc. All rights reserved.

Common verbs not generally used in the progressive tense are listed in the box below.

Common Verbs Not Generally Used in the Progressive

Thoughts, attitudes and desires: agree, believe, imagine, know, like, love, prefer, think, understand, want, wish

Sense perceptions: hear, see, smell, taste

Appearances: appear, seem, look

Possession: belong, have, own, possess

Inclusion: contain, include

Using Gerunds and Infinitives after Verbs

A *gerund* is the *-ing* form of a verb that is used as a noun:

Complaining is my cousin's favorite activity.

(*Complaining* is the subject of the sentence.)

An *infinitive* is *to* plus the basic form of the verb (the form in which the verb is listed in the dictionary), as in **to eat.** The infinitive can function as an adverb, an adjective, or a noun.

We decided **to eat** dinner on the porch.

(*To eat dinner on the porch* functions as an adverb that describes the verb *decided.*)

Simon built a shelf **to hold** his DVD collection.

(*To hold his DVD collection* functions as an adjective describing the noun *shelf.*)

To have good friends is a blessing.

(*To have good friends* functions as a noun—the subject of the verb *is.*)

Some verbs can be followed by only a gerund or only an infinitive; other verbs can be followed by either. Examples are given in the following lists. There are many others; watch for them in your reading.

Verb + gerund (*dislike* + *studying*)
Verb + preposition + gerund (*insist* + *on* + *paying*)

Some verbs can be followed by a gerund but not by an infinitive. In many cases, there is a preposition (such as *for, in,* or *of*) between the verb and the gerund. Following are some verbs and verb-preposition combinations that can be followed by gerunds but not by infinitives:

admit	deny	look forward to
apologize for	discuss	postpone
appreciate	dislike	practice
approve of	enjoy	suspect of
avoid	feel like	talk about
be used to	finish	thank for
believe in	insist on	think about

Incorrect: Sometimes I *enjoy to eat* by myself in a restaurant.
Correct: Sometimes I **enjoy eating** by myself in a restaurant.

Incorrect: Do you *feel like to dance*?
Correct: Do you **feel like dancing**?

Verb + infinitive (*agree* + *to leave*)

Following are common verbs that can be followed by an infinitive but not by a gerund:

agree	decide	manage
arrange	expect	refuse
claim	have	wait

Incorrect: I *agreed taking* Grandma shopping this afternoon.
Correct: I **agreed to take** Grandma shopping this afternoon.

Copyright ©2006 The McGraw-Hill Companies Inc. All rights reserved.

Verb + noun or pronoun + infinitive (*cause + them + to flee*)

Below are common verbs that are first followed by a noun or pronoun and then by an infinitive, not a gerund.

cause	force	remind
command	persuade	warn

Incorrect: The queen *commanded the prince obeying.*

Correct: The queen **commanded the prince to obey.**

Following are common verbs that can be followed either by an infinitive alone or by a noun or pronoun and an infinitive:

ask	need	want
expect	promise	would like

Jerry **would like to join** the army.

Jerry's parents **would like him to go** to college.

Verb + gerund or infinitive (*begin + packing* or *begin + to pack*)

Following are verbs that can be followed by either a gerund or an infinitive:

begin	hate	prefer
continue	love	start

The meaning of each of the verbs above remains the same or almost the same whether a gerund or an infinitive is used.

I prefer **eating** dinner early.

I prefer **to eat** dinner early.

With the verbs below, the gerunds and the infinitives have very different meanings.

forget	remember	stop

Nadia **stopped to put on** makeup.

(She interrupted something to put on makeup.)

Nadia **stopped putting on** makeup.

(She discontinued putting on makeup.)

ACTIVITY

Underline the correct form in parentheses.

1. The police officer (she gave, gave) me a ticket for speeding.

2. The telephone never stops ringing. (Is, It is) driving me crazy.

3. (Are paints and crayons, There are paints and crayons) in that cupboard.

4. That book (contains, is containing) photos of our wedding.

5. My midterm math grade persuaded me (getting, to get) a tutor.

6. After walking in the hot sun, we (very thirsty, were very thirsty).

7. The little girl (talked about to become, talked about becoming) a famous scientist.

8. Lucia (expects earning, expects to earn) a B in the class.

9. The pigeons on the sidewalk (pick up, they pick up) crumbs of food that people drop.

10. For lunch today I (want, am wanting) a big salad.

Copyright ©2006 The McGraw-Hill Companies, Inc. All rights reserved.

Adjectives

Following the Order of Adjectives in English

Adjectives describe nouns and pronouns. In English, an adjective usually comes directly before the word it describes or after a linking verb (a form of *be* or a "sense" verb such as *look*, *seem* and *taste*), in which case it modifies the subject. In each of the following two sentences, the adjective is **boldfaced** and the noun it describes is *italicized*.

That is a **bright** *light.*

That *light* is **bright.**

When more than one adjective modifies the same noun, the adjectives are usually stated in a certain order, though there are often exceptions. Following is the typical order of English adjectives:

Typical Order of Adjectives in a Series

1 **An article or another noun marker:** a, an, the, Joseph's, this, three, your

2 **Opinion adjective:** exciting, plain, annoying, difficult

3 **Size:** enormous, huge, petite, tiny

4 **Shape:** circular, short, round, square

5 **Age:** newborn, recent, old, new, young

6 **Color:** pink, yellow, orange, white

7 **Nationality:** Italian, Chinese, Guatemalan, Russian

8 **Religion:** Buddhist, Catholic, Jewish, Muslim

9 **Material:** plastic, silver, cement, cotton

10 **Noun used as an adjective:** school (as in *school bus*), closet (as in *closet shelf*), birthday (as in *birthday party*)

Here are some examples of the order of adjectives:

> **an interesting old** story
> **the long orange cotton** dress
> **your elderly Hungarian** cousin
> **Rafael's friendly little black** dog

In general, use no more than two or three adjectives after the article or other noun marker. Numerous adjectives in a series can be awkward: **the lovely little old Methodist stone** church.

Using the Present and Past Participles as Adjectives

The present participle ends in *-ing*. Past participles of regular verbs end in *-ed* or *-d*; a list of the past participles of many common irregular verbs appears on pages 413–415. Both types of participles may be used as adjectives. A participle used as an adjective may come before the word it describes:

> It was a **boring** *lecture.*

A participle used as an adjective may also follow a linking verb and describe the subject of the sentence:

> The *lecture* was **boring.**

While both present and past participles of a particular verb may be used as adjectives, their meanings differ. Use the present participle to describe whoever or whatever causes a feeling:

> a **surprising** *conversation*
> (The conversation *caused* the surprise.)

Use the past participle to describe whoever or whatever experiences the feeling:

> the **surprised** *waitress*
> (The waitress *is* surprised.)

Copyright ©2006 The McGraw-Hill Companies, Inc. All rights reserved.

Here are two more sentences that illustrate the differing meanings of present and past participles.

> The mystery movie was **frightening.**
>
> The audience was **frightened.**
>
> (The movie caused the fear; the audience experienced the fear.)

Following are pairs of present and past participles with similar distinctions:

annoying / annoyed	exhausting / exhausted
boring / bored	fascinating / fascinated
confusing / confused	tiring / tired
depressing / depressed	surprising / surprised
exciting / excited	

ACTIVITY

Underline the correct form in parentheses.

1. It was so windy that we had to use stones to hold down the (yellow big plastic, big yellow plastic) tablecloth on the picnic table.

2. At the party, Julie sang a(n) (Vietnamese old, old Vietnamese) song.

3. For her party, the little girl asked if her mother would buy her a (beautiful long velvet, beautiful velvet long) dress.

4. The long walk home from the supermarket left Mira feeling (exhausting, exhausted).

5. The constant barking of our neighbor's dog is very (annoying, annoyed).

Prepositions Used for Time and Place

In English, the use of prepositions is often not based on their common meanings, and there are many exceptions to general rules. As a result, correct use of prepositions must be learned gradually through experience. Following is a chart showing how three of the most common prepositions are used in some customary references to time and place:

Use of *On, In,* and *At* to Refer to Time and Place

Time

On *a specific day:* on Saturday, on June 12, on your birthday
In *a part of a day:* in the morning, in the daytime (but *at* night)
In *a month or a year:* in November, in 1492
In *a period of time:* in a minute, in a couple of days, in a while
At *a specific time:* at 10:00 A.M., at dawn, at sunset, at dinnertime

Place

On *a surface:* on the dresser, on the porch, on the roof
In *a place that is enclosed:* in my bedroom, in the hallway, in the drawer
At *a specific location:* at the pool, at the bar, at the racetrack

---

ACTIVITY

Underline the correct preposition in parentheses.

1. Your next appointment is (on, at) Tuesday.
2. Class begins (on, at) 9 A.M.
3. I plan to watch the game (on, in) a large TV.
4. Sonia is moving to Florida (in, at) a month.
5. The children's birthday party was held (on, at) the bowling alley.

Copyright ©2006 The McGraw-Hill Companies, Inc. All rights reserved.

REVIEW TEST

Underline the correct form in parentheses.

1. When I looked out the window, I was surprised by the deep (snow, snows).

2. (Are, There are) cockroaches in the kitchen.

3. When she did not get the job she wanted, Laura felt (depressing, depressed) for a few days.

4. Owls hunt (at, in) night and sleep most of the day.

5. Larry (postponed to go, postponed going) on vacation because he broke his foot.

6. My English teacher wears a (silver small, small silver) ring in his ear.

7. Marta (has, is having) a very bad cold.

8. (On, In) Valentine's Day, friends and lovers send each other affectionate cards.

9. (Turkey is, Turkeys are) the traditional main course at Thanksgiving dinner.

10. Before the camera was invented, (the paintings, paintings) were the only way to record how people look.

Copyright ©2006 The McGraw-Hill Companies, Inc. All rights reserved.

45 Combined Mastery Tests

Fragments and Run-Ons

■ Combined Mastery Test 1

The word groups below are numbered 1 through 20. In the space provided for each, write C if a word group is a complete sentence, write F if it is a fragment, and write RO if it is a run-on. Then correct the errors.

1. _____
2. _____
3. _____
4. _____
5. _____
6. _____
7. _____
8. _____
9. _____
10. _____
11. _____
12. _____
13. _____
14. _____
15. _____
16. _____
17. _____
18. _____
19. _____
20 _____

[1]I had a frightening dream last night, I dreamed that I was walking high up on an old railroad trestle. [2]It looked like the one I used to walk on recklessly. [3]When I was about ten years old. [4]At that height, my palms were sweating, just as they did when I was a boy. [5]I could see the ground out of the corners of my eyes, I felt a sickening, swooning sensation. [6]Suddenly, I realized there were rats below. [7]Thousands upon thousands of rats. [8]They knew I was up on the trestle, they were laughing. [9]Because they were sure they would get me. [10]Their teeth glinted in the moonlight, their red eyes were like thousands of small reflectors. [11]Which almost blinded my sight. [12]Sensing that there was something even more hideous behind me. [13]I kept moving forward. [14]Then I realized that I was coming to a gap in the trestle. [15]There was no way I could stop or go back I would have to cross over that empty gap. [16]I leaped out in despair. [17]Knowing I would never make it. [18]And felt myself falling helplessly down to the swarm of rejoicing rats. [19]I woke up bathed in sweat. [20]Half expecting to find a rat in my bed.

SCORE   Number correct _____ × 5 = _____ percent

Fragments and Run-Ons

■ Combined Mastery Test 2

The word groups below are numbered 1 through 20. In the space provided for each, write C if a word group is a complete sentence, write F if it is a fragment, and write RO if it is a run-on. Then correct the errors.

1. _____

2. _____

3. _____

4. _____

5. _____

6. _____

7. _____

8. _____

9. _____

10. _____

11. _____

12. _____

13. _____

14. _____

15. _____

16. _____

17. _____

18. _____

19. _____

20 _____

¹My sister asked my parents and me to give up television for two weeks. ²As an experiment for her psychology class. ³We were too embarrassed to refuse, we reluctantly agreed. ⁴The project began on Monday morning. ⁵To help us resist temptation. ⁶My sister unplugged the living room set. ⁷That evening the four of us sat around the dinner table much longer than usual, we found new things to talk about. ⁸Later we played board games for several hours, we all went to bed pleased with ourselves. ⁹Everything went well until Thursday evening of that first week. ¹⁰My sister went out after dinner. ¹¹Explaining that she would be back about ten o'clock. ¹²The rest of us then decided to turn on the television. ¹³Just to watch the network news. ¹⁴We planned to unplug the set before my sister got home. ¹⁵And pretend nothing had happened. ¹⁶We were settled down comfortably in our respective chairs, unfortunately, my sister walked in at that point and burst out laughing. ¹⁷"Aha! I caught you," she cried. ¹⁸She explained that part of the experiment was to see if we would stick to the agreement. ¹⁹Especially during her absence. ²⁰She had predicted we would weaken, it turned out she was right.

SCORE   Number correct _____ × 5 = _____ percent

Verbs

■ **Combined Mastery Test 3**

Each sentence contains a mistake involving (1) standard English or irregular verb forms, (2) subject-verb agreement, or (3) consistent verb tense. Circle the letter that identifies the mistake. Then cross out the incorrect verb and write the correct form in the space provided.

_____ 1. One of my apartment neighbors always keep the radio on all night.

  Mistake in: a. Subject-verb agreement   b. Verb tense

_____ 2. The more the instructor explained the material and the more he wroted on the board, the more confused I got.

  Mistake in: a. Irregular verb form   b. Verb tense

_____ 3. I grabbed the last carton of skim milk on the supermarket shelf, but when I checks the date on it, I realized it was not fresh.

  Mistake in: a. Subject-verb agreement   b. Verb tense

_____ 4. This morning my parents argued loudly, but later they apologized to each other and embrace.

  Mistake in: a. Subject-verb agreement   b. Verb tense

_____ 5. When the bell rang, Mike takes another bite of his sandwich and then prepared for class.

  Mistake in: a. Irregular verb form   b. Verb tense

_____ 6. Someone called Marion at the office to tell her that her son had been bit by a stray dog.

  Mistake in: a. Irregular verb form   b. Verb tense

_____ 7. Because I had throwed away the sales slip, I couldn't return the microwave.

  Mistake in: a. Irregular verb form   b. Verb tense

_____ 8. My dog and cat usually ignores each other, but once in a while they fight.

  Mistake in: a. Subject-verb agreement   b. Verb tense

_____ 9. From the back of our neighborhood bakery comes some of the best smells in the world.

  Mistake in: a. Subject-verb agreement   b. Verb tense

_____ 10. The cost of new soles and heels are more than those old shoes are worth.

  Mistake in: a. Subject-verb agreement   b. Verb tense

SCORE   Number correct _____ × 5 = _____ percent

Copyright ©2006 The McGraw-Hill Companies, Inc. All rights reserved.

Verbs

■ Combined Mastery Test 4

Each sentence contains a mistake involving (1) standard English or irregular verb forms, (2) subject-verb agreement, or (3) consistent verb tense. Circle the letter that identifies the mistake. Then cross out the incorrect verb and write the correct form in the space provided.

_____   1. My friend's bitter words had stinged me deeply.

Mistake in: a. Irregular verb form   b. Verb tense

_____   2. After she poured the ammonia into the bucket, Karen reels backward because the strong fumes made her eyes tear.

Mistake in: a. Subject-verb agreement   b. Verb tense

_____   3. Flying around in space is various pieces of debris from old space satellites.

Mistake in: a. Subject-verb agreement   b. Verb tense

_____   4. Eileen watched suspiciously as a strange car drived back and forth in front of her house.

Mistake in: a. Irregular verb form   b. Verb tense

_____   5. Both crying and laughing helps us get rid of tension.

Mistake in: a. Subject-verb agreement   b. Verb tense

_____   6. All my clothes were dirty, so I stayed up late and washes a load for tomorrow.

Mistake in: a. Subject-verb agreement   b. Verb tense

_____   7. McDonald's has selled enough hamburgers to reach to the moon.

Mistake in: a. Irregular verb form   b. Verb tense

_____   8. When Chen peeled back the bedroom wallpaper, he discovered another layer of wallpaper and uses a steamer to get that layer off.

Mistake in: a. Subject-verb agreement   b. Verb tense

_____   9. Rosie searched for the fifty-dollar bill she had hid somewhere in her dresser.

Mistake in: a. Irregular verb form   b. Verb tense

_____   10. The realistic yellow tulips on the gravestone is made of a weather-resistant fabric.

Mistake in: a. Subject-verb agreement   b. Verb tense

SCORE   Number correct _____ × 5 = _____ percent

Capital Letters and Punctuation

■ Combined Mastery Test 5

Each of the following sentences contains an error in capitalization or punctuation. Refer to the box below and write, in the space provided, the letter identifying the error. Then correct the error.

a. missing capital letter	c. missing quotation marks
b. missing apostrophe	d. missing comma

_____ 1. Maggie's night class has been canceled so she's decided to go to the movies with friends.

_____ 2. "One of the striking differences between a cat and a lie, wrote Mark Twain, "is that a cat has only nine lives."

_____ 3. My uncles checks are printed to look like Monopoly money.

_____ 4. Did you know someone is turning the old school on ninth Street into a restaurant named Home Economics?

_____ 5. My parents always ask me where Im going and when I'll be home.

_____ 6. She doesn't talk about it much, but my aunt has been a member of alcoholics Anonymous for ten years.

_____ 7. The sweating straining horses neared the finish line.

_____ 8. Whenever he gave us the keys to the car, my father would say, Watch out for the other guy."

_____ 9. If you're going to stay up late be sure to turn down the heat before going to bed.

_____ 10. I decided to have a glass of apple juice rather than order a pepsi.

SCORE   Number correct _____ × 5 = _____ percent

Copyright ©2006 The McGraw-Hill Companies, Inc. All rights reserved.

Capital Letters and Punctuation

■ **Combined Mastery Test 6**

Each of the following sentences contains an error in capitalization or punctuation. Refer to the box below and write, in the space provided, the letter identifying the error. Then correct the error.

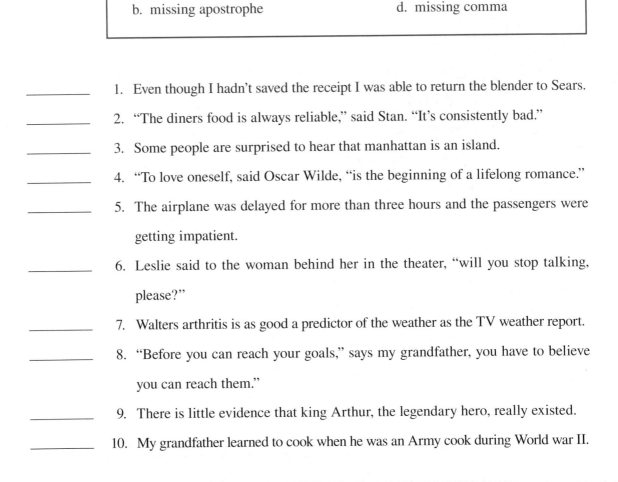

a. missing capital letter	c. missing quotation marks
b. missing apostrophe	d. missing comma

_____   1. Even though I hadn't saved the receipt I was able to return the blender to Sears.

_____   2. "The diners food is always reliable," said Stan. "It's consistently bad."

_____   3. Some people are surprised to hear that manhattan is an island.

_____   4. "To love oneself, said Oscar Wilde, "is the beginning of a lifelong romance."

_____   5. The airplane was delayed for more than three hours and the passengers were getting impatient.

_____   6. Leslie said to the woman behind her in the theater, "will you stop talking, please?"

_____   7. Walters arthritis is as good a predictor of the weather as the TV weather report.

_____   8. "Before you can reach your goals," says my grandfather, you have to believe you can reach them."

_____   9. There is little evidence that king Arthur, the legendary hero, really existed.

_____ 10. My grandfather learned to cook when he was an Army cook during World war II.

SCORE   Number correct _____ × 5 = _____ percent

Word Use

Copyright ©2006 The McGraw-Hill Companies, Inc. All rights reserved.

■ Combined Mastery Test 7

Each of the following sentences contains a mistake identified in the left-hand margin. Underline the mistake and then correct it in the space provided.

Slang

1. Because Nicole has a lot of pull at work, she always has first choice of vacation time.

_____

Wordiness

2. Truthfully, I've been wishing that the final could be postponed to a much later date sometime next week.

_____

Cliché

3. Kate hoped her friends would be green with envy when they saw her new boyfriend.

_____

Pretentious language

4. Harold utilizes old coffee cans to water his houseplants.

_____

Adverb error

5. The sled started slow and then picked up speed as the icy hill became steeper.

_____

Error in comparison

6. When the weather is dry, my sinus condition feels more better.

_____

Confused word

7. If you neglect your friends, their likely to become former friends.

_____

Confused word

8. She's the neighbor who's dog is courting my dog.

_____

Confused word

9. If you don't put cans, jars, and newspapers on the curb for recycling, the township won't pick up you're garbage.

_____

Confused word

10. "Its the most economical car you can buy," the announcer said.

_____

SCORE   Number correct _____ × 5 = _____ percent

Word Use

■ **Combined Mastery Test 8**

Each of the following sentences contains a mistake identified in the left-hand margin. Underline the mistake and then correct it in the space provided.

Slang

1. After coming in to work late all last week, Sheila was canned.

   _____

Wordiness

2. At this point in time, I'm not really sure what my major will be.

   _____

Cliché

3. Jan and Alan knew they could depend on their son in their hour of need.

   _____

Pretentious language

4. I plan to do a lot of comparison shopping before procuring a new dryer.

   _____

Adverb error

5. The children sat very quiet as their mother read the next chapter of *Charlie and the Chocolate Factory.*

   _____

Error in comparison

6. The respectfuller you treat people, the more they are likely to deserve your respect.

   _____

Confused word

7. The dog has lost its' flea collar.

   _____

Confused word

8. "My advise to you," said my grandmother, "is to focus on your strengths, not your fears."

   _____

Confused word

9. The principle advantage of the school cafeteria is that it's three blocks from a Wendy's.

   _____

Confused word

10. My parents mean well, but there goals for me aren't my goals.

    _____

SCORE   Number correct _____ × 5 = _____ percent

46 Editing Tests

The twelve editing tests in this chapter will give you practice in revising for sentence-skills mistakes. Remember that if you don't edit carefully, you run the risk of sabotaging much of the work you have put into a paper. If readers see too many surface flaws, they may assume you don't place much value on what you have to say, and they may not give your ideas a fair hearing. Revising to eliminate sentence-skills errors is a basic part of clear, effective writing.

In half of the tests, the spots where errors occur have been underlined; your job is to identify and correct each error. In the rest of the tests, you must locate as well as identify and correct the errors.

Following are hints that can help you edit the next-to-final draft of a paper for sentence-skills mistakes:

Editing Hints

1   Have at hand two essential tools: a good dictionary (see page 504) and a grammar handbook (you can use Chapter 5 and Part Five of this book).

2   Use a sheet of paper to cover your essay so that you will expose only one sentence at a time. Look for errors in grammar, spelling, and typing. It may help to read each sentence out loud. If a sentence does not read clearly and smoothly, chances are something is wrong.

3   Pay special attention to the kinds of errors you yourself tend to make. For example, if you tend to write run-ons or fragments, be especially on the lookout for those errors.

4   Proofreading symbols that may be of particular help are the following:

	omit	in the ~~the~~ meantime
^	insert missing letter or word	bel*e*ve
cap, lc	Add a capital (or a lowercase) letter	(cap) My persian Çat (lc)

Copyright ©2006 The McGraw-Hill Companies, Inc. All rights reserved.

■ Editing Test 1

Identify the five mistakes in paper format in the student paper that follows. From the box below, choose the letters that describe the five mistakes and write those letters in the spaces provided.

---

a. The title should not be underlined.
b. The title should not be set off in quotation marks.
c. There should not be a period at the end of a title.
d. All the major words in a title should be capitalized.
e. The title should be a phrase, not a complete sentence.
f. The first line of a paper should stand independent of the title.
g. A line should be skipped between the title and the first line of the paper.
h. The first line of a paragraph should be indented.
i. The right-hand margin should not be crowded.
j. Hyphenation should occur only between syllables.

"my candy apple adventure"

It was the best event of my day. I loved the sweetness that filled my mouth as I bit into the sugary coating. With my second bite, I munched contentedly on the apple underneath. Its crunchy tartness was the perfect balance to the smooth sweet-ness of the outside. Then the apple had a magical effect on me. Suddenly I remembered when I was seven years old, walking through the county fairgrounds, holding my father's hand. We stopped at a refreshment stand, and he bought us each a candy apple. I had never had one before, and I asked him what it was. "This is a very special fruit," he said. "If you ever feel sad, all you have to do is eat a candy apple, and it will bring you sweetness." Now, years later, his words came back to me, and as I ate my candy apple, I felt the world turn sweet once more.

1. _____   2. _____   3. _____   4. _____   5. _____

Copyright ©2006 The McGraw-Hill Companies, nc. All rights reserved.

■ Editing Test 2

Identify the sentence skills mistakes at the underlined spots in the paragraph that
follows. From the box below, choose the letter that describes each mistake and write
it in the space provided. The same mistake may appear more than once.

a. fragment	d. apostrophe mistake
b. run-on	e. faulty parallelism
c. mistake in subject-verb agreement	

Looking Out for Yourself

It's sad but true: "If you don't look out for yourself, no one else will." For example,
some people have a false idea about the power of a college <u>degree, they</u> think that once they
<u>possesses</u> the degree, the world will be waiting on their doorstep. In fact, nobody is likely
to be on their doorstep unless, through advance planning, they <u>has</u> prepared themselves
for a career. <u>The kind in which good job opportunities exist.</u> Even after a person has
landed a job, however, a healthy amount of self-interest is needed. People who hide in
corners or <u>with hesitation</u> to let others know about their skills <u>doesn't</u> get promotions or
raises. <u>Its</u> important to take credit for a job well done, whether the job involves writing
a report, <u>organized the office filing system</u>, or calming down an angry customer. Also,
people should feel free to ask the boss for a raise. <u>If they work hard and really deserve it.</u>
Those who look out for themselves get the <u>rewards, people</u> who depend on others to help
them along get left behind.

1. _____ 2. _____ 3. _____ 4. _____ 5. _____

6. _____ 7. _____ 8. _____ 9. _____ 10. _____

■ Editing Test 3

Identify the sentence-skills mistakes at the underlined spots in the paragraph that follows. From the box below, choose the letter that describes each mistake and write it in the space provided. The same mistake may appear more than once.

---

a. fragment

b. run-on

c. mistake in verb tense

d. mistake in irregular verb

e. missing comma after introductory words

f. mistake with quotation marks

g. apostrophe mistake

Deceptive Appearances

Appearances can be deceptive. While looking through a library window yesterday, I saw a neatly groomed woman walk by. Her clothes were skillfully <u>tailored her</u> makeup
<u>was perfect. 1Thinking no one was looking she</u> crumpled a piece of paper in her hand. <u>And
2tossed it into a nearby hedge.</u> Suddenly she no longer <u>looks</u> attractive to me. On another
3   4
occasion, I started talking to a person in my psychology class named Eric. Eric seemed to be a great person. He always got the class laughing with his <u>jokes, on</u> the days when
5
Eric was absent, I think even the professor missed his lively personality. Eric asked me
<u>"if I wanted to eat lunch in the cafeteria with him,"</u> and I felt happy he had <u>chose</u> me to
6   7
be a friend. <u>While we were sitting in the cafeteria.</u> Eric took out an envelope with several
8
kinds of pills inside. "Want one?" he asked. "They're uppers." I didn't want <u>one, I</u> felt
9
disappointed. <u>Erics</u> terrific personality was the product of the pills he took.
10

1. _____   2. _____   3. _____   4. _____   5. _____

6. _____   7. _____   8. _____   9. _____   10. _____

■ Editing Test 4

Identify the sentence-skills mistakes at the underlined spots in the paragraph that follows. From the box below, choose the letter that describes each mistake and write it in the space provided. The same mistake may appear more than once.

a. fragment	e. apostrophe mistake
b. run-on	f. dangling modifier
c. irregular verb mistake	g. missing quotation marks
d. missing comma after introductory words	

A Horrifying Moment

The most horrifying moment of my life occurred in the dark hallway of my building. <u>Which led to my apartment.</u> Though the hallway light was <u>out I</u> managed to find my
1 2
apartment door. However, I could not find the keyhole with my door key. I then pulled

a book of matches from my pocket. <u>Trying to strike a match,</u> the entire book of matches
3
<u>bursted</u> into flames. I flicked the matches away but not before my coat sleeve <u>catched fire.</u>
4 5
Within seconds, my arm was like a torch. <u>Struggling to unsnap the buttons of my coat,</u>
6
flames began to sear my skin. I was quickly going into shock. <u>And began screaming in</u>
7
<u>pain.</u> A <u>neighbors</u> door opened and a voice cried out, <u>My God!</u> I was pulled through an
8 9
apartment and put under a bathroom shower, which extinguished the flames. I suffered

third-degree burns on my <u>arm, I</u> felt lucky to escape with my life.
10

1. _____   2. _____   3. _____   4. _____   5. _____

6. _____   7. _____   8. _____   9. _____   10. _____

Copyright ©2006 The McGraw-Hill Companies, Inc. All rights reserved.

■ Editing Test 5

Identify the sentence-skills mistakes at the underlined spots in the paragraph that follows. From the box below, choose the letter that describes each mistake and write it in the space provided. The same mistake may appear more than once.

---

a. fragment

b. run-on

c. missing capital letter

d. mistake in subject-verb agreement

e. faulty parallelism

f. apostrophe mistake

g. missing quotation mark

h. missing comma after introductory words

Why I Didn't Go to Church

In my boyhood years, I almost never attended church. There was an unwritten code that the guys on the corner <u>was</u> not to be seen in <u>churches'</u>. <u>Although there was</u> many days when I wanted to attend a church, I felt I had no choice but to stay away. If the guys had heard I had gone to church, they would have said things like, <u>"hey,</u> angel, when are you going to <u>fly?</u> With my group of friends, <u>its</u> amazing that I developed any religious feeling at all. Another reason for not going to church was my father. When he was around the <u>house</u> he told my mother, "Mike's not going to church. No boy of mine is a sissy." My mother and sister went to <u>church,</u> I sat with my father and read the Sunday paper or <u>watching television.</u> I did not start going to church until years later. <u>When I no longer hung around with the guys on the corner or let my father have power over me.</u>

1. _____   2. _____   3. _____   4. _____   5. _____

6. _____   7. _____   8. _____   9. _____   10. _____

Copyright ©2006 The McGraw-Hill Companies, Inc. All rights reserved.

■ Editing Test 6

Identify the sentence-skills mistakes at the underlined spots in the paragraph that follows. From the box below, choose the letter that describes each mistake and write it in the space provided. The same mistake may appear more than once.

a. fragment	f. missing comma between two complete thoughts
b. run-on	
c. faulty parallelism	g. missing comma after introductory words
d. missing apostrophe	
e. missing quotation mark	h. misspelled word

Anxiety and the Telephone

Not many of us would want to do without our telephone but there are times when the

                                                                                              1

phone is a source of anxiety. For example, you might be walking up to your front door.

When you hear the phone ring. You struggle to find your key, to unlock the door, and

                 2

getting to the phone quickly. You know the phone will stop ringing the instant you pick up

   3

the receiver, then you wonder if you missed the call that would have made you a millionare

                 4   5

or introduced you to the love of your life. Another time, you may have called in sick to

work with a phony excuse. All day long, youre afraid to leave the house in case the boss

                                          6

calls back. And asks himself why you were feeling well enough to go out. In addition, you

                 7

worry that you might unthinkingly pick up the phone and say in a cheerful voice, "Hello,

                                                                                              8

completely forgetting to use your fake cough. In cases like these having a telephone is more

                 9   10

of a curse than a blessing.

1. _____   2. _____   3. _____   4. _____   5. _____

6. _____   7. _____   8. _____   9. _____   10. _____

■ Editing Test 7

See if you can locate and correct the ten sentence-skills mistakes in the following passage. The mistakes are listed in the box below. As you locate each mistake, write the number of the word group containing that mistake. Use the spaces provided. Then (on separate paper) correct the mistakes.

---

5 fragments   _____   _____   _____   _____   _____

5 run-ons   _____   _____   _____   _____   _____

Family Stories

¹When I was little, my parents invented some strange stories to explain everyday events to me, my father, for example, told me that trolls lived in our house. ²When objects such as scissors or pens were missing. ³My father would look at me and say, "The trolls took them." ⁴For years, I kept a flashlight next to my bed. ⁵Hoping to catch the trolls in the act as they carried away our possessions. ⁶Another story I still remember is my mother's explanation of pussy willows. ⁷After the fuzzy gray buds emerged in our backyard one spring. ⁸I asked Mom what they were. ⁹Pussy willows, she explained, were cats who had already lived nine lives, in this tenth life, only the tips of the cats' tails were visible to people. ¹⁰All the tails looked alike. ¹¹So that none of the cats would be jealous of the others. ¹²It was also my mother who created the legend of the birthday fairy, this fairy always knew which presents I wanted. ¹³Because my mother called up on a special invisible telephone. ¹⁴Children couldn't see these phones, every parent had a direct line to the fairy. ¹⁵My parents' stories left a great impression on me, I still feel a surge of pleasure when I think of them.

■ Editing Test 8

See if you can locate and correct the ten sentence-skills mistakes in the following passage. The mistakes are listed in the box below. As you locate each mistake, write the number of the word group containing that mistake. Use the spaces provided. Then (on separate paper) correct the mistakes.

---

2 fragments _____ _____

2 missing commas between items in a series _____ _____

2 faulty parallelisms _____ _____

2 missing commas around an interrupter _____ _____

1 apostrophe mistake _____

1 run-on _____

A Place of Fear

¹College is supposed to be a place of discovery. ²But for some students can be a place of fear. ³In the classroom for example many students are afraid of appearing dumb in front of their classmates or professors. ⁴Such students often try to hide in class by sitting in the back of the room. ⁵Avoiding eye contact with instructors. ⁶Fear prevents them from raising their hands answering questions or being part of class discussions. ⁷Fear also leads to problems outside the classroom. ⁸Worried that their peers wont like them, many college students smoke or drinking heavily to blend in with the crowd. ⁹They also try drugs or joining in hurtful pranks they may even practice unsafe sex out of fear. ¹⁰Finally, students who get into trouble are often too scared to seek help in solving their problems.

Copyright ©2006 The McGraw-Hill Companies, Inc. All rights reserved.

■ Editing Test 9

See if you can locate and correct the ten sentence-skills mistakes in the following passages. The mistakes are listed in the box below. As you locate each mistake, write the number of the word group containing that mistake. Use the spaces provided. Then (on separate paper) correct the mistakes.

---

2 fragments _____ _____   1 missing comma after introductory

1 run-on _____   words _____

1 irregular verb mistake _____   2 apostrophe mistakes _____ _____

1 missing comma between   1 faulty parallelism _____

   items in a series _____   1 missing quotation mark _____

Fred's Funeral

¹Sometimes when Fred feels undervalued and depression, he likes to imagine his own funeral. ²He pictures all the people who will be there. ³He hears their hushed words sees their tears, and feels their grief. ⁴He glows with warm sadness as the minister begins a eulogy by saying, Fred Grencher was no ordinary man . . . " ⁵As the minister talks on Freds eyes grow moist. ⁶He laments his own passing and feels altogether appreciated and wonderful.

Feeding Time

⁷Recently I was at the cat house in the zoo. ⁸Right before feeding time. ⁹The tigers and lions were lying about on benches and little stands. ¹⁰Basking in the late-afternoon sun. ¹¹They seemed tame and harmless. ¹²But when the meat was brung in, a remarkable change occurred. ¹³All the cats got up and moved toward the food. ¹⁴I was suddenly aware of the rippling muscles' of their bodies and their large claws and teeth. ¹⁵They seemed three times bigger, I could feel their power.

■ **Editing Test 10**

See if you can locate and correct the ten sentence-skills mistakes in the following passage. The mistakes are listed in the box below. As you locate each mistake, write the number of the word group containing that mistake. Use the spaces provided. Then (on separate paper) correct the mistakes.

1 run-on _____	2 missing commas around
1 mistake in subject-verb	an interrupter _____ _____
agreement _____	1 missing comma between items
1 missing comma after	in a series _____
introductory words _____	2 apostrophe mistakes _____ _____
	2 missing quotation marks _____ _____

Walking Billboards

¹Many Americans have turned into driving, walking billboards. ²As much as we all claim to hate commercials on television we dont seem to have any qualms about turning ourselves into commercials. ³Our car bumpers for example advertise lake resorts underground caverns, and amusement parks. ⁴Also, we wear clothes marked with other peoples initials and slogans. ⁵Our fascination with the names of designers show up on the backs of our sneakers, the breast pockets of our shirts, and the right rear pockets of our blue jeans. ⁶And we wear T-shirts filled with all kinds of advertising messages. ⁷For instance, people are willing to wear shirts that read, "Dillon Construction," "Nike," or even I Got Crabs at Ed's Seafood Palace. ⁸In conclusion, we say we hate commercials, we actually pay people for the right to advertise their products.

Copyright ©2006 The McGraw-Hill Companies, Inc. All rights reserved.

■ Editing Test 11

See if you can locate and correct the ten sentence-skills mistakes in the following passage. The mistakes are listed in the box below. As you locate each mistake, write the number of the word group containing that mistake. Use the spaces provided. Then (on separate paper) correct the mistakes.

3 fragments _____   1 mistake in pronoun point

_____ _____   of view _____

2 run-ons _____ _____   1 dangling modifier _____

1 irregular verb mistake _____   1 missing comma between two

1 faulty parallelism _____   complete thoughts _____

Too Many Cooks

¹The problem in my college dining hall was the succession of incompetent cooks who were put in charge. ²During the time I worked there, I watched several cooks come and go. ³The first of these was Irving. ⁴He was skinny and greasy like the undercooked bacon he served for breakfast. ⁵Irving drank, by late afternoon he begun to sway as he cooked. ⁶Once, he looked at the brightly colored photograph on the orange juice machine. ⁷And asked why the TV was on. ⁸Having fired Irving, Lonnie was hired. ⁹Lonnie had a soft, round face that resembled the Pillsbury Doughboy's but he had the size and temperament of a large bear. ¹⁰He'd wave one paw and growl if you entered the freezers without his permission. ¹¹He also had poor eyesight. ¹²This problem caused him to substitute flour for sugar and using pork for beef on a regular basis. ¹³After Lonnie was fired, Enzo arrived. ¹⁴Because he had come from Italy only a year or two previously. ¹⁵He spoke little English. ¹⁶In addition, Enzo had trouble with seasoning and spices. ¹⁷His vegetables were too salty, giant bay leaves turned up in everything. ¹⁸Including the scrambled eggs. ¹⁹The cooks I worked for in the college dining hall would have made Emeril go into shock.

■ Editing Test 12

See if you can locate and correct the ten sentence-skills mistakes in the following passage. The mistakes are listed in the box below. As you locate each mistake, write the number of the word group containing that mistake. Use the spaces provided. Then (on separate paper) correct the mistakes.

2 fragments _____ _____   1 missing comma between two

2 run-ons _____ _____   complete thoughts _____

1 mistake in pronoun   1 missing quotation mark _____

  point of view _____   1 missing comma between items in

1 apostrophe mistake _____   a series _____

                                            1 misspelled word _____

My Ideal Date

[1]Here are the ingredients for my ideal date, first of all, I would want to look as stunning as possible. [2]I would be dressed in a black velvet jumpsuit. [3]That would fit me like a layer of paint. [4]My accessories would include a pair of red satin spike heels a diamond hair clip, and a full-length black mink coat. [5]My boyfriend, Tony, would wear a sharply tailored black tuxedo, a white silk shirt, and a red bow tie. [6]The tux would emphasize Tony's broad shoulders and narrow waist, and you would see his chest muscles under the smooth shirt fabric. [7]Tony would pull up to my house in a long, shiney limousine, then the driver would take us to the most exclusive and glittery nightclub in Manhattan. [8]All eyes would be on us as we entered and photographers would rush up to take our picture for *People* magazine. [9]As we danced on the lighted floor of the club, everyone would step aside to watch us perform our moves. [10]After several bottles of champagne, Tony and I would head to the observation deck of the Empire State Building. [11]As we gazed out over the light's of the city, Tony would hand me a small velvet box containing a fifty-carat ruby engagement ring. [12]And ask me to marry him. [13]I would thank Tony for a lovely evening and tell him gently, "Tony, I don't plan to marry until I'm thirty.

Copyright ©2006 The McGraw-Hill Companies, Inc. All rights reserved.

Sentence-Skills Achievement Test

Part 1

This test will help you measure your improvement in important sentence skills. Certain parts of the following word groups are underlined. Write X in the answer space if you think a mistake appears at the underlined part. Write C in the answer space if you think the underlined part is correct.

The headings ("Fragments," Run-Ons," and so on) will give you clues to the mistakes to look for.

Fragments

_____ 1. After a careless driver hit my motorcycle, I decided to buy a car. At least I would have more protection against other careless drivers.

_____ 2. I was never a good student in high school. Because I spent all my time socializing with my group of friends. Good grades were not something that my group really valued.

_____ 3. The young couple in the supermarket were not a pleasant sight. Arguing with each other. People pretended not to notice them.

_____ 4. Using a magnifying glass, the little girls burned holes in the dry leaf. They then set some tissue paper on fire.

_____ 5. My brother and I seldom have fights about what to watch on television. Except with baseball games. I get bored watching this sport.

_____ 6. My roommate and I ate, talked, danced, and sang at a fish-fry party the other night. Also, we played cards until 3 A.M. As a result, we both slept until noon the next day.

Run-Ons

_____ 7. She decided to quit her high-pressured job, she didn't want to develop heart trouble.

_____ 8. His car's wheels were not balanced properly, for the car began to shake when he drove over forty miles an hour.

_____ 9. I got through the interview without breaking out in a sweat mustache, I also managed to keep my voice under control.

_____ 10. The craze for convenience in our country has gone too far. There are drive-in banks, restaurants, and even churches.

_____ 11. My most valued possession is my stoneware cooker, I can make entire meals in it at a low cost.

_____ 12. The shopping carts outside the supermarket seemed welded together, Rita could not separate one from another.

Standard English Verbs

_____ 13. I am going to borrow my father's car if he agree.

_____ 14. For recreation he sets up hundreds of dominoes, and then he knocks them over.

_____ 15. He stopped taking a nap after supper because he then had trouble sleeping at night.

_____ 16. There was no bread for sandwiches, so he decided to drive to the store.

Irregular Verbs

_____ 17. I learned that Dennis had began to see someone else while he was still going out with me.

_____ 18. That woman has never ran for political office before.

_____ 19. I knowed the answer to the question, but I was too nervous to think of it when the instructor called on me.

_____ 20. They had ate the gallon of natural vanilla ice cream in just one night.

Subject-Verb Agreement

_____ 21. Her watchband have to be fixed.

_____ 22. There is two minutes left in the football game.

_____ 23. He believes films that feature violence is a disgrace to our society.

_____ 24. The plastic slipcovers that she bought have begun to crack.

Copyright ©2006 The McGraw-Hill Companies, Inc. All rights reserved.

Consistent Verb Tense

_____ 25. Myra wanted to watch the late movie, but she <u>was</u> so tired she <u>falls</u> asleep before it started.

_____ 26. When the mailman arrived, <u>I hoped</u> the latest issue of *People* magazine would be in his bag.

_____ 27. <u>Juan ran</u> down the hall without looking and <u>trips</u> over the toy truck lying on the floor.

_____ 28. <u>Debbie enjoys riding</u> her bike in the newly built park, which <u>features</u> a special path for bikers and runners.

Pronoun Agreement, Reference, and Point of View

_____ 29. At the Saturday afternoon movie we went to, children were making so much <u>noise that you</u> could not relax.

_____ 30. <u>We did not return</u> to the amusement park, <u>for we</u> had to pay too much for the rides and meals.

_____ 31. Drivers should check the oil level in <u>their</u> cars every three months.

_____ 32. At the hospital, I saw mothers with tears in their eyes wandering down the hall, <u>hoping that her</u> child's operation was a success.

_____ 33. <u>Sharon's mother was overjoyed when Sharon</u> became pregnant.

_____ 34. You must observe all the rules of the game, even if you do not always agree <u>with it.</u>

Pronoun Types

_____ 35. <u>Nancy and her</u> often go to dance clubs.

_____ 36. No one in the class is better at <u>computers than he.</u>

Adjectives and Adverbs

_____ 37. The little <u>girl spoke so quiet</u> I could hardly hear her.

_____ 38. Lola <u>looks more better</u> than Gina in a leather coat.

Misplaced Modifiers

_____ 39. <u>I saw sharks scuba-diving.</u>

_____ 40. <u>With a mile-wide grin,</u> Betty turned in her winning raffle ticket.

Copyright ©2006 The McGraw-Hill Companies, Inc. All rights reserved.

_____ 41. I bought a beautiful shirt in a local store with long sleeves and French cuffs.

_____ 42. I first spotted the turtle playing tag on the back lawn.

Dangling Modifiers

_____ 43. When seven years old, Jeff's father taught him to play ball.

_____ 44. Running across the field, I caught the baseball.

_____ 45. Turning on the ignition, the car backfired.

_____ 46. Looking at my watch, a taxi nearly ran me over.

Faulty Parallelism

_____ 47. Much of my boyhood was devoted to getting into rock fights, crossing railway trestles, and the hunt for rats in drainage tunnels.

_____ 48. I put my books in my locker, changed into my gym clothes, and hurried to the playing field.

_____ 49. Ruth begins every day with warm-up exercises, a half-hour run, and taking a hot shower.

_____ 50. In the evening I plan to write a paper, to watch a movie, and to read two chapters in my biology text.

Capital Letters

_____ 51. When the can of drano didn't unclog the sink, Hal called a plumber.

_____ 52. I asked Cindy, "what time will you be leaving?"

_____ 53. I have to get an allergy shot once a Week.

_____ 54. Mother ordered a raincoat from the catalog on Monday, and it arrived four days later.

Apostrophe

_____ 55. I asked the clerk if the store had Stevie Wonders latest CD.

_____ 56. He's failing the course because he doesn't have any confidence in his ability to do the work.

_____ 57. Clyde was incensed at the dentist who charged him ninety dollars to fix his son's tooth.

_____ 58. I cant believe that she's not coming to the dance.

Quotation Marks

_____   59. "Don't forget to water the grass, my sister said.

_____   60. Martha said to Fred at bedtime, "Why is it that men's pajamas always have such baggy bottoms?" "You look like a circus clown in that flannel outfit."

_____   61. The red sign on the door read, "Warning—open only in case of an emergency."

_____   62. "I can't stand that commercial," said Sue. "Do you mind if I turn off the television?"

Comma

_____   63. Hard-luck Sam needs a loan, a good-paying job, and someone to show an interest in him.

_____   64. Even though I was tired I agreed to go shopping with my parents.

_____   65. Power, not love or money, is what most politicians want.

_____   66. The heel on one of Lola's shoes came off, so she spent the day walking barefoot.

_____   67. "Thank goodness I'm almost done" I said aloud with every stroke of the broom.

_____   68. I hated to ask Anita who is a very stingy person to lend me the money.

Commonly Confused Words

_____   69. To succeed in the job, you must learn how to control your temper.

_____   70. Fortunately, I was not driving very fast when my car lost it's brakes.

_____   71. Put your packages on the table over their.

_____   72. There are too many steps in the math formula for me to understand it.

_____   73. The counseling center can advise you on how to prepare for an interview.

_____   74. Who's Honda Civic is that in front of the house?

Effective Word Use

_____   75. The teacher called to discuss Ron's social maladjustment difficulties.

_____   76. I thought the course would be a piece of cake, but a ten-page paper was required.

_____   77. When my last class ended, I felt as free as a bird.

_____   78. Spike gave away his television owing to the fact that it distracted him from studying.

Part 2 (Optional)

Do Part 2 at your instructor's request. This second part of the test will provide more detailed information about your improvement in sentence skills. On separate paper, number and correct all the items you have marked with an X. For example, suppose you had marked the word groups below with an X. (Note that these examples are not taken from the test.)

4. If football games disappeared entirely from television. I would not even miss them. Other people in my family would perish.

7. The kitten suddenly saw her reflection in the mirror, she jumped back in surprise.

15. The tree in my cousins front yard always sheds its leaves two weeks before others on the street.

29. When we go out to a restaurant we always order something we would not cook for ourselves.

Here is how you should write your corrections on a separate sheet of paper.

4. television, I

7. mirror, and

15. cousin's

29. restaurant, we

There are more than forty corrections to make in all.

Copyright ©2006 The McGraw-Hill Companies, Inc All rights reserved.

Copyright ©2006 The McGraw-Hill Companies, Inc. All rights reserved.

PART SIX

Seventeen
Reading Selections

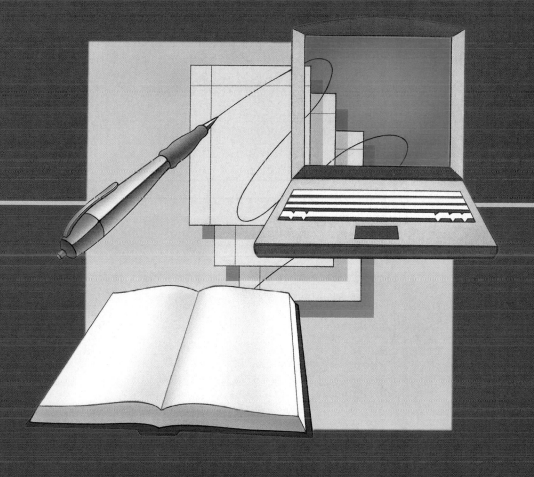

PREVIEW

This book assumes that writing and reading are closely connected skills—so that practicing one helps the other, and neglecting one hurts the other. Part Six will enable you to work on becoming a better reader as well as a stronger writer. Following an introductory section that offers a series of tips on effective reading, there are seventeen reading selections. Each selection begins with an overview that supplies background information about the piece. After the selection are ten questions to give you practice in key reading comprehension skills. A set of discussion questions is also provided, both to deepen your understanding of the selection and to point out basic writing techniques used in the essay. Then come several writing assignments, along with guidelines to help you think about the assignments and get started working on them.

Introduction
to the Readings

Copyright ©2006 The McGraw-Hill Companies, Inc. All rights reserved.

The reading selections in Part Six will help you find topics for writing. Some of the selections provide helpful practical information. For example, you'll learn how to discuss problems openly with others and how to avoid being manipulated by clever ads. Other selections deal with thought-provoking aspects of contemporary life. One article, for instance, dramatizes in a vivid and painful way the tragedy that can result when teenagers drink and drive. Still other selections are devoted to a celebration of human goals and values; one essay, for example, reminds us of the power that praise and appreciation can have in our daily lives. The varied subjects should inspire lively class discussions as well as serious individual thought. The selections should also provide a continuing source of high-interest material for a wide range of writing assignments.

The selections serve another purpose as well. They will help develop reading skills with direct benefits to you as a writer. First, through close reading, you will learn how to recognize the main idea or point of a selection and how to identify and evaluate the supporting material that develops the main idea. In your writing, you will aim to achieve the same essential structure: an overall point followed by detailed, valid support for that point. Second, close reading will help you explore a selection and its possibilities thoroughly. The more you understand about what is said in a piece, the more ideas and feelings you may have about writing on an assigned topic or a related topic of your own. A third benefit of close reading is becoming more aware of authors' stylistic devices—for example, their introductions and conclusions, their ways of presenting and developing a point, their use of transitions, their choice of language to achieve a particular tone. Recognizing these devices in other people's writing will help you enlarge your own range of writing techniques.

The Format of Each Selection

Each selection begins with a short overview that gives helpful background information. The selection is then followed by two sets of questions.

- First, there are ten reading comprehension questions to help you measure your understanding of the material. These questions involve several important reading skills: understanding vocabulary in context, recognizing a subject or topic, determining the thesis or main idea, identifying key supporting points, and making inferences. Answering the questions will enable you and your instructor to check quickly your basic understanding of a selection. More significantly, as you move from one selection to the next, you will sharpen your reading skills as well as strengthen your thinking skills—two key factors in making you a better writer.

- Following the comprehension questions are several discussion questions. In addition to dealing with content, these questions focus on structure, style, and tone.

Finally, several writing assignments accompany each selection. Many of the assignments provide guidelines on how to proceed, including suggestions for prewriting and appropriate methods of development. When writing your responses to the readings, you will have opportunities to apply all the methods of development presented in Part Two of this book.

How to Read Well: Four General Steps

Skillful reading is an important part of becoming a skillful writer. Following are four steps that will make you a better reader—both of the selections here and in your reading at large.

1 Concentrate as You Read

To improve your concentration, follow these tips. First, read in a place where you can be quiet and alone. Don't choose a spot where a TV or stereo is on or where friends or family are talking nearby. Next, sit in an upright position when you read. If your body is in a completely relaxed position, sprawled across a bed or nestled in an easy chair, your mind is also going to be completely relaxed. The light muscular tension that comes from sitting upright in a chair promotes concentration and keeps your mind ready to work. Finally, consider using your index finger (or a pen) as a pacer while you read. Lightly underline each line of print with your index finger as you read down a page. Hold your hand slightly above the page and move your finger

Copyright ©2006 The McGraw-Hill Companies, Inc. All rights reserved

at a speed that is a little too fast for comfort. This pacing with your index finger, like sitting upright on a chair, creates a slight physical tension that will keep your body and mind focused and alert.

2 Skim Material before You Read It

In skimming, you spend about two minutes rapidly surveying a selection, looking for important points and skipping secondary material. Follow this sequence when skimming:

- Begin by reading the overview that precedes the selection.

- Then study the title of the selection for a few moments. A good title is the shortest possible summary of a selection; it often tells you in several words what a selection is about.

- Next, form a basic question (or questions) out of the title. Forming questions out of the title is often a key to locating a writer's main idea—your next concern in skimming.

- Read the first two or three paragraphs and the last two or three paragraphs in the selection. Very often a writer's main idea, *if* it is directly stated, will appear in one of these paragraphs and will relate to the title.

- Finally, look quickly at the rest of the selection for other clues to important points. Are there any subheads you can relate in some way to the title? Are there any words the author has decided to emphasize by setting them off in *italic* or **boldface** type? Are there any major lists of items signaled by words such as *first, second, also, another,* and so on?

3 Read the Selection Straight Through with a Pen Nearby

Don't slow down or turn back; just aim to understand as much as you can the first time through. Place a check or star beside answers to basic questions you formed from the title, and beside other ideas that seem important. Number lists of important points 1, 2, 3. . . . Circle words you don't understand. Put question marks in the margin next to passages that are unclear and that you will want to reread.

4 Work with the Material

Go back and reread passages that were not clear the first time through. Look up words that block your understanding of ideas and write their meanings in the margin. Also, reread carefully the areas you identified as most important; doing so will enlarge your understanding of the material. Now that you have a sense of the whole, prepare a short outline of the selection by answering the following questions on a sheet of paper:

- What is the main idea?

- What key points support the main idea?

- What seem to be other important points in the selection?

By working with the material in this way, you will significantly increase your understanding of a selection. Effective reading, just like effective writing, does not happen all at once. Rather, it is a process. Often you begin with a general impression of what something means, and then, by working at it, you move to a deeper level of understanding of the material.

How to Answer the Comprehension Questions: Specific Hints

Several important reading skills are involved in the ten reading comprehension questions that follow each selection. The skills are:

- Understanding vocabulary in context

- Summarizing the selection by providing a title for it

- Determining the main idea

- Recognizing key supporting details

- Making inferences

The following hints will help you apply each of these reading skills:

- *Vocabulary in context.* To decide on the meaning of an unfamiliar word, consider its context. Ask yourself, "Are there any clues in the sentence that suggest what this word means?"

- *Subject or title.* Remember that the title should accurately describe the *entire* selection. It should be neither too broad nor too narrow for the material in the selection. It should answer the question "What is this about?" as specifically as possible. Note that you may at times find it easier to do the "title" question *after* the "main idea" question.

- *Main idea.* Choose the statement that you think best expresses the main idea or thesis of the entire selection. Remember that the title will often help you focus on the main idea. Then ask yourself, "Does most of the material in the selection support this statement?" If you can answer *Yes* to this question, you have found the thesis.

- *Key details.* If you were asked to give a two-minute summary of a selection, the major details are the ones you would include in that summary. To determine the key details, ask yourself, "What are the major supporting points for the thesis?"

- *Inferences.* Answer these questions by drawing on the evidence presented in the selection and on your own common sense. Ask yourself, "What reasonable judgments can I make on the basis of the information in the selection?"

On page 744 is a chart on which you can keep track of your performance as you answer the ten questions for each selection. The chart will help you identify reading skills you may need to strengthen.

Copyright ©2006 The McGraw-Hill Companies, Inc. All rights reserved.

All the Good Things

Sister Helen Mrosla

Sometimes the smallest things we do have the biggest impact. A teacher's impulsive idea, designed to brighten a dull Friday-afternoon class, affected her students more than she ever dreamed. Sister Helen Mrosla's moment of classroom inspiration took on a life of its own, returning to visit her at a most unexpected time. Her account of the experience reminds us of the human heart's endless hunger for recognition and appreciation.

1 He was in the first third-grade class I taught at Saint Mary's School in Morris, Minnesota. All thirty-four of my students were dear to me, but Mark Eklund was one in a million. He was very neat in appearance but had that happy-to-be-alive attitude that made even his occasional mischievousness delightful.

2 Mark talked incessantly. I had to remind him again and again that talking without permission was not acceptable. What impressed me so much, though, was his sincere response every time I had to correct him for misbehaving—"Thank you for correcting me, Sister!" I didn't know what to make of it at first, but before long I became accustomed to hearing it many times a day.

3 One morning my patience was growing thin when Mark talked once too often, and then I made a novice teacher's mistake. I looked at him and said, "If you say one more word, I am going to tape your mouth shut!"

4 It wasn't ten seconds later when Chuck blurted out, "Mark is talking again." I hadn't asked any of the students to help me watch Mark, but since I had stated the punishment in front of the class, I had to act on it.

5 I remember the scene as if it had occurred this morning. I walked to my desk, very deliberately opened my drawer, and took out a roll of masking tape. Without saying a word, I proceeded to Mark's desk, tore off two pieces of tape and made a big X with them over his mouth. I then returned to the front of the room. As I glanced at Mark to see how he was doing, he winked at me.

6 That did it! I started laughing. The class cheered as I walked back to Mark's desk, removed the tape, and shrugged my shoulders. His first words were, "Thank you for correcting me, Sister."

Copyright ©2016 The McGraw-Hill Companies, Inc. All rights reserved.

At the end of the year I was asked to teach junior-high math. The years flew 7 by, and before I knew it Mark was in my classroom again. He was more handsome than ever and just as polite. Since he had to listen carefully to my instruction in the "new math," he did not talk as much in ninth grade as he had talked in the third.

One Friday, things just didn't feel right. We had worked hard on a new con- 8 cept all week, and I sensed that the students were frowning, frustrated with themselves—and edgy with one another. I had to stop this crankiness before it got out of hand. So I asked them to list the names of the other students in the room on two sheets of paper, leaving a space after each name. Then I told them to think of the nicest thing they could say about each of their classmates and write it down.

It took the remainder of the class period to finish the assignment, and as the 9 students left the room, each one handed me the papers. Charlie smiled. Mark said, "Thank you for teaching me, Sister. Have a good weekend."

That Saturday, I wrote down the name of each student on a separate sheet of 10 paper, and I listed what everyone else had said about that individual.

On Monday I gave each student his or her list. Before long, the entire class 11 was smiling. "Really?" I heard whispered. "I never knew that meant anything to anyone!" "I didn't know others liked me so much!"

No one ever mentioned those papers in class again. I never knew if the stu- 12 dents discussed them after class or with their parents, but it didn't matter. The exercise had accomplished its purpose. The students were happy with themselves and one another again.

That group of students moved on. Several years later, after I returned from 13 a vacation, my parents met me at the airport. As we were driving home, Mother asked me the usual questions about the trip—the weather, my experiences in general. There was a slight lull in the conversation. Mother gave Dad a sideways glance and simply said, "Dad?" My father cleared his throat as he usually did before something important. "The Eklunds called last night," he began. "Really?" I said. "I haven't heard from them in years. I wonder how Mark is."

Dad responded quietly. "Mark was killed in Vietnam," he said. "The funeral is 14 tomorrow, and his parents would like it if you could attend." To this day I can still point to the exact spot on I-494 where Dad told me about Mark.

I had never seen a serviceman in a military coffin before. Mark looked so 15 handsome, so mature. All I could think at that moment was, Mark, I would give all the masking tape in the world if only you would talk to me.

The church was packed with Mark's friends. Chuck's sister sang "The Battle 16 Hymn of the Republic." Why did it have to rain on the day of the funeral? It was difficult enough at the graveside. The pastor said the usual prayers, and the bugler played taps. One by one those who loved Mark took a last walk by the coffin and sprinkled it with holy water.

I was the last one to bless the coffin. As I stood there, one of the soldiers who   17
had acted as pallbearer came up to me. "Were you Mark's math teacher?" he asked. I
nodded as I continued to stare at the coffin. "Mark talked about you a lot," he said.

After the funeral, most of Mark's former classmates headed to Chuck's farm-   18
house for lunch. Mark's mother and father were there, obviously waiting for me. "We
want to show you something," his father said, taking a wallet out of his pocket. "They
found this on Mark when he was killed. We thought you might recognize it."

Opening the billfold, he carefully removed two worn pieces of notebook   19
paper that had obviously been taped, folded and refolded many times. I knew
without looking that the papers were the ones on which I had listed all the good
things each of Mark's classmates had said about him. "Thank you so much for
doing that," Mark's mother said. "As you can see, Mark treasured it."

Mark's classmates started to gather around us. Charlie smiled rather sheep-   20
ishly and said, "I still have my list. It's in the top drawer of my desk at home."
Chuck's wife said, "Chuck asked me to put his list in our wedding album." "I have
mine too," Marilyn said. "It's in my diary." Then Vicki, another classmate, reached
into her pocketbook, took out her wallet, and showed her worn and frazzled
list to the group. "I carry this with me at all times," Vicki said without batting an
eyelash. "I think we all saved our lists."

That's when I finally sat down and cried. I cried for Mark and for all his friends   21
who would never see him again.

■ Reading Comprehension Questions

1. The word *incessantly* in "Mark talked incessantly. I had to remind him again
   and again that talking without permission was not acceptable" (paragraph 2)
   means

   a. slowly.

   b. quietly.

   c. constantly.

   d. pleasantly.

2. The word *edgy* in "We had worked hard on a new concept all week, and I
   sensed that the students were frowning, frustrated with themselves—and
   edgy with one another. I had to stop this crankiness before it got out of hand"
   (paragraph 8) means

   a. funny.

   b. calm.

   c. easily annoyed.

   d. dangerous.

3. Which of the following would be the best alternative title for this selection?
   a. Talkative Mark
   b. My Life as a Teacher
   c. More Important Than I Knew
   d. A Tragic Death

4. Which sentence best expresses the main idea of the selection?
   a. Although Sister Helen sometimes scolded Mark Eklund, he appreciated her devotion to teaching.
   b. When a former student of hers died, Sister Helen discovered how important one of her assignments had been to him and his classmates.
   c. When her students were cranky one day, Sister Helen had them write down something nice about each of their classmates.
   d. A pupil whom Sister Helen was especially fond of was tragically killed while serving in Vietnam.

5. Upon reading their lists for the first time, Sister Helen's students
   a. were silent and embarrassed.
   b. were disappointed.
   c. pretended to think the lists were stupid, although they really liked them.
   d. smiled and seemed pleased.

6. In the days after the assignment to write down something nice about one another,
   a. students didn't mention the assignment again.
   b. students often brought their lists to school.
   c. Sister Helen received calls from several parents complaining about the assignment.
   d. Sister Helen decided to repeat the assignment in every one of her classes.

7. According to Vicki,
   a. Mark was the only student to have saved his list.
   b. Vicki and Mark were the only students to have saved their lists.
   c. Vicki, Mark, Charlie, Chuck, and Marilyn were the only students to have saved their lists.
   d. all the students had saved their lists.

Copyright ©2006 The McGraw-Hill Companies, Inc. All rights reserved.

8. The author implies that

   a. she was surprised to learn how much the lists had meant to her students.

   b. Mark's parents were jealous of his affection for Sister Helen.

   c. Mark's death shattered her faith in God.

   d. Mark's classmates had not stayed in touch with one another over the years.

9. *True or false?*_____The author implies that Mark had gotten married.

10. We can conclude that when Sister Helen was a third-grade teacher, she

    a. was usually short-tempered and irritable.

    b. wasn't always sure how to discipline her students.

    c. didn't expect Mark to do well in school.

    d. had no sense of humor.

■ Discussion Questions

About Content

1. What did Sister Helen hope to accomplish by asking her students to list nice things about one another?

2. At least some students were surprised by the good things others wrote about them. What does this tell us about how we see ourselves and how we communicate our views of others?

3. "All the Good Things" has literally traveled around the world. Not only has it been reprinted in numerous publications, but many readers have sent it out over the Internet for others to read. Why do you think so many people love this story? Why do they want to share it with others?

About Structure

4. This selection is organized according to time. What three separate time periods does it cover? What paragraphs are included in the first time period? The second? The third?

5. Paragraph 8 includes a cause-and-effect structure. What part of the paragraph is devoted to the cause? What part is devoted to the effect? What transition word signals the break between the cause and the effect?

6. What does the title "All The Good Things" mean? Is this a good title for the essay? Why or why not?

About Style and Tone

7. Sister Helen is willing to let her readers see her weaknesses as well as her strengths. Find a place in the selection in which the author shows herself as less than perfect.

8. What does Sister Helen accomplish by beginning her essay with the word "he"? What does that unusual beginning tell the reader?

9. How does Sister Helen feel about her students? Find evidence that backs up your opinion.

10. Sister Helen comments on Mark's "happy-to-be-alive" attitude. What support does she provide that makes us understand what Mark was like?

WRITING ASSIGNMENTS

Assignment 1: Writing a Paragraph

Early in her story, Sister Helen refers to a "teacher's mistake" that forced her to punish a student in front of the class. Write a paragraph about a time you gave in to pressure to do something because others around you expected it. Explain what the situation was, just what happened, and how you felt afterward. Here are two sample topic sentences:

> Even though I knew it was wrong, I went along with some friends who shoplifted at the mall.

> Just because my friends did, I made fun of a kid in my study hall who was a slow learner.

Assignment 2: Writing a Paragraph

Sister Helen's students kept their lists for many years. What souvenir of the past have you kept for a long time? Why? Write a paragraph describing the souvenir, how you got it, and what it means to you. Begin with a topic sentence such as this:

> I've kept a green ribbon in one of my dresser drawers for over ten years because it reminds me of an experience I treasure.

Assignment 3: Writing an Essay

It's easy to forget to let others know how much they have helped us. Only after one of the students died did Sister Helen learn how important the list of positive comments had been to her class. Write an essay about someone to whom you are grateful and explain what that person has done for you. In your thesis statement,

Copyright ©2006 The McGraw-Hill Companies, Inc. All rights reserved.

introduce the person and describe his or her relationship to you. Also include a general statement of what that person has done for you. Your thesis statement can be similar to any of these:

> My brother Roy has been an important part of my life.
>
> My best friend Ginger helped me through a major crisis.
>
> Mrs. Morrison, my seventh-grade English teacher, taught me a lesson for which I will always be grateful.

Use freewriting to help you find interesting details to support your thesis statement. You may find two or three separate incidents to write about, each in a paragraph of its own. Or you may find it best to use several paragraphs to give a detailed narrative of one incident or two or three related events. (Note how Sister Helen uses several separate "scenes" to tell her story.) Whatever your approach, use some dialogue to enliven key parts of your essay. (Review the reading to see how Sister Helen uses dialogue throughout her essay.)

Alternatively, write an essay about three people to whom you are grateful. In that case, each paragraph of the body of your essay would deal with one of those people. The thesis statement in such an essay might be similar to this:

> There are three people who have made a big difference in my life.

Rowing the Bus

Paul Logan

There is a well-known saying that goes something like this: All that is necessary in order for evil to triumph is for good people to do nothing. Even young people are forced to face cruel behavior and to decide how they will respond to it. In this essay, Paul Logan looks back at a period of schoolyard cruelty in which he was both a victim and a participant. With unflinching honesty, he describes his behavior then and how it helped to shape the person he has become.

When I was in elementary school, some older kids made me row the bus. Rowing meant that on the way to school I had to sit in the dirty bus aisle littered with paper, gum wads, and spitballs. Then I had to simulate the motion of rowing while the kids around me laughed and chanted, "Row, row, row the bus." I was forced to do this by a group of bullies who spent most of their time picking on me.

I was the perfect target for them. I was small. I had no father. And my mother,   2
though she worked hard to support me, was unable to afford clothes and sneakers that were "cool." Instead she dressed me in outfits that we got from "the
bags"—hand-me-downs given as donations to a local church.

Each Wednesday, she'd bring several bags of clothes to the house and pull out   3
musty, wrinkled shirts and worn bell-bottom pants that other families no longer
wanted. I knew that people were kind to give things to us, but I hated wearing
clothes that might have been donated by my classmates. Each time I wore something from the bags, I feared that the other kids might recognize something that
was once theirs.

Besides my outdated clothes, I wore thick glasses, had crossed eyes, and spoke   4
with a persistent lisp. For whatever reason, I had never learned to say the "s"
sound properly, and I pronounced words that began with "th" as if they began
with a "d." In addition, because of my severely crossed eyes, I lacked the hand and
eye coordination necessary to hit or catch flying objects.

As a result, footballs, baseballs, soccer balls and basketballs became my ene-   5
mies. I knew, before I stepped onto the field or court, that I would do something
clumsy or foolish and that everyone would laugh at me. I feared humiliation so
much that I became skillful at feigning illnesses to get out of gym class. Eventually
I learned how to give myself low-grade fevers so the nurse would write me an
excuse. It worked for a while, until the gym teachers caught on. When I did have
to play, I was always the last one chosen to be on any team. In fact, team captains
did everything in their power to make their opponents get stuck with me. When
the unlucky team captain was forced to call my name, I would trudge over to the
team, knowing that no one there liked or wanted me. For four years, from second
through fifth grade, I prayed nightly for God to give me school days in which I
would not be insulted, embarrassed, or made to feel ashamed.

I thought my prayers were answered when my mother decided to move during   6
the summer before sixth grade. The move meant that I got to start sixth grade
in a different school, a place where I had no reputation. Although the older kids
laughed and snorted at me as soon as I got on my new bus—they couldn't miss
my thick glasses and strange clothes—I soon discovered that there was another
kid who received the brunt of their insults. His name was George, and everyone
made fun of him. The kids taunted him because he was skinny; they belittled him
because he had acne that pocked and blotched his face; and they teased him
because his voice was squeaky. During my first gym class at my new school, I wasn't
the last one chosen for kickball; George was.

George tried hard to be friends with me, coming up to me in the cafeteria   7
on the first day of school. "Hi. My name's George. Can I sit with you?" he asked
with a peculiar squeakiness that made each word high-pitched and raspy. As I
nodded for him to sit down, I noticed an uncomfortable silence in the cafeteria
as many of the students who had mocked George's clumsy gait during gym class
began watching the two of us and whispering among themselves. By letting him
sit with me, I had violated an unspoken law of school, a sinister code of childhood
that demands there must always be someone to pick on. I began to realize two

Copyright ©2006 The McGraw-Hill Companies, Inc. All rights reserved.

things. If I befriended George, I would soon receive the same treatment that I had gotten at my old school. If I stayed away from him, I might actually have a chance to escape being at the bottom.

Within days, the kids started taunting us whenever we were together. "Who's   8
your new little buddy, Georgie?" In the hallways, groups of students began mumbling about me just loud enough for me to hear, "Look, it's George's ugly boyfriend." On the bus rides to and from school, wads of paper and wet chewing gum were tossed at me by the bigger, older kids in the back of the bus.

It became clear that my friendship with George was going to cause me several   9
more years of misery at my new school. I decided to stop being friends with George. In class and at lunch, I spent less and less time with him. Sometimes I told him I was too busy to talk; other times I acted distracted and gave one-word responses to whatever he said. Our classmates, sensing that they had created a rift between George and me, intensified their attacks on him. Each day, George grew more desperate as he realized that the one person who could prevent him from being completely isolated was closing him off. I knew that I shouldn't avoid him, that he was feeling the same way I felt for so long, but I was so afraid that my life would become the hell it had been in my old school that I continued to ignore him.

Then, at recess one day, the meanest kid in the school, Chris, decided he had had   10
enough of George. He vowed that he was going to beat up George and anyone else who claimed to be his friend. A mob of kids formed and came after me. Chris led the way and cornered me near our school's swing sets. He grabbed me by my shirt and raised his fist over my head. A huge gathering of kids surrounded us, urging him to beat me up, chanting "Go, Chris, go!"

"You're Georgie's new little boyfriend, aren't you?" he yelled. The hot blast   11
of his breath carried droplets of his spit into my face. In a complete betrayal of the only kid who was nice to me, I denied George's friendship.

"No, I'm not George's friend. I don't like him. He's stupid," I blurted out.   12
Several kids snickered and mumbled under their breath. Chris stared at me for a few seconds and then threw me to the ground.

"Wimp. Where's George?" he demanded, standing over me. Someone pointed   13
to George sitting alone on top of the monkey bars about thirty yards from where we were. He was watching me. Chris and his followers sprinted over to George and yanked him off the bars to the ground. Although the mob quickly encircled them, I could still see the two of them at the center of the crowd, looking at each other. George seemed stoic, staring straight through Chris. I heard the familiar chant of "Go, Chris, go!" and watched as his fists began slamming into George's head and body. His face bloodied and his nose broken, George crumpled to the ground and sobbed without even throwing a punch. The mob cheered with pleasure and darted off into the playground to avoid an approaching teacher.

Chris was suspended, and after a few days, George came back to school. I wanted   14
to talk to him, to ask him how he was, to apologize for leaving him alone and for not trying to stop him from getting hurt. But I couldn't go near him. Filled with shame for denying George and angered by my own cowardice, I never spoke to him again.

Several months later, without telling any students, George transferred to   15
another school. Once in a while, in those last weeks before he left, I caught him
watching me as I sat with the rest of the kids in the cafeteria. He never yelled at me
or expressed anger, disappointment, or even sadness. Instead he just looked at me.

In the years that followed, George's silent stare remained with me. It was   16
there in eighth grade when I saw a gang of popular kids beat up a sixth-grader
because, they said, he was "ugly and stupid." It was there my first year in high
school, when I saw a group of older kids steal another freshman's clothes and
throw them into the showers. It was there a year later, when I watched several
seniors press a wad of chewing gum into the hair of a new girl on the bus. Each
time that I witnessed another awkward, uncomfortable, scared kid being tormented,
I thought of George, and gradually his haunting stare began to speak to me. No
longer silent, it told me that every child who is picked on and taunted deserves
better, that no one—no matter how big, strong, attractive, or popular—has the
right to abuse another person.

Finally, in my junior year when a loudmouthed, pink-skinned bully named   17
Donald began picking on two freshmen on the bus, I could no longer deny George.
Donald was crumpling a large wad of paper and preparing to bounce it off the
back of the head of one of the young students when I interrupted him.

"Leave them alone, Don," I said. By then I was six inches taller and, after   18
two years of high-school wrestling, thirty pounds heavier than I had been in my
freshman year. Though Donald was still two years older than me, he wasn't much
bigger. He stopped what he was doing, squinted, and stared at me.

"What's your problem, Paul?"   19

I felt the way I had many years earlier on the playground when I watched the   20
mob of kids begin to surround George.

"Just leave them alone. They aren't bothering you," I responded quietly.   21

"What's it to you?" he challenged. A glimpse of my own past, of rowing the   22
bus, of being mocked for my clothes, my lisp, my glasses, and my absent father
flashed in my mind.

"Just don't mess with them. That's all I am saying, Don." My fingertips were   23
tingling. The bus was silent. He got up from his seat and leaned over me, and I
rose from my seat to face him. For a minute, both of us just stood there, without
a word, staring.

"I'm just playing with them, Paul," he said, chuckling. "You don't have to   24
go psycho on me or anything." Then he shook his head, slapped me firmly on
the chest with the back of his hand, and sat down. But he never threw that wad
of paper. For the rest of the year, whenever I was on the bus, Don and the other
troublemakers were noticeably quiet.

Although it has been years since my days on the playground and the school   25
bus, George's look still haunts me. Today, I see it on the faces of a few scared kids
at my sister's school—she is in fifth grade. Or once in a while I'll catch a glimpse of
someone like George on the evening news, in a story about a child who brought a
gun to school to stop the kids from picking on him, or in a feature about a teenager

Copyright ©2006 The McGraw-Hill Companies, Inc. All rights reserved.

who killed herself because everyone teased her. In each school, in almost every classroom, there is a George with a stricken face, hoping that someone nearby will be strong enough to be kind—despite what the crowd says—and brave enough to stand up against people who attack, tease, or hurt those who are vulnerable.

If asked about their behavior, I'm sure the bullies would say, "What's it to   26 you? It's just a joke. It's nothing." But to George and me, and everyone else who has been humiliated or laughed at or spat on, it is everything. No one should have to row the bus.

■ **Reading Comprehension Questions**

1. The word *simulate* in "Then I had to simulate the motion of rowing while the kids around me laughed and chanted, 'Row, row, row the bus'" (paragraph 1) means

   a. sing.

   b. ignore.

   c. imitate.

   d. release.

2. The word *rift* in "I decided to stop being friends with George. . . . Our classmates, sensing that they had created a rift between George and me, intensified their attacks on him" (paragraph 9) means

   a. friendship.

   b. agreement.

   c. break.

   d. joke.

3. Which of the following would be the best alternative title for this selection?

   a. A Sixth-Grade Adventure

   b. Children's Fears

   c. Dealing with Cruelty

   d. The Trouble with Busing

4. Which sentence best expresses the main idea of the selection?

   a. Although Paul Logan was the target of other students' abuse when he was a young boy, their attacks stopped as he grew taller and stronger.

   b. When Logan moved to a different school, he discovered that another student, George, was the target of more bullying than he was.

Copyright ©2006 The McGraw-Hill Companies, Inc. All rights reserved.

    c. Logan's experience of being bullied and his shame at how he treated George eventually made him speak up for someone else who was teased.

    d. Logan is ashamed that he did not stand up for George when George was being attacked by a bully on the playground.

5. When Chris attacked George, George reacted by

    a. fighting back hard.

    b. shouting for Logan to help him.

    c. running away.

    d. accepting the beating.

6. Logan finally found the courage to stand up for abused students when he saw

    a. Donald about to throw paper at a younger student.

    b. older kids throwing a freshman's clothes into the shower.

    c. seniors putting bubble gum in a new student's hair.

    d. a gang beating up a sixth-grader whom they disliked.

7. *True or false?* _____ After Logan confronted Donald on the bus, Donald began picking on Logan as well.

8. *True or false?* _____ The author suggests that his mother did not care very much about him.

9. The author implies that, when he started sixth grade at a new school,

    a. he became fairly popular.

    b. he decided to try out for athletic teams.

    c. he was relieved to find a kid who was more unpopular than he.

    d. he was frequently beaten up.

10. We can conclude that

    a. the kids who picked on George later regretted what they had done.

    b. George and the author eventually talked together about their experience in sixth grade.

    c. the author thinks kids today are kinder than they were when he was in sixth grade.

    d. the author is a more compassionate person now because of his experience with George.

■ Discussion Questions

About Content

1. Logan describes a number of incidents involving students' cruelty to other students. Find at least three such incidents. What do they seem to have in common? Judging from such incidents, what purpose does cruel teasing seem to serve?

2. Throughout the essay, Paul Logan talks about cruel but ordinary school behavior. But in paragraph 25, he briefly mentions two extreme and tragic consequences of such cruelty. What are those consequences, and why do you think he introduces them? What is he implying?

About Structure

3. Overall, the author uses narration to develop his points. Below, write three time transitions he uses to advance his narration.

   _____   _____   _____

4. Logan describes the gradual change within him that finally results in his standing up for a student who is being abused. Where in the narrative does Logan show how internal changes may be taking place within him? Where in the narrative does he show that his reaction to witnessing bullying has changed?

5. Paul Logan titled his selection "Rowing the Bus." Yet very little of the essay actually deals with the incident the title describes. Why do you think Logan chose that title?

About Style and Tone

6. Paul Logan backs up his point "I was the perfect target for them" (paragraph 2) with solid support. Identify two of the several details that support that point, and write a summary of each below.

   _____

   _____

7. Good descriptive writing involves the reader's senses. Give examples of how Logan appeals to our senses in paragraphs 1–4 of "Rowing the Bus."

   Sight _____

   Smell _____

   Hearing _____

8. What is Logan's attitude towards himself regarding his treatment of George? Find three phrases that reveal his attitude and write them here.

WRITING ASSIGNMENTS

Assignment 1: Writing a Paragraph

Logan writes, " In each school, in almost every classroom, there is a George with a stricken face." Think of a person who filled the role of George in one of your classes. Then write a descriptive paragraph about that person, explaining why he or she was a target and what form the teasing took. Be sure to include a description of your own thoughts and actions regarding the student who was teased. Your topic sentence might be something like one of these:

> A girl in my fifth-grade class was a lot like George in "Rowing the Bus."
>
> Like Paul Logan, I suffered greatly in elementary school from being bullied.

Try to include details that appeal to two or three of the senses.

Assignment 2: Writing a Paragraph

Paul Logan feared that his life at his new school would be made miserable if he continued being friends with George. So he ended the friendship, even though he felt ashamed of doing so. Think of a time when you have wanted to do the right thing but felt that the price would be too high. Maybe you knew a friend was doing something dishonest and wanted him to stop but were afraid of losing his friendship. Or perhaps you pretended to forget a promise you had made because you decided it was too difficult to keep. Write a paragraph describing the choice you made and how you felt about yourself afterward.

Assignment 3: Writing an Essay

Logan provides many vivid descriptions of incidents in which bullies attack other students. Reread these descriptions, and consider what they teach you about the nature of bullies and bullying. Then write an essay that supports the following main idea:

> Bullies seem to share certain qualities.

Identify two or three qualities; then discuss each in a separate paragraph. You may use two or three of the following as the topic sentences for your supporting paragraphs, or come up with your own supporting points:

Copyright ©2006 The McGraw-Hill Companies, Inc. All rights reserved.

Bullies are cowardly.

Bullies make themselves feel big by making other people feel small.

Bullies cannot feel very good about themselves.

Bullies are feared but not respected.

Bullies act cruelly in order to get attention.

Develop each supporting point with one or more anecdotes or ideas from any of the following: your own experience, your understanding of human nature, and "Rowing the Bus."

The Scholarship Jacket

Marta Salinas

All of us have suffered disappointments and moments when we have felt we've been treated unfairly. In "The Scholarship Jacket," originally published in *Growing Up Chicana: An Anthology*, Marta Salinas writes about one such moment in her childhood in southern Texas. By focusing on an award that school authorities decided she should not receive, Salinas shows us the pain of discrimination as well as the need for inner strength.

1   The small Texas school that I attended carried out a tradition every year during the eighth-grade graduation: a beautiful jacket in gold and green, the school colors, was awarded to the class valedictorian, the student who had maintained the highest grades for eight years. The scholarship jacket had a big gold S on the left front side, and the winner's name was written in gold letters on the pocket.

2   My oldest sister, Rosie, had won the jacket a few years back, and I fully expected to win also. I was fourteen and in the eighth grade. I had been a straight-A student since the first grade, and the last year I had looked forward to owning that jacket. My father was a farm laborer who couldn't earn enough money to feed eight children, so when I was six I was given to my grandparents to raise. We couldn't participate in sports at school because there were registration fees, uniform costs, and trips out of town; so even though we were quite agile and athletic, there would never be a sports school jacket for us. This one, the scholarship jacket, was our only chance.

Copyright ©2006 The McGraw-Hill Companies, Inc. All rights reserved.

In May, close to graduation, spring fever struck, and no one paid any attention   3
to class; instead we stared out the windows and at each other, wanting to speed
up the last few weeks of school. I despaired every time I looked in the mirror.
Pencil-thin, with not a curve anywhere, I was called "Beanpole" and "String Bean,"
and I knew that's what I looked like. A flat chest, no hips, and a brain, that's what
I had. That really isn't much for a fourteen-year-old to work with, I thought, as
I absentmindedly wandered from my history class to the gym. Another hour of
sweating during basketball and displaying my toothpick legs was coming up. Then
I remembered my P.E. shorts were still in a bag under my desk where I'd forgotten
them. I had to walk all the way back and get them. Coach Thompson was a real
bear if anyone wasn't dressed for P.E. She had said I was a good forward and once
she even tried to talk Grandma into letting me join the team. Grandma, of course,
said no.

I was almost back at my classroom door when I heard angry voices and argu-   4
ing. I stopped. I didn't mean to eavesdrop; I just hesitated, not knowing what to
do. I needed those shorts and I was going to be late, but I didn't want to interrupt
an argument between my teachers. I recognized the voices: Mr. Schmidt, my history teacher; and Mr. Boone, my math teacher. They seemed to be arguing about
me. I couldn't believe it. I still remember the shock that rooted me flat against the
wall as if I were trying to blend in with the graffiti written there.

"I refuse to do it! I don't care who her father is; her grades don't even begin   5
to compare to Martha's. I won't lie or falsify records. Martha has a straight-A-plus
average and you know it." That was Mr. Schmidt, and he sounded very angry. Mr.
Boone's voice sounded calm and quiet.

"Look, Joann's father is not only on the Board, he owns the only store in   6
town; we could say it was a close tie and—"

The pounding in my ears drowned out the rest of the words, only a word here   7
and there filtered through. ". . . Martha is Mexican . . . resign . . . won't do it. . . ."
Mr. Schmidt came rushing out, and luckily for me went down the opposite way
toward the auditorium, so he didn't see me. Shaking, I waited a few minutes and
then went in and grabbed my bag and fled from the room. Mr. Boone looked up
when I came in but didn't say anything. To this day I don't remember if I got in
trouble in P.E. for being late or how I made it through the rest of the afternoon. I
went home very sad and cried into my pillow that night so Grandmother wouldn't
hear me. It seemed a cruel coincidence that I had overheard that conversation.

The next day when the principal called me into his office, I knew what it   8
would be about. He looked uncomfortable and unhappy. I decided I wasn't going
to make it any easier for him, so I looked him straight in the eye. He looked away
and fidgeted with the papers on his desk.

"Martha," he said, "there's been a change in policy this year regarding the   9
scholarship jacket. As you know, it has always been free." He cleared his throat
and continued. "This year the Board decided to charge fifteen dollars—which still
won't cover the complete cost of the jacket."

I stared at him in shock and a small sound of dismay escaped my throat. I   10
hadn't expected this. He still avoided looking in my eyes.

"So if you are unable to pay the fifteen dollars for the jacket, it will be given   11
to the next one in line."

Standing with all the dignity I could muster, I said, "I'll speak to my grandfa-   12
ther about it, sir, and let you know tomorrow." I cried on the walk home from the
bus stop. The dirt road was a quarter of a mile from the highway, so by the time I
got home, my eyes were red and puffy.

"Where's Grandpa?" I asked Grandma, looking down at the floor so she wouldn't   13
ask me why I'd been crying. She was sewing on a quilt and didn't look up.

"I think he's out back working in the bean field."   14

I went outside and looked out at the fields. There he was. I could see him   15
walking between the rows, his body bent over the little plants, hoe in hand. I
walked slowly out to him, trying to think how I could best ask him for the money.
There was a cool breeze blowing and a sweet smell of mesquite in the air, but I
didn't appreciate it. I kicked at a dirt clod. I wanted that jacket so much. It was
more than just being a valedictorian and giving a little thank-you speech for the
jacket on graduation night. It represented eight years of hard work and expecta-
tion. I knew I had to be honest with Grandpa; it was my only chance. He saw me
and looked up.

He waited for me to speak. I cleared my throat nervously and clasped my   16
hands behind my back so he wouldn't see them shaking. "Grandpa, I have a big
favor to ask you," I said in Spanish, the only language he knew. He still waited
silently. I tried again. "Grandpa, this year the principal said the scholarship jacket
is not going to be free. It's going to cost fifteen dollars and I have to take the
money in tomorrow, otherwise it'll be given to someone else." The last words
came out in an eager rush. Grandpa straightened up tiredly and leaned his chin
on the hoe handle. He looked out over the field that was filled with the tiny green
bean plants. I waited, desperately hoping he'd say I could have the money.

He turned to me and asked quietly, "What does a scholarship jacket mean?"   17

I answered quickly; maybe there was a chance. "It means you've earned it by   18
having the highest grades for eight years and that's why they're giving it to you."
Too late I realized the significance of my words. Grandpa knew that I understood it
was not a matter of money. It wasn't that. He went back to hoeing the weeds that
sprang up between the delicate little bean plants. It was a time-consuming job;
sometimes the small shoots were right next to each other. Finally he spoke again.

"Then if you pay for it, Marta, it's not a scholarship jacket, is it? Tell your   19
principal I will not pay the fifteen dollars."

I walked back to the house and locked myself in the bathroom for a long   20
time. I was angry with Grandfather even though I knew he was right, and I was
angry with the Board, whoever they were. Why did they have to change the rules
just when it was my turn to win the jacket?

It was a very sad and withdrawn girl who dragged into the principal's office   21
the next day. This time he did look me in the eyes.

"What did your grandfather say?"   22

I sat very straight in my chair.   23

"He said to tell you he won't pay the fifteen dollars."   24

The principal muttered something I couldn't understand under his breath,   25
and walked over to the window. He stood looking out at something outside. He
looked bigger than usual when he stood up; he was a tall, gaunt man with gray
hair, and I watched the back of his head while I waited for him to speak.

"Why?" he finally asked. "Your grandfather has the money. Doesn't he own   26
a small bean farm?"

I looked at him, forcing my eyes to stay dry. "He said if I had to pay for it, then   27
it wouldn't be a scholarship jacket," I said and stood up to leave. "I guess you'll
just have to give it to Joann." I hadn't meant to say that; it had just slipped out. I
was almost to the door when he stopped me.

"Martha—wait."   28

I turned and looked at him, waiting. What did he want now? I could feel my   29
heart pounding. Something bitter and vile-tasting was coming up in my mouth;
I was afraid I was going to be sick. I didn't need any sympathy speeches. He
sighed loudly and went back to his big desk. He looked at me, biting his lip, as
if thinking.

"OK, damn it. We'll make an exception in your case. I'll tell the Board, you'll   30
get your jacket."

I could hardly believe it. I spoke in a trembling rush. "Oh, thank you, sir!"   31
Suddenly I felt great. I didn't know about adrenaline in those days, but I knew
something was pumping through me, making me feel as tall as the sky. I wanted
to yell, jump, run the mile, do something. I ran out so I could cry in the hall where
there was no one to see me. At the end of the day, Mr. Schmidt winked at me and
said, "I hear you're getting a scholarship jacket this year."

His face looked as happy and innocent as a baby's, but I knew better. Without   32
answering I gave him a quick hug and ran to the bus. I cried on the walk home
again, but this time because I was so happy. I couldn't wait to tell Grandpa and
ran straight to the field. I joined him in the row where he was working and without saying anything I crouched down and started pulling up the weeds with my
hands. Grandpa worked alongside me for a few minutes, but he didn't ask what
had happened. After I had a little pile of weeds between the rows, I stood up and
faced him.

"The principal said he's making an exception for me, Grandpa, and I'm get-   33
ting the jacket after all. That's after I told him what you said."

Grandpa didn't say anything; he just gave me a pat on the shoulder and a   34
smile. He pulled out the crumpled red handkerchief that he always carried in his
back pocket and wiped the sweat off his forehead.

"Better go see if your grandmother needs any help with supper."   35

I gave him a big grin. He didn't fool me. I skipped and ran back to the house   36
whistling some silly tune.

Copyright ©2006 The McGraw-Hill Companies Inc. All rights reserved.

■ **Reading Comprehension Questions**

1. The word *falsify* in "I won't lie or falsify records. Martha has a straight-A-plus average and you know it" (paragraph 5) means

    a. make untrue.

    b. write down.

    c. keep track of.

    d. sort alphabetically.

2. The word *dismay* in "I stared at him in shock and a small sound of dismay escaped my throat. I hadn't expected this" (paragraph 10) means

    a. joy.

    b. comfort.

    c. relief.

    d. disappointment.

3. Which sentence best expresses the central point of the selection?

    a. It is more important to be smart than good-looking or athletic.

    b. People who are willing to pay for an award deserve it more than people who are not.

    c. By refusing to give in to discrimination, the author finally received the award she had earned.

    d. Always do what the adults in your family say, even if you don't agree.

4. Which sentence best expresses the main idea of paragraph 2?

    a. Marta wanted to win the scholarship jacket to be like her sister Rosie.

    b. The scholarship jacket was especially important to Marta because she was unable to earn a jacket in any other way.

    c. The scholarship jacket was better than a sports school jacket.

    d. Marta resented her parents for sending her to live with her grandparents.

5. Which sentence best expresses the main idea of paragraph 7?

    a. Marta was shocked and saddened by the conversation she overheard.

    b. Marta didn't want her grandmother to know she was crying.

    c. Mr. Schmidt didn't see Marta when he rushed out of the room.

    d. Marta didn't hear every word of Mr. Schmidt's and Mr. Boone's conversation.

6. Marta was raised by her grandparents because

    a. she wanted to learn to speak Spanish.

    b. her father did not earn enough money to feed all his children.

   c. she wanted to learn about farming.

   d. her parents died when she was six.

7. *True or false?* _____ Marta was called by a different name at school.

8. We can infer from paragraph 8 that the principal was "uncomfortable and unhappy" because

   a. the students had not been paying attention in class during the last few weeks before graduation.

   b. his office was very hot.

   c. he was ashamed to tell Marta that she had to pay fifteen dollars for a jacket that she had earned.

   d. Mr. Boone and Mr. Schmidt were fighting in the hallway

9. The author implies that the Board members were not going to give Marta the scholarship jacket because

   a. she was late for P.E. class.

   b. they wanted to award the jacket to the daughter of an important local citizen.

   c. another student had better grades.

   d. they didn't think it was fair to have two members of the same family win the jacket.

10. *True or false?* _____ The author implies that the Board's new policy to require a fee for the scholarship jacket was an act of discrimination.

■ Discussion Questions

About Content

1. Why was winning the scholarship jacket so important to Marta?

2. What seemed to be the meaning of the argument between Mr. Schmidt and Mr. Boone?

3. After Marta's grandfather asks her what the scholarship jacket is, the author writes, "'It means you've earned it by having the highest grades for eight years and that's why they're giving it to you.' Too late I realized the significance of my words." What is the significance of her words?

Copyright ©2006 The McGraw-Hill Companies, Inc. All rights reserved.

About Structure

4. Why do you think Salinas begins her essay with a detailed description of the scholarship jacket? How does her description contribute to our interest in her story?

5. At what point does Salinas stop providing background information and start giving a time-ordered narration of a particular event in her life?

6. In the course of the essay, Salinas rides an emotional roller-coaster. Find and write here three words or phrases she uses to describe her different emotional states:

_____   _____   _____

About Style and Tone

7. As you read the essay, what impression do you form of Salinas's grandfather? What kind of man does he seem to be? What details does Salinas provide in order to create that impression?

8. In paragraph 12, Salinas writes, "Standing with all the dignity I could muster, I said, 'I'll speak to my grandfather about it, sir, and let you know tomorrow.'" What other evidence does Salinas give us that her dignity is important to her?

WRITING ASSIGNMENTS

Assignment 1: Writing a Paragraph

Write a paragraph about a time when you experienced or witnessed an injustice. Describe the circumstances surrounding the incident and why you think the people involved acted as they did. In your paragraph, describe how you felt at the time and any effect the incident has had on you. Your topic sentence could be something like one of the following:

> I was angry when my supervisor promoted his nephew even though I was more qualified.
>
> A friend of mine recently got into trouble with authorities even though he was innocent of any wrongdoing.

Assignment 2: Writing a Paragraph

Marta stresses again and again how important the scholarship jacket was to her and how hard she worked to win it. Write a paragraph about something you worked hard to achieve when you were younger. How long did you work toward that goal?

How did you feel when you finally succeeded? Or as an alternative, write about not achieving the goal. How did you cope with the disappointment? What lessons, if any, did you learn from the experience?

Assignment 3: Writing an Essay

This story contains several examples of authority figures—specifically, the two teachers, the principal, and Marta's grandfather. Write an essay describing three qualities that you think an authority figure should possess. Such qualities might include honesty, fairness, compassion, and knowledge.

In the body of your essay, devote each supporting paragraph to one of those qualities. Within each paragraph, give an example or examples of how an authority figure in your life has demonstrated that quality.

You may write about three different authority figures who have demonstrated those three qualities to you. Alternatively, one authority figure may have demonstrated all three.

Your thesis statement might be similar to one of these:

My older brother, my grandmother, and my football coach have been models of admirable behavior for me.

My older brother's honesty, courage, and kindness to others have set a valuable example for me.

Joe Davis: A Cool Man

Beth Johnson

Copyright ©2006 The McGraw-Hill Companies, Inc All rights reserved.

Drugs and guns, crime and drugs, drugs and lies, liquor and drugs. If there was one constant in Joe Davis's life, it was drugs, the substances that ruled his existence. Personal tragedy was not enough to turn him off the path leading to the brink of self-destruction. Finally Joe was faced with a moment of decision. The choice he made has opened doors into a world that the old Joe barely knew existed.

Joe Davis was the coolest fourteen-year-old he'd ever seen.   1

He went to school when he felt like it. He hung out with a wild crowd. He started   2
drinking some wine, smoking some marijuana. "Nobody could tell me anything," he

says today. "I thought the sun rose and set on me." There were rules at home, but Joe didn't do rules. So he moved in with his grandmother.

Joe Davis was the coolest sixteen-year-old he'd ever seen.   3

Joe's parents gave up on his schooling and signed him out of the tenth grade.   4
Joe went to work in his dad's body shop, but that didn't last long. There were rules there, too, and Joe didn't do rules. By the time he was in his mid-teens, Joe was taking pills that got him high, and he was even using cocaine. He was also smoking marijuana all the time and drinking booze all the time.

Joe Davis was the coolest twenty-five-year-old he'd ever seen.   5

He was living with a woman almost twice his age. The situation wasn't great,   6
but she paid the bills, and certainly Joe couldn't pay them. He had his habit to support, which by now had grown to include heroin. Sometimes he'd work at a low-level job, if someone else found it for him. He might work long enough to get a paycheck and then spend it all at once. Other times he'd be caught stealing and get fired first. A more challenging job was not an option, even if he had bothered to look for one. He couldn't put words together to form a sentence, unless the sentence was about drugs. Filling out an application was difficult. He wasn't a strong reader. He couldn't do much with numbers. Since his drug habit had to be paid for, he started to steal. He stole first from his parents, then from his sister. Then he stole from the families of people he knew. But eventually the people he knew wouldn't let him into their houses, since they knew he'd steal from them. So he got a gun and began holding people up. He chose elderly people and others who weren't likely to fight back. The holdups kept him in drug money, but things at home were getting worse. His woman's teenage daughter was getting out of line. Joe decided it was up to him to discipline her. The girl didn't like it. She told her boyfriend. One day, the boyfriend called Joe out of the house.

Bang.   7

Joe Davis was in the street, his nose in the dirt. His mind was still cloudy from   8
his most recent high, but he knew something was terribly wrong with his legs. He couldn't move them; he couldn't even feel them. His mother came out of her house nearby and ran to him. As he heard her screams, he imagined what she was seeing. Her oldest child, her first baby, her bright boy who could have been and done anything, was lying in the gutter, a junkie with a .22 caliber bullet lodged in his spine.

The next time Joe's head cleared, he was in a hospital bed, blinking up at his   9
parents as they stared helplessly at him. The doctors had done all they could; Joe would live, to everyone's surprise. But he was a paraplegic—paralyzed from his chest down. It was done. It was over. It was written in stone. He would not walk again. He would not be able to control his bladder or bowels. He would not be able to make love as he did before. He would not be able to hold people up, then hurry away.

Joe spent the next eight months being moved between several Philadelphia   10
hospitals, where he was shown the ropes of life as a paraplegic. Officially he was being "rehabilitated"—restored to a productive life. There was just one problem:

Copyright ©2006 The McGraw-Hill Companies Inc. All rights reserved.

Joe. "To be rehabilitated, you must have been habilitated first," he says today. "That wasn't me." During his stay in the hospitals, he found ways to get high every day.

Finally Joe was released from the hospital. He returned in his wheelchair to   11
the house he'd been living in when he was shot. He needed someone to take care of him, and his woman friend was still willing. His drug habit was as strong as ever, but his days as a stickup man were over. So he started selling drugs. Business was good. The money came in fast, and his own drug use accelerated even faster.

A wheelchair-bound junkie doesn't pay much attention to his health or clean-   12
liness. Eventually Joe developed his first bedsore: a deep, rotting wound that ate into his flesh, overwhelming him with its foul odor. He was admitted to Magee Rehabilitation Hospital, where he spent six months on his stomach while the ghastly wound slowly healed. Again, he spent his time in the hospital using drugs. This time his drug use did not go unnoticed. Soon before he was scheduled to be discharged, hospital officials kicked him out. He returned to his friend's house and his business. But then the police raided the house. They took the drugs; they took the money; they took the guns.

"I really went downhill then," says Joe. With no drugs and no money to get   13
drugs, life held little meaning. He began fighting with the woman he was liv-ing with. "When you're in the state I was in, you don't know how to be nice to anybody," he says. Finally she kicked him out of the house. When his parents took him in, Joe did a little selling from their house, trying to keep it low-key, out of sight, so they wouldn't notice. He laughs at the notion today. "I thought I could control junkies and tell them, 'Business only during certain hours.'" Joe got high when his monthly Social Security check came, high when he'd make a purchase for someone else and get a little something for himself, high when a visitor would share drugs with him. It wasn't much of a life. "There I was," he says, "a junkie with no education, no job, no friends, no means of supporting myself. And now I had a spinal cord injury."

Then came October 25, 1988. Joe had just filled a prescription for pills to   14
control his muscle spasms. Three hundred of the powerful muscle relaxants were there for the taking. He swallowed them all.

"It wasn't the spinal cord injury that did it," he says. "It was the addiction."   15

Joe tried hard to die, but it didn't work. His sister heard him choking and called   16
for help. He was rushed to the hospital, where he lay in a coma for four days.

Joe has trouble finding the words to describe what happened next.   17

"I had . . . a spiritual awakening, for lack of any better term," he says. "My   18
soul had been cleansed. I knew my life could be better. And from that day to this, I have chosen not to get high."

Drugs, he says, "are not even a temptation. That life is a thing that happened   19
to someone else."

Joe knew he wanted to turn himself around, but he needed help in knowing   20
where to start. He enrolled in Magee Hospital's vocational rehabilitation program. For six weeks, he immersed himself in discussions, tests, and exercises to help him determine the kind of work he might be suited for. The day he finished the rehab

program, a nurse at Magee told him about a receptionist's job in the spinal cord injury unit at Thomas Jefferson Hospital. He went straight to the hospital and met Lorraine Buchanan, coordinator of the unit. "I told her where I was and where I wanted to go," Joe says. "I told her, 'If you give me a job, I will never disappoint you. I'll quit first if I see I can't live up to it.'" She gave him the job. The wheelchair-bound junkie, the man who'd never been able to hold a job, the drug-dependent stickup man who "couldn't put two words together to make a sentence" was now the first face, the first voice that patients encountered when they entered the spinal cord unit. "I'd never talked to people like that," says Joe, shaking his head. "I had absolutely no background. But Lorraine and the others, they taught me to speak. Taught me to greet people. Taught me to handle the phone." How did he do in his role as a receptionist? A huge smile breaks across Joe's face as he answers, "Excellent."

Soon, his personal life also took a very positive turn. A month after Joe started   21
his job, he was riding a city bus to work. A woman recovering from knee surgery was in another seat. The two smiled, but didn't speak.

A week later, Joe spotted the woman again. The bus driver sensed something   22
was going on and encouraged Joe to approach her. Her name was Terri. She was a receptionist in a law office. On their first date, Joe laid his cards on the table. He told her his story. He also told her he was looking to get married. "That about scared her away," Joe recalls. "She said she wasn't interested in marriage. I asked, 'Well, suppose you did meet someone you cared about who cared about you and treated you well. Would you still be opposed to the idea of marriage?' She said no, she would consider it then. I said, 'Well, that's all I ask.'"

Four months later, as the two sat over dinner in a restaurant, Joe handed   23
Terri a box tied with a ribbon. Inside was a smaller box. Then a smaller box, and a smaller one still. Ten boxes in all. Inside the smallest was an engagement ring. After another six months, the two were married in the law office where Terri works. Since then, she has been Joe's constant source of support, encouragement, and love.

After Joe had started work at Jefferson Hospital, he talked with his supervi-   24
sor, Lorraine, about his dreams of moving on to something bigger, more challenging. She encouraged him to try college. He had taken and passed the high school general equivalency diploma (GED) exam years before, almost as a joke, when he was recovering from his bedsores at Magee. Now he enrolled in a university mathematics course. He didn't do well. "I wasn't ready," Joe says. "I'd been out of school seventeen years. I dropped out." Before he could let discouragement overwhelm him, he enrolled at Community College of Philadelphia (CCP), where he signed up for basic math and English courses. He worked hard, sharpening study skills he had never developed in his earlier school days. Next he took courses toward an associate's degree in mental health and social services, along with a certificate in addiction studies. Five years later, he graduated from CCP, the first member of his family ever to earn a college degree. He went on to receive a

bachelor's degree in mental health from Hahnemann University in Philadelphia and then a master of social work from the University of Pennsylvania.

Today, Joe is the coordinator of "Think First," a violence and injury preven-   25
tion program operated by Magee Rehabilitation Hospital, where he also serves as a case manager for patients with spinal cord injuries. Once a month, he and two other men with such injuries speak to a group of first-time offenders who were arrested for driving under the influence of drugs or alcohol. He talks with government officials about passing stricter gun legislation and installing injury-prevention programs in public schools, and he visits local schools to describe the lessons of his life with students there. In every contact with every individual, Joe has one goal: to ensure the safety and well-being of young people.

At a presentation at a disciplinary school outside of Philadelphia, Joe gazes   26
with quiet authority at the unruly crowd of teenagers. He begins to speak, telling them about speedballs and guns, fast money and bedsores, even about the leg bag that collects his urine. At first, the kids snort with laughter at his honesty. When they laugh, he waits patiently, then goes on. Gradually the room grows quieter as Joe tells them of his life and then asks them about theirs. "What's important to you? What are your goals?" he says. "I'm still in school because when I was young, I chose the dead-end route many of you are on. But now I'm doing what I have to do to get where I want to go. What are you doing?"

He tells them more, about broken dreams, about his parents' grief, about   27
the former friends who turned away from him when he was no longer a source of drugs. He tells them of the continuing struggle to regain the trust of people he once abused. He tells them about the desire that consumes him now, the desire to make his community a better place to live. His wish is that no young man or woman should have to walk the path he's walked in order to value the precious gift of life. The teenagers are now silent. They look at this broad-shouldered black man in his wheelchair, his head and beard close-shaven, a gold ring in his ear. His hushed words settle among them like gentle drops of cleansing rain. "What are you doing? Where are you going?" he asks them. "Think about it. Think about me."

Joe Davis is the coolest forty-eight-year-old you've ever seen.   28

▪ Reading Comprehension Questions

1. The word *immersed* in "For six weeks, he immersed himself in discussions, tests, and exercises to help him determine the kind of work he might be suited for" (paragraph 20) means

   a. totally ignored.

   b. greatly angered.

   c. deeply involved.

   d. often harmed.

Copyright ©2006 The McGraw-Hill Companies, Inc. All rights reserved.

2. Which sentence best expresses the central point of the selection?

 a. Most people cannot improve their lives once they turn to drugs and crime.

 b. Joe Davis overcame a life of drugs and crime and a disability to lead a rich, meaningful life.

 c. The rules set by Joe Davis's parents caused him to leave home and continue a life of drugs and crime.

 d. Joe Davis's friends turned away from him once they learned he was no longer a source of drugs.

3. A main idea may cover more than one paragraph. Which sentence best expresses the main idea of paragraphs 21–23?

 a. First sentence of paragraph 21

 b. Second sentence of paragraph 21

 c. First sentence of paragraph 22

 d. First sentence of paragraph 23

4. Which sentence best expresses the main idea of paragraph 24?

 a. It was difficult for Joe to do college work after being out of school for so many years.

 b. Lorraine Buchanan encouraged Joe to go to college.

 c. Joe's determination enabled him to overcome a lack of academic preparation and eventually succeed in college.

 d. If students would stay in high school and work hard, they would not have to go to the trouble of getting a high school GED.

5. Joe Davis quit high school

 a. when he was fourteen.

 b. when he got a good job at a hospital.

 c. when he was in the tenth grade.

 d. after he was shot.

6. Joe tried to kill himself by

 a. swallowing muscle-relaxant pills.

 b. shooting himself.

 c. overdosing on heroin.

 d. not eating or drinking.

7. According to the selection, Joe first met his wife

 a. in the hospital, where she was a nurse.

 b. on a city bus, where they were both passengers.

     c. on the job, where she was also a receptionist.

     d. at Community College of Philadelphia, where she was also a student.

8. Joe decided to stop using drugs

     a. when he met his future wife.

     b. right after he was shot.

     c. when he awoke after a suicide attempt.

     d. when he was hired as a receptionist.

9. We can conclude from paragraph 26 that

     a. Joe is willing to reveal very personal information about himself in order to reach young people with his story.

     b. Joe was angry at the Philadelphia students who laughed at parts of his story.

     c. Joe is glad he did not go to college directly from high school.

     d. Joe is still trying to figure out what his life goals are.

10. When the author writes "Joe Davis was the coolest fourteen- (or sixteen- or twenty-five-) year-old he'd ever seen," she is actually expressing

     a. her approval of the way Joe was living then.

     b. her envy of Joe's status in the community.

     c. her mistaken opinion of Joe at these stages in his life.

     d. Joe's mistaken opinion of himself at these stages in his life.

■ Discussion Questions

About Content

1. When speaking of his suicide attempt, Joe said, "it wasn't the spinal cord injury that did it. It was the addiction." What do you think Joe meant? Why does he blame his addiction, rather than his disability, for his decision to try to end his life?

2. Why do you think the students Joe spoke to laughed as he shared personal details of his life? Why did they later quiet down? What effect do you think his presentation had on these students?

3. Joe wants young people to learn the lessons he has learned without having to experience his hardships. What lessons have you learned in your life that you would like to pass on to others?

Copyright ©2006 The McGraw-Hill Companies, Inc. All rights reserved.

About Structure

4. Paragraphs 1, 3, 5, and 28 are very similar. In what important way is paragraph 28 different from the others? What do you think Johnson is suggesting by introducing that difference?

5. Johnson tells the story of Joe's shooting briefly, in paragraphs 6–8. She could have chosen to go into much more detail about that part of the story. For instance, she could have described any previous relationship between Joe and the young man who shot him, or what happened to the shooter afterward. Why do you think she chose not to concentrate on those details? How would the story have been different if she had focused on them?

6. In paragraphs 21–23, Johnson condenses an important year in Joe's life into three paragraphs. Locate and write below three of the many transitions that are used as part of the time order in those paragraphs.

_____   _____   _____

About Style and Tone

7. In paragraph 12, Johnson describes Joe's poor physical condition. She could have simply written, "Joe developed a serious bedsore." Instead she writes, "Eventually Joe developed his first bedsore: a deep, rotting wound that ate into his flesh, overwhelming him with its foul odor." Why do you think she provided such graphic detail? What is the effect on the reader?

8. How do you think Johnson feels about Joe Davis? What hints lead you to that conclusion?

WRITING ASSIGNMENTS

Assignment 1: Writing a Paragraph

Like Joe Davis, many of us have learned painful lessons from life. And like him, we wish we could pass those lessons on to young people to save them from making the same mistakes.

Write a one-paragraph letter to a young person you know. In it, use your experience to pass on a lesson you wish he or she would learn. Begin with a topic sentence in which you state the lesson you'd like to teach, as in these examples:

My own humiliating experience taught me that shoplifting is a very bad idea.

I learned the hard way that abandoning your friends for the "cool" crowd will backfire on you.

The sad experience of a friend has taught me that teenage girls should not give in to their boyfriends' pressure for sex.

Dropping out of high school may seem like a great idea, but what happened to my brother should convince you otherwise.

Your letter should describe in detail the lesson you learned and how you learned it.

Assignment 2: Writing a Paragraph

Although Joe's parents loved him, they weren't able to stop him from using drugs, skipping school, and doing other self-destructive things. Think of a time that you have seen someone you cared about doing something you thought was bad for him or her. What did you do? What did you want to do?

Write a paragraph in which you describe the situation and how you responded. Make sure to answer the following questions:

What was the person doing?

Why was I concerned about him or her?

Did I feel there was anything I could do?

Did I take any action?

How did the situation finally turn out?

Assignment 3: Writing an Essay

1. One of Joe's goals is to regain the trust of the friends and family members he abused during his earlier life. Have you ever given a second chance to someone who treated you poorly? Write an essay about what happened. You could begin with a thesis statement something like this: "Although my closest friend betrayed my trust, I decided to give him another chance."

   You could then go on to structure the rest of your essay in this way:

   • In your first supporting paragraph, explain what the person did to lose your trust. Maybe it was an obviously hurtful action, like physically harming you or stealing from you. Or perhaps it was something more subtle, like insulting or embarrassing you.

   • In your second supporting paragraph, explain why you decided to give the person another chance.

Copyright ©2006 The McGraw-Hill Companies, Inc. All rights reserved.

- In your third supporting paragraph, tell what happened as a result of your giving the person a second chance. Did he or she treat you better this time? Or did the bad treatment start over again?
- In your concluding paragraph, provide some final thoughts about what you learned from the experience.

Alternatively, write an essay about a time that you were given a second chance by someone whose trust you had abused. Follow the same pattern of development.

Tickets to Nowhere

Andy Rooney

Who doesn't love a "get rich quick" story? We eagerly read the accounts of lucky people who've become wealthy overnight just by buying the right lottery ticket. The hope that we might do the same keeps many of us "investing" in the lottery week after week. But the syndicated columnist Andy Rooney thinks there's another lottery story that also deserves our attention.

Things never went very well for Jim Oakland. He dropped out of high school because he was impatient to get rich, but after dropping out he lived at home with his parents for two years and didn't earn a dime.

He finally got a summer job working for the highway department holding up a sign telling oncoming drivers to be careful of the workers ahead. Later that same year, he picked up some extra money putting fliers under the windshield wipers of parked cars.

Things just never went very well for Jim, and he was twenty-three before he left home and went to Florida hoping his ship would come in down there. He never lost his desire to get rich; but first he needed money for the rent, so he took a job near Fort Lauderdale for $4.50 an hour servicing the goldfish aquariums kept near the cashier's counter in a lot of restaurants.

Jim was paid in cash once a week by the owner of the goldfish business, and the first thing he did was go to the little convenience store near where he lived and buy $20 worth of lottery tickets. He was really determined to get rich.

A week ago, the lottery jackpot in Florida reached $54 million. Jim woke up nights thinking what he could do with $54 million. During the days, he daydreamed about it. One morning he was driving along the main street in the boss's old pickup truck with six tanks of goldfish in back. As he drove past a BMW dealer, he looked at the new models in the window.

Copyright ©2006 The McGraw-Hill Companies, Inc. All rights reserved.

He saw the car he wanted in the showroom window, but unfortunately he 6
didn't see the light change. The car in front of him stopped short and Jim slammed on his brakes. The fish tanks slid forward. The tanks broke, the water gushed out, and the goldfish slithered and flopped all over the back of the truck. Some fell off into the road.

It wasn't a good day for the goldfish or for Jim, of course. He knew he'd have to 7
pay for the tanks and 75 cents each for the fish, and if it weren't for the $54 million lottery, he wouldn't have known which way to turn. He had that lucky feeling.

For the tanks and the dead goldfish, the boss deducted $114 of Jim's $180 8
weekly pay. Even though he didn't have enough left for the rent and food, Jim doubled the amount he was going to spend on lottery tickets. He never needed $54 million more.

Jim had this system. He took his age and added the last four digits of the 9
telephone number of the last girl he dated. He called it his lucky number . . . even though the last four digits changed quite often and he'd never won with his system. Everyone laughed at Jim and said he'd never win the lottery.

Jim put down $40 on the counter that week and the man punched out his 10
tickets. Jim stowed them safely away in his wallet with last week's tickets. He never threw away his lottery tickets until at least a month after the drawing just in case there was some mistake. He'd heard of mistakes.

Jim listened to the radio all afternoon the day of the drawing. The people at 11
the radio station he was listening to waited for news of the winning numbers to come over the wires and, even then, the announcers didn't rush to get them on. The station manager thought the people running the lottery ought to pay to have the winning numbers broadcast, just like any other commercial announcement.

Jim fidgeted while they gave the weather and the traffic and the news. Then 12
they played more music. All he wanted to hear were those numbers.

"Well," the radio announcer said finally, "we have the lottery numbers some 13
of you have been waiting for. You ready?" Jim was ready. He clutched his ticket with the number 274802.

"The winning number," the announcer said, "is 860539. I'll repeat that. 14
860539." Jim was still a loser.

I thought that, with all the human interest stories about lottery winners, we 15
ought to have a story about one of the several million losers.

■ Reading Comprehension Questions

1. The word *gushed* in "The tanks broke, the water gushed out, and the goldfish slithered and flopped all over the back of the truck" (paragraph 6) means

   a. dripped slowly.

   b. steamed.

   c. poured.

   d. held.

2. The word *digits* in "He took his age and added the last four digits of the telephone number of the last girl he dated" (paragraph 9) means

    a. letters.

    b. single numbers.

    c. rings.

    d. area codes.

3. Which of the following would be the best alternative title for this selection?

    a. A $54 Million Jackpot

    b. An Unnecessary Accident

    c. Foolish Dreams

    d. Moving to Florida

4. Which sentence best expresses the main idea of the selection?

    a. Everyone dreams of winning the lottery.

    b. The more money you invest in lottery tickets, the better your chances of winning.

    c. Jim Oakland's dreams of getting rich by winning the lottery were unrealistic.

    d. Jim Oakland is a very unlucky man.

5. *True or false?* ____ Jim dropped out of school because he was offered a good-paying job in Florida.

6. When Jim lost money as a result of his accident with the goldfish, he

    a. put himself on a strict budget.

    b. spent even more on lottery tickets.

    c. got a second job.

    d. moved back in with his parents to save money.

7. Jim never threw away his lottery tickets

    a. at all.

    b. until his next paycheck.

    c. until at least a month after the drawing.

    d. so that he could write off his losses on his tax return.

8. We can infer from paragraphs 6–7 that

    a. Jim's daydreams about getting rich made him careless.

    b. the driver in front of Jim should have gotten a ticket.

Copyright ©2006 The McGraw-Hill Companies, Inc. All rights reserved.

    c. the brakes on Jim's pickup truck were faulty.

    d. Jim slammed on his brakes because he'd suddenly realized that he'd never win the lottery.

9. In paragraph 9, the author suggests that Jim

    a. was good in math.

    b. did not date very often.

    c. never told anyone about his dreams of winning the lottery.

    d. never dated the same girl for very long.

10. Andy Rooney suggests that

    a. although few people win the lottery, it's still worth trying.

    b. most of what the public hears about lotteries shows how harmful they are.

    c. Jim Oakland gave up playing the lottery after losing the $54 million jackpot.

    d. playing the lottery harms far more people than it helps.

Discussion Questions

About Content

1. Jim Oakland seemed to feel that lotteries were entirely good. Andy Rooney takes a more negative view. What is your opinion? On balance, are lotteries good or bad? On what are you basing your opinion?

2. Do you know anyone like Jim, someone who depends on luck more than on hard work or ability? If so, why do you think this person relies so much on luck? How lucky has he or she been?

3. What would be the good points of suddenly winning a large amount of money? What might be the downside? All in all, would you prefer to win or to earn the money you have? Why?

About Structure

4. As Rooney's piece went on, did you think that it was going to be about Jim Oakland winning the lottery—or losing it? What details contributed to your expectations?

About Style and Tone

5. At only one point in the essay does Rooney use a direct quotation. What is that point? Why do you think he chooses to dramatize that moment with the speaker's exact words?

6. One meaning of *irony* is a contradiction between what might be expected and what really happens. Rooney uses this type of irony in an understated way to contrast Oakland's goal with his actions. For instance, in paragraph 1, he states that Oakland was "impatient to get rich." In the same sentence he states, "he lived at home with his parents for two years and didn't earn a dime." Find one other spot in the selection where Rooney uses irony and write its paragraph number here. _____

7. Rooney refers to himself only one time in the essay, in the final paragraph. Why do you think he chooses to refer to "I" at that point? What is the effect?

8. How do you think Rooney feels about Jim? Does he admire his continued optimism about striking it rich? Does he think Jim is a bad person? Find passages in the essay that support your opinion about how Rooney regards Jim.

WRITING ASSIGNMENTS

Assignment 1: Writing a Paragraph

Write a paragraph about a time when you had good luck. Perhaps you found a twenty-dollar bill, or you happened to meet the person you are currently dating or are married to, or you were fortunate enough to find a job you like. Provide plenty of detail to let readers know why you consider your experience so fortunate. Your topic sentence may begin like this:

A time I had incredibly good luck was the day that _____.

Assignment 2: Writing a Paragraph

As Andy Rooney describes him, Jim is a man who has relied on luck to make good things happen in his life, rather than on hard work or realistic planning. Do you know someone who drifts along in life, hoping for a lucky break but doing little to make it happen? Write a paragraph describing how this person goes about his or her life. Introduce that person in your topic sentence, as in these examples:

My sister's former husband relies on luck, not work or planning, to get ahead in life.

Instead of studying, my roommate hopes that luck will be enough to help her pass her courses.

Then give several specific examples of the person's behavior. Conclude by providing a suggestion about what this person might do in order to take the responsibility of creating his or her own "good luck."

Alternatively, write a paragraph about a person who plans logically and works hard to achieve his or her goals.

Assignment 3: Writing an Essay

Rooney uses just one example—Jim Oakland's story—to suggest the general point that people should not count on the lottery to make them rich. Write an essay in which you, like Rooney, defend an idea that many oppose or have given little thought to. Perhaps you will argue that high schools should distribute birth-control devices to students or that alcohol should be banned on your college campus.

Develop your essay by describing in detail the experiences of one person. Your three supporting paragraphs may be organized by time order, describing the person's experience from an early to a later point; or they may be organized as a list—for example, showing how the person's experience affected him or her in three different ways. In your conclusion, make it clear, as Rooney does, that the one person you're writing about is intended to illustrate a general point.

Here is a sample outline for one such essay:

Thesis statement: Alcoholic beverages should be banned on this campus.
Topic sentence 1: Drinking affected Beverly's academic life.
Topic sentence 2: Drinking also affected Beverly's social life.
Topic sentence 3: Finally, drinking jeopardized Beverly's work life.
Conclusion: Many students, like Beverly, have their lives damaged and even ruined by alcohol.

What Good Families Are Doing Right

Delores Curran

It isn't easy to be a successful parent these days. Pressured by the conflicting demands of home and workplace, confused by changing moral standards, and drowned out by their offspring's rock music and television, today's parents seem to be facing impossible odds in their struggle to raise healthy families. Yet some parents manage to "do it all"—and even remain on speaking terms with their children. How do they do it? Delores Curran's survey offers some significant suggestions; her article could serve as a recipe for a successful family.

Copyright ©2006 The McGraw-Hill Companies, Inc. All rights reserved.

I have worked with families for fifteen years, conducting hundreds of seminars,   1
workshops, and classes on parenting, and I meet good families all the time. They're
fairly easy to recognize. Good families have a kind of visible strength. They expect
problems and work together to find solutions, applying common sense and trying
new methods to meet new needs. And they share a common shortcoming—they
can tell me in a minute what's wrong with them, but they aren't sure what's right
with them. Many healthy families with whom I work, in fact, protest at being called
healthy. They don't think they are. The professionals who work with them do.

To prepare the book on which this article is based, I asked respected work-   2
ers in the fields of education, religion, health, family counseling, and voluntary
organizations to identify a list of possible traits of a healthy family. Together we
isolated fifty-six such traits, and I sent this list to five hundred professionals who
regularly work with families—teachers, doctors, principals, members of the clergy,
scout directors, YMCA leaders, family counselors, social workers—asking them to
pick the fifteen qualities they most commonly found in healthy families.

While all of these traits are important, the one most often cited as central to   3
close family life is communication: The healthy family knows how to talk—and
how to listen.

"Without communication you don't know one another," wrote one family   4
counselor. "If you don't know one another, you don't care about one another, and
that's what the family is all about."

"The most familiar complaint I hear from wives I counsel is 'He won't talk to   5
me' and 'He doesn't listen to me,'" said a pastoral marriage counselor. "And when
I share this complaint with their husbands, they don't hear *me,* either."

"We have kids in classes whose families are so robotized by television that   6
they don't know one another," said a fifth-grade teacher.

Professional counselors are not the only ones to recognize the need. The phe-   7
nomenal growth of communication groups such as Parent Effectiveness Training,
Parent Awareness, Marriage Encounter, Couple Communication, and literally hundreds of others tells us that the need for effective communication—the sharing of
deepest feelings—is felt by many.

Healthy families have also recognized this need, and they have, either instinctively   8
or consciously, developed methods of meeting it. They know that conflicts are to be
expected, that we all become angry and frustrated and discouraged. And they know
how to reveal those feelings—good and bad—to each other. Honest communication
isn't always easy. But when it's working well, there are certain recognizable signs or
symptoms, what I call the hallmarks of the successfully communicating family.

The Family Exhibits a Strong Relationship between the Parents

According to Dr. Jerry M. Lewis—author of a significant work on families, *No*   9
Single Thread—healthy spouses complement, rather than dominate, each other.
Either husband or wife could be the leader, depending on the circumstances. In

the unhealthy families he studied, the dominant spouse had to hide feelings of weakness while the submissive spouse feared being put down if he or she exposed a weakness.

Children in the healthy family have no question about which parent is boss. 10 Both parents are. If children are asked who is boss, they're likely to respond, "Sometimes Mom, sometimes Dad." And, in a wonderful statement, Dr. Lewis adds, "If you ask if they're comfortable with this, they look at you as if you're crazy—as if there's no other way it ought to be."

My survey respondents echo Dr. Lewis. One wrote, "The healthiest families I 11 know are ones in which the mother and father have a strong, loving relationship. This seems to flow over to the children and even beyond the home. It seems to breed security in the children and, in turn, fosters the ability to take risks, to reach out to others, to search for their own answers, become independent and develop a good self-image."

The Family Has Control over Television

Television has been maligned, praised, damned, cherished, and even thrown out. 12 It has more influence on children's values than anything else except their parents. Over and over, when I'm invited to help families mend their communication ruptures, I hear "But we have no time for this." These families have literally turned their "family-together" time over to television. Even those who control the quality of programs watched and set "homework-first" regulations feel reluctant to intrude upon the individual's right to spend his or her spare time in front of the set. Many families avoid clashes over program selection by furnishing a set for each family member. One of the women who was most desperate to establish a better sense of communication in her family confided to me that they owned nine sets. Nine sets for seven people!

Whether the breakdown in family communication leads to excessive viewing 13 or whether too much television breaks into family lives, we don't know. But we do know that we can become out of one another's reach when we're in front of a TV set. The term *television widow* is not humorous to thousands whose spouses are absent even when they're there. One woman remarked, "I can't get worried about whether there's life after death. I'd be satisfied with life after dinner."

In family-communication workshops, I ask families to make a list of phrases 14 they most commonly hear in their home. One parent was aghast to discover that his family's most familiar comments were "What's on?" and "Move." In families like this one, communication isn't hostile—it's just missing.

But television doesn't have to be a villain. A 1980 Gallup Poll found that the 15 public sees great potential for television as a positive force. It can be a tremendous device for initiating discussion on subjects that may not come up elsewhere, subjects such as sexuality, corporate ethics, sportsmanship, and marital fidelity.

Even very bad programs offer material for values clarification if family mem- 16 bers view them together. My sixteen-year-old son and his father recently watched

Copyright ©2006 The McGraw-Hill Companies, Inc. All rights reserved.

a program in which hazardous driving was part of the hero's characterization. At one point, my son turned to his dad and asked, "Is that possible to do with that kind of truck?"

"I don't know," replied my husband, "but it sure is dumb. If that load shifted . . ."   17 With that, they launched into a discussion on the responsibility of drivers that didn't have to originate as a parental lecture. Furthermore, as the discussion became more engrossing to them, they turned the sound down so that they could continue their conversation.

Parents frequently report similar experiences; in fact, this use of television was   18 recommended in the widely publicized 1972 Surgeon General's report as the most effective form of television gatekeeping by parents. Instead of turning off the set, parents should view programs with their children and make moral judgments and initiate discussion. Talking about the problems and attitudes of a TV family can be a lively, nonthreatening way to risk sharing real fears, hopes, and dreams.

The Family Listens and Responds

"My parents say they want me to come to them with problems, but when I do,   19 either they're busy or they only half-listen and keep on doing what they were doing—like shaving or making a grocery list. If a friend of theirs came over to talk, they'd stop, be polite, and listen," said one of the children quoted in a *Christian Science Monitor* interview by Ann McCarroll. This child put his finger on the most difficult problem of communicating in families: the inability to listen.

It is usually easier to react than to respond. When we react, we reflect our   20 own experiences and feelings; when we respond, we get into the other person's feelings. For example:

Tom, age seventeen: "I don't know if I want to go to college. I don't think I'd do very well there."

Father: "Nonsense. Of course you'll do well."

That's reacting. This father is cutting off communication. He's refusing either   21 to hear the boy's fears or to consider his feelings, possibly because he can't accept the idea that his son might not attend college. Here's another way of handling the same situation:

Tom: "I don't know if I want to go to college. I don't think I'd do very well there."

Father: "Why not?"

Tom: "Because I'm not that smart."

Father: "Yeah, that's scary. I worried about that, too."

Tom: "Did you ever come close to flunking out?"

Father: "No, but I worried a lot before I went because I thought college would be full of brains. Once I got there, I found out that most of the kids were just like me."

This father has responded rather than reacted to his son's fears. First, he   22
searched for the reason behind his son's lack of confidence and found it was fear of academic ability (it could have been fear of leaving home, of a new environment, of peer pressure, or of any of a number of things); second, he accepted the fear as legitimate; third, he empathized by admitting to having the same fear when he was Tom's age; and, finally, he explained why his, not Tom's, fears turned out to be groundless. He did all this without denigrating or lecturing.

And that's tough for parents to do. Often we don't want to hear our children's   23
fears, because those fears frighten us; or we don't want to pay attention to their dreams because their dreams aren't what we have in mind for them. Parents who deny such feelings will allow only surface conversation. It's fine as long as a child says, "School was OK today," but when she says, "I'm scared of boys," the parents are uncomfortable. They don't want her to be afraid of boys, but since they don't quite know what to say, they react with a pleasant "Oh, you'll outgrow it." She probably will, but what she needs at the moment is someone to hear and under-stand her pain.

In Ann McCarroll's interviews, she talked to one fifteen-year old boy who said   24
he had *"some* mother. Each morning she sits with me while I eat breakfast. We talk about anything and everything. She isn't refined or elegant or educated. She's a terrible housekeeper. But she's interested in everything I do, and she always listens to me—even if she's busy or tired."

That's the kind of listening found in families that experience real communi   25
cation. Answers to the routine question, "How was your day?" are heard with the eyes and heart as well as the ears. Nuances are picked up and questions are asked, although problems are not necessarily solved. Members of a family who really listen to one another instinctively know that if people listen to you, they are interested in you. And that's enough for most of us.

The Family Recognizes Unspoken Messages

Much of our communication—especially our communication of feelings—is non-   26
verbal. Dr. Lewis defines *empathy* as "someone responding to you in such a way that you feel deeply understood." He says, "There is probably no more impor-tant dimension in all of human relationships than the capacity for empathy. And healthy families teach empathy." Their members are allowed to be mad, glad, and sad. There's no crime in being in a bad mood, nor is there betrayal in being happy while someone else is feeling moody. The family recognizes that bad days and good days attack everyone at different times.

Copyright ©2006 The McGraw-Hill Companies, Inc. All rights reserved.

Nonverbal expressions of love, too, are the best way to show children that   27
parents love each other. A spouse reaching for the other's hand, a wink, a squeeze
on the shoulder, a "How's-your-back-this-morning?" a meaningful glance across
the room—all these tell children how their parents feel about each other.

The most destructive nonverbal communication in marriage is silence. Silence   28
can mean lack of interest, hostility, denigration, boredom, or outright war. On the
part of a teen or preteen, silence usually indicates pain, sometimes very deep pain.
The sad irony discovered by so many family therapists is that parents who seek
professional help when a teenager becomes silent have often denied the child any
other way of communicating. And although they won't permit their children to
become angry or to reveal doubts or to share depression, they do worry about the
withdrawal that results. Rarely do they see any connection between the two.

Healthy families use signs, symbols, body language, smiles, and other gestures   29
to express caring and love. They deal with silence and withdrawal in a positive,
open way. Communication doesn't mean just talking or listening; it includes all
the clues to a person's feelings—his bearing, her expression, their resignation.
Family members don't have to say, "I'm hurting," or, "I'm in need." A quick glance
tells that. And they have developed ways of responding that indicate caring and
love, whether or not there's an immediate solution to the pain.

The Family Encourages Individual Feelings and Independent Thinking

Close families encourage the emergence of individual personalities through open   30
sharing of thoughts and feelings. Unhealthy families tend to be less open, less
accepting of differences among members. The family must be Republican, or
Bronco supporters, or gun-control advocates, and woe to the individual who says,
"Yes, but . . . ."

Instead of finding differing opinions threatening, the healthy family finds   31
them exhilarating. It is exciting to witness such a family discussing politics, sports,
or the world. Members freely say, "I don't agree with you," without risking ridicule or rebuke. They say, "I think it's wrong . . ." immediately after Dad says, "I
think it's right. . ."; and Dad listens and responds.

Give-and-take gives children practice in articulating their thoughts at home   32
so that eventually they'll feel confident outside the home. What may seem to be
verbal rambling by preteens during a family conversation is a prelude to sorting
out their thinking and putting words to their thoughts.

Rigid families don't understand the dynamics of give-and-take. Some label it   33
disrespectful and argumentative; others find it confusing. Dr. John Meeks, medical director of the Psychiatric Institute of Montgomery County, Maryland, claims
that argument is a way of life with normally developing adolescents. "In early
adolescence they'll argue with parents about anything at all; as they grow older,
the quantity of argument decreases but the quality increases." According to Dr.

Meeks, arguing is something adolescents need to do. If the argument doesn't become too bitter, they have a good chance to test their own beliefs and feelings. "Incidentally," says Meeks, "parents can expect to 'lose' most of these arguments, because adolescents are not fettered by logic or even reality." Nor are they likely to be polite. Learning how to disagree respectfully is a difficult task, but good families work at it.

Encouraging individual feelings and thoughts, of course, in no way presumes 34 that parents permit their children to do whatever they want. There's a great difference between permitting a son to express an opinion on marijuana and allowing him to use it. That his opinion conflicts with his parents' opinion is OK as long as his parents make sure he knows their thinking on the subject. Whether he admits it or not, he's likely at least to consider their ideas if he respects them.

Permitting teenagers to sort out their feelings and thoughts in open discus- 35 sions at home gives them valuable experience in dealing with a bewildering array of situations they may encounter when they leave home. Cutting off discussion of behavior unacceptable to us, on the other hand, makes our young people feel guilty for even thinking about values contrary to ours and ends up making those values more attractive to them.

The Family Recognizes Turn-Off Words and Put-Down Phrases

Some families deliberately use hurtful language in their daily communication. 36 "What did you do all day around here?" can be a red flag to a woman who has spent her day on household tasks that don't show unless they're not done. "If only we had enough money" can be a rebuke to a husband who is working as hard as he can to provide for the family. "Flunk any tests today, John?" only discourages a child who may be having trouble in school.

Close families seem to recognize that a comment made in jest can be insult- 37 ing. A father in one of my groups confided that he could tease his wife about everything but her skiing. "I don't know why she's so sensitive about that, but I back off on it. I can say anything I want to about her cooking, her appearance, her mothering—whatever. But not her skiing."

One of my favorite exercises with families is to ask them to reflect upon 38 phrases they most like to hear and those they least like to hear. Recently, I invited seventy-five fourth- and fifth-graders to submit the words they most like to hear from their mothers. Here are the five big winners:

"I love you."

"Yes."

"Time to eat."

Copyright ©2006 The McGraw-Hill Companies, Inc. All rights reserved.

"You can go."

"You can stay up late."

And on the children's list of what they least like to hear from one another are   39
the following:

"I'm telling."

"Mom says!"

"I know something you don't know."

"You think you're so big."

"Just see if I ever let you use my bike again."

It can be worthwhile for a family to list the phrases members like most and   40
least to hear, and post them. Often parents aren't even aware of the reaction of
their children to certain routine comments. Or keep a record of the comments
heard most often over a period of a week or two. It can provide good clues to
the level of family sensitivity. If the list has a lot of "shut ups" and "stop its," that
family needs to pay more attention to its relationships, especially the role that
communication plays in them.

The Family Interrupts, but Equally

When Dr. Jerry M. Lewis began to study the healthy family, he and his staff video-   41
taped families in the process of problem solving. The family was given a question,
such as, "What's the main thing wrong with your family?" Answers varied, but
what was most significant was what the family actually did: who took control,
how individuals responded or reacted, what were the put-downs, and whether
some members were entitled to speak more than others.

The researchers found that healthy families expected everyone to speak   42
openly about feelings. Nobody was urged to hold back. In addition, these family
members interrupted one another repeatedly, but no one person was interrupted
more than anyone else.

Manners, particularly polite conversational techniques, are not hallmarks of   43
the communicating family. This should make many parents feel better about their
family's dinner conversation. One father reported to me that at their table people
had to take a number to finish a sentence. Finishing sentences, however, doesn't
seem all that important in the communicating family. Members aren't sensitive to
being interrupted, either. The intensity and spontaneity of the exchange are more
important than propriety in conversation.

The Family Develops a Pattern of Reconciliation

"We know how to break up," one man said, "but who ever teaches us to make   44
up?" Survey respondents indicated that there is indeed a pattern of reconciliation
in healthy families that is missing in others. "It usually isn't a kiss-and-make-up situation," explained one family therapist, "but there are certain rituals developed
over a long period of time that indicate it's time to get well again. Between husband
and wife, it might be a concessionary phrase to which the other is expected to
respond in kind. Within a family, it might be that the person who stomps off to
his or her room voluntarily reenters the family circle, where something is said to
make him or her welcome."

When I asked several families how they knew a fight had ended, I got remark-   45
ably similar answers from individuals questioned separately. "We all come out of
our rooms," responded every member of one family. Three members of another
family said, "Mom says, 'Anybody want a Pepsi?'" One five-year-old scratched his
head and furrowed his forehead after I asked him how he knew the family fight
was over. Finally, he said, "Well, Daddy gives a great big yawn and says, 'Well . . .'"
This scene is easy to visualize, as one parent decides that the unpleasantness needs
to end and it's time to end the fighting and to pull together again as a family.

Why have we neglected the important art of reconciling? "Because we have   46
pretended that good families don't fight," says one therapist. "They do. It's essential to fight for good health in the family. It gets things out into the open. But we
need to learn to put ourselves back together—and many families never learn this."

Close families know how to time divisive and emotional issues that may cause   47
friction. They don't bring up potentially explosive subjects right before they go
out, for example, or before bedtime. They tend to schedule discussions rather than
allow a matter to explode, and thus they keep a large measure of control over
the atmosphere in which they will fight and reconcile. Good families know that
they need enough time to discuss issues heatedly, rationally, and completely—and
enough time to reconcile. "You've got to solve it right there," said one father.
"Don't let it go on and on. It just causes more problems. Then when it's solved, let
it be. No nagging, no remembering."

The Family Fosters Table Time and Conversation

Traditionally, the dinner table has been a symbol of socialization. It's probably the   48
one time each day that parents and children are assured of uninterrupted time
with one another.

Therapists frequently call upon a patient's memory of the family table during   49
childhood in order to determine the degree of communication and interaction there
was in the patient's early life. Some patients recall nothing. Mealtime was either
so unpleasant or so unimpressive that they have blocked it out of their memories.

Copyright ©2006 The McGraw-Hill Companies, Inc. All rights reserved.

Therapists say that there is a relationship between the love in a home and life around the family table. It is to the table that love or discord eventually comes.

But we are spending less table time together. Fast-food dining, even within   50
the home, is becoming a way of life for too many of us. Work schedules, individual organized activities, and television all limit the quantity and quality of mealtime interaction. In an informal study conducted by a church group, 68 percent of the families interviewed in three congregations saw nothing wrong with watching television while eating.

Families who do a good job of communicating tend to make the dinner meal   51
an important part of their day. A number of respondents indicated that adults in the healthiest families refuse dinner business meetings as a matter of principle and discourage their children from sports activities that cut into mealtime hours. "We know which of our swimmers will or won't practice at dinnertime," said a coach, with mixed admiration. "Some parents never allow their children to miss dinners. Some don't care at all." These families pay close attention to the number of times they'll be able to be together in a week, and they rearrange schedules to be sure of spending this time together.

The family that wants to improve communication should look closely at its   52
attitudes toward the family table. Are family table time and conversation important? Is table time open and friendly or warlike and sullen? Is it conducive to sharing more than food—does it encourage the sharing of ideas, feelings, and family intimacies?

We all need to talk to one another. We need to know we're loved and appre-   53
ciated and respected. We want to share our intimacies, not just physical intimacies but all the intimacies in our lives. Communication is the most important element of family life because it is basic to loving relationships. It is the energy that fuels the caring, giving, sharing, and affirming. Without genuine sharing of ourselves, we cannot know one another's needs and fears. Good communication is what makes all the rest of it work.

■ Reading Comprehension Questions

1. The word *aghast* in "One parent was aghast to discover that his family's most familiar comments were 'What's on?' and 'Move'" (paragraph 14) means
   a. horrified.
   b. satisfied.
   c. curious.
   d. amused.

2. The word *engrossing* in "as the discussion became more engrossing to them, they turned the sound down so that they could continue their conversation" (paragraph 17) means

Copyright ©2006 The McGraw-Hill Companies, Inc. All rights reserved.

   a. disgusting.

   b. intellectual.

   c. foolish.

   d. interesting.

3. Which of the following would be the best alternative title for this selection?

   a. Successful Communication

   b. How to Solve Family Conflicts

   c. Characteristics of Families

   d. Hallmarks of the Communicating Family

4. Which sentence best expresses the article's main point?

   a. Television can and often does destroy family life.

   b. More American families are unhappy than ever before.

   c. A number of qualities mark the healthy and communicating family.

   d. Strong families encourage independent thinking.

5. *True or false?* _____ According to the article, healthy families have no use for television.

6. Healthy families

   a. never find it hard to communicate.

   b. have no conflicts with each other.

   c. know how to reveal their feelings.

   d. permit one of the parents to make all final decisions.

7. The author has found that good families frequently make a point of being together

   a. in the mornings.

   b. after school.

   c. during dinner.

   d. before bedtime.

8. *True or false?* _____ The article implies that the most troublesome nonverbal signal is silence.

9. The article implies that

   a. verbal messages are always more accurate than nonverbal ones.

   b. in strong families, parents practice tolerance of thoughts and feelings.

    c. parents must avoid arguing with their adolescent children.

    d. parents should prevent their children from watching television.

10. From the article, we can conclude that

    a. a weak marital relationship often results in a weak family.

    b. children should not witness a disagreement between parents.

    c. children who grow up in healthy families learn not to interrupt other family members.

    d. parents always find it easier to respond to their children than to react to them.

■ Discussion Questions

About Content

1. What are the nine hallmarks of a successfully communicating family? Which of the nine do you feel are most important?

2. How do good parents control television? How do they make television a positive force instead of a negative one?

3. In paragraph 20, the author says, "It is usually easier to react than to respond." What is the difference between the two terms *react* and *respond?*

4. Why, according to Curran, is a "pattern of reconciliation" (paragraph 44) crucial to good family life? Besides those patterns mentioned in the essay, can you describe a reconciliation pattern you have developed with friends or family?

About Structure

5. What is the thesis of the selection? Write here the number of the paragraph in which it is stated: _____

6. What purpose is achieved by Curran's introduction (paragraphs 1–2)? Why is a reader likely to feel that her article will be reliable and worthwhile?

7. Curran frequently uses dialogue or quotations from unnamed parents or children as the basis for her examples. The conversation related in paragraphs 16–17 is one instance. Find three other dialogues used to illustrate points in the essay and write the numbers below:

Paragraph(s) _____

Paragraph(s) _____

Paragraph(s) _____

About Style and Tone

8. Curran enlivens the essay by using some interesting and humorous remarks from parents, children, and counselors. One is the witty comment in paragraph 5 from a marriage counselor: "And when I share this complaint with their husbands, they don't hear *me,* either." Find two other places where the author keeps your interest by using humorous or enjoyable quotations, and write the numbers of the paragraphs here:

_____   _____

WRITING ASSIGNMENTS

Assignment 1: Writing a Paragraph

Write a definition paragraph on the hallmarks of a *bad* family. Your topic sentence might be, "A bad family is one that is _____, _____, and _____."

To get started, you should first reread the features of a good family explained in the selection. Doing so will help you think about what qualities are found in a bad family. Prepare a list of as many bad qualities as you can think of. Then go through the list and decide on the qualities that seem most characteristic of a bad family.

Assignment 2: Writing a Paragraph

Curran tells us five phrases that some children say they most like to hear from their mothers (paragraph 38). When you were younger, what statement or action of one of your parents (or another adult) would make you especially happy—or sad? Write a paragraph that begins with a topic sentence like one of the following:

A passing comment my grandfather once made really devastated me.

When I was growing up, there were several typical ways my mother treated me that always made me sad.

A critical remark by my fifth-grade teacher was the low point of my life.

My mother has always had several lines that make her children feel very pleased.

You may want to write a narrative that describes in detail the particular time and place of a statement or action. Or you may want to provide three or so examples of statements or actions and their effect on you.

To get started, make up two long lists of childhood memories involving adults— happy memories and sad memories. Then decide which memory or memories you could most vividly describe in a paragraph. Remember that your goal is to help your readers see for themselves why a particular time was sad or happy for you.

Copyright ©2006 The McGraw-Hill Companies, Inc. All rights reserved.

Assignment 3: Writing an Essay

In light of Curran's description of what healthy families do right, examine your own family. Which of Curran's traits of communicative families fit your family? Write an essay pointing out three things that your family is doing right in creating a communicative climate for its members. Or, if you feel your family could work harder at communicating, write the essay about three specific ways your family could improve. In either case, choose three of Curran's nine "hallmarks of the successfully communicating family" and show how they do or do not apply to your family.

In your introductory paragraph, include a thesis statement as well as a plan of development that lists the three traits you will talk about. Then present these traits in turn in three supporting paragraphs. Develop each paragraph by giving specific examples of conversations, arguments, behavior patterns, and so on, that illustrate how your family communicates. Finally, conclude your essay with a summarizing sentence or two and a final thought about your subject.

Do It Better!

Ben Carson, M.D., with Cecil Murphey

If you suspect that you are now as "smart" as you'll ever be, then read the following selection. Taken from the book *Think Big*, it is about Dr. Ben Carson, who was sure he was "the dumbest kid in the class" when he was in fifth grade. Carson tells how he turned his life totally around from what was a path of failure. Today he is a famous neurosurgeon at the Johns Hopkins University Children's Center in Baltimore, Maryland.

"Benjamin, is this your report card?" my mother asked as she picked up the folded white card from the table. 1

"Uh, yeah," I said, trying to sound casual. Too ashamed to hand it to her, I had dropped it on the table, hoping that she wouldn't notice until after I went to bed. 2

It was the first report card I had received from Higgins Elementary School since we had moved back from Boston to Detroit, only a few months earlier. 3

I had been in the fifth grade not even two weeks before everyone considered me the dumbest kid in the class and frequently made jokes about me. Before long I too began to feel as though I really was the most stupid kid in fifth grade. Despite Mother's frequently saying, "You're smart, Bennie. You can do anything you want to do," I did not believe her. 4

No one else in school thought I was smart, either. 5

Now, as Mother examined my report card, she asked, "What's this grade in reading?" (Her tone of voice told me that I was in trouble.) Although I was embarrassed, I did not think too much about it. Mother knew that I wasn't doing well in math, but she did not know I was doing so poorly in every subject. 6

While she slowly read my report card, reading everything one word at a time, I hurried into my room and started to get ready for bed. A few minutes later, Mother came into my bedroom. 7

"Benjamin," she said, "are these your grades?" She held the card in front of me as if I hadn't seen it before. 8

"Oh, yeah, but you know, it doesn't mean much." 9

"No, that's not true, Bennie. It means a lot." 10

Copyright ©2006 The McGraw-Hill Companies, Inc. All rights reserved.

"Just a report card."   11

"But it's more than that."   12

Knowing I was in for it now, I prepared to listen, yet I was not all that interested.   13
I did not like school very much and there was no reason why I should. Inasmuch as
I was the dumbest kid in the class, what did I have to look forward to? The others
laughed at me and made jokes about me every day.

"Education is the only way you're ever going to escape poverty," she said.   14
"It's the only way you're ever going to get ahead in life and be successful. Do you
understand that?"

"Yes, Mother," I mumbled.   15

"If you keep on getting these kinds of grades you're going to spend the rest   16
of your life on skid row, or at best sweeping floors in a factory. That's not the kind
of life that I want for you. That's not the kind of life that God wants for you."

I hung my head, genuinely ashamed. My mother had been raising me and my   17
older brother, Curtis, by herself. Having only a third-grade education herself, she
knew the value of what she did not have. Daily she drummed into Curtis and me
that we had to do our best in school.

"You're just not living up to your potential," she said. "I've got two mighty 18
smart boys and I know they can do better."

I had done my best—at least I had when I first started at Higgins Elementary   19
School. How could I do much when I did not understand anything going on in our
class?

In Boston we had attended a parochial school, but I hadn't learned much   20
because of a teacher who seemed more interested in talking to another female
teacher than in teaching us. Possibly, this teacher was not solely to blame—perhaps
I wasn't emotionally able to learn much. My parents had separated just before we
went to Boston, when I was eight years old. I loved both my mother and father
and went through considerable trauma over their separating. For months afterward, I kept thinking that my parents would get back together, that my daddy
would come home again the way he used to, and that we could be the same old
family again—but he never came back. Consequently, we moved to Boston and
lived with Aunt Jean and Uncle William Avery in a tenement building for two
years until Mother had saved enough money to bring us back to Detroit.

Mother kept shaking the report card at me as she sat on the side of my bed.   21
"You have to work harder. You have to use that good brain that God gave you,
Bennie. Do you understand that?"

"Yes, Mother." Each time she paused, I would dutifully say those words.   22

"I work among rich people, people who are educated," she said. "I watch   23
how they act, and I know they can do anything they want to do. And so can you."
She put her arm on my shoulder. "Bennie, you can do anything they can do—only
you can do it better!"

Mother had said those words before. Often. At the time, they did not mean   24
much to me. Why should they? I really believed that I was the dumbest kid in fifth
grade, but of course, I never told her that.

Copyright ©2006 The McGraw-Hill Companies, Inc. All rights reserved.

"I just don't know what to do about you boys," she said. "I'm going to talk   25
to God about you and Curtis." She paused, stared into space, then said (more to
herself than to me), "I need the Lord's guidance on what to do. You just can't
bring in any more report cards like this."

As far as I was concerned, the report card matter was over.   26

The next day was like the previous ones—just another bad day in school,   27
another day of being laughed at because I did not get a single problem right in
arithmetic and couldn't get any words right on the spelling test. As soon as I came
home from school, I changed into play clothes and ran outside. Most of the boys
my age played softball, or the game I liked best, "Tip the Top."

We played Tip the Top by placing a bottle cap on one of the sidewalk cracks.   28
Then taking a ball—any kind that bounced—we'd stand on a line and take turns
throwing the ball at the bottle top, trying to flip it over. Whoever succeeded got
two points. If anyone actually moved the cap more than a few inches, he won five
points. Ten points came if he flipped it into the air and it landed on the other side.

When it grew dark or we got tired, Curtis and I would finally go inside and   29
watch TV. The set stayed on until we went to bed. Because Mother worked long
hours, she was never home until just before we went to bed. Sometimes I would
awaken when I heard her unlocking the door.

Two evenings after the incident with the report card, Mother came home   30
about an hour before our bedtime. Curtis and I were sprawled out, watching TV.
She walked across the room, snapped off the set, and faced both of us. "Boys," she
said, "you're wasting too much of your time in front of that television. You don't
get an education from staring at television all the time."

Before either of us could make a protest, she told us that she had been praying   31
for wisdom. "The Lord's told me what to do," she said. "So from now on, you will
not watch television, except for two preselected programs each week."

"Just *two* programs?" I could hardly believe she would say such a terrible   32
thing. "That's not—"

"And *only* after you've done your homework. Furthermore, you don't play   33
outside after school, either, until you've done all your homework."

"Everybody else plays outside right after school," I said, unable to think of   34
anything except how bad it would be if I couldn't play with my friends. "I won't
have any friends if I stay in the house all the time—"

"That may be," Mother said, "but everybody else is not going to be as suc-   35
cessful as you are—"

"But, Mother—"   36

"This is what we're going to do. I asked God for wisdom, and this is the answer   37
I got."

I tried to offer several other arguments, but Mother was firm. I glanced at   38
Curtis, expecting him to speak up, but he did not say anything. He lay on the floor,
staring at his feet.

"Don't worry about everybody else. The whole world is full of 'everybody   39
else,' you know that? But only a few make a significant achievement."

The loss of TV and play time was bad enough. I got up off the floor, feeling as 40
if everything was against me. Mother wasn't going to let me play with my friends,
and there would be no more television—almost none, anyway. She was stopping
me from having any fun in life.

"And that isn't all," she said. "Come back, Bennie."   41

I turned around, wondering what else there could be.   42

"In addition," she said, "to doing your homework, you have to read two 43
books from the library each week. Every single week."

"Two books? Two?" Even though I was in fifth grade, I had never read a 44
whole book in my life.

"Yes, two. When you finish reading them, you must write me a book report 45
just like you do at school. You're not living up to your potential, so I'm going to
see that you do."

Usually Curtis, who was two years older, was the more rebellious. But this time 46
he seemed to grasp the wisdom of what Mother said. He did not say one word.

She stared at Curtis. "You understand?"   47

He nodded.   48

"Bennie, is it clear?"   49

"Yes, Mother." I agreed to do what Mother told me—it wouldn't have 50
occurred to me not to obey—but I did not like it. Mother was being unfair and
demanding more of us than other parents did.

The following day was Thursday. After school, Curtis and I walked to the local 51
branch of the library. I did not like it much, but then I had not spent that much
time in any library.

We both wandered around a little in the children's section, not having any 52
idea about how to select books or which books we wanted to check out.

The librarian came over to us and asked if she could help. We explained that 53
both of us wanted to check out two books.

"What kind of books would you like to read?" the librarian asked.   54

"Animals," I said after thinking about it. "Something about animals."   55

"I'm sure we have several that you'd like." She led me over to a section of 56
books. She left me and guided Curtis to another section of the room. I flipped
through the row of books until I found two that looked easy enough for me to
read. One of them, *Chip, the Dam Builder*—about a beaver—was the first one
I had ever checked out. As soon as I got home, I started to read it. It was the
first book I ever read all the way through even though it took me two nights.
Reluctantly I admitted afterward to Mother that I really had liked reading about
Chip.

Within a month I could find my way around the children's section like someone 57
who had gone there all his life. By then the library staff knew Curtis and me and
the kind of books we chose. They often made suggestions. "Here's a delightful
book about a squirrel," I remember one of them telling me.

As she told me part of the story, I tried to appear indifferent, but as soon as 58
she handed it to me, I opened the book and started to read.

Best of all, we became favorites of the librarians. When new books came in 59
that they thought either of us would enjoy, they held them for us. Soon I became
fascinated as I realized that the library had so many books—and about so many
different subjects.

After the book about the beaver, I chose others about animals—all types of 60
animals. I read every animal story I could get my hands on. I read books about
wolves, wild dogs, several about squirrels, and a variety of animals that lived in
other countries. Once I had gone through the animal books, I started reading
about plants, then minerals, and finally rocks.

My reading books about rocks was the first time the information ever became 61
practical to me. We lived near the railroad tracks, and when Curtis and I took the
route to school that crossed by the tracks, I began paying attention to the crushed
rock that I noticed between the ties.

As I continued to read more about rocks, I would walk along the tracks, 62
searching for different kinds of stones, and then see if I could identify them.

Often I would take a book with me to make sure that I had labeled each stone 63
correctly.

"Agate," I said as I threw the stone. Curtis got tired of my picking up stones 64
and identifying them, but I did not care because I kept finding new stones all the
time. Soon it became my favorite game to walk along the tracks and identify the
varieties of stones. Although I did not realize it, within a very short period of time,
I was actually becoming an expert on rocks.

Two things happened in the second half of fifth grade that convinced me of 65
the importance of reading books.

First, our teacher, Mrs. Williamson, had a spelling bee every Friday afternoon. 66
We'd go through all the words we'd had so far that year. Sometimes she also
called out words that we were supposed to have learned in fourth grade. Without
fail, I always went down on the first word.

One Friday, though, Bobby Farmer, whom everyone acknowledged as the 67
smartest kid in our class, had to spell "agriculture" as his final word. As soon as
the teacher pronounced his word, I thought, *I can spell that word.* Just the day
before, I had learned it from reading one of my library books. I spelled it under my
breath, and it was just the way Bobby spelled it.

If I can spell "agriculture," I'll bet I can learn to spell any other word in the 68
world. I'll bet I can learn to spell better than Bobby Farmer.

Just that single word, "agriculture," was enough to give me hope. 69

The following week, a second thing happened that forever changed my life. 70
When Mr. Jaeck, the science teacher, was teaching us about volcanoes, he held up
an object that looked like a piece of black, glass-like rock. "Does anybody know
what this is? What does it have to do with volcanoes?"

Immediately, because of my reading, I recognized the stone. I waited, but 71
none of my classmates raised their hands. I thought, *This is strange. Not even the
smart kids are raising their hands.* I raised my hand.

"Yes, Benjamin," he said. 72

Copyright ©2006 The McGraw-Hill Companies, Inc. All rights reserved.

I heard snickers around me. The other kids probably thought it was a joke, or   73
that I was going to say something stupid.

"Obsidian," I said.   74

"That's right!" He tried not to look startled, but it was obvious he hadn't   75
expected me to give the correct answer.

"That's obsidian," I said, "and it's formed by the supercooling of lava when   76
it hits the water." Once I had their attention and realized I knew information no
other student had learned, I began to tell them everything I knew about the subject of obsidian, lava, lava flow, supercooling, and compacting of the elements.

When I finally paused, a voice behind me whispered, "Is that Bennie Carson?"   77

"You're absolutely correct," Mr. Jaeck said and he smiled at me. If he had   78
announced that I'd won a million-dollar lottery, I couldn't have been more pleased
and excited.

"Benjamin, that's absolutely, absolutely right," he repeated with enthusiasm   79
in his voice. He turned to the others and said, "That is wonderful! Class, this is a
tremendous piece of information Benjamin has just given us. I'm very proud to
hear him say this."

For a few moments, I tasted the thrill of achievement. I recall thinking,   80
*Wow, look at them. They're all looking at me with admiration. Me, the dummy!
The one everybody thinks is stupid. They're looking at me to see if this is really me
speaking.*

Maybe, though, it was I who was the most astonished one in the class.   81
Although I had been reading two books a week because Mother told me to, I
had not realized how much knowledge I was accumulating. True, I had learned to
enjoy reading, but until then I hadn't realized how it connected with my schoolwork. That day—for the first time—I realized that Mother had been right. Reading is the way out of ignorance, and the road to achievement. I did not have to be
the class dummy anymore.

For the next few days, I felt like a hero at school. The jokes about me stopped.   82
The kids started to listen to me. *I'm starting to have fun with this stuff.*

As my grades improved in every subject, I asked myself, "Ben, is there any   83
reason you can't be the smartest kid in the class? If you can learn about obsidian, you can learn about social studies and geography and math and science and
everything."

That single moment of triumph pushed me to want to read more. From then   84
on, it was as though I could not read enough books. Whenever anyone looked for
me after school, they could usually find me in my bedroom—curled up, reading a
library book—for a long time, the only thing I wanted to do. I had stopped caring
about the TV programs I was missing; I no longer cared about playing Tip the Top
or baseball anymore. I just wanted to read.

In a year and a half—by the middle of sixth grade—I had moved to the top   85
of the class.

Copyright ©2006 The McGraw-Hill Companies, Inc. All rights reserved.

■ Reading Comprehension Questions

1. The word *trauma* in "I loved both my mother and father and went through considerable trauma over their separating. For months afterward, I kept thinking that my parents would get back together, . . . but he never came back" (paragraph 20) means

   a. love.

   b. knowledge.

   c. distance.

   d. suffering.

2. The word *acknowledged* in "One Friday, though, Bobby Farmer, whom everyone acknowledged as the smartest kid in our class, had to spell 'agriculture' as his final word" (paragraph 67) means

   a. denied.

   b. recognized.

   c. forgot.

   d. interrupted.

3. Which of the following would be the best alternative title for this selection?

   a. The Importance of Fifth Grade

   b. The Role of Parents in Education

   c. The Day I Surprised My Science Teacher

   d. Reading Changed My Life

4. Which sentence best expresses the main idea of this selection?

   a. Children who grow up in single-parent homes may spend large amounts of time home alone.

   b. Because of parental guidance that led to a love of reading, the author was able to go from academic failure to success.

   c. Most children do not take school very seriously, and they suffer as a result.

   d. Today's young people watch too much television.

5. Bennie's mother

   a. was not a religious person.

   b. spoke to Bennie's teacher about Bennie's poor report card.

   c. had only a third-grade education.

   d. had little contact with educated people.

6. To get her sons to do better in school, Mrs. Carson insisted that they

   a. stop watching TV.

   b. finish their homework before playing.

   c. read one library book every month.

   d. all of the above.

7. *True or false?* _____ Bennie's first experience with a library book was discouraging.

8. We can conclude that Bennie Carson believed he was dumb because

   a. in Boston he had not learned much.

   b. other students laughed at him.

   c. he had done his best when he first started at Higgins Elementary School, but still got poor grades.

   d. all of the above.

9. We can conclude that the author's mother believed

   a. education leads to success.

   b. her sons needed to be forced to live up to their potential.

   c. socializing was less important for her sons than a good education.

   d. all of the above.

10. From paragraphs 70–80, we can infer that

   a. Bennie thought his classmates were stupid because they did not know about obsidian.

   b. Mr. Jaeck knew less about rocks than Bennie did.

   c. this was the first time Bennie had answered a difficult question correctly in class.

   d. Mr. Jaeck thought that Bennie had taken too much class time explaining about obsidian.

■ **Discussion Questions**

About Content

1. How do you think considering himself the "dumbest kid in class" affected Bennie's schoolwork?

2. The author recalls his failure in the classroom as an eight-year-old child by writing, "Perhaps I wasn't emotionally able to learn much." Why does he make

this statement? What do you think parents and schools can do to help children through difficult times?

3. How did Mrs. Carson encourage Bennie to make school—particularly reading—a priority in his life? What effect did her efforts have on Bennie's academic performance and self-esteem?

4. As a child, Carson began to feel confident about his own abilities when he followed his mother's guidelines. How might Mrs. Carson's methods help adult students build up their own self-confidence and motivation?

About Structure

5. What is the main order in which the details of this selection are organized—time order or listing order? Locate and write below three of the many transitions that are used as part of that time order or listing order.

_____   _____   _____

6. In paragraph 65, Carson states, "Two things happened in the second half of fifth grade that convinced me of the importance of reading books." What two transitions does Carson use in later paragraphs to help readers recognize those two events? Write those two transitions here:

_____   _____

About Style and Tone

7. Instead of describing his mother, Carson reveals her character through specific details of her actions and words. Find one paragraph in which this technique is used, and write its number here: _____. What does this paragraph tell us about Mrs. Carson?

8. Why do you suppose Carson italicizes sentences in paragraphs 67, 68, 71, 80, and 82? What purpose do the italicized sentences serve?

WRITING ASSIGNMENTS

Assignment 1: Writing a Paragraph

The reading tells about some of Carson's most important school experiences, both positive and negative. Write a paragraph about one of your most important experiences in school. To select an event to write about, try asking yourself the following questions:

Copyright ©2006 The McGraw-Hill Companies, Inc. All rights reserved.

Which teachers or events in school influenced how I felt about myself?

What specific incidents stand out in my mind as I think back to elementary school?

To get started, you might use freewriting to help you remember and record the details. Then begin your draft with a topic sentence similar to one of the following:

A seemingly small experience in elementary school encouraged me greatly.

If not for my sixth-grade teacher, I would not be where I am today.

My tenth-grade English class was a turning point in my life.

Use concrete details—actions, comments, reactions, and so on—to help your readers see what happened.

Assignment 2: Writing a Paragraph

Reading helped Bennie, and it can do a lot for adults, too. Most of us, however, don't have someone around to make us do a certain amount of personal reading every week. In addition, many of us don't have as much free time as Bennie and Curtis had. How can adults find time to read more? Write a paragraph listing several ways adults can add more reading to their lives.

To get started, simply write down as many ways as you can think of—in any order. Here is an example of a prewriting list for this paper:

Situations in which adults can find extra time to read:
    Riding to and from work or school
    In bed at night before turning off the light
    While eating breakfast or lunch
    Instead of watching some TV
    In the library

Feel free to use items from the list above, but see if you can add at least one or two of your own points as well. Use details such as descriptions and examples to emphasize and dramatize your supporting details.

Assignment 3: Writing an Essay

Mrs. Carson discovered an effective way to boost her children's achievement and self-confidence. There are other ways as well. Write an essay whose thesis statement is "There are several ways parents can help children live up to their potential." Then, in the following paragraphs, explain and illustrate two or three methods parents can use. In choosing material for your supporting paragraphs, you might consider some of these areas, or think of others on your own:

Assigning regular household "chores" and rewarding a good job

Encouraging kids to join an organization that fosters achievement: Scouts, Little League, religious group, or neighborhood service club

Going to parent-teacher conferences at school and then working more closely with children's teachers—knowing when assignments are due, etc.

Giving a child some responsibility for an enjoyable family activity, such as choosing decorations or food for a birthday party

Setting up a "Wall of Fame" in the home where children's artwork, successful schoolwork, etc. can be displayed

Setting guidelines (as Mrs. Carson did) for use of leisure time, homework time, and the like

Draw on examples from your own experiences or from someone else's—including those of Bennie Carson, if you like.

Anxiety: Challenge by Another Name

James Lincoln Collier

What is your basis for making personal decisions? Do you aim to rock the boat as little as possible, choosing the easy, familiar path? There is comfort in sticking with what is safe and well-known, just as there is comfort in eating mashed potatoes. But James Lincoln Collier, author of numerous articles and books, decided soon after leaving college not to live a mashed-potato sort of life. In this essay, first published in *Reader's Digest,* he tells how he learned to recognize the marks of a potentially exciting, growth-inducing experience, to set aside his anxiety, and to dive in.

Copyright ©2005 The McGraw-Hill Companies, Inc. All rights reserved.

Between my sophomore and junior years at college, a chance came up for me   1
to spend the summer vacation working on a ranch in Argentina. My roommate's
father was in the cattle business, and he wanted Ted to see something of it. Ted
said he would go if he could take a friend, and he chose me.

The idea of spending two months on the fabled Argentine pampas* was excit-   2
ing. Then I began having second thoughts. I had never been very far from New
England, and I had been homesick my first weeks at college. What would it be like
in a strange country? What about the language? And besides, I had promised to
teach my younger brother to sail that summer. The more I thought about it, the
more the prospect daunted me. I began waking up nights in a sweat.

In the end I turned down the proposition. As soon as Ted asked somebody   3
else to go, I began kicking myself. A couple of weeks later I went home to my old
summer job, unpacking cartons at the local supermarket, feeling very low. I had
turned down something I wanted to do because I was scared, and I had ended
up feeling depressed. I stayed that way for a long time. And it didn't help when
I went back to college in the fall to discover that Ted and his friend had had a
terrific time.

In the long run that unhappy summer taught me a valuable lesson out of   4
which I developed a rule for myself: *do what makes you anxious, don't do what
makes you depressed.*

I am not, of course, talking about severe states of anxiety or depression,   5
which require medical attention. What I mean is that kind of anxiety we call stage
fright, butterflies in the stomach, a case of nerves—the feelings we have at a job
interview, when we're giving a big party, when we have to make an important
presentation at the office. And the kind of depression I am referring to is that
downhearted feeling of the blues, when we don't seem to be interested in anything, when we can't get going and seem to have no energy.

I was confronted by this sort of situation toward the end of my senior year. As   6
graduation approached, I began to think about taking a crack at making my living
as a writer. But one of my professors was urging me to apply to graduate school
and aim at a teaching career.

I wavered. The idea of trying to live by writing was scary—a lot more scary   7
than spending a summer on the pampas, I thought. Back and forth I went, making
my decision, unmaking it. Suddenly, I realized that every time I gave up the idea of
writing, that sinking feeling went through me; it gave me the blues.

The thought of graduate school wasn't what depressed me. It was giving up   8
on what deep in my gut I really wanted to do. Right then I learned another lesson.
To avoid that kind of depression meant, inevitably, having to endure a certain
amount of worry and concern.

The great Danish philosopher Søren Kierkegaard believed that anxiety always   9
arises when we confront the possibility of our own development. It seems to be a
rule of life that you can't advance without getting that old, familiar, jittery feeling.

Even as children we discover this when we try to expand ourselves by, say, learn-   10
ing to ride a bike or going out for the school play. Later in life we get butterflies

*A vast plain in south-central South America.

Copyright ©2006 The McGraw-Hill Companies, Inc. All rights reserved.

when we think about having that first child, or uprooting the family from the old hometown to find a better opportunity halfway across the country. Any time, it seems, that we set out aggressively to get something we want, we meet up with anxiety. And it's going to be our traveling companion, at least part of the way, in any new venture.

When I first began writing magazine articles, I was frequently required to 11 interview big names—people like Richard Burton, Joan Rivers, sex authority William Masters, baseball great Dizzy Dean. Before each interview I would get butterflies and my hands would shake.

At the time, I was doing some writing about music. And one person I particu- 12 larly admired was the great composer Duke Ellington. On stage and on television, he seemed the very model of the confident, sophisticated man of the world. Then I learned that Ellington still got stage fright. If the highly honored Duke Ellington, who had appeared on the bandstand some ten thousand times over thirty years, had anxiety attacks, who was I to think I could avoid them?

I went on doing those frightening interviews, and one day, as I was getting 13 onto a plane for Washington to interview columnist Joseph Alsop, I suddenly realized to my astonishment that I was looking forward to the meeting. What had happened to those butterflies?

Well, in truth, they were still there, but there were fewer of them. I had 14 benefited, I discovered, from a process psychologists call "extinction." If you put an individual in an anxiety-provoking situation often enough, he will eventually learn that there isn't anything to be worried about.

Which brings us to a corollary to my basic rule: *you'll never eliminate anxiety by avoiding the things that caused it.* I remember how my son Jeff was when I first began 15 to teach him to swim at the lake cottage where we spent our summer vacations. He resisted, and when I got him into the water he sank and sputtered and wanted to quit. But I was insistent. And by summer's end he was splashing around like a puppy. He had "extinguished" his anxiety the only way he could—by confronting it.

The problem, of course, is that it is one thing to urge somebody else to take on 16 those anxiety-producing challenges; it is quite another to get ourselves to do it.

Some years ago I was offered a writing assignment that would require three 17 months of travel through Europe. I had been abroad a couple of times on the usual "If it's Tuesday this must be Belgium"* trips, but I hardly could claim to know my way around the continent. Moreover, my knowledge of foreign languages was limited to a little college French.

I hesitated. How would I, unable to speak the language, totally unfamiliar with 18 local geography or transportation systems, set up interviews and do research? It seemed impossible, and with considerable regret I sat down to write a letter begging off. Halfway through, a thought—which I subsequently made into another corollary to my basic rule—ran through my mind: *you can't learn if you don't try.* So I accepted the assignment.

There were some bad moments. But by the time I had finished the trip I was 19 an experienced traveler. And ever since, I have never hesitated to head for even

*Reference to a film comedy about a group of American tourists who visited too many European countries in too little time.

the most exotic of places, without guides or even advance bookings, confident that somehow I will manage.

The point is that the new, the different, is almost by definition scary. But each time   20
you try something, you learn, and as the learning piles up, the world opens to you.

I've made parachute jumps, learned to ski at forty, flown up the Rhine in a   21
balloon. And I know I'm going to go on doing such things. It's not because I'm braver or more daring than others. I'm not. But I don't let the butterflies stop me from doing what I want. Accept anxiety as another name for challenge, and you can accomplish wonders.

■ Reading Comprehension Questions

1. The word *daunted* in "The more I thought about [going to Argentina], the more the prospect daunted me. I began waking up nights in a sweat" (paragraph 2) means
   a. encouraged.
   b. interested.
   c. discouraged.
   d. amused.

2. The word *corollary* in "Which brings us to a corollary to my basic rule: *you'll never eliminate anxiety by avoiding the things that caused it*" (paragraph 15) means
   a. an idea that follows from another idea.
   b. an idea based on a falsehood.
   c. an idea that creates anxiety.
   d. an idea passed on from one generation to another.

3. Which of the following would be the best alternative title for this selection?
   a. A Poor Decision
   b. Don't Let Anxiety Stop You
   c. Becoming a Writer
   d. The Courage to Travel

4. Which sentence best expresses the main idea of the selection?
   a. The butterflies-in-the-stomach type of anxiety differs greatly from severe states of anxiety or depression.
   b. Taking on a job assignment that required traveling helped the author get over his anxiety.
   c. People learn and grow by confronting, not backing away from, situations that make them anxious.
   d. Anxiety is a predictable part of life that can be dealt with in positive ways.

5. When a college friend invited the writer to go with him to Argentina, the writer
   a. turned down the invitation.
   b. accepted eagerly.
   c. was very anxious about the idea but went anyway.
   d. did not believe his friend was serious.

6. *True or false?* _____ As graduation approached, Collier's professor urged him to try to make his living as a writer.

7. *True or false?* _____ The philosopher Søren Kierkegaard believed that anxiety occurs when we face the possibility of our own development.

8. "Extinction" is the term psychologists use for
   a. the inborn tendency to avoid situations that make one feel very anxious.
   b. a person's gradual loss of confidence.
   c. the natural development of a child's abilities.
   d. the process of losing one's fear by continuing to face the anxiety-inspiring situation.

9. The author implies that
   a. it was lucky he didn't take the summer job in Argentina.
   b. his son never got over his fear of the water.
   c. Duke Ellington's facing stage fright inspired him.
   d. one has to be more daring than most people to overcome anxiety.

10. The author implies that
    a. anxiety may be a signal that one has an opportunity to grow.
    b. he considers his three-month trip to Europe a failure.
    c. facing what makes him anxious has eliminated all depression from his life.
    d. he no longer has anxiety about new experiences.

■ Discussion Questions

About Content

1. Collier developed the rule "Do what makes you anxious; don't do what makes you depressed." How does he distinguish between feeling anxious and feeling depressed?

2. In what way does Collier believe that anxiety is positive? How, according to him, can we eventually overcome our fears? Have you ever gone ahead and done something that made you anxious? How did it turn out?

Copyright ©2006 The McGraw-Hill Companies, Inc. All rights reserved.

About Structure

3. Collier provides a rule and two corollary rules that describe his attitude toward challenge and anxiety. Below, write the location of that rule and its corollaries.

    Collier's rule: paragraph _____

    First corollary: paragraph _____

    Second corollary: paragraph _____

    How does Collier emphasize the rule and its corollaries?

4. Collier uses several personal examples in his essay. Find three instances of these examples and explain how each helps Collier develop his main point.

About Style and Tone

5. In paragraph 3, Collier describes the aftermath of his decision not to go to Argentina. He could have just written, "I worked that summer." Instead he writes, "I went home to my old summer job, unpacking cartons at the local supermarket." Why do you think he provides that bit of detail about his job? What is the effect on the reader?

6. Authors often use testimony by authorities to support their points. Where in Collier's essay does he use such support? What do you think it adds to his piece?

7. In the last sentence of paragraph 10, Collier refers to anxiety as a "traveling companion." Why do you think he uses that image? What does it convey about his view of anxiety?

8. Is Collier just telling about a lesson he has learned for himself, or is he encouraging his readers to do something? How can you tell?

WRITING ASSIGNMENTS

Assignment 1: Writing a Paragraph

Collier explains how his life experiences made him view the term *anxiety* in a new way. Write a paragraph in which you explain how a personal experience of yours has given new meaning to a particular term. Following are some terms you might consider for this assignment:

Failure

Friendship

Copyright ©2006 The McGraw-Hill Companies, Inc. All rights reserved.

Goals

Homesickness

Maturity

Success

Here are two sample topic sentences for this assignment:

I used to think of failure as something terrible, but thanks to a helpful boss, I now think of it as an opportunity to learn.

The word *creativity* has taken on a new meaning for me ever since I became interested in dancing.

Assignment 2: Writing a Paragraph

The second corollary to Collier's rule is "you can't learn if you don't try." Write a paragraph using this idea as your main idea. Support it with your own experience, someone else's experience, or both. One way of developing this point is to compare two approaches to a challenge: One person may have backed away from a frightening opportunity while another person decided to take on the challenge. Or you could write about a time when you learned something useful by daring to give a new experience a try. In that case, you might discuss your reluctance to take on the new experience, the difficulties you encountered, and your eventual success. In your conclusion, include a final thought about the value of what was learned.

Listing a few skills you have learned will help you decide on the experience you wish to write about. To get you started, below is a list of things adults often need to go to some trouble to learn.

Driving with a stick shift

Taking useful lecture notes

Knowing how to do well on a job interview

Asking someone out on a date

Making a speech

Standing up for your rights

Assignment 3: Writing an Essay

Collier describes three rules he follows when facing anxiety. In an essay, write about one or more rules, or guidelines, that you have developed for yourself through experience. If you decide to discuss two or three such guidelines, mention or refer to them in your introductory paragraph. Then go on to discuss each in one or more paragraphs of its own. Include at least one experience that led you to develop a given guideline, and tell how it has helped you at other times in your life. You might end with a brief summary and an explanation of how the guidelines as a group have helped. If you decide to focus on one rule, include at least two or three experiences that help to illustrate your point.

To prepare for this assignment, spend some time freewriting about the rules or guidelines you have set up for yourself. Continue writing until you feel you have a central idea for which you have plenty of interesting support. Then organize that support into a scratch outline, such as this one:

> <u>Thesis:</u> I have one rule that keeps me from staying in a rut—Don't let the size of a challenge deter you; instead, aim for it by making plans and taking steps.
>
> <u>Topic sentence 1:</u> I began to think about my rule one summer in high school when a friend got the type of summer job that I had only been thinking about.
>
> <u>Topic sentence 2:</u> After high school, I began to live up to my rule when I aimed for a business career and entered college.
>
> <u>Topic sentence 3:</u> My rule is also responsible for my having the wonderful boyfriend (*or* girlfriend *or* job) I now have.

Old Before Her Time

Katherine Barrett

Most of us wait for our own advanced years to learn what it is like to be old. Patty Moore decided not to wait. At the age of twenty-six, she disguised herself as an eighty-five-year-old woman. What she learned suggests that to be old in our society is both better and worse than is often thought. This selection may give you a different perspective on the older people in your life—on what they are really like inside and on what life is really like for them.

This is the story of an extraordinary voyage in time, and of a young woman who devoted three years to a singular experiment. In 1979, Patty Moore—then aged twenty-six—transformed herself for the first of many times into an eighty-five-year-old woman. Her object was to discover firsthand the problems, joys, and

1

Copyright ©2005 The McGraw-Hill Companies, Inc. All rights reserved.

frustrations of the elderly. She wanted to know for herself what it's like to live in a culture of youth and beauty when your hair is gray, your skin is wrinkled, and no men turn their heads as you pass.

Her time machine was a makeup kit. Barbara Kelly, a friend and professional makeup artist, helped Patty pick out a wardrobe and showed her how to use latex to create wrinkles and wrap Ace bandages to give the impression of stiff joints. "It was peculiar," Patty recalls, as she relaxes in her New York City apartment. "Even the first few times I went out, I realized that I wouldn't have to act that much. The more I was perceived as elderly by others, the more 'elderly' I actually became. . . . I imagine that's just what happens to people who really are old."   2

What motivated Patty to make her strange journey? It was partly her career—as an industrial designer, Patty often focuses on the needs of the elderly. But the roots of her interest are also deeply personal. Extremely close to her own grandparents—particularly her maternal grandfather, now ninety—and raised in a part of Buffalo, New York, where there was a large elderly population, Patty always drew comfort and support from the older people around her. When her own marriage ended in 1979 and her life seemed to be falling apart, she dived into her "project" with all her soul. In all, she donned her costume more than two hundred times in fourteen states. Here is the remarkable story of what she found.   3

Columbus, Ohio, May 1979. Leaning heavily on her cane, Pat Moore stood alone in the middle of a crowd of young professionals. They were all attending a gerontology conference, and the room was filled with animated chatter. But no one was talking to Pat. In a throng of men and women who devoted their working lives to the elderly, she began to feel like a total nonentity. "I'll get us all some coffee," a young man told a group of women next to her. "What about me?" thought Pat. "If I were young, they would be offering me coffee, too." It was a bitter thought at the end of a disappointing day—a day that marked Patty's first appearance as "the old woman." She had planned to attend the gerontology conference anyway, and almost as a lark decided to see how professionals would react to an old person in their midst.   4

Now, she was angry. All day she had been ignored . . . counted out in a way she had never experienced before. She didn't understand. Why didn't people help her when they saw her struggling to open a heavy door? Why didn't they include her in conversations? Why did the other participants seem almost embarrassed by her presence at the conference—as if it were somehow inappropriate that an old person should be professionally active?   5

And so, eighty-five-year-old Pat Moore learned her first lesson: The old are often ignored. "I discovered that people really do judge a book by its cover," Patty says today. "Just because I looked different, people either condescended to me or totally dismissed me. Later, in stores, I'd get the same reaction. A clerk would turn to someone younger and wait on her first. It was as if he assumed that I—the older woman—could wait because I didn't have anything better to do."   6

New York City, October 1979. Bent over her cane, Pat walked slowly toward the edge of the park. She had spent the day sitting on a bench with friends,   7 but now dusk was falling and her friends had all gone home. She looked around nervously at the deserted area and tried to move faster, but her joints were stiff. It was then that she heard the barely audible sound of sneakered feet approaching and the kids' voices. "Grab her, man." "Get her purse." Suddenly an arm was around her throat and she was dragged back, knocked off her feet.

She saw only a blur of sneakers and blue jeans, heard the sounds of mocking laughter, felt fists pummeling her—on her back, her legs, her breasts, her stomach. "Oh, God," she thought, using her arms to protect her head and curling herself into a ball. "They're going to kill me. I'm going to die. . . ."   8

Then, as suddenly as the boys attacked, they were gone. And Patty was left alone, struggling to rise. The boy's punches had broken the latex makeup on her face, the fall had disarranged her wig, and her whole body ached. (Later she would learn that she had fractured her left wrist, an injury that took two years to heal completely.) Sobbing, she left the park and hailed a cab to return home. Again the thought struck her: What if I really lived in the gray ghetto? . . . What if I couldn't escape to my nice safe home . . . ?   9

Lesson number two: The fear of crime is paralyzing. "I really understand now why the elderly become homebound," the young woman says as she recalls her ordeal today. "When something like this happens, the fear just doesn't go away. I guess it wasn't so bad for me. I could distance myself from what happened . . . and I was strong enough to get up and walk away. But what about someone who is really too weak to run or fight back or protect herself in any way? And the elderly often can't afford to move if the area in which they live deteriorates, becomes unsafe. I met people like this, and they were imprisoned by their fear. That's when the bolts go on the door. That's when people starve themselves because they're afraid to go to the grocery store."   10

New York City, February, 1980. It was a slushy, gray day, and Pat had laboriously descended four flights of stairs from her apartment to go shopping. Once outside, she struggled to hold her threadbare coat closed with one hand and manipulate her cane with the other. Splotches of snow made the street difficult for anyone to navigate, but for someone hunched over, as she was, it was almost impossible. The curb was another obstacle. The slush looked ankle-deep—and what was she to do? Jump over it? Slowly, she worked her way around to a drier spot, but the crowds were impatient to move. A woman with packages jostled her as she rushed past, causing Pat to nearly lose her balance. If I really were old, I would have fallen, she thought. Maybe broken something. On another day, a woman had practically knocked her over by letting go of a heavy door as Pat tried to enter a coffee shop. Then there were the revolving doors. How could you push them without strength? And how could you get up and down stairs, on and off a bus, without risking a terrible fall?   11

Lesson number three: If small, thoughtless deficiencies in design were corrected, life would be so much easier for older people. It was no surprise to Patty that the "built" environment is often inflexible. But even she didn't realize the extent of the problems, she admits. "It was a terrible feeling. I never realized how   12

Copyright ©2006 The McGraw-Hill Companies, Inc. All rights reserved.

difficult it is to get off a curb if your knees don't bend easily. Or the helpless feeling you get if your upper arms aren't strong enough to open a door. You know, I just felt so vulnerable—as if I was at the mercy of every barrier or rude person I encountered."

Fort Lauderdale, Florida, May 1980. Pat met a new friend while shopping, 13 and they decided to continue their conversation over a sundae at a nearby coffee shop. The woman was in her late seventies, "younger" than Pat, but she was obviously reaching out for help. Slowly, her story unfolded. "My husband moved out of our bedroom," the woman said softly, fiddling with her coffee cup and fighting back tears. "He won't touch me anymore. And when he gets angry at me for being stupid, he'll even sometimes . . . " The woman looked down, too embarrassed to go on. Pat took her hand. "He hits me; . . . he gets so mean." "Can't you tell anyone?" Pat asked. "Can't you tell your son?" "Oh, no!" the woman almost gasped. "I would never tell the children; they absolutely adore him."

Lesson number four: Even a fifty-year-old marriage isn't necessarily a good 14 one. While Pat met many loving and devoted elderly couples, she was stunned to find others who had stayed together unhappily—because divorce was still an anathema in their middle years. "I met women who secretly wished their husbands dead, because after so many years they just ended up full of hatred. One woman in Chicago even admitted that she deliberately angered her husband because she knew it would make his blood pressure rise. Of course, that was pretty extreme. . . ."

Patty pauses thoughtfully and continues. "I guess what really made an 15 impression on me, the real eye-opener, was that so many of these older women had the same problems as women twenty, thirty, or forty—problems with men . . . problems with the different roles that are expected of them. As a 'young woman' I, too, had just been through a relationship where I spent a lot of time protecting someone by covering up his problems from family and friends. Then I heard this woman in Florida saying that she wouldn't tell her children their father beat her because she didn't want to disillusion them. These issues aren't age-related. They affect everyone."

Clearwater, Florida, January 1981. She heard the children laughing, but she 16 didn't realize at first that they were laughing at her. On this day, as on several others, Pat had shed the clothes of a middle-income woman for the rags of a bag lady. She wanted to see the extremes of the human condition, what it was like to be old and poor, and outside traditional society as well. Now, tottering down the sidewalk, she was most concerned with the cold, since her layers of ragged clothing did little to ease the chill. She had spent the afternoon rummaging through garbage cans, loading her shopping bags with bits of debris, and she was stiff and tired. Suddenly, she saw that four little boys, five or six years old, were moving up on her. And then she felt the sting of the pebbles they were throwing. She quickened her pace to escape, but another handful of gravel hit her and the laughter continued. They're using me as a target, she thought, horror-stricken. They don't even think of me as a person.

Lesson number five: Social class affects every aspect of an older person's exis-   17
tence. "I found out that class is a very important factor when you're old," says
Patty. "It was interesting. That same day, I went back to my hotel and got dressed
as a wealthy woman, another role that I occasionally took. Outside the hotel, a
little boy of about seven asked if I would go shelling with him. We walked along
the beach, and he reached out to hold my hand. I knew he must have a grandmother who walked with a cane, because he was so concerned about me and
my footing. 'Don't put your cane there, the sand's wet,' he'd say. He really took
responsibility for my welfare. The contrast between him and those children was
really incredible—the little ones who were throwing pebbles at me because they
didn't see me as human, and then the seven-year-old taking care of me. I think
he would have responded to me the same way even if I had been dressed as the
middle-income woman. There's no question that money does make life easier for
older people, not only because it gives them a more comfortable lifestyle, but
because it makes others treat them with greater respect."

New York City, May 1981. Pat always enjoyed the time she spent sitting on the   18
benches in Central Park. She'd let the whole day pass by, watching young children
play, feeding the pigeons and chatting. One spring day she found herself sitting
with three women, all widows, and the conversation turned to the few available
men around. "It's been a long time since anyone hugged me," one woman complained. Another agreed. "Isn't that the truth. I need a hug, too." It was a favorite
topic, Pat found—the lack of touching left in these women's lives, the lack of
hugging, the lack of men.

In the last two years, she found out herself how it felt to walk down Fifth   19
Avenue and know that no men were turning to look after her. Or how it felt to
look at models in magazines or store mannequins and know that those gorgeous
clothes were just not made for her. She hadn't realized before just how much
casual attention was paid to her because she was young and pretty. She hadn't
realized it until it stopped.

Lesson number six: You never grow old emotionally. You always need to feel   20
loved. "It's not surprising that everyone needs love and touching and holding,"
says Patty. "But I think some people feel that you reach a point in your life when
you accept that those intimate feelings are in the past. That's wrong. These women
were still interested in sex. But more than that, they—like everyone—needed to
be hugged and touched. I'd watch two women greeting each other on the street
and just holding onto each other's hands, neither wanting to let go. Yet, I also saw
that there are people who are afraid to touch an old person; . . . they were afraid
to touch me. It's as if they think old age is a disease and it's catching. They think
that something might rub off on them."

New York City, September 1981. He was a thin man, rather nattily dressed, with   21
a hat that he graciously tipped at Pat as he approached the bench where she sat.
"Might I join you?" he asked jauntily. Pat told him he would be welcome and he
offered her one of the dietetic hard candies that he carried in a crumpled paper bag.
As the afternoon passed, they got to talking . . . about the beautiful buds on the

trees and the world around them and the past. "Life's for the living, my wife used to tell me," he said. "When she took sick, she made me promise her that I wouldn't waste a moment. But the first year after she died, I just sat in the apartment. I didn't want to see anyone, talk to anyone or go anywhere. I missed her so much." He took a handkerchief from his pocket and wiped his eyes, and they sat in silence. Then he slapped his leg to break the mood and change the subject. He asked Pat about herself, and described his life alone. He belonged to a "senior center" now, and went on trips and had lots of friends. Life did go on. They arranged to meet again the following week on the same park bench. He brought lunch—chicken salad sandwiches and decaffeinated peppermint tea in a thermos—and wore a carnation in his lapel. It was the first date Patty had had since her marriage ended.

Lesson number seven: Life does go on . . . as long as you're flexible and open   22 to change. "That man really meant a lot to me, even though I never saw him again," says Patty, her eyes wandering toward the gray wig that now sits on a wig stand on the top shelf of her bookcase. "He was a real old-fashioned gentleman, yet not afraid to show his feelings—as so many men my age are. It's funny, but at that point I had been through months of self-imposed seclusion. Even though I was in a different role, that encounter kind of broke the ice for getting my life together as a single woman."

In fact, while Patty was living her life as the old woman, some of her young   23 friends had been worried about her. After several years, it seemed as if the lines of identity had begun to blur. Even when she wasn't in makeup, she was wearing unusually conservative clothing, she spent most of her time with older people, and she seemed almost to revel in her role—sometimes finding it easier to be in costume than to be a single New Yorker.

But as Patty continued her experiment, she was also learning a great deal from   24 the older people she observed. Yes, society often did treat the elderly abysmally; . . . they were sometimes ignored, sometimes victimized, sometimes poor and frightened, but so many of them were survivors. They had lived through two world wars, through the Depression, and into the computer age. "If there was one lesson to learn, one lesson that I'll take with me into my old age, it's that you've got to be flexible," Patty says. "I saw my friend in the park, managing after the loss of his wife, and I met countless other people who picked themselves up after something bad—or even something catastrophic—happened. I'm not worried about them. I'm worried about the others who shut themselves away. It's funny, but seeing these two extremes helped me recover from the trauma in my own life, to pull my life together."

Today, Patty is back to living the life of a single thirty-year-old, and she rarely   25 dons her costumes anymore. "I must admit, though, I do still think a lot about aging," she says. "I look in the mirror and I begin to see wrinkles, and then I realize that I won't be able to wash those wrinkles off." Is she afraid of growing older? "No. In a way, I'm kind of looking forward to it," she smiles. "I know it will be different from my experiment. I know I'll probably even look different. When they aged Orson Welles in *Citizen Kane* he didn't resemble at all the Orson Welles of today."

Copyright ©2006 The McGraw-Hill Companies, Inc. All rights reserved.

But Patty also knows that in one way she really did manage to capture the   26
feeling of being old. With her bandages and her stooped posture, she turned her
body into a kind of prison. Yet inside she didn't change at all. "It's funny, but that's
exactly how older people always say they feel," says Patty. "Their bodies age, but
inside they are really no different from when they were young."

■ Reading Comprehension Questions

1. The word *nonentity* in "But no one was talking to Pat. In a throng of men and
   women who devoted their working lives to the elderly, she began to feel like a
   total nonentity. . . . All day she had been ignored" (paragraphs 4–5) means
   a. expert.
   b. nobody.
   c. experiment.
   d. leader.

2. The word *abysmally* in "society often did treat the elderly abysmally; . . .
   they were sometimes ignored, sometimes victimized, sometimes poor and
   frightened" (paragraph 24) means
   a. politely.
   b. absentmindedly.
   c. very badly.
   d. angrily.

3. Which of the following would be the best alternative title for this selection?
   a. How Poverty Affects the Elderly
   b. Similarities between Youth and Old Age
   c. One Woman's Discoveries about the Elderly
   d. Violence against the Elderly

4. Which sentence best expresses the main idea of the selection?
   a. The elderly often have the same problems as young people.
   b. Pat Moore dressed up like an elderly woman over two hundred times.
   c. By making herself appear old, Pat Moore learned what life is like for the
      elderly in the United States.
   d. Elderly people often feel ignored in a society that glamorizes youth.

5. *True or false?* _____ As they age, people need others less.

6. Pat Moore learned that the elderly often become homebound because of the
   a. fear of crime.
   b. high cost of living.
   c. availability of in-home nursing care.
   d. lack of interesting places for them to visit.

7. One personal lesson Pat Moore learned from her experiment was that
   a. she needs to start saving money for her retirement.
   b. by being flexible she can overcome hardships.
   c. she has few friends her own age.
   d. her marriage could have been saved.

8. From paragraph 2, we can infer that
   a. behaving like an old person was difficult for Moore.
   b. many older people wear Ace bandages.
   c. people sometimes view themselves as others see them.
   d. Barbara Kelly works full-time making people look older than they really are.

9. The article suggests that fifty years ago
   a. young couples tended to communicate better than today's young couples.
   b. divorce was less acceptable than it is today.
   c. verbal and physical abuse was probably extremely rare.
   d. the elderly were treated with great respect.

10. We can conclude that Pat Moore may have disguised herself as an elderly woman over two hundred times in fourteen states because
    a. she and her friend Barbara Kelly continuously worked at perfecting Moore's costumes.
    b. her company made her travel often.
    c. she was having trouble finding locations with large numbers of elderly people.
    d. she wanted to see how the elderly were seen and treated all over the country, rather than in just one area.

■ Discussion Questions

About Content

1. Why did Pat Moore decide to conduct her experiment? Which of her discoveries surprised you?

Copyright ©2006 The McGraw-Hill Companies, Inc. All rights reserved.

2. Using the information Moore learned from her experiment, list some of the things that could be done to help the elderly. What are some things you personally could do?

3. How do the elderly people Moore met during her experiment compare with the elderly people you know?

4. Lesson number seven in the article is "Life does go on . . . as long as you're flexible and open to change" (paragraph 22). What do you think this really means? How might this lesson apply to situations and people you're familiar with—in which people either were or were not flexible and open to change?

About Structure

5. Most of the selection is made up of a series of Pat Moore's experiences and the seven lessons they taught. Find the sentence used by the author to introduce those experiences and lessons, and write that sentence here:

_____

6. The details of paragraph 21 are organized in time order, and the author has used a few time transition words to signal time relationships. Find two of those time words, and write them here:

_____   _____

About Style and Tone

7. What device does the author use to signal that she is beginning a new set of experiences and the lesson they taught? How does she ensure that the reader will recognize what each of the seven lessons is?

8. Do you think Barrett is objective in her treatment of Patty Moore? Or does the author allow whatever her feelings might be for Moore to show in her writing? Find details in the article to support your answer.

WRITING ASSIGNMENT

Assignment 1: Writing a Paragraph

In her experiment, Moore discovered various problems faced by the elderly. Choose one of these areas of difficulty and write a paragraph in which you discuss what could be done in your city to help solve the problem. Following are a few possible topic sentences for this assignment:

Fear of crime among the elderly could be eased by a program providing young people to accompany them on their errands.

The courthouse and train station in our town need to be redesigned to allow easier access for the elderly.

Schools should start adopt-a-grandparent programs, which would enrich the emotional lives of both the young and the old participants.

Assignment 2: Writing a Paragraph

What did you learn from the selection, or what do you already know, about being older in our society that might influence your own future? Write a paragraph in which you list three or four ways in which you plan to minimize or avoid some of the problems often faced by elderly people. For instance, you may decide to do whatever you can to remain as healthy and strong as possible throughout your life. That might involve quitting smoking and incorporating exercise into your schedule. Your topic sentence might simply be: "There are three important ways in which I hope to avoid some of the problems often faced by the elderly."

Assignment 3: Writing an Essay

Lesson number seven in Barrett's article is "Life does go on . . . as long as you're flexible and open to change" (paragraph 22). Think about one person of any age whom you know well (including yourself). Write an essay in which you show how being (or not being) flexible and open to change has been important in that person's life. Develop your essay with three main examples.

   In preparation for writing, think of several key times in your subject's life. Select three times in which being flexible or inflexible had a significant impact on that person. Then narrate and explain each of those times in a paragraph of its own. Here are two possible thesis statements for this essay:

My grandmother generally made the most of her circumstances by being flexible and open to change.

When I was a teenager, I could have made life easier for myself by being more flexible and open to change.

Your conclusion for this essay might summarize the value of being flexible or the problems of being inflexible, or both, for the person you are writing about.

Assignment 4: Writing an Essay Using Internet Research

As Patty Moore studied the elderly people around her, she recognized that some were "survivors"—people who adapted successfully to the challenges of aging—and some were not. What can people do, both mentally and physically, to make their later years active and happy? Use the Internet to see what some experts have suggested. Then write an essay on three ways that people can cope well with old age.

Copyright ©2006 The McGraw-Hill Companies, Inc. All rights reserved.

To access the Internet, use the very helpful search engine Google (*www. google.com*). Try one of the following phrases or some related phrase:

> growing older and keeping active and happy
>
> happy healthy aging
>
> elderly people and healthy living

You may, of course, use a simple phrase such as "growing older," but that will bring up too many items. As you proceed, you'll develop a sense of how to "track down" and focus a topic by adding more information to your search words and phrases.

Let's Really Reform Our Schools

Anita Garland

A few years ago, a National Commission on Excellence in Education published *A Nation at Risk,* in which the commission reported on a "rising tide of mediocrity" in our schools. Other studies have pointed to students' poor achievement in science, math, communication, and critical thinking. What can our schools do to improve students' performance? Anita Garland has several radical ideas, which she explains in this selection. As you read it, think about whether or not you agree with her points.

American high schools are in trouble. No, that's not strong enough. American high   1
schools are disasters. "Good" schools today are only a rite of passage for American
kids, where the pressure to look fashionable and act cool outweighs any concern
for learning. And "bad" schools—heaven help us—are havens for the vicious and
corrupt. There, metal detectors and security guards wage a losing battle against
the criminals that prowl the halls.

Desperate illnesses require desperate remedies. And our public schools are   2
desperately ill. What is needed is no meek, fainthearted attempt at "curriculum
revision" or "student-centered learning." We need to completely restructure our
thinking about what schools are and what we expect of the students who attend
them.

The first change needed to save our schools is the most fundamental one. Not   3
only must we stop *forcing* everyone to attend school; we must stop *allowing* the
attendance of so-called students who are not interested in studying. Mandatory
school attendance is based upon the idea that every American has a right to basic

Copyright ©2006 The McGraw-Hill Companies, Inc. All rights reserved.

education. But as the old saying goes, your rights stop where the next guy's begin. A student who sincerely wants an education, regardless of his or her mental or physical ability, should be welcome in any school in this country. But "students" who deliberately interfere with other students' ability to learn, teachers' ability to teach, and administrators' ability to maintain order should be denied a place in the classroom. They do not want an education. And they should not be allowed to mark time within school walls, waiting to be handed their meaningless diplomas while they make it harder for everyone around them to either provide or receive a quality education.

By requiring troublemakers to attend school, we have made it impossible to deal with them in any effective way. They have little to fear in terms of punishment. Suspension from school for a few days doesn't improve their behavior. After all, they don't want to be in school anyway. For that matter, mandatory attendance is, in many cases, nothing but a bad joke. Many chronic troublemakers are absent so often that it is virtually impossible for them to learn anything. And when they *are* in school, they are busy shaking down other students for their lunch money or jewelry. If we permanently banned such punks from school, educators could turn their attention away from the troublemakers and toward those students who realize that school is a serious place for serious learning.

You may ask, "What will become of these young people who aren't in school?" But consider this: What is becoming of them now? They are not being educated. They are merely names on the school records. They are passed from grade to grade, learning nothing, making teachers and fellow students miserable. Finally they are bumped off the conveyor belt at the end of twelfth grade, oftentimes barely literate, and passed into society as "high school graduates." Yes, there would be a need for alternative solutions for these young people. Let the best thinkers of our country come up with some ideas. But in the meanwhile, don't allow our schools to serve as a holding tank for people who don't want to be there.

Once our schools have been returned to the control of teachers and genuine students, we could concentrate on smaller but equally meaningful reforms. A good place to start would be requiring students to wear school uniforms. There would be cries of horror from the fashion slaves, but the change would benefit everyone. If students wore uniforms, think of the mental energy that could be redirected into more productive channels. No longer would young girls feel the need to spend their evenings laying out coordinated clothing, anxiously trying to create just the right look. The daily fashion show that currently absorbs so much of students' attention would come to a halt. Kids from modest backgrounds could stand out because of their personalities and intelligence, rather than being tagged as losers because they can't wear the season's hottest sneakers or jeans. Affluent kids might learn they have something to offer the world other than a fashion statement. Parents would be relieved of the pressure to deal with their offspring's constant demands for wardrobe additions.

Next, let's move to the cafeteria. What's for lunch today? How about a Milky Way bar, a bag of Fritos, a Coke, and just to round out the meal with a vegetable, maybe some french fries. And then back to the classroom for a few hours of intense mental activity, fueled on fat, salt, and sugar. What a joke! School is an institution of education, and that education should be continued as students sit down to eat. Here's a perfect opportunity to teach a whole generation of Americans about nutrition, and we are blowing it. School cafeterias, of all places, should demonstrate how a healthful, low-fat, well-balanced diet produces healthy, energetic, mentally alert people. Instead, we allow school cafeterias to dispense the same junk food that kids could buy in any mall. Overhaul the cafeterias! Out with the candy, soda, chips, and fries! In with the salads, whole grains, fruits, and vegetables!

Turning our attention away from what goes on during school hours, let's consider what happens after the final bell rings. Some school-sponsored activities are all to the good. Bands and choirs, foreign-language field trips, chess or skiing or drama clubs are sensible parts of an extracurricular plan. They bring together kids with similar interests to develop their talents and leadership ability. But other common school activities are not the business of education. The prime example of inappropriate school activity is in competitive sports between schools.

Intramural sports are great. Students need an outlet for their energies, and friendly competition against one's classmates on the basketball court or baseball diamond is fun and physically beneficial. But the wholesome fun of sports is quickly ruined by the competitive team system. School athletes quickly become the campus idols, encouraged to look down on classmates with less physical ability. Schools concentrate enormous amounts of time, money, and attention upon their teams, driving home the point that competitive sports are the *really* important part of school. Students are herded into gymnasiums for "pep rallies" that whip up adoration of the chosen few and encourage hatred of rival schools. Boys' teams are supplied with squads of cheerleading girls . . . let's not even get into what the subliminal message is *there*. If communities feel they must have competitive sports, let local businesses or even professional teams organize and fund the programs. But school budgets and time should be spent on programs that benefit more than an elite few.

Another school-related activity that should get the ax is the fluff-headed, money-eating, misery-inducing event known as the prom. How in the world did the schools of America get involved in this showcase of excess? Proms have to be the epitome of everything that is wrong, tasteless, misdirected, inappropriate, and just plain sad about the way we bring up our young people. Instead of simply letting the kids put on a dance, we've turned the prom into a bloated nightmare that ruins young people's budgets, their self-image, and even their lives. The pressure to show up at the prom with the best-looking date, in the most expensive clothes, wearing the most exotic flowers, riding in the most extravagant form of transportation, dominates the thinking of many students for months before the prom itself. Students cling to doomed, even abusive romantic relationships rather than risk being dateless for this night of nights. They lose any concept of meaningful values as they implore their parents for more, more, more money to throw into the jaws of the prom god. The adult trappings of the prom—the slinky dresses, emphasis on romance, slow dancing, nightclub atmosphere—all encourage kids to engage in behavior that can have tragic consequences. Who knows how many unplanned pregnancies and alcohol-related accidents can be directly attributed to the pressures of prom night? And yet, not going to the prom seems a fate worse than death to many young people—because of all the hype about the "wonder" and "romance" of it all. Schools are not in the business of providing wonder and romance, and it's high time we remembered that.

We have lost track of the purpose of our schools. They are not intended to be   11 centers for fun, entertainment, and social climbing. They are supposed to be institutions for learning and hard work. Let's institute the changes suggested here—plus dozens more—without apology, and get American schools back to business.

■ Reading Comprehension Questions

1. The word *affluent* in "Kids from modest backgrounds could stand out because of their personalities and intelligence. . . . Affluent kids might learn they have something to offer the world other than a fashion statement" (paragraph 6) means

   a. intelligent.

   b. troubled.

   c. wealthy.

   d. poor.

2. The word *implore* in "They lose any concept of meaningful values as they implore their parents for more, more, more money to throw into the jaws of the prom god" (paragraph 10) means

   a. beg.

   b. ignore.

   c. pay.

   d. obey.

3. Which of the following would be the best alternative title for this selection?

   a. America's Youth

   b. Education of the Future

   c. Social Problems of Today's Students

   d. Changes Needed in the American School System

4. Which sentence best expresses the main idea of the selection?

   a. Excesses such as the prom and competitive sports should be eliminated from school budgets.

   b. Major changes are needed to make American schools real centers of learning.

Copyright ©2006 The McGraw-Hill Companies, Inc. All rights reserved.

    c. Attendance must be voluntary in our schools.

    d. The best thinkers of our country must come up with ideas on how to improve our schools.

5. Garland believes that mandatory attendance at school

    a. gives all students an equal chance at getting an education.

    b. allows troublemakers to disrupt learning.

    c. is cruel to those who don't really want to be there.

    d. helps teachers maintain control of their classes.

6. Garland is against school-sponsored competitive sports because she believes that

    a. exercise and teamwork should not have a role in school.

    b. they overemphasize the importance of sports and athletes.

    c. school property should not be used in any way after school hours.

    d. they take away from professional sports.

7. We can infer that Garland believes

    a. teens should not have dances.

    b. proms promote unwholesome values.

    c. teens should avoid romantic relationships.

    d. proms are even worse than mandatory education.

8. The author clearly implies that troublemakers

    a. are not intelligent.

    b. really do want to be in school.

    c. should be placed in separate classes.

    d. don't mind being suspended from school.

9. *True or false?* _____ We can conclude that the author feels that teachers and genuine students have lost control of our schools.

10. The essay suggests that the author would also oppose

    a. school plays.

    b. serving milk products in school cafeterias.

    c. the selection of homecoming queens.

    d. stylish school uniforms.

■ Discussion Questions

About Content

1. What reforms does Garland suggest in her essay? Think back to your high school days. Which of the reforms that Garland suggests do you think might have been most useful at your high school?

2. Garland's idea of voluntary school attendance directly contradicts the "stay in school" campaigns. Do you agree with her idea? What do you think might become of students who choose not to attend school?

3. At the end of her essay, Garland writes, "Let's institute the changes suggested here—plus dozens more." What other changes do you think Garland may have in mind? What are some reforms you think might improve schools?

About Structure

4. The thesis of this essay can be found in the introduction, which is made up of the first two paragraphs. Find the thesis statement and write it here:

_____

_____

5. The first point on Garland's list of reforms is the elimination of mandatory (that is, required) education. Then she goes on to discuss other reforms. Find the transition sentence which signals that she is leaving the discussion about mandatory education and going on to other needed changes. Write that sentence here:

_____

_____

6. What are two transitional words that Garland uses to introduce two of the other reforms?

_____   _____

About Style and Tone

7. Garland uses some colorful images to communicate her ideas. For instance, in paragraph 5 she writes, "Finally [the troublemakers] are bumped off the conveyor belt at the end of twelfth grade, oftentimes barely literate, and passed into society as 'high school graduates.'" What does the image of a conveyor belt imply about schools and about the troublemakers? What do the quotation marks around *high school graduates* imply?

Copyright ©2006 The McGraw-Hill Companies, Inc. All rights reserved.

8. Below are three other colorful images from the essay. What do the italicized words imply about today's schools and students?

   . . . don't allow our schools to serve as a *holding tank* for people who don't want to be there. (paragraph 5)

   A good place to start would be requiring students to wear school uniforms. There would be cries of horror from the *fashion slaves* . . . (paragraph 6)

   Students are *herded* into gymnasiums for "pep rallies" that whip up adoration of the chosen few . . . (paragraph 9)

9. To convey her points, does the author use a formal, straightforward tone or an informal, impassioned tone? Give examples from the essay to support your answer.

WRITING ASSIGNMENTS

Assignment 1: Writing a Paragraph

Write a persuasive paragraph in which you agree or disagree with one of Garland's suggested reforms. Your topic sentence may be something simple and direct, like these:

> I strongly agree with Garland's point that attendance should be voluntary in our high schools.

> I disagree with Garland's point that high school students should be required to wear uniforms.

Alternatively, you may want to develop your own paragraph calling for reform in some other area of American life. Your topic sentence might be like one of the following:

> We need to make radical changes in our treatment of homeless people.

> Strong new steps must be taken to control the sale of guns in our country.

> Major changes are needed to keep television from dominating the lives of our children.

Assignment 2: Writing a Paragraph

If troublemakers were excluded from schools, what would become of them? Write a paragraph in which you suggest two or three types of programs that troublemakers could be assigned to. Explain why each program would be beneficial to the troublemakers themselves and society in general. You might want to include in your paragraph one or more of the following:

Apprentice programs

Special neighborhood schools for troublemakers

Reform schools

Work-placement programs

Community service programs

Assignment 3: Writing an Essay

Garland suggests ways to make schools "institutions for learning and hard work." She wants to get rid of anything that greatly distracts students from their education, such as having to deal with troublemakers, overemphasis on fashion, and interschool athletics. When you were in high school, what tended most to divert your attention from learning? Write an essay explaining in full detail the three things that interfered most with your high school education. You may include any of Garland's points, but present details that apply specifically to you. Organize your essay by using emphatic order—in other words, save whatever interfered most with your education for the last supporting paragraph.

It is helpful to write a sentence outline for this kind of essay. Here, for example, is one writer's outline for an essay titled "Obstacles to My High School Education."

Thesis: There were three main things that interfered with my high school education.

Topic sentence 1: Concern about my appearance took up too much of my time and energy.
a. Since I was concerned about my looking good, I spent too much time shopping for clothes.
b. In order to afford the clothes, I worked twenty hours a week, drastically reducing my study time.
c. Spending even more time on clothes, I fussed every evening over what I would wear to school the next day.

Topic sentence 2: Cheerleading was another major obstacle to my academic progress in high school.
a. I spent many hours practicing in order to make the cheerleading squad.
b. Once I made the squad, I had to spend even more time practicing and then attending games.
c. Once when I didn't make the squad, I was so depressed for a while that I couldn't study, and this had serious consequences.

Copyright ©2006 The McGraw-Hill Companies, Inc. All rights reserved.

Topic sentence 3: The main thing that interfered with my high school education was my family situation.

  a. Even when I had time to study, I often found it impossible to do so at home, since my parents often had fights that were noisy and upsetting.

  b. My parents showed little interest in my schoolwork, giving me little reason to work hard for my classes.

  c. When I was in eleventh grade, my parents divorced; this was a major distraction for me for a long time.

To round off your essay with a conclusion, you may simply want to restate your thesis and main supporting points.

As an alternative to the above assignment, you can write about current obstacles to your college education.

How They Get You to Do That

Janny Scott

So you think you're sailing along in life, making decisions based on your own preferences? Not likely! Janny Scott brings together the findings of several researchers to show how advertisers, charitable organizations, politicians, employers, and even your friends get you to say "yes" when you should have said "no"—or, at least, "Let me think about that."

The woman in the supermarket in a white coat tenders a free sample of "lite" cheese. A car salesman suggests that prices won't stay low for long. Even a penny will help, pleads the door-to-door solicitor. Sale ends Sunday! Will work for food.   1

The average American exists amid a perpetual torrent of propaganda. Everyone, it sometimes seems, is trying to make up someone else's mind. If it isn't an athletic shoe company, it's a politician, a panhandler, a pitchman, a boss, a billboard company, a spouse.   2

The weapons of influence they are wielding are more sophisticated than ever, researchers say. And they are aimed at a vulnerable target—people with less and less time to consider increasingly complex issues.   3

As a result, some experts in the field have begun warning the public, tipping people off to precisely how "the art of compliance" works. Some critics have taken   4 to arguing for new government controls on one pervasive form of persuasion — political advertising.

The persuasion problem is "the essential dilemma of modern democracy,"   5
argue social psychologists Anthony Pratkanis and Elliot Aronson, the authors of *Age of Propaganda: The Everyday Use and Abuse of Persuasion.*

As the two psychologists see it, American society values free speech and pub-   6
lic discussion, but people no longer have the time or inclination to pay attention. Mindless propaganda flourishes, they say; thoughtful persuasion fades away.

The problem stems from what Pratkanis and Aronson call our "message-dense   7
environment." The average television viewer sees nearly 38,000 commercials a year, they say. The average home receives . . . [numerous] pieces of junk mail annually and . . . [countless calls] from telemarketing firms.

Bumper stickers, billboards and posters litter the public consciousness. Athletic   8
events and jazz festivals carry corporate labels. As direct selling proliferates, workers patrol their offices during lunch breaks, peddling chocolate and Tupperware to friends.

Meanwhile, information of other sorts multiplies exponentially. Technology   9
serves up ever-increasing quantities of data on every imaginable subject, from home security to health. With more and more information available, people have less and less time to digest it.

"It's becoming harder and harder to think in a considered way about any-   10
thing," said Robert Cialdini, a persuasion researcher at Arizona State University in Tempe. "More and more, we are going to be deciding on the basis of less and less information."

Persuasion is a democratic society's chosen method for decision making   11
and dispute resolution. But the flood of persuasive messages in recent years has changed the nature of persuasion. Lengthy arguments have been supplanted by slogans and logos. In a world teeming with propaganda, those in the business of influencing others put a premium on effective shortcuts.

Most people, psychologists say, are easily seduced by such shortcuts. Humans are   12
"cognitive misers," always looking to conserve attention and mental energy—leaving themselves at the mercy of anyone who has figured out which shortcuts work.

The task of figuring out shortcuts has been embraced by advertising agencies,   13
market researchers, and millions of salespeople. The public, meanwhile, remains in the dark, ignorant of even the simplest principles of social influence.

As a result, laypeople underestimate their susceptibility to persuasion, psychologists   14
say. They imagine their actions are dictated simply by personal preferences. Unaware of the techniques being used against them, they are often unwittingly outgunned.

As Cialdini tells it, the most powerful tactics work like jujitsu: They draw their   15
strength from deep-seated, unconscious psychological rules. The clever "compliance professional" deliberately triggers these "hidden stores of influence" to elicit a predictable response.

One such rule, for example, is that people are more likely to comply with a request   16
if a reason—no matter how silly—is given. To prove that point, one researcher tested different ways of asking people in line at a copying machine to let her cut the line.

Copyright ©2006 The McGraw-Hill Companies, Inc. All rights reserved.

When the researcher asked simply, "Excuse me, I have five pages. May I use   17
the Xerox machine?" only 60 percent of those asked complied. But when she
added nothing more than, "because I have to make some copies," nearly everyone agreed.

The simple addition of "because" unleashed an automatic response, even   18
though "because" was followed by an irrelevant reason, Cialdini said. By asking
the favor in that way, the researcher dramatically increased the likelihood of getting
what she wanted.

Cialdini and others say much of human behavior is mechanical. Automatic   19
responses are efficient when time and attention are short. For that reason, many
techniques of persuasion are designed and tested for their ability to trigger those
automatic responses.

"These appeals persuade not through the give-and-take of argument and   20
debate," Pratkanis and Aronson have written. ". . . They often appeal to our deepest fears and most irrational hopes, while they make use of our most simplistic
beliefs."

Life insurance agents use fear to sell policies, Pratkanis and Aronson say. Parents   21
use fear to convince their children to come home on time. Political leaders use
fear to build support for going to war—for example, comparing a foreign leader
to Adolf Hitler.

As many researchers see it, people respond to persuasion in one of two ways: 22
If an issue they care about is involved, they may pay close attention to the arguments; if they don't care, they pay less attention and are more likely to be influenced by simple cues.

Their level of attention depends on motivation and the time available. As   23
David Boninger, a UCLA psychologist, puts it, "If you don't have the time or motivation, or both, you will pay attention to more peripheral cues, like how nice
somebody looks."

Cialdini, a dapper man with a flat Midwestern accent, describes himself as   24
an inveterate sucker. From an early age, he said recently, he had wondered what
made him say yes in many cases when the answer, had he thought about it, should
have been no.

So in the early 1980s, he became "a spy in the wars of influence." He took   25
a sabbatical and, over a three-year period, enrolled in dozens of sales training
programs, learning firsthand the tricks of selling insurance, cars, vacuum cleaners,
encyclopedias, and more.

He learned how to sell portrait photography over the telephone. He took a   26
job as a busboy in a restaurant, observing the waiters. He worked in fund-raising,
advertising, and public relations. And he interviewed cult recruiters and members
of bunco squads.

By the time it was over, Cialdini had witnessed hundreds of tactics. But he   27
found that the most effective ones were rooted in six principles. Most are not
new, but they are being used today with greater sophistication on people whose
fast-paced lifestyle has lowered their defenses.

Copyright ©2006 The McGraw-Hill Companies, Inc. All rights reserved.

Reciprocity.   People have been trained to believe that a favor must be repaid in   28
kind, even if the original favor was not requested. The cultural pressure to return
a favor is so intense that people go along rather than suffer the feeling of being
indebted.

Politicians have learned that favors are repaid with votes. Stores offer free   29
samples—not just to show off a product. Charity organizations ship personalized
address labels to potential contributors. Others accost pedestrians, planting paper
flowers in their lapels.

Commitment and Consistency.   People tend to feel they should be consistent—   30
even when being consistent no longer makes sense. While consistency is easy,
comfortable, and generally advantageous, Cialdini says, "mindless consistency"
can be exploited.

Take the "foot in the door technique." One person gets another to agree   31
to a small commitment, like a down payment or signing a petition. Studies show
that it then becomes much easier to get the person to comply with a much larger
request.

Another example Cialdini cites is the "lowball tactic" in car sales. Offered a   32
low price for a car, the potential customer agrees. Then at the last minute, the
sales manager finds a supposed error. The price is increased. But customers tend
to go along nevertheless.

Social Validation.   People often decide what is correct on the basis of what other   33
people think. Studies show that is true for behavior. Hence, sitcom laugh tracks,
tip jars "salted" with a bartender's cash, long lines outside nightclubs, testimoni-
als, and "man on the street" ads.

Tapping the power of social validation is especially effective under certain   34
conditions: When people are in doubt, they will look to others as a guide; and
when they view those others as similar to themselves, they are more likely to follow their lead.

Liking.   People prefer to comply with requests from people they know and like.   35
Charities recruit people to canvass their friends and neighbors. Colleges get alumni
to raise money from classmates. Sales training programs include grooming tips.

According to Cialdini, liking can be based on any of a number of factors.   36
Good-looking people tend to be credited with traits like talent and intelligence.
People also tend to like people who are similar to themselves in personality, back-
ground, and lifestyle.

Authority.   People defer to authority. Society trains them to do so, and in many   37
situations deference is beneficial. Unfortunately, obedience is often automatic, leaving people vulnerable to exploitation by compliance professionals, Cialdini says.

As an example, he cites the famous ad campaign that capitalized on actor   38
Robert Young's role as Dr. Marcus Welby, Jr., to tout the alleged health benefits of
Sanka decaffeinated coffee.

An authority, according to Cialdini, need not be a true authority. The trap- 39
pings of authority may suffice. Con artists have long recognized the persuasive
power of titles like doctor or judge, fancy business suits, and expensive cars.

Scarcity.   Products and opportunities seem more valuable when the supply is 40
limited.

As a result, professional persuaders emphasize that "supplies are limited." 41
Sales end Sunday and movies have limited engagements—diverting attention
from whether the item is desirable to the threat of losing the chance to experience it at all.

The use of influence, Cialdini says, is ubiquitous.   42

Take the classic appeal by a child of a parent's sense of consistency: "But you 43
said . . ." And the parent's resort to authority: "Because I said so." In addition, nearly
everyone invokes the opinions of like-minded others—for social validation—in
vying to win a point.

One area in which persuasive tactics are especially controversial is political 44
advertising—particularly negative advertising. Alarmed that attack ads might be
alienating voters, some critics have begun calling for stricter limits on political ads.

In Washington, legislation pending in Congress would, among other things, 45
force candidates to identify themselves at the end of their commercials. In that
way, they might be forced to take responsibility for the ads' contents and be
unable to hide behind campaign committees.

"In general, people accept the notion that for the sale of products at least, 46
there are socially accepted norms of advertising," said Lloyd Morrisett, president
of the Markle Foundation, which supports research in communications and information technology.

"But when those same techniques are applied to the political process—where 47
we are judging not a product but a person, and where there is ample room for
distortion of the record or falsification in some cases—there begins to be more
concern," he said.

On an individual level, some psychologists offer tips for self-protection.   48

• Pay attention to your emotions, says Pratkanis, an associate professor of psy- 49
  chology at UC Santa Cruz: "If you start to feel guilty or patriotic, try to figure
  out why." In consumer transactions, beware of feelings of inferiority and the
  sense that you don't measure up unless you have a certain product.

• Be on the lookout for automatic responses, Cialdini says. Beware foolish consistency. 50
  Check other people's responses against objective facts. Be skeptical of authority,
  and look out for unwarranted liking for any "compliance professionals."

Since the publication of his most recent book, *Influence: The New Psychol-* 51
ogy of Modern Persuasion, Cialdini has begun researching a new book on ethical
uses of influence in business—addressing, among other things, how to instruct
salespeople and other "influence agents" to use persuasion in ways that help,
rather than hurt, society.

"If influence agents don't police themselves, society will have to step in to regulate . . . the way information is presented in commercial and political settings," Cialdini said. "And that's a can of worms that I don't think anybody wants to get into." 52

■ Reading Comprehension Questions

1. The word *wielding* in "The weapons of influence they are wielding are more sophisticated than ever" (paragraph 3) means
   a. handling effectively.
   b. giving up.
   c. looking for.
   d. demanding.

2. The word *peripheral* in "As David Boninger . . . puts it, 'If you don't have the time or motivation, or both, you will pay attention to more peripheral cues, like how nice someone looks'" (paragraph 23) means
   a. important.
   b. dependable.
   c. minor.
   d. attractive.

3. Which of the following would be the best alternative title for this selection?
   a. Automatic Human Responses
   b. Our Deepest Fears
   c. The Loss of Thoughtful Discussion
   d. Compliance Techniques

4. Which sentence best expresses the selection's main point?
   a. Americans are bombarded by various compliance techniques, the dangers of which can be overcome through understanding and legislation.
   b. Fearful of the effects of political attack ads, critics are calling for strict limits on such ads.
   c. With more and more messages demanding our attention, we find it harder and harder to consider any one subject really thoughtfully.
   d. The persuasion researcher Robert Cialdini spent a three-year sabbatical learning the tricks taught in dozens of sales training programs.

5. *True or false?* _____ According to the article, most laypeople think they are more susceptible to persuasion than they really are.

Copyright ©2006 The McGraw-Hill Companies, Inc. All rights reserved.

6. According to the article, parents persuade their children to come home on time by appealing to the children's sense of

   a. fair play.

   b. guilt.

   c. humor.

   d. fear.

7. When a visitor walks out of a hotel and a young man runs up, helps the visitor with his luggage, hails a cab, and then expects a tip, the young man is depending on which principle of persuasion?

   a. reciprocity

   b. commitment and consistency

   c. social validation

   d. liking

8. An inference that can be drawn from paragraph 49 is that

   a. Anthony Pratkanis is not a patriotic person.

   b. one compliance technique involves appealing to the consumer's patriotism.

   c. people using compliance techniques never want consumers to feel inferior.

   d. consumers pay too much attention to their own emotions.

9. One can infer from the selection that

   a. the actor Robert Young was well-known for his love of coffee.

   b. Sanka is demonstrably better for one's health than other coffees.

   c. the actor Robert Young was also a physician in real life.

   d. the TV character Marcus Welby, Jr., was trustworthy and authoritative.

10. We can conclude that to resist persuasive tactics, a person must

   a. buy fewer products.

   b. take time to question and analyze.

   c. remain patriotic.

   d. avoid propaganda.

■ **Discussion Questions**

About Content

1. What unusual method did Robert Cialdini apply to learn more about compliance techniques? Were you surprised by any of the ways he used his time during

Copyright ©2006 The McGraw-Hill Companies, Inc. All rights reserved

that three-year period? Have you ever been employed in a position in which you used one or more compliance techniques?

2. What are the six principles that Cialdini identifies as being behind many persuasion tactics? Describe an incident in which you were subjected to persuasion based on one or more of these principles.

3. In paragraph 16, we learn that "people are more likely to comply with a request if a reason—no matter how silly—is given." Do you find that to be true? Have you complied with requests that, when you thought about them later, were backed up with silly or weak reasons? Describe such an incident. Why do you think such requests work?

4. In paragraphs 44–47, the author discusses persuasive tactics in political advertising. Why might researchers view the use of such tactics in this area as "especially controversial"?

About Structure

5. What is the effect of Janny Scott's introduction to the essay (paragraphs 1–2)? On the basis of that introduction, why is a reader likely to feel that the selection will be worth his or her time?

6. Which of the following best describes the conclusion of the selection?

   a. It just stops.

   b. It restates the main point of the selection.

   c. It focuses on possible future occurrences.

   d. It presents a point of view that is the opposite of views in the body of the selection.

   Is this conclusion effective? Why or why not?

About Style and Tone

7. Why might Robert Cialdini have identified himself to the author as an "inveterate sucker"? How does that self-description affect how you regard Cialdini and what he has to say?

8. The author writes, "People defer to authority. Society trains them to do so; and in many situations deference is beneficial." Where does the author himself use the power of authority to support his own points? In what situations would you consider authority to be beneficial?

WRITING ASSIGNMENTS

Assignment 1: Writing a Paragraph

According to the article, "laypeople underestimate their susceptibility to persuasion. . . . They imagine their actions are dictated simply by personal preferences. Unaware of the techniques being used against them, they are often unwittingly outgunned." After having read the selection, do you believe that statement is true of you? Write a paragraph in which you either agree with or argue against the statement. Provide clear, specific examples of ways in which you are or are not influenced by persuasion.

Your topic sentence might be like either of these:

> After reading "How They Get You to Do That," I recognize that I am more influenced by forms of persuasion than I previously thought.

> Many people may "underestimate their susceptibility to persuasion," but I am not one of those people.

Assignment 2: Writing a Paragraph

Think of an advertisement—on TV, or radio, in print, or on a billboard—that you have found especially memorable. Write a paragraph in which you describe it. Provide specific details that make your reader understand why you remember it so vividly. Conclude your paragraph by indicating whether or not the advertisement persuaded you to buy or do what it was promoting.

Assignment 3: Writing an Essay

Robert Cialdini identifies "social validation" as a strong persuasion technique. Social validation involves people's need to do what they hope will get approval from the crowd, rather than thinking for themselves. The essay provides several examples of social validation, such as laughing along with a laugh track and getting in a long line to go to a nightclub.

Choose a person you know for whom the need for social validation is very strong. Write an essay about that person and the impact the need for social validation has in several areas of his or her life. Develop each paragraph with colorful, persuasive examples of the person's behavior. (You may wish to write about an invented person, in which case, feel free to use humorous exaggeration to make your points.)

Here is a possible outline for such an essay:

Thesis statement: My cousin Nina has a very strong need for social validation.

Topic sentence 1: Instead of choosing friends because of their inner qualities, Nina chooses them on the basis of their popularity.

Copyright ©2005 The McGraw-Hill Companies, Inc. All rights reserved.

Topic sentence 2: Nina's wardrobe has to be made up of the newest and most popular styles.

Topic sentence 3: Instead of having any real opinions of her own, Nina adopts her most popular friend's point of view as her own.

End your essay with a look into the future of a person whose life is ruled by the need for social validation.

Alternatively, write about the most independent thinker you know, someone who tends to do things his or her way without worrying much about what others say.

Dealing with Feelings

Rudolph F. Verderber

Do you hide your feelings, no matter how strong they are, letting them fester inside? Or do you lash out angrily at people who irritate you? If either of these descriptions fits you, you may be unhappy with the results of your actions. Read the following excerpt from the college textbook *Communicate!* Sixth Edition (Wadsworth), to discover what the author recommends as a better approach to dealing with your emotions.

An extremely important aspect of self-disclosure is the sharing of feelings. We all   1
experience feelings such as happiness at receiving an unexpected gift, sadness about the breakup of a relationship, or anger when we believe we have been taken advantage of. The question is whether to disclose such feelings, and if so, how. Self-disclosure of feelings usually will be most successful not when feelings are withheld or displayed but when they are described. Let's consider each of these forms of dealing with feelings.

Withholding Feelings

Withholding feelings—that is, keeping them inside and not giving any verbal or   2
nonverbal clues to their existence—is generally an inappropriate means of dealing with feelings. Withholding feelings is best exemplified by the good poker player who develops a "poker face," a neutral look that is impossible to decipher.

The look is the same whether the player's cards are good or bad. Unfortunately, many people use poker faces in their interpersonal relationships, so that no one knows whether they hurt inside, are extremely excited, and so on. For instance, Doris feels very nervous when Candy stands over her while Doris is working on her report. And when Candy says, "That first paragraph isn't very well written," Doris begins to seethe, yet she says nothing—she withholds her feelings.

Psychologists believe that when people withhold feelings, they can develop   3
physical problems such as ulcers, high blood pressure, and heart disease, as well as psychological problems such as stress-related neuroses and psychoses. Moreover, people who withhold feelings are often perceived as cold, undemonstrative, and not much fun to be around.

Is withholding ever appropriate? When a situation is inconsequential, you   4
may well choose to withhold your feelings. For instance, a stranger's inconsiderate behavior at a party may bother you, but because you can move to another part of the room, withholding may not be detrimental. In the example of Doris seething at Candy's behavior, however, withholding could be costly to Doris.

Displaying Feelings

Displaying feelings means expressing those feelings through a facial reaction,   5
body response, or spoken reaction. Cheering over a great play at a sporting event, booing the umpire at a perceived bad call, patting a person on the back when the person does something well, or saying, "What are you doing?" in a nasty tone of voice are all displays of feelings.

Displays are especially appropriate when the feelings you are experiencing   6
are positive. For instance, when Gloria does something nice for you, and you experience a feeling of joy, giving her a big hug is appropriate; when Don gives you something you've wanted, and you experience a feeling of appreciation, a big smile or an "Oh, thank you, Don" is appropriate. In fact, many people need to be even more demonstrative of good feelings. You've probably seen the bumper sticker "Have you hugged your kid today?" It reinforces the point that you need to display love and affection constantly to show another person that you really care.

Displays become detrimental to communication when the feelings you   7
are experiencing are negative—especially when the display of a negative feeling appears to be an overreaction. For instance, when Candy stands over Doris while she is working on her report and says, "That first paragraph isn't very well written," Doris may well experience resentment. If Doris lashes out at Candy by screaming, "Who the hell asked you for your opinion?" Doris's display no doubt will hurt Candy's feelings and short-circuit their communication. Although displays of negative feelings may be good for you psychologically, they are likely to be bad for you interpersonally.

Describing Feelings

Describing feelings—putting your feelings into words in a calm, nonjudgmental   8
way—tends to be the best method of disclosing feelings. Describing feelings not
only increases chances for positive communication and decreases chances for
short-circuiting lines of communication; it also teaches people how to treat you.
When you describe your feelings, people are made aware of the effect of their behavior. This knowledge gives them the information needed to determine whether
they should continue or repeat that behavior. If you tell Paul that you really feel
flattered when he visits you, such a statement should encourage Paul to visit you
again; likewise, when you tell Cliff that you feel very angry when he borrows your
jacket without asking, he is more likely to ask the next time he borrows a jacket.
Describing your feelings allows you to exercise a measure of control over others'
behavior toward you.

Describing and displaying feelings are not the same. Many times people think   9
they are describing when in fact they are displaying feelings or evaluating.

If describing feelings is so important to communicating effectively, why don't   10
more people do it regularly? There seem to be at least four reasons why many
people don't describe feelings.

1. Many people have a poor vocabulary of words for describing the various   11
feelings they are experiencing. People can sense that they are angry; however,
they may not know whether what they are feeling might best be described as
annoyed, betrayed, cheated, crushed, disturbed, furious, outraged, or shocked.
Each of these words describes a slightly different aspect of what many people
lump together as anger.

2. Many people believe that describing their true feelings reveals too much   12
about themselves. If you tell people when their behavior hurts you, you risk their
using the information against you when they want to hurt you on purpose. Even
so, the potential benefits of describing your feelings far outweigh the risks. For
instance, if Pete has a nickname for you that you don't like and you tell Pete that
calling you by that nickname really makes you nervous and tense, Pete may use
the nickname when he wants to hurt you, but he is more likely to stop calling you
by that name. If, on the other hand, you don't describe your feelings to Pete, he is
probably going to call you by that name all the time because he doesn't know any
better. When you say nothing, you reinforce his behavior. The level of risk varies
with each situation, but you will more often improve a relationship than be hurt
by describing feelings.

3. Many people believe that if they describe feelings, others will make them   13
feel guilty about having such feelings. At a very tender age we all learned about
"tactful" behavior. Under the premise that "the truth sometimes hurts" we learned
to avoid the truth by not saying anything or by telling "little" lies. Perhaps when

Copyright ©2006 The McGraw-Hill Companies, Inc. All rights reserved

you were young your mother said, "Don't forget to give Grandma a great big kiss." At that time you may have blurted out, "Ugh—it makes me feel yucky to kiss Grandma. She's got a mustache." If your mother responded, "That's terrible—your grandma loves you. Now you give her a kiss and never let me hear you talk like that again!" then you probably felt guilty for having this "wrong" feeling. But the point is that the thought of kissing your grandma made you feel "yucky" whether it should have or not. In this case what was at issue was the way you talked about the feelings—not your having the feelings.

4. Many people believe that describing feelings causes harm to others or to a   14
relationship. If it really bothers Max when his girlfriend, Dora, bites her fingernails, Max may believe that describing his feelings to Dora will hurt her so much that the knowledge will drive a wedge into their relationship. So it's better for Max to say nothing, right? Wrong! If Max says nothing, he's still going to be bothered by Dora's behavior. In fact, as time goes on, Max will probably lash out at Dora for other things because he can't bring himself to talk about the behavior that really bothers him. The net result is that not only will Dora be hurt by Max's behavior, but she won't understand the true source of his feelings. By not describing his feelings, Max may well drive a wedge into their relationship anyway.

If Max does describe his feelings to Dora, she might quit or at least try to quit biting her nails; they might get into a discussion in which he finds out that   15
she doesn't want to bite them but just can't seem to stop, and he can help her in her efforts to stop; or they might discuss the problem and Max may see that it is a small thing really and not let it bother him as much. The point is that in describing feelings the chances of a successful outcome are greater than they are in not describing them.

To describe your feelings, first put the emotion you are feeling into words. Be   16
specific. Second, state what triggered the feeling. Finally, make sure you indicate that the feeling is yours. For example, suppose your roommate borrows your jacket without asking. When he returns, you describe your feelings by saying, "Cliff, I [indication that the feeling is yours] get really angry [the feeling] when you borrow my jacket without asking [trigger]." Or suppose that Carl has just reminded you of the very first time he brought you a rose. You describe your feelings by saying, "Carl, I [indication that the feeling is yours] get really tickled [the feeling] when you remind me about that first time you brought me a rose [trigger]."

You may find it easiest to begin by describing positive feelings: "I really feel   17
elated knowing that you were the one who nominated me for the position" or "I'm delighted that you offered to help me with the housework." As you gain success with positive descriptions, you can try negative feelings attributable to environmental factors: "It's so cloudy; I feel gloomy" or "When the wind howls through the cracks, I really get jumpy." Finally, you can move to negative descriptions resulting from what people have said or done: "Your stepping in front of me like that really annoys me" or "The tone of your voice confuses me."

Copyright ©2006 The McGraw-Hill Companies, Inc. All rights reserved.

■ Reading Comprehension Questions

1. The word *detrimental* in "For instance, a stranger's inconsiderate behavior at a party may bother you, but because you can move to another part of the room, withholding may not be detrimental" (paragraph 4) means

   a. useful.

   b. private.

   c. helpless.

   d. harmful.

2. The word *wedge* in "Max may believe that describing his feelings to Dora will hurt her so much that the knowledge will drive a wedge into their relationship" (paragraph 14) means

   a. something that divides.

   b. loyalty.

   c. friendship.

   d. many years.

3. Which of the following would be the best alternative title for this selection?

   a. Effective Communication

   b. Negative Feelings

   c. The Consequences of Withholding Feelings

   d. Emotions: When and How to Express Them

4. Which sentence best expresses the article's main point?

   a. Everyone has feelings.

   b. There are three ways to deal with feelings; describing them is most useful for educating others about how you want to be treated.

   c. Withholding feelings means not giving verbal or nonverbal clues that might reveal those feelings to others.

   d. Psychologists have studied the manner in which people deal with their feelings.

5. You are most likely to create physical problems for yourself by

   a. withholding your feelings.

   b. displaying your positive feelings.

   c. describing your positive feelings.

   d. describing your negative feelings.

6. The author uses the term "describing your feelings" to refer to

   a. keeping your feelings inside.

   b. giving a nonverbal response to feelings.

   c. putting your feelings into words calmly.

   d. telling "little" lies.

7. Shouting angrily at a person who has stepped in front of you in line is an example of

   a. withholding feelings.

   b. displaying feelings.

   c. describing feelings.

   d. self-disclosing.

8. From the reading, we can conclude that describing feelings

   a. is usually easy for people.

   b. is often a good way to solve problems.

   c. should be done only for positive feelings.

   d. should make you feel guilty.

9. Which sentence can we infer is an example of describing a feeling?

   a. Although Mrs. Henderson hates going to the mountains, she says nothing as her husband plans to go there for their vacation.

   b. Neil calls Joanna the day after their date and says, "I want you to know how much I enjoyed our evening together. You're a lot of fun."

   c. Raoul jumps out of his seat and yells joyfully as the Packers make a touchdown.

   d. Peggy's office-mate chews gum noisily, cracking and snapping it. Peggy shrieks, "How inconsiderate can you be? You're driving me crazy with that noise!"

10. *True or false?* _____ We can infer that people who describe their feelings tend to be physically healthier than those who withhold feelings.

■ Discussion Questions

About Content

1. What is the difference between describing feelings and expressing them? How might Doris describe her feelings to Candy after Candy says, "That first paragraph isn't very well written" (paragraph 2)?

Copyright ©2006 The McGraw-Hill Companies, Inc. All rights reserved.

2. Why do you think Verderber emphasizes describing feelings over the other two methods of dealing with feelings?

3. What are some examples from your own experience of withholding, expressing or displaying, and describing feelings? How useful was each?

About Structure

4. What method of introduction does Verderber use in this selection?

   a. Broad to narrow

   b. Anecdote

   c. Beginning with a situation opposite to the one he will describe

   d. Question

   Is his introduction effective? Why or why not?

5. Verderber divides the body of his essay into three parts: first about withholding feelings, second about displaying feelings, and finally about describing feelings. He further divides the third part by introducing a list. What is that list about? How many items does he include in it?

6. What devices does the author use to emphasize the organization of his essay?

7. How many examples does Verderber provide for withholding feelings? Displaying feelings? Describing feelings?

About Style and Tone

8. What type of evidence does the author use to back up his points throughout the selection? What other types of support might he have used?

WRITING ASSIGNMENTS

Assignment 1: Writing a Paragraph

Write a paragraph about a time when you withheld or displayed feelings, but describing them would have been a better idea. Your topic sentence might be something like either of these:

> An argument I had with my boyfriend recently made me wish that I had described my feelings rather than displaying them.

> Withholding my feelings at work recently left me feeling frustrated and angry.

Then narrate the event, showing how feelings were withheld or displayed and what the result was. Conclude your paragraph by contrasting what really happened with what *might* have happened if feelings had been described.

Assignment 2: Writing a Paragraph

"Dealing with Feelings" lists and discusses several ways to cope with emotions. Write a paragraph in which you present three ways to do something else. Your tone may be serious or humorous. You might write about three ways to do one of the following:

Cut expenses

Meet people

Get along with a difficult coworker

Ruin a party

Embarrass your friends

Lose a job

Here is a possible topic sentence for this assignment:

To ruin a party, you must follow three simple steps.

Assignment 3: Writing an Essay

At one time or another, you have probably used all three methods of communicating described by Verderber: withholding, displaying, and describing. Write an essay that describes a situation in which you have used each of those methods. In each case, narrate the event that occurred. Then explain why you responded as you did and how you ended up feeling about your response. Finish your essay with some conclusion of your own about dealing with feelings.

Here's a sample outline for such an essay:

Thesis statement: At different times, I have withheld my feelings, displayed my feelings, and described my feelings.

Topic sentence 1: Dealing with a rude store clerk, I withheld my feelings.

Topic sentence 2: When another driver cut me off in traffic, I displayed my feelings.

Topic sentence 3: When my mother angered me by reading a letter I'd left lying on the dining-room table, I described my feelings.

Conclusion: When it comes to dealing with people I care about, describing my feelings works better than withholding or displaying them.

The Most Hateful Words

Amy Tan

Copyright ©2006 The McGraw-Hill Companies, Inc. All rights reserved.

For years, a painful exchange with her mother lay like a heavy stone on Amy Tan's heart. In the following essay, Tan, author of best-selling novels including *The Joy Luck Club* and *The Kitchen God's Wife*, tells the story of how that weight was finally lifted. This essay is from her memoir, *The Opposite of Fate*.

The most hateful words I have ever said to another human being were to my mother. I was sixteen at the time. They rose from the storm in my chest and I let them fall in a fury of hailstones: "I hate you. I wish I were dead. . . ." 1

I waited for her to collapse, stricken by what I had just said. She was still standing upright, her chin tilted, her lips stretched in a crazy smile. "Okay, maybe I die too," she said between huffs. "Then I no longer be your mother!" We had many similar exchanges. Sometimes she actually tried to kill herself by running into the street, holding a knife to her throat. She too had storms in her chest. And what she aimed at me was as fast and deadly as a lightning bolt. 2

For days after our arguments, she would not speak to me. She tormented me, acted as if she had no feelings for me whatsoever. I was lost to her. And because of that, I lost, battle after battle, all of them: the times she criticized me, humiliated me in front of others, forbade me to do this or that without even listening to one good reason why it should be the other way. I swore to myself I would never forget these injustices. I would store them, harden my heart, make myself as impenetrable as she was. 3

I remember this now, because I am also remembering another time, just a few years ago. I was forty-seven, had become a different person by then, had become a fiction writer, someone who uses memory and imagination. In fact, I was writing a story about a girl and her mother, when the phone rang. 4

It was my mother, and this surprised me. Had someone helped her make the call? For a few years now, she had been losing her mind through Alzheimer's disease. Early on, she forgot to lock her door. Then she forgot where she lived. She forgot who many people were and what they had meant to her. Lately, she could no longer remember many of her worries and sorrows. 5

693

"Amy-ah," she said, and she began to speak quickly in Chinese. "Something   6
is wrong with my mind. I think I'm going crazy."

I caught my breath. Usually she could barely speak more than two words at a   7
time. "Don't worry," I started to say.

"It's true," she went on. "I feel like I can't remember many things. I can't   8
remember what I did yesterday. I can't remember what happened a long time ago,
what I did to you. . . ." She spoke as a drowning person might if she had bobbed
to the surface with the force of will to live, only to see how far she had already
drifted, how impossibly far she was from the shore.

She spoke frantically: "I know I did something to hurt you."   9

"You didn't," I said. "Don't worry."   10

"I did terrible things. But now I can't remember what. . . . And I just want to   11
tell you . . . I hope you can forget, just as I've forgotten."

I tried to laugh so she would not notice the cracks in my voice. "Really, don't   12
worry."

"Okay, I just wanted you to know."   13

After we hung up, I cried, both happy and sad. I was again that sixteen-year-   14
old, but the storm in my chest was gone.

My mother died six months later. By then she had bequeathed to me her most   15
healing words, as open and eternal as a clear blue sky. Together we knew in our
hearts what we should remember, what we can forget.

■ Reading Comprehension Questions

1. The word *stricken* in "I waited for her to collapse, *stricken* by what I had just said" (paragraph 2) means
   a. wounded.
   b. amused.
   c. annoyed.
   d. bored.

2. The word *bequeathed* in "By then she had *bequeathed* me her most healing words, those that are as open and eternal as a clear blue sky" (paragraph 15) means
   a. denied.
   b. sold.
   c. given.
   d. cursed.

3. Which sentence best expresses the central idea of the selection?
   a. Because of Alzheimer's disease, the author's mother forgot harsh words the two of them had said to one another.

b. Amy Tan had a difficult relationship with her mother that worsened over the years.

c. Years after a painful childhood with her mother, Amy Tan was able to realize peace and forgiveness.

d. Despite her Alzheimer's disease, Amy Tan's mother was able to apologize to her daughter for hurting her.

4. Which sentence best expresses the main idea of paragraphs 1–2?

a. Amy Tan's mother was sometimes suicidal.

b. Amy Tan wanted to use words to hurt her mother.

c. It is not unusual for teenagers and their parents to argue.

d. Amy Tan and her mother had a very hurtful relationship.

5. Which sentence best expresses the main idea of paragraphs 8–9?

a. The author's mother was deeply disturbed by the thought that she had hurt her daughter.

b. Alzheimer's disease causes people to become confused and unable to remember things clearly.

c. The author's mother could not even remember what she had done the day before.

d. The author's mother had changed very little from what she was like when Tan was a child.

6. After arguing with her daughter, the author's mother

a. would say nice things about her to others.

b. would immediately forget they had argued.

c. would refuse to speak to her.

d. would apologize.

7. When she was a girl, the author swore that she

a. would never forget her mother's harsh words.

b. would never be like her mother.

c. would publicly embarrass her mother by writing about her.

d. would never have children.

8. The first sign that the author's mother had Alzheimer's disease was

a. forgetting where she lived.

b. being able to speak only two or three words at a time.

Copyright ©2006 The McGraw-Hill Companies, Inc. All rights reserved.

     c. forgetting people's identities.

     d. forgetting to lock her door.

9. We can infer from paragraph 2 that

     a. the author wished her mother were dead.

     b. the author immediately felt guilty for the way she had spoken to her mother.

     c. the author's mother was emotionally unstable.

     d. the author's mother was physically abusive.

10. The author implies, in paragraphs 9–15, that

     a. she was pleased by her mother's sense of guilt.

     b. her love and pity for her mother were stronger than her anger.

     c. she did not recall what her mother was talking about.

     d. she was annoyed by her mother's confusion.

■ Discussion Questions

About Content

1. How would you describe Amy Tan's mother? What kind of mother does she appear to have been?

2. In the discussion at the end of the essay, Tan chooses to keep her emotions hidden from her mother. Why do you think she does this?

3. What does Tan mean by her last line, "Together we knew in our hearts what we should remember, what we can forget."

About Structure

4. Tan makes effective use of parallel structure in writing her story. What are two examples of parallelism that help make her sentences clear and easy to read?

5. Tan begins her essay from the point of view of a sixteen-year-old girl but finishes it from the perspective of a woman in her late-forties. Where in the essay does Tan make the transition between those two perspectives? What words does she use to signal the change?

6. Paragraph 5 describes a sequence of events, and the writer uses several transition words to signal time relationships. Locate three of those transitions and write them here:

    _____   _____   _____

Copyright ©2006 The McGraw-Hill Companies, Inc. All rights reserved.

About Style and Tone

7. What effect does Tan achieve by using so many direct quotations?

8. Tan uses images of the weather throughout her essay. Find three instances in which Tan mentions weather and list them below. What does she accomplish with this technique?

_____   _____   _____

WRITING ASSIGNMENTS

Assignment 1: Writing a Paragraph

Despite being an adult, Tan recalls feeling like a sixteen-year-old girl again when she speaks to her mother. Think about something in your life that has the power to reconnect you to a vivid memory. Write a paragraph in which you describe your memory and the trigger which "takes you back" to it. Begin your paragraph with a topic sentence that makes it clear what you are going to discuss. Then provide specific details so that readers can understand your memory. Here are sample topic sentences.

> Whenever I see swings, I remember the day in second grade when I got into my first fistfight.
>
> The smell of cotton candy takes me back to the day my grandfather took me to my first baseball game.
>
> I can't pass St. Joseph's Hospital without remembering the day, ten years ago, when my brother was shot.

Assignment 2: Writing a Paragraph

In this essay, we see that Tan's relationship with her mother was very complicated. Who is a person with whom you have a complex relationship—maybe a relationship you'd describe as "love-hate" or "difficult"? Write a paragraph about that relationship. Be sure to give examples or details to show readers why you have such difficulties with this person.

Your topic sentence should introduce the person you plan to discuss. For example:

> To me, my mother-in-law is one of the most difficult people in the world. (*Or,* My mother-in-law and I have contrasting points of view on several issues.)
>
> While I respect my boss, he is simply a very difficult person.
>
> Even though I love my sister, I can't stand to be around her.

Be sure to provide specific examples or details to help your reader understand why the relationship is so difficult for you. For example, if you decide to write about your boss, you will want to describe specific behaviors that show just why you consider him or her difficult.

Assignment 3: Writing an Essay

Like Tan's mother, most of us have at some time done something we wish we could undo. If you had a chance to revisit your past and change one of your actions, what would it be? Write an essay describing something you would like to undo.

In your first paragraph, introduce exactly what you did. Here are three thesis statements that students might have written:

> I wish I could undo the night I decided to drive my car while I was drunk.

> If I could undo any moment in my life, it would be the day I decided to drop out of high school.

> One moment from my life I would like to change is the time I picked on an unpopular kid in sixth grade.

Be sure to provide details and, if appropriate, actual words that were spoken, so that your readers can "see and hear" what happened. Once you've described the moment that you wish to take back, write three reasons why you feel the way you do. Below is a scratch outline for the first topic.

> I wish I could undo the night I decided to drive my car while I was drunk.
> 1. Caused an accident that hurt others.
> 2. Lost my license, my car, and my job.
> 3. Affected the way others treat me.

 To write an effective essay, you will need to provide specific details explaining each reason you identify. For instance, to support the third reason above, you might describe new feelings of guilt and anger you have about yourself as well as provide examples of how individual people now treat you differently. To end your essay, you might describe what you would do today if you could replay what happened.

The Storyteller

Adapted from H. H. Munro ("Saki")

Copyright ©2006 The McGraw-Hill Companies, Inc. All rights reserved.

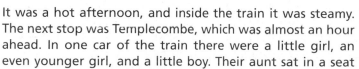
What is a good story for children: one that teaches them a lesson—or one that they enjoy? In the timeless and beloved tale that follows, an aunt learns a lesson herself about storytelling.

It was a hot afternoon, and inside the train it was steamy. The next stop was Templecombe, which was almost an hour ahead. In one car of the train there were a little girl, an even younger girl, and a little boy. Their aunt sat in a seat in the corner. In the opposite corner of the car was a bachelor who didn't know them. The girls and the boy were running all over the train car. Their conversation with their aunt reminded the bachelor of the irritating buzzing of a housefly. Everything the aunt said to the children began with "Don't," while everything the children said to her began with "Why?" The bachelor said nothing. 1

"Don't, Cyril, don't!" exclaimed the aunt, as the boy began hitting the seat cushions, making clouds of dust fly up. "Come over here and look out the window." 2

Reluctantly, the boy went over to the window. "Why are they driving those sheep out of that field?" he asked. 3

"I guess they are being taken to another field that has more grass," said the aunt weakly. 4

"But there's lots of grass in that field," protested the boy. "There's nothing but grass there. Aunt, there's lots of grass in that field." 5

"Maybe the grass in the other field is better," the aunt suggested foolishly. 6

"Why is it better?" came the quick, obvious question. 7

"Oh, look at those cows!" exclaimed the aunt. Almost every field they passed was full of cows, but she sounded as if this was an amazing surprise. 8

"Why is the grass in the other field better?" Cyril kept at her. 9

The frown on the bachelor's face was deepening into a scowl. The aunt noticed, and decided he was a mean, unfriendly man. And she couldn't come up with any good explanation for the little boy about the grass in the field. 10

The younger girl began to entertain herself by reciting a poem. She knew only the first line, but she put that one line to good use, repeating it over and over again in a loud, dreamy voice. The bachelor wondered if someone had bet her she couldn't say that same line two thousand times without stopping. Unfortunately for him, it seemed she was going to win the bet. 11

"Come over here and listen to a story," said the aunt, who had noticed the bachelor glaring at her. He looked as if he might complain to the train conductor. 12

The children moved over toward the aunt without any enthusiasm. It was 13 clear she didn't have a very good reputation as a storyteller.

In a quiet voice that was often interrupted by loud questions from the chil- 14 dren, the aunt started a dreadfully boring story about a little girl who was good. Because she was so good, she made a lot of friends, and was finally saved from a wild bull by people who admired how good she was.

"Wouldn't they have saved her if she hadn't been good?" demanded the older 15 of the little girls. That was exactly the question the bachelor had wanted to ask.

"Well, yes," answered the aunt lamely, "but I don't think they would have run 16 so fast to help her if they hadn't liked her so much."

"It's the stupidest story I've ever heard," said the older of the little girls. 17

"I didn't even listen after the first part because it was so stupid," said Cyril. 18

The younger girl didn't comment on the story. Minutes earlier she had stopped 19 listening and started repeating the line from the poem.

"You don't seem to be a very successful storyteller," said the bachelor suddenly. 20

The aunt became defensive at this unexpected attack. "It's very difficult to tell 21 stories that children will understand and enjoy," she said stiffly.

"I don't agree with you," said the bachelor. 22

"Maybe you'd like to tell them a story," the aunt shot back. 23

"Tell us a story!" demanded the older of the little girls. 24

"Once upon a time," began the bachelor, "there was a little girl called Ber- 25 tha, who was very, very good."

The children's temporary interest started fading immediately. To them, all 26 stories seemed boring and the same, no matter who told them.

"She did everything she was told to do. She always told the truth and kept 27 her clothes neat and clean. She ate food that was good for her instead of junk food and sweets, got good grades in school, and was polite to everyone."

"Was she pretty?" asked the older little girl. 28

"Not as pretty as any of you," said the bachelor, "but she was horribly good." 29

The children became more enthusiastic. The word *horrible* in connection with 30 goodness was something new, and they liked it. It seemed real and true, unlike the aunt's stories about children.

"She was so good," continued the bachelor, "that she won several medals 31 for goodness, which she always wore pinned to her dress. There was a medal for following rules, one for being on time, and one for general good behavior. They were large metal medals and they clicked against each other when she walked. No other child in her town had three medals, so everyone knew that she must be an extra good child."

"Horribly good," repeated Cyril. 32

"Everybody talked about how good she was, and the prince of the country heard 33 about it. He decided she was so good that he would let her walk once a week in his park just outside the town. It was a beautiful park, and no children had ever been allowed in it before. So it was a great honor for Bertha to be allowed to go there."

"Were there any sheep in the park?" demanded Cyril. 34

"No," said the bachelor, "there were no sheep."   35

"Why weren't there any sheep?" came the unavoidable question.   36

The aunt grinned, looking forward to seeing the bachelor trapped.   37

"There were no sheep in the park," said the bachelor, "because the prince's   38
mother had once had a dream that her son would be killed either by a sheep or
by a clock falling on him. So the prince never kept sheep in his park or a clock in
his palace."

The aunt gasped in admiration at how well the bachelor had answered the   39
question.

"Was the prince killed by a sheep or a clock?" asked Cyril.   40

"He is still alive, so we don't know if the dream will come true," said the   41
bachelor. "Anyway, there were no sheep in the park, but there were lots of little
pigs running all over the place."

"What color were they?"   42

"Black with white faces, white with black spots, black all over, gray with white   43
patches, and some were white all over."

The storyteller stopped to let the children imagine all of the wonderful things   44
about the park, and then started again: "Bertha was sad to find that there were
no flowers in the park. She had promised her aunts, with tears in her eyes, that
she wouldn't pick any of the flowers. She wanted to keep her promise, so it made
her feel silly that there weren't any flowers to pick."

"Why weren't there any flowers?"   45

"Because the pigs had eaten all of them," said the bachelor. "The gardeners   46
told the prince he couldn't have both pigs and flowers, so he decided to keep the
pigs and forget the flowers."

The children looked pleased with the prince's choice; so many people would   47
have chosen the flowers instead of the pigs.

"There were lots of other delightful things in the park. There were ponds   48
with gold, blue, and green fish in them; and trees with beautiful talking parrots;
and hummingbirds that could hum popular music. Bertha walked around, enjoying herself greatly. She thought, 'If I weren't so very good, they wouldn't have
let me come to this beautiful park and enjoy everything in it.' Her three medals
clinked against each other as she walked and again reminded her how good she
was. But just then, a very big wolf came prowling into the park to hunt for a fat
little pig for its supper."

"What color was it?" asked the children, who were now very interested in   49
the story.

"Mud-colored all over, with a black tongue and pale gray eyes that gleamed   50
fiercely. The first thing it saw in the park was Bertha. Her dress was so spotlessly
white and clean that you could see it from far away. Bertha saw the wolf creeping
toward her, and she wished she had never been invited to the park. She ran as fast
as she could, but the wolf came after her with huge leaps and bounds. She managed to reach some bushes, and she hid in them. As the wolf sniffed the bushes,
she could see its black tongue hanging out of its mouth and its cold gray eyes.

Copyright ©2006 The McGraw-Hill Companies, Inc. All rights reserved.

Bertha was very frightened, and thought, 'If I had not been so very good, I would be safe back in town right now.'

"However, the smell of the bushes was so strong and the branches were so 51 thick that the wolf couldn't smell or see Bertha, so it decided to give up and go catch a pig instead. Bertha was so scared of the wolf that she was shaking, and her medals for goodness started clinking together. The wolf was just moving away when it heard the medals clinking and stopped to listen. When they clinked again, it dived into the bush with its gray eyes shining fiercely. It dragged Bertha out and ate her all up. All that was left were her shoes, scraps of clothing, and the three medals for goodness."

"Were any of the pigs killed?"   52

"No, they all escaped."   53

"The story started badly," said the younger girl, "but it had a beautiful ending." 54

"It is the most beautiful story I have ever heard," said the older little girl 55 seriously.

"It is the *only* beautiful story I have ever heard," said Cyril.   56

The aunt disagreed. "That is a most inappropriate story to tell young chil- 57 dren! You may have ruined years of careful teaching!"

"Anyway," said the bachelor, gathering his belongings together so he could 58 get off the train, "I kept them quiet for ten minutes, which was more than you could do."

"Poor woman!" he thought to himself as he walked down the platform of 59 Templecombe station. "For the next six months those children will beg her in public for an inappropriate story!"

■ Reading Comprehension Questions

1. The word *glaring* in "'Come over here and listen to a story,' said the aunt, who had noticed the bachelor glaring at her. He looked as if he might complain to the train conductor" (paragraph 12) means

   a. staring angrily.

   b. smiling.

   c. yelling.

   d. laughing.

2. The word *defensive* in "The aunt became defensive at this unexpected attack. 'It's very difficult to tell stories that children will understand and enjoy,' she said stiffly" (paragraph 21) means

   a. amused.

   b. self-protecting.

   c. sad.

   d. confused.

3. Which sentence best expresses the central point of the selection?

   a. An aunt traveling with nieces and a nephew tells them a story that taught a lesson.

   b. A bachelor on a train ride tells a story to three children he doesn't know.

   c. Children bored by an aunt's story about goodness listen happily to a bachelor's awful and surprising tale.

   d. It is not right to tell stories to children in which the good character ends up being eaten up by a wolf.

4. Which sentence best expresses the main idea of paragraph 51?

   a. The bush had such thick branches and a strong smell that the wolf couldn't find Bertha.

   b. Bertha was so frightened by the wolf that she was shaking.

   c. By the time the wolf left, only scraps of clothing, shoes, and the medals remained.

   d. Though Bertha hid in thick bushes, the wolf found her when her medals clinked, and then ate her up.

5. The aunt offered to tell the children a story when the

   a. little girl began reciting poetry.

   b. children began running around the train car.

   c. children asked the bachelor for a story.

   d. bachelor glared at the aunt.

6. The children first began to show real interest in the bachelor's story when he

   a. referred to Bertha as "horribly good."

   b. mentioned the wolf.

   c. explained why there were no sheep in the park.

   d. told about Bertha's medals.

7. As Bertha was hiding in the bushes, she thought

   a. of a plan for escaping from the wolf.

   b. that the prince should not have allowed a wolf in his park.

   c. that if she had not been so good, she would be safe.

   d. that the wolf would probably go away and eat a little pig.

8. When Bertha discovered that there were no flowers in the park, she felt

   a. relieved, because she would not be tempted to pick them.

   b. sad, because she had made a promise that was now useless.

Copyright ©2006 The McGraw-Hill Companies, Inc. All rights reserved.

      c. angry, because she thought the prince should have provided flowers.

      d. happy, because she did not like flowers.

9. The author implies that the bachelor

      a. wanted something bad to happen to the children on the train.

      b. understood children better than the aunt did.

      c. actually was acquainted with the children and their aunt.

      d. told a true story.

10. The author implies that

      a. the children had very good manners.

      b. the aunt had not spent much time with the children before.

      c. the aunt would not be taking the children on any more trips.

      d. the children were tired of their aunt's stories about perfect children.

■ Discussion Questions

About Content

1. Why do you think the children preferred the bachelor's story to the aunt's?

2. When you were little, who was your favorite storyteller? Was it an adult in your life such as a parent or teacher, or was it a friend of yours, or was it a TV personality? What stories do you remember him or her telling or reading?

3. Did your parents (or other adults in your life) ever hold up other children as examples to you? What qualities did they admire in the other children? How did you respond to being compared with other kids?

About Structure

4. Saki describes the aunt's story in just one paragraph (14). He spends many paragraphs on the bachelor's story, providing every word that the bachelor and the children said. Why do you think he gives the two stories such unequal treatment?

5. The bachelor makes his story very specific. Name three details he provides that you feel are especially effective.

6. Find an example of how the aunt responds to a question from the children; then find an example of how the bachelor responds to one. How do the two contrast with each other?

Copyright ©2006 The McGraw-Hill Companies, Inc. All rights reserved.

About Style and Tone

7. What are a few words you think the author would probably use to describe the aunt? Find evidence in the story to support your opinion.

8. As the bachelor's story goes on, how can you tell that the children are becoming increasingly enthusiastic about it? What hints does the author give you?

WRITING ASSIGNMENTS

Assignment 1: Writing a Paragraph

The children in "The Storyteller" will probably never forget their meeting with the bachelor on the train. Write a paragraph about a brief but memorable encounter you've had with a stranger. Include some direct quotations as well as descriptive details that appeal to several senses (sight, hearing, smell, touch) so that the reader can clearly "see" the stranger as you did. Begin your paper with a main point like this:

> I'll never forget a conversation I had with a homeless man last winter.
>
> I had a brief but interesting encounter with a woman I met in a doctor's waiting room.
>
> Standing in line to buy tickets for a concert, I met a girl whom I've remembered ever since.

Assignment 2: Writing a Paragraph

The aunt in "The Storyteller" probably means well, but she doesn't seem to understand children or how to relate to them. Think of a person you've observed who didn't seem to understand how to relate to someone else. Maybe it was an adult with a child, a parent with a teenager, or a teacher with a student. Write a paragraph about the lack of connection between those two people. Begin with a sentence that sums up your observations. Here are some examples:

> Watching my grandfather and my sister's little boy makes it clear that Grandpa doesn't know much about babies.
>
> A mother I saw in a toy store didn't seem to understand how to relate to her little girl.
>
> A waitress at the diner I go to doesn't seem to understand how to deal with customers.

In your paper, include direct quotations and specific details that illustrate the poor communication you observed.

Assignment 3: Writing an Essay

Favorite stories help families and friends form strong bonds. When people get together, familiar stories are often told. Even though everyone present may already know a story, we enjoy retelling and rehearing it.

Write an essay in which you tell three stories that involve your family or friends, or both. Your thesis statement might be something like one of these:

> Of all the stories my relatives tell when they get together, my favorite three involve my dad, my aunt Rosa, and my cousin José.

> When I think about my high school friends, I remember three special stories. Two of them were funny, and one was sad.

In the body of your essay, devote one paragraph to telling each of your stories. Remember to explain briefly who each character is and provide any background information your reader will need in order to understand what is happening. Be sure to include the elements that make each story memorable. If one involves a funny conversation, for instance, be sure to quote that conversation directly. If one focuses on something physical, be sure to describe what happened in enough detail so that your reader can clearly envision it. In your concluding paragraph, make a few final remarks about why the three stories are memorable to you.

Alternatively, tell one long story that naturally divides itself into two or three parts. Each of those parts can be one of the supporting paragraphs in your essay.

Rudeness at the Movies

Bill Wine

When you're at a movie theater, do loud conversations, the crinkling of candy wrappers, and the wailing of children make you wish you'd gone bowling instead? Do you cringe when your fellow viewers announce plot twists moments before they happen? If so, you'll find a comrade in suffering in the film critic and columnist Bill Wine, who thinks people have come to feel far too at home in theaters. In the following essay, which first appeared as a newspaper feature story, Wine wittily describes what the moviegoing experience all too often is like these days.

Copyright ©2006 The McGraw-Hill Companies, Inc. All rights reserved.

Is this actually happening or am I dreaming?　　1

I am at the movies, settling into my seat, eager with anticipation at the prospect of seeing a long-awaited film of obvious quality. The theater is absolutely full for the late show on this weekend evening, as the reviews have been ecstatic for this cinema masterpiece.　　2

Directly in front of me sits a man an inch or two taller than the Jolly Green Giant. His wife, sitting on his left, sports the very latest in fashionable hairdos, a gathering of her locks into a shape that resembles a drawbridge when it's open.　　3

On his right, a woman spritzes herself liberally with perfume that her popcorn-munching husband got her for Valentine's Day, a scent that should be renamed "Essence of Elk."　　4

The row in which I am sitting quickly fills up with members of Cub Scout Troop 432, on an outing to the movies because rain has canceled their overnight hike. One of the boys, demonstrating the competitive spirit for which Scouts are renowned worldwide, announces to the rest of the troop the rules in the Best Sound Made from an Empty Good-n-Plenty's Box contest, about to begin.　　5

Directly behind me, a man and his wife are ushering three other couples into their seats. I hear the woman say to the couple next to her: "You'll love it. You'll just love it. This is our fourth time and we enjoy it more and more each time. Don't we, Harry? Tell them about the pie-fight scene, Harry. Wait'll you see it. It comes just before you find out that the daughter killed her boyfriend. It's great."　　6

The woman has more to say—much more—but she is drowned out at the moment by the wailing of a six-month-old infant in the row behind her. The baby is crying because his mother, who has brought her twins to the theater to save on babysitting costs, can change only one diaper at a time.　　7

Suddenly, the lights dim. The music starts. The credits roll. And I panic.　　8

I plead with everyone around me to let me enjoy the movie. All I ask, I wail, is to be able to see the images and hear the dialogue and not find out in advance what is about to happen. Is that so much to expect for six bucks, I ask, now engulfed by a cloud of self-pity. I begin weeping unashamedly.　　9

Then, as if on cue, the Jolly Green Giant slumps down in his seat, his wife removes her wig, the Elk lady changes her seat, the Scouts drop their candy boxes on the floor, the play-by-play commentator takes out her teeth, and the young mother takes her two bawling babies home.　　10

Of course I am dreaming, I realize, as I gain a certain but shaky consciousness. I notice that I am in a cold sweat. Not because the dream is scary, but from the shock of people being that cooperative.　　11

I realize that I have awakened to protect my system from having to handle a jolt like that. For never—NEVER—would that happen in real life. Not on this planet.　　12

I used to wonder whether I was the only one who feared bad audience behavior more than bad moviemaking. But I know now that I am not. Not by a long shot. The most frequent complaint I have heard in the last few months about the moviegoing experience has had nothing to do with the films themselves.　　13

No. What folks have been complaining about is the audience. Indeed, there   14
seems to be an epidemic of galling inconsiderateness and outrageous rudeness.

It is not that difficult to forgive a person's excessive height, or malodorous   15
perfume, or perhaps even an inadvisable but understandable need to bring very
young children to adult movies.

But the talking: that is not easy to forgive. It is inexcusable. Talking—loud,   16
constant, and invariably superfluous—seems to be standard operating procedure
on the part of many movie patrons these days.

It is true, I admit, that after a movie critic has seen several hundred movies   17
in the ideal setting of an almost-empty screening room with no one but other
politely silent movie critics around him, it does tend to spoil him for the packed-
theater experience.

And something is lost viewing a movie in almost total isolation—a fact that   18
movie distributors acknowledge with their reluctance to screen certain audience-
pleasing movies for small groups of critics. Especially with comedies, the infec-
tiousness of laughter is an important ingredient of movie-watching pleasure.

But it is a decidedly uphill battle to enjoy a movie—no matter how suspenseful or   19
hilarious or moving—with nonstop gabbers sitting within earshot. And they come
in sizes, ages, sexes, colors, and motivations of every kind.

Some chat as if there is no movie playing. Some greet friends as if at a picnic.   20
Some alert those around them to what is going to happen, either because they
have seen the film before, or because they are self-proclaimed experts on the
predictability of plotting and want to be seen as prescient geniuses.

Some describe in graphic terms exactly what is happening as if they were   21
doing the commentary for a sporting event on radio. ("Ooh, look, he's sitting
down. Now he's looking at that green car. A banana—she's eating a banana.")
Some audition for film critic Gene Shalit's job by waxing witty as they critique the
movie right before your very ears.

And all act as if it is their constitutional or God-given right. As if their admission   22
price allows them to ruin the experience for anyone and everyone else in the
building. But why?

Good question. I wish I knew. Maybe rock concerts and ball games—both envi-   23
ronments which condone or even encourage hootin' and hollerin'—have conditioned
us to voice our approval and disapproval and just about anything else we can spit
out of our mouths at the slightest provocation when we are part of an audience.

But my guess lies elsewhere. The villain, I'm afraid, is the tube. We have seen   24
the enemy and it is television.

We have gotten conditioned over the last few decades to spending most of   25
our screen-viewing time in front of a little box in our living rooms and bedrooms.
And when we watch that piece of furniture, regardless of what is on it—be it
commercial, Super Bowl, soap opera, funeral procession, prime-time sitcom,
Shakespeare play—we chat. Boy, do we chat. Because TV viewing tends to be an
informal, gregarious, friendly, casually interruptible experience, we talk whenever
the spirit moves us. Which is often.

All of this is fine. But we have carried behavior that is perfectly acceptable in 26 the living room right to our neighborhood movie theater. And that *isn't* fine. In fact, it is turning lots of people off to what used to be a truly pleasurable experience: sitting in a jammed movie theater and watching a crowd-pleasing movie. And that's a first-class shame.

Nobody wants Fascist-like ushers, yet that may be where we're headed of 27 necessity. Let's hope not. But something's got to give.

Movies during this Age of Television may or may not be better than ever. 28 About audiences, however, there is no question.

They are worse.   29

■ Reading Comprehension Questions

1. The word *ecstatic* in "The theater is absolutely full . . . as the reviews have been ecstatic for this cinema masterpiece" (paragraph 2) means

   a. clever.

   b. disappointing.

   c. a little confusing.

   d. very enthusiastic.

2. The word *malodorous* in "It is really not that difficult to forgive a person's . . . malodorous perfume" (paragraph 15) means

   a. pleasant.

   b. expensive.

   c. bad-smelling.

   d. hard-to-smell.

3. Which of the following would be the best alternative title for this selection?

   a. Television-Watching Behavior

   b. Today's Movie Audiences

   c. Modern Films

   d. The Life of a Movie Critic

4. Which sentence best expresses the main idea of the selection?

   a. Ushers should now make movie audiences keep quiet.

   b. People talk while they watch television or sports.

   c. Rude audiences are ruining movies for many.

   d. Films have changed in recent years.

Copyright ©2006 The McGraw-Hill Companies, Inc. All rights reserved.

5. The author states that in his dream
    a. he had come to the movies with a friend.
    b. he wore a tall hat and sat in front of a person shorter than he is.
    c. the Cub Scouts stopped making noises with empty candy boxes.
    d. the popcorn was too salty.

6. *True or false?* _____ The experience that Wine describes in the first eight paragraphs of this article is typical of what really happens at the movies today.

7. The most frequent complaint the author has heard about movies is that
    a. they are too long.
    b. they are too expensive.
    c. the audiences are too noisy.
    d. the audiences arrive too late.

8. The author suggests that watching television
    a. has affected the behavior of movie audiences.
    b. should be done in silence.
    c. is more fun than seeing movies in a theater.
    d. is a good model for watching movies in theaters.

9. From the selection, we can conclude that the author feels
    a. films aren't as good as they used to be.
    b. teenagers are the rudest members of movie audiences.
    c. talking during a movie is much more common now than it used to be.
    d. tall people should be seated in the back of a theater.

10. In paragraph 27, the author implies that unless audiences become quieter,
    a. movie theaters will be closed.
    b. everyone will watch less television.
    c. movies will get worse.
    d. ushers will have to force talkers to be quiet or leave.

■ Discussion Questions

About Content

1. According to Wine, what are some possible causes for people's rude behavior at movies? Of these, which does Wine consider the most likely cause?

Copyright ©2006 The McGraw-Hill Companies, Inc. All rights reserved.

2. Do you agree with Wine's theory about why some people are rude at the movies? Why or why not? What might theater operators and other audience members do to control the problem?

3. Have you noticed the problem of noisy audiences in a movie theater? If so, what exactly have you experienced? What, if anything, was done about the problems you encountered?

About Structure

4. Wine writes about a problem. Write here the paragraphs in which Wine presents details that explain and illustrate what that problem is: paragraphs _____ to

_____.

5. Wine discusses reasons for the problem he writes about. Write here the paragraphs in which he discusses those reasons: paragraphs _____ to _____.

6. Wine suggests one possible but unwelcome solution for the problem he writes about. Write here the number of the paragraph in which he mentions that solution: _____.

About Style and Tone

7. Wine provides exaggerated descriptions of audience members—for example, he refers to the tall man sitting in front of him as "an inch or two taller than the Jolly Green Giant." Find two other examples of this humorous exaggeration.

_____

_____

Besides making readers smile, why might Wine have described the audience in this way?

_____

_____

8. Wine tends to use informal wording and sentence structure. In paragraphs 22–26, for instance, find two examples of his informal wording.

_____

_____

In the same paragraphs, find an example of his informal sentence structure.

_____

WRITING ASSIGNMENTS

Assignment 1: Writing a Paragraph

Which do you prefer—watching a movie on your DVD player (or VCR) at home or seeing it in a movie theater? Drawing on your own experiences, write a paragraph in which you explain why you prefer one viewing location over the other. Provide a strong example or two for each of your reasons. For instance, below is one reason with a specific example to support it.

> *Reason:* One reason I prefer going to a movie theater is that it is definitely more peaceful than watching a film at home.
>
> *Supporting example:* For instance, when I tried watching *Titanic* at home the other night, I had to check on a crying baby or a fussy toddler every ten minutes. Can you imagine what it is like just as two pairs of lips on the screen are getting close enough to meet, to hear, "Mommy, my tummy hurts." If I go out to the movies, I leave my kids and their diapers in the care of my husband or mother.

Assignment 2: Writing a Paragraph

Using exaggeration and humor, Wine gives his impressions of people's looks and behavior at a movie theater. Write a paragraph describing your impressions of people's looks and behavior at a specific event or place. For instance, you might describe how people look and act at a rock concert, in an elevator, in a singles' hangout, or in a library. Like Wine, use colorful descriptions and quotations. Your topic sentence might be similar to the following:

> How people behave on an elevator reveals some key personal qualities.

Try listing ideas to develop your supporting details. For example, below is a list of possible supporting points for the topic sentence above.

> Shy people tend to avoid eye contact.
>
> Very friendly people smile and may say something.
>
> Helpful people will keep the elevator from leaving when they see someone rushing toward it.
>
> A romantic couple won't notice anyone else on the elevator.
>
> Impatient people may push the number of their floor more than once.

Assignment 3: Writing an Essay

Rudeness, unfortunately, is not limited to the movie theater. We have all observed rude behavior in various places we often go to. Write an essay on this topic. You might use one of the following thesis statements:

Rude behavior is all too common in several places I often go to.

A common part of life at my neighborhood supermarket is the rude behavior of other shoppers.

In an essay with the first central point, you could write about three places where you have seen rude behavior. Develop each paragraph with one or more vivid examples.

In an essay on the second central point, you would need to come up with two or three general types of rude behavior to write about. Below is one student's outline for an essay with that topic sentence.

<u>Central idea:</u> A common part of life at my neighborhood supermarket is the rude behavior of other shoppers.

(1) Getting in the way of other shoppers
    Blocking the aisle with a cart
    Knocking things down and not picking them up
    "Parking" in front of all the free samples

(2) Misplacing items
    Putting unwanted frozen food on a shelf instead of back in a freezer
    Putting unwanted meat on a shelf instead of in a refrigerated section

(3) Unreasonably making others wait at the checkout line
    Bringing a bulging cartload to the express line
    Keeping a line waiting while running to get "just one more thing" (instead of stepping out of line)
    Keeping a line waiting while deciding what not to buy to keep the total price down (instead of keeping track while shopping)

Copyright ©2006 The McGraw-Hill Companies, Inc. All rights reserved.

Bullies in School

Kathleen Berger

How serious a problem is bullying in schools? Is it a rite of passage, a normal part of childhood that every kid has to go through? Should adults intervene, or is the bully-victim relationship something children need to work out for themselves? And what influences create a bully or a victim? In this selection, Kathleen Berger reports on the work of a researcher who has come up with some surprising—even alarming—findings about bullies. Read it and see if the researcher's conclusions correspond with what you have observed or experienced.

Bullying was once commonly thought to be an unpleasant but normal part of   1
children's play, not to be encouraged, of course, but of little consequence in the
long run. However, developmental researchers who have looked closely at the
society of children consider bullying to be a very serious problem, one that harms
both the victim and the aggressor, sometimes continuing to cause suffering years
after the child has grown up.

One leading researcher in this area is Dan Olweus, who has studied bullying   2
in his native country of Norway and elsewhere for twenty-five years. The cruelty, pain, and suffering that he has documented in that time are typified by the
examples of Linda and Henry:

> Linda was systematically isolated by a small group of girls, who pressured
> the rest of the class, including Linda's only friend, to shun her. Then the
> ringleader of the group persuaded Linda to give a party, inviting everyone.
> Everyone accepted; following the ringleader's directions, no one came. Linda
> was devastated, her self-confidence "completely destroyed."
>
> Henry's experience was worse. Daily, his classmates called him "Worm,"
> broke his pencils, spilled his books on the floor, and mocked him whenever
> he answered a teacher's questions. Finally, a few boys took him to the bath-
> room and made him lie, face down, in the urinal drain. After school that day
> he tried to kill himself. His parents found him unconscious, and only then
> learned about his torment.

Following the suicides of three other victims of bullying, the Norwegian   3
government asked Olweus in 1983 to determine the extent and severity of the
problem. After concluding a confidential survey of nearly all of Norway's 90,000
school-age children, Olweus reported that the problem was widespread and serious;
that teachers and parents were "relatively unaware" of specific incidents of bullying; and that even when adults noticed bullying, they rarely intervened. Of all
the children Olweus surveyed, 9 percent were bullied "now and then"; 3 percent
were victims once a week or more; and 7 percent admitted that they themselves
sometimes deliberately hurt other children, verbally or physically.

As high as these numbers may seem, they are equaled and even exceeded in   4
research done in other countries. For instance, a British study of eight- to nine-year-
olds found that 17 percent were victims of regular bullying and that 13 percent
were bullies. A study of middle-class children in a university school in Florida found
that 10 percent were "extremely victimized." Recently, American researchers have
looked particularly at sexual harassment, an aspect of childhood bullying ignored
by most adults. Fully a third of nine- to fifteen-year-old girls say they have experienced sexual teasing and touching sufficiently troubling that they wanted to
avoid school, and, as puberty approaches, almost every boy who is perceived as
homosexual by his peers is bullied, sometimes mercilessly.

Researchers define bullying as repeated, systematic efforts to inflict harm on   5
a particular child through physical attack (such as hitting, punching, pinching, or

Copyright ©2006 The McGraw-Hill Companies, Inc. All rights reserved.

kicking), verbal attack (such as teasing, taunting, or name-calling), or social attack (such as deliberate social exclusion or public mocking). Implicit in this definition is the idea of an unbalance of power: victims of bullying are in some way weaker than their harassers and continue to be singled out for attack, in part because they have difficulty defending themselves. In many cases, this difficulty is compounded by the fact that the bullying is being carried out by a group of children. In Olweus's research, at least 60 percent of bullying incidents involved group attacks.

As indicated by the emphasis given to it, the key word in the preceding defini- 6 tion of bullying is "repeated." Most children experience isolated attacks or social slights from other children and come through them unscathed. But when a child must endure such shameful experiences again and again—being forced to hand over lunch money, or to drink milk mixed with detergent, or to lick someone's boots, or to be the butt of insults and practical jokes, with everyone watching and no one coming to the child's defense—the effects can be deep and long-lasting. Not only are bullied children anxious, depressed, and underachieving during the months and years of their torment, but even years later, they have lower self-esteem as well as painful memories.

The picture is somewhat different, but often more ominous, for bullies. Contrary 7 to the public perception that bullies are actually insecure and lonely, at the peak of their bullying they usually have friends who abet, fear, and admire them, and they seem brashly unapologetic about the pain they have inflicted, as they often claim, "all in fun." But their popularity and school success fade over the years, and especially if they are boys, they run a high risk of ending up in prison. In one longitudinal study done by Olweus, by age twenty-four, two-thirds of the boys who had been bullies in the second grade were convicted of at least one felony, and one-third of those who had been bullies in the sixth through the ninth grades were already convicted of three or more crimes, often violent ones. International research likewise finds that children who are allowed to regularly victimize other children are at high risk of becoming violent offenders as adolescents and adults.

Unfortunately, bullying during middle childhood seems to be universal: it occurs 8 in every nation that has been studied, is as much a problem in small rural schools as in large urban ones, and is as prevalent among well-to-do majority children as among poor immigrant children. Also quite common, if not universal, is the "profile" of bullies and their victims. Contrary to popular belief, victims are not distinguished by their external traits: they are no more likely to be fat, skinny, or homely, or to speak with an accent, than nonvictims are. But they usually are "rejected" children, that is, children who have few friends because they are more anxious and less secure than most children and are unable or unwilling to defend themselves. They also are more often boys than girls and more often younger children.

Bullies have traits in common as well, some of which can be traced to their 9 upbringing. The parents of bullies often seem indifferent to what their children do outside the home but use "power-assertive" discipline on them at home. These children are frequently subjected to physical punishment, verbal criticism, and displays of dominance meant to control and demean them, thereby giving them a vivid model, as well as a compelling reason, to control and demean others. Boys who are bullies are often above average in size, while girls who are bullies are often above average in verbal assertiveness. These differences are reflected in bullying tactics: boys typically use force or the threat of force; girls often mock or ridicule their victims, making fun of their clothes, behavior, or appearance, or revealing their most embarrassing secrets.

What can be done to halt these damaging attacks? Many psychologists have   10 attempted to alter the behavior patterns that characterize aggressive or rejected children. Cognitive interventions seem particularly fruitful: some programs teach social problem-solving skills (such as how to use humor or negotiation to reduce a conflict); others help children reassess their negative assumptions (such as the frequent, fatalistic view of many rejected children that nothing can protect them, or the aggressive child's typical readiness to conclude that accidental slights are deliberate threats); others tutor children in academic skills, hoping to improve confidence and short-circuit the low self-esteem that might be at the root of both victimization and aggression.

These approaches sometimes help individuals. However, because they target   11 one child at a time, they are piecemeal, time-consuming, and costly. Further, they have to work against habits learned at home and patterns reinforced at school, making it hard to change a child's behavior pattern. After all, bullies and their admirers have no reason to learn new social skills if their current attitudes and actions bring them status and pleasure. And even if rejected children change their behavior, they still face a difficult time recovering accepted positions in the peer group and gaining friends who will support and defend them. The solution to this problem must begin, then, by recognizing that the bullies and victims are not acting in isolation but, rather, are caught up in a mutually destructive interaction within a particular social context.

Accordingly, a more effective intervention is to change the social climate   12 within the school, so that bully-victim cycles no longer spiral out of control. That this approach can work was strikingly demonstrated by a government-funded awareness campaign that Olweus initiated for every school in Norway. In the first phase of the campaign, community-wide meetings were held to explain the problem; pamphlets were sent to all parents to alert them to the signs of victimization (such as a child's having bad dreams, having no real friends, and coming home from school with damaged clothes, torn books, or unexplained bruises); and videotapes were shown to all students to evoke sympathy for victims.

The second phase of the campaign involved specific actions within the schools.   13 In every classroom, students discussed reasons for and ways to mediate peer conflicts, to befriend lonely children, and to stop bullying attacks whenever they saw them occur. Teachers were taught to be proactive, organizing cooperative learning groups so that no single child could be isolated, halting each incident of name-calling or minor assault as soon as they noticed it, and learning how to see through the bully's excuses and to understand the victim's fear of reprisal. Principals were advised that adequate adult supervision during recess, lunch, and bathroom breaks distinguished schools where bullying was rare from those where bullying was common.

If bullying incidents occurred despite such measures, counselors were urged to intervene, talking privately and seriously with bullies and their victims, counseling their parents, and seeking solutions that might include intensive therapy with the bully's parents to restructure family discipline; reassigning the bully to a different class, grade, or even school; and helping the victim strengthen skills and foster friendships. 14

Twenty months after this campaign began, Olweus resurveyed the children in forty-two schools. He found that bullying had been reduced overall by more than 50 percent, with dramatic improvement for both boys and girls at every grade level. Developmental researchers are excited because results such as these, in which a relatively simple, cost-effective measure has such a decided impact on a developmental problem, are rare. Olweus concludes, "It is no longer possible to avoid taking action about bullying problems at school using lack of awareness as an excuse. . . . it all boils down to a matter of will and involvement on the part of the adults." Unfortunately, at the moment, Norway is the only country to have mounted a nationwide attack to prevent the problem of bullying. Many other school systems, in many other nations, have not even acknowledged the harm caused by this problem, much less shown the "will and involvement" to stop it. 15

■ Reading Comprehension Questions

1. The word *compounded* in ". . . victims of bullying . . . continue to be singled out for attack, in part because they have difficulty defending themselves. In many cases, this difficulty is compounded by the fact that the bullying is being carried out by a group of children" (paragraph 5) means

   a. reduced.

   b. increased.

   c. solved.

   d. forgiven.

2. The word *unscathed* in "Most children experience isolated attacks . . . from other children and come through them unscathed. But when a child must endure such shameful experiences again and again . . . the effects can be deep and long-lasting" (paragraph 6) means

   a. unharmed.

   b. unpleasant.

   c. unknown.

   d. uncertain.

Copyright ©2006 The McGraw-Hill Companies, Inc. All rights reserved.

3. Which of the following would be the best alternative title for the selection?

    a. Bullies: Why Do They Act That Way?

    b. The Pain of Being Bullied

    c. Bullies in Norway

    d. Bullying: A Problem Too Serious to Ignore

4. Which sentence best expresses the selection's main point?

    a. Certain types of children are inclined to become either bullies or victims.

    b. To combat the problem of bullying in Norway, a researcher designed an innovative program for all of its schools.

    c. Researchers consider bullying a very serious problem, one that harms both victims and bullies.

    d. Researchers have concluded that bullying is a very serious problem that can be solved only by changing the social climate in which it develops.

5. One thing many bullies have in common is that they

    a. are harshly punished at home.

    b. have few friends.

    c. are often apologetic after they've acted in a bullying way.

    d. are often from poor immigrant families.

6. *True or false?* _____ Victims of bullies tend to be physically unattractive.

7. Parents of a bully

    a. are usually anxious to stop their child's bullying behavior.

    b. were often victims of bullies themselves.

    c. often seem unconcerned about their child's behavior away from home.

    d. actively encourage their child to be a bully.

8. A study done by Dan Olweus of what happens in later years to boys who are bullies showed that

    a. a high proportion become teachers.

    b. a high percentage end up in prison.

    c. they have trouble finding and keeping jobs.

    d. their suicide rate is higher than average.

9. Boy and girl bullies

    a. differ: girls tend to mock their victims, while boys are more likely to use force.

    b. bully their victims in just about the same ways.

Copyright ©2006 The McGraw-Hill Companies, Inc. All rights reserved.

c. differ: girls tend to be bigger than average, while boys are more verbally assertive than average.

d. differ: girls tend to use force on their victims, while boys are more likely to mock them.

10. If a teacher witnessed an incident of bullying, we can infer that Olweus (the designer of the Norwegian program) would advise him or her to

a. ignore it, letting the students involved settle the matter themselves.

b. privately encourage the victim to fight back.

c. transfer the victim to another class.

d. immediately confront the bully.

Discussion Questions

About Content

1. Olweus describes two specific incidents of bullying, involving Linda and Henry. Did those incidents remind you of anything that ever occurred at your own school? Who were the bullies? Who were the victims? Describe the incident. What, if any, role did you play in such events?

2. What are some of the measures Olweus recommends be taken in a school and community to stop bullying? Do you think such measures would have been helpful in your school? If you are a parent, would you support such programs in your child's school?

3. Olweus concludes that bullying is a very serious problem, with effects that carry over for years into the lives of both bullies and victims. Do you agree? Or do you think Olweus is exaggerating the problem?

4. Olweus reports that, although bullying is a widespread and serious problem, most teachers and parents are "relatively unaware" that bullying is going on. How can this be? What is it about the dynamics of the relationship between bully and victim that can make it both a serious problem and one that is nearly invisible to adults?

About Structure

5. What combination of methods does Berger use to introduce this selection?

a. Broad to narrow; quotation

b. Anecdote; question

c. Beginning with opposite; anecdotes

d. Quotation; question

Is this introduction effective? Why or why not?

6. This selection can be divided be into five parts. Fill in the following blanks to show which paragraphs are included in each part:

(1) Berger's introduction of the topic: paragraph _____

(2) Two examples of bullying typical of the consequences Olweus reports on: paragraph _____

(3) Findings of Olweus's government-sponsored study and other research: paragraphs _____ to _____

(4) Ways to halt bullying: paragraphs _____ to _____

(5) Olweus's follow-up study and the author's brief conclusion: paragraph

_____

About Style and Tone

7. Find three places in the selection where statistics are cited. Why would a selection like this use so many statistics? What do statistics accomplish that anecdotes cannot?

8. The author's tone can be described as a combination of

a. horror and fear.

b. concern and objectivity.

c. bewilderment and pleading.

d. curiosity and excitement.

Find examples in the selection that illustrate this tone.

WRITING ASSIGNMENTS

Assignment 1: Writing a Paragraph

Write a paragraph describing a bully you have been acquainted with. Focus on three aspects of the person: his or her appearance, actions, and effects on others. Help your reader vividly imagine the bully by providing concrete details that illustrate each aspect. Your topic sentence might be similar to this:

In junior high school, I became familiar with a bully and the pain he caused one student.

Copyright ©2006 The McGraw-Hill Companies, Inc. All rights reserved.

Assignment 2: Writing a Paragraph

The social aspect of school is hard for many students, even if they are not victims of bullies. Write a paragraph about another reason or reasons that school was difficult for you or for people you observed. Was it the pressure to wear a certain kind of clothing? Be involved in sports? Use drugs and drink? Become sexually active? Hang out with a "cool" crowd? Provide details that help your reader understand how difficult pressures at school can be.

Assignment 3: Writing an Essay

Think of a time when you were on the giving end or the receiving end of an act of bullying. (The incident could fall into any of the categories mentioned in paragraph 5 of the reading—a physical, verbal, or social attack.) If you cannot think of an incident that involved you, think of one that you witnessed. Write an essay describing the incident. In your essay, be sure to cover the following points: How did the bully behave? How did the victim respond? And how did any onlookers react to what was going on? For an example of one author's clear, detailed narrative of such an incident, read Paul Logan's essay "Rowing the Bus" (page 598).

Assignment 4: Writing an Essay Using Internet Research

Victims of bullying often need help for two reasons. They have to stand up to the bullies who are tormenting them, and they also have to deal with negative feelings about themselves. Use the Internet to research methods recommended by experts for helping victims of bullying. Then write an essay that describes in detail three methods that can help victims cope with their own negative self image or with the bullies themselves.

   To access the Internet, use the very helpful search engine Google (*www.google. com*). Try one of the following phrases or some related phrase:

   coping with bullies

   victims of bullying

   bullies and coping and victims

You may, of course, use a single keyword such as "bullies," but that will bring up too many items. By using a phrase such as one of the above, you can begin to limit your search. As you proceed, you'll develop a sense of how to "track down" and focus a topic by adding more information to your search words and phrases.

A Drunken Ride, a Tragic Aftermath

Theresa Conroy and Christine M. Johnson

Have you ever sat behind the wheel of your car after drinking? Have you ever assured yourself, "I haven't had too much. I'm still in control"? If you have, you're not alone. The large number of arrests for drunk driving proves that plenty of drivers who have been drinking thought they were capable of getting home safely. After all, who would get into a car with the intention of killing himself or herself or others? Yet killing is exactly what many drunk drivers do. If all drivers could read the following selection—a newspaper report on one tragic accident—perhaps the frequent cautions about drinking and driving would have some impact. Read the article and see if you agree.

When Tyson Baxter awoke after that drunken, tragic night—with a bloodied head, broken arm, and battered face—he knew that he had killed his friends.   1

"I knew everyone had died," Baxter, eighteen, recalled. "I knew it before anybody told me. Somehow, I knew."   2

Baxter was talking about the night of Friday, September 13, the night he and seven friends piled into his Chevrolet Blazer after a beer-drinking party. On Street Road in Upper Southampton, he lost control, rear-ended a car, and smashed into two telephone poles. The Blazer's cab top shattered, and the truck spun several times, ejecting all but one passenger.   3

Four young men were killed.   4

Tests would show that Baxter and the four youths who died were legally intoxicated.   5

Baxter says he thinks about his dead friends on many sleepless nights at the Abraxas Drug and Alcohol Rehabilitation Center near Pittsburgh, where, on December 20, he was sentenced to be held after being found delinquent on charges of vehicular homicide.   6

"I drove them where they wanted to go, and I was responsible for their lives," Baxter said recently from the center, where he is undergoing psychological treatment. "I had the keys in my hand, and I blew it."   7

The story of September 13 is a story about the kind of horrors that drinking and driving is spawning among high school students almost everywhere, . . . about parents who lost their children in a flash and have filled the emptiness with hatred, . . . about a youth whose life is burdened with grief and guilt because he happened to be behind the wheel.   8

Copyright ©2006 The McGraw-Hill Companies, Inc. All rights reserved.

It is a story that the Baxter family and the dead boys' parents agreed to tell 9
in the hope that it would inspire high school students to remain sober during this
week of graduation festivities—a week that customarily includes a ritual night of
drunkenness.

It is a story of the times. 10

The evening of September 13 began in high spirits as Baxter, behind the wheel of 11
his gold Blazer, picked up seven high school chums for a drinking party for William
Tennent High School students and graduates at the home of a classmate. Using
false identification, according to police, the boys purchased one six-pack of beer
each from a Warminster Township bar.

The unchaperoned party, attended by about fifty teenagers, ended about 12
10:30 P.M. when someone knocked over and broke a glass china cabinet. Baxter
and his friends decided to head for a fast-food restaurant. As Baxter turned onto
Street Road, he was trailed by a line of cars carrying other partygoers.

Baxter recalled that several passengers were swaying and rocking the high- 13
suspension vehicle. Police were unable to determine the vehicle's exact speed, but,
on the basis of the accounts of witnesses, they estimated it at fifty-five miles per
hour—ten miles per hour over the limit.

"I thought I was in control," Baxter said. "I wasn't driving like a nut; I was 14
just . . . driving. There was a bunch of noise. Just a bunch of noise. The truck was
really bouncing.

"I remember passing two [cars]. That's the last I remember. I remember a big 15
flash, and that's it."

Killed in that flash were: Morris "Marty" Freedenberg, sixteen, who landed 16
near a telephone pole about thirty feet from the truck, his face ripped from his
skull; Robert Schweiss, eighteen, a Bucks County Community College student,
whose internal organs were crushed when he hit the pavement about thirty feet
from the truck; Brian Ball, seventeen, who landed near Schweiss, his six-foot-seven-
inch frame stretched three inches when his spine was severed; and Christopher
Avram, seventeen, a premedical student at Temple University, who landed near
the curb about ten feet from the truck.

Michael Serratore, eighteen, was thrown fifteen feet from the truck and 17
landed on the lawn of the CHI Institute with his right leg shattered. Baxter, who
sailed about ten feet after crashing through the windshield of the Blazer, lost
consciousness after hitting the street near the center lane. About five yards away,
Paul Gee Jr., eighteen, lapsed into a coma from severe head injuries.

John Gahan, seventeen, the only passenger left in the Blazer, suffered a broken 18
ankle.

Brett Walker, seventeen, one of several Tennent students who saw the car- 19
nage after the accident, would recall later in a speech to fellow students: "I ran
over [to the scene]. These were the kids I would go out with every weekend.

"My one friend [Freedenberg], I couldn't even tell it was him except for his 20
eyes. He had real big, blue eyes. He was torn apart so bad . . . ."

Francis Schweiss was waiting up for his son, Robert, when he received a telephone   21
call from his daughter, Lisa. She was already at Warminster General Hospital.

"She said Robbie and his friends were in a bad accident and Robbie was not   22
here" at the hospital, Schweiss said. "I got in my car with my wife; we went to the
scene of the accident."

There, police officers told Francis and Frances Schweiss that several boys had   23
been killed and that the bodies, as well as survivors, had been taken to Warminster
General Hospital.

"My head was frying by then," Francis Schweiss said. "I can't even describe   24
it. I almost knew the worst was to be. I felt as though I were living a nightmare. I
thought, 'I'll wake up. This just can't be.'"

In the emergency room, Francis Schweiss recalled, nurses and doctors were scram-   25
bling to aid the injured and identify the dead—a difficult task because some bodies
were disfigured and because all the boys had been carrying fake drivers' licenses.

A police officer from Upper Southampton was trying to question friends   26
of the dead and injured—many of whom were sobbing and screaming—in an
attempt to match clothing with identities.

When the phone rang in the Freedenberg home, Robert Sr. and his wife, Bobbi,   27
had just gone upstairs to bed; their son Robert Jr. was downstairs watching a
movie on television.

Bobbi Freedenberg and her son picked up the receiver at the same time. It   28
was from Warminster General. . . . There had been a bad accident. . . . The family
should get to the hospital quickly.

Outside the morgue about twenty minutes later, a deputy county coroner   29
told Rob Jr., twenty-two, that his brother was dead and severely disfigured; Rob
decided to spare his parents additional grief by identifying the body himself.

Freedenberg was led into a cinder-block room containing large drawers   30
resembling filing cabinets. In one of the drawers was his brother, Marty, identifi-
able only by his new high-top sneakers.

"It was kind of like being taken through a nightmare," Rob Jr. said. "That's   31
something I think about every night before I go to sleep. That's hell. . . .That whole
night is what hell is all about for me."

As was his custom, Morris Ball started calling the parents of his son's friends after   32
Brian missed his 11:00 P.M. curfew.

The first call was to the Baxters' house, where the Baxters' sixteen-year-old   33
daughter, Amber, told him about the accident.

At the hospital, Morris Ball demanded that doctors and nurses take him to his   34
son. The hospital staff had been unable to identify Brian—until Ball told them that
his son wore size fourteen shoes.

Brian Ball was in the morgue. Lower left drawer.   35

"He was six foot seven, but after the accident he measured six foot ten,   36
because of what happened to him," Ball said. "He had a severed spinal cord at

the neck. His buttocks were practically ripped off, but he was lying down and we couldn't see that. He was peaceful and asleep.

"He was my son and my baby. I just can't believe it sometimes. I still can't 37 believe it. I still wait for him to come home."

Lynne Pancoast had just finished watching the 11:00 P.M. news and was curled up 38 in her bed dozing with a book in her lap when the doorbell rang. She assumed that one of her sons had forgotten his key, and she went downstairs to let him in.

A police light was flashing through the window and reflecting against her 39 living room wall; Pancoast thought that there must be a fire in the neighborhood and that the police were evacuating homes.

Instead, police officers told her there had been a serious accident involving 40 her son, Christopher Avram, and that she should go to the emergency room at Warminster General.

At the hospital she was taken to an empty room and told that her son was 41 dead.

Patricia Baxter was asleep when a Warminster police officer came to the house 42 and informed her that her son had been in an accident.

At the hospital, she could not immediately recognize her own son lying on a 43 bed in the emergency room. His brown eyes were swollen shut, and his straight brown hair was matted with blood that had poured from a deep gash in his forehead.

While she was staring at his battered face, a police officer rushed into the 44 room and pushed her onto the floor—protection against the hysterical father of a dead youth who was racing through the halls, proclaiming that he had a gun and shouting, "Where is she? I'm going to kill her. I'm going to kill him. I'm going to kill his mother."

The man, who did not have a gun, was subdued by a Warminster police offi- 45 cer and was not charged.

Amid the commotion, Robert Baxter, a Lower Southampton highway patrol 46 officer, arrived at the hospital and found his wife and son.

"When he came into the room, he kept going like this," Patricia Baxter said, 47 holding up four fingers. At first, she said, she did not understand that her husband was signaling that four boys had been killed in the accident.

After Tyson regained consciousness, his father told him about the deaths. 48

"All I can remember is just tensing up and just saying something," Tyson Bax- 49 ter said. "I can remember saying, 'I know.'

"I can remember going nuts." 50

In the days after the accident, as the dead were buried in services that Tyson Baxter 51 was barred by the parents of the victims from attending, Baxter's parents waited for him to react to the tragedy and release his grief.

"In the hospital he was nonresponsive," Patricia Baxter said. "He was home 52 for a month, and he was nonresponsive.

Copyright ©2006 The McGraw-Hill Companies, Inc. All rights reserved.

"We never used to do this, but we would be upstairs and listen to see if Ty responded when his friends came to visit," she said. "But the boy would be silent. That's the grief that I felt. The other kids showed a reaction. My son didn't." 53

Baxter said, however, that he felt grief from the first, that he would cry in the quiet darkness of his hospital room and, later, alone in the darkness of his bedroom. During the day, he said, he blocked his emotions. 54

"It was *just* at night. I thought about it all the time. It's still like that." 55

At his parents' urging, Baxter returned to school on September 30. 56

"I don't remember a thing," he said of his return. "I just remember walking around. I didn't say anything to anybody. It didn't really sink in." 57

Lynne Pancoast, the mother of Chris Avram, thought it was wrong for Baxter to be in school, and wrong that her other son, Joel, a junior at William Tennent, had to walk through the school halls and pass the boy who "killed his brother." 58

Morris Ball said he was appalled that Baxter "went to a football game while my son lay buried in a grave." 59

Some William Tennent students said they were uncertain about how they should treat Baxter. Several said they went out of their way to treat him normally, others said they tried to avoid him, and others declined to be interviewed on the subject. 60

The tragedy unified the senior class, according to the school principal, Kenneth Kastle. He said that after the accident, many students who were friends of the victims joined the school's Students Against Driving Drunk chapter. 61

Matthew Weintraub, seventeen, a basketball player who witnessed the bloody accident scene, wrote to President Reagan and detailed the grief among the student body. He said, however, that he experienced a catharsis after reading the letter at a student assembly and, as a result, did not mail it. 62

"And after we got over the initial shock of the news, we felt as though we owed somebody something," Weintraub wrote. "It could have been us and maybe we could have stopped it, and now it's too late. . . . 63

"We took these impressions with us as we then visited our friends who had been lucky enough to live. One of them was responsible for the accident; he was the driver. He would forever hold the deaths of four young men on his conscience. Compared with our own feelings of guilt, [we] could not begin to fathom this boy's emotions. He looked as if he had a heavy weight upon his head and it would remain there forever." 64

About three weeks after the accident, Senator H. Craig Lewis (D., Bucks) launched a series of public forums to formulate bills targeting underage drinking. Proposals developed through the meetings include outlawing alcohol ads on radio and television, requiring police to notify parents of underage drinkers, and creating a tamperproof driver's license. 65

The parents of players on William Tennent's 1985–1986 boys' basketball team, which lost Ball and Baxter because of the accident, formed the Caring Parents of William Tennent High School Students to help dissuade students from drinking. 66

Several William Tennent students, interviewed on the condition that their names not be published, said that, because of the accident, they would not drive 67

Copyright ©2006 The McGraw-Hill Companies, Inc. All rights reserved.

after drinking during senior week, which will be held in Wildwood, N.J., after graduation June 13.

But they scoffed at the suggestion that they curtail their drinking during the celebrations. 68

"We just walk [after driving to Wildwood]," said one youth. "Stagger is more like it." 69

"What else are we going to do, go out roller skating?" an eighteen-year-old student asked. 70

"You telling us we're not going to drink?" one boy asked. "We're going to drink very heavily. I want to come home retarded. That's senior week. I'm going to drink every day. Everybody's going to drink every day." 71

Tyson Baxter sat at the front table of the Bucks County courtroom on December 20, his arm in a sling, his head lowered, and his eyes dry. He faced twenty counts of vehicular homicide, four counts of involuntary manslaughter, and two counts of driving under the influence of alcohol. 72

Patricia Ball said she told the closed hearing that "it was Tyson Baxter who killed our son. They used the car as a weapon. We know they killed our children as if it were a gun. They killed our son. 73

"I really could have felt justice [was served] if Tyson Baxter was the only one who died in that car," she said in an interview, "because he didn't take care of our boys." 74

Police officers testified before Bucks County President Judge Isaac S. Garb that tests revealed that the blood-alcohol levels of Baxter and the four dead boys were above the 0.10 percent limit used in Pennsylvania to establish intoxication. 75

Baxter's blood-alcohol level was 0.14 percent, Ball's 0.19 percent, Schweiss's 0.11 percent, Avram's 0.12 percent, and Freedenberg's 0.38 percent. Baxter's level indicated that he had had eight or nine drinks—enough to cause abnormal bodily functions such as exaggerated gestures and to impair his mental faculties, according to the police report. 76

After the case was presented, Garb invited family members of the dead teens to speak. 77

In a nine-page statement, Bobbi Freedenberg urged Garb to render a decision that would "punish, rehabilitate, and deter others from this act." 78

The parents asked Garb to give Baxter the maximum sentence, to prohibit him from graduating, and to incarcerate him before Christmas Day. (Although he will not attend formal ceremonies, Baxter will receive a diploma from William Tennent this week.) 79

After hearing from the parents, Garb called Baxter to the stand. 80

"I just said that all I could say was, 'I'm sorry; I know I'm totally responsible for what happened,'" Baxter recalled. "It wasn't long, but it was to the point." 81

Garb found Baxter delinquent and sentenced him to a stay at Abraxas Rehabilitation Center—for an unspecified period beginning December 23—and community service upon his return. Baxter's driver's license was suspended by the judge for an unspecified period, and he was placed under Garb's jurisdiction until age twenty-one. 82

Baxter is one of fifty-two Pennsylvania youths found responsible for fatal 83
drunken-driving accidents in the state in 1985.

Reflecting on the hearing, Morris Ball said there was no legal punishment 84
that would have satisfied his longings.

"They can't bring my son back," he said, "and they can't kill Tyson Baxter." 85

Grief has forged friendships among the dead boys' parents, all of whom blame 86
Tyson Baxter for their sons' deaths. Every month they meet at each other's homes,
but they seldom talk about the accident.

Several have joined support groups to help them deal with their losses. Some 87
said they feel comfortable only with other parents whose children are dead.

Bobbi Freedenberg said her attitude had worsened with the passage of time. 88
"It seems as if it just gets harder," she said. "It seems to get worse."

Freedenberg, Schweiss, and Pancoast said they talk publicly about their sons' 89
deaths in hopes that the experience will help deter other teenagers from drunken
driving.

Schweiss speaks each month to the Warminster Youth Aid Panel—a group 90
of teenagers who, through drug use, alcohol abuse, or minor offenses, have run
afoul of the law.

"When I talk to the teens, I bring a picture of Robbie and pass it along to 91
everyone," Schweiss said, wiping the tears from his cheeks. "I say, 'He was with us
last year.' I get emotional and I cry. . . .

"But I know that my son helps me. I firmly believe that every time I speak, he's 92
right on my shoulder."

When Pancoast speaks to a group of area high school students, she drapes her 93
son's football jersey over the podium and displays his graduation picture.

"Every time I speak to a group, I make them go through the whole thing 94
vicariously," Pancoast said. "It's helpful to get out and talk to kids. It sort of helps
keep Chris alive. . . . When you talk, you don't think."

At Abraxas, Baxter attended high school classes until Friday. He is one of three youths 95
there who supervise fellow residents, who keep track of residents' whereabouts, attendance at programs, and adherence to the center's rules and regulations.

Established in Pittsburgh in 1973, the Abraxas Foundation provides an alter- 96
native to imprisonment for offenders between sixteen and twenty-five years old
whose drug and alcohol use has led them to commit crimes.

Licensed and partially subsidized by the Pennsylvania Department of Health, 97
the program includes work experience, high school education, and prevocational
training. Counselors conduct individual therapy sessions, and the residents engage
in peer-group confrontational therapy sessions.

Baxter said his personality had changed from an "egotistical, arrogant" teen- 98
ager to someone who is "mellow" and mature.

"I don't have quite the chip on my shoulder. I don't really have a right to be 99
cocky anymore," he said.

Baxter said not a day went by that he didn't remember his dead friends.   100

"I don't get sad. I just get thinking about them," he said. "Pictures pop into   101
my mind. A tree or something reminds me of the time. . . . Sometimes I laugh. . . .
Then I go to my room and reevaluate it like a nut," he said.

Baxter said his deepest longing was to stand beside the graves of his four friends.   102

More than anything, Baxter said, he wants to say good-bye.   103

"I just feel it's something I *have* to do, . . . just to talk," Baxter said, averting   104
his eyes to hide welling tears. "Deep down I think I'll be hit with it when I see the
graves. I know they're gone, but they're not gone."

▪ Reading Comprehension Questions

1. The word *fathom* in "Compared with our own feelings of guilt, [we] could not
   begin to fathom this boy's emotions" (paragraph 64) means

   a. choose.

   b. understand.

   c. mistake.

   d. protest.

2. The word *dissuade* in "The parents . . . formed the Caring Parents of William
   Tennent High School Students to help dissuade students from drinking"
   (paragraph 66) means

   a. discourage.

   b. delay.

   c. organize.

   d. frighten.

3. Which of the following would be the best alternative title for this selection?

   a. The Night of September 13

   b. A Fatal Mistake: Teenage Drinking and Driving

   c. The Agony of Parents

   d. High School Drinking Problems

4. Which sentence best expresses the main idea of the selection?

   a. Teenagers must understand the dangers and consequences of drinking and
      driving.

   b. Tyson Baxter was too drunk to drive that night.

   c. The Abraxas Foundation is a model alternative program to imprisonment
      for teenagers.

   d. Teenagers are drinking more than ever before.

Copyright ©2006 The McGraw-Hill Companies, Inc. All rights reserved.

5. The hospital had trouble identifying the boys because

    a. officials could not find their families.

    b. the boys all had false licenses and some of their bodies were mutilated.

    c. there weren't enough staff members on duty at the hospital that night.

    d. everyone was withholding information.

6. Tyson Baxter feels that

    a. the judge's sentence was unfair.

    b. he will never graduate from high school.

    c. he is responsible for the whole accident.

    d. he should not be blamed for the accident.

7. *True or false?* _____ Because of the accident, all the seniors promised that they would not drink during senior week.

8. The authors imply that the parents of the dead boys felt that

    a. Tyson should not be punished.

    b. their boys shared no blame for the accident.

    c. Tyson should have come to the boys' funerals.

    d. Tyson should be allowed to attend graduation.

9. The authors imply that most of the parents' anger has been toward

    a. school officials.

    b. Senator H. Craig Lewis.

    c. their local police.

    d. Tyson Baxter.

10. The authors imply that Tyson

    a. behaved normally after the accident.

    b. will always have a problem with alcohol.

    c. no longer thinks about his dead friends.

    d. is benefiting from his time at Abraxas.

■ Discussion Questions

About Content

1. Why do the authors call their narrative "a story of the times"?

2. Exactly why did four teenagers die in the accident? To what extent were their deaths the driver's fault? Their own fault? Society's fault?

3. What effect has the accident had on other Tennent students? In view of the tragedy, can you explain the reluctance of the Tennent students to give up drinking during "senior week"?

4. How would you describe the attitude of Tyson Baxter after the accident? How would you characterize the attitude of the parents? Whose attitude, if any, seems more appropriate under the circumstances?

About Structure

5. The lead paragraphs in a newspaper article such as this one are supposed to answer questions known as the *five W's:* who, what, where, when, and why.

   Which paragraphs in the article answer these questions? _____

6. The authors *do not* use transitional words to move from one section of their article to the next. How, then, do they manage to keep their narrative organized and clear?

About Style and Tone

7. Why do the authors use so many direct quotations in their account of the accident? How do these quotations add to the effectiveness of the article?

8. What seems to be the authors' attitude toward Tyson Baxter at the end of the piece? Why do you think they end with Tyson's desire to visit his dead friends' graves? What would have been the effect of ending with Lynne Pancoast's words in paragraph 94?

WRITING ASSIGNMENTS

Assignment 1: Writing a Paragraph

While drunk drivers are of all ages, a large percentage of them are young. Write a paragraph explaining what you think would be one or more *effective* ways of dramatizing to young people the dangers of drunk driving. Keep in mind that the young are being cautioned all the time, and that some of the warnings are so familiar that they probably don't have any impact.

What kind of caution or cautions would make young people take notice? Develop one approach in great detail or suggest several approaches for demonstrating the dangers of drunk driving to the young.

Assignment 2: Writing a Paragraph

Tyson Baxter's friends might still be alive if he had not been drunk when he drove. But there is another way their deaths could have been avoided—they might have refused to get into the car. Such a refusal would not have been easy; one does not,

Copyright ©2006 The McGraw-Hill Companies, Inc. All rights reserved.

after all, want to embarrass a person who has given you a ride to some event. At the same time, it may be absolutely necessary to make such a refusal. Write a paragraph suggesting one or more ways to turn down a ride from a driver who may be drunk.

Assignment 3: Writing an Essay

A number of letters to the editor followed the appearance of "A Drunken Ride, a Tragic Aftermath." Here are some of them:

To the Editor:

I am deeply concerned by the June 8 article, "A Drunken Ride, a Tragic Aftermath," not because of the tragedy it unfolds, but because of the tragedy that is occurring as a result.

It is an injustice on the part of the parents whose children died to blame Tyson Baxter so vehemently for those deaths. (I lost my best friend in a similar accident eight years ago, and I haven't forgotten the pain or the need to blame.) All the youths were legally intoxicated. None of them refused to go with Mr. Baxter, and I submit that he did not force them to ride with him.

Yes, Mr. Baxter is guilty of drunk driving, but I would like the other parents to replace Mr. Baxter with their sons and their cars and ask themselves again where the blame lies.

Tyson Baxter did not have the intent to kill, and his car was not the weapon. All these boys were Mr. Baxter's friends. The weapon used to kill them was alcohol, and in a way each boy used it on himself.

If we are to assign blame, it goes far beyond one drunk eighteen-year-old.

The answer lies in our society and its laws—laws about drinking and driving, and laws of parenting, friendship, and responsibility. Why, for instance, didn't the other youths call someone to come get them, or call a taxi, rather than choose to take that fatal ride?

These parents should be angry and they should fight against drunk driving by making people aware. But they shouldn't continue to destroy the life of one boy whose punishment is the fact that he survived.

Elizabeth Bowen
Philadelphia

To the Editor:

I could not believe the attitude of the parents of the boys who were killed in the accident described in the June 8 article "A Drunken Ride, a Tragic Aftermath." Would they really feel that justice was done if Tyson Baxter were dead, too?

Copyright ©2006 The McGraw-Hill Companies, Inc. All rights reserved.

Tyson Baxter is not the only guilty person. All the boys who got into the vehicle were guilty, as well as all the kids at the party who let them go. Did any of the parents question their children earlier that fateful night as to who would be the "designated driver" (or did they think their sons would never go out drinking)?

How would those parents feel if their son happened to be the one behind the wheel?

I do not want to lessen the fact that Tyson Baxter was guilty (a guilt he readily admits to and will carry with him for a lifetime). However, should he have to carry his own guilt and be burdened with everyone else's guilt as well?

Andrea D. Colantti
Philadelphia

To the Editor:

Reading the June 8 article about the tragic aftermath of the drunken-driving accident in which high school students were killed and injured, I was aware of a major missing element. That element is the role of individual responsibility.

While we cannot control everything that happens to us, we can still manage many of the events of our lives. Individual responsibility operates at two levels. First is the accountability each person has for his own actions. To drink, or not to drink. To drink to excess, or to remain sober. To ride with someone who has been drinking, or to find another ride.

Second is the responsibility to confront those who are drinking or using drugs and planning to drive. To talk to them about their alcohol or drug consumption, to take their keys, call a cab, or do whatever else a friend would do.

The toughest, most punitive laws will not prevent people from drinking and driving, nor will they rectify the results of an accident. The only things we can actually control are our personal choices and our responses.

Don't drink and drive. Don't ride with those that do. Use your resources to stop those who try.

Gregory A. Gast
Willow Grove

To the Editor:

After reading the June 8 article about the tragic accident involving the students from William Tennent High School, my heart goes out to the parents of the boys who lost their lives. I know I can't begin to understand the loss they feel. However, even more so, my heart goes out to them for their inability to forgive the driver and their ability to wish him dead.

I certainly am not condoning drunk driving; in fact, I feel the law should be tougher.

But how can they be so quick to judge and hate this boy, when all their sons were also legally drunk, some more so than the driver, and any one of them could have easily been the driver himself? They all got into the car knowingly drunk and were noisily rocking the vehicle. They were all teenagers, out for a night of fun, never thinking of the consequences of drunk driving.

I would view this differently had the four dead boys been in another car, sober, and hit by a drunk driver. However, when you knowingly enter a car driven by someone who is drunk and are drunk yourself, you are responsible for what happens to you.

Tyson Baxter, the driver, needs rehabilitation and counseling. He will live with this for the rest of his life. The parents of the four boys who died need to learn about God, who is forgiving, and apply that forgiveness to a boy who desperately needs it. He could have easily been one of their sons.

Debbie Jones
Wilmington

To the Editor:

The June 8 article "A Drunken Ride, a Tragic Aftermath" missed an important point. The multiple tragedy was a double—a perhaps needless—tragedy because the young men were not belted into their seats when the Blazer crashed.

All of those who were killed and severely injured had been thrown out of the vehicle; the only one left inside suffered a broken ankle. Had all been properly belted, all or most would probably have survived with similar minor injuries.

As much as this article points up the dangers of drunken driving, it also points up the absolute need for a mandatory seat-belt law strictly enforced. Two other points reinforce this. With eight people, the Blazer was overloaded by a factor of two. Also, Tyson Baxter, the driver, stated that his passengers were bouncing about and making the vehicle rock, a dangerous situation even when the driver is stone cold sober; being belted in puts a real damper on this sort of thing.

Roy West
Philadelphia

Copyright ©2006 The McGraw-Hill Companies, Inc. All rights reserved.

These letters make apparent a difference of opinion about how severely Tyson Baxter should be punished. Write an essay in which, in an introductory paragraph, you advance your judgment about the appropriate punishment for Tyson Baxter. Then provide three supporting paragraphs in which you argue and defend your opinion. You may use or add to ideas stated in the article or the letters, but think through the ideas yourself and put them into your own words.

Assignment 4: Writing an Essay Using Internet Research

The tragic deaths of Tyson Baxter's four friends highlight the problem of drinking and driving. What can be done to get drunken drivers off the road? Use the Internet to research the topic. Then write an essay that explains three ways to get intoxicated drivers off the road. These could include ways to prevent people from drinking and driving in the first place, or ways to keep a person convicted of drunken driving from doing it again.

To access the Internet, use the very helpful search engine Google (*www.google.com*). Try one of the following phrases or some related phrase:

keeping drunk drivers off the road

drunk drivers and prevention

successful prevention programs for drunk driving

As you proceed, you'll develop a sense of how to "track down" and focus a topic by adding more information to your search words and phrases

Answers and Charts

Copyright ©2006 The McGraw-Hill Companies, Inc. All rights reserved.

PREVIEW

This Appendix provides answers for the Sentence-Skills Diagnostic Test on pages 355–360 and for the Introductory Projects in Part Five. It also contains four useful charts: an assignment chart, a spelling list, and a reading comprehension chart, to be filled in by the student, and a general form for planning a paragraph.

Answers to Sentence-Skills Diagnostic Test and Introductory Projects

Sentence-Skills Diagnostic Test (pages 355–360)

Fragments

1. X
2. C
3. X
4. X
5. C
6. X

Run-Ons

7. C
8. X
9. X
10. X
11. C
12. X

Standard English Verbs

13. C
14. C
15. X
16. X

Irregular Verbs

17. X
18. C
19. C
20. X

Subject-Verb Agreement

21. X
22. X
23. C
24. X

Consistent Verb Tense

25. X
26. C
27. C
28. X

Pronoun Agreement, Reference, and Point of View

29. X
30. C
31. X
32. C
33. X
34. C

Pronoun Types

35. X
36. C

Adjectives and Adverbs

37. X
38. X

Misplaced Modifiers

39. X
40. C
41. X
42. X

Dangling Modifiers

43. C
44. X
45. C
46. X

Faulty Parallelism

47. X
48. C
49. X
50. C

Capital Letters

51. X
52. X
53. C
54. X

Apostrophe

55. C
56. X
57. X
58. C

Quotation Marks

59. C
60. X
61. X
62. C

Comma

63. X
64. X
65. C
66. X
67. C
68. X

Commonly Confused Words

69. X
70. X
71. C
72. X
73. X
74. C

Effective Word Use

75. X
76. X
77. X
78. X

Copyright ©2006 The McGraw-Hill Companies, Inc. All rights reserved.

Introductory Projects

Fragments *(page 369)*

1. thought
2. subject
3. verb
4. subject

Run-Ons *(page 386)*

1. period
2. *but*
3. semicolon
4. *When*

Standard English Verbs *(page 402)*

enjoyed . . . enjoys; started . . . starts;
cooked . . . cooks
1. past . . . *-ed*
2. present . . . *-s*

Irregular Verbs *(page 412)*

1. crawled, crawled (regular)
2. brought, brought (irregular)
3. used, used (regular)
4. did, done (irregular)
5. gave, given (irregular)
6. laughed, laughed (regular)
7. went, gone (irregular)
8. scared, scared (regular)
9. dressed, dressed (regular)
10. saw, seen (irregular)

Subject-Verb Agreement *(page 420)*

The second sentence in each pair is correct.

Pronoun Agreement and Reference *(page 427)*

The second sentence in each pair is correct.

Misplaced Modifiers *(page 445)*

1. Intended: A young man with references is wanted to open oysters.
   Unintended: The oysters have references.
2. Intended: On their wedding day, Clyde and Charlotte decided to have two children.
   Unintended: Clyde and Charlotte decided to have two children who would appear on their wedding day.
3. Intended: The students who failed the test no longer like the math instructor.
   Unintended: The math instructor failed the test.

Dangling Modifiers *(page 449)*

1. Intended: My dog sat with me as I smoked a pipe.
   Unintended: My dog smoked a pipe.
2. Intended: He was busy talking on a cell phone.
   Unintended: His car was talking on a cell phone.
3. Intended: A beef pie baked in the oven for several hours.
   Unintended: Grandmother baked in the oven.

Capital Letters *(page 459)*

All the answers to questions 1 to 13 should be in capital letters.
14. The   15. I   16. That

Copyright ©2006 The McGraw-Hill Companies, Inc. All rights reserved.

Apostrophe (page 472)

1. The purpose of the *'s* is to show possession (Larry owns the motorcycle, the boyfriend belongs to the sister, Grandmother owns the shotgun, the room belongs to the men).
2. The purpose of the apostrophe is to show the omission of one or more letters in a contraction—two words shortened to form one word.
3. In each of the second sentences, the *'s* shows possession: the body of the vampire; the center of the baked potato. In each of the first sentences, the *s* is used to form a simple plural: more than one vampire; more than one potato.

Quotation Marks (page 481)

1. The purpose of quotation marks is to set off the exact words of a speaker. (The words that the young man actually spoke aloud are set off with quotation marks, as are the words that the old woman spoke aloud.)
2. Commas and periods go inside quotation marks.

Comma (page 489)

1. a. Frank's interests are Maria, television, and sports.
   b. My mother put her feet up, sipped some iced tea, and opened the newspaper.
2. a. Although they are tiny insects, ants are among the strongest creatures on Earth.
   b. To remove the cap of the aspirin bottle, you must first press down on it.
3. a. Kitty Litter and Dredge Rivers, Hollywood's leading romantic stars, have made several movies together.
   b. Sarah, who is my next-door neighbor, just entered the hospital with an intestinal infection.
4. a. The wedding was scheduled for four o'clock, but the bride changed her mind at two.
   b. Verna took three coffee breaks before lunch, and then she went on a two-hour lunch break.
5. a. Lola's mother asked her, "What time do you expect to get home?"
   b. "Don't bend over to pat the dog," I warned, "or he'll bite you."
6. a. Roy ate seventeen hamburgers on July 29, 2003, and lived to tell about it.
   b. Roy lives at 817 Cresson Street, Detroit, Michigan.

Other Punctuation Marks (page 499)

1. pets: holly
2. freeze-dried
3. Shakespeare (1564–1616)
4. Earth; no
5. proudly—with

Commonly Confused Words (page 525)

1. Your   4. to
2. There   5. It's
3. then

Effective Word Choice (page 536)

1. "Flipped out" is slang.
2. "Few and far between" is a cliché.
3. "Ascertained" is a pretentious word.

Charts

Assignment Chart

Use this chart to record daily or weekly assignments in your writing class. You might want to print writing assignments and their due dates in capital letters so that they stand out clearly.

Date Given	Assignment	Date Due

Spelling List

Enter here the words that you misspelled in your papers (note the examples). If you add to and study this list regularly, you will not repeat the same mistakes in your writing.

Incorrect Spelling	Correct Spelling	Points to Remember
alright	all right	two words
ocasion	occasion	two "c"s

Copyright ©2006 The McGraw-Hill Companies, Inc. All rights reserved.

Reading Comprehension Chart

Write an X through the numbers of any questions you missed while answering the comprehension questions for each selection in Part Six, Seventeen Reading Selections. Then write in your comprehension score. To calculate your score for each reading, give yourself 10 points for each item that is *not* X'd out. The chart will make clear any skill question you get wrong repeatedly, so that you can pay special attention to that skill in the future.

Selection	Vocabulary in Context	Subject, Thesis, or Main Idea	Key Details	Inferences	Comprehension Score
Mrosla	1 2	3 4	5 6 7	8 9 10	%
Logan	1 2	3 4	5 6 7	8 9 10	%
Salinas	1 2	3 4 5	6	7 8 9 10	%
Johnson	1	2 3 4	5 6 7 8	9 10	%
Rooney	1 2	3 4	5 6 7	8 9 10	%
Curran	1 2	3 4	5 6 7	8 9 10	%
Carson	1 2	3 4	5 6 7	8 9 10	%
Collier	1 2	3 4	5 6 7 8	9 10	%
Barrett	1 2	3 4	5 6 7	8 9 10	%
Garland	1 2	3 4	5 6 7	8 9 10	%
Scott	1 2	3 4	5 6 7	8 9 10	%
Verderber	1 2	3 4	5 6 7	8 9 10	%
Tan	1 2	3 4 5	6 7 8	9 10	%
Saki	1 2	3 4	5 6 7 8	9 10	%
Wine	1 2	3 4	5 6 7	8 9 10	%
Berger	1 2	3 4	5 6 7 8 9	10	%
Conroy/Johnson	1 2	3 4	5 6 7	8 9 10	%

Form for Planning a Paragraph

To write an effective paragraph, first prepare an outline. Often (though not always) you may be able to use a form like the one below.

Copyright ©2006 The McGraw-Hill Companies, Inc. All rights reserved.

Topic sentence: _____

_____

_____

Support (1): _____

_____

Details:

Support (2): _____

_____

Details:

Support (3): _____

_____

Details:

Acknowledgments

Text and Illustrations

Katherine Barrett, "Old Before Her Time." From *Ladies' Home Journal* magazine. Copyright 1983 by Meredith Corporation. All rights reserved. Used with the permission of *Ladies' Home Journal.*

Kathleen Stassen Berger and Ross A. Thompson, "Bullies in School." Excerpt from *The Developing Person through the Life Span* by Kathleen Stassen Berger and Ross A. Thompson, ©1998 by Worth Publishers. Used with permission.

Ben Carson, M.D., with Cecil Murphey, "Do It Better!" Excerpt from *Think Big,* copyright ©1992 by Benjamin Carson, M.D. Used by permission of Zondervan Publishing House.

James Lincoln Collier, "Anxiety: Challenge by Another Name." Originally published in *Reader's Digest,* December 1986. Reprinted by permission of the author.

Theresa Conroy and Christine M. Johnson, "A Drunken Ride, A Tragic Aftermath." From *The Philadelphia Inquirer.* Copyright ©1986, The Philadelphia Inquirer. Reprinted by permission.

Delores Curran, "What Good Families Are Doing Right," from *McCall's,* March 1983. Reprinted by permission.

Anita Garland, "Let's Really Reform Our Schools." Copyright ©1994. Reprinted by permission of the author

Google home page. Reproduced with permission of Google Inc.

Beth Johnson, "Joe Davis: A Cool Man." Beth Johnson lives in Harleysville, Pennsylvania. Reprinted by permission of the author.

Paul Logan, "Rowing the Bus." Copyright ©1997. Reprinted by permission of the author.

Sister Helen Mrosla, "All the Good Things." Originally published in *Reader's Digest,* October 1991. Reprinted by permission.

Andy Rooney, "Tickets to Nowhere." Originally published in the *San Francisco Chronicle,* Sept. 25, 1988. ©Tribune Media Services, Inc. All Rights Reserved. Reprinted with permission.

Marta Salinas, "The Scholarship Jacket." Excerpt from *Nosotros: Latina Literature Today,* edited by Maria del Carmen Boza, Beverly Silva, and Carmen Vale. Copyright ©1986. Reprinted with permission of Bilingual Press/Editorial Bilingüe and Arizona State University, Tempe, AZ.

Janny Scott, "How They Get You to Do That." Originally published in the *Los Angeles Times,* July 23, 1992. Copyright 1992, Los Angeles Times. Reprinted by permission.

Copyright ©2006 The McGraw-Hill Companies, Inc. All rights reserved.

Amy Tan, "The Most Hateful Words." Copyright © 2003 by Amy Tan. Originally published in *The New Yorker.* Reprinted by permission of the author and the Sandra Dijkstra Literary Agency.

Rudolph F. Verderber, "Dealing with Feelings." Excerpt from *Communicate, 6th Edition,* by Rudolph F. Verderber, ©1990. Reprinted with permission of Wadsworth, an imprint of the Wadsworth Group, a division of Thomson Learning.

Bill Wine, "Rudeness at the Movies." Copyright 1989. Reprinted by permission of the author.

Photos

192: © Jeffrey Greenberg/PhotoEdit; **202:** © David Young Wolff/PhotoEdit; **215:** © Photodisc; **219:** © Stephanie Carter/Photodisc; **231:** © Craig Lovell/Corbis; **243:** © David Young Wolff/PhotoEdit; **256:** © Karl Weatherly/Getty Images; **267:** © Richard Hutchings/Corbis; **280:** © Russell Underwood/Corbis; **293:** © Spencer Grant/PhotoEdit; **306:** © Photodisc; **332:** © Jeff Greenberg/PhotoEdit; **592:** Courtesy of the Franciscan Sisters of Little Falls, Minnesota; **613:** © Paul Kowal; **622:** © AP Photo/Jim Cooper; **641:** © Joe Giza/Corbis; **651:** By permission of James Lincoln Collier; **676:** © Mark Peterson/Corbis SABA; **693:** © Frank Capri/Hulton Archive/Getty Images; **699:** © Time Life Pictures/Mansell/Getty Images; **706:** © Kelly & Massa; **713:** By permission of Kathleen Berger

Index

Copyright ©2006 The McGraw-Hill Companies, Inc. All rights reserved.

Copyright ©2006 The McGraw-Hill Companies, Inc. All rights reserved.

Copyright ©2006 The McGraw-Hill Companies, Inc. All rights reserved.

Copyright ©2006 The McGraw-Hill Companies, Inc. All rights reserved.